Temperature Conversions

Degrees Fahrenheit (°F.)	Degrees Celcius (°C.)
32	0
40	4
140	60
150	65
160	70
170	75
212	100
275	135
300	150
325	165
350	175
375	190
400	205
425	220
450	230
475	245
500	260

I(T)P® an International Thomson Publishing Company
The ITP logo is a registered trademark used herein under license

Printed in the United States of America

For more information, contact:

Van Nostrand Reinhold
115 Fifth Avenue
New York, NY 10003

Chapman & Hall GmbH
Pappelallee 3
69469 Weinheim
Germany

Chapman & Hall
2-6 Boundary Row
London
SE1 8HN
United Kingdom

International Thomson Publishing Asia
221 Henderson Road #05-10
Henderson Building
Singapore 0315

Thomas Nelson Australia
102 Dodds Street
South Melbourne, 3205
Victoria, Australia

International Thomson Publishing Japan
Hirakawacho Kyowa Building, 3F
2-2-1 Hirakawacho
Chiyoda-ku, 102 Tokyo
Japan

Nelson Canada
1120 Birchmount Road
Scarborough, Ontario
Canada M1K 5G4

International Thomson Editores
Seneca 53
Col. Polanco
11560 Mexico D.F. Mexico

2 3 4 5 6 7 8 9 10   QEB-FF   01 00 99 98 97 96

Library of Congress Cataloging-in-Publication Data

Rubash, Joyce.
    The master dictionary of food and wine/Joyce Rubash; illustrations by
Benchmark Productions, Inc.
    p. cm.
    ISBN 0-442-02242-5
    1. Food—Dictionaries.   2. Cookery—Dictionaries.
3. Wine and wine making—Dictionaries.   I. Title.
TX349.R83   1996   96-15811
641.3' 003—dc20   CIP

The *Master Dictionary*

of *Food*

and *Wine*

Joyce Rubash, R.D., L.D.

Illustrations by

Benchmark Productions, Inc.

VAN NOSTRAND REINHOLD
I(T)P® A Division of International Thomson Publishing Inc.

New York • Albany • Bonn • Boston • Detroit • London • Madrid • Melbourne
Mexico City • Paris • San Francisco • Singapore • Tokyo • Toronto

Contents

Preface

Word from VNR for revision of *Master Dictionary of Food and Wine* for a second edition came at a difficult and stressful time in my life—we were building our retirement home and I was general contractor for the job! I could not see how I could do both, but I consented to the revision.

This second edition retains the characteristics of the first edition: accurate, simply written, brief in definition, and self-pronouncing. Users of this book will find it is still simple to use, and words and terms are easy to find and pronounce.

Three people in particular were of considerable help to me with pronunciations of the varietals and cheeses. Many thanks go to Oliver Kielwasser, Perishables Buyer for Auchan's Hypermart in Houston, who spent several hours of his valuable time pronouncing the names of cheeses. Thanks also go to Herman Key and Charles Jenkins, both Wine Consultants for Spec's Liquor Stores in Houston for helping with the pronunciations of the names of grape varieties. Thanks also go to Melissa Rosati, my editor, for allowing me some extra time to get the job done due to my house-building.

How to Use This Book

The *Master Dictionary of Food and Wine* is patterned after the standard dictionary format of word, pronunciation, word origin, and definition. For example,

> **ärter med fläsk** (EHR-ter med flesk). Swe. Yellow pea soup.
>
> **baccalà** (bahk-kah-LAH). Ita. Salt cod.

Word entries are listed alphabetically and set in **bold** type, followed by the pronunciation in parentheses, then the country of origin abbreviated and, lastly, the definition. Guide words are printed at the tops of facing pages, indicating the entries falling alphabetically between them.

Pronunciations

The pronunciations are transliterations. These imitated pronunciations are to be read as if in English. Accented syllables are shown simply and clearly in capital letters. You will see that in some languages only part of a syllable is accented and that French words have no accented syllables.

No two languages are exactly the same. Some languages have sounds that do not appear in the English language. However, if the transliterated syllables are sounded out as if in English, and accents placed as indicated, the sounding of the word should be accurate, or in the case of a difficult language, close enough to be understood.

A few rules to remember when pronouncing these transliterations:

• When *ah, eh, ih,* and *oh* are presented together in a word or syllable, this forms the short sound of that vowel; that is, *a* as in *cat, e* as in *elephant, i* as in *fill,* and *o* as in *hot.*

• Any vowel presented alone before consonants is to be pronounced in its long sound; that is, *a* as in *cake, e* as in *emit, i* as in *item,* and *o* as in *Ohio.*

• Two transliterated sounds that appear in several languages, but not in English, and when presented in the following combinations, are to be pronounced as follows: *ahng* as in *hang,* but barely sounding the *g,* and *awng* as in *pong,* but barely sounding the *g.*

• Multiple *r*'s indicate trilling; that is, *rr* slightly trilled, *rrr* heavily trilled.

• Double *o* (*oo*) used in a word is pronounced as in *boo.*

Word Origins

The following is a list of the abbreviations used for the word origins:

Afr	African	Fin	Finnish
Ara	Arabic	Fre	French
Bri	British	Ger	German
Chi	Chinese	Gre	Greek
Cze	Czechoslovakian	Hun	Hungarian
Dan	Danish	Ice	Icelandic
Dut	Dutch	Ind	Indian

Ino	Indonesian	Nor	Norwegian
Iri	Irish	Phi	Philippine
Ita	Italian	Pol	Polish
Jap	Japanese	Por	Portuguese
Jew	Jewish	Rus	Russian
Kor	Korean	Sco	Scottish
Lao	Laotian	Swe	Swedish
Mal	Malayan	Thi	Thai
Mex	Mexican	Tur	Turkish
NZe	New Zealand	USA	American (USA)

Definitions

The definitions given are concise and uncomplicated. Cross references, synonyms, and alternative spellings have been included to clarify some definitions. For example, malfatti is defined as "Gnocchi of spinach and ricotta," and gnocchi is cross referenced in its alphabetical place with its pronunciation, origin, and definition. Likewise, palsterzipfel is defined as "An Austrian jam filled turnover" and turnover is listed and defined, or agnolotti is defined as "Squares of pasta stuffed with meat filling, such as ravioli, tortelli, tortellini," and ravioli, tortelli, and tortellini are listed and defined. Cross references appear in **bold face.** Variations for terms found in the book are set in italics within a definition.

Commonly used synonyms are also listed for many entries. For example, the entry for baked custard indicates "Also called cup custard"; for field lettuce, "Also called lamb's lettuce"; for hazelnut, 'Also known as filbert"; and for annatto, "Also known as bixin." And many languages have more than one spelling for numerous words; when known, these alternative spellings are listed as in the following examples: corvina, "Also spelled corbina"; kugelhopf, "Also spelled kugelhoph"; matzo, "Also spelled matzoh"; and panocha, "Also spelled penuche."

Agurk - Danish, Norwegian - Cucumber

A

Aal (arl). Ger, Dut. **Eel.**

aal og rørawg (awl oa RUR-rehg). Dan. **Eel** with scrambled **eggs.**

aam (ahm). Ind. Ripe **mango** fruit.

aara (AH-dah). Ind. **Flour, whole wheat flour.**

aardappelen (AHR-dahp-pul). Dut. **Potatoes;** *gebakken* (khuh-BAHK-kuh) fried; *gekookt* (khuuh-KOHKT) boiled; *purée* (pew-RAY) mashed.

aardbeien (AHR-bay-uh). Dut. **Strawberries.**

abacate (ah-bah-KA-ta). Por. **Avocado.**

abacaxi (ah-bah-kah-SHEE). Por. **Pineapple.**

abaissage (ah-bay-sahzj). Fre. Rolling out pastry **dough.**

abaisse (ah-bess). Fre. A thin, rolled-out **biscuit** or pastry; a thin bottom crust.

abalone (ah-bah-LOHN-e). USA. A **mollusk** whose large adductor muscle is edible; used fresh, dried, canned; especially in Japanese and Chinese cooking; called *ormer* in Europe.

abatis (ah-bah-tee). Fre. External poultry trimmings such as wing tips, necks, feet.

abats (ah-bahts). Fre. **Giblets;** edible internal organs such as liver, heart, **sweetbreads,** etc.

abbacchio (ahb-bahk-KEE-o). Ita. A very young suckling lamb.

abborre (AH-bor-rer). Swe. **Perch.**

abbrusttolito (ahb-broost-too-LEE-to). Ita. Toasted.

Aberdeen Crowdie (AAH-behr-den Krew-de). Bri. A fresh, unripened cheese similar to **cottage cheese** that sometimes contains **caraway** seeds; made in England and Scotland.

Abertam (Ah-behr-tohn). Ger. A Bohemian hard cheese made of ewe's milk.

à blanc (ah blahnk). Fre. A method of cooking **veal, pork,** or **poultry** in **stews** and pot **roasts,** in which raw meat is placed directly in boiling stock, without first browning the meat.

ablette (ahb-leht). Fre. A type of **carp.**

abóbora (ah-BAW-boh-rah). Por. **Pumpkin, squash,** vegetable **marrow.**

aborinha (ah-bo-RI-nyah). Por. Zucchini.

abricot (ahb-re-coh). Fre. **Apricot.**

abrikoos (ahb-ri-KO-zen). Dut. **Apricot.**

abrikos (ah-bre-KO-ssi). Rus. **Apricot.**

abruzze (ah-BROOZ-dze). Ita. In the Abruzzi way; with hot red **peppers** and, sometimes, **ham.**

absinthe (AHB-senth). Gre. A green **liqueur** with **wormwood** leaves and **anise;** highly intoxicating.

abuñolado (ah-bhoo-no-LAH-do). Spa. Fried in **batter.**

abura (ah-BOO-rah). Jap. Oil; *sarada* for salads, **tempura** for frying, **goma** (sesame oil) for seasoning.

aburage (ah-BOO-rah-geg). Jap. **Deep-fried tōfu.**

açafrão (a-sa-frahng). Por. **Saffron.**

acciughe (aht-CHOO-gay). Ita. **Anchovies.**

aceite (ah-SAY-tay). Spa. Oil.

aceituna (ah-say-TOO-nah). Spa. **Olive.**

acelga (ah-THEHL-gah). Spa. **Beet.**

acepipes (a-se-PE-pesh). Por. **Hors d'oeuvres.**

acerola (ah-se-ROLL-ah). USA. A small, soft, juicy, thin-skinned fruit that is crimson when mature and has orange-yellow flesh; richest known source of vitamin C; a sweet flavor; used fresh, in **preserves, purées** and **desserts.** Also known as **Barbados cherry,** *West Indian cherry.*

acetary (ASS-e-tah-ree). USA. Acidic fruit pulp.

acetic acid (a-SE-tik ASS-ehd). USA. The acid in **vinegar** that is produced by a second fermentation.

aceto (ah-CHEH-toh). Ita. **Vinegar.**

aceto balsamico (ah-CHEH-toh bahl-sah-MEH-co). Ita. A very fine Italian **vinegar** with a dark, mellow, subtle flavor.

aceto-dolce (ah-CHEH-toh-DOAL-chay). Ita. A sweet-sour mix of **vegetables** and **fruits** used as an **antipasto.**

acetosella (ah-SE-toh-sehl-lah). Ita. **Sorrel.**

achar (ah-CHAR). Ind. **Pickle.**

achiote (ah-shee-O-teh). Spa. A red dye from fruit used to color **cheese, butter,** and **confectionary.**

acidophilus milk (ass-ceh-DOHF-eh-lus mehlk). USA. Slightly soured **milk** that is both easy to digest and healthful.

acidulated water (ah-SEHD-u-la-ted WAIIT-er). USA. Water with **lemon** juice or **vinegar** added to prevent **fruits** and **vegetables** from discoloring; also used to blanch certain foods.

acini di pepe (ah-CHEE-nee dee PE-pee). Ita. Tiny squares or rounds of **pasta** used in **soup.**

açorda (a-SOR-dah). Por. **Garlic** bread **porridge.**

acorn squash (A-korn squash). USA. Acorn-shaped dark green winter **squash** with a ridged surface and sweet yellow-orange flesh; also called *Table Queen, Danish,* or *Des Moines.*

acqua (AHK-kwah). Ita. Water.

acquacotta (AHK-kwah-KOT-toh). Ita. A **soup** made with stale bread, into which an **egg** is added to each serving.

active dry yeast (AHK-tehv dri yest). USA. Granular form of **yeast;** usually packaged in an air-tight, moisture-proof envelope containing one ounce yeast.

açúcar (a-SOO-kar). Por. **Sugar.**

açúcar granulado (a-SOO-kar gra-noo-LAH-doo). Por. **Granulated sugar.**

adas (AH-dahs). Ara. Lentils.

adega (ah-DE-ja). Por. Storage cellar, usually above ground.

aderezo (ah-deh-REH-soh). Spa. **Salad dressing.**

adobo (ah-DOH-boh).   Phi. A **stew** with thick spicy sauce made piquant with **vinegar;** usually made with **pork** or **game;** sometimes with **chicken** or **seafood.**

adobo (ah-DOH-boh).   Spa. Seasoning paste or sauce made of **chilies, herbs,** and **vinegar.**

adrak (ah-DAH-rahk).   Ind. Fresh **gingerroot.**

advocaat (ahd-vo-KAHT).   Dut. **Eggnog** eaten with a spoon in The Netherlands.

aebleflaesk (EHB-blerr-FLEHSK).   Dan. Fried **salt pork** or **bacon** with fried **apples.**

aeblegrød (EHB-lerr-grurdh).   Dan. **Applesauce.**

aeblekage (EHB-ler-kaaer).   Dan. **Apple cake.**

aeblemost (EHB-ler-most).   Dan. Sweet **cider.**

aeblepidsvin (ehb-lerr-PIDS-vin).   Dan. A **dessert** of **apples, lemon** juice, and toasted **almonds.**

aebleskiver (eh-bleh-SKEE-vor).   Dan. **Doughnuts.**

aeg (ehg).   Dan. **Egg;** *blødkogt aeg* (BLURDH-kot ehg) soft-boiled egg; *hårdkogt* (HAWR-kot) **omelet;** *pocheret* (poa-SHAYR-et) **poached;** *røraeg* (RURR-ehg) **scrambled eggs;** *spejlaeg* (SPIGH-ehg) fried eggs.

aemono (ah-moh-nah).   Jap. Cold, dressed, salad-like foods.

aerter (AIR-terr).   Dan. **Peas.**

affettato (ahf-feht-TAA-toh).   Ita. Cold cuts.

affogato (ahf-foa-GAA-toh).   Ita. **Poached** or **steamed.**

affumicato (ahf-foo-mee-KAA-toh).   Ita. **Smoked.**

áfonya (A-fawn-ya).   Hun. **Blueberries.**

agar-agar (ah-gahr-ah-gahr).   Chi. A **gelatin** made of **seaweed** that does not melt at room temperature and has remarkable absorption capability.

agave (ah-GAH-veh).   Mex. A cactus known as century plant.

age (ah-GOH-eh).   Jap. **Deep-fried.**

agemono (AH-ge-mo-no).   Jap. **Fried.**

agerhøne (AAERR-hur-ner).   Dan. **Partridge.**

ägg (ehg).   Swe. Egg; *kokt* (KOO-kah) **boiled;** *stekt* (STA-kaht) fried; *äggröra* (ehg-RURR-ah) **scrambled;** *förlorade* (fur-LOO-rah-der)

poached; *löskokt* (LURS-kookt) soft; *lagom* (LA-gom) medium; *håardkokt* (HOARD-kokt) hard cooked.

agi (aji). Spa. Red-hot **pepper** used in spicy dishes.

aging (AJ-ing). USA. A method of maturing a food, such as wine, **cheese, game,** beef to improve its flavor.

agiter (azh-ee-tay). Fre. To stir.

agliota (AH-ly-o-to). Ita. A sauce consisting of **garlic** slices, bread crumbs, and **vinegar.**

aglio (AH-ly-o). Ita. **Garlic.**

agneau (ahn-yoh). Fre. Lamb.

agnello (ahn-NYEHL-loa). Ita. Lamb.

agnolotti (ahn-nyoa-LOT-tee). Ita. Squares of **pasta** stuffed with meat filling, such as **ravioli,** tortelli, **tortellini.**

agresto (ah-GREHZ-toa). Ita. The juice of unripe **grapes,** used occasionally in some sauces instead of **vinegar.**

agrimony (ah-GRIM-o-nee). Bri. An **herb** whose dark green, downy leaves used in **tea** blends and wines have a flavor reminiscent of **apricot.** The plant yields a golden yellow dye.

agrio (AH-greeh-oh). Mex. Sour.

agriões (a-gree-AWNGSH). Por. **Watercress.**

agrodolce (ah-roh-DOL-chay). Ita. Sharp and sweet, pertains to the flavoring of a dish.

agua (AH-gwah). Spa. Water.

água (AH-gwah). Por. Water.

aguacate (ah-gwah-KAH-tay). Spa. **Avocado.**

água gelo (AH-gwah ZHAY-loo). Por. Ice water.

àgua mineral (AH-gwah mee-nay-RAHL). Por. **Mineral water.**

aguardiente (ah-wahr-DEHN-tay). Spa. A very strong Spanish **liqueur.**

aguglie (ah-GOO-ly-ay). Ita. Garfish.

agurk (ah-GOORK). Dan, Nor. **Cucumber.**

ahp sun (AHP sun). Chi. Dried **duck** gizzard.

ahtapot (okh-tu-BOOT). Ara. **Octopus.**

ahven (AHH-vayn). Fin. **Perch;** used in **soup** or served in **lemon-butter.**

aiglefin (ehg-ler-fang). Fre. **Haddock.**

aigre (ay-zhreh). Fre. Bitter, sour, possibly tart.

aïgroissade (ah-ee-grwah-sahd). Fre. Cooked **vegetables** mixed with a garlicky **mayonnaise.**

aiguillette (eh-gew-ee-ley). Fre. A very thin, lengthwise-cut strip of meat or **poultry.**

ail (ahy). Fre. **Garlic.**

ailerons (ahy-rohn). Fre. **Chicken** wings.

aillade (ahy-lee-dah). Fre. Sauce of **garlic, onion, chive, leek, herbs,** spices, and oil.

aïoli (ahj-o-lee). Fre. A thick **mayonnaise** strongly flavored with **garlic,** served with **seafood.**

aipo (IE-poh). Por. **Celery.**

airelle (a-rehl). Fre. **Bilberry,** a variety of **blueberry.**

airelle rouge (a-rehl roozh). Fre. **Cranberry.**

aisu kohi (ah-EES koh-hee). Jap. Iced **coffee.**

aisu ti (ah-EES tee). Jap. Iced **tea.**

ajam panggang (au-AUM PAH-yahng). Dut. **Grilled chicken** flavored with **ginger, saffron, garlic, chili peppers.**

aji (AH-jee). Jap. Horse **mackerel.**

aji (AH-khee). Spa. **Chili peppers.**

ajin (ah-JEEN). Ara. **Dough.**

ajo (AH-khoa). Spa. **Garlic.**

ajonjoli (ah-hohn-hoh-LEE). Mex. **Sesame.**

ajouter (ah-zju-tay). Fre. To add an ingredient.

ajwain (AHJ-wahne). Ind. **Celery-seed**-sized spice with flavor of **anise, oregano,** and **black pepper.**

ajwi (AHJ-wee). Ara. **Dates.**

akee (AH-kee). Afr. A West African **fruit** that is one of the most strikingly beautiful and delicious of fruits; however, unless it has ripened to the point of voluntary opening, it is a deadly poison. All seeds must be removed as they are poison. When picked ripe, hulled, and completely seeded, it may be eaten raw or cooked; parboiled it may be used hot or cold.

akni (ACK-nee).   Ind. A delicate, aromatic **broth** used to **poach** or flavor certain foods.

akule (ah-KUHLE).   USA. A Hawaiian food fish, usually salted and dried, also known as bigeye scad.

akuri (ah-KUH-dree).   Ind. Spiced **scrambled eggs.**

akvavit (ahk-vah-VEET).   Dan. A strong, colorless liquor distilled from **grain** or **potatoes;** flavored with **caraway;** served very cold before or with a meal. See **aquavit.**

ål (awl).   Nor. **Eel.**

ål (oal).   Swe. **Eel.**

à la (ah lah).   Fre. In the style of.

à la Broche (a lah brosh).   Fre. **Roast** in front of the fire on a spit or **skewer.**

à la carte (ah lah kahrt).   Fre. According to a menu that prices items separately.

à la mode (ah lah mod).   USA. "According to the fashion"; topped with **ice cream.** See **beef à la mode** and **tripe à la mode de Caen.**

al burro (ahl BOOR-roa).   Ita. A style of serving **pasta;** after the pasta has been cooked and drained, it is tossed in **butter** and served without out a sauce.

al dente (ahl-DEN-tay).   Ita. **Pasta** that is firm to the bite, chewy, slightly undercooked.

al forno (ahl FOR-noa).   Ita. **Baked; roasted.**

al funghetto (ahl foon-GHEHT-toa).   Ita. A method of cooking **vegetables** quickly over high heat and using an **herb;** so called after a method of cooking **mushrooms.** Vegetables usually cooked al funghetto are **eggplant** and zucchini.

al horno (ahl HOR-noh).   Mex. **Baked** or **roasted** in an oven.

al sangue (ahl SAHNG-goo-ay).   Ita. Rare; describing the degree of cooking of meat.

alajú (ah-lah-KHOO).   Spa. Pastry of **sugar, nuts,** and **ginger.**

alalunga (ahl-ah-LOON-gah).   Ita. White **tuna.**

albedo (ahl-BED-o).   USA. The white inner peel of **oranges** and other **citrus fruit.**

albicocca (ahl-bee-KOK-kah).   Ita. **Apricot.**

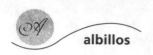

albillos (AHL-bee-lious). Spa. White **grapes.**

albóndigas (ahl-BOHN-dee-gahs). Spa. Spicy **meatballs** of **pork,** beef; also a **dumpling.**

albuiéra (ahl-bew-fay-rah). Fre. A **suprême sauce** with meat **glaze** and **pimento butter.**

albumen (ahl-BU-mehn). USA. The protein portion of **egg** white; also found in **milk,** some plants, and seeds.

alcachofa (ahl-cah-CHOH-fah). Spa. **Artichoke.**

alcaparras (ahl-cah-PAH-rrahs). Spa. **Capers.**

alcaravia (al-cah-RA-vjah). Por. **Caraway.**

alcohol (AHL-co-hol). USA. A colorless, flammable liquid. Whiskey.

ale (ael). USA. Bittersweet **malt** beverage.

Alemtejo (ah-lem-TAH-ho). Por. A rather soft **cheese** made mostly from ewe's milk, but goat's milk is often added; cylindrical in shape, made in three sizes: two ounces, one pound, and four pounds; also called *Alemtejo.*

aletria (ah-le-TREE-ah). Por. **Vermicelli,** sometimes used as **dessert** in a **pudding.**

alewife (AL-wif). USA. A food fish of the **herring** family; abundant on the Atlantic coast.

alewife caviar (AL-wif CAH-vee-ahr). USA. An inexpensive **caviar** substitute; made from a **herring** whose **roe** is processed.

alface (ahl-FAH-say). Por. **Lettuce.**

alfajores (ahl-fah-HOA-rehs). Spa. Sweet pastry made with **corn** and **honey.**

alfalfa (ahl-FAHL-fah). USA. A **legume** widely grown for hay and forage, whose seeds are used as sprouts in salads.

alföldi marharostélyos (OL-furl-dee MOR-hor-rawsh-tay-yawsh). Hun. Steak Alföldi style, with a rich sauce and stewed **vegetables.**

alfostigo (al-fos-TEE-goo). Por. **Pistachio nut.**

algérienne (ahl-ger-een). Fre. **Garnished** with **tomatoes braised** in oil and **sweet potato croquettes.**

algin (AHL-gehn). USA. A thickening agent derived from **seaweed,** used mostly in processed foods.

alheira (al-EIH-rah). Por. **Sausage** of smoked **ham, nuts,** and **garlic.**

alho (AHL-yoh). Por. **Garlic.**

alho franceses (AL-yoosh fran-SES-esh). Por. **Leeks.**

alic (ahl-EE-chay). Ita. **Anchovy.**

alici (ahl-EE-chee). Ita. **Anchovies** in **salt.**

alicot (ah-lee-koht). Fre. **Giblets.**

aliñado (ah-lee-NAH-doh). Spa. Seasoned.

aliño (ahl-lee-NOH). Spa. Seasoning.

aliolo (ah-lee-OO-loa). Spa. A thick **mayonnaise** strongly flavored with **garlic,** served with **seafood.**

alkannet (AHL-kahn-neht). USA. Natural food additive used to color fats and cheeses.

Allgaüer (ahl-GOA-ah). Ger. A type of **Swiss cheese** produced in the fertile Allgaü region just north of Switzerland.

all'olio (ahl OL-yoa). Ita. In oil.

all-purpose flour (ahl-PUHR-puhs flowr). USA. A blend of soft and hard wheat **flours,** bleached or unbleached, that has many general uses including thickening.

alla griglia (AHL-lah GREE-lyah). Ita. **Grilled.**

alla parmigiana (AHL-lah pahr-mee-JAH-nah). Ita. A description used for **vegetables** that are **boiled** and served with melted **butter** and grated **Parmesan cheese;** also for **veal scallops** sautéed in **butter** and finished with **Parmesan.**

allemande sauce (ahl-MAHND saus). Fre. Smooth **white sauce** with **butter, egg yolk** added; a basic classical sauce; an **egg**-thickened **velouté.**

alligator (AHL-lee-ga-tohr). USA. A large reptile of the Gulf Coast swamplands whose tail meat is particularly relished and used in stews.

alloro (ahl-LOH-roa). Ita. **Bay leaves,** laurel.

allspice (AHL-spis). USA. A mildly aromatic spice tasting like a combination of **clove, nutmeg,** and **cinnamon.**

allumette (ahl-lee-meht). Fre. A strip of puff pastry with a sweet or savory **filling** or **garnish;** also **potatoes,** peeled and cut into match-stick-size strips.

almamártás (OL-mom-maar-taash). Hun. **Applesauce.**

almás palacsinta (OL-maash PO-lo-cheen-to). Hun. **Apple** pancake.

almejas (ahl-MEH-hah). Spa. **Clams.**

almendrado (ahl-meh-DRAH-doz). Spa. **Macaroon.**

almendras (ahl-MEHN-drah). Spa. **Almonds.**

almond (AH-mund). USA. Edible kernel of the **fruit** of the almond tree, used as a **nut.**

almôndegas (ahl-MOHN-day-gahss). Por. **Meatballs, croquettes.**

almond oil (AH-mund oyl). USA. Yellow-white oil extracted from **almonds** that is odorless and has mild nutty flavor.

almond powder (AH-mund pouw-dehr). USA. Very finely ground **almonds,** used in Chinese **desserts.**

almuerzo (ahl-MWER-soh). Mex. Late breakfast or brunch.

aloo (AH-loo). Ind. **Potato.**

aloo bokhara (AH-loo bahk-HA-row). Ind. Sour, dried **plums** or **prunes.**

alose (ah-lo-seh). Fre. **Shad.**

alouettes (al-wets). Fre. Larks, a great delicacy.

aloyau (al-wa-jo). Fre. **Sirloin,** always beef.

alperche (al-PAIR-sesh). Por. **Apricot.**

alphabets (AHL-fah-behts). USA. Tiny **pasta** letters.

Alpin (Ahl-pahn). Fre. A variant of Mont d'Or **cheese** made in the Alpine region of France of goat's milk; also known as Clérimbert.

alsacienne (ahl-sah-cyeen). Fre. Garnished with **sauerkraut** and **ham** or **sausages,** or with other Alsatian specialties.

Altenburger (AHL-tehn-berg-er). Ger. A soft, uncooked **cheese** made from goat's milk that has a delicate white mold on the exterior and a creamy, smooth, flavorful interior.

alubia (ah-LOO-bee-ah). Spa. **Bean;** same as shell beans.

alum (AH-lum). USA. Astringent compound used as a preservative, such as in **pickles.**

amadai (ah-MAH-dah-ee). Jap. Red **tilefish.**

amai (ah-mah-ee). Jap. Sweet.

amalgamer (ah-mahl-gah-meh). Fre. Blend or combine ingredients.

amande (ahm-end). Fre. **Almond.**

amandel (um-MUN-del). Dut. **Almonds.**

amandine (ahm-ah-deen). Fre. Made or garnished with **almonds.**

amaranth (AHM-ah-ranth). USA. A **vegetable** with edible dark green leaves and stems like **asparagus;** taste is a cross between **spinach** and mild-tasting **cabbage.**

amarelles (ahm-ah-REHLZ). USA. Cultivated, sour **cherries** with colorless juice.

amaretti (ahm-ah-REHT-tee). Ita. Crisp **macaroons** made with **bitter almonds.**

amaretto (ahm-ah-REHT-o). Ita. A sweet, **almond**-flavored **liqueur.**

amassada (ah-mah-SAH-dah). Por. **Mashed,** as in **potatoes.**

amatriciana (ah-mah-tree-CHAH-nah). Ita. With **tomatoes, ham,** and **Pecorino cheese.**

amazu shoga (AH-mah-zoo SHO-gah). Jap. Pink, **pickled ginger,** usually eaten with **sushi.**

Ambert (ohm-bear). Fre. A **Roquefort**-type **cheese** made to a limited extent of cow's milk that differs from other Roquefort-type cheeses in that the **salt** is mixed with the curd instead of being rubbed on the surface of the cheese; also called **Forez.**

ambrosia (ahm-BRO-zha). Ita. A **dessert** made of **oranges** and shredded **coconut.**

ambrosia (ahm-BRO-zah). Mex. An **herb** with an extremely sweet scent, whose leaves are used in cold beverages in the same way that **mint** is used.

amchoor (AHM-choor). Ind. Dried slices and powder of sour, unripe **mangos,** used for a sweet-sour taste.

amêijoas (ah-MAY-zho-ahs). Por. Small, succulent **clams.**

ameixas (a-MAY-shash). Por. **Plums.**

amêndoas (ah-MEN-doh-ahs). Por. **Almonds.**

amendoim (ah-men-doh-EE). Por. **Peanut.**

américaine (ah-mer-ee-cahn). Fre. Garnished with **lobster** tail and **truffles.**

American cheese (ah-MEHR-eh-kahn cheez). USA. An American-made **cheddar,** both natural and processed. Eighty percent of all cheese consumed by Americans is classified as **cheddar.**

amiral (am-eh-rehl). Fre. Garnish of **mussels, oysters, crayfish,** and **mushrooms.**

amontillado (ah-mon-tee-LAH-doa).   Spa. A medium sherry.

amóras (ah-MAW-rahs).   Por. **Berries.**

amoroso (AH-moa-ROA-soa).   Spa. A dark, sweet sherry.

amorphous sugar (ah-MOR-fuss SCHU-gahr).   USA. Sucrose melted, allowed to dry, then crystallize, making a very brittle, very hard, solid, transparent mass; rock **candy.**

Amsterdamse korsties (AHM-stehr-dahm KOHR-sjuh).   Dut. Spice **cake.**

an (ahn).   Jap. Sweet red-**bean** past; azuki **beans** boiled with sugar that comes in two textures: *koshi-an,* smooth puree, and *tsubushi-an,* chunky texture.

anadama (ah-nah-DAY-mah).   USA. A **yeast bread** made from white **flour** with **cornmeal** and **molasses.**

anago (ah-NAH-goh).   **Jap.** Conger **eel.**

Anaheim chili (AN-ah-heim CHIL-ee).   Mex. A fairly hot greenish-yellow **chili pepper** that is generally used fresh, toasted, canned, but never dried. Also known as **güero, Californian chili,** or sweet **green pepper.**

ananas (ah-nah-nahs).   Fre, Ger, Dut, Swe. **Pineapple.**

ananas (ah-nah-NAHS).   Rus. **Pineapple.**

ananás (UN-ah-nus).   Por. **Pineapple.**

ananasso (AH-nah-nahs-soa).   Ita. **Pineapple.**

ananász (Oon-non-naas).   Hun. **Pineapple.**

anardana (ahn-NAHR-dahn-nah).   Ind. Dried seeds from sour **pomegranates** used in Indian cooking.

anatra (An-nah-trah).   Ita. **Duck;** also spelled **anitra.**

ancho (AHN-choh).   Mex. A deep-red **chili pepper,** mild in flavor. Used **dried,** not fresh.

anchoaïde (anh-shwah).   Fre. Mashed **anchovy** spread on toast.

anchoas (ahn-CHO-ahss).   Spa. **Anchovies.**

anchois (ahn-swa).   Fre. **Anchovy.**

anchova (ahn-SHOH-vahss).   Por. **Anchovy.**

anchovy (ahn-CHO-vee).   USA. Any of numerous small fishes resembling **herring** used for making **sauces, salads,** and **relishes.**

Ancien Impérial (Ahn-syen aim-pehr-yahl).   Fre. A two-inch square fresh **cheese** much like **Neufchâtel.**

ancienne (ahn-syen). Fre. In the old way; with white **rice, béchamel sauce,** and **mushrooms.**

and (ung). Dan. **Duck.**

anda (AHN-dah). Ind. **Egg.**

andalouse (ahn-dah-loos). Fre. **Garnished** with **tomatoes,** sweet red **peppers, eggplant.**

andijvie (ahn-DAY-vee). Dut. **Endive.**

andouille (ahn-doo-ee). Fre. **Smoked** pure **pork sausage,** usually served cold as an **hors d'oeuvre.**

añejo (ah-NAY-khoa). Spa. Ripe, as referring to **cheese.**

anellini (ahn-nah-LEE-nee). Ita. **Pasta** in the shape of little rings.

aneth (ah-neht). Fre. **Dill.**

aneto (ah-NEH-toa). Ita. **Dill.**

angel cake (ANG-jel CAK). USA. A sponge **cake** made with stiffly beaten **egg** whites, producing a white, airy cake.

angel flake coconut (ANG-jel FLAK CO-co-nuht). USA. **Coconut** flakes cut wider than the standard cut, making it moister, used in **confections** and **baking.**

angel food cake (ANG-jel food CAK). USA. See **angel cake.**

angel hair (ANG-jel haer). USA. The thinnest **pasta** made.

angelica (ahn-JEL-eh-cah). USA. An **herb** of the **parsley** family, used to flavor **liqueurs** and **confections;** imparts a green color.

angélique (an-geh-leek). Fre. Angelica.

Angelot (Awhn-gjee-lo). Fre. A **cheese** said to be the same as Pont-L'Evêque.

angels on horseback (AHN-jels ohn HORS-bahk). USA. An **hors d'oeuvre** of **oysters** wrapped in **bacon, skewered, broiled.**

anglaise (ang-glayz). Fre. In English style, that is plainly **boiled, roasted, fried.**

angler (AHN-glur). USA. **Monkfish.**

Angostura bitters (anj-goh-STUHR-rah BIHT-tuhrs). USA. Reddish-brown aromatic **bitters** produced in Trinidad, used primarily in making **cocktails.**

anguila (ahn-GEE-lah). Spa. **Eel.**

anguilla (ahng-goo-EEL-lah). Ita. **Eel.**

anguille (ahng-geey). Fre. **Eel.**

anguilles à l'escaveche (ahng-geey ah les-kah-vehsh). Fre. **Pickled eels,** first **fried** in oil, then cooled in **aspic.**

anguria (ahng-GOO-ree-ah). Ita. One of the names for **watermelon.**

anho (ah-nyoo). Por. Lamb.

anhydrated (ahn-HIY-dra-ted). USA. **Dehydrated; dried.**

anice (AH-nes). Ita. **Anise.**

anijs (ah-NIS). Dut. **Anise.**

animelle (ah-nee-MEHL-lay). Ita. **Sweetbreads.**

animelle (ahn-ee-mehl). Fre. Testicles of animals, usually bull, pig, lamb.

anise (ahn-ess). Fre. An **herb** of the **carrot** family having carminative aromatic seeds; similar to the flavor of **licorice.**

aniseed oil (AHN-eh-seed oyl). USA. Oil from the aniseed; gives the **licorice** flavor to **anisette.**

anisette (ahn-ei-set). Fre. A colorless sweet **liqueur** flavored with aniseed.

anitra (A-nah-trah). Ita. **Duck,** also spelled **anatra.**

Anjou (ahn-zju). Fre. A variety of **pear,** very sweet, used fresh as **dessert** or with **cheese.**

anka (AHNG-kah). Swe. **Duck.**

ankerias (AHN-kay-ri-ahss). Fin. **Eel.**

anlann (AN-lan). Iri. **Sauce.**

annatto (ahn-NAHT-toh). USA. Food-coloring agent derived from the seeds of a Central American plant, used to color **butter** and **cheese.** Also known as **bixin.**

anraith (AHN-reeh). Iri. **Soup.**

anraith glasraí (AHN-reeh GLAHS-ree). Iri. **Vegetable soup.**

anschovis (ahn-SHO-fiz). Ger. **Anchovies.**

ansjos (ahn-SHOOS). Nor. **Anchovy.**

ansjovis (ahn-SHOO-vihs). Swe. **Anchovies; marinated sprats.**

antioxidant (AHN-tee OHX-ee-dehnt). USA. A substance that inhibits the browning process of **fruits** and **vegetables** when exposed to the air.

antipasto (ahn-tee-PAHS-toh).   Ita. The appetizer or first course served that may consist of **prosciutto** or other **hams, salami** or other **sausages,** stuffed **eggs, pickled** and fresh **vegetables,** fish, and **seafood.**

antojito (ahn-toh-HEE-toh).   Mex. "Little whim"; **hors d'oeuvre;** small snack food.

aonegi (hoh-SOH-neh-gee).   Jap. **Spring onion, green onion.**

ao-togarashi (oh-TOH-gah-rah-shee).   Jap. Small **green peppers.**

apaz onion (ah-PAHZ UN-yun).   USA. Edible wild **onion** that looks and tastes similar to pearl onions.

apee (A-Pee).   USA. A **cookie** made from **butter, sugar,** and **sour cream** created by Ann Page, who carved her initials AP on top of each cookie.

apelsin (ah-perl-SSEEN).   Swe. **Orange.**

apel'sin (ah-pyeel'SEE-ni).   Rus. **Oranges.**

apenoten (AH-puh-no-tuh).   Dut. **Peanuts.**

apéritif (ahp-ree-teef).   Fre. Wine or spirits served as an **appetizer.**

aperitivo (ah-pay-ree-TEE-voa).   Ita. Wine or spirits served as an **appetizer.**

aperitívet (O-pah-ree-tee-veht).   Hun. **Aperitif.**

aperitivo (ah-peh-ree-TEE-voh).   Mex. **Appetizer.**

Apfel (AH-pferl).   Ger. **Apple.**

Apfel pfannkuchen (AH-pferl PFAHN-eh-KU-chuhn).   Ger. **Apple pancakes.**

Apfelbröïsï (AH-pferl-brur-ihs-ee).   Ger. **Bread pudding** with **apples,** sultana **raisins.**

Apfelmus (AH-pferl-mus).   Ger. **Applesauce.**

Apfelsaft (AH-pferl-zaft).   Ger. **Apple** juice.

Apfelschmitzchen (AH-pferl schneht-zhen).   Ger. **Apple fritters.**

Apfelsine (ah-pferl-ZEE-ner).   Ger. **Orange.**

Apfelstrudel (AH-pferl-shtroo-derl).   Ger. **Apple strudel.**

Apfeltorte (AH-pferl-TOHR-tah).   Ger. **Apple cake.**

Apfelwein (AH-pferl-vain).   Ger. **Apple cider.**

aphrodisiac (ahf-roh-DE-zee-ahk).   USA. A food or drink, usually believed to arouse the sexual appetite.

apio (AH-pyoh). Spa. **Celery.**

apio (AH-pee-oo). Por. **Celery.**

appalam (AHP-blahm). Ind. Lentil wafers.

appareil (ah-par-e-zj). Fre. A ready-mix for use in a preparation.

appelbeignets (AHP-pul-bayn-yays). Dut. **Apple fritter.**

appelen (AHP-puln). Dut. **Apples.**

äppelfläsk (EHP-pehl-flehsk). Swe, Dan. A dish of **apples, onions,** and **Canadian bacon.**

äppelformar (EHP-pehl-FOR-mar). Swe. **Apple muffins.**

äppelkaka med vaniljsås (EH-perl-kaa-kah mayd vah-NILY-soass). Swe. **Apple** cake with **vanilla custard.**

appelmoes (AHP-pul-moos). Dut. **Applesauce.**

äppelmos (ehp-lay-MOOS). Swe. **Applesauce.**

appelsap (AHP-pul-sahp). Dut. **Cider.**

appelsiini (AHP-pay-lseeni). Fin. **Orange.**

appelsiinimehua (AHP-pay-lseeni-MAY-hoon). Fin. **Orange** juice.

appelsinsaft (ah-berl-SEEN-sahft). Dan, Nor. **Orange** juice.

appeltaart (AHP-pul-tahrt). Dut. **Apple** cake.

appelvin (EHP-lay-veen). Swe. **Apple cider.**

Appenzell (AHP-en-zell). Ger. A whole-milk firm buttery, piquant **cheese** of cow's milk made in large flat, 12-inch wheels in Switzerland; it is straw-colored with holes and a brownish-yellow rind.

Appenzellerbitter (AHP-pen-zehl-er-beht-ter). Ger. A Swiss flowery **liqueur.**

Appetitost (Ah-peh-TEE-toast). Dan. A semi-soft **cheese** made from buttermilk; has a nutlike flavor; sometimes contains caraway.

appetizer (ahp-eh-TI-zohr). USA. A food or drink that stimulates the appetite and is usually served before a meal.

apple (AHP-pul). USA. **Fruit** of the apple tree that may be eaten raw or cooked, made into **sauce, preserves,** or juice, and used in cooking and **baking.** Some comon varieties include Baldwin, Cortland, Gravenstein, Jonathan, and McIntosh, which are all-purpose apples; Delicious, Golden Delicious, and Winesap, which are table apples; and Rome Beauty and York Imperial, which are cooking apples.

äpple (EHP-ler). Swe. **Apple.**

apple brown betty (AHP-pul brown BEHT-tee). USA. A dessert of layered **apples** and buttered crumbs.

apple butter (AHP-pul BUHT-er). USA. A **preserve** of **apples** that has been slowly cooked for a long time until reduced to a spicy, thick, dark spread.

apple charlotte (AHP-pul CHAHR-laht). USA. A dessert of cooked **apples** and bread slices; of French origins.

apple pandowdy (AHP-pul pahn-DOW-dee). USA. A homely, humble dish of spiced, sliced **apples** covered with a crust.

apple schnitz (AHP-pul schnetz). USA. Dried **apple** slices used in Pennsylvania German cooking.

apple snow (AHP-pul snoa). USA. A once-popular dessert of **egg** whites, **sugar, applesauce,** and served with whipped **cream** or **custard sauce.**

applejack (AHP-pul-jahk). USA. A **brandy** distilled from fermented **cider.**

applesauce (AHP-pul-saus). USA. A **purée** of **apples, sugar,** and usually spices.

apricot (AP-ri-coht). USA. Orange-colored fruit of the apricot tree, resembling the **peach** and **plum** in flavor.

aprikos (ah-pri-KOOS). Swe. **Apricot.**

Aprikosen (Ahp-ree-KOAZ-zern). Ger. **Apricot.**

a puntino (ah poon-TEE-noa). Ita. Medium well-done; describing the degree of cooking of meat.

aquavit (ah-kar-VEET). Nor, Swe. A strong, colorless liquor distilled from **grain** or **potatoes** flavored with **caraway,** served very cold as an **appetizer** or with meals.

arabic gum (AHR-ah-bihk guhm). USA. See **gum arabic.**

Arabica (ah-RAB-i-kah). USA. Fine Columbian **coffee;** first discovered in Arabia; today, the finest coffee available.

arachide (ah-rah-szwid). Fre. **Peanut.**

arachide (ah-RAH-kee-day). Ita. **Peanuts.**

arachis huile (ah-rah-szwis weel). Fre. **Peanut oil.**

aragosta (ah-rah-GOS-stah). Ita. Spiny **lobster.**

arak (A-ra). Ara. A strong, **anise**-flavored **liqueur.**

arán (ar-ANN). Iri. **Bread.**

arán coirce (ar-ANN KUR-ka). Iri. **Oat bread.**

arán cruitbneachta (ar-ANN krih-NAKH-ta). Iri. **Wheat bread.**

arán donn (ar-ANN dunn). Iri. Brown **bread.**

arán prátí (ar-ANN PRA-tee). Iri. **Potato bread.**

arán rósta (ar-ANN RAW-sta). Iri. Toast.

arància (ah-RAHN-chah). Ita. **Orange.**

aranygaìuska (O-rrohn-gol-loosh-koa). Hun. Sweet **dumpling.**

araq (AH-rok). Ara. **Anise**-flavored wine.

arare (ah-lah-la). Jap. A small, crispy wheat **cracker** that can be sweet or savory with **soy sauce, sesame, seaweed.**

arbi (AHLR-bee). Ind. Indian starchy root **vegetable.**

Arborio rice (ar-boh-REE-oh RIS). Ita. Short, fat-grained Italian **rice,** used for **risotto.**

Arbroath smokies (AR-brohth SMO-kees). Sco. Small **haddock** that are gutted, **salted,** and **smoked,** but not split until **broiling** before serving.

Arbuckle's (AHR-buck-uhls). USA. A name synonymous with **coffee** in the Old West, much as Kleenex™ is for tissue today.

arbuz (ahr-BOOZ). Rus. **Watermelon.**

archiduc (ahr-schwe-dehk). Fre. Seasoned with **paprika** and blended with **cream.**

Ardennes Hervé (AHR-dehnz Er-vay). Bel. A velvet-smooth **dessert cheese.**

ardishawki (ah-dee-SHO-kee). Ara. **Artichoke.**

arenque (ah-REHN-kayss). Spa, Por. **Herring.**

Argenteuil (ar-zjen-teel). Fre. **Garnished** with **asparagus.**

arhar dal (ahr-HAHR dahl). Ind. Yellow lentils.

aringa (ah-REENG-gah). Ita. **Herring.**

arista (ah-REES-tah). Ita. **Roast loin** of **pork,** usually seasoned with a mixture of **garlic, pepper,** and **rosemary.**

arlésienne (ahrl-ehs-yehng). Fre. A **garnish** containing **tomatoes.**

armadillo (ahr-mah-DEHL-lo). USA. An armored-plated mammal, mostly of the Southwest, whose meat is rarely eaten in the United States today, except for some westerners who consider it an unusual delicacy to be stewed.

Armagnac (ahr-mahg-yahk). Fre. A dry, smooth, dark, aromatic **brandy.**

Armavir (Ah-mah-veer). Rus. A sour-milk **cheese** made in the western Caucasus from ewe's milk and sour **buttermilk** or whey; ripened in a warm place.

Arme Ritter (AHR-mee REET-ter). Ger. **French toast.**

Armenian Bole (ar-MEHN-e-uhn Bol). USA. Ferric oxide, an additive used to color food.

Armenian cucumber (ar-MEHN-e-uhn KU-kuhm-ber). USA. A coiled-shape **cucumber** 10–18 inches long, with a mellow-sweet taste, ridges, and edible skin.

Armenian wax pepper chili (ar-MEHN-e-uhn wahx PEHP-per chihl-ee). USA. Elongated, shiny yellow **chili pepper** with a mild, sweet taste; used fresh or **pickled.**

armorlcalne (ahr-mor-ree-kehn). Fre. In the Breton way; with **brandy,** white wine, **onion, tomatoes, herbs.**

aromatic (ahr-oh-MAH-tik). USA. A pleasantly scented plant or **herb** used to flavor food or drink.

aromatic rice (ahr-oh-MAH-tik RIS). USA. **Rice** with a natural aroma and flavor similar to that of roasted **popcorn** or **nuts;** fragrant rice.

arnab (ARR-nahb). Ara. **Rabbit.**

arrack (A-ra). Ara. A strong **anise**-flavored **liqueur;** same as **arak.**

arraia (ah-RAI-ah). Por. **Skate,** ray.

arrôs (ah-ROHSS). Por. **Rice.**

arroser (ah-roh-zer). Fre. To **baste** or moisten.

arrosto (ahr-ROA-stoa). Ita. **Roast,** roasted.

arrowroot (AHR-row-root). USA. An easily digested flour or starch used as a thickening agent in **soups** and **gravies** that remains clear when cooked; sometimes called Chinese potato.

arruz (ah-RROS). Spa. **Rice.**

arroz blanco (ah-RRROS BLAHN-koh). Spa. Plain boiled white **rice.**

arroz con leche (ah-RRROS kohn LEH-cheh). Spa. **Rice pudding.**

arroz con pollo (ah-RRROS kohn POH-yoh). Mex. A dish of **chicken** with **rice, tomatoes, peas,** or **asparagus,** cooked together.

arroz refogado (ah-RRROS ree-foh-GAH-dohz). Por. Savory **rice.**

arsekka (ahr-SEHK-kah). Ita. **Mussel.**

arselle (ahr-SEHL-lay). Ita. **Scallops, a mollusk.**

ärter (AER-toor). Swe. **Peas.**

ärter med flask (AER-toor med flesk). Swe. Yellow **pea soup.**

artichaut (ahr-tee-shoa). Fre. **Artichoke.**

artichoke (R-tee-chok). USA. Globe or French; bud of a thistle plant, served **boiled** with leaves pulled off, dipped into **sauce,** and the tender bottom portion eaten.

Artischocke (ar-tee-sho-KE). Ger. **Artichoke.**

artisjok (AHR-tee-schok). Dut. **Artichoke.**

ärtsoppa (AERT-sop-pah). Swe. Yellow **pea soup** with smoked **salt pork,** traditionally served on Thursday in winter.

arugula (ah-roo-GOO-lah). Ita. A peppery, piquant, aromatic salad **lettuce**-type **herb** loved by Italians; also called **roquette, rugola,** and **misticanza,** but not to be confused with a poisonous weed called **rocket.**

arum root (ah-room root). Jap. A root used to make a translucent **cake** called **konnyaku** and translucent noodles called **shirataki.**

arwa chawal (AHR-wa CHAH-vahl). Ind. Long grain **rice.**

Asadero (Oh-sah-DEH-ro). Mex. A white braided **cheese** that melts easily; the name *asadero* means "fit for baking"; also called *Oaxaco.*

asado (ah-SAHR-doh). Spa. **Roasted** or **broiled.**

asadura (ah-sah-DOO-rah). Spa. **Offal;** liver, **lights,** and **chitterlings.**

asafetida (ah-sah-feh-TEE-dah). Ind. A brown, smelly resin used in small quanities in cooking partly for flavor and mostly for its digestive properties.

asakusa nori (ah-SAH-koo-sah NOH-lei). Jap. Crisp, paper-thin, edible **seaweed;** sea **lettuce.**

asar (ah-SAHR). Mex. To **roast** or **broil.**

asciutta (ahs-chee-OOT-toa).   Ita. A dry **pasta** that can be served stuffed or in a **sauce.**

ascorbic acid (ah-SCOR-bek AHS-ehd).   USA. Vitamin C; used as an **antioxidant** to retard spoilage and to preserve the red color of fresh or preserved meats.

Ashley bread (ASH-lee brehd).   USA. A southern batter **bread** made with **rice flour,** similar to **spoon bread.**

Asiago d'Allevo (Ah-zee-AA-goa d'Ahl-LEH-voa).   Ita. A cheese made of skim milk and aged up to two years; it is pale yellow and smooth, with holes and a thin brownish rind.

Asian pear (A-zuhn pehr).   USA. Apple-like in shape; skin may be green yellow or russet; crisp like an **apple;** juicy flavor of a **pear;** eaten fresh or **baked;** the oldest cultivated pear known.

asier (ah-SEE-yor).   Dan. Sweet-sour **pickled cucumber garnish.**

Asin (Ah-zehn).   Ita. A sour-**milk,** washed-curd **cheese;** soft, whitish, buttery; also called Water cheese.

asparagi (as-SPAH-rah-jee).   Ita. **Asparagus.**

asparagus (ah-SPAR-ah-gus).   USA. A perennial plant of the lily family widely cultivated for its green young shoots that have minute scale-like leaves. White asparagus is regular asparagus that is heavily mulched before cutting to prevent it from ever getting the sunlight that causes it to turn green.

asparagus beans (ah-SPAR-ah-gus bens).   USA. Oriental **green bean** that grows about 12–15 inches long with flavor somewhat stronger than ordinary green beans. Also called **long beans, yard-long beans.**

asparges (ah-SPAHRS).   Dan. **Asparagus.**

asparges (as-SPAHR-ggerss).   Nor. **Asparagus.**

aspargesbønner (ah-SPAHR-ggerss-BURN-nerr).   Nor. **String beans.**

aspartame (AHS-pahr-tahme).   USA. Artificial sweetener that is 200 times sweeter than **sugar** and tastes very much like sugar.

asperge (ahs-spehr-rez).   Fre. **Asparagus.**

aspergesoep (ahs-PEHR-zhuh soop).   Dut. **Asparagus soup.**

aspic (ahs-pehk).   Fre. A gelatinous substance used in molds of decorative shapes in which slices or pieces of food are placed.

aspide (AHS-pee-duh). Por. **Aspic.**

assado (ah-SAH-doh). Por. **Roast.**

assaisonnement (ahs-eh-zon-mehn). Fre. Seasoning, **condiment,** or **dressing.**

Assam (ahs-SAHN). Ind. A **tea** from India that is strong and pungent, used to blend with milder teas.

assiette anglaise (ahs-zjet ahn-glez) Fre. Plate of assorted cold meats.

assiette volantes (ahs-zjet vo-lahn-tehs). Fre. The small entrees and **hors d'oeuvres** that a plate will hold.

Asturias (ahs-TOU-ree-ahs). Spa. A strong sharp-flavored **cheese** from Spain.

asupara (ah-SOO-pah-prah). Jap. **Asparagus.**

ásványvizet (AHSH-vahn-vee-zeht). Hun. **Mineral water.**

ata (AH-tah). Ind. **Chappati flour;** very finely ground **whole wheat flour** of low **gluten,** used in making Indian breads.

atemoyua (ah-tee-MOU-yah). USA. A gray-green, thick-skinned, heart-shaped **fruit** with a pudding-like pulp with black seeds; very sweet taste, slightly juicy, melting texture.

athénienne (ah-tee-neen). Fre. Garnished with **onion, eggplant, tomato,** and sweet red **pepper** fried in **olive oil.**

atholl brose (AH-thohl broz). Sco. A famous drink of heather **honey,** whiskey, and the creamy liquor of strained **oatmeal paste;** recipe is at least 500 years old.

atole (ah-TOH-leh). Mex. A thick beverage made with **masa** and flavored with **sugar, fruit, chocolate,** and sometimes **chili.**

attelet (aht-teh-leh). Fre. A small **skewer** with an ornamental top used to thread **garnishments** for decorating hot or cold dishes served in a grand style.

attereau (aht-teh-roa). Fre. **Skewer;** refers to alternating food pieces on a skewer, usually coated in **batter** and **deep-fat fried.**

attorta (aht-TOAR-tah). Ita. Delectable pastry filled with toasted **almonds, chocolate,** and candied **fruit.**

atum (a-TOOM). Por. **Tuna** fish.

atún (ah-TOON). Spa. **Tuna** fish.

Auberginen (oa-ber-ZHEE-nern). Ger. **Eggplant.**

aubergine (oa-BEHR-zheen). Fre, Ita, Bri. **Eggplant.**

au beurre (oa burr). Fre. Cooked in or with **butter sauce** or browned **butter.**

au bleu (oa blu). Fre. Plain **boiled;** used with reference to freshwater fish.

Auflauf (AUF-lauf). Ger. **Souffle.**

au four (oa fur). Fre. **Baked** in the oven.

Aufschnitt (AUF-schneht). Ger. Cold cuts.

au gras (oa graws). Fre. Cooked in fat or a rich meat **gravy.**

au gratin (oa graw-tehn). Fre. Made with crumbs, scalloped, often with a **cheese sauce.**

augurken (ow-KHOOR-kuh). Dut. **Pickles.**

au jus (oa zhus). Fre. Served with the meat's natural juices.

au lait (oa leh). Fre. Served with added **milk.**

au maigre (oa meg-re). Fre. Served without meat.

au naturel (oa nat-eh-rel). Fre. Plainly cooked or served raw.

aurore (oa-ror). Fre. **Béchamel sauce** made pink with **tomato puree.**

au ruban (oa rew-bahng). Fre. Describes **sugar syrup** during the **crystallization** process when the syrup reaches the stage of forming a ribbon when dropped from a spoon.

Ausbackteig (AUS-bahk-tahg). Ger. **Dough; paste.**

Auster (AUS-ter). Ger. **Oyster.**

autrichienne (oa-tree-shyen). Fre. Austrian style, flavored with **caraway seeds** and **paprika.**

Auvergne (Oh-vehr-nenr). Fre. A blue-veined cow's-milk cheese, sometimes called Bleu d'Auvergne.

aux croutons (oa kroo-toa). Fre. Food served with dried bread cubes, the **croutons.**

avêia (ah-VAY-yah). Por. **Oatmeal.**

aveline (ahv-eh-leen). Fre. **Hazelnut, filbert.**

avella (ah-VEHL-lah). Ita. **Hazelnut.**

avellanas (ahb-hay-LYAH-nahss). Spa. **Filberts, hazelnuts.**

aves (AH-vehs). Mex. Birds.

aves de corral (AH-vehs da kah-RAHL). Mex. **Chickens, poultry.**

avgolemono (ahv-gho-LEH-mohn-no). Gre. A soup made with **egg** yolks and **lemon** juice. Also can be a **sauce.**

avocado (av-oh-KAH-do). USA. A dark green pear-shaped **fruit** with a large pit and pulpy yellow-green flesh, served **peeled, sliced, cubed, puréed** in **salads** and **dips.**

avond koffie (AH-vuns KAWF-fee). Dut. Evening **coffee** served with **cookies, cake.**

avond thee (AH-vuns tay). Dut. Evening **tea** served with **cookies, cake.**

awabi (AH-wah-bee). Jap. **Abalone.**

Awenda bread (AH-wehn-dah brehd). USA. A bread of American Indian origin made of **hominy grits.**

ayu (AH-yoo). Jap. Freshwater **trout.**

azafrán (ah-thah-FRAHN). Spa. **Saffron.**

azeda (ah-ZAY-dah). Por. Sour.

azedinha (ah-zay-DEE-nyah). Por. **Sorrel.**

Azeitão (ah-zay-TAHNG). Por. Rich, "fat" **cheese** with creamy **paste;** made of sheep's milk.

azeite (a-ZAYT). Por. **Olive oil.**

azeitonas (ah-ZAY-toh-nahss). Por. **Olives.**

azijn (ah-ZEYN). Dut. **Vinegar.**

azúcar (ah-THOO-kahr). Spa. **Sugar.**

azuki (ah-ZOO-kee). Jap. A dried **bean** prized for its sweet flavor; when **powdered** it is used in **confections** and **puddings** in China and Japan.

azyme (ah-zim). Fre. Unleavened **bread.**

B

baadhinjaana (bi-din-GEHN). Ara. **Eggplant.**

baak guo (bahk gwoah). Chi. **Ginkgo nut;** ginnan; the **fruit** of the mature female ginko tree; raw **nuts** are white but turn pale green when cooked; mild flavor; eaten **raw, grilled, deep fried,** or in one-pot dishes.

baars (bahrs). Dut. **Bass.**

baba (bah-bah). Fre. **Baba au rhum.**

baba au rhum (bah-bah oh rum). Fre. A **yeast cake** with **raisins** baked in a cylindrical mold and soaked with a rum **syrup.**

babaco (BAH-bah-ko). NZe. A **fruit** with the appearance of a large star and a flavor similar to **strawberries** with a hint of **papaya** and **pineapple;** when ripe its skin is a soft gold; eat **raw** or cooked.

baba ghanoush (BAH-bah gehn-OOSCH). Ara. **Eggplant purée** flavored with **lemon, olive oil, garlic,** and crushed **sesame** seeds called **tahini.**

babao fàn (ba-bao fan). Chi. Glutinous **rice pudding.**

baba rannouj (Bah-bah rahn-NOOG). Ara. **Roast eggplant** with **tahini.**

babbelaars (BAH-bah-lahrs). Dut. Buttercake.

babeurre (bah-buhr). Fre. **Buttermilk.**

babka (bahb-kah). Fre. **Baba.**

baby beef (BA-bee bef). USA. Meat from a calf younger than 12 months old.

bacalao (bah-kah-LAH-oh). Spa. **Salt cod, codfish.**

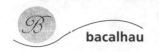

bacalhau (ba-cal-YAH-oo). Por. **Salt codfish;** prepared at least 1,001 ways.

baccalà (bahk-kah-LAH). Ita. **Salt cod.**

bachelor's button (BAHCH-lohrz BUHT-tohn). USA. A **cookie** with a **cherry** on top.

Bachforelle (bahk-fo-REH-lo). Ger. Brook **trout.**

backen (BAH-kern). Ger. To **bake.**

Bäckerei (beh-ker-RIGH). Ger. Pastries.

Backhuhn (BAHK-hoon). Ger. **Chicken** rolled in bread crumbs, then **fried.**

backobst (BAHK-obst). Ger. **Dried fruit.**

backpflaume (BAHK-pflauma). Ger. **Prune.**

Backsteiner (BAHK-stin-ehr). Ger. A Bavarian **cheese** that is similar to **Limburger** cheese, but firmer in texture.

Backwerk (BAHK-verk). Ger. **Cakes,** pastries.

baclava (bak-LEH-wah). Ara. **Baklava.**

bacon (BA-kuhn). USA. A cut from the side of **pork;** can be **fresh, cured,** and/or **smoked;** generally used **sliced.**

bacon (ba-kohn). Fre. **Salt pork.**

bacon og aeg (BA-kohn oa ehg). Dan. **Bacon** and **egg.**

badaam (bah-DAHM). Ind. **Almond.**

bade (ba-RRAY). Ind. Small **doughnut**-shaped fried **bean dumpling.**

badi elaich (ba RREE eh-LIE-ee-jee). Ind. Black **cardamom** pods.

bagda jheengari (BAHG-da JEEN-ga-ree). Ind. Giant **prawns.**

bagel (BA-guhl). Jew. A **doughnut**-shaped roll that is **boiled,** then **baked,** giving it a hard crust and a soft interior.

bagesse (bahzh-jehs). Fre. **Sugar cane.**

baghar (bag-HAAR). Ind. Spice-perfume **butter** used for flavoring **yogurt, dals, vegetables, relishes,** and some meats.

bagna (bah-nah). Fre. Beach **bread;** a crusty loaf of bread coated with olive oil and filled with hard-boiled **eggs, anchovies, tomatoes, onions, sweet peppers, radishes,** ripe **olives;** prepared by hotels and restaurants along the Riviera to be eaten on the sands as a picnic lunch.

bagña cauda (BAA-nah KAH-oo-dah). Ita. A **garlic** and **anchovy sauce** served warm over **raw vegetables.**

Bagnes (bah-nyees). Fre. A hard, delicately flavored **cheese** of Switzerland.

Bagozzo (Bah-gots-soh). Ita. A hard, yellow, rather sharp **cheese** whose surface is often colored red; similar to **Reggiano** and **Parmigiano.**

baguette (bahg-eht). Fre. A long, thin loaf of French bread.

bagún (ba-GOON). Iri. **Bacon.**

baht ghok (baht goak). Chi. **Star anise.**

bái cài (bay tsay). Chi. **Chinese cabbage, bok choy.**

bái cù (baak chou). Chi. White **vinegar.**

bai fan (baak fahn). Chi. Plain **rice.**

bai fun (baak fuhn). Chi. Translucent **noodles.**

bái-án-di-jiu (bai-laan-dee-jyoe). Chi. **Brandy.**

baigan (BAYN-guhn). Ind. **Eggplant.**

bain-marie (banc-mah-ree). Fre. A container to provide a hot-water bath for keeping cooked food hot.

bainne (BAN-ya). Iri. **Milk.**

bainne gabhair (BAN-ya GO-wayr). Iri. Goat's **milk.**

bajai halászlé (BO-yo-ee HO-llaas-lay). Hun. Fish and **potato soup.**

ba jiao (bah jee-aw). Chi. Seed from the magnolia family with **anise** flavor; **Chinese anise; star anise.**

bake (bak). USA. To cook by dry heat, usually in an oven; when applied to meat is referred to as **roasting.**

bake blind (bak blind). USA. To partially **bake** a pastry shell unfilled and weighted.

Baked Alaska (bakd Ah-LAHS-kah). USA. **Dessert** of ice cream set on sponge **cake,** covered with **meringue,** and quickly **browned** in a very hot oven.

baked custard (bakd KUS-tahrd). USA. **Custard baked** in an oven, usually in heavy ceramic cup. Also called **cup custard.**

bakelse (BAA-kerl-see). Swe. Pastry, fancy **cake.**

Baker's Cheese (BAY-kerz chez). USA. A special sour **cheese** used by bakers, similar to **cottage cheese,** but smoother and softer.

baking chocolate (BA-kehng CHOK-o-leht). USA. The bitter, or unsweetened, **chocolate** used in pastries and **confections.**

baking powder (BA-kehng POW-der). USA. A leavening agent for pastry goods and quick **breads.**

baking soda (BA-kehng SO-dah). USA. Sodium bicarbonate; a leavening agent used with acid such as sour **milk.**

baklava (BAHK-lah-vah). Ara. A sweet pastry made with **phyllo dough,** chopped **nuts, honey,** and **butter,** usually cut into diamond shapes.

bakonyi betyárleves (BOK-kawn-yee BEHT-yaar-leh-vehsh). Hun. **Soup** Bakony style: a mix of **chicken,** beef chunks, thin **noodles, mushrooms,** and **vegetables,** richly spiced. Also called Outlaw soup.

bakonyi gombamártás (BOK-kawn-yee GAWM-bom-maar-taash). Hun. **Mushroom soup.**

balachan (BAH-lah-chahn). Mal. A salty, pungent Malaysian condiment of fermented **shrimp** or other seafood. Also spelled *balchan.*

ballottine (bahl-lot-teen). Fre. Stuffed boneless meat, **poultry,** fish, or **game** that is rolled into a bundle.

baloney (bah-LO-nee). USA. An American variation of **bologna;** not to be confused with Italian bologna.

balsamella (bahl-sah-MAL-lah). Ita. **Béchamel sauce.**

balsamic vinegar (bahl-SAHM-ic VEHN-eh-gar). USA. A very fine Italian **vinegar** with a dark, mellow, subtle flavor.

balsam pear (BAHL-sum pahr). USA. **Bitter melon,** a Chinese fruit.

balut (bah-oot). Phi. A fertilized duck **egg** nearly ready to hatch, a delicacy to Filipinos.

bamboo shoots (BAHM-boo shuht). USA. **Sprouts** of young bamboo plants, used in Chinese cooking.

bami (BAH-mee). Dut. Indonesian **noodle** dish made of **pork, shrimp, eggs, onions,** and **vegetables** such as **green beans, peas, cabbage, cauliflower, leeks, celery;** various combinations can be expected.

bami goreng (BAH-mee GOR-eng). Ino. **Noodles** used to replace **rice** in a recipe.

bamyi (BAM-ya). Ara. **Okra.**

banan (bah-NAHN). Rus. **Banana.**

banán (BO-nnaan). Hun. **Banana.**

banana (BAH-nah-nah). Jap. **Banana.**

banana (bah-NAH-nah). USA. Tropical **fruit** that is long, usually with yellow skin; grows in clusters; use **raw** or cooked.

banana fig (bah-NAH-nah feeg). USA. **Banana** slices that are sun-dried without preservative, dark and sticky, resembling figs in appearance.

banana pepper (bah-NAH-nah PEHP-pehr). USA. A mild, yellow-green pepper, three to four inches long; good in **salads** or filled with a savory stuffing.

banana squash (bah-NAH-nah squash). USA. A winter **squash** shaped like a banana; long, cylindrical shape with a pale orange to creamy white exterior and orange to yellow flesh with a hearty, mildly sweet flavor; can weigh 10–70 pounds.

banane (bah-NAA-nah). Ita, Ger. **Banana.**

banane (bah-nan). Fre. **Banana.**

Banbury (BAHN-bur-ree). Bri. A soft, rich **cheese** of England; cylindrical in shape and about one inch thick.

Banbury cake (BAHN-bur-ree kak). Bri. An oval flaky pastry filled with **currants, lemon** peel, and spices.

bancha (bahn-CHAH). Jap. A coarse, cheap grade of green **tea.**

bànbàng ji (bong-bong jee). Chi. Cold **chicken** spiced with **sesame.**

banger (BAHN-jehr). Bri. Slang for **sausage** made of ground **pork** and bread crumbs.

banira (bah-NEE-rah). Jap. **Vanilla** (the flavor), as **vanilla ice cream.**

bankebiff (BAHN-keh-biff). Nor. Beefsteak **browned** in lots of butter, then simmered in **stock.**

bankekød (BON-kay-kerth). Dan. **Stewed** beef.

banket letter (bahn-KEHT LEH-tehr). Dut. French flake pastry with **almond paste** filling.

bannock (BAHN-uhk). Sco. A large, round **cake** of **barley, wheat,** or **oatmeal.**

Banon (bahn-no). Fre. A French firm sheep **cheese,** sprinkled with **brandy** and wrapped in fresh **grape leaves.**

bao (ba-aw). Chi. **Abalone.**

baobab (ba-OH-bahb). Afr. A **fruit** called **monkey bread** from a tree in central Africa.

bap (bahp). Bri. A small round loaf of soft, white bread eaten at breakfast in Scotland and England.

Baptist cake (BAHP-tihst kak). USA. A New England **deep-fried doughnut**-like **confection** made of **yeast** dough. Also known as **hustlers, holy pokes,** and **huff juffs.**

baqdunis (bahk-DOO-nees). Ara. **Parsley.**

baqlawa (bahk-LAH-wah). Ara. Var. **baklava.**

baqli (BAHK-lee). Ara. **Herbs.**

bar (bahr). Fre. **Sea bass.**

bär (bah). Swe. **Berry.**

bara jheenga (BAH-ra JEEN-gah). Ind. **Lobster.**

bárányhúst (BAA-raan-yhoost). Hun. Lamb.

baraquille (bah-rah-kee-yuh). Fre. A triangular stuffed pastry **hors d'oeuvre.**

barashek (bah-RAH-shash). Rus. Lamb.

barbabietola (bar-bah-bee-EH-to-lah). Ita. **Beetroot, beets.**

Barbacena (Bahr-bah-CHEE-nah). Brz. A firm white **cheese.**

barbacoa (bahr-bah-KO-ah). Mex. Meat cooked in a **barbecue** pit.

Barbados cherry (Bahr-BA-dohs CHEH-ree). USA. **Acerola.**

Barbados sugar (bahr-BA-dohs SCHOO-gahr). USA. **Brown sugar.**

barbecue, barbeque (BAHR-bee-qu). USA. to **roast** or **broil** on a rack over hot coals; usually in a highly seasoned **vinegar sauce.**

Barberey (or Barberry) (Bahr-beh-ree). Fre. French **cheese** similar to **Camembert,** but more pungent; sometimes called *Fromage de Troyes.*

barberry (BAHR-beh-ree). USA. Red **berries** from the barberry tree that are **pickled** or ripened and made into preserves, syrup, and wine; acidic. Also called *Oregon grapes.*

barbo (bahr-boo). Nor. Barbel, a freshwater fish of the **carp** family.

barbue (bahr-bew). Fre. A European **flatfish** of the **flounder** family.

bardé (bahr-day). Fre. **Larded;** covered with **salt pork** or slices of **bacon.**

barfi (BAHR-fee). Ind. **Fudge.**

barigoule (bah-ree-gouw). Fre. **Artichokes blanched** and stuffed, wrapped in **bacon, braised** in white wine, and served with the reduced **broth.**

barista (bahr-RIH-stah). Ind. Crisp **fried onion** shreds used in Moslem cooking.

bar-le-Düc (bahr-luh-duk). Fre. A **preserve** originally made of selected whole white **currants** seeded by hand with the aid of knitting needles; now **gooseberries, strawberries,** or other **berries** are used; often served with the **cheese** course of a meal.

barley (BAHR-lee). USA. A **grain** used in **soups,** as a **cereal,** and for making **malt** for **beer, ale,** and whiskey.

barley flour (BAHR-lee flowr). USA. A **flour** made by pulverizing **barley** grains.

barley pearl (BAHR-lee perl). USA. Polished **barley** used in cooking.

barm (bahrm). USA. **Yeast;** formed on fermenting **malt** liquors.

barmbrack (bahrm-brahk). Iri. **Bread** speckled with dried **fruits.**

baron (BAHR-ohn). Bri. An extra large cut of beef that includes part of the **ribs** and both **sirloins.**

Baron (bah-rowng). Fre. The **saddle** and two legs of lamb.

barquette (bahr-keht). Fre. A boat-shaped pastry shell filled and baked as an **hors d'oeuvre** or sweet; also **vegetable** cases for stuffing, such as **squash.**

basala (BA-sol). Ara. **Onions.**

Basbousa (bas-BOO-sa). Ara. **Semolina** baked in the oven, often with **nuts,** and steeped in **syrup.**

bascoutou (bahs-KOO-tee). Ara. Sweet **crackers.**

baskoot (bahs-KOOT). Ara. **Biscuit, cookie.**

basil (BAZ-uhl). USA. A sweet, pungent **herb** of the **mint** family much used in Mediterranean cooking; the basis of **pesto.** Varieties include

    African basil (camphor-like scent),

cinnamon basil (medium leaves, wonderful cinnamon aroma),

clove basil (clove pungency),

holy basil (spicy clove scent, used in the cuisines of India),

lemon basil (sharp citrus essence),

lettuce leaf basil (fruity scent),

opal basil (heavy perfume scent),

purple basil (leaves add color as well as a sweet, lavender perfume essence to a salad),

sweet basil (fruity fragrance).

basilic (bah-see-leek).   Fre. Food in a sauce seasoned with **basil.**

basilico (bah-ZEE-lee-koa).   Ita. **Basil.**

basmati rice (baz-MAH-tee rice).   Ind. A long-grain **rice** that is aromatic and delicate; flavor, texture, and aroma complement western and European foods.

bass (bahs).   USA. A name for many unrelated fish.

baste (bast).   USA. To moisten with a liquid such as melted fat, meat drippings, or water at intervals during cooking.

baster (BAS-stur).   USA. A ladle, cup, or syringe used to pour liquid or fat over cooking food.

básu oíngguo (ba-sse ping-guo).   Chi. Hot candied **apples.**

batarde (bah-tahrd).   Fre. A **sauce** of white **roux** with water, **egg yolks, butter,** and **lemon** juice; means "bastard," for its indirect relationship to other classic sauces.

batata (ba-TAA-tis).   Ara. **Potato.**

batatas (ba-TA-tash).   Por. **Potatoes.**

Batavian endive (bah-TA-vee-un EHN-dive).   USA. Similar to **curly endive** with broader, paler, less highly crimped leaves, and less bitter. Also known as *escarole* or **chicory escarole.**

Bath cheese (bahth chez).   Bri. A delicate-flavored, ripened, soft **cream cheese** made in the City of Bath, England.

batinjan (bi-din-GEHN).   Ara. **Eggplants.**

baton, batonnet (bah-toh, bah-toh-nah).   Fre. Little sticks of **vegetables** or **potatoes;** larger than **julienne.**

bat out (baht awt).   USA. To flatten slices of raw meat with a cutlet bat.

Battelmatt (Baht-tehl-mout). Swi. A **cheese** somewhat like **Tilsiter** in flavor with the same kind of holes as **Emmentaler,** but smaller and softer.

batter (BAHT-tuhr). USA. A mixture of liquid and **flour** that can be poured, spooned, or dipped.

batter bread (BAHT-tuhr brehd). USA. An unsweetened **bread** from southern United States made of white **cornmeal** and **eggs.** Also called **spoon bread.**

batter-dip (BAHT-tur-dip). USA. Pieces of food that are dipped in **batter,** then **baked** or **fried.**

battiykha (baht-TEEKH). Ara. **Watermelon.**

battuto (bah-TOO-toa). Ita. A base for **stews** and **soups: onion, garlic, celery,** and **herbs,** cooked in oil.

baudroie (boa-drwah). Fre. **Monkfish.**

bauern (BOW-errn). Ger. Peasant or country-style.

Bauernbrot (BOW-errn-brot). Ger. Peasant rye **bread.**

Bauernfrühstück (BOW-errn-fry-styk). Ger. A lunch dish of **fried potatoes** topped with scrambled **eggs, ham,** and **cucumber.**

Bauernomelett (BOW-errn-ohm-leht). Ger. **Bacon** and **onion omelet.**

Bauernschmaus (BOW-errn-schmowss). Ger. Austrian dish of **sauer-kraut, pork, sausages,** and **dumplings.**

Bauernsuppe (BOW-ween-zupp-e). Ger. A peasant **soup** of **bacon, vegetables,** and **legumes.**

bauletti (ba-oo-LEHT-tee). Ita. **Veal** roll-ups; **saltimbocca.**

Baumkuchen (baum-KU-zon). Ger. A Christmas **cake** traditionally baked tall in may layers to resemble the rings of a tree trunk and iced with **chocolate** to resemble bark.

Bavarian Cream (bah-VAHR-ree-ahn krem). USA. A French dessert of cold **custard** and **gelatin** with whipped **cream** folded in as it begins to stiffen.

Bavarois (bav-ar-waz). Fre. Bavarian.

bavaroise (bav-vah-rwaz). Fre. A sweetened **tea** drink enriched with **egg** yolks, **milk,** and **citrus.**

bavette (bah-veht). Fre. **Flank** steak; **sirloin tip.**

bavosa (bah-VOA-sah). Ita. Liquid in the center, reference to a **frittata** or **omelet.**

bawd (bawd). Sco. **Hare, rabbit.**

bayd (beyd). Ara. **Eggs.**

Bayer (BAH-yerr). Nor. A dark-colored, light-tasting **beer.**

bay leaf (bay lef). USA. The dried leaf of the European **laurel.**

Bayrischer Bierkäse (Ba-RISH-er BEER-kaz-zah). Ger. A Bavarian **cheese** that is usually dunked in **beer** before eating.

bazilla (bi-SIHL-la). Ara. **Peas.**

bean (ben). USA. Numerous varieties available worldwide. See specific types, i. e., **lima, green, fava,** etc.

bean curd (ben kuhrd). USA. **Tofu.**

bean flour (ben flawr). USA. **Soybean flour.**

bean sprouts (ben sprouts). USA. Tiny tender, green, young shoots of the **mung bean, alfalfa** seeds, **radish** seeds.

bean threads (ben threds). USA. Translucent **noodles** made from **mung beans** used in Chinese cooking.

beard (berd). USA. To remove the beard from **oysters** or **mussels.**

béarnaise (bay-ahr-nayz). Fre. A classic French **sauce** of reduced wine **vinegar, shallots** and **tarragon, egg** yolks, and **butter** served on **grilled** meat and fowl.

beat (bet). USA. To mix by stirring vigorously, resulting in a smooth, light, and fluffy texture.

Beaufort (boa-foa). Fre. A whole-milk **cheese** similar to **Gruyère.**

Beauges (Baugz). Fre. A **cheese** of the Tomme family; see **Tomme.**

Beaumont (Bo-mahnt). Fre. A semisoft cheese much as **Brie** and **Port du Salut.**

becasse (bay-kahss). Fre. Woodcock.

beccaccia (bayk-KAHT-chah). Ita. Woodcock.

beccafico (bech-kah-FEE-koa). Ita. **Game** birds.

béchamel sauce (bay-scha-mel saus). Fre. **Cream sauce** made with **chicken broth** instead of **milk;** one of the basic sauces.

bêche de mer (behsh dah meh). Fre. A sea slug relished for its gelatinous texture. Also called **sea cucumber.**

beckasin (bah-kah-SIN). Swe. Snipe.

bécsi heringsaláta (BAY-chee HEHR-eeng-shol-laa-to). Hun. **Herring salad** with **vinegar.**

beechnut (BECH-nuht). USA. The **fruit** of the beech tree; flavor is midway between that of the **hazelnut** and the **chestnut;** slightly astringent taste that is dispelled with **roasting.**

beechnut oil (BECH-nuht oil). USA. Oil extracted from the **beechnut;** has a distinctive, but not unpleasant flavor.

beef à la mode (bef ah lah mod). Fre. A well-**larded** large cut of beef cooked slowly in water with **vegetables,** similar to **braised** beef.

beef cotto (bef KOHT-o). USA. Low-calorie cooked **salami** that is coarse-cut; contains whole **peppercorns** as seasoning.

beef-ham (BEF-hahm). Bri. Rump of beef **salted** and **cured** like **hams.**

beef pudding (bef PUHD-eng). Bri. A meat pie that has been **boiled** or **steamed.**

beef Stroganoff (bef STROH-gah-nohf). USA. Beef strips sautéed with chopped **mushrooms** and **onions,** then thickened with **sour cream.**

beef tea (bef tee). USA. An **extract** made by stewing beef in water for several hours.

beef Wellington (bef WEHL-ehng-tuhn). USA. Beef **filet** covered with **chicken liver pâté** topped with **sauce perigueux.**

beer (behr). USA. Alcoholic beverage, amber in color, made from various **grains,** water, and **yeast.**

beet (bet). USA. A gaden plant with thick, long-stalked edible leaves and a swollen round root; also called **beetroot;** a close relative is the **gold beet.**

Beetensuppe (BET-en-zup). Ger. **Borsch.**

beetroot (bet-ruht). Bri. **Beets.**

beet sugar (bet SCHU-gahr). USA. Sucrose from the **sugar beet.**

beignets (ben-yea). Fre. **Fritters.**

beignets (ben-YEAZ). Bri. A kind of **pancake, fried** in deep fat.

beignets de bénichon (ben-yeaz dah bee-nee-shon).   Fre. Very thin Swiss **fritters**, rich with **eggs, cream,** and **kirsch.**

Beijing kao ya (bay-jing kao ya).   Chi. **Peking roast duck;** an elaborate and famous dish eaten with the fingers.

Beilagen (beil-AG-en).   Ger. Accompanying dishes.

Beinwurst (BEN-voorst).   Ger. Popular Swiss **sausage.**

békacomb gombával és rákkal (BAY-kots-awmb GAWM-baa-vol aysh RAAK-kol).   Hun. Frog legs with freshwater **crabmeat** and **mushrooms.**

bekon (BEH-kohn).   Jap. **Bacon.**

bekon to tamago (BEH-kohn oh tah-MAH-goh).   Jap. **Bacon** and **eggs.**

Bel Lago (Behl Lah-go).   Swi. A semisoft **cheese** with a delicate, distinctive flavor.

Bellelay (Bel-leh-lay).   Swi. A semisoft, buttery **cheese,** similar to **Gruyére** in flavor; sometimes called **Tête de Moine.**

Bel Paese (behl pah-AY-zay).   Ita. A semisoft, rich, creamy, mild-flavored cow's milk **cheese.**

belegtes Brot (be-LAYK-tes broat).   Ger. Open-face **sandwich.**

Belgian endive (BEHL-gjun EHN-div).   USA. A specially cultivated **chicory** whose leaves are cut off and shielded from the light so that new pale yellow leaves grow back in their characteristic cigar shape; used fresh in **salads** or **braised** in various preparations. Also called *wiltoff chicory* and *French endive.*

bellevue (behl-vu).   Fre. Food enclosed in **aspic** through which it can be plainly seen.

bell pepper (behl PEHP-ur).   USA. Large, sweet apple-shaped **green pepper** used fresh or cooked; also available in red and gold.

Belon oysters (beh-loh OY-sturs).   USA. Choice **oysters** from the river Belon.

beluga caviar (beh-LU-gah KAH-vee-ahr).   USA. Choicest Russian **caviar** from the white **sturgeon;** has largest **egg,** gray in color. Also **beluge** (Iranian).

ben cotto (bain KOT-to).   Ita. Well done, as for steak.

Bénédictine (bay-nay-dehk-tang). Fre. A **liqueur** made principally at the Abbey of Fecamp in Normandy, France.

beni shoga (beh-nee shoh-gah). Jap. **Pickled** or **vinegared ginger;** natural color is white, may be bought tinted pink or red.

benitade (beh-nee-TAH-deh). Jap. Red benitade **sprouts,** used in **salads.**

benløse fugle (BERN-lur-say FOO-lee). Nor, Dan. Beef "birds" rolled around **pork** and **onions,** with a spicy **gravy.**

Bercy (burr-cay). Fre. A sauce of white wine and fish **fumet,** or meat **glaze** and beef **marrow,** reduced with **shallots, butter,** and **parsley.**

berenjena (behr-ehn-HEH-nah). Spa. **Eggplant.**

bergamot orange (BEHR-zhah-mo OHR-ahnj). USA. Bitter, pear-shaped, very acid French **orange,** but with a very pleasant taste; oil extracted from the rind is used in **confectionery,** as well as perfumery and pharmaceuticals.

bergamot pear (BEHR-zhah-mo pehr). USA. A particular variety of **pear.**

Bergkäse (berg-KAHZ-zah). Ger. A hard, yellow **cheese** from the Bavarian Alps.

Berliner Kuhkäse (behr-LEE-ner Koo-kahz-zah). Ger. A soft hand **cheese** made of cow's milk with **caraway** seeds.

Berliner Pfannkuchen (behr-LEE-ner pfan-koo-khern). Ger. Fancy jelly **doughnuts.**

Berliner Weisse (behr-LEE-ner veissr). Ger. A pale, tart, low-alcohol **ale,** usually drunk with a dash of **raspberry syrup.**

berlingela (bay-reen-ZHEN-lah). Por. **Eggplant.**

Berlingozzo (bay-leen-GOZ-zah). Ita. **Cream cake.**

Bermuda onion (behr-MUD-dah UHN-yuhn). USA. Large, brown-skinned and mild-flavored **onion.** Also known as **Spanish onion.**

Bernarde (Behr-NAHR-dah). Ita. A **cheese** made from cow's whole milk with added goat's milk, light saffron in color; surface rubbed with dry salt.

Berner Platte (BEHR-nerr PLAH-ter). Ger. A Swiss speciality; a copious mound of **sauerkraut** or **green beans** topped with a variety of meats, such as **bacon, ham, pork** chops, **pigs feet, sausages,** or **ribs.**

berry (BEHR-ree). USA. General term for all **fruits** that contain seeds in the pulp, such as **blackberries, strawberries.** Technically, a **tomato** is a berry.

berry sugar (BEHR-ree SCHU-gahr). USA. A finer grind of granulated **sugar,** still coarse enough to discern individual crystals; best used in **meringues** and for sweetening drinks and **fruits.**

Bertolli (burr-TO-lee). Ita. A firm, pale yellow sheep's milk **cheese** with a delightfully piquant flavor.

besan (BAY-sahn). Ind. **Chickpea flour.**

beschuit (buh-SKHIRT). Dut. Holland **rusk,** double toasted.

beschuittaart (buh-SKHIRT-tahrt). Dut. **Rusk cake.**

besciamella (bay-chee-MAYL-lah). Ita. **Béchamel sauce.**

bessenvla (BEHS-sen-vlah). Dut. **Currant pudding.**

betasuppe (bay-ter-SSEW-per). Nor. **Mutton broth.**

betterave (beh-ter-rahv). Fre. **Beetroot; beets.**

beurre (berr). Fre. **Butter;** au beurre nois, "with butter sauce **browned** in a pan."

beurré (berr-ay). Fre. Buttered.

beurre blanc (berr blahnk). Fre. A white **sauce** for seafood, **poultry,** or **vegetables** made of white wine, **shallots,** and **butter.**

beurre Chivry (berr sheev-reh). Fre. **Butter** flavored with **parlsey, tarragon, chives,** and **shallots.**

beurre fondue (berr fawng-dew). Fre. Melted **butter.**

beurre manie (berr mah-neeh). Fre. Equal parts of **butter** and **flour,** kneaded into a **paste** to thicken **sauces** and **gravies; kneaded butter.**

beurre noir (berr nohr). Fre. A fish **sauce** of browned **butter, capers, parsley,** and **venegar.**

Beuschls (BOY-sherlz). Ger. Stewed calves' lungs with a sweet-sour tang; usually served with **Knödel.**

bhara (BAH-rah). Ind. Stuffed.

bharat (BHAH-raht). Ara. A blend of seasonings.

bharta (BHAR-rah). Ind. **Smoked eggplant fried** with **onions, tomatoes,** and **herbs.**

bhatoora (bheh-TOO-rah). Ind. Leavened **dough** made of **yogurt, potatoes,** and white **flour,** rolled into circles, then **deep-fried.**

bhindi (BHIN-dee). Ind. **Okra.**

bhojia (BHOO-jee-ah). Ind. Highly spiced stir-fried **vegetables.**

bhona (BOU-nah). Ind. **Fried.**

bhorji (BHOOR-jee). Ind. **Scrambled,** generally applied to **scrambled eggs.**

bianco d'uovo (bee-AHNG-koa d-WAW-vah). Ita. **Egg** white.

bianchetti (bee-ahn-KAYT-tee). Ita. **Whitebait;** fish.

bian dòu (bien doh). Chi. **Beans.**

bias (BI-uhs). USA. In a slanting manner, e.g., cutting **celery** stalks on the bias.

biatas (bee-a-tahs). Iri. **Beetroot.**

bibb lettuce (bihb LEHT-us). USA. A **salad** green of the butterhead family, considered the finest grown anywhere; the prime variety of **butterhead lettuce.**

bicarbonate of soda (bi-CAHR-boh-neht of SO-dah). USA. A leavening agent used with sour **milk.**

bicchiere (bee-kee-AY-ree). Ita. A measuring cup.

biefstuk (BEEF-sterk). Dut. **Sirloin tip** or **bottom round** of beef.

biefstuk van de haas (BEEF-sterk vahn deh hahs). Dut. **Filet mignon.**

bien cuit (byang kwee). Fre. Well done, as referring to steak.

bienenstich (byang-ah-steesh). Fre. A **glazed,** filled coffee **cake.**

bier (beer). Dut. **Beer.**

Bierkaltschale (BEHR-kahlt-scarler). Ger. Cold **beer soup;** favorite in summer.

Bierkäse (Behr-kahz-zah). Ger. **Cheeses** similar to **Limburger,** pungent, smelly; semisoft; often dissolved in beer.

Bierplinsen (BEHR-plen-zen). Ger. Cooked meats or **sausages** dipped in a **beer batter** and **deep-fried.**

Bierwurst (BEHR-voorst). Ger. A fat, reddish brown **sausage** of **pork,** pork fat, and beef.

bieten (BEE-tehn). Dut. **Beets.**

bietola (bee-ay-TO-lah). Ita. **Swiss chard.**

bietoline (bee-ay-to-LEE-nay). Ita. **Erbette;** a vegetable similar to **spinach** or **beet** greens; having an elongated smallish leaf and a slim tender green stalk.

bife (BEE-fay). Por. Beefsteak.

biff (bif). Nor. Beefsteak.

biff à la lindstrom (bif ah lah lend-STRUM). Swe. Chopped beef, similar to **hamburger** patties, but with chopped **potatoes, beets,** and **onions** mixed in.

biffstek (BEHF-stayk). Swe. Beefsteak.

Bifrost (Bee-fohst). Nor. A white goat **cheese;** both natrural and processed.

biftec (beef-TAYK). Spa. Beefsteak; sometimes spelled **bistec.**

bifteck (beef-tehk). Fre. Beefsteak.

bifuteki (bee-FOO-teh-kee). Jap. Beefsteak.

bigarade (bee-gah-rahd). Fre. A brown **sauce** for roast **duck** made of caramelized **sugar, lemon** and **orange** juice, **demi-glace,** and **stock.**

bigoli (bee-GO-lee). Ita. A large form of **spaghetti,** homemade, using only water, **flour,** and a small amount of **egg.**

bijane (bee-zhahn). Fre. A cold **soup** prepared by putting crumbled **bread** into sweetened red wine.

bikesmad (BEHK-sey-meth). Dan. Beef **hash** served with a fried **egg.**

bilberry (BIHL-behr-ree). USA. **Blueberry.**

Billy Bi (beh-lee bee). Fre. A **mussel soup** with **cream** and white wine.

bind (bind). USA. Add a liquid, **egg,** or melted fat to a dry mixture to cause to stick together; to form a cohesive mass.

Bing cherry (behng CHEHR-ree). USA. A variety of **cherry** that is round, plump, and a dark red, almost black color. Flesh is purple-red with dark purple juice.

bing-gan (bing-gaan). Chi. **Crackers.**

bing-jí-líng (bing-gee-ling). Chi. **Ice cream.**

bing zhèn píjiu (bing dzen pee-jiu). Chi. Iced **beer.**

birch beer (burch beer). USA. Carbonated soft drink made from the sap of the black birch tree.

bird's nest (burdz nehst). USA. **Yan cai;** the nest of cliff-dwelling birds, soaked in water to restore its gelatinous texture and used to garnish **soups** at banquets and special occcasions; very expensive.

bird's nest (burdz nehst). USA. Straw **potatoes** deep fried in a special holder to form a nest, filled with other food, such as **peas.**

birne (BEER-ner). Ger. **Pear.**

birnenbrot (BEER-nen-broat). Ger. Sweet **bread,** rather like a **fruit-cake** full of dried **fruits.**

biryani (beh-ree-YON-nee). Ind. A **pilaf-**type **rice** dish; the national dish of India.

Bischofsbrot (BISH-ofs-broat). Ger. A **cake** of dried **fruit** and **choco-late** drops; bishop's bread.

biscoitos (bees-KOY-tohss). Por. **Cookies.**

biscotte (bees-kott). Fre. **Rusk; biscuit.**

biscotti (bee-SKOT-tee). Ita. **Cookies; biscuits.**

biscotti di prato (bee-SKOT-tee dee PRAH-toa). Ita. Hard-textured, sweet **cookies** with **almond** pieces; often eaten dipped in vin santo.

biscuit (BEHS-kiht). USA. A small **quickbread** made from **dough** that has been rolled out and cut, or dropped from a spoon, and baked.

biscuit (BEHS-kiht). Bri. A wide variety of small flat **cakes, cookies, breads.**

biscuit (bees-kwee). Fre. A wide variety of small flat **cakes, cookies, breads.**

biscuit a la cuillere (bees-kwee ah lah cwee-yehr). Fre. **Ladyfingers.**

biscuit tortoni (BEHS-kiht tohr-TOHN-ee). USA. A frozen **dessert** made with **cream, eggs,** and crushed **macaroons.**

bishop's cake (BEHS-shup's kak). USA. A light **cake** with **almonds** and **raisins.**

biskopskake (BEH-skop-kar-keh). Nor. **Bishop's cake.**

Biskote (bee-SKOT-teh). Ger. **Ladyfinger.**

biskvit (bees-KVEET). Rus. **Sponge cake.**

Bismark herring (BIZ-mawrk HEH-renj). Ger. **Herring** marinated in **vinegar, filleted** and split, seasoned with **onion,** and eaten with **sour cream.**

bisque (bihsk). Frc. A thick **soup** usually made with **cream, egg yolks,** and fish or shellfish; made with a fairly dark **roux** if it's **Cajun.**

bissar (BEHS-sahr). Afr. Dried **beans** cooked in water and oil until a jelly is formed; eaten cold or hot.

bistec (beef-TAYK). Spa. Beefsteak. Sometimes spelled **biftec.**

bistecca (bee-STAYK-kah). Ita. Beefsteak.

biswa tulsi (BEHS-wah TUHL-see). Ind. **Sweet basil.**

bitter almond oil (BEHT-ter AH-mohnd oil). USA. The oil extracted from **bitter almonds;** has a high concentration of prussic acid; is considered poisonous by some authorities; others advise using a very minute amount to flavor; not available in the American markets.

bitter almonds (BEHT-ter AH-mondz). USA. Used only as flavoring; called for in some classic European recipes; bitterness is caused by the relatively considerable amount of prussic acid contained in these **nuts.**

bitterballen (bee-teht-BAHL-lehn). Dut. Tiny, **croquette**-like **meatballs** eaten as a **canapé** with drinks; not at all bitter.

bitterkoekjes (BEE-tur-kook-yus). Dut. **Macaroons.**

bitterkoekjespudding (BEE-tur-kook-yus-pood-ing). Dut. **Pudding** with **raisins, fruit,** rum or wine, and **macaroons.**

bitter melon (BIHT-ter MEHL-uhn). USA. The Chinese melon, **foo gwah;** zucchini-shaped, green, crocodile-skinned; bitter; silvery-green flesh, pale brown seeds; only used cooked.

bitter orange (BIHT-ter OHR-ahnj). USA. **Seville orange;** a bitter **orange** with a thin skin that is much used in making **marmalade;** used to lend piquancy to meat, fish dishes, and various drinks.

bitters (BIHT-ters). Bri. An alcoholic solution of bitter, aromatic plant products used as flavoring in mixed drinks; also, a very dry, heavily hopped ale.

bittersweet (BIHT-ter-sweet). USA. Being at once pleasantly bitter and sweet; as **chocolate** prepared with very little **sugar.**

Bitto (BEHT-toe). Swi. A hard **cheese** similar to **Fontina;** semifirm, bland, with big eyes when young; after two years of ripening the eyes get smaller, the cheese harder and sharper.

bivalve (BI-valv). USA. Animal with hinged two-valve shell, such as **clam, scallop, oyster.**

biwa (BEE-wah). Jap. **Loquats.**

bixin (BEHX-un). USA. Another name for **annatto,** a coloring agent for **butter** and **cheese.**

bizcocho (beeth-KO-choa). Spa. **Biscuit, cake, ladyfinger.**

bizcochos borrachos (beeth-KO-choa boh-RRAH-choh). Spa. Sugared **sponge cake,** splashed with wine and sprinkled with **cinnamon.**

björnbär (BURRN-baar). Swe. **Blackberry.**

bjørnebaer (BYUR-ner-baer). Nor. **Blackberry.**

blåbar (BLAW-baer). Nor. **Blueberries; huckleberries;** popular in **pancakes** and in cold **soup.**

blåbär (BLOA-baer). Swe. **Blueberry.**

black bass (blahk bahs). USA. A small freshwater fish with firm, lean, delicate white flesh; skin must be removed before cooking to eliminate objectionable mossy, weedy flavor.

black beans (blahk bens). USA. **Frijoles negros;** dried **beans** from Mexico that resemble the red **kidney bean,** sweet in taste, ebony in color; used in **rice** dishes, **stews,** and **soups.**

blackberry (BLAHK-behr-ree). USA. A purplish-black **berry** that is juicy, sweet, but seedy; used in **cobblers, pies, tart** and **turnover** fillings.

black-bottom pie (blahk-BOHT-um pi). USA. A **custard** pie with a layer of heavy **chocolate custard** on the bottom.

black cabbage (blahk KAHB-bahj). USA. An Italian **vegetable** with very dark-colored, elongated leaves.

black chanterelle (blahk chan-ter-REHL). USA. A European wild **mushroom** with an earthy flavor; grayish-black, fluted in shape; should be eaten cooked.

blackened (BLAHK-und). USA. A **Cajun** method of cooking fish and meats, using an intensely hot cast iron skillet, to capture the taste of cooking directly over an open fire.

black-eyed peas (BLAHK-iyd pez). USA. tiny, off-white African **beans** with a black "eye"; used fresh or dried; an essential ingredient in **Hopping John.**

black Mike (blahk Mik). USA. A term used by loggers for **stew** of meat and **vegetables.**

black mission fig (blahk MEHSH-shun fihg). USA. A variety of **fig** with sweet flavor, purple-black skin, crimson flesh; eat fresh or cooked.

black pepper (blahk PEHP-purr). USA. A pungent, East Indian condiment that is the dried, unripened fruit of a semiwoody vine, ground with the outer black coating still on.

black pudding (blahk PUHD-eng). USA. **Blood sausage.**

black sea bass (blahk SE-bahs). USA. A small saltwater fish with lean, delicate white flesh; used widely in Chinese cuisine; also called **sea bass.**

blackstrap molasses (BLAHK-strahp mo-LAHS-esz). USA. Unrefined, dark, thick **syrup** produced in **sugar** refining.

black turnip (blahk TUHR-nuhp). USA. A large, black Italian **vegetable** resembling a **turnip;** has white interior, sharp, pungent flavor, crisp texture; must be peeled before eating.

black walnut (blahk WAHL-nuht). USA. The oily, edible nut of the black walnut tree.

blakhan (BLA-kahn). Ind. A salty, pungent **shrimp paste,** related to other Oriental fermented fish **condiments.**

blanc (blahng). Fre. A cooking **stock** of flour and water, in which certain foods, such as **mushrooms** and **artichokes,** are cooked to retain their color.

blanch (blahnch). USA. To plunge into boiling water (or fat) for very short time, usually in preparation for further cooking by another method or to loosen skins of fruits and vegetables.

blancmange (BLAHNG-mahnzh). Fre. A **pudding** or **custard.**

blandad frukt (BLAHN-dahd frewkt). Swe. Mixed **fruit.**

blandad grönsaker (BLAHN-dahdb GRURN-saak). Swe. Mixed **vegetables.**

blanquette (blang-ket). Fre. A white **stew** of **veal,** lamb, or **chicken** in an **egg-yolk**-thickened **cream sauce.**

bláthach (bla-akh). Iri. **Buttermilk.**

Blau (blaus). Ger. Same as the French au bleu. See **bleu, au.**

blawn fish (blown fish). Bri. Fish that has been hung in a breezy place to get a fresh, outdoorsy flavor.

blaze (blaz). USA. To pour liquor over food and ignite.

ble (blee). Fre. **Wheat.**

bleek (blak). Dut. Pascal-type **celery.**

blend (blehnd). USA. To mix two or more ingredients thoroughly until uniform.

blended flour (BLEHND-ehd flaur). USA. Two or more classes of **flours** blended for specific purposes, such as for making pretzels.

bleu (bluh). Fre. Blue; or very rare, as for steak.

bleu, au (oa bluh). Fre. A method of preparing fish, especially **trout,** by plunging the fish, absolutely fresh if not actually alive, into a boiling water and **vinegar** mixture, seasoned with **salt,** and spiced with **thyme** and **bay leaf,** which causes the skin of the fish to take on a bluish color; served with melted **butter** or **hollandaise sauce.**

Bleu d'Auvergne (blur d`oa-veh-awng-yeh). Fre. A cow's whole-milk soft, blue **cheese** with a distinctive flavor.

blinde vinken (BLIN-duh VING-kuh). Dut. Stuffed **veal** or beef.

blind Huhn (blint Hoon). Ger. A casserole of **beans, bacon,** dried **apples,** and various **vegetables.**

blinis (blyee-NI). Rus. **Pancakes,** of a light **batter,** served with **caviar** and **sour cream.**

blintz (blehnz). USA. A thin **pancake,** rolled or folded, with a filling, usually **cheese.**

bloater (BLOW-ter). Bri. A large, fat, salted **herring,** usually whole and ungutted, then cold-smoked to a pale gold color; gutted just prior to serving.

blockwurst (BLOHK-vurst). Ger. A **salami**-like **sausage** of **pork** and beef.

blodfersk (BLEWD-fehrshk). Nor. Blood-fresh, an expression used to denote freshness of fish.

blodkorv (BLOOD-korv). Swe. **Black (blood) pudding,** a type of **sausage.**

bloedworst (BLOOT-worst).   Dut. **Sausage** made with blood, **oat bran, raisins,** pork fat; served boiled, broiled, or fried.

bloemkool (BLOOM-kohl).   Dut. **Cauliflower.**

blomkål (BLOOM-koal).   Nor, Swe. **Cauliflower.**

blomkaal (BLOAM-kawl).   Dan. **Cauliflower.**

blommer (BLOAM-err).   Dan. **Plums.**

blond de veau (blon de vo).   Fre. White **veal stock.**

blonmd de volaille (blon de voh-laj).   Fre. Clear **chicken stock.**

blondir (blohn-deer).   Fre. To cook lightly in fat.

blood (bluhd).   USA. Used as a thickening agent for a **sauce** when made to accompany a meat dish, usually **game** or **fowl.**

blood orange (bluhd OHR-ahnj).   USA. A member of the **orange** family, with pulp that is rust, scarlet, garnet, or purple, and a dramatically sanguine juice with overtones of **raspberries;** skin is orange or red-flecked; resembles a **valencia orange.**

blood pudding (bluhd PUHD-eng).   USA. Same as **blood sausage.**

blood sausage (bluhd SAW-sahj).   USA. A **sausage** of diced pork fat and blood from freshly killed pigs, **herbs,** spices, and **onions;** black in color. Also known as **black pudding, blood pudding.**

bløtkake (blurdh-kaa-ker).   Nor. A layer **cake** with a rich filling of whipped **cream, egg yolks,** and **nuts.**

Blue (blu).   USA. Blue-veined cow's milk **cheeses** that have been inoculated with Penicillium rogueforti.

blueberry (BLU-behr-ree).   USA. The blue or black, small, round **fruit** of the blueberry bush; eaten fresh or cooked in **jellies, syrups,** and baked products.

Blue cheese (blu chez).   USA. **Cheese** injected with mold to form the blue veining that gives the cheese its characteristic flavor. Blue-veined cheeses include French **Roquefort,** American **Maytag Blue,** and Italian **Gorgonzola.**

blue crabs (blu krahbz).   USA. A variety of **crab** best known in its soft-shell stage.

Blue Dorset (Blu DOOR-seht).   Bri. An aged **cheese,** chalk-white; has a streak of bright blue horizontally across the center made by the innoculation of a special mold; made from partly skimmed cow's milk. Also called **Blue Vinney.**

bluefish (BLU-fisch).   USA. An important food dish related to the **pompanos** found off the Atlantic coast; bluish above and silvery below; has a delicate flavor when gutted, scaled, and iced immediately after being taken from the water; pan-**fry** small blues; **fillet,** then **bake** or **broil** the larger.

blue meat (blu met).   USA. A term used to designate the meat of an unweaned calf.

Blue Point (Blu Point).   USA. An outstanding species of **oyster** found off the coast of Long Island; served **raw.**

Blue Vinney (blu VEHN-ney).   Bri. A cheese the same as **Blue Dorset.**

Blumenkohl (BLOO-mern-kohl).   Ger. **Cauliflower.**

Blutwurst (BLOOT-voorst).   Ger. **Blood sausage.**

bobi (bah-BI).   Rus. **Broad beans.**

bobotee (BOH-boh-tee).   USA. A **pudding**-like dish of **milk,** bread crumbs, **almonds, onions,** and **hot sauce.**

bócài (baw tsai).   Chi. **Spinach.**

Bock (bohk).   Ger. A dark, strong Bavarian **beer.**

böckling (BURK-ling).   Swe. Small **smoked herring.**

Bockwurst (BOHK-voorst).   Ger. **Sausage** of **pork, veal, lemon** juice, **eggs, milk;** eaten in the spring.

bodega (bo-DEE-go).   Spa. Wine cellar.

boerenkool (BOOR-uh-kohl).   Dut. **Kale.**

boerenkool metroke worst (BOOR-uh-kohl met rohk worst).   Dut. A hotch-potch of crispy **kale** and **potatoes** served with **smoked sausage.**

boeuf (buhf).   Fre. Beef; boeuf à la jardinière, **braised** beef with **vegetables;** boeuf roti, **roast beef.**

boeuf à la mode (buhf ah lah mod).   Fre. **Pot roast** deluxe; meat sliced very thin and even, covered with **sauce,** and platter garnished with beautifully arranged **vegetables.**

boeuf bouilli (buhf bu-ji).   Fre. Boiled beef.

boeuf salé (buhf sah-lee).   Fre. **Corned beef.**

bøf (burf).   Dan. Beef.

bogavente (boa-ghah-BEN-tay).   Spa. Large-clawed **lobster.**

bohne (BOA-nern).   Ger. **Bean.**

boil (boyl).   USA. To bring a lizuid to the boiling point, which is 212°F for water.

boiled custard (boyld KUS-tahrd).   USA. **Custard** cooked on top of the stove, as opposed to custard **baked** in an oven.

boiled icing (boyld I-ceng).   USA. The product of whipping hot **sugar syrup** into beaten **egg** whites; Italian **meringue.**

boiler onion (BOY-luhr UN-yun).   USA. Small, round, tender; white **onion** with mild flavor, used in **casseroles, soups, stews,** or creamed.

bok choy (bahk chee).   Chi. A clump of snow-white stalks ending in wide, dark green leaves, related to **Chinese cabbage;** used alone or in **stir-fry.** Also known as **baak choy, pak choi, celery mustard,** and **Chinese mustard.**

bok goh (baak gqoak).   Chi. **Ginko nut.**

bokking (BAWK-king).   Dut. Red **herring;** a **bloater.**

bola (BOH-lah).   Mex. Ball; shape such as **meatball.**

bola (BOH-lah).   Jew. A cut of Kosher forequarter meat.

Bola (BOH-lah).   Por. A ball-shaped cow's-milk **cheese** that is semi-firm, crumbly, and yellow.

bolacha (boh-LAH-shah).   Por. **Crackers.**

boletus (boh-le-tus).   Fre. A genus of wild **mushroom,** whose most prized edible varieties are bolete, **cèpe,** and **porcini;** have fleshy caps and stems and range from white to very dark brown; eaten fresh or dried.

bolillo (boh-EE-yoh).   Mex. Small, hard **roll.**

bolita (boh-LEE-tah).   Mex. Little ball; such as shape of little ball.

bölledünne (BURL-leh-dewn-neh).   Ger. A Swill **onion custard pie.**

boller (BOAL- er).   Dan. **Meatballs** or fish balls.

bollito (bo-LEE-toa).   Ita. A meat dish made up of various kinds of **boiled** meats, served with a green **parsley sauce.**

bollo (BOH-yoh).   Spa. Small loaf or **roll.**

bolo (BOH-loh).   Por. **Cake.**

bologna (bo-LON-yah).   Ita. A large **sausage** of ground **pork** with cubes of white fat, seasoned with **coriander, pistachio nuts,** and wine; not akin to U.S. **baloney.**

boluó (baw-luo).   Chi. **Pineapple.**

bomba di riso (BOM-bah dee REE-zoa).   Ita. A molded **bombe** of **rice** with a rich filling of **ground** meat, **herbs, mushrooms,** diced **cheese,** or **ham.**

Bombay duck (Bohm-BAY duhk).   USA. **Bombil.**

bombe (baumb).   Fre. A frozen **dessert** made of a combination of two or more frozen mixtures packed in a round or melon-shaped mold. **Bombe glacé.**

bombil (BOHM-behl).   Ind. A fish that is split, boned, **filleted,** and **dried;** used to flavor **curry** dishes. Also known as **Bombay duck.**

bombons (bohm-BOHSS).   Por. **Candy.**

böna (BUR-nah).   Swe. Bean.

Bonbel (bohn bell).   Fre. A semisoft, pale yellow, bland cheese that resembles American **Munster** in flavor; excellent with sherry.

bonbon (bahn bahn).   Fre. **Candy, confections.**

Bondane (bohn-dahn).   Fre. A skimmed- or whole-milk **cheese** of the **Tomme** family.

Bondon (Bohn-dohn).   Fre. A small, unripened, whole-milk **cheese,** similar to **Neufchâtel.**

Bondost or Bundost (Bohn-DOST).   Swe. A firm, mellow **cheese** often flavored with **caraway** and sometimes **cumin.** A Bondost is also made in Wisconsin.

bone (bon).   USA. To remove the bones from meat or fish.

bone broth (bon brohth).   USA. Soup made from **boiling** cracked bones.

boned and rolled (bond and rold).   USA. Meat cuts that are boned by the butcher, rolled up, and tied for roasting.

bonen (bo-nehn).   Dut. **Beans.**

boniatos (bou-nee-AH-tos).   Spa. **Sweet potatoes.**

boniatos confitadas (boa-nee-AH-tos kon-fee-TAY-dos). Spa. Candied **sweet potatoes.**

bonita (boh-NEE-tah). USA. **Bonito.**

bonite (boh-nee-teh). Fre. **Bonito.**

bonito (boh-NEE-toa). Jap. A small member of the **tuna** family, used primarily in Japanese cooking, **dried, salted,** or **flaked.**

bonne femme (bong fam). Fre. In simple home style; for example, **soups, stews,** and **casseroles.**

bønner (BURN-err). Dan. **Beans.**

bönor (BUR-noor). Swe. **Beans.**

boova shenkel (BOO-vah SHEHN-kehl). USA. A **stew** and **dumpling** dish from the Pennsylvania Dutch.

boquerones (boa-kay-RON-nayss). Spa. Fresh **anchovies; whitebait.**

borage (BOU-raj). USA. An **herb** whose young leaves are used to flavor **vegetables** and in **salads.** The tiny flowers can be used in beverages, or when dipped in **egg** white, sugared, and dried, can be used as **cake** and **confection** decorations.

borda (BAWR-do). Hun. **Chop.**

bordelaise (bor-dah-lays). Fre. A brown **sauce** in which Bordeaux or Burgundy is one of the ingredients.

bordure (bvoar-dewr). Fre. Mashed **rice** or **potato** used to border or decorate hot foods.

Borelli (Bohr-eh-lee). Ita. A small **cheese** made of buffalo's milk.

Borjú (BAWR-yoo). Hun. **Veal.**

borjúpaprikás (BAW-ryoopo-pree-kaash). Hun. **Veal fricassee** with **onions, pepper rings, tomatoes,** and a seasoning of **paprika** and **garlic.**

borlotto bean (boar-LOHT-toa ben). Ita. A common dried **bean,** splotched brown, and used in **soups** or cooked to a smooth **paste.**

Bornholmeraeggekage (born-HAHL-meyr-egg-gee-kay-yee). Dan. **Omelet** with Bornhol smoked **herring, radishes,** and **chives.**

borracho (boh-RRAH-choh). Mex. Cooked with wine, liquor.

borsch (bohrsh). Rus. A soup made with **beets,** meat **broth,** and **vegetables** and always served with **sour cream.**

borscht (bohrsh). Pol. **Borsch.**

borsot (BAWR-shawt). Hun. **Black pepper.**

borstplaat (BAWRST-plaht). Dut. **Sugar candy;** hard-baked **fondant.**

borststuk (BAWRST-stook). Dut. **Brisket.**

bosbessen (BOS-bessen). Dut. **Blueberries.**

Boston baked beans (BOHS-tohn bakd benz). USA. **Navy beans** flavored with **molasses** and **salt pork, baked** in an earthenware pot.

Boston brown bread (BOHS-tohn brahn brehd). USA. A sweet, rye **bread** flavored with **molasses.**

Boston cracker (BOHS-tohn krahk-er). USA. A large, thin, slightly sweet **cracker,** similar to the **common cracker.**

Boston cream pie (BOHS-tohn crem pi). USA. A round **cake,** split and filled with a **custard** or **cream** filling, topped with **chocolate icing.**

Boston lettuce (BOHS-tohn LEHT-uhs). USA. A **salad lettuce** with a small, slightly loose head; dark green outer leaves, pale green inner leaves; a variety of **butterhead lettuce.**

bot (bawt). Dut. **Flounder.**

boter (BO-tur). Dut. **Butter.**

boterham (BO-tur-ahm). Dut. Cold cuts.

botifarra (boo-ti-FAR-rah). Spa. Spiced **sausage.**

bottagio (bo-tah-JEE-o). Ita. **Pork stew.**

bottarga (bo-TAHR-jah). Ita. **Mullet roe,** used in **antipasto.**

bottom round (BAHT-tuhm round). USA. The cut of beef from the hindquarter that is adjacent to the tip, being the lower portion of the round.

bouchees (boo-shay). Fre. A mouthful; small puff-paste patties.

boucher (bu-cher). Fre. Butcher.

bouchon (bu-shon). Fre. Cork.

Boudanne (Bohr-dawng). Fre. A cheese made from cow's milk, either whole or skim.

boudin (BOO-downg). USA. A **Cajun sausage** with **rice** mixed with the stuffing; white boudin is made with **pork;** red boudin has pork blood added; other meats as well as **seafood** can also be used.

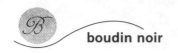

boudin noir (boo-den nwar). Fre. **Blood sausage.**

bouillabaisse (boo-yah-behss). Fre. The national soup of France; a highly seasoned fish **soup** made especially at Marseilles; served in plates with dry toast.

bouilli (BOO-yee). USA. A classic **Cajun soup** made with the internal organs of beef.

bouilli (bu-jee). Fre. Fresh **boiled** beef or other meat.

bouillir (bu-jir). Fre. To **boil.**

bouillon (boo-yawn). Fre. **Broth** or unclarified **stock** made from beef, **veal,** or **chicken;** concentrated **brown stock.**

boula (BOO-lah). USA. A green pea and green turtle soup, flavored with sherry, usually topped with **cheese** and sometimes **whipped cream.**

boulage (bu-lajz). Fre. To shape **dough** for **baking.**

boulangère, à la (bu-lahn-zehr). Fre. A **garnish** of **braised potatoes** and **onions.**

boule-de-neige (bul-de-nejg). Fre. A round, **dessert** pastry covered in **whipped cream** to resemble snowballs.

boulette (boo-leht). Fre. **Meatballs** or anything formed in a sphere, then cooked, usually **fried.**

bouquet (boo-keh). Fre. Volatile oils from **herbs** and plants that give aroma.

bouquet garni (boo-keh gahr-nee). Fre. **Herbs** and seasonings, usually includes **parsley, thyme, bay leaf,** among others, tied in cheesecloth and used to flavor **sauces** and **soups;** removed before serving. Also known as fagot.

bouquetiere, à la (bu-keh-tyehr). Fre. **Garnishes** of **vegetables** arranged on the meat platter.

bouquettes (boo-kehtt). Fre. **Buckwheat pancakes** with **raisins** in the **batter,** serfed in Belgium.

Bourgain (Bohr-gwang). Fre. A very soft, perishable **cheese** of the fresh **Neufchâtel** type; low fat content, not salted.

bourgeoise (bohr-zhwaz). Fre. Usually means served with **vegetables.**

bourguignon (bohr-ghee-n'yang). Fre. A classic **stew** of beef braised in red wine with **onions** and **mushrooms.**

bourride (boo-reed). Fre. A garlicky fish **stew;** served on crusty **bread.**

Boursin (Boor-sahn). Fre. A triple-créme **cheese;** soft, fresh, delicate.

Box (firm) (Boux). Ger. Cow's milk **cheese** similar to Brick; mild, piquant flavor, saffron colored.

Box (soft) (Boux). Ger. A **cheese** made from partly skimmed cow's milk, colored witrh **saffron.**

boysenberry (BOYZ-un-behr-ree). USA. A **berry** that looks like a large **blackberry** and tastes like a **raspberry.**

Bra (Brah). Ita. A firm **cheese** made in the Piedmont; also a soft, creamy cheese cured in brine.

braciola (brah-cee-OHL-lah). Ita. A chop or **cutlet.**

braciola di maiale (brah-CHOA-lah dee ma-ee-A-lay). Ita. **Pork** chop.

braciolette ripiene (brah-choa-LAH-tay ree-pee-EH-nay). Ita. Stuffed **veal** rolls; veal birds.

braciolini (brah-chee-o-LEE-nee). Ita. Beef rolls stuffed with bits of **pork** or **sausage.**

bräckkorv (BREHK-korv). Swe. **Smoked pork sausage.**

bradán (brad-dan). Iri. **Salmon.**

brændende kærlighed (BRAY-ne-ne KAYHR-li-heth). Dan. Literally, "burning love", mashed **potato** with **bacon.**

Bragenwurst (BRAH-gun-voorst). Ger. A long, thin, **smoked sausage** made of pig's brains, **onions, flour,** and **oats.**

brains (brans). USA. Usually from a calf or lamb. To prepare, **blanch** in acidulated water, then **poach** in court-boullion or **fry** in **butter,** serve with **brown butter;** also cooked in **scrambled eggs.**

braise (braz). USA. To cook by **browning** or **scaring** in fat, then cooking tightly covered in small amount of liquid at low temperature, either in the oven or over direct heat.

brak geal (brak gyal). Iri. **Sea trout.**

bramble jelly (BRAHM-buhl JEHL-lee). USA. A jelly made from **crab apples** and **blackberries.**

bramble pie (BRAHM-bul pi). Bri. A deep dish **pie** made from wild **blackberries.**

bran (brahn). USA. The outer covering of a **cereal grain;** one of the beneficial fiber foods.

brandade (brahng-dahd). Fre. **Salted codfish puréed** with oil and seasoned with **garlic.**

Brandkäse (Brahn-KAHZ-zah). Ger. A sour-milk **cheese** whose curd is mixed with **butter** before being pressed into bricks, then ripened in old beer kegs and occasionally moistened with **beer.** Also called **Brand.**

brandon puff (BRAHN-dohn puhf). USA. A **muffin** made with **corn-meal** and **flour.**

brandy (BRAHN-dee). Dut. An alcoholic liquor distilled from wine.

bran flour (brahn flowr). USA. **Flour** made from finely ground **wheat bran.**

brasato (brah-SAA-toa). Ita. **Braised.**

Braskartofler (brahs-kahr-TOF-lerr). Dan. **Fried potatoes.**

Braten (BRART-ern). Ger. **Braised** or **roasted** meat.

Brathandl (BRART-hehndl). Ger. **Roast chicken.**

Brathering (brart-HAY-ring). Ger. **Grilled** or **fried herring,** which is **pickled;** served cold.

Brathuhn (BRART-thoon). Ger. **Roast chicken.**

Bratwurst (BRART-voorst). Ger. A **sausage** of spiced **pork.**

Bräune Tunke (BROY-neh TOON-kay). Ger. **Brown sauce.**

Braunschweiger (BROWN-schvahg-er). Ger. Liver **sausage;** rich flavor, smooth consistency; made from **pork,** pork liver, **smoked bacon;** delicately seasoned with **coriander, ginger, mustard, onion, pepper,** other seasonings.

Braunsweiger Kuchen (BROWN-schvahg-er KOOK-hern). Ger. Brunswick cake, rich in b**utter, eggs, raisins, currants,** and **almonds.**

brawn (brahvn). Ger. **Head cheese,** a jellied loaf made from the edible meat of a pig or calf head.

Brazil nut (BRAH-zeel nuht). USA. The three-sided **nut** of a wild Brazilian tree; the nutmeat is white, creamy, and high in fat.

brazo de gitano (BRAH-soh del gee-TAH-noh). Spa. "Gypsy's arm", a **jelly roll.**

breac (brak). Iri. **Trout.**

bread (brehd). USA. To dip a food into an **egg-milk** mixture, then coat with fine breadcrumbs prior to cooking.

bread flour (brehd flowr). USA. Made from hard **wheat** with high **gluten** content that gives structural support to products; gives elasticity to the **dough,** allows it to expand and hold the gas liberated by the **yeast;** feels gritty to touch; one of the world's basic foods.

bread fruit (brehd froot). USA. Sweet, starchy, green, tropical, round **fruit** with pulp similar to bread when baked.

bread sauce (brehd saus). Bri. A **sauce** for **poultry** and **game,** made with milk thickened with bread crumbs.

bread stick (brehd stehk). USA. A **yeast**-bread product that is eight to ten inches long, and about one inch in diameter when baked; crispy texture.

breakfast cream (brehk-fahst krem). USA. **Light cream.**

bream (brehm). USA. Various species of fish throughout the world; best known are the American **porgy** and the Mediterranean **gilthead;** a small freshwater fish used mostly in **stews.**

bree (broo). Sco. **Soup.**

bréme (braym). Fre. **Bream.**

Bremer Kükenragout (Breh-mer KOOK-hern-rah-goo). Ger. **Stewed chicken** and **vegetables** in **cream sauce.**

brennevin (BROWN-veen). Nor. **Brandy.**

Brennsuppe (BREHN-zuppe). Ger. **Brown soup;** made of **flour browned** in the oven or dry skillet, flavored with **onions** and wine.

Bresse Bleu (Bres Blur). Fre. A blue **cheese** made in the district of Bresse.

bretone (bray-TOU-nay). Spa. **Brussel sprouts.**

bretonne (breh-ton). Fre. A garnish of red white **haricot beans.**

brew (broo). USA. To cook or heat in liquid to extract flavor, as in preparing **tea.**

brewer's rice (BROO-ehrz ris). USA. Broken grains of rice used as an ingredient in **beer brewing.**

brewer's yeast (BROO-ehrz yest). USA. High-protein **yeast** used in brewing beer; used as nutritional supplement.

Brezel (BRET-sehl).   Ger. **Pretzel.**

Brick (brehk).   USA. A cow's whole-milk **cheese** whose taste and texture is similar to cheddar; brick-shaped; made mostly in Wisconsin.

Brickbat (Brehk-baht).   Bri. A **cheese** made of fresh cow's milk to which a little cream has been added; cures for one year before eating.

Bricotta (Breh-kah-tah).   Fre. A Corsican semisoft, salty sheep cheese; often blended with **sugar** and rum and used as a **dessert.**

brider (bree-dayr).   Fre. To truss.

Brie (bree).   Fre. A **cheese** with a smooth buttery interior; a fine aroma and taste; white surface, ripened rind; made in flat disc. Widely imitated, true Brie is made only in France.

brigidini (bree-gee-DEE-nee).   Ita. **Anise**-flavored **cookies.**

brik (breek).   Ara. **Phyllo;** leaf-thin pastry sheets, made from **flour** and water; used for sweet and savory dishes by layering with fillings. Also known as **filo, yukka. malsouka.**

brill (brehl).   USA. An European **flatfish** of the **flounder** family.

Brillat-Savarin (Bree-yuawng-Sah-vah-rahn).   Fre. A white, delighful, delicate **dessert cheese** named for the famed French gourmand.

Brindza (BREHND-zah).   Hun. A cousin to Greek Feta, this sheep or goat **cheese** is made throughout the Balkans and Hungary. Some is stored in brine, and some is pressed between layers of pine bark, giving it a resinous flavor. This is the cheese used in making the Romanian dish mamaliga.

brine (brin).   USA. Solution of **salt** and water; used to draw natrural **sugars** and moisture from food to preserve it.

bringa (BRING-ah).   Swe. **Brisket,** breast.

bringebaer (BRING-er-bahr).   Nor. **Raspberry.**

brinjal (BREEN-jahl).   Ind. **Eggplant.**

brioche (bree-ohsh).   Fre. A slightly sweetened, rich bread of French origin; baked in a fluted mold with a button on top.

brisket (BRIHS-ket).   USA. An economical cut of meat from the breast, including part of the ribs and shoulder.

brisler (BREESS-lerr).   Dan. **Sweetbreads.**

brisling (brehz-leng).   USA. A small fish similar to the **herring; sprat.**

brisquet (brehs-keet). Fre. **Brisket.**

Bristol cream (Brehs-tohl krem). Bri. A **dessert** sherry; one of the most elegant.

brittle (BRIH-tehl). USA. **Candy** made by caramelizing **sugar,** usually adding **nuts,** spread in thin sheets to cool; used powdered, crumbled, and cracked in many desserts.

broa (broah). Spa. **Cornbread.**

broad beans (brawhd bens). USA. **Fava beans;** large, meaty bean that is light green when fresh; eaten **raw,** cooked fresh, **dried,** or **canned;** important nutritionally; used worldwide.

Broccio (Brogh-cho). Fre. A Corsican sheep's-or goat's-milk **cheese** similar to **Bricotta.**

broccoli (BROH-klee). USA. A green **vegetable** of Italian origin that is a type of **cauliflower.** Used cooked or **raw** in **salads** and with **dips.**

broccoli rabe (BROK-ko-lee RAH-beh). Ita. **Broccoli.**

brochan (BROX-ehn). Sco. **Porridge, gruel.**

broche (brosh). Fre. **Skewer;** cooked on a skewer.

brochet (bro-sheh). Fre. **Pike.**

brochette (bro-shet). Fre. A **skewer** for **grilling** chunks of meat and vegetables; **kabobs.**

brocoli (brohc-co-lay). Fre. **Broccoli.**

bróculo (BROK-ko-lo). Nor. **Broccoli.**

bröd (brurd). Swe. Bread.

brød (brur). Dan, Nor. Bread.

brodettato (braw-dayt-TAH-toa). Ita. **Stewed.**

brodetto (braw-DAYT-toa). Ita. Fish **stew** or **soup.**

brodo (BRAW-doa). Ita. **Broth.**

brodo ristretto (BRAW-doa reez-TRAYT-toa). Ita. **Consommé.**

broil (broyl). USA. To cook under a direct flame or over a charcoal fire.

Broiler (Broh-ee-lah). Ger. A cow's whole-milk **cheese** similar to **Limburger.**

broiler (broyl-ehr).   USA. As a food, refers to a young **chicken** of either sex that weighs about 2 ½ pounds. See also **fryer, roaster, stewing chicken, capon, stag chicken,** and **cock.**

bromelain (BRO-mch-lynn).   USA. Enzyme from the **pineapple** used to tenderize meat.

bronzino (brahn-DZEE-noa).   Ita. **Sea bass.**

brood (broht).   Dut. Bread; *bruin* (brirn) brown; *krenten* (KREN-tuh) raisin; *rogge* (RAWKH-uh) rye; *roosteren* (ROHS-turtn) toast; *wit* (vit) white.

broodbeleggingen (brot-BEH-lahg-ghen-en).   Dut. Toppings for **sandwiches;** anyuthing to be put on a slice of bread.

broodje (BROHT-yus).   Dut. **Sandwich roll.**

broodmaaltyd (brot-MAHL-tayd).   Dut. A bread meal, or rather a meal of **sandwiches.**

broodpap (BROHT-pahp).   Dut. Bread **pudding.**

broonie (BEOO-nee).   Bri. **Oatmeal gingerbread cookies.**

broqueta (broh-KAY-tah).   Mex. **Skewer; brochette.**

Broschen (BRO-shehn).   Ger. **Sweetbreads.**

Brot (broat).   Ger. Bread.

Brotchen (BROAT-khern). Ger. **Rolls.**

broth (brauth).   USA. The clear liquor in which meat or **vegetables** have been cooked.

Brotkoch (BROAT-kokh).   Ger. Molded bread **pudding.**

Brotsuppe (BROAT-zuppe).   Ger. Bread **soup;** a way to use stale bread tastily by combining with meat **stock** and flavoring with **nutmeg.**

Brottorte (BROAT-tor-ter).   Ger. A **torte** of breadcrumbs, **eggs, almonds,** with hot wine bath poured slowly over entire **cake** while hot.

brou (broo).   Fre. A liquor made from green **walnuts,** flavored with **cinnamon** and **coriander.**

brouille (broo-yay).   Fre. **Scrambled.**

brown (braughn).   USA. To cause the surface of food to turn dark brown by using high heat, leaving the inside moist; accomplished by **frying, broiling, grilling.**

brown and serve (braughn ahnd suhrv). USA. A term used to indicate that a product has been baked to the point of doneness, but not browned; browning is done just prior to serving; usually refers to bread products.

brown betty (braughn BEHT-tee). USA. A **pudding** of **apples,** bread crumbs, spices, and **sugar.**

browned flour (braughnd flawr). USA. Used as a **sauce** enhancer and thickener; has a nutty and baked aroma.

brownie (BRAUGH-nee). USA. A rich **chocolate confection,** usually frosted with chocolate, and cut in squares.

brown onion sauce (braughn UN-yun saus). USA. **Lyonnaise sauce.**

brown rice (braughn ris). USA. Unpolished **rice** having only the hull removed; usually long grain; the least processed form of rice.

brown sauce (braughn saus). USA. **Sauce Espagnole;** the French basic **brown sauce,** used in many other sauces; made of brown **roux, brown stock,** brown **mirepoix, tomatoes,** and **herbs** slowly cooked together and **strained.**

brown stock (braughn stohk). USA. Thin liquid from simmering roasted meat in water with seasonings for several hours.

brown sugar (braughn SCHU-gahr). USA. A soft **sugar** whose crystals are covered with a coating of **molasses.**

brugnon (brew-nawng). Fre. **Nectarine;** a smooth-skinned **peach.**

Brühne (BREW-er). Ger. **Consommé.**

bruin brood (BRIRN broht). Dut. **Whole wheat** bread.

bruiss (brus). USA. A dish of boiled **milk** and bread.

brûlant (brew-lahngt). Fre. Flaming; **flambé;** drenched in **brandy,** set aflame.

brule (brew-leh). Fre. Caramelized as in **Crème Brûlée,** or flamed as in burnt **brandy.**

brun (brang). Fre. Method of **braising** in which meat is **seared** first.

bruna bönor (brewna BUR-noor). Swe. **Brown beans.**

brunekager (BROON-kaaer). Dan. Brown spice **cookies.**

brunfisksuppe (brewn FISK-ssewp-per). Nor. Fish **soup** darkened with browned **flour** and **butter.**

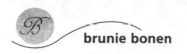
brunie bonen (brirn BOH-nuh). Dut. **Kidney** or brown **beans.**

brunkaalssupe (broon-KAHL-soo-bber). Dan. Brown **cabbage soup.**

Brunnenkresse (broo-nen-KRE-seh). Ger. **Watercress.**

brunoise (broo-noyz). Fre. Very small diced or shredded **vegetables** such as **celery, carrots, leeks,** and **turnips** cooked for **soups, sauces.**

Brunstück (BROON-stewk). Ger. **Brisket.**

brunsviger kager (BROONZ-veeg-err kaaer). Dan. Brunswick **cookies;** rich in **butter** and **sugar,** topped with **almonds** and **cinnamon.**

Brunswick stew (BRUHNZ-wehk stu). USA. A **stew** of **chicken** and various **vegetables.**

bruschetta (broo-SKEHT-tah). Ita. Coarse textured bread, toasted over coals and liberally dressed with extra virgin **olive oil.** Also known as *fett'unta* or *fregolotta.*

brush (bruhsh). USA. To coat food with melted fat or liquid.

brush roast (bruhsh rost). USA. A dish of **oysters** cooked over a wood fire on wire and served with **chowchow, butter,** and corn **bread.**

brussels lof (BROOS-suls lawf). Dut. **Endive.**

Brussels sprouts (BRUHS-ul sprouts). USA. Small green **vegetable** resembling a tiny **cabbage.**

brut (broot). Fre. Unsweetened; having a natural flavor.

brylépudding (bru-LEPU-ding). Swe. **Caramel cream.**

brysselkål (BREW-serl-koal). Swe. Brussels sprouts.

bubble and squeak (BUB-uhl ahnd squek). Bri. Boiled beef **fried** with **cabbage** and **potatoes.**

bubbly jock (BUHB-bly jahk). Sco. **Turkey.**

bucatini (bou-cah-TEE-nee). Ita. A medium-size **macaroni**-shaped **pasta.**

buccellato (book-chahl-LAH-toa). Ita. **Cake** with **currants** and flavored with **anise** seed.

bûche de Noël (bush-dah-No-ehl). Fre. Yule log; rtaditional Christmas **dessert; genoise** decorated with **buttercream** to resemble a log.

buck and breck (buhk ahnd brehk). USA. A **pickled condiment,** similar to **chowchow;** served cold.

Bückling (BEWK-ling). Ger. **Smoked herring.**

buckwheat flour (BUHK-whet flowr). USA. **Flour** made from the seed of the **buckwheat cereal grain.**

budding (BOOTH-eng). Dan. **Pudding.**

budin (boo-DEEN). Spa. **Pudding.**

bùding (boo-DING). Chi. **Pudding.**

budino (boo-DEE-noa). Ita. **Pudding.**

budino di pasta (boo-DEE-noa dee PAHS-toa). Ita. **Noodle pudding.**

budino di ricotta (boo-DEE-noa dee ree-KOT-tha). Ita. **Cheese pudding.**

budino torinese (boo-DEE-noa taw-ree-NAY-zeh). Ita. **Chestnut pudding.**

budo (boo-DOH). Jap. **Grapes.**

bue (BOO-eh). Ita. Beef.

buey (bway). Spa. Beef.

buffalo wings (BUHF-fah-lo wengs). USA. **Deep-fried chicken wings** brushed with **hot sauce; a** fiery dish.

buffet (boo-fah). Fre. A table displaying a variety of foods.

buisson (bwee-sawng). Fre. A **garnish** of small groups of **shrimp, cray-fish;** also a method of twisting pastry to a pointed end.

bulger (BULL-jger). Ara. **Cracked wheat;** precooked and prepared **wheat;** oldest known processed food.

buljong (BUL-jong). Swe, Nor. Beef **broth.**

bulka (BOOL-koo). Rus. **Roll.**

bullabesa (BOOL-yah-beh-sah). Spa. Fish **stew.**

bul'on (bool'YON). Rus. **Broth.**

bun (buhn). USA. Any of various sweet or plain small flatish, round **roll.**

Bundkuchen (bunt-KOO-khern). Ger. **Gugelhupf;** a sweet yellow **cake.**

Bundnerfleisch (BEWND-nerr-flighsh). Ger. Very thinly sliced, cured, air-dried beef.

Bunter Hans (BEWNT-nerr hahnz).   Ger. A large bread **dumpling** cooked in a napkin to hold its shape, then served with cooked **vegetables** or stewed **fruits.**

buñuelo (boo-NYUE-loh).   Spa. **Fritter;** crisp, puffy round coated with **sugar** and **cinnamon.**

burdock (BUHR-dahk).   Jap. A long, slender, neutral tasting root used for its crunchy texture; **gobo.**

burghul (burr-ghul).   Ara. Crushed wheat; usually come in fine (#1), medium (#2), and coarse (#3); not to be confused with **cracked wheat** or **bulgur.**

burgonyakrémleves (BOOR-gawn-yok-ray-leh-vehsh).   Hun. **Cream** of **potato soup.**

burgonyát (BOOR-gawn-yaat).   Hun. **Potatoes.**

burgoo (BUHR-goo).   USA. Meat and vegetable **stew** thickened with **okra.**

Burgos (BOOR-goass).   Spa. A ewe's-milk **cheese;** rindless, mild, soft, pleasant; often served for **dessert.**

Burgundy (Buhr-guhn-dee).   Fre. A soft, white, loaf-shaped **cheese** also known in France as *Fromage de Bourgogne.*

buri (boo-ree).   Jap. Yellowtail, a food fish.

Burmeister (BUHR-my-stehr).   USA. The trade name of a ripened, soft, Brick-type **cheese** made in Wisconsin.

burnet (BUHR-net).   USA. An **herb** whose leaves impart a delicate **cucumber** flavor to winter **salads;** the leaves become tough in hot weather and taste of **watermelon;** use in **salad, vinegars, soups,** and with **asparagus, celery, beans,** and **mushrooms.**

burrida (boor-REE-dah).   Ita. Fish **stew** with **garlic,** oil, **tomatoes, dried mushrooms, onions, celery, saffron.**

burrito (boo-RREE-toh).   Spa. Warm, soft flour **tortilla** filled with savory ingredients such as hot and spicy meats, **beans, cheese, tomatoes,** and **green onions,** topped with **guacamole** and **sour cream.**

burro (BOOR-roa).   Ita. **Butter.**

burro banana (BOUR-roh bah-NAH-nah).   Mex. A variety of **banana** with a tangy lemon-banana flavor, a flat, square appearance; eat fresh or use in **fruit salads** and in **desserts.** Also known as *chunky banana.*

burtugaala (bor-too-KOHD). Ara. **Orange.**

busecca (boo-ZAYK-kah). Ita, Swe. A thick **tripe soup** usually made with **beans** and always with **onions.**

bushmills (BUSH-mehlz). Iri. A smoky-flavored whiskey.

Busserl (BOOS-sehrl). Ger. "Kiss", small pastries.

bustard (BUH-stahrd). Afr. A game bird; a food bird.

buster (Buhs-tuhr). USA. A shedding **crab** whose shell has "busted" loose.

buta (boo-TAH). Jap. **Pork.**

butaniku (boo-TAH-nee-koo). Jap. **Pork.**

buterbrod (boo-teer-BROD). Rus. **Sandwich.**

butifarra (boo-teh-FAH-rah). Spa. Catalonian **sausage.**

butirro (boo-TEER-roa). Ita. Small ball of **cheese** formed around a lump of **butter;** served sliced.

butter (BUHT-ehr). USA. A solid emulsion made by churning **cream;** used as a food spread, as a seasoning, for **sautéeing,** in **baking.**

Butter (BOOT-er). Ger. **Butter.**

butter bean (BUHT-ehr ben). USA. **Lima bean.**

buttercream (BUHT-ehr-krem). USA. Used to ice **cakes** and **confections;** and to decorate or **garnish.** Mixture of **butter, sugar,** and **egg yolk,** variously flavored.

buttercrunch lettuce (BUHT-ehr-krunch LEHT-uhs). USA. A **salad lettuce** with a small, slightly loose head; dark green outer leaves, pale green inner leaves; a variety of **butterhead lettuce.**

buttercup squash (BUHT-ehr-kuhp-squash). USA. A turban-shaped winter **squash** with a distinctive pale "beanie"; heavy rind, deep ivy-green, marked with uneven, narrow striped the color of the cap; medium-sweet orange flesh is fine-textured, creamy, and mild.

butterfly (BUHT-ehr-fli). USA. To cut open, but not completely through, spread apart or flat; usually meat or fish.

butterhead lettuce (BUHT-ehr-hehd LEHT-uhs). USA. A **salad** green lettuce with a small, slightly loose, soft head that has delicate leaves

that are dark green on the outside and pale yellowesh green on the inside; has a buttery taste. Varieties include Boston, buttercrunch, bibb, White Boston, May King, and Manoa.

Buttermllch (BOO-tur-milc). Ger. **Buttermilk.**

Buttermilk Cheese (BUHT-ehr-mehlk chez). USA. A **cheese** made from the curd of **buttermilk;** resembles **cottage cheese** but with a finer grain.

buttermilk (BUHT-ehr-melk). USA. Liquid remaining after **butter** has been churned; contains no butter fat.

butternut (BUHT-ehr-nuht). USA. Large edible nut or kernel from the white walnut tree; a **walnut.**

Butternut squash (BUHT-tehr-nuht skwosh). USA. A hard rind, winter **squash** with a buttery taste; must peel before using; has smooth, buff-colored skin, yellow-orange flesh; 9–12 inches long and shaped like a giant pear.

butter swirls (BUHT-ehr swehrls). USA. The result of a technique to slightly thicken a **sauce** by swirling unsalted **butter** in the sauce, bit by bit, making a visible spiral in the hot sauce as it melts.

Butterreis (BOO-tur-rais). Ger. **Rice.**

Butterteig (BOO-tur-taik). Ger. **Puff pastry.**

button mushroom (BUHT-uhn MUHSH-rohm). USA. A variety of cultivated **mushroom** with pure white flesh and a round, half-ball-shaped smooth cap.

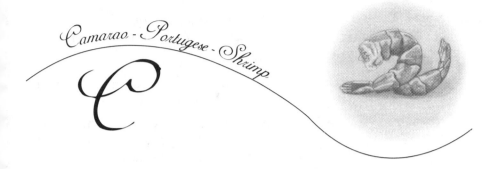

Camarao - Portugese - Shrimp

cabbage (KAH-bahj). USA. A leafy garden plant with a short stem and a dense globular head; eaten **raw** or cooked. Varieties include green, **Chinese,** celery, red, savoy, **bok choy, Swiss chard,** pe tsai.

Cabecou (Cahb-ah-koo). Fre. A **cheese** that is the same as **Chabichou.**

cabello de ángel (kah-BHAY-loh day AHN-khayl). Spa. "Angel's Head"; a **squash pudding.**

cabidela (kah-bee-DAY-lah). Por. **Sauce** made with **chicken** blood.

cabillaud (kah-bee-yoa). Fre. Fresh **cod.**

cabra (KAH-brah). Spa, Por. Goat.

Cabrales (kah-BRAH-lays). Spa. A goat's milk **cheese,** blue-veined, earthy, pungent, mellow.

Cabreiro (Cah-BRA-oh). Por. A **cheese** made of mixed ewe's and goat's milk; delicate in flavor when young; very sharp and pungent when aged.

Cabrinneti (Cab-bree-NEHT-tee). Dan. A delicate, soft **dessert cheese.**

Cabrion (Cah-bree-ohn). Fre. A goat's milk **cheese** soaked in **eau de vie** and ripened between layers of grape skins.

cabrito (kah-BREE-toh). Spa, Por. Kid, young goat.

caca (CAH-ssa). Por. Wild **game.**

cacao (kah-kah-oa). Fre, Ita, Dut. **Cocoa.**

cacao (kah-KA-oh). USA. The **dried,** partially **fermented** fatty seeds of the cacao tree, used for making **chocolate, cocoa,** and **cocoa butter.**

cacau (ka-KA-oo). Por. **Cocoa,** usually made very sweet.

cacciagione (kaht-chah-JOA-nay). Ita. **Game.**

cacciatora (koch-a-TOR-ree). Ita. Prepared in a spicy **tomato sauce** with a minimum number of ingredients such as a hunter would have on hand.

cacerola (kah-seh-ROH-lah). Mex. **Casserole.**

Cachat (Cah-cha). Fre. A soft, creamy **cheese** made with sheep's or goat's milk; sometimes blended with **brandy** or wine.

Caciocavallo (kah-choa-kah-VAHL-loa). Ita. A cow's whole-milk **cheese,** straw-colored, delicate and sweet to pungent depending on age; good as table cheese or for cooking; sometimes **smoked.**

caciucco (kah-cee-OOK-choa). Ita. Highly seasoned fish **soup** served with rounds of **garlic-**flavored toast.

cadas (ahds). Ara. Lentils.

Caerphilly (Cah-PHEHL-lee). Bri. A semisoft, cow's milk **cheese,** moist, slightly sour, mild, crumbly; made in Wales.

Caesar salad (CEE-zuhr SAHL-lahd). USA. A tossed **salad** of **romaine, garlic, anchovies, croutons;** served with a dressing of **olive oil,** coddled **egg, lemon** juice, and grated **Parmesan cheese.**

café (kah-fay). Fre, Por. **Coffee.**

café (kah-FEH). Spa. **Coffee.**

café au lait (kaf-fay oa leh). Fre. **Coffee** with hot **milk.**

café cargado (kaf-FEH kar-GAH-doh). Spa. Strong **coffee.**

café Carioca (kah-FEH ca-ree-O-ca). Por. **Coffee** diluted with hot water.

café com crême e açúcar (kah-FEH com krem eh a-SOO-kar). Por. **Coffee** with **cream** and **sugar.**

café com leite (kah-FEH com late). Por. **Coffee** with hot **milk.**

café complet (kah-fay kom-pleh). Fre. The traditional continental breakfast of **coffee** and **rolls.**

cafè con panna e zucchero (kahf-FAI kon PAHN-nah un TSOOK-kay-roa). Ita. **Coffee** with **cream** and **sugar.**

café dé bil (kaf-FEH day behl). Spa. Weak **coffee.**

café double (kah-fay dewbl). Fre. Double-strength **coffee.**

café frappé (kah-fay frah-pay). Fre. Iced **coffee.**

café noir (kah-fay nwahr). Fre. Black **coffee;** after-dinner coffee.

café simples (kah-FEH SEE-plesh). Por. Black **coffee.**

cafézinho (kah-feh-ZEE-nyoh). Por. Small cup of black **coffee.**

caffè (kahf-FAI). Ita. **Coffee.**

caffè espresso (kahf-FAI ex-SPREHS-soa). Ita. An especially strong **coffee** prepared by forcing steam under pressure through the powdered coffee, causing the moisture to fall into the cup, then condense to form the beverage; requires a special espresso maker.

caffelatte (kahf-fai-LAHT-tay). Ita. **Coffee** with hot **milk.**

caffè nero (kahf-FAI NAY-roa). Ita. Black **coffee.**

caife (KA-fee). Iri. **Coffee.**

cai juan (caeh juan). Chi. A **pancake**-like wrapper around a filling of finely chopped **pork, shrimp, vegetables,** bean **sprouts, water chestnuts,** grated fresh **ginger,** seasoned with **soy sauce,** then **fried.** Also known as **egg roll.**

caille (kahy). Fre. **Quail.**

caillé (kah-yea). Fre. **Curd.**

cáis (kaash). Iri. **Cheese.** Also spelled *cáise.*

caju (kah-ZHU). Por. **Cashew nut.**

Cajun (KAY-gjuhn). USA. A hot, spicy cuisine famous in southern Louisiana.

cake (kak). USA. A leavened sweet **batter** or **dough** put into small flat pans, then baked; usually stacked in layers and covered with **icing** or **frosting.**

cake (kak). Dut. **Cake.**

cake flour (kak flowr). USA. Milled from soft **wheat;** very fine granulation; low protein content; low **gluten** content; bakes to a crumbly texture.

calabacita (kah-lah-bah-SEE-tah). Spa. Zucchini.

calabash (KAH-lah-bahsh). Spa. **Passion fruit.**

Calabaza (Kah-lah-BAH-tha). Spa. **Pumpkin;** any large **squash;** bright orange usually, may also be green, yellow, or cream-colored on outside with brilliant orange meat; moist and sweet in flavor.

calamaretti (kah-lah-mah-RAYT-tee). Ita. Small **squid.**

calamari (kah-lah-MAH-ree). Ita. **Squid.**

calamondin (kahl-eh-MAHN-dehn). USA. A Philippine variety of **tangerine,** the size of a **kumquat.**

calas (KAH-lahs). USA. A breakfast confection of **rice** mixed with **flour,** spices, and **sugar,** dropped from a spoon and **deep-fried;** a New Orleans specialty.

Calcagno (Kahl-kahg-noh). Ita. A hard **cheese** of ewe's milk, made in Sicily, suitable for **grating.**

calcium chloride (KAHL-ce-um CHLO-rid). USA. A firming compound used by commercial canners, especially in tomatoes.

caldeirada (kahl-day-RAH-dah). Por. Fish **soup** with different kinds of fish, **onions, potatoes,** and **olive oil;** the Portugese **bouillabaisse.**

calderata (kahl-deh-RAH-tah). Spa. A thick fish **stew.**

caldo (KAHL-doa). Ita. Hot.

caldo (KAHL-doh). Spa. **Broth.**

caldo de carne (KAHL-doo duh KAHR-nee). Por. Meat **bouillon.**

caldo de gallina (kahl-doh day gahl-LEE-nah). Spa. **Chicken broth.**

caldo verde (KAHL-doo vaird). Por. Green **soup;** made with mashed **potatoes** and finely chopped green **vegetables.**

calibougas (kah-lee-BOO-gahs). USA. A beverage of rum, spruce **beer,** and **molasses.**

caliente (kahl-LEEN-tah). Spa. Hot.

California dry chili (Cahl-eh-FORN-yah dri CHIHL-ee). USA. A long **chili** pepper that has been left on the vine to dry; turns red.

Californian chili (Cahl-eh-FORN-eh-un CHIHL-ee). USA. A fairly hot, greenish-yellow Mexican **chili** pepper; used fresh or canned, but never **dried.** Also known as **güero, sweet green pepper.**

calimyrna fig (kahl-eh-MURN-ah fehg). USA. A small, amber-skinned **fig** with a sweet, nut-like flavor; eaten fresh, in fruit salads, or in **preserves** and **chutney;** goes well with **poultry,** lamb, and **rice** dishes.

callaloo (cahl-LAH-loh). Spa. A Carribean **stew** of the leafy green tops of **taro,** cooked with **okra, eggplant, tomatoes, onions, garlic, chilies,** spices, **herbs,** meat, **crab,** and **coconut** milk.

callos (KAH-lyoss). Spa. **Tripe.**

calmar (kahl-mahr). Fre. **Squid.**

Calvados (kahl-vah-doa). Fre. **Apple brandy.**

calzone (KAHL-zon). Ita. A savory stuffed **turnover** made of **pizza dough.**

camarão (kah-mah-ROW). Por. **Shrimp.**

camarón (kah-mah-ROH-neh). Spa. **Shrimp.**

cambric tea (KAHM-brehk tee). USA. A drink of hot water, **milk, sugar,** and maybe a dash of **tea;** a thin, white beverage, as cambric is a thin, white fabric; usually given to children to make them feel part of the social gathering.

Cambridge (KAHM-brehg). Bri. A soft, cow's milk **cheese,** also known as York cheese.

Cambridge sauce (KAM-brehg saus). Bri. A **mayonnaise**-based **sauce** of sieved hard-boiled **egg yolks, anchovies, capers, chives, chervil, mustard,** and spices; served with cold meat.

Camembert (kahm-ehm-behr). Fre. One of the world's most renowned **cheeses;** a cow's milk cheese, pale yellow, soft, creamy, rich; crusty exterior; has white mold rind.

Camosun (KAHM-oh-sohn). USA. A semisoft, open-textured **cheese** resembling Gouda and Monterey; developed at Washington State College to utilize surplus milk on farms.

camote (kah-MOH-teh). Spa. **Sweet potato.**

campagnola (kahm-pahg-NOA-lah). Ita. Country style.

Canadian bacon (kah-NA-dee-un BA-kohn). USA. Cut from the boned **pork loin,** which is **cured,** then **smoked,** fully cooked, and **sliced.** Also known as *Canadian-style bacon.*

canapé (kahn-nah-pay). Fre. **Appetizer** served either hot or cold as an **hors d'oeuvre** and eaten with fingers.

canapé (kah-nah-PEH). Mex. **Appetizer, hors d'oeuvre.**

canard (kahn-nahrd). Fre. **Duck.**

canard sauvage (kahn-nahrd soa-vahjg). Fre. Wild **duck.**

candito (kahn-DEE-toa). Ita. Candied.

candy (KAN-dee). USA. To **preserve** or cook with heavy **syrup.** To cook with **sugar** and fat to achieve a **glaze,** as with **carrots** and **sweet potatoes.** A **confection.**

canela (kah-NEH-lah). Spa. **Cinnamon.**

Canestrato (kah-neh-STRAH-toa). Ita. A strong-flavored popular Sicilian **cheese;** bright yellow in color; made of ewe's milk, ripened, then aged.

cane syrup (kan SEHR-up). USA. **Syrup** made from the concentrated sap of **sugar cane;** can be substituted for **molasses.**

caneton (kahn-er-tawng). Fre. Duckling.

cangrejo (kahn-GREH-khoa). Spa. **Crab.**

canistel (kah-NEHS-stuhl). USA. An egg-shaped **fruit** with a thin, glossy skin covering pumpkin-colored flesh that is somewhat flaky; flavor similar to **sweet potato** mixed with heavy **cream;** mixes well fresh with **orange slices, almonds,** and **coconut.**

canja de galinha (KAHN-zah duh gah-LEE-nah). Por. A rich **chicken soup.**

Canned Cheese (Kahnd Chez). USA. Refers to packaging, not kind of cheese; usually is American Cheddar.

canned ham (kahnd hahm). USA. Various **ham** cuts that have been processed and completely cooked before canning.

cannèlla (kahn-NEHL-lah). Ita. **Cinnamon.**

cannelle (kahn-nehl). Fre. **Cinnamon.**

cannellini (kahn-eh-LEE-nee). Ita. White **kidney beans.**

cannelloni (kahn-eh-LON-ee). Ita. **Pasta** tubes with a savory stuffing, baked in a **sauce.**

cannoli (kah-NO-lee). Ita. Deep-fried horn-shaped pastry stuffed with **cheese, chocolate, pudding,** or **whipped cream.**

Canquillote (Kah-kee-oat). Fre. A skim-milk **cheese** made in eastern France.

Cantal (cahn-tah). Fre. A cow's-milk **cheese** with a nutty, full flavor, cylindrical in shape; similar to Cheddar; has been made for more than 2,000 years; semifirm and golden in color; unique taste.

cantaloupe (KAN-tah-lop). USA. **Muskmelon.**

canterellen (kahn-tuh-REL-luh). Dut. **Chanterelles.**

cantucci (kahn-TOO-cee). Ita. Hard-textured sweet **cookies** with **almond** pieces. Also called *cantuccini, biscotti di prato.*

cao-mí (tsao may). Chi. **Strawberries.**

caoireoil (KEE-ry-awil). Iri. **Mutton.**

capão (kah-PAHNG). Por. **Capon.**

capeado (kah-pay-AH-doh). Spa. Dipped in **batter** and **fried.**

capelan (kah-peh-lah). Fre. Fish resembling **smelts** but of the **cod** family.

capelli d'angelo (kahp-PAYL-lee dahn-GEHL-o). Ita. Fine **angel hair pasta.**

capellini (kah-payl-LEE-nee). Ita. The thinnest cut of **pasta.**

capers (KA-purs).   USA. The flower buds of the caper plant, **pickled** for use as a **garnish** or flavoring.

capilotade (kahp-ee-loa-tahd).   Fre. A kind of hashed **game** or **chicken.**

capirotada (kah-pee-roh-TAH-dah).   Mex. Bread **pudding.**

capitone (kah-pay-TO-nee).   Ita. Large conger **eel.**

capocollo (kah-poa-KOL-loa).   Ita. Cooked, boneless **pork** butt that has been rolled in spices and pepper and is served in thin slices.

capon (KA-pahn).   USA. A castrated male **chicken;** well fattened; distinctive taste. Also see **broiler, fryer, roaster, stewing chicken, stag chicken,** and **cock.**

caponata (kah-poa-NAH-tah).   Ita. A vegetable salad of **fried eggplant, onions, tomatoes, anchovies, capers,** and **olives.**

capozella (kah-poa-ZEHL-lah).   Ita. Lamb's head.

cappelletti (cahp-ah-LEHT-tee).   Ita. A moist, stuffed **pasta** usually served in **soup;** said to resemble "little hats"; similar to **tortellini.**

capperi (kahp-PAY-ree).   Ita. **Capers.**

cappone (kahp-PO-nay).   Ita. **Capon.**

cappon magro (KAHP-pohn MAHG-roa).   Ita. An elaborate **salad** of cooked **vegetables, anchovies, fish, lobster,** and **garlic**-rubbed **biscuits.**

cappuccino (kahp-pook-CHEE-noa).   Ita. **Espresso coffee** with hot frothy **milk,** sprinkled with **cinnamon** and **cocoa.**

câpres (kah-preh).   Fre. **Capers.**

capretto (kah-PREH-toa).   Ita. Kid, young goat.

Caprino Formaggio (kah-PREE-noa Foar-MAHD-joa).   Ita. A goat's-milk **cheese.**

capriolo (kah-pree-O-loa).   Ita. **Roebuck, deer.**

capsicum (KAP-ci-kohm).   USA. A genus of **chili** peppers.

caracoles (kahr-rah-LOHL-ehs).   Spa. **Snails.**

carambola (kah-rahm-BO-lah).   USA. A tropical **fruit** with glossy, yellow, waxy skin; very juicy, crisp, almost translucent flesh; has five longitudinal ribs, when sliced across is star-shaped. Also called **starfruit.**

caramel (kahr-a-mehl).   Fre. A coloring substance made by boiling **sugar** in water until a rich dark brown color; used in **candy, desserts, sauces, stocks.**

caramelize (KAR-mah-liz). USA. To heat **sugar** until a brown color and a characteristic flavor develops.

caramelized sugar (KAR-mah-lizd SCHU-gahr). USA. The seventh stage of **sugar crystallization:** begins at 310° F to 338° F, between these temperatures syrup turns dark golden, but it will turn black at 350° F.

caramella (kah-rah-MEHL-lah). Ita. **Caramel,** or any hard **candy.**

caramelo (kah-rah-MAY-loo). Por. **Caramel.**

caranguejo (kah-rehn-GAY-zhoh). Por. **Crab.**

Caraway (KAHR-ah-way). USA. A hard **cheese** that contains **caraway** seeds; one of the spiced cheeses.

caraway (KAHR-ah-way). USA. An **herb** that produces a black, ribbed seed used for brewing **tea, baking,** flavoring meats and **vegetables,** and flavoring the **liqueur kümmel;** leaves used in **salads** and **soups.**

carbonado (kahr-boh-NAH-doh). Spa. An Argentine **stew** made of beef, **apples, pears, potatoes, tomatoes,** and **onions.**

carbonara (kahr-bo-NAHR-ah). Ita. A spaghetti sauce made of **cream, bacon,** eggs, and **Parmesan.**

carbonnade (kahr-bon-nahd). Fre. **Stewed** or **braised** meat.

carbonnade flamande (kahr-bon-nahd flah-mahngd). Fre. A beef **stew** made of **bacon, onions,** and **brown sugar** and simmered in **beer.**

carciòfi (kah-CHO-fee). Ita. **Artichokes.**

cardamom (KAHRD-ah-mahm). USA. A Middle Eastern **herb** of the **ginger** family with an aromatic **fruit** whose seeds are used as a **condiment** and a flavoring.

cardinal (kahr-dee-nahl). Fre. A red-colored sauce used for fish **garnish;** made of **mushrooms, truffle** slices; usually hen **lobsters** are used instead to get the naturally red tint.

cardinal fish (KAHR-dee-null fesch). USA. A red **mullet** found in the Mediterranean, called king of the mullets; very similar to the redfish found on the East and Gulf Coasts of United States.

cardinal suppe (kahr-dee-NAHL ssewpper). Nor. Creamy **soup** with bits of **ham** and **noodles.**

cardon (kahr-dawng). Fre. **Cardoon.**

cardoni (kar-DOHN-nee). USA. A member of the thistle family; looks somewhat like **celery;** has **artichoke**-like flavor; use cooked, **diced** in **salads, deep fried,** or **marinated.**

cardoon (kahr-dawng).   Fre. A **vegetable** grown for its fleshy, silver-gray stalks that grow in bunches, like **celery;** stalks are flat, long, wide, with notched sides, suede-like finish; a relative of the **artichoke;** also spelled **cardon.**

cari (kah-ree).   Fre. **Curry;** many times spelled *curry.*

carmine (kahr-meen).   Fre. Red coloring used in **confectionery.**

carnab (AR-nab).   Ara. **Rabbit.**

carne (KAHR-neh).   Ita, Spa, Por. Meat.

carne asada en horno (KAHR-neh ah-SAH-dah en OHR-noh).   Spa. **Baked** meat.

carne asada en parrilla (KAHR-neh ah-SAH-dah en pahr-REE-yah).   Spa. **Boiled** meat.

carne de cerdo (KAR-neh dah SEHR-doh).   Mex. **Pork, corn.**

carne de porco à Algarvia (KAHR-nuh duh POR-koo ah al-GAHR-vee-ah).   Por. **Fried pork** and **clams.**

carne de vinha de Alhos (KAHR-nuh duh VEE-nyah duh AH-lious).   Por. **Pickled pork** dish.

carne in umido (KAHR-nay un OO-mee-doa).   Ita. **Stewed** beef.

carneiro (kahr-NAY-roh).   Por. **Mutton.**

carne lessa (KAHR-nay LAYS-sah).   Ita. **Boiled** beef.

carne picada (KAHR-nuh peek-AH-dah).   Por. **Chopped** or **minced** meat.

carne tritata (KAHR-nay tray-TAH-toa).   Ita. **Minced** meat.

carob (KAHR-uhb).   USA. Pods of the Mediterranean evergreen locust tree, high in protein and **sugar,** eaten fresh and **dried;** used as a **chocolate** substitute; **locust bean.**

carob flour (KAHR-uhb flowr).   USA. A **chocolate**-flavored **flour** or **powder** milled from the **carob** tree pod; a nutritious, low-fat substitute for chocolate.

Carolina rice (kahr-oh-LI-nah ris).   USA. A variety of **rice,** long-grained, angular, white, bright, and shiny.

caroline (kah-o-leen).   Fre. Small **éclair,** served as an **hors d'oeuvre.**

carota (kah-RAW-tah).   Ita. **Carrots.**

carottes (kah-rot).   Fre. **Carrots.**

carottes Flamandes (kah-rot flah-mohnd).   Fre. Creamed **carrots,** in the Flemish style.

carp (karp).   USA. A freshwater fish, found in Asia, Europe, and United States; unless farmed has a muddy taste.

carpa (KAHR-pah).   Ita. **Carp.** Also called *carpione.*

carpaccio (kahr-paak-CHEE-o).   Ita. Raw beef filet **sliced** very, very thin; served with **mustard sauce,** or oil and **lemon** juice.

carp caviar (kahrp kah-vee-AHR).   USA. A **caviar** substitute; the **roe** or eggs of the **carp.**

carpe (kahrp).   Fre. **Carp.**

carpeau (kahrp-oa).   Fre. Small **carp.**

carpione (kahr-pee-O-neh).   Ita. **Carp.** Also called **carpe.**

carrageenan (KAHR-ah-ghee-nohn).   USA. A **seaweed** of North America and northern Europe; reddish-purple, white when dried; eaten fresh or dried; excellent source of **gelatin;** used in sweet and savory dishes; **Irish moss.**

Carré (kah-ray).   Fre. A small, rich **cheese** of the **Neufchâtel** type; also known as *Double Crème Carré* and *Fromage Double Crème.*

carré d'agneau (kah-ray dah-noa).   Fre. **Rack** of lamb.

Carré de l'Est (Kahr-reh doo lehst).   Fre. A **cheese** described as a cross between **Brie** and **Camembert;** made of **raw** or **pasteurized** cow's whole milk; soft in texture; always sold in small boxes; has a crust that may be eaten unless yellow or orange in color.

carrelet (kah-reh-leh).   Fre. **Flounder, plaice.**

carrettes (KAHR-rhehtz).   USA. Small very sweet **carrots** about one to two inches long. Also known as *French carrots.*

carrot (KAHR-roht).   USA. A root **vegetable** that is orange; has mild, sweet taste; use cooked or **raw** in **salads.**

carrots Vichy (KAHR-rohtz VEE-chee).   USA. **Pared** and **sliced carrots** prepared in **Vichy water** and **glazed.**

carte du jour (cahrt dew zuhr).   Fre. The bill of fare for the day.

casaba (kah-SAH-bah).   Ara. A Turkish, globular-shaped winter **melon** with chartruse-yellow rind that wrinkles at the pointed end; flesh is thick, soft, creamy white, sweet, and juicy.

casal (AH-sal).   Ara. **Honey.**

casalinga (kah-sah-LEEN-gah). Ita. Homemade.

cascabel (KAHS-sah-behl). Mex. A small, round, dried **chili** pepper with reddish-brown skin; fairly hot; the seeds rattle in the dried pod.

Casera or Cashera (Cah-see-rah or Cah-shah-rah). Tur. A sharp, firm, salty, white goat's-milk cheese that is crumbly; when young, soft enough to spread; firm and zesty when aged.

cashew (KASH-u). USA. A kidney-shaped **nut** favored in Indian, Asian, and South American cooking; used to make wine, **vinegar,** and **liqueur.**

Cashkavallo or Caskcaval (Kahs-kah-VAHL-lo). Ita. Balkan version of **cheese** known as *Caciocavallo.*

casing (KA-sing). USA. A natural or synthetic membranous case used for **sausage forcemeat.**

casiyr (a-SEER). Ara. Juice.

cassata (kahs-SAH-tah). Ita. A rich **chocolate** dessert of **sponge cake,** cut in layers, filled with a mixture of **ricotta cheese,** candied **fruits,** chopped **chocolate,** and a **liqueur.**

cassava (kah-SAH-vah). Spa. A tropical tree whose root is used to make **flour** for bread and **tapioca** pearls for thickening **soups** and **puddings;** a pure starch.

casserole (cahss-rohl). Fre. A dish served in a bowl or pan, made with **rice,** pastry crust, or **pasta,** and filled with **minced** meat, **vegetables, seafood,** or **cheese,** that is usually **baked,** then served.

casseruola (kas-say-RWO-lah). Ita. **Casserole.**

cassia (KASH-e). USA. A reddish-brown spice often confused with **cinnamon.**

cassis (kahs-seess). Fre. Black **currant liqueur.**

cassoulet (kass-oo-leht). Fre. **Garlic**-flavored **bean stew** usually containing **sausages, poultry,** and meat.

castagna (kah-STAA-nah). Ita. **Chestnut.**

castagnaccio (kah-staa-nahk-CHEE-o). Ita. A sweet **cake** made with **chestnut flour, pine** kernels, and **currants.**

castagnaci (kah-staa-NAH-chee). Ita. **Fritters** or **waffles** made of **chestnut flour.**

castagnoles (kahs-tahg-nyohl). Fre. **Batter fritters.**

castanhas (kahss-TAH-nyahss). Por. **Chestnuts.**

castigane alla fiamma (kah-stee-GAH-nay AHL-lah fee-AHM-mah). Ita. **Brandied chestnuts.**

castor sugar (KAHS-tohr SCHU-gawr). Bri. **Superfine sugar.**

castradina (cah-strah-DEE-nah). Ita. **Mutton.** Also called **castrato.**

castrato (kah-STRAH-toa). Ita. **Mutton.** Also called **castradina.**

catalane, à la (kah-tahl-ahn). Fre. A **garnish** of **sautéed eggplants** and **rice pilaf** served on large cuts of meats.

catfish (KAT-fehsh). USA. A fresh and saltwater fish with no scales, whiskers, delicate flesh, and very few bones.

caudle (KAHU-duhl). Bri. A hot spice drink of wine or **ale** with bread or **gruel, eggs,** and **sugar** added.

caul (kahl). Fre. The thin, fatty, lacy membrane from a pig's or lamb's intestines, used to contain and cover pâtés or **roasts;** melts away during cooking.

cauliflower (KAUL-ee-flawr). USA. A garden plant grown for its compact, edible head of white undeveloped flowers.

cavallucci di siena (kah-vahl-LOO-chee dee cee-EHN-ah). Ita. Small **cakes** made of **honey,** candied **fruit,** and **nuts.**

cavatelli (cah-vah-TEHL-lee). Ita. **Pasta** in shape of curled shells with about three ridges.

caveau (kah-voh). Fre. A little cellar for keeping fine wines.

caviale (kah-vee-AH-lay). Ita. Dried fish **roe;** a local **caviar** substitute.

caviar (kav-ee-AHR). Fre. The salted **roe** or **eggs** of the **sturgeon** or other large fish, pressed, and used as **relish.** See also specific varieties: **beluga, malosol, oscietr, pausnaya, sevruga, sterlet,** and **ship;** caviar substitutes: **carp, herring, hon-tarako, karasumi,** and **lumpfish** are listed in this volume.

cavolfiore (kah-vol-fee-OA-ray). Ita. **Cauliflower.**

cavolfiore alla romana (kah-vol-fee-OA-ray AHL-loa roa-MAH-nah). Ita. **Cauliflower** in oil.

cavolfiore alla villeroy (kah-vol-fee-OA-ray AHL-loa veel-lay-ROA-ee). Ita. **Cauliflower** with **lemon sauce.**

cavolfiore indorato e fritto (kah-vol-fee-OA-ray een-doa-RAH-toa ay FREET-toa). Ita. Breaded, fried **cauliflower.**

cavolini di bruxelles (kah-vo-LEE-nee dee broos-SAYL). Ita. **Brussels sprouts.**

cavolo (KAH-voa-loa). Ita. **Cabbage.**

cavolrapa (kah-vol-RAH-pah). Ita. **Kohlrabi.**

cavroman (kahv-RO-mahn). Ita. **Mutton** or lamb **stew,** with **potatoes, peppers,** and **onions.**

cayenne pepper (ki-AHN PEHP-per). Mex. **Dried** red **chili** pepper, finely **ground;** also used fresh.

cazuela (kah-SWEH-lah). Spa. Earthenware **casserole.**

cebiche (theh-BEE-cheh). Spa. Raw fish or **shellfish marinated** in **lime** juice; not cooked by heat, but by chemical reaction of lime juice.

cebolas (say-BOH-lah). Por. **Onions.**

cebolla (theh-BOH-lah). Spa. **Onion.**

Cebreto (theh-BREH-toa). Spa. A blue-veined **cheese;** yellow rind; creamy paste.

ceche (CHEE-cay). Ita. Very tiny, young **eels, fried** with **garlic** and **sage,** or mixed with **eggs** and **flour** and served as little **pancakes.**

ceci (CHAY-chee). Ita, Spa. **Chickpeas; garbanzo beans.**

cefalo (kay-FAH-lee). Ita. Gray **mullet.**

celeriac (seh-LEHR-ee-ahk). USA. **Celery root;** a variety of **celery** having a large edible root.

céleri-rave (seh-ler-ree-rahv). Fre. **Celery root.**

celery (SEHL-ree). USA. An herb of the **carrot** family with leafstalks eaten **raw** or cooked.

celery root (SEHL-ree root). USA. A large, bulb-type root with light brown skin and white flesh; eaten raw or cooked; also known as **celeriac.**

celery seed (SEHL-ree seed). USA. The seed of the **celery** plant; used in the **pickling** process as a seasoning.

celestine (see-les-teen). Fre. A **garnish** for clear **soup,** consisting of fine strips of **fried pancakes.**

cellophane noodles (cehl-lo-FAN NOO-duhls). USA. Oriental translucent **noodles** made from **mung beans.**

celtuce (cehl-TUHS). USA. A stem **lettuce;** use only the stem or seedstalk; use **raw** or **braised,** as **water chestnuts;** very high vitamin C content.

cenci (CHEH-chee). Ita. **Fried** sweets.

cenders (sohn-druh). Fre. **Baked** in hot ashes.

cenouras (seh-NOH-rahss). Por. **Carrots.**

centollos (theen-TOHL-loas). Spa. **Crabs.**

cèpe (sehp). Fre. **Boletus mushroom.**

cerdo (THEHR-doa). Spa. **Pork;** used interchangably with *puerco.*

cerdo (SAYR-doo). Por. Wild boar.

cereal (CEH-ree-uhl). USA. **Grain** suitable for food; also prepared foodstuff made of grain, such as **oatmeal, grits,** cornflakes, or branflakes; eaten hot or cold.

cereal cream (CEH-ree-uhl krem). USA. **Cream** containing 10.5–18% milk fat; same as **half-and-half.**

cerejas (say-RAY-zhahss). Por. **Cherries.**

cerezas (thay-RAY-thahss). Spa. **Cherries.**

cerfeuil (sehr-fuhy). Fre. **Chervil.**

ceriman (CEH-ree-muhm). USA. The **fruit** of the subtropical plant commonly known as the split-leaf philodendron; has a cucumbershaped fruit, covered with tiny hexagonal plateelets that fall off when ripe; soft, juicy flesh tastes like fresh **pineapple** and ripe **banana;** eat fresh or use as a **chutney** base. Also known as *monstera.*

cerise (suh-reez). Fre. **Cherry.**

cernaux confits (sehr-noh kon-fees). Fre. Pickled green **walnuts.**

cervelas (sehr-veh-la). Fre. A **garlic**-flavored **pork sausage.**

Cervelatwurst (SEHR-veh-layt-voorst). Ger. Spiced beef and **pork sausage.**

cervelles (sehr-vehl). Fre. Brains, usually from calf or **veal.**

cerveza (thayr-BHAY-thah). Mex. **Beer.**

cèrvo (CHEH-voa). Ita. **Venison.**

cestino da viaggio (cheh-STEE-noa dah vee-ahg-JEE-o). Ita. Picnic lunch to take on a trip.

cetriòlo (chay-tree-O-loa-nee). Ita. **Cucumber.**

cha (chah). Jap. **Tea.**

chá (shah). Por. **Tea.**

chá (tsah). Chi. **Tea.**

Chabichou (shah-bee-shoo). Fre. A soft, mild goat's-milk **cheese,** conical or cylindrical in shape; smooth and delicious; shape of small ball covered with a blue-green mold; excellent with Madeira.

chah (chah). Ind. **Tea.**

chahr ziu (chaah dsda-ow). Chi. **Barbecued pork.**

chai (CHYAH-yoo). Rus. **Tea.**

chair blanc (shehr blan). Fre. White meat.

chair noire (shehr nawr). Fre. Dark meat.

challah (HKAH-lah). Jew. A braided **egg** bread, traditional on the Sabbath.

chalota (shah-LOU-tah). Por. **Green onion.**

chalupa (chah-LOO-pah). Mex. Oval or boat-shaped **tortilla dough,** pinched up around edge and filled.

chamomile (KAHM-oh-mehl). USA. A small fragrant plant with daisylike flowers that produce a delightful apple-scented **tea.**

champ (chahmp). Iri. Mashed **potatoes** beaten to a light foam, combined with some cooked **vegetables** (usually **cabbage** or **onions),** and served with a huge dollop of melting **butter** in the center.

champagne grapes (sham-PAN grapz). USA. A variety of **grapes** that are tiny, like **currants,** with a very sweet flavor; used as **garnish** on plates, on beverage glasses, or on cheese boards; not the wine grape.

champanhe (sham-PAH-nyay). Por. **Champagne.**

champignons (shahng-peen-yawn). Fre, Ger, Dut. **Mushrooms.**

champiñon (sham-pee-NYOHN). Mex. **Mushroom.**

Champoléon (Chah-poh-lee-owng). Fre. A skim-milk, hard **cheese;** also known as Queyras.

channa (CHAH-nah). Ind. **Chickpeas.**

chanquettes (chahn-KAH-tays). Spa. Tiny, fried fish.

Chantelle (Shahn-tee). Fre. A semisoft, ripened **cheese** with a pale golden interior; delicious with **pears** or fresh, ripe **pineapple.**

chanterelle (shang-tee-rell). Fre. A golden-orange, apricot-scented, trumpet-shaped, wild **mushroom** with a ruffled edge.

Chantilly (Shawn-tee-e). Ita. A soft, ripe cream **cheese** sometimes flavored with **chives.**

chantilly (shang-tee-yeh). Fre. Served with **whipped cream.**

chantilly cream (shang-tee-yeh krem). Fre. Sweetened and flavored **whipped cream.**

chao (tsao). Chi. To **stir-fry; sauté.**

chao fan (tsao fan). Chi. **Fried rice.**

chao gwoo (tsao gwu). Chi. Straw **mushrooms;** a bud containing a miniature mushroom; fresh, canned, **dried.**

chao jidàn (tsao gee-dan). Chi. Scrambled **eggs.**

chao miàn (chow mein). Chi. **Fried noodles.**

Chaource (shah-oorceh). Fre. A soft, creamy, whole-milk **cheese** with a mild, fruity taste, and is produced in the Champagne district.

chao yùlánpiàn donggu (tsao yoo lan pien doong gu). Chi. Black **mushrooms sautéed** with **bamboo shoots.**

chap (shah). Fre. The lower jaw, or half of cheek of a pig.

chapati (cha-PAH-tee). Ind. Thin griddle-baked **whole wheat** bread.

chapelure (sha-pehl-lewr). Fre. Bread crumbs made by crushing oven-dried bread with a rolling pin and passing through a sieve.

chapon (shah-pawng). Fre. The heel of bread rubbed with **garlic,** seasoned with oil and **vinegar,** added to **salad.**

char (shahr). USA. A fat fish with very firm, delicate, white to deep red flesh; found in various deep lakes and rivers in the northern hemisphere; superior to **salmon** in taste.

charcoal-grilled (CHAR-koal-grield). USA. To cook over glowing charcoal embers, to impart that special flavor, usually done out-of-doors.

charcuterie (shahr-kew-ter-ree). Fre. Meat specialities of French butcher shops, such as **sausages, ham, galantines, pâtés, rillettes.**

charcutière (shahr-kew-tehr). Fre. A sauce of sautéed **onions,** white wine, **vinegar, demi-glace, mustard,** with **julenne gherkins** added before serving; served with meats.

chard cabbage (chard CAHB-bahg). USA. **Chinese cabbage.**

charentais (shahr-ahng-tehs). Fre. A **melon** of yellow-green ribbed skin, orange flesh; sweet, succulent.

charlotte (shahr-loht). Fre. A dish of **custard.**

charlotte russe (shahr-loht rews). Fre. A **dessert** made in a mold lined with **cake** slices or **ladyfingers,** filled with a **custard, whipped cream,** and **strawberries** on top.

charni (CHAR-nee). Ind. **Chutney.**

Chartreuse (shahr-truz). Fre. **Liqueur** made of **angelica** leaves, **hyssop, cinnamon** bark, balm, **mace,** and **saffron.**

chartreuse ragoût (shahr-truz raa-GOO). Dan. A **casserole** of prettily arranged **carrots, cabbage,** and meat or **chicken.**

chá shao bao (cha shaoo baoo). Chi. **Steamed** bun stuffed with **roast pork.**

chasseur (shahs-sur). Fre. A **garnish** of **mushrooms, sliced** and **sautéed,** flavored with **shallots** and moistened with white wine.

chat (chaht). Ind. A cold dish made with **vegetables, fruits,** and spices; eaten as a snack or **appetizer.**

châtaignes (shah-tayg-nehs). Fre. **Chestnuts.**

chateaubriand (shah-toa-bree-ahng). Fre. A superb, thick **filet** steak, served with a **brown sauce** of fat, **lemon, parsley,** seasonings, and **Spanish sauce.**

château potatoes (SHAH-toa po-TA-tos). USA. **Potatoes** cut in long strips and cooked in **butter.**

charni (CHAR-nee). Ind. **Chutney.**

chaud (sho). Fre. Hot.

chaud-froid (sho-fro). Fre. **Chicken fricassee** served cold, covered with its **gravy,** glazed with **aspic.**

chaunk gobhi (chawnk GOHB-hee). Ind. **Brussels sprouts.**

chausson aux pommes (sho-so oa pom). Fre. **Apple turnover.**

Chavignol (shah-vee-nah). Fre. A small, soft goat's-milk **cheese;** semi-hard to hard; aging brings out goaty flavor.

chawal (CHAH-val). Ind. **Rice.**

chayote (chah-YOH-teh). Mex. **Pear**-shaped **vegetable.**

Cheddar (CHEHD-ehr). Bri. A cow's whole-milk, hard **cheese** with a smooth texture, orange color, and a flavor ranging from mild to sharp, depending on age; the name covers 80% of all USA cheeses, both natural and pasteurized.

cheese (chez). USA. A generic term for the products made from **milk curd** separated from **whey,** sometimes **fermented,** usually molded under presssure, and ripened for use as food; countless varieties worldwide.

cheesecake (CHEZ-kak). USA. A **cake** made with a mixture of beaten **eggs, cream cheese** or **cottage cheese, sugar,** flavorings; baked in a mold lined with sweet crumbs.

chef's salad (chehfs SAH-lahd). USA. Mixed green **salad** with hard-boiled **egg** and **julienne** meats added.

chemise (sher-meez). Fre. With skins on; generally applies to **potatoes; ice cream** covered with a thin coating.

chemiser (shuh-mee-zyay). Fre. To coat a mold; with **aspic,** bread crumbs, **ice cream,** and so forth.

chenna (CHAY-nah). Ind. Indian **cheese.**

cherba-bel-frik (SHUR-ba-beel-freek). Afr. Green **corn soup.**

chereshnya (VEESH-nyee). Rus. **Cherry.**

cherimoya (che-ree-MOY-a). Spa. A low acid, sweet tasting **fruit** with silky smooth, juicy, and cream-colored flesh that is slightly granular like a custard of fine pears; also known as custard apple and white sapote.

Cherries Jubilee (CHEH-reez JUB-eh-lee). USA. An elegant **dessert** of **vanilla ice cream** topped with a flaming sweet-**cherry sauce.**

cherry (CHEH-ree). USA. The fruit of a cherry tree; sour or **pie** cherries are of the Morello and Montmorency varieties; sweet cherries the Black Tartarian and Napoleon.

Cherry Heering (chehr-ree heer-eng). Dan. **Cherry brandy.**

cherry tomatoes (CHEH-ree toh-MAH-tohs). USA. A variety of **tomatoes** that is tasty, globular, about one inch in diameter; available in red, pink, or yellow.

chervil (CHUR-vul). USA. An **herb** of the **parsley** family; delicate flavor; slightly **anise**-like; use fresh for fullest flavor.

Cheshire (SHEHS-shur). Bri. A hard cow's-milk **cheese,** made in colors: red, white, blue; called **Chester** on the continent; one of the most famous of English cheeses; made before the arrival of the first Roman legions.

Chester (chehs-ter). Fre. **Cheshire cheese.**

chestnut (CHEHS-nuht). USA. The edible **nut** of the chestnut tree; used for various culinary preparations and in the **confection** of sweets and pastries.

cheston crappin (TSHEHS-tuhn KRAHP-pen). Sco. **Chestnut** stuffing.

cheveaux d'ange (sheh-voh danj). Fre. **Angel hair pasta,** the thinnest **vermicelli.**

Chèvre (shevr). Fre. Goat's-milk **cheese** that is soft and fresh.

Chevret (Shuhr-vah). Fre. A chalky white, delicate goat's-milk **cheese;** sometimes spelled *Chevreton;* also called **Chevrotin.**

chevreuil (sherv-rery). Fre. **Venison.**

Chevrotin (sheh-vroh-teen). Fre. A **cheese** the same as **Chevret.**

Chhena (CHAY-nah). Ind. A very fine-grained, fresh **cheese** made from curdled milk; used for making Indian milk sweets; also spelled **Chenna.**

Chiavari (Cheh-VAHR-ree). Ita. A sour-milk **cheese** made from cow's whole milk.

chícharo (CHEE-chah-roh). Mex. **Pea.**

chicharroón (chcc-char-RROHN). Mex. Crisp-fried **pork** rind.

chicken (CHEH-kehn). USA. The common domestic **fowl** whose flesh is used for food. Also see **broiler, pullet, fryer, roaster, stewing chicken, capon, stag chicken, cock.**

chicken cacciatore (CHEH-kehn kotch-ah-TOR-ree). USA. A dish in which the **chicken** is cooked with **tomatoes** and **mushrooms.**

chicken-fried steak (CHEH-kehn-frid stahk). USA. Steak rolled in **flour,** dipped in **egg batter,** rolled in flour again, and **fried** crisp.

chicken Kiev (CHEH-kehn KEE-ehv). USA. **Chicken** breast spread with herb **butter,** rolled, dipped in **egg batter,** rolled in bread crumbs, and deep fried.

chicken of the woods (CHEH-kehn of the woods). USA. A **mushroom** that is rather large and fan-shaped; flesh is white or salmon-orange, with deep orange to yellow skin; must be cooked.

chicken paprika (CHEH-kehn pahp-REE-kah). USA. The Hungarian dish, **paprikas csirke,** of **chicken** braised with **onions** and **garlic,** with plenty of **paprika** and **sour cream.**

chicken steak (CHEH-kehn stahk). USA. A cut of beef from the **chuck,** in small individual portions with a characteristic white streak down the center.

chicken tetrazzini (CHEH-kehn tet-tra-ZEE-neh). USA. Strips of cooked **chicken** and **spaghetti** in a sherry-flavored **cream sauce** with grated Parmesan.

chickpea (CHEHK-pee). USA. A round **legume, dried** or fresh; used extensively in Mediterranean, Middle Eastern, Indian, and Mexican cooking; an important ingredient in **couscous, hummus,** and many **soups** and **stews.**

chicorée frisée (sheek-or-ray fri-zay). Fre. Curly-leaf **chicory.**

chicória (shee-KOU-ree-ah). Por. **Chicory.**

chicory (CHICK-oh-ree). USA. A plant whose long, tight-fitting, bleached white leaves are used as a **salad** green; roots are commonly **roasted, ground,** mixed with **coffee,** or used alone as a coffee substitute. Also called **curly endive.**

chicory escarole (CHICK-oh-ree EHS-cah-role). USA. Batavian **endive;** a bitterish **salad** green with closely packed greenish-white outer leaves that may look like **celery ribs.**

chiffon (schef-FAHN). Fre. Having a light, delicate texture achieved by adding whipped **egg** whites or whipped **gelatin.**

chiffonade (sher-fon-NAHD). Fre. **Minced** or **shredded vegetables** or meat sprinkled over **soups** or **salads.**

chih mah (zhi ma). Chi. **Sesame** seeds, white or black.

chikin sarada (chee-KEEN sah-rah-dah). Jap. **Chicken salad.**

chikin supu (chee-KEEN soo-poo). Jap. **Chicken soup.**

chikuwa (che-KUH-wah). Jap. Fish **paste.**

chilaquiles (CHEE-lah-KEE-lehs). Mex. Dish made with stale **tortillas.**

chili (CHIHL-ee). USA. The **fruit** of the Capsicum family, **pepper** plants; many varieties from mild to fiery hot; used in many cuisines throughout the world.

chili con carne (CHIHL-ee kohn KAR-neh). USA. A spicy **stew** of **ground beef, minced chilies, chili powder,** with or without **beans.**

chili con queso (CHIHL-ee kohn kaa-so). USA. Melted **cheeses** seasoned with finely chopped **chilies;** served very hot with **tortilla** chips.

chili powder (CHIHL-ee POW-der). Mex. A mixture of various dried **herbs** and spices and **chili peppers** used for seasoning; always includes **cumin, oregano, coriander.**

chilindrón (chee-leen-DROHN). Spa. A garnish of sweet red **peppers, onions, tomatoes, garlic,** and **ham.**

chill (chehl). USA. To reduce the temperature of a food by refrigerating until thoroughly cold.

chimichanga (chee-mee-CHAHN-gah). Mex. Like a **burrito,** but deep-fried.

chine (chin). USA. The bony part, or backbone, adhering to the **filet;** usually cut away, leaving only the muscle.

Chinese anise (chi-NEEZ AHN-ehs). USA. An **herb** whose star-shaped seeds are used for flavoring many Oriental foods, meats, **curries, confections, pickles;** the oil is used for flavoring baked goods and **ice cream.** Also called **star anise.**

Chinese artichoke (chi-NEEZ AR-tee-chok). USA. A tuber that produces a mint-like plant; tuber is white, thin, and crisp-fleshed; can be eaten **raw** or cooked.

Chinese beans (chi-NEEZ benz). USA. **Long beans;** bright **green beans,** about a foot long, flavor stronger than ordinary green beans. Also called **asparagus beans.**

Chinese cabbage (chi-NEEZ CAHB-bahg). USA. A Chinese **vegetable** that is slightly elongated, but chunky, with fairly white and wide ribs and frilly dark green leaves; also known as **dà báicài,** chad cabbage, **Chinese mustard, shirona, bok choy, bái cài.** Use alone or **stir-fry.**

Chinese cinnabar melon (chi-NEEZ CEN-nee-bahr MEII-lun). USA. A **melon** with a deep red color, smooth texture; sweet, subtle flavor; ideal breakfast fruit or use in fresh **fruit salads.**

Chinese gooseberry (chi-NEEZ GOUS-behr-ree). USA. **Kiwi fruit.**

Chinese mustard (chi-NEEZ MUHST-urd). USA. **Chinese cabbage.**

Chinese naval orange (chi-NEEZ NA-vuhl OHR-ahnj). USA. A sweet-flavored orange with a low acid content; eaten fresh.

Chinese okra (chi-NEEZ OH-krah). USA. A dark green, heavily ridged **okra,** about 10–12 inches long, one-inch diameter.

Chinese parsley (chi-NEEZ PARS-lee). USA. **Coriander.**

Chinese pea pods (chi-NEEZ pee pohds). USA. **Snow peas.**

Chinese red stew (chi-NEEZ rehd stu). USA. Meats cooked without **browning** in liquid that is half **soy sauce** and half water, seasoned with **ginger, scallions,** and **sherry;** meat is colored during cooking; of Chinese origin.

Chinese sausages (chi-NEEZ sau-SAHGE). USA. Spicy **pork sausages,** about five inches long, reddish in color; sometimes **dried.**

Chinese spinach (chi-NEEZ SPEHN-ihch). USA. A dark green leafy **vegetable.** Also called **tampala.**

chingchao mingzia (ching-tsao ming-sia). Chi. **Sautéed prawns.**

chinook (sheh-NOOK). USA. Member of the **salmon** family; most prized of North American species; tasty flesh, large flakes, high oil content, soft texture; best eaten **au naturel.**

chinquapin (CHEHNK-ah-pehn). USA. **Pine nut.** Also known as **crenata, pignola, piñon, Indian nut.**

chiodi di garofano (kee-O-dee dee gah-RO-fah-noh). Ita. **Cloves.**

chipolata (kee-poa-LAH-tah). Ita. Small Italian **sausages.**

chipolatas (shee-po-lah-tahs). Fre. Small **pork sausages.**

chipotle (chee-POT-tleh). Mex. Name of a **smoked chili.**

chipped beef (chehpt bef). USA. Flakes of dried beef; used to flavor foods and in **cream sauce.**

chips (chehpz). Bri. **Deep-fried potato** pieces.

chiqueter (shee-kwee-teh). Fre. To flute the rim or edge of pastry with a special knife or the fingertips.

chirashi zushi (chee-RAH-shee SOO-shee). Jap. A type of **sushi** that consists of **rice** filled or topped with bits or slices of various **vegetables** and **seafood,** arranged in a lacquer box.

chitarra (chee-TAHR-rah). Ita. This square **spaghettini** was originally cut with guitar (chitarra) strings.

chitterling (CHEHT-ehr-lehng). USA. The small intestines of pigs when prepared as food; commonly called *chitlings* or *chitlins.*

chives (chivz). USA. An **herb** of the **onion** family; has tiny tubular leaves, delicate onion-like flavor; use finely chopped and **raw.**

chi zhi (cheh dzi). Chi. **Black bean sauce.**

chlodnik (CLOHD-nehk). Pol. A warm-weather **borsch** made with **beets, onions, cucumbers,** seasonings; served cold with dollop of **sour cream.**

chocola (sho-ko-LAH). Dut. **Chocolate.**

chocolat (shok-kol-lah). Fre. **Chocolate;** used as a beverage.

chocolate (CHOHK-o-laht). USA. **Ground roasted cacao beans** prepared for use as beverage, **confection,** coloring agent; available in several forms: candy coating, chips, squares, flakes, powder, blocks, sweet, semisweet, unsweetened; see **white chocolate;** also known as *schokolade, cioccolata, chocolat, chocolade.*

chocos (SHOU-koos). Por. **Squid.**

chokladglass (shook-LAAD-glahss). Swe. **Chocolate ice cream.**

chokoreto (choh-KOH-reh-toh). Jap. **Chocolate;** (the flavor), as chocolate **cake.**

cholent (HKOHL-lehnt). Jew. A slowly cooked dish of **brisket, potatoes, barley,** and **lima beans.**

chongos (CHOAN-gos). Spa. A **custard** seasoned with **lemon** and **cinnamon.**

chop (chohp). USA. Cutting food into pieces less than ¼ inch with a knife or sharp tool. See **cube, dice,** and **mince.**

chorizo (choh-REE-soh). Mex. Spicy **sausage.**

choron (shoa-rawng). Fre. A **bearnaise sauce** colored pink with **tomato purée.**

chota piaz (CHO-tah pih-YAZ). Ind. **Shallot.**

choti elaichi (CHO-tee ee-LIE-a-chee). Ind. Green **cardamom;** also *white bleached cardamom.*

chou (shoo). Fre. **Cabbage.**

choucroute (shoo-kroot). Fre. **Sauerkraut.**

chou farci (shoo fahr-see). Fre. Stuffed **cabbage.**

choufleur (shoo-flurr). Fre. **Cauliflower.**

chou rouge (shoo roozh). Fre. Red **cabbage.**

chouriço (shoh-REE-soh). Por. **Pork sausage;** one of numerous varieties.

choux de Bruxelles (shoo der brews-sehl). Fre. **Brussels sprouts.**

choux paste (shoo past). USA. Cream **puff pastry;** a simple paste of **flour,** boiling water, beaten **eggs, butter;** pâté à choux.

chowchow (CHOW-chow). USA. A mustard-flavored **vegetable pickle.**

chowder (CHOW-dehr). USA. A thick **soup** of fish, meat, or **vegetables,** to which **salt pork,** milk, **diced vegetables,** even bread and **crackers** may be added.

chow fun (chow fuhn). Chi. Wide, flat **rice noodles.**

chow mein (chow men). USA. A dish made of **stewed vegetables** and meat with **fried noodles.**

choysum (choy-sum). Chi. **Chinese chard; bok choy** heart; more tender than **bok choy.**

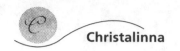

Christalinna (Chreh-tah-lee-nah). Swi. A hard **cheese** made of cow's milk.

Christian IX (KREISH-tee-ahn IX). Dan. A semifirm, **caraway**-seed **cheese; slices** easily; Also called *King Christian IX.*

chub (chuhb). USA. A member of the **whitefish** family; correctly known in United States as the **cisco.**

chuck (chuhk). USA. A cut of beef from between the neck and shoulder.

chuka bifun (CHOO-koo BEE-fuhn). Jap. Thin, translucent, Chinese-style **rice noodles.**

chukandar (choo-KAHN-dahr). Ind. Red **beets.**

chukar (chuh-KAHR). USA. A gray and black **partridge** native to India and introduced into dry parts of western USA.

chuleta (choo-LEH-tah). Spa. A chop.

chun juan (chwon jwahn). Chi. **Spring roll;** a thin pastry wrapper stuffed variously, rolled up, deep-fat fried.

churrasco (shoo-RRAHSS-koh). Por. **Barbecue.**

churros (choo-roz). Spa. **Deep-fried dough,** flavored with **cinnamon,** rolled in **sugar** while hot.

chutney (CHUT-nee). Ind. A **condiment,** with a puréed texture; made of **raisins, garlic, shallots, pimentos, apples, mustard, brown sugar** pounded together in a mortar, then cooked in boiling **vinegar.**

cialde (chee-AHL-dey). Ita. Wafers.

ciboulette (cee-boo-layt). Fre. **Chives.**

cibreo (chee-RAY-oa). Ita. An ancient dish of cocks' combs and **sweet-breads,** served with a molded **vegetable timbale.**

cicely (SIHS-eh-le). USA. An **herb** of the **parsley** family; **anise**-flavored leaves, stems, and seeds used in **salads** and **bouquet garnis.** Also called **sweet cicely.**

cichorei (see-cho-RYE). Dut. **Chicory.**

cicoria (chee-koa-REE-ah). Ita. **Chicory; endive.**

cider (SI-dehr). USA. Unfermented **apple** juice.

cider vinegar (SI-dehr vehn-eh-gur). USA. **Fermented apple** juice with varying alcoholic content and often sparkling; 5–6% acetic acid; full-bodied.

cigala (thee-GAH-lahss). Spa. Saltwater **crayfish.**

cilantro (cee-LAHN-tro). USA. Fresh **coriander.**

cilantro (thee-LAHN-tro). Spa. Fresh **coriander** (leaves and stems).

ciliègia (chee-lee-AY-jay). Ita. **Cherry.**

cima ripiena (chee-mah ree-PEE-nah). Ita. **Veal** breast with a pocket cut and stuffed with various fillings.

Cincho (THEEN-cho). Spa. A hard and pungent ewe's-milk **cheese.**

cinghiale (chee-ng-gee-AA-lay). Ita. Boar, usually **braised,** served with a sweet and sour sauce of **vinegar** and **chocolate.**

cinnamon (SIHN-ah-muhn). USA. The highly aromatic bark of a tree of the laurel family used as a spice.

cioccolata (choak-koa-LAA-tah). Ita. **Chocolate.**

cioppino (cheh-PEE-noh). USA. A fisherman's **stew** made with fish, **lobster, shrimp, crab, mussels, clams, mushrooms,** and seasonings; *California fish stew.*

cipollines (chee-pol-LEE-neez). Ita. Pearl **onions,** round in shape, belonging to **shallot** and **garlic** family.

ciruelas (thee-RWAY-lahss). Spa. **Plums.**

ciruelas pasa (thee-RWAY-lahss PAH-ssahss). Spa. **Prunes.** Also called *ciruelas secas.*

cisco (SIS-coa). USA. A member of the **whitefish** family, usually **smoked.** Commonly called **chub.**

ciseler (cee-zur-lay). Fre. To make incisions on the back of a fish to hasten its cooking; to cut in **julienne** strips, or to **shred.**

citroen (see-TROO-nuh). Dut. **Lemon.**

citrom (TSEE-trawm). Hun. **Lemon.**

citron (CEH-tron). USA. A type of **lemon** cultivated for its very thick skin, usually **preserved** and used in **cake** making and **confectionery.**

citron (cee-troa). Fre, Dan, Swe. **Lemon.**

citron fromage (see-TROON froam-aa-sher). Dan. **Lemon**-flavored **dessert.**

citron kram (see-TROON kraam). Swe. **Lemon dessert.**

citronne (cee-tro-nay). Fre. Anything with the taste or flavor of **lemon.**

citron vert (cee-tro vehr). Fre. **Lime.**

citrus (SIHT-truhs). USA. Any of a genus of often thorny trees and shrubs of the rue family grown in warm regions for their edible fruit

with firm, thick rind and pulpy flesh. Includes **orange, grapefruit, lemon, lime, ugli fruit, tangerine, mandarin, citron,** as well as any of these crossbred, such as **tangelo** or **temple orange.**

ciuppin (thee-OO-peen). Ita. Variety of fish **stew.**

civet (cee-veh). Fre. A **stew** using furred **game,** cooked in red wine.

civet de lièvre (cee-veh der ljehvr). Fre. **Hare** or **rabbit** stewed in wine and **herbs;** commonly referred to as "jugged and stewed."

civette (cee-veht). Fre. **Chives.**

Clabber (KLAH-behr). USA. A very soft **cheese** of sour milk that has thickened and curdled but not separated from the **whey;** also called **pot cheese.**

clafouti (clah-foo-tee). Fre. A fruit pastry made of **cherries** baked in **custard.**

clam (klahm). USA. Bivalve **mollusk** of many varieties; includes hard-shell (e.g., **quahog** and cherrystones) and soft-shell.

Clamart (clah-mahr). Fre. A **garnish** of **peas.**

clambake (KLAHM-bak). USA. Process of **steaming** an assortment of foods, such as **clams, lobsters, chicken,** unhusked **corn,** and whole **potatoes,** in a pit dug in the beach, layered with hot rocks, and covered with **seaweed;** cooks by steam of seaweed and hot rocks; originated in New England.

clapshot (KLAHP-shoat). Bri. Mashed **potatoes** and mashed **turnips** with chopped **chives** and **butter** or **bacon** drippings.

clarified butter (klar-eh-FIED BUHT-ehr). USA. **Butter** that has been heated gently until the milky solids separate, then the clear liquid poured off, discarding the milky solids. Also called **drawn butter.**

clarify (KLAR-ih-fi). USA. To make clear or pure by skimming or adding **egg** white and straining.

clavo (KLAH-voh). Mex. **Clove.**

clementine (KLEHM-ehn-tin). USA. A virtually seedless North African **orange** of the Mandarin family; very flavorful, juicy, a refreshing bittersweet zip.

cloche (klosh). Fre. Under cover.

clooty dumpling (KLUT-tee DUHM-pleng). Sco. A type of **plum pudding.**

clos de girofle (cloa day zhee-roafl). Fre. **Clove.**

clotted cream (KLOHT-ted krem). Bri. Thick **cream** made by slowly heating whole **milk** on which the cream has been allowed to rise, then skimming the cooled cream from the top.

cloudberry (KLOWD-behr-ree). USA. Arctic **berry** that resembles a yellow **raspberry,** with a sweet, mossy taste.

cloud ear (klowd ear). USA. A crinkly fungus, black when dried; has a crisper texture than **dried mushrooms** after soaking in water; swells to an "ear" when soaked.

cloute (clew-teh). Fre. Studded, as with **cloves.**

clove (klov). USA. The dried flower bud of a tropical tree of the myrtle family; used as a spice and a source of an oil.

cloverleaf roll (KLO-vehr-lef rol). USA. **Yeast roll** made by putting three small balls of dough in a muffin tin, letting them rise, then baking; shape of baked roll looks like a cloverleaf.

club steak (klub stak). USA. A tender and flavorful cut of beef from the **loin** between the **T-bone** and the **rib** section.

cluck and grunt (kluhk ahnd gruhnt). USA. An old West term for **eggs** and **bacon.**

coarsely chop (KORS-lee chohp). USA. Cutting food into small pieces, about ³⁄₁₆ inch.

coarse salt (kors sawlt). USA. A squarish-grained **salt;** sprinkled on meats, **pretzels, rolls,** and breads before baking; not to be confused with rock salt, which is inedible; also known as **kosher salt** or **sea salt.**

coat (koht). USA. To cover entire surface with **flour,** fine bread crumbs, **sauce, batter,** or other food as required.

cobbler (KOHB-lehr). USA. A deep dish **fruit pie** with a **biscuit dough** top.

cocada (koa-KAH-dah). Spa. **Coconut custard.**

cochineal (kosh-ee-nehl). Fre. A liquid red coloring agent used for coloring **icing, sauces.**

cochinillo (koa-chee-NEE-lyoa). Spa. Suckling pig.

cochino (koa-CHEE-noa). Spa. Pig.

cochon (ko-shawng). Fre. Pig. Also **porc.**

cochon de lait (ko-shawng dehr leh). Fre. Suckling pig.

cocido (koa-THEE-dhoa). Spa. **Stew.** Also means cooked, as opposed to fresh.

cock (kohk).   USA. A male **chicken** that is too old to roast, but makes a well-flavored adjunct for the stock pot; also see **broiler, capon, fryer, roaster, stag chicken,** and **stewing chicken.**

cock-a-leekie (kohk-ah-LEE-ke).   Sco. A **soup** made of **chicken** boiled with **leeks.**

cockles (KOHK-uls).   Bri. European bivalve **mollusk** similar to **oysters.**

cocktail (KOHK-tal).   USA. An **appetizer,** either a beverage or a light, highly seasoned food, served before a meal.

cocktail avocado (KOHK-tal ah-vah-KAH-doh).   USA. A small, buttery flavored, seedless fruit of the Fuerte **avocado;** often treated as a **vegetable;** use fresh in **salads, dips, sandwiches, soups,** or eaten out of hand.

coco (KOH-koh).   Mex, Por. **Coconut.**

cocoa (KO-koa).   Spa. **Chocolate** with part of the fat removed, then pulverized to **powder** form.

cocoa (KO-ko).   USA. A hot beverage made with **cocoa** powder, **milk,** and **sugar.**

cocomero (ko-KO-may-roa).   Ita. **Watermelon.**

cocomoka (KOH-koh-moh-kah).   USA. A beverage, served hot or cold, combining **coffee** and **cocoa** as the base.

coconut (KO-koh-nuht).   USA. Edible seed-nut of the palm tree with brown, shaggy, hard, bark-like shell; meat is white and flavorful, and can be used raw or cooked in dishes; cavity is filled with a milky liquid.

coconut oil (KO-koh-nuht oyl).   USA. An almost colorless oil extracted from fresh **coconuts;** liquid and semisolid forms.

cocotte (koh-koht).   Fre. **Casserole;** food prepared and served in the same dish.

cocozelle (kok-ah-ZEL-leh).   USA. A summer **squash** resembling the zucchini; also called *Italian marrow.*

coctel (KOK-tehl).   Mex. **Cocktail.**

cod (kahd).   USA. A food-fish family of the North Atlantic with numerous members; flesh is lean, firm, white, mild, large flakes. **Haddock, pollock,** and **hake** are of the cod family.

coda di bue (koa-dah dee BOO-ee).   Ita. **Oxtail.**

coddes (KAH-dees).   USA. Codfish cakes, breaded and **deep-fried;** especially in Maryland.

coddle (KAH-dle). USA. To simmer gently, below the boiling point, in liquid for a short time.

codorniz (koa-doarn-NEETH). Spa, Por. **Quail.**

coelho (koh-AYL-yoh). Por. **Rabbit.**

coeur (kurr). Fre. Heart.

Coeur à la Crème (Kurr ah lah krehm). Fre. A very simple, classic **dessert cheese** pressed from **curds** of naturally soured whole milk and **heavy cream,** then molded in a heart-shaped basket that allows the **whey** to drain off; it is unmolded, garnished with **strawberries** or other **berries,** and served as **dessert.**

coffee (KAUF-fee). USA. A beverage made from roasted and ground **coffee** beans.

coffee cream (KAUF-fee krem). USA. **Cream** containing 18–30% milk fat; widely used in **coffee;** also called **light** or **table cream.**

Cognac (kon-yahk). Fre. **Brandy** from the French town of the same name.

cogumelo (koh-goo-MEH-lohss). Por. **Mushrooms.**

coing (kawhn). Fre. **Quince.**

Coimbra (Ko-EM-brah). Por. A sharp, salty, semifirm **cheese** usually made with goat's milk.

Cointreau (Kwahn-tro). Fre. A colorless, sweet, **orange**-flavored **liqueur.**

col (kohl). Spa. **Cabbage.**

Colbert, à la (koh-behr). Fre. A preparation for fish in which the fish is dipped in **egg,** bread crumbed, **fried,** and served with a **butter** mixed with chopped **parsley** and **tarragon.**

Colby (KOL-bee). USA. **Cheese,** similar to **Cheddar,** but softer body and more open texture; mild to mellow flavor; light cream to orange color.

colcannon (kohl-CAHN-un). Iri. A dish of **cabbage, leeks, potatoes,** and **milk,** served with a hidden "treasure" within.

Colchesters (KOAL-chuh-strs). Bri. **Oysters** from the famous beds of Colchester.

colère, en (ahng ko-lehr). Fre. Fish, usually **whiting,** cooked with its tail in its mouth, giving it a so-called angry look; often dipped in **egg batter,** rolled in bread crumbs, and **deep-fried.**

coleslaw (KOL-slahw). USA. A **vegetable** dish used as a **salad** made basically of **shredded cabbage;** other **vegetables** and **fruits** such as

grated carrots, finely chopped apples, chopped celery, nuts, may be mixed with a slaw dressing.

coliflor (ko-lee-FLOR). Spa. **Cauliflower.**

colin (ko-lahnk). Fre. **Hake.**

colinabo (ko-lee-NAH-boa). Spa. **Turnip.**

collards (KAH-lards). USA. Collard greens; a vegetable with dark green, paddle-like leaves resembling **cabbage,** on long, heavy, tough stalks; taste between **cabbage** and **kale.**

collè (koal-lay). Fre. **Gelatin** added.

collop (KOHL-luhp). Bri. A thin **slice** of meat; same as the French **scallop.**

Colorado Blackie (kohl-o-RAH-do Blah-kee). USA. A natural **cheese** of the **Cheddar** family; has a black outer wrapping.

colza (KOL-za). Ita. An **herb** of the **mustard** family whose seeds yield oil for **salads** and **frying** and blending with **butter;** the leaves and young shoots can be braised as a **vegetable.** Generally known as *rapeseed.*

comfrey (KOHM-free). USA. A medicinal **herb** used to make a **tea;** fresh young leaves have been eaten for centuries, sparingly, in **salads,** or cooked as greens. It is now known that they contain small amounts of an alkaloid that can cause liver damage; use sparingly.

comino (koh-MEE-noh). Mex. **Cumin.**

Commission (Koh-meh-shea-owng). Dut. A **cheese** made from slightly skimmed milk; similar to **Edam** but twice the size.

common cracker (KOHM-mohn KRAHK-kehr). USA. Very crisp, hard, thick **wheat flour crackers;** used split in half.

composé (kom-po-say). Fre. A **salad** that is arranged in the bowl or plate, rather than tossed.

compota (kohm-PO-tah). Spa. **Stewed fruits; preserves.**

compote (kohm-poo-tay). Fre. **Stew** of **fruits** or **vegetables,** often flavored with spices and **liqueur,** served cold.

compound butter (KOHM-pound BUHT-ehr). USA. **Butter** seasoned with **herbs, shallots,** and wine.

compressed yeast (KOHM-prehsd yest). USA. A small cake of **yeast** weighing ⅗ ounce; light greyish-tan in color; used in **baking.**

Comté (kom-tee). Fre. An ivory yellow **cheese** with holes the size of **cherries;** rind is usually dark yellow; high butter fat content makes it equally suitable for cooking and eating plain; has legendary keeping qualities.

concasse (kon-kaas). Fre. Coarsely chopped, such as **tomatoes** or **parsley.**

concasser (kon-kaas-say). Fre. Rough **chopping** with a knife, or breaking up in a mortar.

conch (kohnk). USA. A **mollusk** whose muscle is made into **chowder, fritters,** used in **salads,** or **breaded** and **fried.**

conchiglia (koa-keej-LEE-ah). Ita. **Shellfish;** also **pasta** shells.

conchiglia rigate (koa-keej-LEE-ah ree-GAH-teh). Ita. Medium-sized **pasta** shells.

conchiglioni (koa-keej-lee-AHN-nee). Ita. Jumbo **pasta** shells.

conchigliette piccole (koa-keej-lee-eht PEEK-koa-lay). Ita. Small **pasta** shells.

concombre (kawng-kawng-br). Fre. **Cucumber.**

Condé (kawng-day). Fre. A **pâtisserie** of leftover flaky pastry rolled out in strips and used variously for sweet or savory dishes; traditionally strips are covered with royal **almond icing,** sprinkled with **powdered sugar,** and **baked.**

condensed milk (kohn-DENSD mehlk). USA. **Milk** with its water content reduced by one-half, and **sugar** added in the ratio for 18 pounds to 100 pounds of milk. Also called *sweetened condensed milk;* not to be confused with **evaporated milk.**

condimento (koan-dee-MAYN-toh). Ita. Seasonings.

condiments (KOHN-de-munts). USA. Seasonings that enhance the flavor of foods: spices, **herbs, sauces, pickles, relishes.**

conejo (koa-NAY-khoh). Spa. **Rabbit.**

coney (KOHN-nee). USA. A hot dog.

confectioners' sugar (kon-FEHC-shun-ehrs' SCHU-gahr). USA. Very finely ground **sugar** with **cornstarch** added; quick dissolving. Also known as **powdered sugar** and, in France, **icing sugar.**

confectionery (kohn-FEHC-shun-ar-ee). USA. The transformation of **sugar** into sweets.

confeitado (kon-fay-TAH-doo). Por. Candied. Sometimes called **conservado.**

confeito (kon-FAY-too). Por. **Candy.**

confiserie (kawng-fee-ser-ree). Fre. **Confectionery.**

confit (kawng-fee). Fre. Meat or **poultry** cooked and preserved in its own fat; **fruits** or **vegetables** cooked and **preserved** in **brandy** or liquor **syrup.**

confit d'oie (kawng-fee dwah). Fre. Slices of goose preserved in goose fat, a rare delicacy.

confiture (kawng-fee-tewr). Fre. **Preserves** or **jam** made from **fruit.**

cong (tsoong). Chi. **Scallions.**

congbào yángròu (tsoong-bao yang-row). Chi. A dish of lamb quick-fried with **scallions.**

congeal (kohn-GEEL). USA. To change a liquid into a solid by lowering the temperature of the food sufficiently to bring about gelation.

congo eel (KOHNG-go eeul). Bri. One of the names for the ocean pout, a fish of the eelpout family whose flesh is sweet, white, and has few bones.

congre (kong-reh). Fre. Large sea **eel.**

coniglio (koa-NEE-lyoh). Ita. **Rabbit.**

conserva de fruta (kohn-SER-vah duh FRU-tah). Por. **Jam.**

conservado (kon-ser-VAH-doo). Por. Candied. Sometimes called **confeitado.**

conserves (KOHN-servs). USA. Glorified **jams** made from a mixture of **fruits,** usually including **citrus; raisins** and **nuts** are frequently added.

consommé (kawngs-som-may). Fre. Clarified double-strength **brown stock** made from two or three kinds of meats; a clear brown **broth** to which various savories may be added: See specific types listed below.

> **consommé Alexandra** (ah-lehx-ahn-drah). **Chicken broth** with chicken balls and **lettuce.**
>
> **consommé allemande** (ahl-mangd). Strong beef **broth** with slices of **frankfurter.**
>
> **consommé Alsacienne** (ahl-sah-ceene). Beef **broth** with **noodles.**
>
> **consommé Bellevue** (bel-ve). Combination of **chicken consommé** and **clam broth.**
>
> **consommé cardinal** (kahr-dee-nahl). Fish **broth** with pink **lobster** balls.
>
> **consommé colbert** (coa-bahr). **Broth** with a soft-poached **egg** in it.

consommé soubrette (soo-breht).   **Chicken broth** garnished with green **peas** and **chopped shrimp.**

consommé vaudoise (vahn-dwah).   Beef **broth** with **julienne vegetables.**

converted rice (kohn-VEHR-tehd ris).   USA. **Rice** that has been **steamed** and **dried** before milling for higher nutritional content and easier processing.

cooked cheese (kuhkd chez).   USA. A **cheese** made by "cooking" cheese **curd** from skim milk; also called in USA *cup cheese* and Pennsylvania **pot cheese;** in northern Germany, it is called **Topfen** and in Sardinia, **Fresa.**

cookie (KUHK-kee).   USA. Any of various small sweet flat or slightly raised **cakes** in a multitude of shapes and flavors; called **biscuits** throughout most of the world.

cooking salt (KUHK-eng sawlt).   USA. A finely ground, free-flowing **salt** used in food preparation; **table salt.**

cool (koul).   USA. Allow to come to room temperature.

copeaux (koo-po).   Fre. Pastry twists.

Coon (koon).   USA. A **cheese,** well-aged, vey sharp, piquant, natural **Cheddar**-type, almost white in color; slightly crumbly; has black-cloth covering.

Cooper (KOO-pehr).   USA. A mild Vermont **Cheddar cheese.**

copeaux en chocolat (koo-po ahng shok-kol-lah).   Fre. **Chocolate** shavings.

coppa (KO-pah).   Ita. **Cured pork** shoulder.

coppa gelata (KO-pah jay-LAH-to).   Ita. Mixed **ice cream dessert.**

coq au bruyère (kok-oa brwee-yehr).   Fre. Wood grouse; prepared like **pheasant.**

coq au vin (kok-oa-vang).   Fre. Cut-up **chicken** braised in red wine with **onions** and **mushrooms.**

coquillage (kok-kee-lazg).   Fre. **Shellfish.**

coquille (kok-kee).   Fre. Served in a **scallop** shell.

coquille Saint Jacques (kok-kee sang zhahk).   Fre. **Scallops** in **cream sauce** on half shell.

coquina (koh-KEEN-ah).   USA. A periwinkle **clam.**

coral (KAH-rahl). USA. **Lobster roe;** turns a bright reddish color when cooked; used for **sauces** and **butters.**

coratèlla (koa-rah-TAYL-lah). Ita. Organ meats such as liver, heart, **sweetbreads.**

corbina (korh-BEE-nah). USA. **Corvina;** a fish of the **drum** family.

cordeiro (coor-DAY-roo). Por. Lamb.

cordero (kohr-DEH-roh). Spa. Lamb.

cordero lechazo (kohr-DEH-roh lay-CHAH-thoh). Spa. Suckling lamb.

cordial (KOHR-duhl). USA. A sweet, syrupy **liqueur.**

core (kohr). USA. To remove the core from a **fruit.**

coriander (KOH-ree-ahn-dehr). USA. An **herb** used for its leaves and seeds; dried seeds have a warm, nutty flavor and aroma; leaves have strong, musty flavor. Also known as **cilantro.**

corn (korn). USA. A sweet, yellow food **grain** eaten as a **vegetable** while still in its soft stage of growth, either with the loose kernels removed from the cob or cooked on the cob. **Maize.**

cornbread (KORN-brehd). USA. A **quick bread** of **cornmeal** and **flour.**

corn dog (korn dawg). USA. A **frankfurter**-on-a-stick, dipped in **cornmeal batter, fried** till crisp on outside.

corned beef (kornd bef). USA. Cuts of beef including the **plate, chuck, brisket,** and **round** that are boned, trimmed, seasoned with **bay leaves** and whole **peppers,** then **cured** or **corned.**

corned bief (KOHR-nehd bef). Dut. **Corned beef.**

Cornell bread (kohrn-NEHL brehd). USA. A high-protein bread developed by Cornell University made by substituting part of the unbleached white **flour** with one tablespoon each of soya flour and **wheat germ,** and one teaspoon of nonfat dry milk.

cornet (kohr-nah). Fre. Horn or cornucopia shaped; as a pastry stuffed with a cream filling; slices of meat rolled into a cone and stuffed.

corn flour (korn flowr) Bri. **Cornstarch;** a very fine **flour** milled from **corn;** a thickening agent.

corn flour (korn flowr). USA. Milled of white or yellow **corn;** fine granulation; if used in **baking,** must be mixed with other flours.

Cornhusker (korn HUHS-kehr). USA. A soft **Cheddar**-type **cheese** made in Nebraska.

cornichons (korn-ee-shawng). Fre. **Pickles;** tiny, slender pickled **gherkins,** commonly served alongside French **patés, terrins,** and with Swiss **paclette;** used thinly cut as fans for **garnishes.**

Cornish hen (KORN-esh hehn). Bri. A crossbreed **chicken** with delicate flesh; Rock Cornish game hen.

Cornish pastry (KORN-esh PAS-tree). Bri. A pastry **turnover** stuffed with meat or vegetable filling.

cornmeal (KORN-mehl). USA. Coarsely ground white or yellow **corn;** if used in **quick** or **yeast cornbreads,** must be mixed with other **flour.**

corn oil (korn oyl). USA. A pale yellow, fatty oil obtained from the **corn** kernel; liquid and semisolid forms.

corn pone (korn pon). USA. A flat bread made of **cornmeal dough, fried** or **baked.**

corn salad (korn SAHL-ahd). USA. A **salad** green, used **raw** in salad or cooked like **spinach.** Aso known as **lamb's lettuce, mache.**

cornstarch (KORN-starch). USA. Very finely milled white **corn flour,** used as thickening agent and in **baking.**

corn sugar (korn SCHU-gahr). USA. A crystallized dextrose-glucose obtained by hydrolizing **cornstarch** with acid; less sweet than sucrose sugars.

corn syrup (korn SEHR-uhp). USA. A syrup of **dextrose** and **glucose;** generallly used in canning and jelly making; available in a mild-tasting light and a stronger-tasting dark.

corvina (kohr-VEE-nah). USA. A catchall name for fish of the **drum** family. Also spelled **corbina.**

cos (kos). Bri. **Romaine lettuce.**

còscia (KOAS-chee-ah). Ita. Thigh; as thigh of **chicken.**

coscia de montone (KOS-chee-ah da moan-TO-nay). Ita. Leg of lamb. Also called **cosciotto.**

cosciotto (koa-SHAWT-to). Ita. Leg of lamb. Also called **coscia de montone.**

costata (kos-TOA-to). Ita. **Rib** chop.

costela (coosh-too-LAY). Por. **Rib.**

costeleta (coosh-too-LET-ash). Por. **Cutlet;** chop.

costeletas de carneiro (coosh-too-LET-ash der car-NAY-roo). Por. **Mutton** chops.

costeletas de porco (coosh-too-LET-ash der POR-coo). Por. **Pork** chops.

costillas (kohs-TEE-yahs). Spa. **Ribs,** chops.

costmary (KOHS-mah-ree). USA. An **herb** with a minty taste and bitter overtones; use sparingly in **sauces, soups, stuffings.**

costole (KOS-to-lay). Ita. **Ribs.**

costoletta (koas-to-LAYT-tah). Ita. **Cutlet.**

côte (koat). Fre. **Rib.**

cotechino (koa-teh-KEE-no). Ita. A large **pork sausage** seasoned with **nutmeg** and **cloves;** delicate to spicy.

cotellette (kot-toh-LEHT). Dut. **Cutlet.**

côtelette (kot-ter-leht). Fre. Chops.

Cotherstone (KOWTH-ehr-stohn). Bri. A blue-veined **cheese** made of cow's milk; also known as **Yorkshire-Stilton.**

cotogno (koa-TO-nyah). Ita. **Quince.**

cotoletta (koa-toa-LAH-tah). Ita. **Braised** chop or **cutlet.**

cotriade (cot-ree-ahd). Fre. Fish **soup.**

Cotronese (KO-trah-ne-seh). Ita. A ewe's-milk **cheese** similar to **Moliterno;** sometimes seasoned with pepper.

cottage cheese (KAHT-tehgj chez). USA. A soft, bland, creamy white, uncurded **cheese** made from soured skim milk; the simplest form of cheese; also known as *Dutch cheese,* **pot cheese.**

cottage potatoes (KAHT-tehgj po-TA-tos). USA. **Potatoes** cooked and cold, then **sliced** or **diced, sautéed** in **butter** without stirring to get a golden-brown crust, then turned to brown on other side. Also called **country-fried.**

cottage pudding (KAHT-tehgj PUHD-eng). USA. Plain **cake** covered with a hot, sweet, **pudding**-like **sauce.**

Cottenham (KOHT-tehn-hahm). Bri. A semifirm, double cream **cheese** that is creamier and richer than **Stilton;** sometimes blue-veined.

còtto (KO-toa). Ita. Cooked.

cottonseed flour (KAHT-tuhn-sed flowr). USA. With at least four times the protein value of **wheat,** this **flour** is often used to enrich breads.

cottonseed oil (KAHT-tuhn sed oyl).   USA. A pale yellow, fatty oil obtained from the cottonseed; liquid and semisolid form.

couche-couche (COUS-cous).   USA. A **Cajun fried corn dough,** served with **preserves** or **cane syrup.**

coulibiac (cool-ee-bee-ak).   Fre. A hot fish **pie** filled with layers of **salmon** or fish, **rice, mushrooms, herbs, onions.**

coulis (koo-lees).   Fre. A thick liquid **sauce** made by **puréeing vegetables, fruit,** fish, **chicken, crustaceans,** and **game;** used over meat, **chicken,** or fish entree as a low-calorie garnish.

coulis (koo-lees).   Fre. The juices that run out of meat during the cooking process.

Coulommiers (coo-loa-mee-ah).   Fre. A cow's whole-milk, velvety soft **cheese** with white rind flora, creamy white and flavorful interior; when well ripened, develops a strong **almond**-like flavor with a crust that is snowy white. According to some authorities, Coulommiers and the smaller **Brie** are identical, but according to other authorities, it is similar to **Brie** and **Camembert,** but is ripened for a shorter period.

country captain (KOUN-tree KAHP-tahn).   USA. A curried **chicken** dish with **bacon strips, onions, garlic, celery, tomatoes,** and seasoned with **orange juice, curry** powder, and **thyme.**

country-fried potatoes (KOUN-tree-frid po-TA-tos).   USA. **Cottage potatoes.**

country ham (KOUN-tree hahm).   USA. A **ham** that has been dry **cured** and heavily **salted;** requires soaking followed by long simmering. **Smithfield** is one type of country ham.

country style spareribs (KOUN-tree stil SPAR-rihbs).   USA. The backbones of **pork** from the shoulder end of the **loin.**

coupe (koop).   Fre. **Ice cream dessert.**

coupe Jacques (koop zhahk).   Fre. **Lemon** and **strawberry ices** with **fruit** steeped in **cherry brandy.**

courgette (koor-zheht).   Fre. Zucchini.

couronne, en (ahng ky-rohn).   Fre. In the shape of a ring.

court-bouillon (kort boo-yon).   Fre. A highly seasoned **broth** in which fish has been boiled.

cous cous (koos koos).   Afr. A grain; a type of hardwheat **semolina;** use same as **rice.**

couscous (KOOS-koo-see).   Ara. An ancient North African dish made with **millet flour** or crushed **rice** steamed in the top of a two-part pot with meat such as **mutton, chicken, stewed** in the bottom part; served together with **hot sauce.**

couve (koh-vay).   Por. **Cabbage.**

couve de Bruxelas (koh-vay duh broo-SAY-lahsh).   Por. **Brussels sprouts.**

couve flor (koh-vay FLOR).   Por. **Cauliflower.**

couve Lombarda (koh-vay lom-BAHR-dah).   Por. **Collard** greens.

cowpeas (KOW-pez).   USA. **Black-eyed peas.**

cozida (kou-ZEE-dah).   Por. **Boiled.**

cozida de Portuguesa (kou-ZEE-da duh por-too-GAY-zah).   Por. Traditional mixture of **boiled** beef, **vegetables, potatoes, rice, sausages.**

cozza (KOT-say).   Ita. **Mussel.**

crab (krahb).   USA. Clawed **crustacean** with many edible varieties; delicate, white flesh; very versatile to use.

crab apple (krahb AHP-puhl).   USA. A tiny, round, very tart **apple** with yellow skin with red to maroon blush; must be cooked as apple **jelly, tarts, apple butter,** or use as **garnish.**

crab butter (krahb BUHT-tehr).   USA. The white-yellow fat inside the back shell of crabs, used in **dressings** or **sauces.**

crab claws (krahb claus).   USA. The large pinchers at the end of the two legs on either side of the mouth; a delicacy.

crabe (krahb).   Fre. **Crab.**

crab legs (krahb lehgs).   USA. The first three or four legs on either side of the body of the Alaskan king **crab;** boiled or steamed and served with melted butter.

crabmeat (KRAHB-met).   USA. The meat of crabs; best from the claws.

cracked wheat flour (krahkd whet flowr).   USA. In this flour, the **wheat** has been cut rather than **ground.** It gives up little of its starch as a binder and must be used with all-purpose or **whole wheat flour.**

cracker (KRAHK-kehr).   USA. A dry, thin, crisp bakery product that may be leavened or unleavened, made in various shapes and variously flavored.

cracker flour (KRAHK-kehr flowr).   USA. Flour milled from soft **wheat;** has low water-absorbing capacity.

crackling (KRAHK-lens). USA. Crispy, **fried** pieces of fresh **pork** fatback. Also called *cracklins.*

cracknels (KRAHK-nehls). USA. Hard, crisp **biscuits;** *cracklings.*

crackseed (KRAHK-sed). USA. A Hawaiian speciality; various seeds of fruit that have been smashed and **preserved** with **salt;** salty-sweet taste that hints of **licorice.**

cranberry (KRAHN-behr-ree). USA. A red, acidic **berry** used in **sauce,** baked goods, meat **garnishes.**

crapaudine (krah-poo-deen). Fre. Method of preparing **fowl,** usually **pigeon,** giving the appearance of a toad.

crapaudine sauce (krah-poo-dee-nay saus). Fre. Tangy **sauce** with **onions, pickles, mushrooms, mustard,** and wine.

crappin (KRAHP-pen). Sco. **Stuffing.**

crauti (krah-OO-tee). Ita. **Sauerkraut.**

cravo (KRAH-voo). Por. **Clove.**

crawfish (CRAHW-fisch). USA. **Cajun** pronunciation for **crayfish.**

crayfish (KRA-fisch). USA. A freshwater **crustacean** of many species, resembling a small **lobster** with firm flesh and subtly, but delicately flavored.

cream (krem). USA. That part of the milk that rises to the top; butterfat, milk fat. Terms used to describe cream include **half-and-half, cereal, light, coffee, table, whipping, whipped.**

cream (krem). USA. To mix fat and sugar, or fat and eggs, until soft, smooth, and creamy.

cream cheese (krem cheez). USA. A cow's soft whole-milk **cheese;** delicate, slightly acid flavor; creamy, bland in taste; never ripened.

cream of tartar (krem uv TAHR-tahr). USA. A white crystalline **salt** used in **baking powder.**

cream puff (krem puhf). USA. A round shell of pastry that creates an internal hollow space when baked, filled with various flavored **custards** or **creams.**

cream puff pastry (krem puhf PA-stry). USA. A simple paste of **flour,** boiling water, **eggs, butter** that puffs up on baking, leaving a cavity that is generally filled with a flavored **cream filling.**

cream soup (krem soop). USA. A thick **soup** to which **cream, butter** have been added, and usually **vegetables.**

Crécy, à la (kray-cee). Fre. With **carrots.**

crema (KRAI-mah). Ita, Spa. **Cream.**

crema batida (KRAI-mah bah-TEE-dhah). Spa. **Whipped cream.**

crema di pollo (KRAI-mah day POL-lo). Ita. **Cream** of **chicken soup.**

crema di verdura (KRAI-mah day veh-DOO-rah). Ita. **Purée** of **vegetables,** often with **milk** or **cream,** and sometimes thickened with puréed **potatoes** or sieved cooked **rice.**

crema española (KRAI-mah ays-pah-NOH-lah). Spa. A **dessert** made of **milk, gelatin,** and **eggs.**

crema rovesciata (KRAI-mah ro-vays-chee-AH-to). Ita. **Baked custard.**

crème (KREH-may). Por. **Cream.**

crème (krehm). Fre. **Cream.**

crème a l'anglaise (krehm lahng-las). Fre. **Custard.**

crème bachique (krehm bac-ee-shah). Fre. **Custard** flavored with **cinnamon** and **Sauternes.**

crème beurre (krehm burr). Fre. **Hard sauce.**

crème brûlée (krehm brew-lah). Fre. A rich **custard** with a **caramelized brown sugar** crust.

Crème Chantilly (Krehm Shang-tee-ye). Fre. Although this name is usually given to simple **whipped cream** in France, it is also a soft, delicate-flavored **dessert cheese.**

crème chantilly (krehm shang-tee-ye). Fre. Sweetened **whipped cream,** flavored with **vanilla** or **liqueur.**

crème chiboust (krehm chee-boos). Fre. Crème pastry with sweetened **egg** whites added.

crème choisy (krehm shwah-see). Fre. **Lettuce soup.**

crème de cassis (krehm deh kahs-seess). Fre. A **liqueur** made from black **currants,** used to make **aperitifs.**

Crème de Gruyére (Krehm deh Gru-yer). Fre. A soft, ripened **cheese** with the flavor of **Gruyére** but the consistency of **Camembert;** used a spread for crisp **crackers** or topping for fresh **fruit.**

crème de menthe (krehm deh menthe). Fre. A **liqueur** made from peppermint; flavoring for food and drink; **aperitifs.**

crème d'orge (krehm doarj). Fre. **Soup** made with fine **barley.**

crème fouette (krehm foo-eh-tay).   Fre. **Whipped cream.**

crème fraiche (krehm fraysh).   Fre. A cultured **heavy cream** with a tangy taste.

crème frite (krehm freet).   Fre. **Fried cream;** a cream filling chilled until it can be cut in squares, **dipped** in finely crushed cake crumbs, **deep-fried,** and sprinkled with **powdered sugar** and rum.

crème glacée (krehm glahs-say).   Fre. **Ice cream;** sometimes means a sundae.

crème pâtissière (krehm pah-tees-syehr-ree).   Fre. Variously flavored pastry **cream** used to fill **tarts, cream puffs, éclairs,** pastries.

crème pralinée (krehm prah-lee-neh).   Fre. **Crème pâtissière** flavored with **powdered praline,** used to fill pastries.

crème renversée (krehm rehn-vehr-seh).   Fre. **Custard** baked in **caramel**-lined mold, chilled, and served by inverting on plate.

crenata (koo-leh-NAH-tah).   Jap. **Pine nut.**

crenshaw melon (KREHN-shaw MEHL-uhn).   USA. A **melon** with a golden netless rind at its peak of ripeness; has a slightly wrinkled stem end, gold-pink flesh, and a rich aroma.

Creole (KREE-ol).   USA. A soft, unripened cheese made in Louusiana of equal parts **cottage cheese** and **cream.**

creole (KREE-ol).   USA. Made with **tomatoes, peppers, onions,** seasonings; any **soups, garnishes, sauces** so prepared.

creole mustard (KREE-ol MUHS-tahrd).   USA. A hot, spicy mustard made from mustard seeds marinated in vinegar.

crêpe (krayp).   Fre. A small, very thin, and crisp **pancake** served for **tea** or **dessert.**

crepes (KRAH-payz).   Ita. **Pancakes.**

crepes do ceu (KRAY-puhsh do SAY-oo).   Por. **Pancakes** richly filled with **whipped cream** and candied **fruit.**

crêpes parmentier (krayp pahr-mehn-teh).   Fre. **Potato pancakes.**

crêpes suzette (krayp su-zeht).   Fre. **Crêpes** with an **orange sauce,** orange-flavored **liqueur,** heated and flambéed.

crépine (kreh-pee-neh).   Fre. Pig's **caul;** a fatty, lacy membrane enclosing the paunch, which melts away when cooked.

crépinette (kreh-pee-neht).   Fre. Small **pork sausage** wrapped in **caul** instead of a casing.

crescent (krehss-SCEHNT). USA. A curve-shaped **roll** of butterflake pastry.

Crescenza (krehz-CHAY-tsah). Ita. An uncooked, cow's-milk **cheese** that is rindless, buttery, smooth, delicate, mildly sweet, yellowish; also called **Stracchino.**

crescione (krays-chee-OA-nay). Ita. **Watercress.**

crespella (krehz-PAYL-lah). Ita. A stuffed, thin **pancake; a crepe.**

cresson (krehs-sawng). Fre. **Watercress.**

crêtes de coq (creh-tehs der kok). Fre. Cocks combs, a great delicacy.

Creuse (Kohyz). Fre. A skim-milk **cheese;** when aged a year or more is very dry and firm; or it may be put into tightly closed containers lined with straw to ripen, in which case it becomes soft and yellow and has a very pronounced flavor.

crevette (krer-veht). Fre. **Shrimp.**

criadillas (kree-ah-DHEE-lyahss). Spa. **Sweetbreads.**

crisp (krihsp). USA. To make foods brittle and firm, as in chilling vegetables or heating **cereals** or **crackers** in the oven to remove excessive moisture.

crisphead lettuce (KRIHSP-hehd LEHT-uhs). **Iceberg lettuce.**

crispito (KRIHS-pee-toa). Mex. A **corn tortilla** tightly rolled and **fried;** used with dipping **sauces.**

croaker (KRO-kehr). USA. One of the many members of the **drum** family having delicate, finely flavored flesh.

crocchette (kroa-KAYT-tay). Ita. **Croquettes.** Also **croche.**

croche (KRO-kay). Ita. Croquettes. Also **crocchette.**

croche di riso alla torinese (KRO-kay dee REE-zoa ahl-lay toa-ree-NAY-zay). Ita. **Rice fritters.**

croissant (krwa-sahng). Fre. **Crescent;** applies to **rolls** and **confectionery** of crescent shape.

Croissant Demi-sel (Krwa-sahng deh-me-sehl). Fre. A double-crème **dessert cheese** molded in crescent shape and lightly salt-cured.

cromesquis (kroam es-kee). Fre. Finely **ground poultry** or **shellfish** rolled in thin **bacon** slices, **dipped** in **batter, fried** in deep fat.

croquants (kroa-kough). Fre. **Confections** that crunch between the teeth.

croque madame (kroak mah-dahm). Fre. **Chicken** and **cheese sand-wich.**

croquembouche (kroa-kough-boosh). Fre. A pyramid of bite-size **cream puffs,** held together with **sugar glaze,** and covered with **caramel.**

croque monsieur (kroak mer-syur). Fre. **Grilled ham** and **cheese sand-wich.**

croquesignole (krook-SIN-yawl). USA. A **Cajun doughnut,** without a hole, sometimes square.

croquetes (krou-KAY-tuhsh). Por. **Croquettes.**

croquetes de Camarão (krou-KAY-tuhsh duh kah-mah-RAHNG). Por. **Croquettes** made of **shrimp,** usually part of the **appetizer** course.

croquetjes (croh-ket-YER). Dut. **Croquettes.**

croquette (kroa-keht). Fre. A **savory** or pattie prepared with **minced** meat, **fowl,** or fish with **sauce** to **bind,** shaped variously, then **egged, crumbed,** and **fried.**

cròsta (KROZ-tah). Ita. Crust.

crostacei (kro-sta-KAY-ee). Ita. **Shellfish.**

crostata (kro-STAH-tah). Ita. **Pie.**

crostata di fragole (kro-STAH-tah dee FRAH-goa-lay). Ita. **Strawberry pie.**

crostatina (kro-stah-TEE-nah). Ita. **Tart.**

crostini (kro-STEE-nee). Ita. **Crouton;** toasted bread cubes.

crostini alla fiorentina (kro-STEE-nee AHL-lah fee-oa-ray-TEE-nah). Ita. **Toasted** bread spread with a **chicken** liver mixture.

crostini alla napoletana (kro-STEE-nee AHL-lah nah-poa-lay-TAH-nah). Ita. **Fried** or **toasted** bread spread with **tomatoes** and **anchovies.**

crostini alla Parmigiana (kroa-STEE-nee AHL-lah Pahr-mee-jaa-AHN-ah). Ita. **Toasted** bread with **cheese** and **anchovies.**

crostini di mare (kro-STEE-nee dee MAH-ray). Ita. **Fried** or **toasted** bread spread with **minced shellfish.**

croustade (kroos-tahd). Fre. A **toasted** shape or shell of bread in which various mixtures are served.

croûte (kroot).   Fre. Bread or pastry in which a meat is **baked,** then served.

croûte au pot (kroot oa po).   Fre. Beef-vegetable **soup,** topped with a thick slice of bread and **grated cheese.**

croute aux morilles (kroot oa mohr-ree).   Fre. **Morels** on **toast.**

croûton (kroo-to).   Fre. Small **cube** of **fried** or **toasted** bread used for **garnishing** dishes or **salads.**

crowdie (KREW-dee).   Sco. A breakfast dish made of finely **ground oatmeal** with **buttermilk.**

crown roast (krown rost).   USA. **Loin** from the **rib** section of beef, **pork,** lamb, tied into a crown shape, and **roasted;** paper frills placed on end of bones before serving; center cavity filled with **stuffing** or **vegetables.**

cru (krew).   Fre, Por. **Raw.**

crudités (krew-dee-tay).   Fre. **Raw vegetables** used as **appetizers.**

crudo (KROO-doa).   Ita, Spa. Fresh; **raw.**

cruller (KRUEL-lehr).   Dut. A rich **doughnut** in the form of a twisted strip **fried** in deep fat.

crumb (kruhmb).   USA. To cover with crumbs; to break bread, **crackers, cookies** into small particles.

crumpet (KRUHM-pet).   Bri. A **muffin** similar to **English muffins,** except the batter is more liquid; muffin rings must be used when preparing in order to define the shape.

crush (kruhsh).   USA. Press to extract juice or oils; usually in a mortar or with side of knife.

crustacean (kruhs-STA-shun).   USA. Water dwelling anthropods, with a hard shell: **lobster, shrimp, crab, crayfish.**

crystallize (KRIHS-tahl-lize).   USA. to cause to form crystals, as in making **fudge.**

császärkörte (CHEH-ssaar-kurr-tae).   Hun. Type of **pear.**

cseresznye (CHEH-rehsn-yeh).   Hun. **Cherries.**

csirkét (CHEE-rkayt).   Hun. **Chicken.**

csuka (CHOO-ko).   Hun. **Pike.**

cú (chu).   Chi. **Vinegar.**

cuaresmeño (thoo-ahays-MEEN-yo).   Mex. A dark green, round, hot **chili pepper.**

cube (kub).   USA. Cutting food into shapes the same width, depth, and thickness; usually ⅜ inch or larger, depending on the dish in which it is to be used. See **dice, chop,** and **mince.**

cucumber (QUE-kuhm-behr).   USA. A vine-**vegetable** related to the gourd family; a basic **salad** ingredient; dark green skin, white flesh with a pale greenish cast, crisp texture; also used for **pickles** and **relishes.**

cuìpí ji (tswei pee jee).   Chi. **Chicken** cooked to have a crispy skin.

cuisine minceur (kwee-zeen mahns-uhr).   Fre. Low-calorie cuisine.

cuisse (kwees).   Fre. Drumstick.

cuisseau (kwee-so).   Fre . Leg of **veal.**

cuisses de grenouille (kweess dar grer-nooy).   Fre. **Frog legs.**

cuissot (kwee-so).   Fre. Haunch of **venison.**

cukrot (TSOO-krawt).   Hun. **Sugar.**

cullen skink (KUHL-lehn skehnk).   Sco. **Creamed haddock.**

culotte (koo-loht).   Fre. **Rump** of beef.

Cumberland sauce (KUHM-behr-luhnd saus).   USA. **Red currant jelly** thinned with **port,** flavored with **shallots, orange** zest, **mustard** and served with **game.**

cumin (QU-mehn).   USA. An **herb** grown for its seeds, which give **chili** its characteristic flavor; used whole, **roasted,** and **ground;** important in the cuisines of India, the Middle East, and Mexico; major ingredient in **curry** powders.

cuore (koo-OA-ray).   Ita. Heart.

cupcake (KUHP-kak).   USA. An individual portion of **cake** baked in a muffin tin, usually frosted with **icing** or dusted with **powdered sugar.**

cup custard (kuhp KUHS-tahrd).   USA. **Baked custard.**

Curaçao (KYUR-dah-so).   Dut. A **liqueur** made from the dried peel of the green sour **orange.** Sold as **Cointreau, triple sec,** and **Grand Marnier.**

curd (kuhrd).   USA. The thick, casin-rich part of coagulated **milk.**

curdle (KUHR-dle). USA. The separation of a **sauce** or **pudding** containing **eggs** into a watery liquid with thick, almost solid, particles in it. The sauce is still edible, but the appearance is unpleasant.

cure (keur). USA. A process of preserving by **aging, drying, salting,** or **smoking.**

curly endive (KUHR-lee EHN-div). USA. A bitter, green plant with sticky leaves; used in salads; cooked as a vegetable. Also known as **chicory.**

currant (KUHR-ruhnt). USA. Small black, seedless **raisin** used in **cakes, jellies, syrups, liqueurs;** used fresh in ice **cream, yogurt, sorbets.** See also **red currants.**

curry (KUHR-ree). USA. Highly spiced **condiment** from India; a **stew** seasoned with curry.

cuscinetti (kooz-chee-NAYT-tee). Ita. **Fried cheese sandwiches.**

cush (koosh). USA. A **cornmeal pancake.**

cushaw (koo-SHAH). USA. A variety of large crookneck **squash.**

Cussy (key-see). Fre. An elaborate garnish of **mushrooms** stuffed with **puréed chestnuts, giblets,** and **truffles.**

custard (KUHS-tahrd). USA. A sweet **pudding**-like mixture made of **eggs** and **milk** that can be **baked** or cooked. Also called **baked custard, cup custard, boiled custard.**

custard apple (KUHS-tahrd AHP-puhl). USA. A tropical **fruit** with jade green peel, sweet, low-acid flesh that is silky smooth and juicy, cream-colored, with a slight granular finish, like a custard of fine pears. Also known as **cherimoya, white sapote.**

custard marrow (KUST-tahrd MAR-row). USA. A pear-shaped **vegetable** of the **melon** family, with green, prickly, ribbed skin. Also called **chayote** and **mirliton.**

cut in (kuht ihn). USA. To cut a solid fat into flour with knives or pastry blender until fat particles are the desired size.

cutlet (KUHT-leht). USA. Thin **slice** of meat, a **scallop.**

cygne (sig-nah). Fre. A swan-shaped pastry filled with **crème Chantilly.**

cymling (SEHM-len). USA. A yellow or white round summer **squash** with a scalloped edge. Also known as **pattypan.**

dà báicài (da bai tsai). Chi. **Chinese cabbage.**

dab (dahb). Fre. A **flatfish** of the **sole** family; flesh is white, rather soft, easily digested.

dacquoise (dah-kwahs). Fre. A pastry made of **meringue** with **ground nuts,** baked in flat discs, filled with flavored **whipped cream** or **buttercream** and **berries.**

dadar-isi (DAII-dahr EE see). Dut. Indonesian stuffed **omelet.**

dadels ((DAH-dehls). Dut. **Dates.**

dadlar (DAH-dlahr). Swe. **Dates.**

dà-dòu (dah-doe). Chi. **Soy beans.**

daging smor (DAHKH-ingh smor). Dut. Indonesian stewed meat in a rich black sauce.

dagmarsuppe (DAHG-mahr-ssuppe). Nor. A **soup** made with **cream, sherry,** and tiny green **peas.**

Dagwood sandwich (DAHG-wood SAHND-wihch). USA. A **sandwich** made of many slices of bread filled with a variety of meats, **lettuce, tomatoes, pickles,** and such.

dahchini (DAH-chee-nee). Ind. **Cinnamon** or **cassia.**

dahi bhalle (da-HEE BHAH-lay). Ind. **Fried bean dumplings** in spice and herb-laced **yogurt.**

dai choy goh (dah-ee choy gwa). Chi. A **gelatin** made from **seaweed;** does not melt at room temperature.

daikon (DAH-ee-kohn). Jap. A giant, white **radish;** very crisp, tender, mild, sweet; eaten raw or cooked like **turnips;** at least a foot in length.

Daisy (DAY-zee). USA. A mild, firm **Cheddar cheese.**

daizu (DAH-ee-zoo). Jap. **Dried soybeans.**

dajaaj (da-JEHJ). Ara. **Chicken.**

dal (dahl). Ind. **Legumes:** lentils, dried **peas** and **beans.**

dalchini (dahl-CHEE-nee). Ind. **Cinnamon.**

damascos (dah-MAHSS-kohss). Por. **Apricots.**

Damen (DAH-mehn). Hun. A soft, uncured **cheese** made from cow's milk; sometimes called *Gloire des Montagnes.*

Dampfbraten (Dampf-BRAHT-un). Ger. Beef **stew.**

Dampfnudeln (Dampf-NOOD-eln). Ger. Sweetened **yeast dumplings;** served with stewed **fruit** or **jam.**

dan (dahn). Chi. **Egg.**

Danablu (DAAN-aa-bloo). Dan. A cow's whole-milk blue **cheese;** the sharpest of the blues; creamy white with a flaky texture.

Danbo (DAAN-boo). Dan. A **cheese** that is mild, smooth, semifirm, and pale golden in color; often contains **caraway** seeds; usually square in shape.

dàn-gao (daan-gau). Chi. **Cake.**

Danish Blue (DAAN-ish Blu). Dan. See **Danablu.**

Danish Crème Special (DAAN-ish krehn speh-shuhl). Dan. A triple-crème **dessert cheese;** soft, delicious, and very delicate.

Danish Export (Dane-esh X-port). Dan. A **cheese** made from skim milk and **buttermilk,** small, flat, and cylindrical.

Danish pastry (DAN-ish PA-stre). USA. A **yeast** pastry filled variously with **fruit, cheese, custard,** and served at breakfast.

dariole (dah-ree-ool). Fre. A small cylindrical mold; also the little **cakes** baked in this mold.

Darjeeling (dahr-jee-lehng). Ind. A variety of **tea,** used as a beverage.

darne (dahrn). Fre. A thick slice of a large fish; fish steak.

d'Artois (dahr-twah). Fre. A pastry of **puff-paste** and **jam.**

dasheen (dah-sheen). Chi. **Taro.**

dashi (dah-SHEE). Jap. Fish **stock** made of dried **bonito** and **seaweed.**

dates (datz). USA. Edible **fruit** of the palm tree, by composition, about half sugar. Of Arabian origins, three varieties are now grown in United States: Medjool, Deglet Noor, and Khadrawy.

dátiles (DAH-tee-layss). Spa. **Dates.**

Datteln (DAH-terln). Ger. **Dates.**

datteri (DAHT-tay-ree). Ita. **Dates.**

dattero di mare (DAH-tay-roa dee MAH-ray). Ita. Date **mussel,** a type of **shellfish.**

dattero farciti (DAH-tay-roa fahr-CHEE-tee). Ita. Stuffed **dates.**

dattes (daht). Fre. **Dates.**

daube (doab). Fre. **Stew.**

Dauphin (doug-fahng). Fre. A **cheese** flavored with **tarragon** and **powdered cloves;** molded in half-moon shape.

dauphine, a la (doa-fawng). Fre. **Puff paste** withj **potato purée,** shaped into balls or piped in shapes, and **deep-fried.**

dauphinois (doa-fee-nwah). Fre. A dish of **potatoes** prepared using **Gruyère.**

daurade (doa-rahd). Fre. **Gilthead;** a food fish of the **bream** family.

dà xia (da siah). Chi. Prawn; large **shrimp.**

dayolya (DOT-taw-yo). Hun. **Dates.**

De Arbol chile (De AHR-bol chihl-ee). USA. A small, long, and thin dried **chili** with brilliant red, thin shiny skin; very hot; should be used with caution.

debrecziner (DAEB-rae-sseen-eer). Hun. A spicy, coarse textured **sausage** resembling the **frankfurter.**

decouper (deh-koo-peh). Fre. To carve; to cut in pieces.

deem sum (dihm suhm). Chi. A snack or appetizer. See **dim sum.**

deep-fry (dep fri). USA. A method of immersing food in deep boiling fat to seal the exterior while keeping the interior moist. Also known as *deep fat frying* and French frying.

deer (dehr). USA. A highly desirable **game** animal.

deghi mirch (DAY-ghee meerch). Ind. Indian **paprika** made from mild Kashmiri pepper pods.

déglaçage (deh-glah-ssahj). Fre. The operation of pouring any liquid into the pan in which food has been cooked in butter or other fat; **deglaze.**

deglaze (dee-glaz). USA. To dilute with liquid, such as wine, **stock,** or **cream,** the concentrated juices left in the pan when meat, fish, or **poultry** has been **roasted, braised,** or **fried.**

degorger (deh-gor-jeh). Fre. To soak food for a variable time to cleanse it of any impurities.

degraisser (deh-grese). Fre. To remove excess fat from the surface of a liquid or a joint of meat.

degrease (dee-GREEZ). USA. To remove accumulated fat from surface of hot liquid.

degustation (deh-gys-tah-ssyoh). Fre. Tasting.

dehydrate (dee-HI-drate). USA. To render dry by removing water content.

déjeuner (day-zhuh-nay). Fre. Lunch; the meal in the middle of the day.

de la maison (der lah meh-sawng). Fre. Specialty of the house.

Delft (Dehlft). Dut. A spiced cheese made from partly skimmed milk; almost exactly like **Leyden.**

del giorno (dayl jee-OAR-no). Ita. Of the day; same as the French **du jour.**

Delicata (dehl-eh-KAH-tah). USA. Small, slender **squash** with green, cream, and orange striped exterior and yellow flesh; meat is golden yellow with mild flavor.

Delikatessaufschnitt (deh-li-kah-tess-OWF-schnitt). Ger. Assorted cold cuts.

Delmonico (dehl-MOHN-ee-koa). USA. A boneless steak cut from the **rib** section of beef. Also a **Spencer steak.**

Delmonico potatoes (dehl-MOHN-ee-ko po-TAT-tos). USA. **Potato** balls **boiled,** tossed in **butter, lemon** juice, **parsley, pepper,** and **salt.**

Demeltorte (deh-mehn-tohrt). Fre. An Austrian pastry filled with candied **fruit.**

demerara sugar (deh-MEHR-ah-rah SCHU-gahr). Bri. Raw **cane sugar,** partially refined, naturally light brown; very similar to **turbinado.**

demi (deh-me). Fre. Half.

demi-deuil (deh-me douj). Fre. Half-mourning, q. v.

demi-glace (deh-me glas). Fre. Brown **sauce** mixed in **veal stock,** reduced in half, flavored with **madeira** or **sherry.**

demi-loaf (DEHM-ee lohf).   USA. A term to describe a small, individual-size loaf of bread.

Demi-Sel (deh-me-sehl).   Fre. A square, soft, fresh, slightly salted cow's whole-milk **cheese.**

demitasse (deh-mee-tahss).   Fre. After-dinner **coffee** served in small cups; usually black and strong.

denerver (deh-nehr-veh).   Fre. The removal of tendons, gristle, membranes from meat, **game,** and **poultry.**

dent-de-lion (dehnt-deh-lee-o).   Fre. Dandelion.

dentice (DEHN-tee-chay).   Ita. Any of several white-fleshed fish found mostly along the Riviera.

depecer (deh-peh-seh).   Fre. To carve.

depouiller (deh-puj-ch).   Fre. To skim fat or scum off the surface of a **sauce** or **stock.**

Derby (DAHR-bee).   Bri. A large flat cow's whole-milk **cheese,** uncooked, pale, mild, hard, sweet.

desayuno (deh-sah-YOO-noh).   Mex. Light Breakfast.

deshebrar (dehs-ay-BRAHR).   Spa. To **shred.**

dëshydrate (day-zi-drat).   Fre. **Dehydrate.**

désossé (day-zose).   Fre. Boneless.

dessert (deh-SZEHRT).   USA, Fre. The last course of a meal; usually sweetmeats or **fruit** are served.

dessert (des-SAIRT).   Dut. **Dessert.**

detrempe (day-trup-eh).   Fre. A mixture of **flour** and water used in the preparation of flaky pastry.

Deventer koek (DAY-vun-tur kook).   Dut. Spice **cake** (from Deventer).

devil (DEH-vehl).   USA. To prepare food with hot seasonings such as **cayenne** or **mustard,** or serve with hot sauce.

devil's food cake (DEH-vehlz food kak).   USA. A rich, light, moist, very **chocolate cake.**

Devonshire cream (DEH-vun-shurr krem).   Bri. A thick **cream** made by slowly heating whole **milk** on which the cream has been allowed to rise, then skimming the cooled cream from the top.

Devonshire Cream Cheese (DEH-vuhn-shurr Krem Chez). Bri. A **cheese** made from cow's whole-milk as is **Devonshire cream,** except the skimmed, cooled cream is put into small molds, placed on straw mats, allowed to drain until hard enough to retain their shape.

dewberry (DU-behr-ree). USA. A sweet, edible **berry** related to the **blackberry.**

dextrose (DEHX-stros). USA. Grape **sugar;** used to thicken and sweeten baked goods, **candy, caramels.**

dhania (DHAH-nee-yah). Ind. **Coriander.**

dhan-sak masala (DHAHN-sahk ma-SAH-la). Ind. Spice blend used for making **Dhan-sek,** a **chicken,** lentil, and **vegetable stew.**

diablé (dee-ahb-lay). Fre. **"Devil";** any dish with sharp and hot seasonings.

diable (dj-ahbl). Fre. A strongly flavored **sauce** containing **herbs, vinegar,** white **wine,** and **shallots.**

diablo (dee-AHB-loh). Mex, Spa. **"Devil";** with sharp and hot seasonings.

diablotins (dj-ahb-bleh-tehn). Fre. Cheese-flavored **croutons,** for **garnishing soup.**

diavolini (dee-ah-oh-voh-LEE-nee). Ita. Short lengths of medium-sized hollow **pasta** tubes.

dibs (dehbs). Ara. **Carob syrup.**

dice (dics). USA. To cut in ¼ inch cubes. See **cube, chop,** and **mince.**

dick (dik). Ger. Thick.

dieppoise (deh-pwah-say). Fre. Saltwater fish garnished with **mussels** and **crayfish** in white wine reduction **sauce.**

Dijon (deh-zjohn). Fre. A white-wine-based **mustard.**

dijonnaise (deh-zjoh-naz). Fre. **Mustard-**flavored **sauce.**

dilan (dehl-LAHN). Ara. **Ribs,** as for meat or leafy **vegetables.**

dill (dehl). USA. An ancient **herb** whose seeds are baked in breads; whose leaves are used fresh, **dried,** frozen in **salads, soups, sauces;** and whose flowers flavor **pickles** and **vinegars.**

dillilammas (dil-li-LAHM-mah-stah). Fin. **Boiled mutton** in **dill sauce.**

dillkött (DIL-chot). Swe. **Boiled veal** with **dill sauce.**

dillsås (DILL-soass). Swe. **Dill sauce.**

dilute (deh-LUT). USA. To diminish the strength or flavor of a mixture, usually with water.

dim sum (dehm suhm). Chi. Small dishes eaten as snacks, or **hors d'oeuvres,** such as **fried shrimp** balls, hargow, **spring rolls, won ton.**

dinde (dahnd). Fre. **Turkey hen.**

dindon (dahn-dun). Fre. Tom **turkey.**

dindonneau (dahn-dun-noa). Fre. Young **turkey.**

dîner (deh-na). Fre. Dinner; to dine.

dió (DEE-aw). Hun. **Walnuts.**

dip (dehp). USA. A **sauce** of soft mixture, savory or sweet, into which food may be dipped.

diplomat pudding (DEH-plo-maht PUHD-eng). Bri. A **dessert** of **ladyfingers** and candied **fruit** soaked in **brandy** or **liqueur,** alternately layered in a mold with **custard.**

diplomat sauce (DEH-plo-maht saus). Bri. **Sauce normande** with **lobster butter, garnished** with **truffles,** diced lobster.

dirty rice (DEHR-tee ris). USA. A **Cajun** dish of **rice** cooked with **chicken** gizzards and livers.

disjoint (dehs-JOINT). USA. To cut chicken, turkey, or other poultry into pieces at the joints.

disossato (dee-soas-ZAH-to). Ita. Boned.

dissolve (dih-SOHLV). USA. To cause a dry substance to pass into solution in a liquid.

disznóhúst (DEES-naw-hoosht). Hun. **Pork.**

ditali (dee-TAH-lee). Ita. **Pasta** in form of tiny thimbles.

ditalini (dee-tah-LEE-nee). Ita. A tubular-shaped **pasta** about ¼ inch both in diameter and length, usually used in soups.

divinity (deh-VIN-eh-tee). USA. A white **fudge candy** made of whipped **egg** whites, **sugar,** and usually **nuts.**

djaj (da-JEHJ). Ara. **Chicken.**

Dobbeltøl (doubled-erl). Dan. Nonalcoholic dark **beer.**

Dobosch torte (doa-BAHSH tor-tah). Ger. Rich towering 10-layer **cake** with **mocha cream** filling.

Dobostorta (DAW-bawsh-tawr-to). Hun. A **caramel glazed dessert** of stacked layers of **sponge cake** spread with **chocolate cream.**

dobrada (dou-BRAH-dah). Por. **Tripe.**

dobrada com feijão branco (dou-BRAH-da kom fay-ZHAHNG BRAHN-koo). Por. **Tripe, sausages,** and **white beans** in a savory **stew.**

D'Oka (do-kah). Fre. A **cheese** similar to **Port du Salut,** formerly made by Trappist monks in Canada; no longer produced.

dolce (DOL-chay). Ita. Sweet, as in sweet taste.

dolceforte (dol-chay-FOAR-tah). Ita. Sweet and strong; pertains to a method of flavoring a dish.

Dolcelatte (Dol-chay-LAHT-tah). Ita. A young, sweet, mild blue-veined **cheese.**

dolci (DOL-chee). Ita. Sweet or **dessert.**

dolma (dol-MAH). Gre. Stuffed **grape leaf** using **ground meat, rice, onions, mint, lemon.**

Domiati (doh-MAH-tee). Egy. A **cheese** made of whole or partly skimmed cow's or buffalo's milk; soft, white with no openings, mild and salty in flavor when fresh, and cleanly acid when cured.

Donaukarpfen (do-now-KAHR-pfern). Ger. Danube river **carp.**

donburi (don-BUR-ee). Jap. A bowl of hot, boiled **rice** topped with meat, fish, **egg,** or **vegetables,** colorful **garnishes,** and spicy **condiments.**

dòng de (doong de). Chi. Frozen.

dong gu (doong goo). Chi. Smoky flavored, **dried,** black **mushrooms.**

dong gua (doong gwa). Chi. **Winter melon.**

donut (DO-nuht). USA. **Doughnut.**

doodh (doohdt). Ind. **Milk.**

doperwtjes (doap-efr-vwtys). Dut. **Green peas.**

Doppelbock (Dohp-pul-bok). Ger. Extra strong Bock **beer.**

dorata (doa-RAH-tah). Ita. **Gilthead;** a food fish of the sea **bream** family.

dorato (doa-RAH-to). Ita. Dipped in **egg batter** and **fried** light golden brown.

doreshingu (doh-REHSH-sheen-goo). Jap. **Salad dressing.**

Doreye au riz (doa-reh-yeh oa ree). Fre. Belgium **rice tarts;** many different versions.

Doria (dohr-ree-ah). Fre. A classical **garnish** for fish of **cucumbers** simmered in **butter.**

Dorsch (dorsch). Ger. **Cod.**

Dorset (dough-SAY). Bri. See **Blue Dorset.**

dorure (dohr-ewr). Fre. A beaten **egg** mixture for gilding pastry.

dosai (DOH-sah). Ind. **Yeast pancakes.**

dot (daht). USA. To scatter small bits of **butter** or **margarine** over the surface of food.

Dotter (Dough-tehr). Ger. A **cheese** made of skim milk and egg yolks.

dou (doh). Chi. **Bean.**

Double Crème (DUH-buhl Krem). USA. Any soft, ripened **cheese** in which the **milk** is enriched with added **cream** containing 60% butterfat.

Double Gloucester (DUH-buhl GLOH-stehr). Bri. A deep yellow, cow's whole milk **cheese** with a rich, mellow flavor, dense texture, made in large flat rounds.

douce (doos). Fre. Sweet; also called **doux.**

dou fu (doh foo). Chi. **Bean curd;** similar to **tofu,** but drier and firmer.

dòufù (doh-foo). Chi. **Bean curd.**

dough (doh). USA. A mixture of **flour,** liquid, and other ingredients, thick enough to roll or knead.

doughnut (DO-nuht). USA. A small ring-shaped **cake** made of **yeast dough,** usually **fried.**

dòu sha bao (doh sha bao). Chi. Sweet bean buns.

doux (doo). Fre. Sweet. Also called **douce.**

dou zhi (doh ya). Chi. Black **beans.**

dòuyá (doh dz). Chi. **Bean sprouts.**

Dover sole (Do-ver sohl). Bri. A member of the **flatfish** family; considered by many the best fish ever to eat.

dow ghok (doh gohk). Chi. Very thin **beans,** sometimes 18 inches long; taste is stronger than ordinary **green beans.** Also called **long beans, asparagus beans, yard-long beans.**

dow see (doh see).   Chi. Salty fermented **black beans** used for **sauces.**

dragée (drah-zhee).   Fre. A silver-coated **nut** or **sugar** bead used for decorating cakes.

deagoncello (drah-goan-CHAYL-lo).   Ita. **Tarragon.**

drain (dran).   USA. To place food in colander or strainer.

dram (drahm).   Nor. **Aquavit.**

Drambuie (drahm-BOO-ee).   Sco. A heather **honey**-flavored **liqueur** made from Scotch **malt** whiskey.

dranken (DRAHN-kehn).   Dut. Drinks; beverages.

drawn (drahn).   USA. A method of dressing fish by scaling and gutting, but leaving head, tail, and fins intact.

drawn butter (drahn BUHT-ehr).   USA. Clear, melted **butter** from which the milky solids have been removed.

dredge (drehg).   USA. To thoroughly cover a food by coating or sprinkling with **flour** or other fine substance.

Dresden dressing (DREHZ-dehn DREHS-seng).   USA. A cold **sauce,** made of hard-boiled **eggs, onions, mustard,** and other seasonings, that accompanies meats.

dress (drehs).   USA. To mix with some sauce or flavoring just before serving, as to dress cooked **vegetables** with melted **butter** or to dress fresh greens with **salad dressing.**

dried (drid).   USA. To remove moisture by means of heat.

dried beef (drid bef).   USA. Beef rounds **cured** with **salt** and **sugar,** **sliced** paper thin, then **dried, smoked,** and **pressed;** often referred to as *smoked* or *sliced beef.*

dried fruit (drid froot).   USA. **Fruit** that has had part of the water content removed to preserve it, such as **figs, prunes, apricots, peaches, pears,** and additional specialty fruits.

drikker (DRIK-kehr).   Nor. Drinks.

drippings (DREHP-engs).   USA. Fat and liquid residue from frying or roasting meat or poultry.

dronningsuppe (DRON-neng-ssew-pper).   Nor. Chicken **broth** fortified with **sherry, egg yolks, cream,** and **forcemeat** balls.

druiven (DRIR-vuh).   Dut. **Grapes.**

drum (druhm). USA. A large family of fish, sometimes called **croaker,** of the Atlantic.

drupe (droop). USA. A general term for a **fruit** with a single stone.

Dry Cheese (Dri Chez). USA. American name for **Sperrkäse** and **Trockenkäse;** made in the Bavarian Alps and the Tyrol only in winter and for home consumption.

dry heat (dri het). USA. A method of cooking, particularly meats, requiring no liquid in the cooking process; **roasting, broiling,** pan broiling, and cooking with fat.

dry milk solids (dri melk SAH-lehds). USA. Pasteurized **milk** particles, air-dried to remove most of the moisture.

drypasilla chili (dri-pah-SEE-ah CHILL-ee). Mex. A round, flatish **chili pepper** with a rich, sweet taste; mild to medium hot.

Dubarry (Doo-bah-rcc). Fre. Small flowerettes of **cauliflower,** covered with **mornay sauce,** sprinkled with **grated cheese,** bread crumbs, and **browned.**

dubbele boterham (dub-AY-lee BO-tehr-ruhm). Dut. A **sandwich** made with two pieces of bread, such as is made in United States.

dubbelsmörgås (dew-behl-SMURR-goass). Swe. **Sandwich.**

Dublin Bay prawn (DUB-lehn Bay prahn). Bri. Saltwater **crayfish.**

duchesse, a la (duh-shees). Fre. Boiled **potatoes, puréed** with **eggs** and **butter,** then piped through a pastry tube as a garnish.

Duel (Dooel). Aus. A soft, cured, cow's-milk **cheese.**

duck (duhk). USA. Any of various edible swimming game birds, with short legs and neck, and webbed feet. For domesticated duck, see **Long Island duck.**

duck sauce (duhk saus). USA. **Suan mei jiang,** a Chinese sauce.

du corps (doo kowr). Fre. Good body, as applies to **sauces** or **soups.**

due (doo-ey). Dan. **Pigeon (squab).**

duff (duhff). USA. A steamed **pudding** with **fruit,** such as *plum duff* or *cranberry duff.*

duglère (doog-lahr). Fre. Indicates the use of **tomatoes.**

du jour (doo-zhoor). Fre. "Of the day," soup du jour is **soup** of the day.

dulce (DOOL-seh). Mex. Sweet.

dulces (DOOL-sehs).   Spa. Sweets; **desserts.**

dulse (dehls).   Bri. A coarse, edible **seaweed** used for **gelatin.**

dumpling (DUM-pleng).   USA. A lump of **dough** steamed on top of a liquid, such as **soup** or **stew.**

Dundee cake (DEHN-dee-kek).   Sco. A **fruit cake** with a topping of **almonds.**

Dungeness crab (DUN-gehn-ess krab).   USA. The most popular of the Pacific crabs; pinkish-green and yellow before cooking, it becomes a brilliant red when cooked.

dunkeles Bier (DUNG-klerss beer).   Ger. Dark, heavy **beer.**

Dunlop (DUHN-loap).   Sco. A cow's-milk **cheese,** moderately soft, moist, flaky, sharp, almost white in color; an excellent cocktail cheese.

dünsten (DEWN-shtehn).   Ger. To **steam** or **stew,** either **fruit** or meat.

dur (dyr).   Fre. Hard; as hard boiled, of **eggs.**

duranzo (doo-RAHS-zoh).   Mex. **Peach.**

durchgebraten (DURKH-geh-braat-en).   Ger. Well done, as of steak.

durian (DUHR-ree-un).   Mal. A large, oval, tasty, but foul-smelling **fruit** with a prickly rind; the large seeds are roasted and eaten like **nuts.**

duro (DOO-ro).   Ita. Hard, as hard crust.

Dürre Runde (DEW-reh roont).   Ger. A **dried sausage.**

durham wheat (DUHR-um whet).   USA. A very hard **wheat** whose **grain** is made into **semolina flour.**

dust (duhst).   USA. To sprinkle lightly with **flour, cornmeal,** or **sugar.**

duva (du-va).   Swe. **Pigeon.**

duxelles (dews-sehl).   Fre. A kind of **mushroom hash,** used for seasoning **sauces** and as a spread.

dynya (DI-nyah).   Rus. **Melon.**

dyreryg (DEWR-rewg).   Nor. **Venison** that has been **marinated,** then cooked in **sour cream.**

dyrestek (DEWR-stehkt).   Nor. **Roast venison.**

Dyrlaegens natmad (dewr-leh-yahns nat-meth).   Dan. "Veterinarian's Midnight Snack"; a smørrebrød of dark rye bread, spread with spiced **lard,** liver **paste,** jellied **consommé, veal.**

Elote - Mexican - Fresh Corn

eau de vie (oh duh vee).   Fre. **Fruit brandy;** many varieties, **Kirschwasser** being best known.

eau sucrée (oh su-crae).   USA. A **Creole** word for "sugar water"; supposedly aids digestion and promotes sleep.

ebi (eh-BEE). Jap. **Shrimp.**

ebi suimono (eh-BEE soo-EE-moh-noh). Jap. Clear **soup** with **shrimp.**

ebis wantan men (eh-BEES wahn-tahn mehn).   Jap. Curled white **noodles** plus dried Chinese-style **won ton.**

ecarlate (ay-kahr-laht). Fre. Scarlet; a red **sauce** containing **lobster roe,** red tongue, and so forth.

Eccles cake (EK-kuhls kak). Bri. A small **cake** of **puff pastry** filled with **currants** and sprinkled with **sugar.**

ecetes torma (eht-seh-tehsh TAW-rmo). Hun. **Horseradish sauce.**

ecetet (eht-seh-teht). Hun. **Vinegar.**

echalote (ee-shah-lot). Fre. **Shallot.**

echaude (eh-shoad). Fre. Pastry made of **dough,** then **poached** in water and **baked** in the oven.

éclair (ay-klahr).   Fre. A finger-shaped pastry filled with **cream** or **custard.**

éclanche (ay-klahn-sheh). Fre. Shoulder of **mutton.**

écrevisse (ay-krey-vehs). Fre. **Crayfish.**

Edam (ee-duhm). USA. A round Dutch "cannon ball" **cheese** of partly skimmed cows' milk with a mellow, nut-like flavor. It has the texture of firm, yellow paste with red wax cover.

eda mame (eh-DAH mah-meh). Jap. Green soy **bean pods,** used as a smack or **appetizer.**

Edammer (ay-DAHM-mur). Dut. **Edam cheese.**

eddik (EHD-dik). Nor. **Vinegar.**

eddike (EHDH-eegger). Dan. **Vinegar.**

Edelpilzkäse (A-dehl-pe-kahz-zah). Aus. A high-butterfat, blue-veined **cheese** that is soft when young, but firm and crumbly when aged.

édeskömény (AY-dehsh-kur-mayny). Hun. **Caraway** seeds.

édespaprika (AY-dehsh-pop-ree-ko). Hun. **Milk paprika.**

édességet (AY-dehsh-shy-geht). Hun. **Dessert.**

Edinburgh fog (EHD-en-bherg fawg). Bri. **Whipped cream** flavored with **sugar** and **vanilla** and mixed with **ratafia biscuits** and **chopped almonds.**

Edinburgh rock (EHD-en-bherg rahk). Bri. **Sugar candy** with a mellow texture.

Edirne (A-DEE-ohn). Tur. A sheep's-milk **cheese,** white, semifirm; very good in or with green **salads.**

eel (ehl). USA. A snake-like fish, with delicate flesh when caught in fast-flowing water.

een broodje ei (AYn brood-yeh ay). Dut. **Egg sandwich.**

eend (aynt). Dut. **Duck.**

eendje (AYnd-yeh). Dut. Duckling.

efterrätt (AYF-terr-reht). Swe. **Dessert,** sweet.

egg cheese (ehg). Fin. A **cheese** made with fresh **milk** and fresh **eggs.**

egg (ehg). USA. The hard-shelled reproductive body produced by a domestic **fowl. Chicken eggs** are most commonly used in cooking.

egg (ehg). Nor. **Egg;** *eggerøre* (EHGG-errurrer) scrambled egg; *hård-kokt* (HAWR-kookt) hard-boiled; *kokt* (kookt) boiled; and *litekokt* (lite-kookt) soft-boiled egg.

egg and crumb (ehg ahnd krum). USA. To dip food into diluted, slightly beaten **egg,** then dredge or sprinkle with crumbs.

egg foo yung (ehg foo yuhng). USA. A rich **omelet** made with the addition of Chinese **vegetables,** fish, and meat.

eggnog (EHG-naug).   USA. A drink consisting of beaten **eggs, milk** or **cream, sugar,** spices, and usually rum or **brandy.**

egg noodles (ehg nood-dles).   USA. **Pasta** in short, flat ribbons.

egg og bacon (ehg o BAY-kern).   Nor. **Bacon** and **eggs.**

egg pie (ehg pi).   Bri. A baked **savory** that is an ordinary **pie** crust filled with beaten or whole **eggs** and crumbled bits of crisp **bacon.**

eggplant (EHG-plahnt).   USA. A perennial plant that yields a blackish-purple ovoid **fruit,** used as a **vegetable,** known as **aubergine.**

egg roll (ehg rohl).   USA. **Cai juan; pancake**-like "skin" wrapped around a filling in the shape of a roll, then fried.

eggs Benedict (ehgs BEHN-ee-dehkt).   USA. One half of an **English muffin** topped with a slice of **Canadian bacon, poached egg,** and **hollandaise sauce.**

eggs Sardou (ehgs SAHR-doh).   USA. **Poached eggs** with **artichoke** hearts, **anchovies, chopped ham, truffle,** and **hollandaise sauce.**

egg wash (ehg-wahsh).   USA. Beaten **egg** diluted with a liquid, used to dip food in preparation for crumbing.

egg yolks (ehg-uohlk).   USA. The yellow of the **egg** used to thicken **sauces,** enrich foods, add color to foods; high fat content.

églefin (ehg-ler-fang).   Fre. **Haddock.** Also spelled **égrefin, aiglefin.**

egres (eh-grahsh).   Hun. **Gooseberries.**

Égyptienne (ay-zgeep-sjen).   Fre. Egyptian style: with lentils.

ei (ege).   Dut. **Egg.**

Eier (IGH-err).   Ger. Eggs; **Hartgekocht Eier** (HAHRT-ger-KOKHT) hard-cooked; **Rühreier** (REWR-igherr) scrambled; **Verloren Eier** (fehr-LO-rehm IGH-err) eggs poached in **vinegar; Weich Gekochte** (vighkh ger-KOKH-ter IGH-err) soft-boiled.

Eiercrème (IGH-err-krem).   Ger. **Custard.**

eieren (AY-uh-ruh).   Dut. **Eggs;** *gekookte eieren* (khuh KOHKTAY-uh-run) boiled; *harde eieren* (hart AY-uh-run) hard-cooked; *harde gekookte eieren* (hart khuh-KOKH-tuh AY-uh-ruh) hard-boiled; *spiegeleiren* (SPEE-khul-ay-uh-ruh) fried.

eieren met ham (AY-uh-ruh-met-HAHM).   Dut. Ham and **eggs.**

eieren met spek (AY-uh-ruh-met-SPEK).   Dut. **Bacon** and **eggs.**

eierenpannekoeken (AY-uh-ruh-PAHN-nuh-koo-kuh). Dut. **Pancakes.**

eiergehak (AY-uh-khuh-haak). Dut. **Eggs** with **ground** meat added.

Eierkuchen (IGH-err-ku-xon). Ger. **Omelet.**

Eier mit Speck (AIN-meht-shpehk). Ger. **Bacon** and **eggs.**

Eieröhrli (IGH-err-oh-rurht-lee). Ger. Zürich carnival **cakes, fried** in **butter;** very, very thin but rich.

Eierpflanzen (IGH-err-phlant-zen). Ger. **Eggplant.**

Eierspeisen (IGH-err-shpai-zen). Ger. **Egg** dishes.

Eierteigwaren (IGH-err-taik-vaar-en). Ger. **Egg noodles, spaghetti, macaroni.**

einbern (AIN-bern). Jew. A brown **roux.**

Eingemacht (AIN-ga-mahk-ta). Ger Preserved, such as preserved **fruits.**

Eintopf (AIN-topf). Ger. One-dish meal.

Eis (eyess). Ger. **Ice cream.**

Eisbein (IGHS-bighn). Ger. **Pickled pork** knuckles.

éisc (ayshk). Iri. Fish, plural; one fish is **isac.**

Eisschokolade (eyess-shok-o-LAAD-eh). Ger. Iced **chocolate.**

ejotes (e-HOH-tehs). Mex. **Green beans.**

elaichi (ee-LIE-a-chee). Ind. **Cardamom.**

Elbing or Elbinger (EL-beng). Ger. A **cheese;** hard, crumbly, and sharp.

elderberry (EL-dur-behr-ree). USA. A blackish-purple **berry** of the elder tree, used in fruit **soups, jellies,** homemade wines; must be cooked.

eleesh (EH-lesh). Ind. Fatty fish found in Hooghly River.

elephant garlic (EHL-eh-fahnt GAHR-lick). USA. A very large, mild-flavored **vegetable** with a mild **garlic** flavor; does not have a strong garlic odor; looks similar to common garlic; whole cloves can be prepared like **potatoes** and **onions;** also use **raw** in **salads.**

elft (elft). Dut. **Shad.**

elg (ehlg). Nor. **Elk.**

elixir (ee-LEHCK-sur).   USA. A liquid made by dissolving various edible substances in alcohol or wine with high alcoholic content.

elöetelt (eh-lur-ayehlt).   Hun. **Appetizer.**

elote (eh-LOH-teh).   Mex. Fresh **corn.**

embutidos (ehm-boo-TEE-dous).   Spa. **Pork sausages.**

Emiliano (Eh-mehl-ee-AHN-no).   Ita. A very hard **cheese** of the **Parmesan type;** used for **grating.**

emince (eh-manss).   Fre. Thinly sliced leftover meat, covered with a seasoned **sauce** and heated through.

Emmentaler (AHH-mehn-tahl-lehr).   Ger. The world-renowned, big-holed **Swiss cheese;** a cow's whole-milk cheese made in Switzerland, with a hard brown rind, golden interior with large holes; mellow, rich, nutty taste; large wheels. Also known as Swiss cheese.

empada (em-PAH-dah).   Por. **Pie.**

empadinhas de camarão (em-pah-DEEN-yash deh cam-a-ROWNSH).   Por. Little **shrimp pies.**

empanada (ehm-pah-NAH-dah).   Spa. A **tart** with various fillings; a **turnover.**

empandita (ehm-pahn-DEE-tah).   Spa. A pastry **turnover** with various savory fillings.

empanizado (ehm-pah-NEE-zah-doh).   Spa. Breaded.

em sangue (ehm SAN-guh).   Por. Rare, as in preparing steak.

emulsion (e-MUHL-shun).   USA. The dispersion of small droplets of one liquid into a second liquid with which it is incapable of mixing or attaining homogeneity without the use of an emulsifier, for example, the use of **eggs** in making **mayonnaise.**

en brochette (ahng broh-sheh).   Fre. **Broiled** on a **skewer.**

enchiladas (en-chee-LAH-dah).   Mex. **Tortillas** filled variously with meat, **cheese, chilies,** then rolled and served with **sauce.**

en cocotte (ahng-koh-koht).   Fre. In individual **casserole.**

en croute (ahng-kroot).   Fre. Wrapped and **baked** in pastry.

encurtidos (ehn-koor-TEE-doh).   Spa. **Pickles.**

endive (EHN-div). USA. A **salad** green with a bunchy head and narrow, curly, sticky leaves; center is yellow-white; taste is mildly astringent in center, outer green leaves tend to be slightly bitter.

endomame (en-DOH-mah-meh). Jap. **Peas.**

Engardine (ehn-gahr-deen). Swi. A **cheese** made from cow's milk.

Engadiner Nusstorte (ehn-gun-DEE-ner NEUSS-tortr). Ger. Rich, flat Swiss **cake** filled with **nuts** and **honey.**

Engelsk bøf (EHNG-erlsk burf). Dan. English beefsteak; **filet** of beef.

English Dairy (EHNG-glesh DEH-ree). USA. A very hard **cheese,** made similar to **Cheddar** except cooked much longer.

English muffin (EHNG-glesh muhf-fehn). USA. A round, slightly coarse-textured, flat **muffin,** usually split and **grilled** or **toasted.**

enguias (ehn-GHEEAHSH). Por. **Eels.**

en jalea (ayn KHAY-leh). Spa. Jellied.

enoki (ee-NOH-kee). Jap. An abbreviated word for **enokitake.**

enokitake (ee-NOH-kee-tah-kee). Jap. Wild **mushroom** with tiny caps and thin stems; mild-flavored, pleasant crispness and aroma; use in **soups** and one-pot dishes; also called **enoki.**

en papillote (ahng pah-pee-yoa). Fre. Meat, fish, **poultry,** and/or **vegetables** cooked in a parchment bag.

enriched rice (ehn-REHCHD ris). USA. **Rice** that has some of the nutrients replaced that were lost during milling.

enrollado (ehn-roh-LAH-doh). Mex. Rolled.

ensalada (een-sah-LAH-tah). Spa. **Salad.**

ensalada de pepino (een-sah-LAH-tah daa pah-PEE-noh). Spa. **Cucumber salad.**

ensalads de San Isidro (een-sah-LAH-tah daa Sahn Ehs-ee-droh). Spa. **Lettuce** and **tuna** fish **salad.**

ensalada variada (een-sah-LAH-tah BEHR-deh). Spa. Mixed green **salad.**

ensopado (ehn-sou-PAH-doo). Por. Thick, hearty **soup** of bread and meat.

Ente (EHN-ter). Ger. **Duck.**

Entenbrüstchen (ehnt-en-BRUST-khen). Ger. Breast of duckling.

Entenweissauer (ehnt-en-VIHSS-owehr). Ger. Duckling in **aspic.**

entrecôte (ahngtr-kot). Fre, Ita. A steak cut from between the **ribs.**

entrecôte château (ahngtr-kot sha-toah). Fre. A large steak.

entrecôte minute (ahngtr-kot meen-ewt). Fre. Small steak.

entrecuisse (ahngtr-khis). Fre. The fleshy thigh joint of **poultry** or **game** birds.

entree (ahng-tray). Fre. Th first course of a meal.

entree (ahng-tray). USA. The main course of the meal.

entremeses (ehn-treh-MEH-sehs). Spa. **Hors d'oeuvres.**

entremets (ehm-tray-mais). Fre. Dainty dishes of **vegetables** served as a second course; hot or cold sweets and after-dinner **savories** served as a second course.

epaule (ay-pohl). Fre. Shoulder.

epazote (eh-pah-SOH-teh). Mex. An **herb** used in cooking.

eper (eh-oehr). Hun. **Strawberries.**

éperlan (ay-pehr-lahng). Fre. **Smelt.**

épice (ay-pis). Fre. Spice

épices composes (ay-pees kom-poz). Fre. A classic combination of **herbs** and spices for seasoning; dried **thyme, bay leaves, basil, sage, coriander, mace,** and **black pepper.** Also called *spice Parisienne.*

epigramme (eh-pee-grahm). Fre. Slices of breast of **lamb,** dipped in **egg,** rolled in bread crumbs, and **fried** in **butter** or **grilled.**

èpinard (ay-pee-nahr). Fre. **Spinach.**

eple (EHP-ler). Nor. **Apple.**

eplesnø (EHP-le-snur). Nor. **Apple snow pudding.**

eplucher (eh-plew-sheh). Fre. To **peel.**

Epoisses (Eh-pwass). Fre. A **cheese,** usually soft, but may be semifirm when aged; can be flavored with **black pepper, cloves,** or **fennel** seeds and soaked in white wine.

eponger (eh-poan-zhah). Fre. To drain **vegetables** on a towel.

Erba (EHR-bah). Ita. **Herb.**

erbetté (ehr-BEHR-tah). Ita. A **vegetable** similar to **spinach** or **beet** greens; has an elongated smallish leaf and a slim tender green stalk; also called **bietoline.**

Erbo (Ehr-bow). Ita. A **cheese** sometimes compared to **Gargonzola.**

Erbsen (EHRP-sern). Ger. **Peas.**

Erdapfel (EHRT-ah-pferl). Ger. **Potato.**

Erdapfelnudeln (EHRT-ah-pferl-NOOD-len). Ger. Very small, oblong Austrian **potato dumplings** rolled in fat-fried bread crumbs.

Erdberren (EHRT-bay-ren). Ger. **Strawberries.**

erter (AE-terr). Nor. **Peas.**

ertesuppe (ae-terr-SEWP-per). Nor. A hearty **pea soup.**

ervanço (ehr-VAHN-soo). Por. **Chick peas; garbanzo bean.**

ervilhas (ehr-VEEL-yahss). Por. **Peas.**

Ervy (Ehr-vay). Fre. A soft **cheese** similar to **Camembert.**

erwtensoep (EHR-tuh-soop). Dut. Famous split **pea soup.**

erwtjes (EHR-tyus). Dut. **Peas.**

escabeche (ehs-kah-BEH-cheh). Spa **Pickling marinade.**

escalfado (ehsh-kahl-FAH-doo). Por. **Poached.**

escalibada (ays-kah-LAY-bah-dah). Spa. A mixture of **vegetables grilled** over charcoal.

escalopado (ehsh-kah-loh-PAH-doh). Mex. Escalloped.

escalope (eh-skah-lop). Fre. Thin slices of meat or fish.

escalloped (eh-SKAHL-lahped). USA. Baked in a sweet or savory **sauce,** usually covered with bread crumbs.

escargot (ays-skahr-go). Fre. **Snail.**

escarole (ES-kar-roll). Ita. A broad-leaf type of **endive;** slightly bitter; the leaves do not curl at the ends; foliage is deep green, slightly crumpled and closely bunched; use in **salads.**

espadon (eh-spohd-oa). Fre. **Swordfish.**

espagnole (ay-spah-nyol). Fre. Brown **sauce.**

espargos (ess-PAHR-gohss). Por. **Asparagus.**

espárrago (ehs-PAHRR-ah-goh). Spa. **Asparagus.**

espinaca (ehs-prr-NAH-kahs). Spa. **Spinach.**

espinafres (ess-pee-NAH-fray). Por. **Spinach.**

espresso (eh-SPREHS-o). Ita. **Coffee** made by forcing steam through finely ground, darkly roasted coffee beans.

esqueixada (es-quah-ZAH-dah). Spa. Fish **salad.**

Esrom (Ehs-rohm). Dan A semisoft **cheese,** sweet and buttery; rind may be eaten with the velvety interior.

essence (EHS-ehns). USA. A concentrated substance that resembles an **extract** in possessing a quality in concentrated form; that is fish essence, banana essence.

Essig (EHS-sikh). Ger. **Vinegar.**

essigfleisch (ICS-seg-flesh). Jew. Sweet and sour meat.

Essigkren (EHS-sikh-ren). Ger. **Horseradish** in **vinegar, sugar,** and spices.

Esterhazy Rostbraten (ehs-tehr-HAHT-cee hurst-BRAR-tern). Ger. **Filet** of beef with a rich **stuffing, roasted** with a chopped-**vegetable sauce** and basted with **Madeira;** an Austrian dish.

estofado (ehs-toh-FAH-doh). Spa. **Stew.**

estouffade (ehs-toh-fahd). Fre. Food cooked by slowly **stewing;** also, a clear brown **stock** used to dilute **sauces** and moisten **braised** dishes.

estragon (eh-strah-gohn). Fre. **Tarragon.**

etamine (eh-tah-meen). Fre. A cloth for straining **sauces** or **stocks.**

etikkasilli (ay-tahk-kah-SIL-li). Fin. **Pickled herring.**

étolajat (AY-taw-loyot). Hun. **Dessert.**

etouffée (ay-too-fay). Fre. Literally translated "smothered"; a **Cajun stew** of **crawfish** or **shrimp** served over **rice;** made by cooking very slowly in a lidded pot, condensing the food juices into a delicious residue, which when **degreased** if necessary, then **deglazed,** forms the **sauce** for the dish.

etuvee (eh-too-veh). Fre. A method of cooking food with little or no liquid.

evaporated milk (e-VAHP-oh-rat-ed mehlk). USA. Milk with half of its water content removed, then sterilized; has a caramelized taste.

Exeter stew (EHX-eh-tehr stu). Bri. A **stew** of beef, **onions,** and **dumplings.**

exhausting (ehx-ZAUST-eng). USA. A term used in canning food meaning to drive out enough air to make the desired vacuum.

export (EKS-poht). Nor. Potent lager-type **beer.**

expresso (ehx-SPREHS-so). Ita. **Espresso.**

extract (EHX-strack). USA. A product obtained by evaporating animal or vegetable juice.

extruded (ehx-STRU-dehd). USA. To shape by forcing, pressing, or pushing through a die or sieve.

eye of the round (eye ovf the rahund). USA. The round muscle in the center of the **round** section of the hindquarter of beef.

Fasol - Russian - Bean

faakiha (FAK-ha). Ara. **Fruit.**

faaswulyaa (fa-SUL-yah). Ara. **Beans.**

fabada asturiana (fah-BAH-dah ahs-too-ree-AH-nah). Spa. A hearty stew of **fava beans,** meats, and **onions.**

fadøl (fah-durl). Dan. Draught **beer.**

fagiano (fah-JAA-no). Ita. **Pheasant.**

fagioli (fah-JOA-lee). Ita. **Beans,** usually **kidney beans.**

fagioli assolutti (fah-JOA-lee ahs-zoa-LOOT-tee). Ita. **Kidney beans fried** with **garlic** in oil.

fagiolini (fah-joa-LEE-nee). Ita. **Green beans.**

fagot (FAHG-gaht). USA. **Herbs** and seasoning **vegetables** tied together in a small cheesecloth bundle; usually called **bouquet garni.**

fagylaltot (FOD-ylol-tawt). Hun. **Ice cream.**

fah chiu (fah chiu). Chi. A hot **pepper** for seasoning.

faht choy (faht choy). Chi. A hair-like **seaweed.**

faisan (feh-zahng). Fre. **Pheasant.**

faisan (figh-SSAHN). Spa. **Game** birds.

faisão (fay-ZAHNG.) Por. **Pheasant.**

fajita (fah-HEE-tah). Mex. Warm, soft **tortilla** rolled with **grilled** spicy meats, **chopped lettuce, tomatoes, green onions, grated cheeses,** topped with **sour cream.**

falafel (fah-LAH-fahl). Ara. **Chickpea** patties made of ground **peas** mixed with **herbs** and spices, then **fried.**

fàn (fahn). Chi. **Rice.**

fannings (FAHN-engz). USA. Broken leaves from which a quick, strong **tea** is brewed.

får (fohr). Swe. **Mutton.**

faraona (fah-rar-OA-nah). Ita. **Guinea hen** roasted in clay to seal in juices and flavor.

farce (fahr-ceh). Fre. **Forcemeats** or **stuffings.**

farci (fahr-cee). Fre. **Cabbage** stuffed with **sausage** meat or other **forcemeat**, wrapped in muslin, and cooked in **stock.**

farcito (fah-CHEE-to). Ita. Stuffed.

farefrikassée (FAWR-freek-ahs-see). Nor. **Fricasseed lamb.**

fårestek (FAWR-sstayk). Nor. **Roast** leg of lamb.

farahin (fahr-fah-HEHN). Ara. The **herb purslane.**

farfalle (fah-FAHL-lay). Ita. Butterfly- or bowtie- shaped **pasta.**

farfel (FAHR-fehl). Jew. **Dried, grated egg dough;** used as **garnish** in **soup.**

fårikål (FAY-nah-lawr). Nor. **Lamb stewed** with **cabbage.**

farina (fah-REE-nah). Ita. **Flour.**

farina (fah-REE-nah). USA. A creamy colored, granular, protein-rich **meal** made from **hard wheat** other than **durum,** with the **bran** and most of the **germ** removed.

farinacceous (fah-ree-nank-chay-OA-ooz). Ita. Starchy; made of **flour,** meat, **grains.**

farinha de avêa (fah-REE-nyah duh ah-VAY-ah). Por. **Oatmeal.**

Farmer cheese (FAHR-mehr chez). USA. A **cheese** of cow's partly skimmed milk, similar to **cottage cheese.** known in France as **Farm Cheese, Fromage à la Pie, Mou, Maiagre,** and **Ferme.**

farsh (fahrsh). Rus. **Stuffing.**

fårsj oxbringa (fahrsk OOKS-BRING-a). Swe. **Boiled** beef.

färsk sill (faersk sil). Swe. Fresh **herring.**

fårstek (fooaar stayk). Swe. Leg of **mutton.**

fasan (fa-SAHN). Swe. **Pheasant.**

fasan (fah-SAAN). Dan. **Pheasant.**

Fasan (fah-ZARN) Ger. **Pheasant.**

Faschierter Braten (fah-SHEER-terss BRAR-tern). Ger. Meatloaf.

Fasnacht (FAAS-nakht). USA. Pennsylvania Dutch diamond-shaped **potato dough yeast** pastry that is fried, traditionally eaten on Shrove Tuesday.

fasol (fah-SSOL). Rus. **Haricot bean, green bean, French bean.**

fasulya (fah-SUL-ya). Ara. **Lima beans.**

fatia (fah-TEE-ah). Por. **Slice.**

fatias frias (fah-TEE-ahss FREE-ahss). Por. Cold cuts.

fatir (fi-TERR). Ara. **Pancakes,** often served with **jam** or **honey.**

fatta (FAHT-tah). Ara. **Mutton** stewed in **broth** with bread and **rice.**

fåttiga riddare (FOAR-ti RID-ahrer). Swe. **French toast.**

fatto in casa (FAHT-toa een KAH-sah). Ita. Homemade.

fausse tortue (fos tohr-ty). Fre. Mock turtle.

fava bean (FAV-ah ben). USA. A broad **bean** of Mediterranean origin; large, meaty, pale green with large green pods; used fresh, **dried,** and canned; important worldwide for its nutritional value.

favas (FAH-vahsh). Por. **Fava beans; broad beans.**

fave (FAH-vay). Ita. **Broad beans.**

fazan (FAH-zhan). Rus. **Pheasant.**

fazant (fah-ZAHNT). Dut. **Pheasant.**

febras de porco (FAY-bahsh duh POUR-koo). Por. Leg of **pork,** cooked in red wine and **brandy,** seasoned with **cloves, garlic, cumin.**

fécule (fehk-eul). Fre. Refined **potato** starch used as thickener.

fedelini (fay-dee-LEE-nee). Ita. **Pasta** that is thin, fine **spaghetti;** larger than **capellini.**

fegatelli (fay-gah-TAYL-lee). Ita. **Pork** liver.

fegatini (fay-gah-TEE-nee). Ita. **Chicken** livers.

fegato (fay-GAH-toa). Ita. Liver.

fegato d'oca (fay-GAH-toa dOA-kah). Ita. Goose liver.

fehérhagyma mártás (feh-HAYR-rod-ymo MAAR-taash). Hun. **Onion sauce.**

Feigen (FAIG-ahn). Ger. **Figs.**

feijão (fay-ZHOW). Por. **Beans.**

feijão de vagens (fay-ZHOW dat VAH-zhayz). Por. **Green beans.**

feijoa (fay-HO-a). Spa. A slightly bumpy, thin-skinned, green **fruit** of South America, with a cream-colored granular, slightly soft flesh, like a **pear;** tart and perfumy; use fresh in **salads** or make into preserves. Also known as **pineapple guava.**

feijoada (fay-zhoh-AH-dah). Por. A hearty, soupy **stew** made of **pork,** beef, **black beans, rice,** seasoned with **peppers, garnished** with **oranges.**

Feingeback (FYENT-bak). Ger. Pastry.

fejes-salátát (feh-yaysh SHOL-laa-taat). Hun. **Lettuce.**

Felchen (FEHL-chehn). Ger. A kind of freshwater **trout.**

fenalår (FAY-nah-lawr). Nor. **Smoked** leg of **mutton.**

fennel (FEHN-nul). USA. An **anise**-flavored, **celery-like** herb, whose seeds and leaves are used for seasoning and whose stems, and in some varieties whose bulbous base, are edible.

fenouil (fah-nujz). Fre. **Fennel.**

fen si (fen see). Chi. Translucent **noodles** made from **mung beans.**

fenugreek (FEHN-uh-grek). Ind. An ancient **herb** whose maple-flavored leaves are used as a **vegetable**, in **curry powder,** as an artificial maple flavoring in **candies** and **syrup;** its **celery**-flavored seeds are used whole and **ground.**

feoil (fy-AWIL). Iri. Meat.

feoil mhairt (fy-AWIL-wartch). Iri. Beef.

féra (fah-rah). Fre. A variety of **salmon.**

fermentation (fuhr-mehn-TA-shun). USA. A chemical change brought about by the action of bacteria, **yeast,** or mold.

fermiere (fayr-myahr). Fre. In plain, country style.

ferri (FEHR-ree). Ita. **Grilled** over an open fire.

fersken (FAYRSK-nerr). Dan. **Peach.**

fersk røget laks (fayrsk ROI-ert lahks). Dan. Fresh smoked Nova Scotia **salmon.**

Feta (FEH-tah).   Gre. A crumbly, salty, white, rindless ewe's-milk **cheese;** semisoft; excellent as **hors d'oeuvre** when accompanied by black Kalamata **olives** and glasses of Greek **retsina** wine.

fett'unta (feht-t'OON-tah). Ita. A favorite Tuscany dish of coarse-textured bread, **toasted** over coals and liberally dressed with extra virgin **olive oil**. Also called **fregolotta** or **bruschetta**.

fetta (FAYT-tah). Ita. A **slice.**

fettuccine (fayt-toot-CHEE-nay).   Ita. **Egg pasta** in long, thin, flat strips. Also known as **tagliatelle, pappardelle.**

fettuccine verdi (fayt-toot-CHEE-nay vehr-dee). Ita. **Pasta** in form of flat ribbons made green by adding **spinach.**

feuilles de betteraves (furee-lehs der beh-ter-rahv). Fre. **Beet** greens.

feuilletage (fuhy-leh-tah-zhay). Fre. **Puff pastry;** flaky, leafy.

feuilletée (fuhy-leh-tay). Fre. In leaves; said of very thin sheets of pastry, similar to **phyllo.**

fèves (fehv). **Broad beans.**

fiambres (FYAHM-brayss).   Spa. Cooked meats served cold; **boiled ham.**

fichi (FEE-kee). Ita. **Figs.**

fichi secchi (FEE-kee sAY-chee). Ita. **Dried figs.**

fiddlehead (FEHD-uhl-hehd).   USA. The young sprouts of certain ferns, harvested while young and tender, used as a **vegetable** and for **garnishes.**

fideos (fee-DHAY-oass). Spa. **Spaghetti; noodles.**

field lettuce (feeld LEHT-uhs). USA. A loose-leaf **lettuce** found in the wild in United States; clusters are small with smooth green leaves; sometimes cooked as **vegetable.** Also called **lamb's lettuce.**

field peas (feeld pes). USA. A small, edible **pea** grown for food and forage.

figado (FEE-gah-doh). Por. Liver.

figos (FEE-gohss). Por. **Figs.**

figs (fihgz). USA. The **pear**-shaped, edible **fruit** of the fig tree; eaten fresh and **dried.**

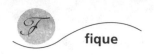
fique (fig). Fre. **Fig.**

fijn brood (fine broht). Dut. Fine bread.

fikon (FEE-kon). Swe. **Figs.**

filbert (FIHL-behrt). USA. The nut of a hazel shrub; round or slightly oval and flat on one end, amber colored; flavor is sweet; texture firm, rich in oil; pleasant to taste; used in confectionary. Also known as **hazelnut.**

filbunke (FIL-bewnk). Swe. Clabbered **milk, junket.** Not to be mistaken for **yogurt.**

filé (FEE-lay). Hun. **Filet.**

filé (fee-LEH). Por. **Filet; tenderloin** steak.

filé powder (fee-LAY). USA. **Ground** young, dried sassafras leaves, used to flavor and thicken **gumbos** in **Creole** cooking. Also called **gumbo fileé.**

filet (fee-leh). Fre. Boneless piece of red meat or beef; not to be confused with **fillet,** which refers to fish or **poultry.**

filete (fi-LEH-teh). Spa. **Filet.**

filete de vaca (fi-LEH day vau-kah). Spa. Beef **tenderloin.**

filet mignon (fee-leh mee-nyon). Fre. A small **slice** from the thick end of the **tenderloin.**

filetto (fee-LEHT-toa). Ita. **Fillet.**

filfil (FIL-fil). Ara. **Pepper.**

filhó (fee-lee-OO). Por. **Fritter, pancake.**

Filled Cheese (filld chez). USA. A **cheese** made from whole or skim milk to which a foreign fat has been added.

fillet (FIHL-eht). USA. Boneless piece of fish or **poultry;** not to be confused with **filet,** which refers to beef or red meat.

filling (FIHL-eng). USA. A food mixture to fill pastries or **sandwiches.**

filmjölk (FIL-myohlk). Swe. Sour **milk,** similar to **yogurt.**

filo (FEE-lo). Gre. **Phyllo.**

filosoop (FEE-loh-sooph). Dut. "Philosopher's Dish"; made of **minced** meat, mashed **potato,** and **onions,** similar to **shepherd's pie.**

financiere (fee-nahng-syenr). Fre. A meat or **poultry garnish** of cocks' combs and kidneys, **truffles, sweetbreads, mushrooms,** and **olives.**

finanziere (fee-nahn-ZEE-rah). Ita. Cibreo; a dish of cocks' combs and **sweetbreads,** served with **vegetable timbales.**

finely chop (fin-lee chahp). USA. Cutting food into very small pieces, less than ⅛ inch.

fine marineret sild (fin maaree-NAYT-ert seel). Dan. Fine **pickled herring.**

fine herbes (feen-zehrb). Fre. A combination of finely **chopped** fresh **herbs.**

finik (Fee-nyee-kee). Rus. **Dates.**

finocchio (feen-NOK-kee-o). Ita. **Fennel.**

finocchiona (feen-nok-kee-OAN-ah). Ita. **Fennel**-flavored **salami;** never allowed to age.

fiocchi d'avena (fee-OAK-kee dAHV-ay-nah). Ita. **Oatmeal.**

fiocchi di granturco (fee-OAK-kee day grahn-TOOR-ko). Ita. Cornflakes.

Fior di Latte (FEE-oar day LAHT-tay.) Ita. A cow's-milk **cheese** similar to **Mozzarella.**

fiore de zucchine ripiene (fee-O-ray day tsook-CHEE-nay kree-pee-AY-nay). Ita. **Stuffed** zucchini flowers.

fiore mollo (fee-O-ray MOAL-lo). Ita. **Saffron**-tinted **cheese,** soft and well flavored.

fiorentina (fee-o-rayn-TEE-nah). Ita. **Florentine** style, usually with **spinach.**

fiorentina, bistecca (fee-o-rayn-TEE-nah bee-stayk-kah). Ita. **T-bone steak grilled** over charcoal, in the **florentine** style—rare and plain, but moistened after grilling with a few drops of **olive oil.**

fiori di zucca (fee-O-ray day ZOO-kah). Ita. **Batter dipped** and **fried squash** blossoms.

Fiore Sardo (FEE-oar Sahr-do). Ita. Ewe's-milk **cheese,** eaten fresh as table cheese; when aged, it is hard and used for grating.

firm-ball stage (FURM-bahl staj). USA. The third stage of **sugar crystallization:** begins at 244°F. The **syrup,** when dropped in a glass of

water, will form a ball that will not flatten unless squeezed between the fingers.

firni (FIHR-nee). Ind. **Pudding** made with **rice flour, almonds,** and **creamy milk.**

Fisch (fish). Ger. Fish.

Fischbeuschlsuppe (fish-BOY-sherl-zup-per). Ger. A thick Austrian **soup** with lively flavoring; made from the lungs of freshwater fish.

Fischcrouton (fish-kroo-TONG). Ger. Fish balls.

Fischhackbraten (fish-HANK-brar-tern). Ger. Baked fish loaf.

Fisch mit Kümmelkraut (fish met KEW-mehl-kroet). Ger. Fish with **caraway**-seasoned **cabbage.**

Fish mit Feinen Kräuten (fish met FIGH-nern KROET-ehn). Ger. Austrian dish of fish seasoned with **chopped herbs.**

Fischrogen (FISH-roa-gehn). Ger. **Roe.**

Fischschüssel (Fish-SHEWSS-el). Ger. **Bacon** and **fish pie.**

fish muddle (fesch MUHD-duhl). USA. Fish **stew.**

fisk (feesk). Dan. Fish.

fisk (fisk) Nor, Swe. Fish.

fiskbuller (FUSK-bew-lahr). Swe. Codfish balls.

fiskeboller (FISK-bool-lehr). Nor. Fish balls.

fiskefars (FEESK-fars). Dan. **Minced** fish.

fiskefrikadellar (feesk-free-kah-DAY-ler). Dan. Fish balls

fiskegrateng (FISK-graa-tteng). Nor. Fish **soufflé.**

fiskepudding (FISK-pewd-ding). Nor. Fish **pudding.**

fiskfärs (FISK-faer). Swe. **Minced** fish.

fiskkroketter (fiak-kroat-KEET-terr). Swe. Fish cakes; **croquettes.**

fisk med fyllning (fisk mayd FEWL-ning). Swe. With **filling; stuffing.**

fish og skalldur (fisk o SKAHL-dewr). Nor. **Seafood.**

fisk på fat (fisk paw faht). Nor. "Fish on a platter"; **fried,** then **baked** in a **sauce.**

fisksnäcka (fisk-SNAHK-kah). Swe. Fish served in the shell.

fisksoppa (FISK-SO-pa). Swe. Fish **soup.**

five-spice powder (fiv-spic POW-dehr). USA. A spicy Chinese seasoning consisting of **ground cloves, fennel** seeds, **star anise, cinnamon,** and Sichuan **peppercorns** or **licorice root.**

fjærkre (FYEHR-kreh). Nor. **Poultry.**

fläderbär (FLA-dehr-BAHR). Swe. **Elderberries.**

flaesk (flehsk). Dan. **Pork, bacon.**

flaeskesteg (FLEHSK-stayg). Dan. **Roast pork.**

flaeskesteg med Svaer (FLEHS-ker-stayg mahdh svaer). Dan. **Roast pork** with red **cabbage.**

flageolet (FLA-zoe-lay). Fre. A very small **green bean** suitable as a **garnish** for meats or as a delicately flavored **purée.**

flake (flak) USA. To break into small pieces, usually with a fork.

flake salt (flak sawlt). USA. A **flake** form of **pickling salt.**

flamande (fla-mahnd). Fre. A **garnish** of braised **cabbage,** diced **pork** belly, **carrots,** and **potatoes;** a **hot pot.**

flambé (flahm-BAY). Fre. Served flaming; to douse with **brandy, rum, cognac,** or other liquors, then ignite.

flameado (flah-meh-AH-doh). Spa. Served flaming.

flan (flahn). Fre, Bri. An open **fruit tart** in **sponge cake** or pastry crust.

flan (flahn). Spa. A **caramel cream custard** that is baked.

flanchet (flahn-sheht). Fre. **Flank** steak.

flank (flahnk). USA. A cut of meat from between the ribs and the hip; the cut for **London broil.**

flapjack (FLAHP-jahc). USA. **Pancake.**

fläsk (flahsk). Swe. **Pork.**

flatfish (flaht-fisch). USA. Any saltwater fish that, as an adult, has both eyes on one side: **flounder, sole, turbot, halibut,** and the European flounder, **plaice.**

flatbrød (FLAHT-brur). Nor. Very thin, crisp flat bread made of wheat, rye, barley **flours.**

flauta (FLAH-OO-tah). Mex. A large **tortilla,** or two overlapping, filled and folled in a narrow long shape.

Fleisch (fleyesh). Ger. Meat.

Fleischbrühe (fleyesh-BRY-eh). Ger. Meat **consommé.**

Fleischgerichte (fleyesh-GEH-richt). Ger. Meat dishes.

Fleischkase (fleyesh-KEH-zeh). Ger. **Meat loaf.**

Fleischklösse (fleyesh-KLOHS). Ger. **Meatballs.**

Fleischkuchen (fleyesh-KU-sehn). Ger. Meat **pies.**

flensje (FLEN-shus). Dut. Thin **pancakes; crèpes suzettes.**

fleskepannekake (flehs-PAHN-ner-kkaaker). Nor. **Pancakes** with **pork.**

fleskepølse (flehs-PURLSS-err). Nor. **Pork sausages.**

flet (fleh). Fre. **Flounder.**

fleurette (flew-reht). Fre. Sweet **cream.**

fleurons (flew-rawng). Fre. Small half-moon shapes of **puff paste, baked,** used for **garnishing entrees.**

flitch (flehch). USA. A side of **bacon, smoked.**

floating island (FLOT-eng I-luhn). USA. A **dessert** of clumps of **meringue** in **custard.**

flødekage (FLURDH-er-kaaer). Dan. Layer cream **cake.**

flødeskum (FLURDH-er-skoom). Dan. **Whipped cream.**

flødeost (FLURDH-oast). Dan. **Cream cheese.**

fløode (FLURDH-er). Dan. **Cream.**

florentine (FLOOR-en-teen). Fre. Prepared with **spinach.**

Fløte (FLUR-ter). Nor. **Cream.**

Fløtekaker (FLUR-ter-kaaker). Nor. **Cream cakes.**

Fløtesuppe (FLUR-ter-sewpper). Nor. **Cream Soup.**

Fløtevafler (FLUR-ter-vaaf-lerr). Nor. **Cream waffles.**

Fløtost (FLUR-tost). Nor. A boiled-whey **cheese.**

flounder (FLAHN-dehr). USA. One of the **flatfish;** has delicate, soft flesh.

flundra (FLEWN-drah). Swe. **Flounder.**

flour (flowr). USA. Finely **ground meal** of various **grains.** See specific name.

flour, to (flowr). USA. To coat with **flour.**

flour paste (flowr pahst). USA. A thickener of two parts liquid to one part **flour,** used for thickening **sauces.**

Flower (flowr). Bri. A soft, cured **cheese** from cow's milk that contains the petals of various flowers, such as roses or marigolds.

flummery (FLUM-mree). Bri. Cold sweet dish, mainly of **oatmeal** set in a mold, chilled, and turned out on a plate to be eaten with wine, cider, **milk,** or a **sauce.**

flummery (FLUM-ree). USA. A **fruit pudding** thickened with **cornstarch.**

Flunder (FLUHN-der). Ger. **Flounder.**

flute (fluht). USA. To make a grooved pattern on **vegetables, fruit,** or the edge of **pie** crust.

focaccia (fo-chah-CHEE-ah). Ita. Flat, round bread seasoned with **sage** and **bacon.**

focaccia di vitello (fo-chah-CHEE-ah day vee-TAYL-lo). Ita. **Veal** patties.

foderare (foa-day-RAH-ray). Ita. To line a mold or pan with **dough** or **sponge cake slices** or **biscuits.**

fodros fehér kalács (FAW-drawsh FEH-hayr KOL-laach). Hun. Spongy white milk-bread, available as **rolls** or in **slices.**

fofas de bacalhau (FOU-fahsh duh bah-kah-lee-YAU). Por. Codfish balls.

fogas (FAW-gosh). Hun. A local fish of the **pike-perch** family.

fogasszeletek Gundel módra (FAW-gosh-sehlehtehk GOON-dehl MAW-dro). Hun. Slices of **fogas** prepared Gundel style: breaded **fillet** of **pike.** Gundel was a famous Hungarian restauranteur.

Foggiano (fo-jgee-AHN-no). Ita. A ewe's-milk **cheese** similar to **Cotronese** and **Moliterno.**

fogosch (FOA-goash). Ger. Austrian freshwater **trout**-like fish.

foie (fwa). Fre. Liver.

foie de veau (fwa du vu). Fre. Calf's liver.

foie gras (fwa-grah). Fre. The liver of fat geese for making **pâté de foie gras,** which is cooked livers seasoned with **truffles,** wine, and aromatics.

fokhagymás mártás (FAWK-hody-maash MAAR-tash).   Hun. **Garlic sauce.**

folares (fou-LAH-ruhsh).   Por. **Eggs** backed in nests of bread.

fold in (fold ehn).   USA. To incorporate into a mixture by repeated gentle overturnings without beating or stirring. Also called *folding.*

foncer (fohs-jer).   Fre. To line the botton of a pan with **slices** of **ham** or **bacon.**

fond (fahn).   Fre. Strong **gravy** or **meat stock.**

fondant (FAHN-dant).   Fre. **Icing** mixture used as coating for pastries and **confections.**

fond d'artichaut (fon d'ahr-tee-choh).   Fre. **Artichoke** heart.

fondre, faire (fehr fon-druh).   Fre. To "melt"; to cook **vegetables** very gently until softened, especially **onions, leeks,** and **garlic.**

fondue (FONG-du).   Fre. Melted or blended **cheese.**

fonduta (foan-DOO-tah).   Ita. A dish of melted **Fontina cheese** with **eggs** and sliced **truffles.**

fontana (foan-TAH-nah).   Ita. The method of mixing **pasta;** putting the flour in the shape of a fountain on the table, into which **eggs** or liquid required to make the **pasta** or **dough** are placed.

Fontel (FOAN-tayl).   Ita. A cow's whole-milk cheese similar to **Fontina.**

Fontina (Foan-TEE-nah).   Ita. A cow's whole-milk, pale yellow **cheese** with brown crust, creamy, mild, nutty; semisoft, melts easily; when aged, becomes semifirm with slighty smoky taste.

Fontinella (Foan-tee-NELL-ah).   Ita. A **cheese** of the same family as **Fontina** but firm enough to grate; has a sharper, zestier flavor. An excellent Fontinella is made in Wisconsin.

foo gwah (foo gwah)   Chi. **Bitter melon;** the size of a **cucumber,** brilliant green, has a bitter flavor; **stuffed** or **stir-fried** with meat.

fool (fuool).   Bri. **Puréed fruit** mixed with **cream** and **sugar.**

foon tiu meen (foon tiu meen).   Chi. Wide, flat **noodles.**

foo yung (foo yung).   Chi. An **omelet** made with meat, **poultry, seafood, vegetables,** or just **eggs.**

forcemeat (FOHRS-met).   Fre. Finely chopped, highly seasoned meat or fish; served alone or as a **stuffing.** Also called **farce.**

forel (fah-REHL). Rus. **Trout.**

forel (fo-REL). Dut. **Trout.**

forell (fo-RAYL). Swe. **Trout.**

Forelle (foh-REL-ea). Ger. **Trout.**

forestiere (for-ees-tee-air). Fre. A **garnish** of **sautéed morels, diced bacon** and **potatoes;** served with small cuts of meat and **poultry.**

Forez (Fohr-rehz). Fre. A cow's-milk **cheese;** if of good quality resembles **Roquefort** in flavor; also called *d'Ambert.*

forloren skildpadde (far-LAUREN skil-PAHD-deh). Dan. "Mock Turtle"; a very complicated dish made from calf's head, tongue, brains, **meatballs,** fish balls, and hard-boiled **eggs.**

forlorent (fo-LOOR-ernt). Nor. **Poached.**

Formagelle (fohr-mah-JELL-ee). Ita. A small, soft **cheese** made from goat's or ewe's milk; may or may not be **salted;** always eaten fresh.

Formaggini (fohr-mah-JEE-nee). Ita. Local Italian **cheeses,** soft and usually eaten dressed with **olive oil.**

formaggio (fohr mah JEE oh). Ita. **Cheese.**

forno (FOHR-no). Ita. **Roasted, baked.**

forrett (FOR-reht). Nor. **Appetizer.**

fortune cookie (FOHR-chuhn KOHK-kee). USA. Of Chinese origin, a thin **cookie** that is folded around a slip of paper on which is printed a proverb or humorous saying.

fouet (fweh). Fre. Whisk.

foul (fool). Ara. **Fave beans; broad beans.**

four, au (foor). Fre. **Baked** in the oven.

Fourme d'Ambert (furm d'am-bear). Fre. A cow's skimmed-milk **cheese;** creamy with blue veins, dry rind, tall, cylindrical shape.

fourrage (foo-RAJ). Fre. **Stuffing; filling.**

fourré (foo-RA). Fre. Coated with **sugar, cream.**

four spices (for SPI-cehz). USA. A French formula for seasoning sweets and meats, consisting of one teaspoon each **cloves, nutmeg, ginger,** and one tablespoon **cinnamon** when used with sweet, or **white pepper** when used with savory dishes. Also called **quatre épices.**

fózeléket (FURZ-ehlay-keht). Hun. **Vegetables.**

fragole (FRAA-goa-lay). Ita. **Strawberries.**

fragole di bosco (FRAA-goa-lay day boaz-ko). Ita. Wild **strawberries.**

fraiche (frehsh). Fre. Fresh. Also spelled **frais.**

frais (freh). Fre. Fresh. Also spelled **fraiche.**

fraisage (fray-swagh). Fre. A technique for kneading **dough** by smearing it across the breadboard with the heel of the hand, then forming the mass into a ball.

fraise (frehz). Fre. **Strawberry.**

fraise des bois (frehz day bwah). Fre. Wild **strawberry.**

framboezas (frum-BOZ-en). Por. **Raspberries.**

framboise (frahn-bwahz). Fre. **Raspberry.**

frambozen (frahm-BO-zuh). Dut. **Raspberries.**

frambuesa (frahm-BWAY-ssahss). Spa. **Raspberry.**

franconia (fran-CON-i-a). Ger. **Browned,** as Franconia potatoes: whole **potatoes browned** with the **roast.**

Frangelico (fron-JELL-ee-co). Ita. **Hazelnut liqueur.**

frangipane (fronz-pahn). Fre. A type of **puff pastry.**

frangipane creme (fronz-pahn krehm). Fre. A substitute for **custards** that is made of **eggs, milk,** some **flour** with **lemon** peel, rum, **brandy, vanilla** to flavor.

frango (FRAN-goo). Por. Young **chicken, broiler.**

frango com ervilhas (FRAN-goo com ehr-VEEL-yahss). Por. **Chicken** prepared with **olive oil** and **butter, port wine,** tiny **peas,** and **onions.**

frango guisado (FRAN-goo ghee-ZAH-doh). Por. **Chicken stewed** with **onions** and **tomatoes.**

frankfurter (FRAHNK-fuhr-tehr). Ger. Small **sausage.**

franks (frankz) USA. The abbreviated term for **frankfurters.**

franskbröd (FRAHNSK-brurd). Swe. French bread, **roll.**

franskbrød (FRAHNSK-brurdh). Dan. French bread.

frappé (fra-PAY). Fre. Beaten and iced; applies to water ice frozen to mush while stirring; usually drunk rather than eaten with a spoon or fork.

Frascati, a la (frah-scah-tee).   Fre. A classic **garnish** for meat dishes, consisting of thin **slices** of **foie gras, mushrooms, truffles,** and **asparagus** tips.

fraughan (fraun).   Bri. Irish **blueberries.**

freddo (FRAYD-do).   Ita. Cold.

freezer burn (FRE-zehr buhrn).   USA. The dry, fibrous, and discolored food product resulting from inadequate packaging and protection against moisture loss that occurs in the freezing process.

fregolotta (fray-goa-LOT-tah).   Ita. A popular Tuscan dish of coarse-textured bread, **toasted** over coals and liberally dressed with extra virgin **olive oil.** Also called **fett'unta** and **bruschetta.**

French fry (frehnch fri).   USA. To deep-fat **fry.**

French icing (frehnch I-ceng).   USA. A cooked **icing** using **confectioners' sugar** instead of granulated, with **butter, egg,** and flavoring.

French toast (frehnch tost).   USA. Slices of day-old bread, dipped in sweetened **egg batter,** then pan-**fried** in shallow oil.

Fresa (FRAY-ssahss).   Ita. A mild, sweet, soft, cooked **cheese** made of cow's milk in Sardinia.

fresa (FRAY-ssahss).   Spa. **Strawberry.**

fresca (FREHS-kah).   Mex. Fresh.

fresco (FRAYZ-ko).   Ita. Spa, Por, Fresh.

fresh ham (fresch hahm).   USA. The hind leg of a pig that has not been **cured** or **smoked.**

Fresno chili (FREHZ-noh-CHIHL-lee).   Mex. A fairly hot, small, conical, light green to greenish-yellow **chili pepper.**

fressure (fray-suhr).   Fre. Edibel **offal;** liver, heart, brains, **tripe.**

friandise (frcc-uhn-deez).   Fre. Small **confections.**

Fribourg (Free-bower).   Ita. A hard, cooked-curd **cheese** similar to **Spalen** or **Sbrinz.**

fricadelles (frick-ah-dell).   Fre. **Croquettes.**

fricassee (frick-ah-see).   Fre. A white **stew** of **chicken** or **veal.**

fricassee (FRICK-ah-see).   USA. A light brown **stew** made by browning in a small amount of fat, pieces of **fowl** or **veal,** then **stewing** or **steaming** in a small amount of liquid.

Fridatten (frid-DAH-tern).   Ger. Small Austrian **pancakes** cut in thin strips, used as **garnish** on **soups.**

fried cream (fryd krem).   USA. A thick **custard,** thoroughly chilled, cut in squares, dipped in beaten **eggs,** rolled in finely crushed cake crumbs, **deep-fried,** sprinkled with **powdered sugar** and rum.

Friese (FREE-sah).   Dut. A cow's-milk **cheese;** very hard; spiced with **cloves** and **cumin;** strong flavor.

Friesian Kaas (free-ZEE-ayn Kahz).   Dut. A **cheese** flavored with **cumin** and **cloves;** also called *Friesian Clove.*

friggere (free-JAY-reh).   Ita. **Deep-fat frying.**

frijoles (free-HOH-lehs).   Spa. **Beans.**

frijoles blancos (free-HOH-lehs blahn-kohs).   Spa. **Navy beans.**

frijoles negros (free-HOH-lehs KNEE-grros).   Spa. **Black beans.**

frijoles refritos (free-HOH-lehs re-FREE-tohs).   Spa. **Refried beans.**

frijoles rojos (free-HOH-lehs-roa-hohs).   Spa. **Kidney beans.**

Frikadellen (frik-kah-DEH-lern).   Ger. **Meatballs** served cold.

frikadeller (free-kah-DAYL-err).   Dan. A famous Danish dish of finely ground **pork, veal,** bread crumbs and **onions,** shaped into **cakes** and **sautéed** in **butter.**

frikadeller (FRIK-kah-del-lah).   Swe. **Meatballs.**

frio (FREE-ah).   Spa. Cold.

frire (freer).   Fre. To **fry.**

frisee (freh-zay).   Fre. **Endive;** a **salad** green with curly, short, white inner leaves and greener outer leaves; taste is light and tart.

frit (free).   Fre. **Fried.**

frito (FREE-toh).   Spa. **Fried.**

frittata (free-TAT-tah).   Ita. Flat, open-faced **omelet.**

frittella (free-TELL-lah).   Ita. **Fritter.**

fritter (FREHT-tehr).   USA. Meat, **vegetable,** or **fruit** dipped in **batter** and **fried.**

fritto (FREET-toh).   Ita. **Fried.**

fritto misto (FREET-toa meez-toh).   Ita. Meat and **vegetable** dipped in **batter** and **fried** and served together.

fritura (FREE-tu-rah).   Spa. **Fried** food.

friture (free-tewr).   Fre. **Fried** food.

frituurvet (FREET-tuhr-faht).   Dut. Oil.

frivolitées (free-vol-ee-tees).   Fre. Testicles of a bull, pig, or lamb, breaded and **fried.** Also called **animelles, lamb fries, mountain oysters, Rocky Mountain oysters.**

frizzle (frehz-ul).   USA. To pan **fry** until edges curl.

frog legs (frawg lehgs).   USA. The hind legs of a frog, prepared by cutting off the feet and skinning the leg from the large end to the small end.

froid (frwah).   Fre. Cold.

fromage (froh-mahzh).   Fre. **Cheese.**

Fromage à la Crème (froh-mahzh ah lah Krehm).   Fre. French **cream cheese;** a soft, rich cheese eaten fresh without ripening.

fromage de tete de porc (fro-majz day tet day pohr).   Fre. Hog's **head cheese.**

Fromage de Troyes (fro-majz day twah).   Fre. Same as **Barberey.**

Fromage Fort (Fro-majz Four).   Fre. A cooked **cheese** made of skim milk.

fromage glace (fro-mazj glas).   Fre. A dish of **ice cream** in a cheese-like shape, or anything **glazed** with **cheese.**

fromager (fro-mah-zjer).   Fre. To add **grated cheese.**

Froschschenkel (FROSH-shehnker).   Ger. **Frog legs.**

frossen fløde (FROA-sseen flurdh).   Dan. Frozen **whipped cream,** served molded on fresh **fruit.**

frosted (FROHS-tehd).   USA. A refreshing beverage made by whirling frozen **citrus** juices in a blender.

frosting (FROHS-teng).   USA. Covering for cakes, pastries, made of **sugar, butter,** flavorings; cooked or uncooked; used in **confectionery** of all kinds; interchanges with **icing.**

Frucht (frukht).   Ger. **Fruit.**

Fruchteis (FRUKHT-eyess).   Ger. **Fruit ice.**

Fruchtpastete (frookht-pahs-TAY-teh).   Ger. **Fruit pie.**

Fruchtsalat (frukht-sah-LAHT). Ger. **Fruit salad.**

fructose (FRUCK-tos). USA. The natural **sugar** in **fruit;** sweeter than **sucrose** sugars by 1.7 to 1.

frugt (froogt). Dan. **Fruit.**

frugtcreme (FROOGT-krehm). Dan. **Fruit pudding;** a type of **porridge.**

frugtsuppe (FROOGT-soo-bber). Dan. **Fruit soup** of various dried fruits, often **prunes** and **apricots,** served hot or cold.

Frülingskäse (fre-LINJ-kaiz). Ger. "Spring cheese"; Austrian **cottage cheese** mixed with **cream, chives, parsley, caraway** seeds; served on black bread garnished with stuffed **olives** and **cucumber slices.**

Fruhlingsuppe (fry-LINJ-zupe). Ger. A **soup** of meat **stock** with spring **vegetables.**

Frühstück (fre-stook). Ger. A small, **Limburger**-type **cheese** made from whole or partly skimmed cow's milk.

fruit (froot). USA. The edible reproductive body of a seed plant, having a sweet pulp associated with the seed, used chiefly in **desserts** or a sweet course.

fruit (frirt) Dut. **Fruit.**

fruitcake (FROOT-kak). USA. Basically a butter **cake,** with just enough batter to bind the candied **fruits,** dried fruits, **nuts** together; baked in tube pan or loaf pan; generally flavored with a **brandy.**

fruit cocktail (froot KOHK-tal). USA. A mixture of slightly cooked **diced** or **cubed fruits** in a thick or thin sweet **syrup;** a commercially canned product, usually used in **gelatin salads** and **desserts,** and in baked goods.

fruit cuit (frwee-cuhi). Fre. **Stewed fruit.**

fruits de mer (frwee der mehr). Fre. **Seafood.**

frukt (FROOK-ti). Rus. **Fruit.**

Frukt (frewkt). Nor, Swe. **Fruit.**

frukt-kräm (FREWKT-kraim). Swe. **Puréed fruit pudding.**

fruktsoppa (FREWKT-sop-ah). Swe. **Soup** made from dried **fruits.**

fruktvin (FREWKT-veen). Nor. **Fruit** wine.

frumenty (FROU-men-tee). Bri. A **porridge** of **wheat** or **oatmeal,** boiled in **milk,** and served with **raisins,** spices, **sugar.**

frushie (FRUSH-ee). Sco. Crumbly **fruit tart** eaten with rich **cream.**

fruta (FROO-tah). Spa. **Fruit.**

fruta azucarada (FROO-tah ah-THOO-kah-rah-dah). Spa. Candied **fruit.**

frutta (FROO-tah). Ita. **Fruit.**

frutta di mare (FROOT-tee dee MAA-ray). Ita. **Seafood.**

fry (fri). Bri. A savory mixture of heart, **lights,** liver, and **sweetbreads.**

fry (fri) USA. To cook by plunging in hot fat until done.

fryer (FRI-ehr). USA. A young **chicken** of either sex that weights 2 ½ to 3 ½ pounds; usually cut into serving size pieces, egg-and-crumbed or floured, then **deep-fried.**

fu (foo). Jap. **Wheat gluten,** used in **soups, noodle broths,** and one-pot dishes; high in protein, low in starch.

fudge (fuhdg). USA. A semisoft, **chocolate candy,** usually with nutmeats added.

fugu (foo-goo). Jap. **Blowfish;** has poisonous organs that must be removed by a licensed chef before being prepared.

fugu ryori (foo-goo-ryoh-ree). Jap. Meals featuring **blowfish,** from which the poisonous organs have been removed by licensed chefs.

fuki (foo-kee). Jap. Coltsfoot; plant with large rounded leaves resembling the foot of a colt; light **celery** taste.

ful (fool). Ara. **Fava beans.**

Fullung (FOO-loong). Ger. **Stuffing.**

ful medames (fool MAY-da-mez). Ara. Egypt's national dish; cooked brown **beans** with a wide variety of seasonings.

fumé (foo-may). Fre. **Smoked.**

fumet (foo-maht). Fre. The flavor or **essence** of **game,** fish, or any highly flavored concentrated substance used to impart a rich flavor.

funghi (FOONG-gee). Ita. **Mushrooms.**

funnel cake (FUHN-nehl Kak). USA. A Pennsylvania Dutch **deep-fried** pastry made from **batter** dripped through a funnel, swirling in spiral form in the hot fat; served with **sugar** or **maple syrup.**

furn (furn). Ara. Commercially made bread.

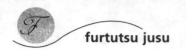

furtutsu jusu (foo-ROO-tsoo joo-soo).   Jap. **Fruit** juice.

fusilli (foo-SEEL-lee).   Ita. Very thin, extra long, twisted, hollow spiral strips of **pasta.**

fyldt (fewlt).   Dan. **Filled, stuffed.**

Fyll (fewl).   Nor. **Stuffing.**

fyllda mandelkakor   (fewld MAHN-dayl-KAA-roor).   Swe. **Filled almond** buns.

fyllkålhode (fewl kawl-hooder).   Nor. **Stuffed** head of **cabbage.**

Gaasesteg (GAWSS-stayg). Dan. **Roast** goose.

Gabelfrühstück (gaa-berl-FREW-shtewk). Ger. "Fork breakfast," meaning that hot foods, such as **eggs** and **ham,** will be served.

gädda (yeh-dah). Swe. **Pike.**

gaffelbitar (GA-fehl-BI-tar). Swe. **Herring** tidbits.

gahwa (Ah-wa). Ara. **Coffee.**

gai choy (gcc-ah chee). Chi. **Mustard cabbage.**

gaika (GRYEHT-skee). Rus. **Nut.**

gairleog (garl-yog). Iri. **Garlic.**

Gaiskasli (Guiss-KAHS-lee). Ger, Swi. A goat's-milk **cheese,** soft, delicately flavored.

gajar (GAH-jar). Ind. **Carrot.**

gajjar (GUH-JUK). Ind. **Sesame brittle.**

galamb (GOL-lomb). Hun. Pigeon.

galanga root (gah-LAHN-gah root). USA. A root of the **ginger** family, used fresh, **dried,** or **powdered** to flavor foods in Southeast Asia.

galantina (gal-lahn-TEE-nah). Ita. Jellied meat, **fowl,** or fish.

galantine (gal-ahn-teen). Fre. **Fowl** or breast of **veal,** boned, stuffed with **forcemeat,** tongue, **truffle,** rolled, covered in **aspic,** and served cold.

galette (gah-leht). Fre. A light, French breakfast **roll.**

galinha (gah-LEE-nyah). Por. **Chicken.**

galinha recheada (gah-LEE-nyah ray-SHAY-dao). Por. **Chicken** stuffed with **eggs** and **olives.**

galinha salteada (gah-LEE-nyah sahl-TEE-ah-dah). Por. **Sautéed chicken.**

galinhola (gah-lee-NYOU-lah). Por. Woodcock.

gambas (GAHM-bahs). Spa. **Shrimps, prawns.**

gamberetti (gahm-bay-RAYT-tee). Ita. Small **shrimp.**

gamberi (gahm-BAH-ree). Spa. **Crayfish.**

gambero (gahm-BAY-roh). Ita. **Shrimp.**

game (gahm). USA. Wild fish, **fowl,** animals hunted for sport, whose flesh is edible.

Gammelost (GAHM-mer-loost). Nor. A cow's soured skimmed-milk **cheese;** light yellow-brown with blue-green veins, crumbly texture; strong aroma.

gammon (GAHM-muhn). Bri. A very lean **bacon; ham.**

ganache (gah-nasch). Fre. A rich **chocolate filling** for pastry.

ganbian sijidou (gan-bien shi-jee-doh). Chi. **Sautéed string beans.**

Gans (gahns). Ger. Goose.

gans (khahns). Dut. Goose.

Gänsebraten (GEHN-zerbraa-tern). Ger. Roasted goose.

Gänsebrust (GEHN-zerbrust). Ger. Breast of goose.

Gänseleberpastete (GEHN-zert-lay-berr-pah-stayter). Ger. Goose liver **pâté.**

ganth gobhi (gahnt GOHB-hee). Ind. **Kohlrabi.**

ganzi (gan dze). Chi. **Orange.**

gao-yáng-ròu (gau-yaang-roe). Chi. **Lamb.**

garam masala (gahr-RAHM mahs-SAH-lah). Ind. An aromatic mixture of spices that supposedly "heats" the body, sprinkled over a dish before serving.

garbanzo (gar-BAHN-zo). Spa. A **pea** that is round, beige-yellow with a soft texture; a nutty flavor reminiscent of **chestnuts;** known as **chickpea.**

garbure (gahr-bewr). Fre. A thick **soup** of meat, **potatoes,** and **vegetables** served with toasted bread.

Garda (GAHR-dah).   Ita. A soft **dessert cheese** with an edible crust.

garden cress (GAHR-dehn krehs).   USA. A green plant used in **salads** and savory fillings; has very tiny leaves and frequently is used combined with baby **mustard greens.**

gardon (gahr-doh).   Fre. A variety of **carp.**

garganelli (gahr-gahn-NEHL-lee).   Ita. Homemade **macaroni.**

gari (GAH-ree).   Jap. Sushi-shop jargon for **vineyard ginger.** Also known as **beni-shoga.**

garlic (GAHR-lehk).   USA. An **herb** of the **onion** family with an odor that remains when used raw but disappears when cooked slowly; late garlic has firm bulbs and strong flavor; early garlic has large, flattened bulbs; covered with an off-white, paper-like sheathing.

garlic chives (GAHR-lehk chivz).   USA. An **herb** of the **onion** family; coarser, flatter, broader leaves than regular **chives;** garlic flavor.

garmugia (gahr-moo-GEE-ah).   Ita. Beef **stew** with **artichokes.**

garnacha (gar-NAH-chah).   Mex. A small round of **tortilla dough** filled with a savory **stuffing** and cooked; an **appetizer** or **entree.** Also known as **picada.**

garnale (khahr-NAH-luh).   Dut. Tiny **shrimps.**

Garnelen (gahr-NAY-lern).   Ger. **Shrimps, prawns.**

garni (gahr-nee).   Fre. **Garnished.**

garnish (GAHR-nehsh).   USA. An embellishment or trimming; to decorate, usually with other foods.

gås (goass).   Swe. Goose.

gåsestak (gawss-stayk).   Nor. **Roast** goose.

gâteau (gau-toe).   Fre. A round, flat butter**cake,** generally decorated.

gateaux (gah-toah).   Ara. A Lebanese **cake** of the **sponge cake** family made with stiffly beaten egg whites, **raisins,** and **nuts** folded into the **batter,** flavored with **nutmeg, baked** in a tube pan, and served unfrosted.

gaufre (goo-freh).   Fre. **Waffle.**

gauloise (goa-lwahs).   Fre. A **garnish** of cocks' combs and kidneys for clear **soup.**

Gautrias (Gou-tree-awng).   Fre. A **cheese** similar to **Port du Salat.**

Gavot (Gah-voh). Fre. A **cheese** made from cow's, goat's or ewe's milk.

gayette (gay-eht). Fre. An **hors d'oeuvre;** a flat **sausage** of pig's liver and **bacon** encased in **caul** and cooked in an oven.

gazpacho (gahs-PAH-choh). Spa. A cold vegetable **soup** of **tomatoes, garlic, olive oil.**

geans (jeans). Bri. Wild **cherries.**

Gebäck (ger-BAHK). Ger. Pastry.

gebäcken (ger-BAHKN). Ger. **Baked.**

gebak (khuh-BAHK). Dut. Pastry.

gebakken (khuh-BAHK-kuh). Dut. **Fried.**

gebonden soep (khuh-BOH-den). Dut. **Cream soup.**

gebraden (khuh-BRAH-duh). Dut. **Roast.**

Gebraden kip (khuh-BRAH-duh kip) Dut. **Fried chicken.**

gebraten (ger-BRAA-tern). Ger. **Roasted.**

gebunden (ger-BUHN-dehn). Ger. **Thickened.**

Gedampfte Ente (ger-DEHMPFT EHN-ter). Ger. Steamed **duck.**

Gedampfte Rinderbrust (ger-DEHMPFT RINT-err-breast). Ger. Wine-marinated beef slowly cooked with **onions** and **carrots.**

Gedünstete Gurke (ger-DOON-sterter goork). Ger. Stewed **cucumbers** in **sour cream sauce.**

Gedünstete Ochsenschlepp (ger-DOON-sterter OK-sern-sch-lehp). Ger. **Braised oxtail.**

gee choy (tze chee). Chi. Paper-thin rectangles of dried purple-black **laver seaweed** used for wrapping food.

gefilte fish (gah-FEHL-tah fesch). Jew. A mixture of **ground** fish, **eggs,** and **matzo meal,** shaped into balls or flat loaves, cooked in fish **broth,** served hot or cold.

Geflügel (ger-FLEW-gerl). Ger. **Poultry.**

Geflügelfrikassee (ger-FLEW-gerl-fri-kah-sser). Ger. **Chicken fricassee.**

Geflügelklein (ger-FLEW-gerl-klahn). Ger. **Chicken giblets.**

Geflügelleber (ger-FLEW-gerl-leh-behr). Ger. **Chicken** livers.

Geflügelragout (ger-FLEW-gerk-rah-goo). Ger. An Austrian **stew** of **chicken** and **giblets.**

gefüllt (ger-FEWLT).   Ger. **Stuffed.**

Gefüllter Gänsehals (ger-FEWLT gahns-hahls).   Ger. **Stuffed** skin of goose neck.

Gefüllte Kartoffeln (ger-FEWLT kahe-TOF-ferln).   Ger. **Stuffed baked potatoes.**

gegrillt (ger-GRILT).   Ger. **Grilled.**

gehakt (khuh-HAHKT).   Dut. **Chopped** meat.

gehaktballetjes (khuh-HAHKT-bahl-let-yus).   Dut. **Meatballs.**

Geheimrath (Gjee-heim-rahth).   Dut. A deep yellow **cheese** that resembles **Gouda;** made in small quantities.

Geitost (YAYT-oost).   Nor. A ewe's-milk **cheese** with a rich brown color and sweet flavor; brick shape.

gekocht (ger-KOKHT).   Ger. **Boiled,** cooked.

gekookt (khuh-KOHKT).   Dut. **Boiled.**

gekootke eieren (khuh-KOHKT AY-uh-ruh).   Dut. **Boiled eggs.**

gekristalliseerde gember (ghei-KRYS-tahl-ez-zeer dah CHEHM-behr).   Dut. **Crystalized ginger.**

gelado (zhe-LAH-doo).   Por. **Ice cream;** frozen **dessert.**

gelatin (JEHL-ah-tehn).   USA. A glutinous material obtained from animal bones, cartilege, tendons by **boiling.** See other types of gelatins: **agar-agar, carrageenan, gum tragacanth, irish moss,** and **rennet.**

gelatina (jehl-ah-TEE-nah).   Ita, Spa. **Jelly.**

gelato (jah-LAHT-to).   Ita. **Ice cream.**

gelé (shay-LAY).   Swe. **Jelly.**

geléa (zheh-LAY-ah).   Por. **Jelly.**

gelée (zhay-LAY).   Fre. **Aspic.**

gelinotte (zhay-lee-nott).   Fre. Hazel **hen.**

gelo (ZHAY-loh).   Por. **Ice.**

gemischt (ger-MISHT).   Ger. Mixed.

Gemischt Kalter Braten (ger-MISHT KALT-ehr BRAA-tern).   Ger. Assorted cold **roast** meats.

Gemischt Salat (ger-MISHT zah-LAAT).   Ger. Mixed **salad.**

Gemüse (ger-MEW-zer). Ger. **Vegetables.**

Gemüseplatte (ger-MEW-zer plah-ter). Ger. **Vegetable** plate.

Genever (yuh-NAY-vur). Dut. Dutch gin. Also spelled **Jenever.**

genevoise (zheh-nayv-wahss). Fre. A **sauce** served only with fish that is made of **salmon stock,** red wine, **herbs,** and **anchovy.**

gengibre (zhehn-ZHEE-bruh) Por. **Ginger.**

genièvre (zhew-neehv). Fre. **Juniper berry.**

genip (heh-NEEP). Spa. A one-inch round **fruit** from the Carribean islands eaten fresh, like **grapes.** Sometimes called **Spanish limes.**

genmai cha (jehn-mah-ee chah). Jap. A green **tea** made of toasted glutinous **rice.** Some rice grains that have exploded and look like little popcorn are left in with the tea leaves and give the beverage a sweet and nutty flavor.

genoise (ZGEN-ah-swoy). Ita. A rich, moist **sponge cake.**

geranium (JEHR-ran-e-uhm). USA. A sweet-scented **herb** having many-flavored leaves; use in pound **cakes, jellies, compotes.**

geräuchert (ger-ROT-khert). Ger. **Smoked.**

German chocolate (JUHR-muhn CHOHK-o-laht). USA. A cooking **chocolate** that has sugar, milk, vanilla added and has been conditioned against heat.

Géromé (GEHR-ro-may). Fre. A whole-milk, semisoft, ripened **cheese** with a brick-red rind; may contain **fennel, anise,** or **cumin** seeds.

gerookte (jer-ROKE-ter). Dut. **Smoked.**

geroosterd brood (khuh-ROHS-turt broht). Dut. Toast.

geröstete (ger-RUR-sterter). Ger. **Broiled** or **grilled.**

geröstete Mehlsuppe (ger-RUR-sterter MAYL-zupper). Ger. Swiss **gravy soup.**

gerst (chehrst). Dut. **Barley.**

Gerstensuppe (GER-stehn-zupper). Ger. **Barley soup.**

Gervaise (gehr-vazz). Fre. A double-crème, soft, delicate, ripened **cheese;** has a piquant flavor; a variation of **Petit-Suisse.**

geschabt (ger-SCHAHBT). Ger. **Grated, ground,** scraped.

geschmort (ger-SCHMOART). Ger. **Braised.**

Geschmorte Kalbshaxe (ger-SCHMOART KAHLP-hahkser). Ger. **Braised veal** with **vegetables.**

Geschnetzeltes (ger-SHNEH-tsert-terss). Ger. Small bits of **veal** served in **wine sauce.**

Geselchtes (ger-ZEHLKH-terss). Ger. South German word for **smoked pork** of any kind.

Gesottenes Rindfleisch (ghee-SORT-tahn-ness RHEND-flehsh). Ger. **Boiled beef.**

gestoofde (khuh-STOHF-duh). Dut. **Stewed.**

gestoofde pruimen (khuh-STOHF-duh PRIR-muh). Dut. **Stewed prunes.**

geung (jiaang). Chi. **Ginger root.**

gevogelte (her-VOH-helter). Dut. **Poultry.**

gevulde (her-VOOL-duh). Dut. **Stuffed.**

gevulde boterkoek (her-VOOL-duh BO-tur-kook). Dut. Butter**cake** with **almond paste** filling.

gevulde broodjes (her-VOOL duh brote-yers). Dut. **Rolls stuffed** with **salad,** meats, fish, and so forth.

gevulde kool (her-VOOL-duh kohl). Dut. Meat-stuffed **cabbage** leaves.

gevulde kalfsborst (her-VOOL-duh kulfs-bawrst). Dut. **Stuffed veal breast.**

Gewürz (ger-VEWRTS). Ger. Spice.

Gewürzkuchen (ger-vewrts-KOOK-hern). Ger. Spice **cakes.**

Gex (Zherx). Fre. A hard, cow's-milk blue **cheese.**

ghee (khee). Ind. **Clarified butter.**

gherkin (guhr-KEHN). USA. A small **cucumber** used for **pickling.**

ghiaccio (gee-AHT-choa). Ita. **Ice,** as for beverages; "on the rocks."

giardiniera (jee-ahrd-EEN-ehrah). Ita. Mixed **vegetables, sliced.**

gibelotte (zhee-beh-loat-teh). Fre. **Rabbit stew** with **butter, onions,** and **potatoes.**

gibier (zhee-behr). Fre. **Game.**

giblets (JEHB-lehts). USA. The edible viscera of **fowl:** heart, liver, gizzard, head, feet wing tips, cocks' comb, kidneys.

gigot (zhee-goa). Fre, Bri. Leg of **mutton.**

gigot d'agneau (zhee-goa d'ah-noh). Fre. Leg of **lamb.**

gigue (zhee-gew). Fre. **Venison** or boar haunch.

gilthead (GEHLT-hehd). USA. A Mediterranean fish of the **bream** family, having white, fine, firm flesh.

ginepro (jee-NEH-proa). Ita. **Juniper berry.**

ginestrata (jeen-eh-STRAH-dah). Ita. A light, creamy, nutritious **soup** of **chicken broth, egg yolks, butter,** white wine, gentle spices.

gingelly (JIN-jeh-lee). Ind. Light **sesame oil.**

gingembre (zheen-zhehm-breh). Fre. **Ginger.**

ginger (GEHN-gher). USA. A cultivated spice with a pungent flavor and sweet aroma; used fresh **preserved,** or **dried** and **ground;** used throughout the world to season dishes from **curries** to **desserts.**

ginger beer (GEHN-gehr behr). USA. A nonalcoholic beverage flavored with fermented **ginger.**

gingerbread (GEHN-gher-brehd). USA. A **cake** or **cookie** flavored with **ginger** and other spices.

ginger champagne (GEHN-gher chahm-pan). USA. A nonalcoholic cocktail made with **ginger** flavoring.

ginger root (GEHN-gher root). USA. A gnarled, knobby, fibrous root with light brown skin; use **grated** for seasoning **sauces, chicken** and fish dishes, **salad dressings, fruit desserts.**

gingersnap (GEHN-gher-schnahp). USA. A crisp, thin **cookie** made with **molasses** and flavored with **ginger.**

ginkgo nut (GHEEN-koh nuht). USA. The **fruit** of the mature female ginkgo tree; raw nuts are white but turn pale green when cooked; mild flavor; eaten **raw, grilled, deep-fried,** or in one-pot dishes.

ginnan (GEEN-nahn). Jap. **Ginkgo nut.**

ginseng (zehn-sehng). Kor. A highly prized root used fresh for **salads** and to flavor **soups** and **stews,** used **dried** to make **tea,** and used for many medicinal purposes.

giri (KEE-ree). Jap. A cut of the knife; stroke.

girolle (zhee-rol-leh). Fre. **Chanterelle.**

gishta (ISH-ta). Ara. **Cream.**

gist (jeest).   Dut. **Yeast.**

gîte à la noix (zheh-tay ah lah nwah).   Fre. A cut of beef from the **rump** of the carcas. Same as **silverside.**

Gjetost (Yeht-ost).   Nor. A **cheese** made of the whey of goat's milk, brown in color, confectionery sweet; usually sliced thin and served with dark Norwegian **flat bread.**

glaçage (glah-sahzhg).   Fre. **Browning** or **glazing.**

glace (glahss).   Fre. Cake **icing; ice cream; ice.**

glacé (glahs-say).   Fre. **Iced,** frozen, **glazed, frosted,** candied, **crystalized.**

glacé fruit (glahs-say frwee).   Fre. **Fruit dipped** in a hot **syrup** that has been cooked to a hard-crack stage.

glamorgan sausages (glah-MOHR-gun SAUS-ahg-jehz).   Bri. Fried **rolls** made of bread crumbs and **cheese** and seasoned with **onions** and **herbs;** vegetarian Welsh **sausages.**

glass (glahss)   Swe. **Sherbet** or **ice cream.**

glassato (glah-SAH-toh).   Ita. **Glazed.**

Glasur (GLAU-seur).   Ger. **Icing.**

glaze (glaz).   USA. To make a smooth, shiny surface that can be decorated variously: **stock** or **gravy** reduced to the thickness of **jelly** that is used to cover meats, or a thin sugar **syrup** on certain **rolls,** pastries, and **confections.**

glazun'ya (yee-EESH-nyee-tsoo).   Rus. **Fried eggs.**

glazuur (glah-ZUHR).   Dut. **Glazed.**

gliomach (glim-makh).   Iri. **Lobster.**

glister pudding (GLEHS-stur PUHD-deng).   Bri. Steamed **pudding** with **marmalade, lemon** juice, and **ginger** seasoning.

glögg (glurgg)   Swe. A hot and spicy wine drink, flavored with **almonds, raisins,** and **brandy.**

Gloucester (Glou-shehs-tehr).   Bri. A firm, velvety textured, mild-flavored **cheese;** the best "red" cheese of England; lower in butterfat than **Double Gloucester.**

glucose (GLU-kos).   USA. **Dextrose;** a natural **sugar** widely distributed in **fruits, honey,** and some **vegetables.**

Glühwein (glew-vighn).   Ger. Mulled wine.

gluten (GLU-tuhn).   USA. The tenacious and elastic substance formed when **wheat flour** is stirred or kneaded with a liquid.

gluten flour (GLU-tuhn flawr).   USA. A starch-free, high-protein **flour** made by washing the starch from hard **wheat flour;** the residue is dried and ground; gluten will not develop except in the presence of moisture and when agitated, as in kneading.

glutinous rice (GLU-tuhn-ous ris).   USA. A short-grained **rice** that is sweet, sticky, and opaque.

glycerin (GLEH-sehr-ehn).   USA. A sweet, clear liquid of syrup-like consistency, used to retain moisture in certain kinds of **confectionery,** such as cake **icing,** and to sweeten and preserve foods.

gnocchette (n-yoc-CHEHT-tee).   Ita. Small, ridged **pasta** shells shaped to resemble **potato gnocchi.**

gnocchi (n-YOC-kee).   Ita. A small **dumpling** of **potato, spinach,** or other ingredients, poached in water, and served in **sauce,** in **soup,** or covered with **grated Parmesan cheese;** discs of **semolina** and **polenta.**

gobhi (GOHB-hee).   Ind. **Cauliflower.**

gobo (goh-BOH).   Jap. **Burdock** root.

gochian (GOO-chee-an).   Ind. Black beehive-shaped **mushrooms** from Kashmir region, similar to **morels.**

goed door bakken (khoot dohr BRAH-duh).   Dut. Well done.

Goetta (GHER-tah)   Ger. A molded meat dish, served **sliced** and **fried,** made of finely chopped **boiled pork** scraps, including heart, liver, and tongue, oats, and seasonings. If made of **corn meal,** it is called **scrapple.**

gohan (GOH-hahn).   Jap. Cooked **rice,** served on a plate Western style; see **ratsu, kome.**

gold beet (gohld bet).   USA. Looks like a red **beet** except the bulbs are golden yellow; taste is a bit sweeter than the red beet; can be eaten **raw** or cooked.

golden buck (GOHL-dehn buhk).   Bri. **Welsh rarebit** on toast, topped with a **poached egg.**

golden mountain oyster (GOHL-dehn MAHN-tehn OEHS-tehr).   USA. A light brown, fan-shaped **mushroom,** with a meaty flavor.

Golden Nugget (GOHL-dehn NUH-geht).   USA. Small, round **squash** with orange-colored ridged exterior; bright orange, slightly sweet flesh; resembles small **pumpkin.**

golden oak mushroom (GOHL-dehn oak MUHSH-room). USA. A dark brown **mushroom** with a woodsy-fruity flavor and smooth velvety caps that have a light pinky-beige meat. Also known as **shiitake.**

golden syrup (GOHL-dehn SEHR-uhp). USA. A mild-flavored residual **molasses** that is clarified and decolorized.

goma (GOH-mah). Jap. **Sesame** seeds, either white or coal-black.

goma abura (GOH-mah ah-BOO-rah). Jap. **Sesame oil.**

gomba (GAWM-bo). Hun. **Mushrooms.**

gombaleves (GWAM-bol-leh-vehsh). Hun. **Mushroom soup.**

Gomost (Go-moost). Nor. A **cheese** usually made from whole cow's milk, but could use goat's milk; has buttery consistency.

gongbao rou ding (goong-bao row ding). Chi. A dish or **diced pork** with hot **peppers.**

gongbao xiaren (goong-bao sia ren). Chi. A **shrimp** dish with hot **peppers.**

Gonterser Bok (gun-ter-SAUR bohk). Ger. A Swiss dish of **batter**-dipped hard-boiled **eggs, fried** in **butter.**

goober (GOO-ber). Afr. **Peanut.**

gooseberry (GOOS-behr-ree). USA. A large green **berry** sometimes streaked in red; popular in France and England for use in **pies, preserves,** or as a **sauce** for **mackerel** in France. Also known as *green gooseberry.*

goosefish (GOOS-fesch). USA. A fish whose tail section has firm, white flesh similar in flavor to **lobster;** can be **sautéed, baked, broiled, poached,** or cut in fingers and **deep-fat fried.** Known by many names, including **monkfish.**

gorchitsa (gahr-CHYEE-tsi). Rus. **Mustard.**

gorda (GOHR-dah). Mex. A thick **cake** of **maize dough** and **lard.**

gordita (gohr-DEE-tah). Mex. **Dough** of **cornmeal** and **potato,** flavored with **cheese, fried** in **lard,** and served with **ground pork** and **guacamole.**

Gorgonzola (goar-goan-DZO-lah). Ita. A cow's whole-milk blue **cheese** with a rough reddish rind and a creamy white interior veined with blue-green mold; less salty than **Roquefort.**

gorokh (gah-ROKH). Rus. **Peas.**

gosht (gohsht).   Ind. Meat.

Gouda (GOO-dah).   USA. A Dutch **cheese** of cow's whole milk; creamy yellow, firm; young cheeses have yellow wax covering, older cured cheeses have black wax covering; *Holland Gouda* has a golden rind, *Baby Gouda* has a red rind; shape is usually round with flattened top and bottom; some aged Goudas are collector's items; piquant, flaky.

Goudsa kaas (KHOWT-suh kahs).   Dut. **Gouda** cheese.

gougère (goo-zhryehr).   Fre. A savory pastry, made in a ring, baked, then chilled; served as a light meal.

gougnettes (goo-zhneht).   Fre. A type of **doughnut** sprinkled with **sugar.**

goujon (gou-zhawng).   Fre. Highly esteemed fish of the **carp** family.

goujonette (goo-zhawng-neht).   Fre. **Deep-fried** strips of breaded **sole** that resemble little fishes.

goulash (GOO-lahsh).   Bri. A Hungarian **stew** of beef, **veal,** or **pork** with **onions, potatoes, tomatoes, peppers,** and **dumplings,** heavily seasoned with **paprika, caraway** seeds, and **garlic.**

Gournay (Gohr-nay).   Fre. A soft **cheese** of the fresh **Neufchâtel** type, round and flat; has the flavor of **Camembert.**

govyading (gah-VYAH-dyee-nah).   Rus. Beef.

Goya (Gau-yah).   Arg. A hard **cheese,** pale gold in color with delicately nutty flavor; used for grating.

grädde (GREH-der).   Swe. **Cream.**

gräddevåfflor (greh-der-VOF-lah).   Swe. **Sour cream waffles.**

Gräddost (grahd-oost).   Swe. A mild, sweet **cheese,** semisoft or hard; irregular holes.

Graeskar (GRAIS-kahr).   Dan. Marrow **squash.**

graham flour (grahm flawr).   USA. Whole **wheat flour** containing the **bran** of the wheat kernel.

graisse (grohss).   Fre. Fat; also **gras.**

Grana (GRAH-nah).   Ita. Hard, dry, crumbly, long-lasting **cheeses,** used grated on **pastas** or in cooking. **Parmesan** is of this type.

granada (grah-NAH-dah).   Spa. **Pomegranate.**

granadilla (grah-nah-DEHL-lah).   Ita. The purple egg-sized tropical **fruit** whose sweet, yellow flesh is eaten raw with the small black seeds or squeezed for juice; has sweet-acid flavor. Also known as **passion fruit.**

granatina (grah-nah-TEE-nah). Ita. **Pomegranate syrup.**

granceole (grahn-ceh-OAL-eh). Ita. Large **crabs,** cooked in shells, and seasoned with oil and **lemon.**

granchi (GRAHNG-kee). Ita. **Crabs.**

grand mère (groh-mehr). Fre. A **garnish** of pearl **onions,** olive-shaped **potatoes, parsley, lemon** juice, and browned **butter.**

grandville (groh-vil). Fre. A sauce of white wine, **truffles, mushrooms,** and **shrimp.**

granita (grah-NEE-tah). Ita. A fruit **ice (sherbet)** intentionally made so that its ice crystals have a grainy texture.

granturco (grahn-TOOR-coa). Ita. **Corn.**

Granular cheese (GRAHN-u-lahr chez). USA. Similar to **Cheddar** and **Colby;** made from raw or pasteurized cow's milk.

granulated sugar (GRAHN-u-la-ted SCHU-gahr). USA. White **sucrose** crystals of a fine granulation that dissolve rapidly; a general-purpose **sugar.**

grape (grap). USA. A vine-produced **fruit** that is a smooth-skinned, juicy, greenish-white to deep red or purple berry. Other than wine grapes, there are three types distinguished by their use: grapes for making juice, grapes for making raisins, and grapes for the table. See specific names.

grapefruit (GRAP-froot). USA. A large **citrus fruit** with a bitter yellow rind and inner skin; highly flavored, somewhat acidic, juicy pulp.

grapefruktjuice (GRAYP-frukt-YOO-SS). Swe. **Grapefruit** juice.

grape leaves (grap leevz). USA. Leaves of **grape** vines, cleaned and packed in brine; rolled with savory stuffings; used in Greek cookery.

gras (groh). Fre. Fat; also **graisse.**

gras, au (ah groh). Fre. Dressed with rich meat **gravy.**

gras-double (groh-dubl). Fre. **Tripe.**

graslök (graiss-lurk). Swe. **Chive.**

grasshopper (GRAHS-hohp-pehr). USA. A flavor combination, always green; usually either a **pie** or a drink containing the cordials green creme de menthe and colorless creme de cocoa.

grate (grat).   USA. To reduce to small pieces by rubbing on something rough.

gratin (GRA-tain).   Dan. **Soufflé,** often cooked with **vegetables.**

gratin, au (GRAW-ten).   Fre. A term for certain dishes prepared with **sauce, garnish,** and bread crumbs, **baked** until brown, and served in the baking dish.

gratin, au (GRAW-tehn).   USA. Refers to a dish prepared with **cheese sauce,** or having **grated cheese** sprinkled on top and **baked.**

gratinée (grah-teen-ay).   Fre. To brown in a hot oven or under a broiler; a food topped with bread crumbs, **cheese,** or **sauce.**

Gratiniert (gra-teen-NEYRT).   Ger. Covered with bread crumbs or **cheese** and oven-browned.

gravad lax (GRAH-vayd lahks).   Swe. **Salmon marinated** in **dill.**

gravlax (GRAHV-lahks).   Nor. Raw, salt-, and sugar-**cured salmon fillets,** seasoned with **crushed dill.**

gravy (GRA-vee).   USA. A **sauce** made from the juices of cooked meat, usually **thickened** and seasoned.

Gray (Graha).   Ger. A pleasant-tasting **cheese** made of sour skim milk with a grayish color interior.

grease (grez).   USA. Top rub lightly with fat.

grecque, à la (greh-kew).   Fre. Prepared in the Greek style; usually **vegetables** such as **artichokes, mushrooms,** cooked in **olive oil, lemon** juice, water, and seasonings.

green beans (gren bens).   USA. An edible and nutritious seed pod, 4–5 inches long, of a species of cultivated **beans;** bright green with about 8–10 immature beans within.

Green Goddess dressing (gren GOHD-dehss drehss-eng).   USA. A **salad dressing** made of **mayonnaise, minced green onions, chives, parlsey, tarragon,** and **anchovy fillets.**

Green Goddess salad (gren GOHD-dehss SAH-lahd).   USA. A **salad** of chopped **romaine, escarole,** and **chicory** mixed with **minced anchovy fillets, green onions, parlsey,** and **tarragon;** then tossed with **mayonnaise, tarragon vinegar,** and **chopped chives;** served in a bowl rubbed with **garlic,** then topped with **chicken, crab,** or **shrimp.**

green gooseberry (gren GOOS-behr-ree).   USA. **Gooseberry.**

green leaf lettuce (gren lef LEHT-uhs). USA. A variety of **lettuce** whose leaves are not tightly bunched in a head.

green mango (gren MAHN-go). USA. The unripe **fruit** of tropical evergreen tree of the sumac family; pectin-rich, sour taste; basis of most Indian **chutneys** and **pickles.**

green onion (gren UN-yun). USA. A garden **vegetable** with a slender white sheath for the bulb and slender, round dark green leaves; widely used in **salads** and as seasoning.

green peppercorns (gren PEHP-pur-kornz). USA. **Berries** of the **black pepper** vine picked while immature; more subtle flavor than traditional black peppercorn; available freeze-dried or **preserved** in **brine** or wine **vinegar.**

green peppers (gren PEHP-pehrs). USA. **Bell peppers.**

green plantain (gren PLAHN-tehn). USA. A very hard and starchy **banana-vegetable** with little banana flavor and no sweetness; used as a staple starch or main dish in many parts of the world.

greens (grenz). USA. Plants with large, green leaves used as vegetable: **collards, dandelion greens, kale, mustard greens,** and **swiss chard** are the major varieties.

green sauce (gren saus). USA. **Mayonnaise** flavored with finely minced **spinach, watercress, parsley, tarragon,** which colors the sauce green; **mayonnaise verte.**

grelhados (gray-LEEAH-doosh). Por. **Grilled.**

grelos (GRAY-loosh). Por. **Dandelion greens.**

gremolada (greh-mo-LAH-dah). Ita. The aromatic **garnish** of **chopped parsley, garlic,** and **grated lemon** zest sprinkled over **osso buco.**

grenade (greh-nahd). Fre. **Pomegranate.**

grenadine (GREN-a-deen). USA. **Pomegranate syrup,** used for flavoring and coloring.

grenadins (greh-nah-danh). Fre. Small **filets** of **veal** or **fowl** that are **braised.**

grenouilles (gruh-nuhy). Fre. **Frog legs.**

gretskii orekh (GRYEHTS-kee-yeh ah-RYWH-khee). Rus. **Walnut.**

grib (gree-BEE). Rus. **Mushrooms.**

gribiche (gree-beesh).   Fre. A **sauce** of **mayonnaise,** hard-boiled **eggs, capers, chopped gherkins, herbs;** served cold with cold fish.

griesmeelpap (GREES-mehl-pahp).   Dut. **Semolina porridge.**

Gries Pudding (grees PUHD-deng).   Ger. Chilled **farina pudding** of Switzerland.

Griessklösschen (GREES-kloss-khern).   Ger. **Semolina dumplings.**

grill (grihl).   USA. To cook by intense direct heat, over flames or embers or under a broiler.

grillades (gree-yahds).   Fre. Small pieces of **grilled** meat, usually lean, boneless **pork.**

grillé (gree-yay).   Fre. **Grilled.**

grilleret lammehoved (gril-YAYR-ert LAHM-hov-erd).   Dan. **Grilled lamb's** head.

grind (grind)   USA. To reduce to small particles or to powder form by putting through a grinder or food chopper.

grinder (GRIND-ehr).   USA. **Hoagie.**

Gris de Lille (Gree du lil-le).   Fre. A **cheese** that is a variety of **Maroilles.**

grisfötter (GREESS-foot-ter).   Swe. Pig's feet.

griskott (GREESS-tyurt).   Swe. **Pork;** also **fläsk.**

grissini (gris-SEE-nee).   Ita. **Breadsticks.**

grits (grehts).   USA. Coarsely **ground** hulled **grain,** specifically **hominy grits.**

grive (greev).   Ita. Thrushes, often stewed with myrtle leaves.

grives (greev).   Fre. Thrushes; tasty birds.

groats (grots).   USA. Hulled **grain,** more coarsely ground than **grits.**

Grød (grurdh).   Dan. **Porridge.**

Grødaertesuppe (GRURDH-aerterr-soo-bber).   Dan. **Green pea soup.**

groente (KHROON-tuh).   Dut. **Vegetables.**

groentesoep (KHROON-tuh-soop).   Dut. **Vegetable soup.**

grog (grohg).   Bri. A drink made of rum, **lemon, sugar,** and hot water; other spirits are also used.

grönar bönar (GRO-nah BO-nor).   Swe. **Green beans.**

grønlangkaal (GRURN-lahng-kawl). Dan. Creamed **cabbage.**

grønsagsfromage (GRURN-saaerr-froa-maash-er). Dan. An elegant **vegetable soufflé.**

grønsaker (GRURN-ssah-kerr). Nor, Swe. **Vegetables.**

grønsakssoppa (GRON-sa-ks-SO-pa). Swe. **Vegetable soup.**

grønsallad (GRURN-sahl-ahd). Swe. Green **salad,** usually **lettuce** only.

groseille à maquereau (gro-zehyah mah-kar-roa). Fre. **Gooseberry.**

groseilles (gro-zehy). Fre. **Red currants.**

groselhas (gros-ssay-lee-AHOO). Por. **Currants.**

grosellas (groa-SSAY-lyahss). Spa. **Currants.**

ground beef (grownd bef). USA. Beef that has been put through a meat grinder; if coarse ground, it is called *chili meat.*

grouper (GRU-pehr). USA. A fish of the **seabass** family that has firm, moist, lean flesh.

grouse (grawhus). USA. A **game** bird with very delicate flesh and a pronounced pine flavor. Also known as **partridge, prairie chicken.**

grovbrød (GROHV-brur). Nor. Rye bread.

gruel (grool). USA. A thin **porridge** made from granules of **cereal** cooked in three times the normal amount of liquid and twice the normal length of time; strained before serving.

Grüne Bohnen (grew-ner BOA-nern). Ger. **Green beans.**

Grüne Erbsen (grew-ner EHR-psern). Ger. **Green peas.**

Grüne Fisolen (grew-ner fee-ZOA-lern). Ger. **Green beans** flavored with **fennel.**

Grüne Gurke (grew-ner GOOR-kern). Ger. **Cucumber.**

grunt (gruhnt). USA. A very old colonial dessert made with **berries** and **steamed dough.**

grusha (GROO-shah). Rus. **Pear.**

Grützwurst (GREWTZ-voorst). Ger. A **smoked sausage** made of **buckwheat, oat,** and **rye groats** with **minced bacon.**

Gruviera (groo-vee-EHR-ah). Ita. Mild-flavored **Swiss cheese.**

Gruyère (Gru-yer). Fre. A world renowed **cheese;** pale yellow; has a nutlike, salty flavor, similar to **Swiss** but sharper; firm, smooth texture with small holes or eyes; also known as **Groyer.**

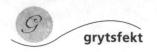

grytsfekt (GREWT-staykt).   Swe. **Pot roast** with **vegetables.**

gua (hwah).   Chi. **Melon.**

guacamole (gua-kah-MOH-leh).   Mex. Mashed **avacado,** seasoned with **lime** juice, finely **chopped onions, chopped tomatoes, chilies.**

guaiweiji (gwai wei jee).   Chi. "Strange tasting chicken"; **chicken slices marinated** in **soy sauce** and **garlic.**

guajillo (gwa-HEEL-loh).   Mex. A long, reddish brown, thin, dried, very hot **chili pepper.**

guajolote (gwa-hoh-LOH-teh).   Mex. Wild **turkey.**

guanciale (gwan-CEE-ahl).   Ita. Pig's cheek; a much sought-after delicacy that is **cured** with **salt** and **pepper** in the same way as **pancetta;** rarer and more choice than pancetta.

guarnito (gwar-NEE-toh).   Ita. **Garnished.**

guastelle (gwa-STAHL-lee).   Ita. **Rolls.**

guava (GWAH-vah).   Mex. The **fruit** of a tropical bush used to make pinkish-orange jellies; fruit pulp is delicious, but poor traveler. Not to be confused with the olive green, elongated egg-shaped fruit found in most of United States, the true guava is little known outside its native habitat.

güero (GWEH-roh).   Mex. A fairly hot, greenish yellow **pepper,** used fresh, **toasted,** or canned, but never **dried.** Also known as **California pepper.**

Gugelhopf (GOO-gerl-hupf).   Ger. A sweet, yellow, bread-type **cake** containing **raisins** or **currants** baked in a fluted tube pan; the traditional Name Day cake. Sometimes spelled **Kugelhoph.**

gui choy (jie cai).   Chi. **Mustard greens.**

guimauve (gee-mov).   Fre. **Marshmallow.**

guinea (GHEEN-neh).   Afr. A **fowl** with delicate-tasting flesh when young; resembles that of a **pheasant.** Also know as *Bohemian pheasant* and **pintade.**

guisado (ghee-SAH-doh).   Spa. **Stewed, ragoût, fricassee.**

guisado (ghee-ZAH-doh).   Por. **Stew.**

guisantes (ghee-SAHN-tehs).   Spa. **Green peas.**

gujjia (goo-jee-ah).   Ind. Crescent-shaped sweet pastry filled with **nuts** and **coconut.**

gulab (Goo-lab).   Ind. **Rosewater** flavoring.

Gulasch (GOO-lahsh).   Ger. **Goulash.** Also called **Gulyas.**

gule aerter (GOO-ler AER-terr).   Dan. Yellow split **pea soup** served with **salt pork.**

gulerødder (GOOL-er-rurd-herr).   Dan. **Carrots.**

gulrøtter (GEWL-rurt-terr).   Nor. **Carrots.**

gulyás (GOO-yaash).   Hun. **Goulash.**

Gulyas (GOO-lahsh).   Ger. **Goulash.** Also called **Gulasch.**

gulyash (goo-LYAHSH).   Rus. **Goulash.**

gulyásleves (GOO-yaash-leh-vehsh).   Hun. **Goulash.**

gum arabic (guhm AHR-ah-behc).   USA. **Vegetable gum** used as emulsifier and thickener in some processed foods.

gum tragacanth (guhm TRAHG-ah-cahnth).   USA. **Vegetable** gum used as an emulsifier and thickener in processed foods.

gumbo (GUM-bo).   USA. A rich, thick **Cajun soup** containing **okra** with a variety of meats, **seafood,** and **vegetables.**

gumbo filé (GUM-bo fee-LAY).   USA. **Filé powder.**

Gudel palacsinta (GOON-dehl POL-lo-cheen-to).   Hun. **Pancake** with **nut**-cream and **raisin filling, flambéed.**

guojiang (guop jiang).   Chi. **Jam.**

guotie (guo tieh).   Chi. **Fried dumpling.**

gur (gour).   Ind. A form of raw lump **sugar,** honey-brown in color; **jaggery.**

gurepufuruto (goo-REH-poo-foo-ROO-tsoo).   Jap. **Grapefruit.**

gurka (GEWR-kah).   Swe. **Cucumbers.**

Gurke (GOOR-kern).   Ger. **Cucumber.**

gus (goos).   Rus. Goose.

Güssing (Goos-eng).   Aus. A skim-milk **cheese** that very much resembles the **Brick cheese** made in the USA.

Gut Durchgebraten (goot-DOORCH-ger-braa-tern).   Ger. Well done, cooked thoroughly.

gyokuro (ryoh-KOO-chah).   Jap. Extremely fragrant and tender, very expensive grade of green **tea.**

gyudon (gyoo-dohn). Jap. A bowl of **rice** with **stir-fried** beef and **onions,** topped with a **sauce** and served with green **tea;** fast food item in Japan.

gyümölcslét (DYEW-murl-chlayt). Hun. **Fruit** juice.

gyümölcsöt (DYEW-murl-churt). Hun **Fruit.**

gyuniku (gyoo-nee-koo). Jap. Beef.

Halyun - Arabic - Asparagus

haagsche hopjes (HAHKH-skhuh HAWP-yus). Dut. **Coffee**-flavored hard **candy.**

haagse bluf (HAH-sexh bleuf). Dut. A light, fluffy **dessert** of **egg** whites and **red currant** juice.

haar chee meen (shah tze mian). Chi. **Shrimp noodles;** noodles colored brown and flavored with shrimp.

Haas (hahs). Dut. **Hare.**

habañero (ah-bhah-NAYR-ro). Mex. A very hot **chili pepper,** green, smooth skin; also available red or yellow.

habas (AH-bhahss). Spa. Broad beans; **fava beans.**

habash (HAH-bash). Ara. **Turkey.**

habichuelas (ah-bee-CHWEH-lah). Spa. **Kidney beans.**

habichuelas verdes (ah-bee-CHWEH-lah BEHR-deh). Spa. **String beans.**

Hable Crème Chantilly (Hah-blah Krehm Shawng-tee-yeh). Swe. A soft, ripened **dessert cheese;** rich and delicious.

haché (hah-shay). Dut. **Hashed** meat.

hachée (a-she-ay). Fre. **Sauce** for minced and leftover meats; made of **butter, chopped shallots, onions, tomato purée, mushrooms, capers,** seasonings.

hacher (ah-shay). Fre. To **chop; mince.**

hachis (ah-shee) Fre. **Hash.**

hachis (hah-SHEES). Dan. **Hash.**

hackad (HAHK-ahd). Swe. **Chopped.**

hackad biff mid lök (HAHK-ahd bif med lurk). Swe. **Chopped** beef with **onions.**

hackat kalvfilet (HA-kat kahlv-fee-lay). Swe. **Chopped veal.**

Hackbraten (HAHK-braa-tern). Ger. **Meat loaf.**

hacken (HA-ken). Ger. **Mince.**

Hackfleisch (HAK-flyesh). Ger. **Ground beef.**

haddock (HAHD-dohk). USA. A small member of the **codfish** family.

Hafer (HAH-fer). Ger. **Oats.**

Haferbrei (HAH-fer-brye). Ger. **Porridge.**

haggis (HAHG-gees). Sco. The national dish of Scotland; sheep stomach stuffed with **minced chopped** liver, heart, **onion,** and **oatmeal,** then **steamed** like a **pudding.**

hagyma (HOD-ymo). Hun. **Onions.**

hahm dahn (sheen DAHN). Chi. Salted duck eggs; **brine** cured about 40 days; used hot with **rice** or cold as a **relish.**

Hahn (hain). Ger. **Cock.**

Hähnchen (HAIN-khern). Ger. Rooster, cockeral, as spoken in the Frankfort area.

hahni (HAHN-hi). Fin. **Goose.**

hai shen (hah sind). Chi. A marine creature. Also called **sea cucumber** or **sea slug,** relished as a delicacy for its gelatinous texture.

hai wèi (hai wei). Chi. **Seafood.**

haizhé pí (hai dze pee). Chi. Jellyfish.

hajikami shoga (hah-jee-KAH-mee SHO-gah). Jap. "Blushing ginger"; pink, pickled **ginger** shoots eaten with **grilled** foods.

hak chih mah (hay tse mah). Chi. Black **sesame** seeds; spicy hot in taste.

hake (hak). USA. A small fish of the **cod** family whose flesh is tender, white, flaky, and easy to digest.

hakkebøf (HAHGG-er-burf). Dan. Chopped beefsteak, **hamburger** meat, **ground beef.**

hakket aeg og sild (HAHGG-ert ehg oa seel). Dan Smørrebrød of hard-boiled **eggs** and **smoked herring** minced together.

hakusai (hah-kuh-SIGH-ee). Jap. **Chinese cabbage;** also called **wong nga bok, siu choy.**

halat (HOL-lot). Hun. Fish.

halb durchgebraten (halp DOORCH-ger-braa-tern). Ger. Cooked medium-rare.

halb roh (halp roa). Ger. Rare; half **raw.**

halbran (HAHL-brahn). USA. A very young **duck,** before the age of being called a duckling.

haldi (HAHL-dee). Ind. **Turmeric.**

halewiyyaat (ha-la-wee-YEHT). Ara. **Confectionery, candies,** sweets.

half-and-half (hahlf-ahnd-hahlf). Bri. A drink of half porter and half pale **ale.**

half-and-half (hahlf-ahnd-hahlf). USA. A mixture of **cream** and **milk,** containing 10.5% to 18% milk fat. Also called **cereal cream.**

halfatányéros (HOL-fot-taan-yay-rawsh). Hun. Assorted fish, some **breaded,** some **fried,** served on a wooden plate, accompanied by **tarter sauce.**

half-mourning (hahlf-MOORN-eng). USA. **Poached poultry** and **braised sweetbreads,** masked with **Supreme Sauce,** and garnished with **truffles** placed under the skin; **demi-deuil.**

halib (hah-LEEB). Ara. **Milk.**

halibut (HAHL-eh-but). USA. A **flatfish** of the **flounder** family whose flesh is white, firm, and blandly sweet.

haliyb (hah-LEEB). Ara. **Milk.**

hälleflundra (HAH-leh-FLUN-dra). Swe. **Halibut.**

hallon (HAH-lon). Swe. **Raspberry.**

halmajonéz (HOL-moyaw-nayz). Hun. An **appetizer** of fish with **mayonnaise.**

halozun (hah-loo-SOON). Ara. **Snails.**

Hälsingeost (HAHL-sing-eh-OOST). Swe. A semisoft **cheese** made of cow's and goat's milk.

halstra (HAHL-strah). Swe. **Roast.**

halstrad (HAHL-strahd). Swe. **Broiled.**

halvah (HA-la-weeh). Ara. A Turkish **candy** made of crushed **sesame** seeds, cooked **chickpeas,** and **honey.**

halwa (HAL-vah). Ind. **Vegetables,** lentils, **nuts, fruits,** cooked with **sugar** and **ghee** to consistency of **plum pudding.**

halwah (HAHL-wah). Ara. Sweets; usually **candy** made of crushed **sesame** seeds, cooked **chickpeas,** and **honey.**

halyun (hahl-YUUN). Ara. **Asparagus.**

ham (hahm). USA. A hind leg of **pork, cured** and **smoked.**

Ham (hum). Dut. **Ham.**

hamaguri (hah-MAH-goo-ree). Jap. Hard-shell **clams.**

Haman's ears (HAY-muhn's eehrs). Jew. Ear-shaped pastries that are **deep-fried** and served with **honey.**

hamburger (HAHM-buhr-gehr). USA. A **sandwich** of a **broiled** or **grilled ground beef** patty on a split bun; ground beef patty.

hamburgerbringa (HAHM-boo-rer-bring-ah). Swe. **Smoked** ox breast.

hamburgerryg (HAHM-boo-rer-rewg). Dan. **Smoked loin** of **pork** in a **sauce** of currant **jelly, mustard, grated onion.**

Hämchen (HAHM-shun). Ger. Pig's knuckles and **sauerkraut.**

Hammel (HAH-merl). Ger. Mutton. Also called *Hammelfleisch.*

Hammelkeule (HAH-merl-kohul). Ger. Leg of **mutton.**

Hammelschulter (HAH-merl-shul-ter). Ger. Shoulder of **mutton.**

Hammelwürste (HAH-merl-voorst). Ger. **Sausages** of **minced mutton, garlic, pork,** seasonings.

Hammelzungen in Aspik (HAH-merl-tsun-gern im ahs-peek). Ger. Sheep's tongue in **aspic.**

hampurilainen (HAHM-poo-ril-lah-nayn). Fin. **Hamburger.**

hamu (HAH-moo). Jap. **Ham.**

hamu eggu (HAH-moo egg-oo). Jap. **Ham** and **eggs.**

hanagatsuo (hah-nah-GOT-soo-oh). Jap. **Dried bonito flakes.**

hanatsuki kyuri (hah-nah-tsu-KEE qoo-lei). Jap. Flowering baby **cucumbers,** used as a **garnish.**

Hand Cheese (Hahnd Chez).   USA. Skim-milk, semifirm **cheese,** usually molded by hand; flavored with **caraway;** has a pungent flavor.

Handkäse (hant-kahz-zah).   Ger. A cow's skimmed milk **cheese** that is pungent and acidic.

hangop (hahng-AWP).   Dut. "Hang up"; a **dessert** of thick **buttermilk** and **sugar.**

hangtown fry (HAHNG-town fri).   USA. An **omelet** with bread crumbed **oysters** and **fried bacon.**

hanjuku tamago (HAHN-joo-koo TAH-mah-gog).   Jap. Soft-boiled **eggs.**

háoyóu gàilán (hao yoh gai lan).   Chi. **Broccoli** in **oyster sauce.**

háoyóu niúròu (hao yoh niu row).   Chi. Beef with **oyster sauce.**

hapankaali (HAH-pahn-KAA-li).   Fin. **Sauerkraut.**

häränfilee (HAE-raen-fil-lay).   Fin. **Filet** of beef.

häränhäntäliemi (HAE-rae-HAEN-tea-LAY-mi).   Fin. **Oxtail soup.**

hara piaz (Ha-rah pih-YAZ).   Ind. **Scallion.**

harcsa (HOR-cho).   Hun. Wels, an extremely large and only member of the **catfish** family found in Europe; not to be confused with the wolffish, which is called **catfish** in Europe.

hard-ball stage (HAHRD-bahl staj).   USA. The fourth stage of **sugar crystallization;** begins at 250°F and forms a firm ball between the fingers when immersed in cold water.

hard-crack stage (HAHRD-krahk staj).   USA. The sixth stage of **sugar crystallization;** begins at 300°F and forms brittle threads and sheets when immersed in cold water.

hard sauce (hahrd saus).   USA. **Sugar** and **butter creamed** till fluffy and flavored with liquor.

hardtack (HAHRD-tahk).   USA. A hard **biscuit** made with **flour** and water but no **shortening** or **yeast.** Also called **sea biscuit, sea bread, ship biscuit, pilot bread,** and **pilot biscuit.**

hare (har).   USA. A wild **rabbit** eaten for its dark meat with gamy flavor.

hare (HAA-rer).   Nor. **Hare, rabbit.**

hareng (ah-rahng).   Fre. **Herring.**

hareragu (HAA-rer-rahg-GEW). Nor. **Jugged hare; rabbit** stewed in red wine, **onion,** various **vegetables,** and seasonings.

haresteg (HAAR-er-staigt). Dan. **Roast hare.**

haricot (ah-ree-koa). Fre. **Bean;** *fresh* (frais), *dried* (sec), *white* (blanc). *pale green* (flageolet), *red kidney* (rouge), *green string* (verte).

haricot de mouton (ah-ree-koa day moo-tom). Fre. **Mutton stew** with **potatoes, turnips,** but no **beans.**

haricots (ahr-ee-ko). Bri. **Dried beans.**

hari gobhi (HA-ree GOHB-hee). Ind. **Broccoli.**

hari mirch (HA-ree meerch). Ind. **Green pepper.**

harina (ah-REE-nah). Spa. **Flour.**

haring (HAH-ring). Dut. **Herring.**

Haringsla (HAH-ring-slah). Dut. **Herring salad.**

hart (hart). Dut. Heart.

harusame (hah-roo-SAH-mee). Jap. Translucent **noodles.**

Harvard beets (hahr-vuhd bets). USA. A dish of **beets, sliced, diced or julienne,** cooked in **vinegar, sugar,** and **cornstarch.**

Harzerkäse (Hahr-zehr-kahz-zer). Ger. A semisoft, skim-milk **cheese** usually flavored with **caraway** seeds, quite as "smelly" as **Limburger.**

Hase (HAA-zer). Ger. **Hare; rabbit.**

Hase im Topf (HAA-zer im tohpf). Ger. Potted **rabbit** in wine.

Hasehendl (HAA-zer-hehndl). Ger. **Chicken,** as spoken in the Frankfort area.

Haselnuss (HAA-zeri-newsser). Ger. **Hazelnut.**

Hasenbraten (HAA-zern-braa-tern). Ger. **Roast hare.**

Hasenpfeffer (HAA-zern-pfeh-ferr). Ger. **Stew** of **rabbit** braised in red wine, flavored with **pepper** and spices.

Haselhühner (HAA-zerl-hoon-nerr). Ger. Hazel **hen.**

hash (hahsch) USA. Chopped leftover or scrap meats mixed with a **sauce** and seasonings.

ha-shoga (hai-SHO-gah). Jap. **Ginger shoots.**

hashwi (HASH-wee). Ara. **Stuffing.**

haslett (haas-leht).   Iri. The Irish version of the Scottish **haggis.**

hasselnöt (HAHSS-erl-nurt).   Swe. **Hazelnut.**

hasty pudding (Ha-stee PUHD-eng).   USA. **Cornmeal pudding** with **molasses** and spices. Also called **Indian pudding.**

hasu (hah-SOO).   Jap. A **lotus root.**

hattit kit (HEHT-teh keht).   Sco. A high-calorie drink made of **buttermilk,** very fresh new **milk, double cream, sugar,** seasoned with **nutmeg.**

hauki (HAHoo-ki).   Fin. **Pike.**

haunch (hahnch).   USA. Hindquarter of deer or wild **game.**

Hauptel Salat (HOWP-tel zah-LAART).   Ger. Austrian wilted **lettuce salad.**

Hausfrauenart (hahus-FRAUHEN-art).   Ger. With **sour cream** and **pickles.**

hausgemacht (howus-ger-MAKAHT).   Ger. Homemade.

Hauskäse (Hawus-kahz-zeh).   Ger. A **Limburger** type **cheese** made in dish-shape about 10-inches in diameter.

Havarti (haa-VAHR-tee).   Dan. A cow's skim-milk **cheese,** pale, mild, semihard, piquant flavor, many small holes.

Havermout (HAH-vehr mauw-tah).   Dut. **Oatmeal.**

Hay (Hi).   Fre. A skim-milk **cheese** ripened on fresh-cut hay, which gives a characteristic aroma to the cheese.

hazel hen (HA-zehl hehn).   USA. A tender, tasty game bird, related to the **grouse.**

hazelnut (HA-zehl-nuht).   USA. The **nut** of a hazel shrub; round or slightly oval and flat on one end, amber colored; flavor is sweet; texture firm; rich in oil, pleasant to taste; used in confectionery. Also known as **filbert.**

headcheese (HEHD-chez).   USA. A jellied meat dish made of the meat of a pig's head, boiled, chopped, highly seasoned, molded, and chilled.

heavenly hash (HEHV-ehn-lee hahsh).   USA. A **dessert** of vanilla wafers and **whipped cream.** A **confection** of **marshmallows** and **nuts** covered with melted milk **chocolate,** then cut in squares.

heavy cream (HEHV-ee krem).   USA. Cow's milk cream that contains 36–40% milk fat, used for **whipping cream.**

heavy syrup (HEH-vee SEHR-uhp).   USA. Two parts **sugar** dissolved in one part water.

hechima (heh-chee-MAH).   Jap. Sponge gourd, about a foot long, green, with deep grooves. Also known as **Chinese okra** or **luffa.**

Hecht (hehkht).   Ger. **Pike.**

hedelmä (HAY-dayl-miae).   Fin. **Fruit.**

hedelmäkakku (HAY-dayl-mae-KAHK-koo).   Fin. **Fruit cake.**

hedelmäkeitto (HAY-dayl-mae-KAYT-toa).   Fin. Cold **fruit soup.**

hedelmäsalaatti (HAY-dayl-mae-SAH-laat-ti).   Fin. **Fruit salad.**

hedgehog mushroom (HEHDG-hawg MUHSH-room).   USA. A **mushroom** with a sweet, hearty mushroom flavor that has a buff-orange cap with white tooth-like projections under it.

Hefe (HAY-fe).   Ger. **Yeast.**

Hefekranz (HAY-fer-krahnts).   Ger. A ring-shaped **cake** of **yeast dough** with **almonds** and candied **fruit.**

Heidelbeeren (HIGH-derl-bay-rern).   Ger. **Blueberries.**

Heilbot (HAYL-bawt).   Dut. **Halibut.**

Heilbutt (HIGHL-but).   Ger. **Halibut.**

heiss (hais).   Ger. Hot.

helados (ay-LAH-dhoass).   Spa. **Ice cream.**

heldersoep (HEL-dur-eh-soop).   Dut. Clear **soup.**

helgeflundra (HEHL-yer-flewnd-rah).   Swe. **Halibut.**

hellefisk (HEHL-ler-fisk).   Nor. **Halibut.**

helleflynder (HAYL-er-flew-nerr).   Dan. **Halibut.**

Helles Bier (HEH-lerss beer).   Ger. Light **beer.**

helstekt (HEHL-stehkt).   Nor. **Fried.**

hen (hehn).   USA. A female **chicken** over a year old; best used **stewed.**

Hendel (hehndl).   Ger. Austrian **chicken.**

Henne (HEHN-neh).   Ger. **Hen.**

Henry IV (auhn-ray IV).   Fre. A classic **garnish** of **artichoke** hearts, **potatoes,** and **bearnaise sauce.**

herb (ehrb or hehrb). USA. An aromatic plant used for flavoring and seasoning foods.

herb salts (ehrb sawltz). USA. A combination of non-iodized **salt** and **crushed herbs;** used for seasoning savory dishes.

herb vinegar (ehrb VEHN-eh-gahr). USA. Any **vinegar** with **herbs** such as **tarragon** or **burnet** placed in vinegar and allowed to develop the flavor of the herb.

Hering (HAY-ring). Ger. **Herring.**

Hering Hausfrauenart (HER-ring hahus-FRAUHEN-art). Ger. **Fillet** of **herring** in **sour cream** with **onions.**

Heringskartoffeln (HAY-ring-kahr-TOF-ferln). Ger. **Casserole** consisting of layers of **herring** alternating with **potatoes.**

Herkimer (HEHR-kee-mehr). USA. A natural **Cheddar,** flaky, sharp, and pale yellow with a dark cloth rind; made to a limited extent, if at all, in Herkimer County, New York.

herkkusienikastike (HAYRK-koo-SAY-ni-KAHS-tik-kay). Fin. **Mushroom sauce.**

herkkusienikeitto (HAYRK-koos-ayni-KAYT-toa). Fin. Cream of **mushroom soup.**

hermit crab (HEHR-meht-krahb). USA. A small **crab** found in vacated univalve shells; eaten **deep-fat fried** or **sautéed,** never eaten raw.

herneet (HAYR-nayt). Fin. **Peas.**

hernekeitto (HAYR-nay-KAYT-toh). Fin. Green **pea soup,** the national dish.

hero (HEE-roh). USA. **Hoagie.**

Herrgårdôost (HAER-goar-oost). Swe. A hard **cheese** with a mild to slightly strong flavor, similar to **Swiss.** Also called *Herrgard.*

herring (HEHR-rehng). USA. A flavorful, nutritious fish that in adult state is **smoked** or **salted,** and in young state is canned and sold as **sardines.**

herring caviar (HEHR-rehng kah-vee-ahr). USA. A **caviar** substitute; the **roe** of the alewife **herring** is processed and used as caviar.

herring rollmop (HAY-ring roll-mohp). Ger. **Raw, filleted herring** rolled around an **onion** or **pickle,** fastened with pick or **clove,** and

packed in **vinegar,** served with a **sauce** such as **horseradish, tomato,** or **mustard;** if fried before packing, known as *bratrollmops.*

Hervé (ehr-va).   Bel. A cow's whole-milk **cheese;** soft, rich, pungent, reddish brown rind.

hervir (ayr-BEER).   Spa. To **poach.**

Herzogin Kartoffeln (hay-TSO-geen kahr-TOF-ferln).   Ger. Mashed **potatoes** browned in the oven.

hé táo (huh tao).   Chi. **Walnuts.**

hé táo zhá jipiàn (huh tao dzah jee pien)   Chi. Deep-fried **chicken** with **walnuts.**

Hete Bliksem (HAA-tah-BLENK-som).   Dut. "Hot Lightning"; spicy mixture of **potatoes, pork** chops, and **apples.**

hickory nut (HEHK-oh-ree nuht).   USA. A variety of **walnut;** the edible **nut** of the hickory tree; rich nut encased in a very hard shell.

hielo (YEH-loh).   Spa. **Ice.**

hierbas finas (YAYR-bahss FEE-nahss).   Spa. Mixture of **herbs.**

higaditos de pollo (ee-gah-DHEE-toass day POL-lyoa).   Spa. **Chicken** livers.

hígado (EE-gah-doh).   Spa. Liver.

higos (EE-goass).   Spa. **Figs.**

hijiki (HEE-gee-kee).   Jap. A calcium-rich edible sea **vegetable** that resembles strands of black twine in its dried form.

hijiso (hee-GEE-soh).   Jap. Shiso seed pods; **pepper;** used for seasonings.

hikiniku (hee-KEE-nee-koo).   Jap. **Ground beef.**

hilloa (HIL-loah).   Fin. **Jam.**

Himbeeren (HIM-bay-rern).   Ger. **Raspberries.**

himmelsk lapskaus (HIM-melsk LAPS-kewss).   Nor. "Heavenly potpourri"; fresh **fruit** and **nuts** with brandied **egg sauce.**

Himmel und Erde (HIM-ehl unt ert).   Ger. "Heaven and Earth"; **apples** and **potatoes** with **onions** and **sausage.**

hina (hee-NAH).   Jap. A young **chicken** 3–4 months of age; **fryer.**

hindbaer (HEEN-baer).   Dan. **Raspberry.**

hindbi (HEEN-bee). Ara. **Dandelion greens.**

hinojo (ee-NOU-hoh). Spa. **Fennel.**

hinta (HEN-tah). Ara. **Wheat grain.**

hirame (hee-RAH-meh). Jap. **Flounder.**

Hirn (hehrn). Ger. Brains.

hirondelles (ee-rohn-dehls). Fre. Swallows.

Hirsch (heersh). Ger. Stag, **venison.**

Hirschbraten (heersh-BRAA-tern). Ger. Roast **venison.**

hirvi (HIR-vay-ni). Fin. Elk.

hjärta (YAHR-ta). Swe. Heart.

hjerte (YAIR-ter). Dan, Nor. Heart.

hjort (yoort). Swe. Deer; **roebuck.**

hjortetakk (YOOR-teh-tahkk). Nor. Special Christmas **doughnuts.**

hjortron (YOORT-ron). Swe. Arctic **cloudberry.**

hjorstek (yoort-stehk). Swe. **Venison** steak. Also called **rådjursstek.**

hoagie (HO-ghe). USA. A glorified **sandwich** made on a long, split **roll** generously filled with cold cuts, **cheeses, onion, lettuce, tomatoes, pickles.** Also called **grinder, hero, Italian sandwich, po boy, poor boy, sub, submarine, torpedo.**

hoagie roll (HO-ghe rol). USA. An oblong yeast-dough **roll** about six inches long, used for a glorified **sandwich** called a **hoagie.**

hoarhound (hoahr-houhnd). USA. An **herb** of the mint family that produces a bitter taste; its stems and leaves are used to make **teas, syrups, candy,** and cough drops.

hochepot (osh-eh-poa). Fre. A thick **stew** of less desirable cuts of meats and winter **vegetables.**

hodesalat (HOO-der-ssah-laat). Nor. **Lettuce.**

hodge-podge (hohdg-pohdg). Sco. A thick **stew** of less desirable cuts of meats and winter **vegetables.**

hodgels (HAHD-gehls). Sco. **Chive**-flavored **oatmeal dumplings** boiled in meat **broth.**

hoecake (HO-kak). USA. A **pancake** of **cornmeal,** originally cooked using a hoe as a griddle; **johnny cake.**

hoh laan dow (how lahn dahw). Chi. Edible-pod **peas; snow peas, sugar pea pods, Chinese pea pods.**

hoh yow (hoa yoh). Chi. **Oyster sauce.**

Hohle Schokoladenhippen (ho-leh shok-eh-LA-den-hep-en). Ger. Hollow tubes of **chocolate** filled with **cream.**

hoi sin jeung (hai sheen gee-ong). Chi. A **bean sauce,** reddish, slightly sweet, seasoned with **garlic** and **chilies;** canned as well as made fresh.

hoja de laurel (OA-khah day lahoo-RAYL). Spa. **Bay leaf.**

Holländische Sosse (HOH-lehn-dish ZOH-seh). Ger. **Hollandaise sauce.**

hollandaise (hol-uhn-daz). Fre. A classic rich **sauce** made of **butter, egg yolks,** and **lemon** juice or **vinegar.**

Holsteiner Magerkäse (HOL-shtigh-nerr Mah-gehr-kahz-zeh). Ger. A **cheese** made from skim milk and buttermilk; semifirm and usually comes in 12 to 14-pound sizes.

Holsteiner Schnitzel (HOL-shtigh-nerr SHNIT-serl). Ger Breaded **veal escallope** topped with fried **egg;** may be garnished with one of the following: **vegetables,** bread, **butter, anchovies, mussels,** and **smoked salmon.**

homard (om-mahr). Fre. **Lobster.**

homard à l'américaine (omahr ah lah-may-ree-kehn). Fre. **Sautéed diced lobster,** flamed in cognac, simmered in wine, aromatic **vegetables, herbs,** and **tomatoes.**

hominy (HOHM-eh-nee). USA. Inner kernel of **corn** that has been processed to remove the outer covering; used whole as is or ground into **grits.**

homogenized milk (hoh-MAH-gehn-izd mehlk). USA. A fresh, fluid **milk,** with 3.25% milk fat and 8.25% protein, **lactose,** and minerals; has no **cream** line; fat particles are broken up so finely during the process that they remian uniformly dispersed throughout the milk. Also called *homo.*

höna (HUR-nah). Swe. **Chicken.**

høne (hur-ner). Dan **Chicken.**

høne bryst (hur-ner brewst). Dan. White meat of **chicken.**

hønekødsuppe (HUR-ner-kurdh-soo-bber). Dan. **Chicken** and **vegetable soup.**

honey (HUHN-ee). USA. A sweet, viscous liquid manufactured by honey bees; used for centuries as a sweetening agent in food and drink.

honeybun (HUHN-e buhn). USA. A flat, **yeast-dough** breakfast **roll** or "bun," basted with **honey** before baking.

honeydew melon (HUHN-e-deu MEHL-uhn). USA. A **melon** with a semihard, creamy, yellow-green rind; flesh is delicate green, juicy, fine-grained, and sweet; used in salads and desserts; the basic ingredient in the **liqueur** called Madori.

hóng chá (hoong chah). Chi. Black **tea.**

hong joh (hoong jo). Chi. Patent-leathery, maroon colored, "red **dates**"; dried, used to flavor.

hongos (OHN-goh). Spa. **Mushrooms.**

hongroise (ahng-grwah). Fre. In the Hungarian way; **eggs,** meats, fish, **poultry** cooked in a **cream sauce** seasoned with **paprika.**

Honig (HOA-nikh). Ger. **Honey.**

honing (HO-ning). Dut. **Honey.**

honingkoek (HO-ninh-kook). Dut. **Honey cake.**

honning (HON-ning). Nor. **Honey.**

honningkake (HON-ning-kaa-ker). Nor. **Honey cake.**

hønsekødsuppe (HRUNSS-er-kurdh-soo-bber). Dan. **Chicken-vegetable soup.**

hønsessup (HURN-sser-ssew-pper). Nor. **Chicken soup.**

hon shimeji (hon SHEE-meh-jee). Jap. A **mushroom** that comes in clusters with small caps and has a lobster-like flavor; entire mushroom cap, stem, and most of the cluster base are edible.

hons med ris (hurn maey reess). Nor. **Chicken** with **rice.**

hönssoppa (HONS-SOOpa). Swe. **Chicken soup.**

hon tarako (hon TAH-rah-koh). Jap. A product made from the **roe** of **cod** that has been **salted** and dyed red; a **caviar** substitute.

honung (HOA-newng). Swe. **Honey.**

Hop (hohp). Ger. A **cheese** the same as **Hopfenkäse.**

Hopfenkäse (HOP-pfen-kahz-zah). Ger. A **cheese** cured between layers of **hops,** often blended with **caraway** seeds, milk, or **beer.**

Hopjes (HAWP-yus). Dut. **Coffee**-flavored **candy.**

Hoppel-poppel (HOP-perl-POP-perl). Ger. Scrambled **eggs** with **bacon** or **sausages** and **potatoes.**

hopping John (HOHP-eng John). USA. A dish of **rice** and **black-eyed peas.**

hops (hahps). USA. The edible tips of the panicle (male plant) are broken awaw from the woody stem in the same manner as asparagus tips, then boiled in salted water with **lemon** juice and served with **butter, cream** or **gravy.** The ripe pistillate, or ovum-bearing catkin of the plant, is used dried to impart a bitter taste to **malt** liquors.

horchata (oar-CHAH-tay). Spa. A beverage made of **almond** or **pumpkin** seeds.

horehound candy (HOR-hownd KAHN-dee). USA. A **candy** made from the aromatic plant **hoarhound;** shaped as balls, drops, or squares; often used to treat sore throats.

horenso (hoh-rehn-soh). Jap. **Spinach;** mild taste and sweet.

Hörnchen ((HERN-shen). Ger. Crescent-shaped, slightly sweet **rolls.**

horno (OAR-no). Spa. **Baked.**

hors d'oeuvre (ohr-durv). Fre. **Canapé, appetizer,** side dish, or **relish** served at the beginning of a meal.

hors d'oeuvres (awr-DER-vruh). Dut. **Hors d'oeuvres.**

horseradish (HORS-rahd-disch). USA. A zesty-flavored **herb** of the **mustard** family; can be used as a **salad** green; its white-fleshed roots are ground up to make a pungent, hot-tasting condiment.

hortalizas (oar-tah-LEE-thays). Spa. Greens.

hortelã pimenta (or-TAY-LAHN pee-MEHN-tah). Por. **Peppermint.**

hortobágyi ropstélyos (HAWR-taw-baad-yee RAWSH-tay-yawsh). Hun. Steak Hortobágy style: **braised** in a mix of **stock** and **bacon** bits and accompanied by a large **semolina dumpling.**

hot chocolate (haht CHOHC-oh-laht). USA. A tasty **chocolate** drink, always served hot, and usually garnished with **marshmallows** or **whipped cream.**

hotch-potch (HAHTCH-pahtch).   Sco. A thick **stew** of less desirable cuts of meats and winter **vegetables.**

hot cross buns (haht krahs buhns).   Bri. A round, sweet **yeast roll** with a white cross in **icing** marking the top.

hot dog (haht dawg).   USA. A long bun split on one side only, stuffed with a boiled weiner or **frankfurter,** seasoned with **mustard,** catsup, **chopped onions, pickle relish.**

hot fudge (haht fujg).   USA. A thick topping of **chocolate, butter,** and **sugar,** used hot on **ice cream** and **desserts.**

hot house cucumbers (haht haus QU-kohm-behrz).   USA. Also known as European and burpless, these **cucumbers** are hydroponically grown; have a mild cucumber flavor and cook like common cucumbers; excellent eaten fresh.

hot pack (haht pahk).   USA. A canning term, referring to food that is precooked a little or fully and packed into canning jars or cans while very hot, then sealed and processed in a boiling-water bath.

hot pot (haht paht).   Bri. A thick **stew** of less desirable cuts of meats and winter **vegetables.**

hot sauce (hoht saus).   USA. Any of various commercially made seasoning sauces containing **chili peppers, salt,** and **vinegar.**

hottokeki (ah-TSOO-keh-kee).   Jap. **Hotcakes.**

hotto kokoa (ah-TSOO KOH-koh-ah).   Jap. **Hot chocolate.**

hovdessert (HOHVOdes-SEHR).   Swe. **Meringues** with **chocolate sauce.**

hua jiao (hwa jiao).   Chi. A reddish brown **peppercorn** that is very hot, used in **dipping sauce.**

hua juan (hwa juan).   Chi. Steamed **rolls.**

huachinango (wah-chee-NAHN-goh).   Mex. **Red snapper.**

huánggua (hwang gwa).   Chi. **Cucumber.**

huáng-yóu (hwaang-yo).   Chi. **Butter.**

huángyú (huang yu).   Chi. **Sturgeon.**

huasheng (hwa sheng).   Chi. **Peanuts.**

Hubbard squash (HUHB-bahrd squawsh).   USA. A large, round winter **squash;** hard-skinned; warty exterior; may be golden, grey-blue, or

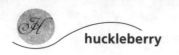

green; rich-flavored but dry, stringy yellow to orange flesh; bake, boil, or steam.

huckleberry (HUHCK-kle-behr-ree).   USA. An edible dark bluish-black **berry** resembling **blueberries;** has 10 large seed (nutlets); acidic taste.

huevos (WEH-vohs).   Spa. **Eggs;** *huevo* is singular.

huevos al horno (WEH-cohs ahl OAR-noh).   Spa. Baked **eggs.**

huevos al nido (WEH-vohs ahl NEE-dho).   Spa. "**Eggs** in a nest"; **egg yolks** set in small soft **rolls,** then **fried** and covered with egg white.

huevos al trote (WEH-vohs ahl TROA-tay).   Spa. Boiled **eggs** filled with **tuna** and dressed with **mayonnaise.**

huevos com jamón (WEH-vohs kohn khak-MON).   Spa. **Ham** and **eggs.**

huevos duros (WEH-vohs DOO-roh).   Spa. Hard-cooked **eggs.**

huevos escaljados (WEH-vohs ehs-kahl-KHAH-do).   Spa. Shirred **eggs.**

huevos flamenco (WEH-vohs flah-mehn-ko).   Spa. **Eggs** baked with **tomato, onion,** and **diced ham;** garnished with **asparagus** tips, **red peppers,** spicy **pork sausage.**

huevos fritos (WEH-vohs FREE-toss).   Spa. Fried **eggs.**

huevos medio cocidos (WEH-vohs MEH-dyoh koh-see-doh).   Spa. Poached **eggs.**

huevos pasados por agua (WEH-vohs pah-SSAH-dhoa por AHG-wah).   Spa. Soft-boiled **eggs.**

huevos rancheros (WEH-vohs rahn-CHER-ohs).   Spa. **Eggs** with a hot spicy **sauce,** served with **tortillas.**

huevos revueltos (WEH-vohs ray-BHWAYL-toss).   Spa. Scrambled **eggs.**

Huhn (hoon).   Ger. **Chicken.**

Hühnerbein (HEW-nerr-bine).   Ger. **Chicken** leg.

Hühnerbraten (HEW-nerr BRAA-tern).   Ger. **Baked chicken.**

Hühnerbrühe mit Nudeln (HEW-nerr-brew-er mit NOO-derln).   Ger. **Chicken broth** with **noodles.**

Hühnerbrust (HEW-nerr-brust).   Ger. **Chicken** breast.

Hühnerfrikassee (HEW-nerr-free-kah-zee). Ger. **Chicken fricassee.**

Hühnerleber (HEW-nerr-LAY-berr). Ger. **Chicken** livers.

Huhn mit Käsesaus (hoon mit KAIZ-saus). Ger. Boiled **chicken** with **cheese sauce;** a Swiss dish.

huile (lweel) Fre. Oil.

huile d'olive (lweel doll-eev). Fre. **Olive oil.**

huitlacoche (wee-tlah-KOH-cheh). Mex. A fungus that grows on green **corn** cobs, making a favorite stuffing for **quesadillas** or **soup;** the fungus makes the kernels grow large, black, and deformed, but tastes delicious.

huître (weetr). Fre. **Oyster.**

hú-jiao-miàr (hoo-gee-ow-mee-ar). Chi. **Pepper.**

hull (huhl). USA. The outer covering of a seed or nut, or pith of a **strawberry.**

húluóbò (hoo luo bo). Chi. **Carrots.**

humble pie (UM-ble pi). Bri. **Pie** once made from sundry parts of the deer and fed to the servants at hunting feasts while the wealthy ate the **venison.**

Humboldt dressing (HUHM-bohlt DREHS-seng). USA. A dressing of **crab butter, mayonnaise,** and seasonings; served mixed with a dish of crabs.

Hummer (HUM-merr). Ger. **Lobster.**

hummer (HOOM-merr). Nor, Dan. **Lobster.**

hummer (HEW-merr). Swe. **Lobster.**

hummer I gelé (HOOM-merr ee sheh-LAY). Nor. **Lobster** in **aspic** jelly.

hummeri (HOOM-mayri). Fin. **Lobster.**

Hummerkrabben (HUM-merr-krah-bern). Ger. Large **prawns;** large **shrimp.**

hummerstuvning (HU-mehr-STOO-veng). Swe. **Lobster Newberg.**

hummus (HUM-muhs). Ara. A paste of mashed **chickpeas** with **lemon** juice, **garlic,** seasonings.

hún tún (hwen tuen). Chi. A **wonton noodle;** used as a **dough** wrapper in making **wonton.**

huo-tui (huo-tway).   Chi. **Ham.**

hush puppies (huhsh PUH-pees).   USA. A deep-fried **cornmeal** bread, shaped like a **dumpling,** seasoned with finely chopped **onion;** eaten with fried fish.

hussaini kabab (hoo-SIE-nee ka-BAHB).   Ind. **Ground meat** shaped into thin **sausages,** stuffed with **nuts** and **raisins,** and **panfried** or **broiled.**

húst (hoost).   Hun. Meat.

Hutspot (HUHTS-poht).   Dut. A dish of **potatoes, onions,** and **carrots.**

Hutspot met Klapstuk (HUHTS-poht meet KLAHP-stahk).   Dut. **Stewed** lean beef with **potatoes, onions,** and **carrots.**

Hüttenkäse (HOO-ten-kayz).   Ger. **Cottage cheese.**

Hutzelbrot (HOOT-serl-broat).   Ger. **Fruit** bread.

Huzarensla (hew-ZAH-ruh-slah).   Dut. Hussars salad; a complete meal in itself consisting of bits of meat, **pickles, diced apples, potatoes,** and **beets,** and all bound together with **mayonnaise.**

hvalkkjøtt (VAAL-khurt).   Nor. Whale meat.

hveteboller (VAY-teh-bohl-lehr).   Nor. Sweet **rolls.**

hvide bønner (VEEDH-er BURN-err).   Dan. **Kidney beans.**

hvidløg (VEEDH-lurg).   Dan. **Garlic.**

hvidløgssmør (VEEDG-lurg-ssmurr).   Dan. **Garlic butter.**

hvidtøl (VEEDH-turl).   Dan. Nonalcoholic **malt beer** used in øllebrød.

hvidvinssovs (VEEDH-veen-soooss).   Dan. White wine **sauce.**

hvitkålsalat (VEET-kawl-ssah-LAAT).   Nor. **Cole slaw.**

hvitløk (VEET-lurk).   Nor. **Garlic.**

hvitting (VIT-ting).   Nor. **Whiting.**

hylderbaersuppe (HEW-derr-bear-soap-pey).   Dan. **Elderberry soup.**

hyse (HEW-sser).   Nor. **Haddock.**

hyssop (HEHSS-uhp).   USA. A minty, spicy, somewhat bitter **herb** used sparingly in **salads** and **fruits;** its dried flowers are used in **soups** and **tisanes.**

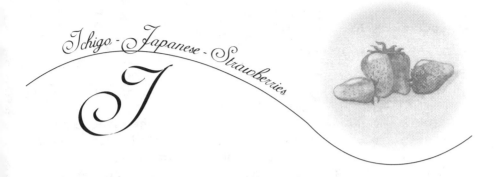

Ichigo - Japanese - Strawberries

iasc (ee-ask). Iri. Fish; more than one fish is **éisc.**

ice (is). USA. **Glacé; water ice;** made of **fruit** juice, **sugar,** and water; flavored variously as **lemon** juice, **coffee,** or **liqueur;** frozen smooth but without addition of egg white; related to **sherbet, granita, spoom, spuma,** but each is different.

ice cream (is krem). USA. A frozen **dessert** of **cream, milk, eggs, sugar,** flavoring, with or without **fruit** or **nuts.**

ice glazing (is GLAHZ-eng). USA. A method of freezing food, particularly fish, meats, and **poultry,** by dipping, brushing, or spraying with water to form a thin shield of ice; preserves freshness and flavor.

iceberg lettuce (IS-burg LEHT-uhs). USA. A **salad lettuce** with a large firm head, crisp, brittle, tightly packed; outer leaves medium green, inner leaves are pale green and chunky; the most common variety of lettuce used in the United States. Also called **crisphead lettuce.**

icebox pie (IS-bohx pi). USA. A crusted **pie** with a creamy **filling** that is frozen or chilled until firm.

Icelandic Banquet (is-LAHN-dehk BAHN-queht). Ice. A firm, delicately flavored **cheese,** much like **Mozzarella;** melts easily.

ichimi (ee-CHEE-mee). Jap. **Red pepper flakes.**

ichigo (ee-CHEE-goh). Jap. **Strawberries.**

icing (IS-eng). USA. Covering for **cakes,** pastries, made of **sugar, butter,** flavorings, cooked or uncooked; used in **confectionery** of all kinds; interchanges with **frosting.**

icing sugar (IS-eng SCHU-gahr). Bri. **Confectioners' sugar.**

i dolce (ee DOAL-chay). Ita. **Desserts.**

iets vooraf (eets fohrd-aff). Dut. **Appetizer.**

ijji (ah-JEE). Ara. **Omelet.**

ijs (eys). Dut. **Ice; ice cream.**

ika (ee-KAH). Jap. **Squid.**

île flottante (eel floh-tahng). Fre. Floating islands; **meringue** "islands" floating on a sea of **custard;** also sliced **sponge cake** layered in a deep bowl, sprinkled with **liqueur,** spread with **jam, nuts,** dried **fruits,** topped with **Chantilly Creme,** decorated, then covered with a chilled **vanilla**-flavored **custard.**

Ilha (EEL-yah). Por. A **Cheddar**-like **cheese** made in the Azores.

im (im). Iri. **Butter.**

imum bayildi (AH-mahm by-yahl-deh). Ara. A cold **vegetable** dish of **sautéed eggplant, garlic, tomatoes, parlsey.**

im baile (im BA-la). Ire. Homemade **butter.**

imbiss (em-BEHSS). Ger. A snack.

imbottini delizia (eem-bou-TEE-nee day-LEE-tsja). Ita. **Veal rolls** stuffed with **ham, cheese,** and **truffles.**

imbottito (eem-boa-TEE-to). Ita. **Stuffed.**

imli (IM-lee). Ind. **Tamarind.**

impanato (eem-pah-NAH-toa). Ita. **Breaded.**

impériale (eem-pay-ree-ahl). Fre. A garnish of **truffles,** cocks' comb, kidneys, **sweetbreads, foie gras,** and **Madeira sauce.**

Incanestrato (een-kah-nehs-STRAH-toh). Ita. A sharp, hard, grating **cheese;** made with ewe's milk usually, but can be made with a mixture of ewe's, goat's, and cow's milk. *Pepato Incanestrato* has **black pepper** added. *Majocchino* has **olive oil** added to the **curd.**

incasciata (een-kahs-cee-AH-tah). Ita. **Noodles** mixed with hard-boiled **eggs** and meat.

Indian bread (EN-de-uhn brehd). USA. **Cornmeal bread.**

Indianerkrapfen (en-dee-AHN-nehr-KRAP-fen). Ger. Indian Cruller Balls; a rich **dessert** of hollow **sponge cake** balls, filled with **whipped cream,** then rolled in **chocolate icing.**

Indian nut (EN-dee-uhn nuht). USA. The edible seed from any of several pine trees. Also called **piñon, pignola, pine nut, chinquapin, crenata.**

Indian pudding (EN-dee-uhn PUHD-eng). USA. An American Indian **pudding** of **cornmeal, molasses,** spices; **hasty pudding.**

indienne (en-dee-ahng). Fre. "In the style of India"; served with boiled **rice, currey** dishes usually.

indo-Chinese rice (EN-doh-CHI-nez ris). USA. **Rice** that is smaller than Indian Rice, is excellent and cooks perfectly without breaking up.

indyuk (een-DYAY-kah). Rus. **Turkey.**

infuse (en-FUZ). USA. To steep or soak **herbs,** spices, or **vegetables** in boiling water to **extract** their **essence.**

ingefaer brød (EEN-sheh-fah-eer brurdh). Dan. **Gingerbread.**

ingefära (I-nger-fae-rah). Swe. **Ginger.**

ingemaakte vruchten (een-gehr-MAAK-teh FRUHK-ten). Dut. Canned **fruit.**

ingen (ENG-ghen). Jap. **String beans.**

Ingwerbrot (INH-vehr-broat). Ger. **Gingerbread.**

Ingwer kuche (INJ-vehr koo-chee). USA. A Pennsylvania Dutch **ginger cake.**

inhame (ee-NYAH-muh). Por. **Yam.**

inlagd sil (IN-lagd SIL). Swe. **Pickled herring.**

insalata (een-sah-LAH-tah). Ita. **Salad.**

insalata mista (een-sah-LAH-tah MEE-stah). Ita. Combination **salad.**

insalata paesana (een-sah-LAH-tah paeh-SAH-nah). Ita. **Potato, egg,** and **vegetable salad.**

insalata verde (en-sah-LAH-tah vehr-day). Ita. Green **salad;** usually only one green is used (**lettuce, escarole,** or **lamb's lettuce**) and extra virgin **olive oil, salt,** and **vinegar.**

instant breakfast (EHN-stahnt BREHK-fahst). USA. A drink with a **milk** basis, having nutrients added, that is drunk in place of eating usual breakfast items.

instant coffee (EHN-stahnt KAWF-fee). USA. Brewed **coffee** that has been **dehydrated** and pulverized, stored, then can be rehydrated quickly in hot water.

instant flour (EHN-stahnt flowr). USA. A specialty **flour** used in making **gravies** and **sauces.**

instant rice (EHN-stahnt rics). USA. **Rice** that has been partially cooked and spit open.

instant tea (EHN-stahnt tee). USA. Brewed **tea** that has been **dehydrated** and pulverized, stored, then can be rehydrated in hot water quickly.

interlard (EHN-tehr-lahrd). USA. To **lard;** to thread strips of fat through meat or other flesh for the purpose of **basting** during cooking.

intingolo (een-teen-GOA-lou). Ita. **Sauce.**

in umido (een OO-mee-doa). Ita. **Braising; stewing.**

invert sugar (EHN-vehrt SCHU-gahr). USA. Simple **sugar;** blended from **dextrose** and **fructose;** used in **candy** making, soft drinks, **confections.**

involtini (een-voul-TEE-nee). Ita. **Rolls.**

involtini di vitello (een-voul-TEE-nee dee vee-TEHL-lou). Ita. **Veal** birds; **meat rollups; scallops** of meat, usually **veal, stuffed,** rolled, and cooked; **saltimbocca.**

iodized salt (I-oh-dizd sawlt). USA. Table **salt** with added iodine, an essential trace element.

iota (EEO-tah). Ita. **Jota;** a robust **soup** of **beans, potatoes, bacon, sauerkraut** slowly cooked.

iqdi safra (AH-dee SAH-frah). Ara. **Saffron.**

Irish coffee (I-rehsh CAHF-fee). USA. Hot sugared **coffee** with Irish whiskey and **whipped cream.**

Irish Mist (I-rehsh mehst). USA. Irish whiskey flavored with heather **honey;** a **liqueur.**

Irish moss (I-rehsh mahss). USA. A **seaweed** that needs to be well purified; used as an emulsifier, stabilizer, and thickener in a variety of foods; **carrageenan.**

Irish soda bread (I-rehsh so-da brehd). USA. A traditionally Irish free-form round bread, leavened with **baking soda** and **buttermilk,** not **yeast.**

Irish stew (I-rehsh stu). USA. A **stew** of meat, **potatoes,** and **onions** in thick **gravy.**

irlandaise (leer-lahng-daise). Fre. Irish style; i.e., with **potatoes.**

is (eess). Dan, Swe. **Ice.**

iscas de figado (EESH-kahs duh FEE-gah-doo). Por. Thin **slices** of calf's liver, cooked in oil and wine, and seasoned with **garlic.**

Ischlertörtchen (ISH-lehr-turt-chern). Ger. A **biscuit** spread with **jam.**

ise ebi (ee-SEH ee-bee). Jap. **Lobster.**

Isigny (E-zeen-ney). USA. A **cheese** said to be of American origin, but named for a town in France; has same shape as **Camembert;** flavor and aroma like a milk **Limburger.**

isinglass (i-seng-glahs). Fre. A pure, transparent **gelatin** obtained from the air bladder of fish, particularly the **sturgeon.**

iskaffe (ICS-KAH-feh). Swe. Iced **coffee.**

iskiriym (ays-KREEM). Ara. **Ice cream.**

Island of Orléans (i-luhnd au Or-lay-ahng). Fre. This **cheese** has been made by farmers on the Island of Orléans since 1679; a whole cow's-milk cheese, soft, piquant with a strong, characteristic flavor.

isleta bread (cs LEH-tah brehd). USA. Bread shaped like a bear's claw; a Pueblo Indian product.

Ismail Bayaldi (es-mayl By-yahl-dee). Fre. A classic **garnish** of Turkish origin; sliced **fried eggplant, crushed tomatoes, rice pilaf,** and **sauce portugaise.** Also known as **iman bayildi.**

ispíní (ish-PEE-nee). Ira. **Sausages.**

iste (ics-teh). Swe. Iced **tea.**

isvann (EESS-vahn). Nor. Ice water.

Italian meringue (Ih-TAHL-ee-ahn meh-RAHNG). USA. **Meringue** made by whipping hot **sugar syrup** into stiffly beaten **egg** whites; used to lighten **buttercreams,** pastry, **sherbets, soufflés,** to frost pastries.

Italian parsley (Ih-TAHL-ee-un PAHR-slee). USA. **Parlsey;** the every-day, grocery store variety; also called *neopolitan parlsey.*

Italian sandwich (Ih-TAHL-ee-uhn SAHND-wehch). USA. **Hoagie.**

Italian sausage (Ih-TAHL-ee-ahn SAW-sahg). USA. An Italian **pork sausage** in two forms, hot and sweet.

itir (AH-tahr). Ara. Syrup made from rose **geranium** leaves; **rosewater** or **orange essence** can be substituted.

ito-kanten (EE-toh AHN-ten). Jap. Thread **agar-agar.**

ivoire (ee-vwahr) Fre. A white **supreme sauce** with meat **glaze** for poultry.

iwahsi (ee-WAH-shee). Jap. **Sardines.**

izer cookie (EHS-zehr KOO-kee). USA. A **cookie** baked on a special iron with figures and designs, much like a waffle iron.

jäätellö (YEE-tay-lur). Fin. **Ice cream.**

jabali (khah-bhah-LEE). Spa. Wild boar.

jaboticaba (zheh-buht-eh-KOHB-eh). Por. A **fruit,** native to Brazil, with a **grape**-like appearance; dark maroon skin with a muscadine flavor; use fresh in **salads, sherbets;** cooked in **cobblers, jams, jellies.**

Jachtschotel (YAHT-skoh-tehl). Dut. **Casserole** dish of meat, **potatoes, onions;** traditional hunting dish.

Jack cheese (jahk chez). USA. **Monterey Jack cheese.**

jagaimo (GAH-ee-moh). Jap. **Potato.**

Jägerart (YAG-er-art). Ger. In the hunter's style; with **mushrooms** and a wine **sauce.**

Jägert (YAG-ert). Ger. **Sautéed** with **onions.**

jaggery (JAHG-geh-ree). Ind. A form of raw, lump, **honey**-colored **sugar.**

jaiba (HAHY-bah). Mex. Small, hard-shell **crab.**

jaiphul (JAY-fehl). Ind. **Nutmeg.**

jalapeño (hah-lah-PEH-nyoh). Mex. Small, plump, **green chili.**

Jalapeño (Hah-lah-PEH-nyoh). Mex. A semisoft **cheese** that is white and creamy and has chopped **jalapeño** peppers.

jalea (khah-LAY-ah). Spa. **Jelly.**

jalousie (ZAH-luh-zee). Fre. Little flaky pastries made in strips, resembling a venetian blind.

jam (jahm). USA. Made from crushed or ground **fruit;** almost holds its shape, but is not jelly-firm.

jambalaya (djahm-buh-LIE-yuh). USA. A **Cajun** dish or **rice** with **ham, shellfish, chicken, sausage, beans,** seasoned with **vegetables** and spices.

jambon (zhahng-bawng). Fre. **Ham.**

jambon d'Ardennes (zhahng-bawng dahr-dehnz). Fre. The famous Belgian **ham** of the Ardennes, served cut in very thin **slices** as an **appetizer.**

jamón (ah-NOHN). Spa, Mex. **Ham.**

jamu (JAH-moo). Jap. **Jam.**

jan hagel (yahn HEH-yehl). Dut. **Cookies** garnished with **almonds.**

jan in de zak (yahn een de zahk). Dut. **Steamed pudding** with **currants** and **raisins.**

jänis (YAE-niss). Finland. **Hare.**

Janssons frestelse (yahn-SOHNS FREES-tel-seh). Swe. Popular Swedish **casserole** of **potatoes, onions,** and **anchovies.**

Japanese cucumbers (JAHP-ahn-neez QU-kuhm-behrs.). USA. A seedless **cucumber,** nine to ten inches long with prickly skin.

Japanese eggplant (JAHP-ahn-neez EHG-plahnt). USA. A small, slender, purple **eggplant,** sweeter than the American variety; use **baked, sautéed, stir-fried, grilled,** or in **casseroles.**

Japanese rice (JAHP-ahn-neez ris). USA. A greyish-white, shiny, short-grain **rice** with regular oval grains, hard, translucent with a dark mark at the center.

japonaise (zhah-pawng-ayz). Fre. A garnish with Japanese or Chinese **artichokes** and **potato croquettes.**

jardinière (zhar-de-nayr). Fre. A dish of mixed **vegetables.**

Jarlsberg (YAHRLZ-behrg). Nor. A cow's partially skim milk **cheese;** hard; nutty and sweet with irregular holes.

jarret (zhah-reh). Fre. A part of the leg of an animal behind the knee joint; hock or knuckle.

Javaanse Sla (yah-VAHD-sah schlah). Dut. An exotic Indonesian **salad.**

javali (jah-vah-LEE).   Por. Wild boar.

Java rice (JAH-vah ris).   USA. Flat, transparent, shiny rice with elongated grains.

javitri (ja-VIH-tree).   Ind. **Mace.**

jazara (GA-zar).   Ara. **Carrot.**

jeera (JEE-rah).   Ind. Cumin.

jellied soup (JEL-leed soop).   USA. A **soup** made from gelatinous knuckle bones, clarified and used as is or with added **gelatin.**

Jell-o (JEHL-o).   USA. A trademark of General Foods Corporation for a **gelatin** product used for **salads** and **desserts.**

jelly (JEHL-lee).   Bri. **Jello®**; any **gelatin dessert.**

jelly (JEHL-lee).   USA. Soft food product made from **fruit** juice and thickened with **gelatin** or **pectin;** clear and firm; quiveringly, it holds its shape when turned out of the jar.

jelly bean (JEHL-lee ben).   USA. An oblong-shaped **candy** with a chewy texture and a semifirm coating, variously flavored and colored.

jelly roll (JEHL-lee rol).   USA. A **sponge cake,** baked in a special rectangular pan, spread with **jelly,** then rolled and sprinkled with **confectioners' sugar.**

Jenever (YAH-neh-vahy).   Dut. Dutch gin; also spelled **Genever.**

jerky (JEHR-kee).   USA. Preserved beef that has been cut in strips and dried in the sun.

Jerusalem artichoke (jeh-RUZ-ah-lehm AHR-tee-chok).   USA. The edible tuber of a sunflower used as a vegetable. Also called **sunchoke.**

jets d'houblon (zjah du'blowng).   Fre. **Hop sprouts** eaten as a vegetable.

jewfish (GEU-fisch).   USA. Giant **sea bass.**

ji (jee).   Chi. **Chicken.**

jian (jien).   Chi. Fry, as in **panfry** or **deep-fry.**

jiang (jiang).   Chi. **Ginger root.**

jiàng niúuròu (jiang niu row).   Chi. **Marinated** beef.

jiàng yóu (jiang yoh).   Chi. **Soy sauce.**

jiaozi (jiao dze). Chi. **Dumpling.**

jibn (GIB-na). Ara. **Cheese.**

jícama (HEE-kah-mah). Mex. A bulbous root with crisp white flesh.

jidàn (JEE-dan). Chi. **Eggs;** *chao jidàn* (tsao jee-dan). scrambled eggs; *jianjidàn* (jien jee dan) fried eggs; *zhu jidàn* (dzoo jee dan) boiled eggs.

jiè-mo (JYEAH-mwaw). Chi. Mustard.

ji rou (jee row). Chi. **Chicken** meat.

ji tang (gee taang). Chi. **Chicken soup.**

jit choh (geo choo). Chi. A red **vinegar** used as a **dipping sauce.**

Jockberg (YOAK-behrg). Ger. A **cheese** made of mixed cow's and goat's milk in the Tyrol mountains.

Joe Mazzetti (Joh Mah-ZHET-ee). USA. **Sloppy** Joe with an Italian seasoning.

Joghurt (YOA-goort). Ger. **Yogurt.**

Johannisbeer Sosse (you-HAH-nis-bay-rern ZO-seh). Ger. **Red currant jelly** made into a **sauce.**

John Dory (John DOU-ree). USA. Better known as St. Peter's fish; the classic ingredient of **bouillabaisse;** flesh is firm, white, and finely flaked; also known as **Saint-Pierre.**

johnny cake (JOHN-nee kak). USA. A **cornmeal pancake.**

Joinville (zwhy-veel). Fre. A **garnish** of **sauce normandie,** finely **diced shrimp, truffles,** and **mushrooms;** served with **fillet** of **sole.**

Jókai bableves (YAWKO-ee BOB-leh-vehsh). Hun. **Bean soup** Jókai style (Jókai was a famous Hungarian writer): a mix of smoked pig's knuckles, butter **beans,** and **carrots,** seasoned with **pepper, garlic, paprika,** and **parsley.**

jolly boy (JOHL-lee boy). USA. A **fried cake** made from a **cornmeal dough, baked,** split in half, buttered, and served with **maple syrup.**

Jonagold apple (JOHN-ah-gohld AHP-pul). USA. A large, hybrid **apple** with yellow skin having a red blush; has a subtle tart-sweet flavor; good eaten fresh or cooked; a cross between the Jonathan and Golden Delicious apples.

jonatán alma (YAW-not-taan OL-mo). Hun. Jonathan **apple.**

jordbaer (YOOR-baer). Dan, Nor. **Strawberry.**

jordgubbar (YOORD-gew-ber). Swe. **Strawberries.**

jordnötter (YOORD-NOH-ter). Swe. **Peanuts.**

Josephine (YOA-soh-feen). Ger. A rather soft **cheese** made of whole cow's milk formed in cylindrical shape.

jota (ee-OA-tah). Ita. A robust soup of **beans, potatoes, bacon, sauerkraut** slowly cooked. Also spelled *iota.*

juan canary melon (waun ka-NAHR-ree MEL-uhn). USA. An oblong **melon** that is canary yellow; flesh is sweet and white with a tinge of pink around the seed cavity.

judia (khoo-DHEE-ahss). Spa. **Kidney beans.**

judiás blancas (khoo-DHEE-ahss BLAHN-ahss). Spa. White **beans.**

judiás verdes (khoo-DHEE-ahss BEHR-dayss). Spa. **Green string beans.**

jugged hare (JUHG-gehd hahr). USA. **Rabbit** stewed in red wine, **onion,** various **vegetables,** and seasonings.

jugo (KHOO-goa). Spa. Juice.

jugo de naranja (KHOO-goa day nah-RAHN-khah). Spa. **Orange** juice.

jugurttia (YOO-goort-tiah). Fin. **Yogurt.**

jujube (joo-JOO-bee). Jap. A **fruit** about the size and shape of an olive; apple-prune flavor; sweet to acidic; flesh is white and pithy; has brown skin; picked ripe; eaten fresh, candied, or **dried.**

julekake (YEWL-kaa-ker). Nor. A fancy Christmas **cake.**

julienne (dzhu-lee-ayn). Fre. **Vegetables** cut into thin strips.

jumble (JUHM-buhl). USA. A cookie with **coconut, rosewater,** and **walnuts** mixed in the **dough.**

Junges Huhn (YOON-gees hoon). Ger. Spring **chicken.**

Junges Zwiebeln (YOON-gees TSVEE-berln). Ger. **Spring onions.**

juniper berries (jun-eh-purr behr-reez). USA. The **fruit** of an evergreen shrub of the pine family; used to add flavor to marinades, as seasoning for certain foods (**sauerkraut,** blackbirds, thrushes), and in the distillation of gin.

junket (JUHN-keht). Bri. **Milk curds** formed with **rennet** and made into a **custard**-like dessert.

jus (zhoo). Fre, Dut. Juice or **gravy.**

jus de viande (zhoo day vee-ahnd). Fre. **Gravy.**

juusto (YOOS-toa). Fin. **Cheese.**

juzi (ju-DZE). Chi. **Tangerine.**

jú-zi (jyew-dz). Chi. **Orange.**

Kaalsi - Finish - Cabbage

K

kaal (kawl). Dan. **Cabbage.**

kaaldolmer (koal-DULL-mah). Dan. **Stuffed cabbage.**

kaali (KAA-li). Fin. **Cabbage.**

kaalikääryleet (KAA-li-KAE-rew-layt). Fin. **Stuffed cabbage** leaves.

kaalipiiras (KAA-li-PRR-rah-kkah). Fin. **Cabbage**-filled pastry, served cold or hot.

kaas (kahs). Dut. **Cheese.**

kaassaus (KAUS-sows). Dut. **Cheese sauce.**

kabab (kah-BAHB). Ara. Squares of **mutton** braised in **butter,** seasoned, and served with **sliced onions** and **parsley.**

kabachok (kah-bahch-KEE). Rus. **Squash.**

Kabeljau (KAH-behl-yow). Ger. **Cod.**

kabeljauw (kah-bul-YOW). Dut. **Codfish.**

kabis (kah-BEEC). Ara. **Pickled, preserved.**

kabocha (kah-BOW-cha). Jap. A deep green-skinned, turban or flattened drum shape **squash,** with exceptionally fine flavor, rich sweetness, and almost fiberless, yellow-orange flesh.

kabu (kah-BOO). Jap. **Turnip.**

kachauri (ka-CHAW-ree). Ind. Fried puffy bread stuffed with spicy **bean** mixture.

kachoomar (ka-CHOO-mahr). Ind. **Chopped** or **sliced onions, tomatoes,** and **green pepper,** flavored with **lemon** juice.

kacsa (KO-cho). Hun. **Duck.**

kadhi (kahr-HEE). Ind. **Dumplings** made with **chickpea flour** and simmered in **yogurt** with spices and **vegetables.**

kaerlinghedskranse (KAYH-lee-heths-kroan-see). Dan. A Danish pastry; "Love Rings."

kaernemaelk (KAYHR-nah-meylk). Dan. **Buttermilk.**

kaernemaelkskoldskaal (KEHR-neh-MELK-skolk-skol). Dan. Cold **buttermilk soup.**

kafe (KO-fyeh). Rus. **Coffee.**

kafei (kay fay). Chi. **Coffee.**

kaffee (KAHF-er). Dan. **Coffee.**

Kaffee (kah-FAY). Ger. **Coffee;** afternoon coffee with sweets and **sandwiches,** similar to English high tea. See **Schwarzer Kaffee.**

kaffee (KAH-fay). Swe. **Coffee.**

kaffee (KAWF-fee). Dut. **Coffee.**

kaffeebröd (KAH-fay-brurd). Swe. **Coffee cake.**

kaffee complet (KAWF-fee koam-PLEHT). Dut. **Coffee,** usually with **whipped cream,** and **jam** and **rolls.**

Kaffee Haag (kah-FAY-hahk). Ger. Decaffeinated **coffee.**

Kaffeekuchen (kah-FAY-KOO-khern). Ger. Coffee **cake.**

Kaffee mit Sahne und Zucker (KAH-fay mit ZAA-ner unt TSUK-kerr). Ger. **Coffee** with **cream** and **sugar.**

Kaffee Verkehrt (kah-FAY FEHR-kert). Ger **Coffee** with more **milk** than coffee.

kafta (KAHF-tah). Ara. Finely **ground** lean meat.

kage (KAA-er). Dan. **Cake.** See also **flødkage, lagkage, småkage,** and **tørkage.**

Kahlua (kah-LOO-ah). Mex. **Coffee**-flavored **liqueur.**

kahvi (KAHH-vi). Fin. **Coffee.** See also **mustaa kahvia** and **maitokahvi.**

kahvi kerman ja sokerin kera (KAHH vi KAYR-mahn yah SOA-kay-riah KAY-rah). Fin. **Coffee** with **cream** and **sugar.**

kaibashira (kah-EE-bah-shee-rah). Jap. **Scallops.**

kail (kal). Bri. **Kale.**

kailkenny (KEHL-kahn-nee). Sco. A dish of **cabbage, potatoes, leeks,** and **milk,** similar to the Irish **colcannon.**

kaiseki ryori (kah-EE-seh-kee ryoh-ree). Jap. Originally part of the **tea** ceremony, now a succession of many small dishes served in a formal style. The ingredients change with the seasons and may include **fowl** or **seafood,** but no meat.

Kaiserfleisch (KIGH-zerr-flighsh). Ger. "Meat for the Emperor", a special **smoked pork.**

Kaiserkäse (KAI-zehr-KAHZ-zeh). Ger. A bright yellow, firm, mellow **cheese.**

Kaiser Koch (KIGH-zerr kohx). Ger. Emperor's Pudding; **rice pudding** with **almonds.**

Kaiserschmarren (KIGH-zerr-shmah-rern). Ger. Emperor's Dessert Omelet; **shredded pancake** with **raisins** served with **syrup** or **jam.**

kaitsuki nagareko (kai-IETS-soo-kee nah-GAH-lei-koh). Jap. Canned baby **abalone** in the half shell, seasoned with **soy sauce.**

kajiki (KAH-jee-kee). Jap. **Swordfish.**

Kajmak (KA-ee-muk). Tur. A sheep's milk cream **cheese,** soft and buttery, sometimes called "Serbian butter."

kajmak (KA-ee-muk). Yug. A fluffy creamed **cheese** dish of **feta** and creamed cheeses beaten with **butter;** served as an **appetizer** with bread and **roasted peppers.**

kajoo (KA-joo). Ind. **Cashew nuts.**

kak (kahk). Ara. Hard **rolls** or small **cakes;** similar to **doughnuts.**

kaka (KAA-kah). Swe. **Cake.**

kakao (kah-KAH-o). Rus. **Cocoa.**

kakao (KAA-kao). Swe. **Cocoa.**

kaki (kah-kee). Fre. **Persimmon,** usually served in **kirsch.**

kaki (kah-KEE). Jap. **Persimmon.**

kaki (KAH-kee). Jap. **Oysters.**

kakku (KAHK-kooah). Fin. **Cake.**

kakukkfú (KOK-kook-few). Hun. **Thyme.**

kål (koal). Swe. **Cabbage.**

kål (kawl). Dan, Nor. **Cabbage.**

kala (KAH-laa). Fin. Fish.

kalakakot (KAH-lah-kah-kot). Fin. Fish **cakes.**

kalakeitto (KAH-lah-KAYT-toa). Fin. Fish **soup.**

kalakukko (KAH-lah-KOOK-koa). Fin. "Fish fowl"; a famous dish consisting of a hollowed loaf of bread filled with layers of fish and **pork** or **bacon;** somewhat fish-shaped.

kala namak (dKA-lah NEH-mek). Ind. Black **salt.**

Kalb (lahlp). Ger. **Veal.**

Kalsbraten (KAHLP-braa-tern). Ger. **Roast veal.**

Kalbsbratwurst (KAHLP-braat-voorst). Ger. **Veal sausage.**

Kalbsbries (KAHLP-breece). Ger. **Sweetbreads.**

Kalbsbrust (KAHLP-brust). Ger. Breast of **veal.**

Kalbfleisch (KAHLP-flighsh). Ger. **Veal.**

Kalbfüsse (KAHLP-fooss). Ger. Calf's feet.

Kalbsfrikassee (KAHLP-frik-ah-see). Ger. **Veal fricassee.**

Kalbschnitzel (KAHLP-shnit-serl). Ger. **Veal cutlet sautéed** in **butter.**

Kalbshaxe (KAHLP-hahk-ser). Ger. Leg of **veal.**

Kalbskotelett (KAHLP-kot-leht). Ger. Veal **cutlet.**

Kalbsleber (KAHLP-lay-berr). Ger. Calfe's liver.

Kalbsleberwurst (KAHLP-ley-berr-voost). Ger. **Veal** liver **sausage.**

Kalbslende (KAHLP-lahn-der). Ger. **Filet** of **veal.**

Kalbsrippchen (KAHLP-rip-khern). Ger. **Veal** chop.

Kåldomber (KOHL-dohl-mar). Swe. **Stuffed cabbage.**

kaldt kjøtt (kahlt khurt). Nor. Cold meats, cold cuts.

kale (kal) USA. A **vegetable** that has loose, ruffly, green or dusky bluish leaves; resembles a giant sprig of **parsley;** a member of the **cabbage** family, kale has a mild cabbage flavor.

kalflsapjes (kawlf-LAP-pen). Dut. **Veal** steaks.

kalfslappen (kawlfs-LAHP-pen). Dut. **Veal cutlets.**

kalfsoesters (kawlfs-OOS-tur). Dut. Small, very tender **veal cutlets;** a delicacy.

kalfsvlees (KAWLFS-vlays). Dut. **Veal.**

kalfszwezerik (KAWLF-swear-iek). Dut. **Sweatbreads.**

kali mirch (KA-lee meerch). Ind. **Black pepper.**

kalja (KAHL-yah). Fin. Home-brew **beer;** nonalcoholic.

kalkeon (kal-KOON). Dut. **Turkey.**

kalkun (KAHLK-koonah). Fin. **Turkey.**

kalkon (kal-KOONN). Swe. **Turkey.**

kalkun (kahl-KOON). Dan. **Turkey.**

kalkunragout (kahl-KOON-raa-goo). Dan. Jugged **turkey** in a sweet-sour **gravy,** served with mashed **potatoes** or **chestnut purée.**

kall (kahl). Swe. Cold.

kalocsai halászlé (KOL-law-cho-ee HOL-leh-vehsh). Hun. Fish **soup** in red wine.

kalops (ka-LOPS). Swe. **Scallops** of beef simmered in a rich **sauce** seasoned with **allspice** and **bay leaf.**

kålrouletter (kawl-ru-LEHT-ehr). Nor **Stuffed cabbage.**

kalt (kehlt). Ger. Cold.

Kalteschale (KAHLT-shaaler). Ger. Cold **fruit soup.**

Kalte Speisen (kehlt SHPE-yeen). Ger. Cold dishes.

kalv (kaalv). Dan, Swe. **Veal.**

kalvbräss (KALV-brahs). Swe. **Sweetbreads.**

kalvbrissel (KAAL-ver-bree-sserl). Dan. **Veal sweetbreads.**

kalvekotelett (KAHLV-er-kot-ter-leht). Nor. **Veal** chops.

kalvelever (KAALV-leh-ver). Dan. Calf's liver.

kalvemedaljong (KAHLV-may-dahl-yoon). Nor. **Roast veal.**

kalvenyrestek (KAHLV-crn-ewrer-sstayk). Nor. **Loin** of **veal.**

kalvkotlett (KALV-kot-LAHT). Swe. **Veal cutlets.**

kalvkyckling (KAHLV-tyewk-ling). Swe. **Veal** birds.

kalvstek (KAHLV-stayk). Swe. **Roast veal.**

kamaboko (KAH-mah-boo-koh). Jap. **Steamed** fish cake, served cold as a side dish.

kamasu (KAH-mah-soo). Jap. A long slender fish called saury **pike.**

kaminari-jiru (KAH-mee-NAH-lei joo-loo). Jap. Thunder **soup,** with **bean curd** and **vegetables.**

kampyo (KAHM-puo). Jap. Dried gourd shavings, which look like strips of rawhide packaged in cellophane.

kana (KAH-nah). Fin. **Chicken;** sometimes called **kananpoika;** see also **paistettu kana.**

kananpoika (KAH-nahn-KOA-pi). Fin. **Chicken** leg.

Kaneel (kah-NAIL). Dut. **Cinnamon.**

kanel (kah-NAYL). Swe. **Cinnamon.**

kami (kah-NEE). Jap. **Crab.**

kaniini (KAH-nee-ee-nee). Fin. **Rabbit.**

kanin (kah-NEEN) Swe. **Rabbit.**

Kaninchen (kah-NEEN-khern). Ger. **Rabbit.**

kanin i flødepeberrod (kah-NEEN ee FLURDH-er-pehoo-rroadh). Dan. **Jugged rabbit** in a **horseradish-cream dressing** with **mushrooms** and **onions.**

kanten (KAHN-tain). Jap. **Gelatin** made from **seaweed;** does not melt at room temperature. Also called stick **agar-agar.**

kao (kao). Chi. To **roast** or **bake.**

kao-miàn-bao (kao-mien-bao). Chi. Toast.

Kapaun (kah-POWN). Ger. **Capon.**

Kapern (KAA-pern). Ger. **Capers.**

kaperssovs (KAH-pehr-soavs). Dan. **Caper sauce.**

kapormártás (KOP-pawr-maar-taash). Hun. **Dill** sauce.

káposzta (KAA-paw-sto). Hun. **Cabbage.**

kappan (KOP-pon). Hun. **Capon.**

kapros túrós rétes (KOP-rawsh TOO-rawsh RAY-tehsh). Hun. **Curds strudel** with **dill.**

kapucineres felfújt (KOP-poot-seen-eh-rehsh FEHL-fooyt). Hun. **Mocha soufflé.**

kapucyners (KAHP-u-seinus). Dut. Grey brown **peas.**

kapusta (kah-POOS-tah). Rus. **Cabbage.**

Karamel (kah-rah-MEHL). Ger. **Caramel.**

karamelbudding (kah-rah-MAYL-booth-eng).   Dan. **Caramel pudding.**

karamelrand (kah-rah-MAYL-rahn).   Dan. **Caramel custard.**

karashi (kah-RAH-shee).   Jap. Very strong dry, **ground mustard;** prepared by mixing with water, not **vinegar.**

karashina (kah-LAH-see-nah).   Jap. **Mustard cabbage;** a clump of fat, apple-green stalks with darker green leaves; milder flavor than ordinary mustard greens; can be purchased **pickled.**

karasumi (kah-LAH-see-mee).   Jap. A **caviar** substitute; the **roe** of **mullet** that has been **salted.**

karbonader (kar-bo-NAYTH-ehr).   Dan. **Fried pork** and **veal** patties.

karbonader (kahr-bohn-NAHD).   Dut. Ready-to-cook rolled **roast** with spices.

kardemommekaker (kahr-dehr-MAHN-meh-kak-ker).   Dut. **Cardamom-**spiced **cookies.**

kardi (KAHR-dee).   Ind. Yogurt-base **sauce** that contains **curry** leaves and spices.

karei (KAH-lae).   Jap. **Sole.**

Karfiol (kahr-fi-OAL).   Ger. **Cauliflower.**

karhu (KAHR-hoon).   Fin. Bear.

karhunkinkku (KAHR-hoon-KINK-koo).   Fin. **Smoked** bear **ham.**

karhunliha (KAHR-hoon-LI-hah).   Fin. Bear steak.

kari (kah-ree).   Fre. **Curry.**

kari (KAH-ree).   Ind. **Curry** seasoned **sauce.**

karicollen (KAH-ree-koo-leng).   Ger. Tiny steamed **snails;** usually purchased from pushcart vendors in Belgium.

karjalanpaisti (KAHR-yah-lahn-PAH-ste).   Fin. A dish of **mutton, pork,** and **veal** slowly simmered together.

karljohanssvamp (kaar-yoh-HAH-niss-vahmph).   Swe. **Boletus mushroom.**

karnemelk (kahr-nuh-MEL-uk).   Dut. **Buttermilk.**

Karotten (kah-ROT-tern).   Ger. **Carrots.**

karp (kahrp).   Rus. **Carp.**

karpalo (KAHR-pah-loa).   Fin. **Cranberry.**

karpalo kiisseli (KAHR-pah-loa KEES-sayli).   Fin. **Cranberry pudding.**

karper (KAHR-perr). Dut. **Carp.**

Karpfen (KAHR-pfern). Ger. **Carp.**

kärrmjölk (TYARR-myurlk). Swe. **Buttermilk.**

karry (KAAR-ee). Dan. **Curry.**

karrysalat (KAR-rew-sa-LAHT). Dan. **Curried macaroni salad.**

kartofel (kahr-TO-fyehl). Rus. **Potatoes.**

Kartoffel (kahr-TOF-ferln). Ger. **Potato;** *Kartoffelbrei* (kahr-TOF-ferl-brigh) mashed potatoes; *Kartoffelklösse* (kahr-TOF-ferl-klurss-er) potato **dumplings;** *Kartoffelpuffer* (kahr-TOF-ferl-puff-err) potato **fritters.**

kartofler (kahr-TOAF-lerr). Dan. **Potatoes.**

kartoflermos (kahr-TOAF-lerr-muss). Dan. **Potato** puffs; also mashed **potato stuffing.**

Käse (KAHZ-zher). Ger. **Cheese.**

Käsekuchen (KAHZ-zaeh-koo-khern). Ger. **Cheese cakes.**

Käsestangen (KAHZ-zehr-schtanj-ehn). Ger. **Swiss cheese** twists.

Käseteller (KAHZ-zehr-teh-lerr). Ger. **Cheese** plate.

Käsetorte (KAHZ-zahr-tor-ter). Ger. **Cheesecake.**

kasha (KAH-shi). Rus. **Groats** that are hulled, crushed, and cooked; **buckwheat; porridge.**

Kashkaval (KAHSH-ko-vahl). Gre. A **cheese** made from sheep's or goat's milk; creamy when young, firm enough to grate when aged; slightly smoky flavor. Also called *Kashcavallo, Kachavelj,* and *Katschkawalj.*

kasnudeln (KAH-noo-derln). Ger. Stuffed **noodles,** either savory sweet.

Kasseler Rippenspeer (KAH-sseh-ler RIP-pern-shpayr). Ger. **Pork loin, cured** and **smoked,** served on **sauerkraut,** with mashed **potatoes, apples** or red **cabbage, potato dumplings,** with a **gravy** of **sour cream** and red wine; a favorite German meal.

Kastanienreis (kass-STAHN-yen-rice). Ger. An Austrian **dessert** of **puréed chestnuts** and **whipped cream** made into a very rich **pudding.**

kastanier (KAHS-tahn-yerr). Dan. **Chestnut.**

kastaniesovs (kah-STAHN-yer-soooss). Dan. **Chestnut sauce,** flavored with **Madeira.**

kastanjat (KAHS-tahn-yaht). Fin. **Chestnuts.**

kastanjer (kahss-TAHNY). Swe. **Chestnuts.**

Kastlerribchen (KAH-ssehlerr-rip-skhern). Ger. A Belgium dish of **smoked pork loin** cooked with **sauerkraut,** white wine, and **juniper berries.**

Kasutado (kahs-TAH-doh). Jap. **Custard.**

kaszinó tojás (KOS-see-naw TAW-yaash). Hun. An **appetizer** of **eggs** with **mayonaisse.**

katakuriko (kah-TAH-koo-lee-koh). Jap. **Potato** starch, similar to **cornstarch.**

katch (kahch). Ind. **Lamb.**

kateh (kah-HEHT). Ara. Plain **boiled rice** cooked with a crust. Also called **Persian-style rice.**

katella (kah-TEL-lah). Dut. **Sweet potatoes.** Also called **obi.**

Katenschinken (KAA-tern-shin-kern). Ger. **Smoked** country **ham.**

Katenwurst (KAA-tern-voorst). Ger. **Smoked sausage.**

katkaravut (KAHT-kah-RAH-voot). Fin. **Shrimp.**

katrinplommen (kaht-REEN-PLOO-mon). Swe. **Prunes.**

Katschkawalj (KAHSH-koh-vohl). Rum., Bul. A plastic-curd, **Caciocavallo**-type **cheese** made from ewe's milk.

katsuobushi (kah-TSU-oh-boo-shee). Jap. **Dried bonito** fish, one of the two essential ingredients of basic **soup stock; dashi.**

Katzenjammer (KAHT-sehn-jahmm-ehrn). Ger. Slices of cold beef in **mayonnaise** with **cucumbers.**

kavamelon (KAH-vah-mehl-uhn). USA. A member of the **muskmelon** family; taste of **honeydew,** texture of **watermelon,** size of a football.

kávét (KAA-vayt). Hun. **Coffee.**

kaviaari (KAH-viaari). Fin. **Caviar.**

kaviar (KAHV-eeahr). Dan. **Caviar.**

kaviar (kah-vee-AAR). Nor. **Caviar.**

kaviar (KAH-vi-yahr). Swe. **Caviar.**

kaviár (KOV-vee-aar). Hun. **Caviar.**

kazu no ko (kah-ZOO-noh-kon). Jap. **Herring roe.**

kebab (kah-BEHB). Ara. Small **slices** of meat on **skewers, grilled** or **braised.**

kebob (keh-BOHB).   USA. **Kebab.**

kechappu (keh-CHAHP-poo).   Jap. Catsup.

kecsege (KEH-chehgah).   Hun. **Sterlet.**

kecskeméti barack-puding (KEHCH-keh-may-tee BOR-rotsh-pudding).   Hun. **Apricot pudding** with **vanilla cream.**

kedgeree (KUH-jree).   Ind. A breakfast dish of **curried rice,** lentils, spices, fish, and hard-boiled **eggs.**

keema (KEE-mah).   Ind. **Ground meat.**

Kefalotyri (Kah-fahl-o-TAHR-ree).   Gre. A hard, salty **cheese** used for **grating,** made from sheep's and goat's milk.

kefir (ke-FEHR).   Rus. Fermented camel's **milk** that is thick, frothy, slightly alcoholic, and healthful; slightly effervescent.

kefta (KEHF-tah).   Ara. **Mutton, chopped** and **spiced,** then shaped into **rissoles** and **grilled.**

keditetyt (KAY-teh-tewt-RA-voot).   Fin. **Boiled crayfish.**

keitto (KAYT-toaah).   Fin. **Soup.**

kekada (KAY-krah).   Ind. **Crab.**

keki (KEH-kee).   Jap. **Cake.**

Keks (KEE-kss).   Ger. **Biscuit.**

kelbimbó (KEHL-beem-baw).   Hun. **Brussels sprouts.**

kelp (kehlp).   USA. **Seaweed;** several varities harvested for food, dried, then processed in various ways: leaf form, thread form, sheet form; used as a **cracker,** for seasoning, to wrap various savory and sweet foods; **konbu.**

kenyér (KEHN-yeh).   Hun. Bread.

képviselófák (KAYP-veesh-ehl-ur-faank).   Hun. **Cream puff.**

kerma (KAYR-mahn).   Fin. **Cream.**

kermakakku (KEHR-ma-kahk-koo).   Fin. **Sour cream** pound **cake.**

kermakastiketta (KAYR-mah-KAHS-tik-kay).   Fin. **Cream sauce.**

kerre (KEHR-ruh).   Dut. **Curry.**

kerrieryst (KEHR-ruh-rayst).   Dut. **Curried rice.**

kersen (KEHR-suh).   Dut. **Cherries.**

kesäkeitto (KAY-ssae-KAYT-toa).   Fin. Summer **vegetable soup.**

kesar (KAY-sahr).   Ind. **Saffron.**

keta (kee-TAH). Rus. Siberian **salmon.**

ketchup (KEHT-chuhp). USA. Catsup.

ketchupot (KEH-chur-purt). Hun. Catsup.

ketelkoek (KAY-tel-kook). Dut. **Steamed pudding.**

ketsup (KET-soop). Dut. Catsup.

kex (kayks). Swe. Unsweetened **cracker.**

khali (kah-lee). Ara. Dried **mutton,** cooked in oil and fat to preserve it.

khall (khahll). Ara. **Vinegar.**

khas-khas (KAS-kas). Ind. White **poppy seeds.**

khass (khass). Ara. **Lettuce.**

kheer (keerh). Ind. **Pudding, rice pudding.**

kheera (KEER-ah). Ind. **Cucumber.**

khiyaar (khi-YAAR). Ara. **Cucumber.**

khleb (KHLYEH-bah). Rus. Bread.

khoobani (koo-BAH-nee). Ind. **Apricot.**

khowkha (khohkh). Ara. **Peach.**

khoya (KOY-yah). Ind. **Milk "fudge",** very thick and reduced.

khren (khryehn). Rus. **Horseradish.**

khubz (khubz). Ara. Bread, usually Oriental bread.

khudar (khi-daar). Ara. **Vegetable.**

khyar (khyahr). Ara. **Cucumber.**

kibbi (KIHB-bee). Ara. **Baked minced meat** with cracked **wheat** and spices.

kidney (KEHD-nee). USA. One of the edible, internal organs of **veal, lamb,** beef; used **sautéed, broiled, braised.**

kidney bean (KEHD-nee behn). USA. A large, dark red, edible, nutritious, common **bean,** usually used **dried.**

kielbasa (keel-BAH-sah). Pol. **Sausages** of very long links of coarsely **ground smoked pork,** flavored with **garlic.**

kieli (KAY-li). Fin. Tongue.

kiev (kee-EHV) Rus. A method of preparing **chicken** breasts by rolling seasoned **butter** into pounded breast **filets,** rolling in bread crumbs, and **frying** or **baking.**

kikuna (kee-koo-NAH). Jap. Edible chrysanthemum leaves; have a distinct fragrance, light, astringent flavor; used fresh only.

kikurage (kee-KOO-lah-gay). Jap. A crinkly, dried black fungus; crisp texture; use in **stir-fry** and lightly vinegared **salads.** Also known as **cloud ear.**

Kim (kehm). Kor. Toasted laver **seaweed** eaten like a **cracker** or crumbled over food.

Kim Chee (kehm chee). Kor. A fermented **vegetable pickle,** served with most meals as well as cooked in many dishes.

kinako (KEE-maj-koh). Jap. **Soy flour** made by grinding roasted **soybeans;** nutty and fragrant; used in many traditional sweet dishes.

king, a la (kehng). Fre. Served in **cream sauce** containing **green pepper, pimento,** and **mushrooms.**

King Christian IX (Keng KREHS-tee-un). Dan. A **cheese** also called **Christian IX.**

king crab (keng krahb). USA. A large **crab** of the northern Pacific waters. Also called **Alaska king crab, Japanese crab.**

Kingdom of Fire pie (KENG-dum ouv fireh pie). Sco. Dish of **pickled pork, rabbit,** and **forcemeat** balls spiced with **nutmeg,** served in a rich **gravy** topped with **puff pastry.**

king salmon (keng SAHM-mohn). USA. **Chinook,** or **royal chinook;** most highly prized of U.S. salmon; flesh separates into very large flakes, high fat content, soft texture.

kinku (KINK-koo). Fin. **Ham.**

kinoko (KEE-noh-koh). Jap. An edible fungi, with a woodsy fragrance and gentle flavor; used fresh, **dried,** and canned.

kinome (KEE-noh-mah). Jap. Fragrant young leaves of the prickly ash, plucked for use as an aromatic and colorful **garnish;** bright, with a mild hint of mint.

kip (kip). Dut. **Chicken;** *kip aan't spit* (kip ahnt SPIT) broiled chicken.

Kipferl (KEEP-fell). Ger. A sweet, doughy, crescent-shaped **roll.**

kip met kerrysaus (kip mayt KEHR-ruh-sows). Dutch. **Curried chicken fricassee.**

kippelever (KIP-pah-laver). Dut. **Chicken** liver.

kippensoep (KIP-puh-soop). Dut. **Chicken soup.**

kipper (KEHP-ehr). Bri. Lightly **salted** and **smoked herring.**

Kir (keer). Ger. A **liqueur** made from **black currants; Cassis.**

kiriboshi daikon (kee-LEE-she DI-ee-kon). Jap. Dried **daikon** shavings, used to flavor savory dishes.

Kirschen (KEER-shern). Ger. **Cherries.**

Kirschwasser (KERSCH-wass-ser). Ger. A colorless **liqueur** distilled from wild **cherries** and used to flavor **confectionery** and pastry. Often called *kirsch.*

Kirsebaer (KEER-sser-baer). Dan. **Cherries.**

kirsebaer koldskål (KHEESH-er-baer kolt-skawl). Nor. Chilled **cherry soup.**

kirsikkat (KEER-sik-kaht). Fin. **Cherries.**

kishk (keehk). Ara. **Yogurt** and crushed **wheat fermented** together, **dried,** and **ground.**

kishka (KEHSH-kah). USA. A Jewish-American **sausage** made by baking meat, flour, and spices.

kissel (kee-SSYEHL). Rus. A **berry pudding;** when thinned, used as a **dessert sauce.**

kisu (KU-suh). Jap. A small white fish.

kitcheri (KITCH-ehr-dree). Ind. A breakfast dish of cooked **rice,** lentils, spices with fish, hard-cooked **eggs,** and **curry; kedgeree.**

kitcheri (KITCH-ehr-ee). Bri. A breakfast dish of cooked **rice,** lentils, spices, with fish, hard-boiled **eggs,** and **curry.**

kited fillet (KI-ted FIHL-eht). USA. Fish cut through at the backbone, filleted but left attached at the belly.

kiwano (kee-WAHN-noh). USA. An oblong **fruit,** horned, golden-orange skin; subtle flavor of cucumbers, bananas, and limes; flat, white seeds encased in juicy green pulp with jelly-like texture; eaten out of shell or added to desserts.

kiwi fruit (KEE-wee froot). Nze. A plum-shaped **fruit** with a brown, fuzzy outer covering and soft green flesh with small black seeds. Also called **Chinese gooseberry** and *kiwi berry.*

kizbara (KEHZ-bah-rah). Ara. **Coriander.**

kjeks (khehks). Nor. **Crackers; cookies.**

kjøtt (khurt). Nor. Meat.

kjøttboller (KHURT-bol-lerr).   Nor. **Croquettes.**

kjøttfarse (KHURT-fawr-ser).   Nor. **Hamburger; ground meat.**

kjøttpudding (KHURT-pewd-ding).   Nor. Meat **pudding; meatloaf.**

kjøttsuppe (KHURT-ssewpper).   Nor. **Bouillion;** meat **broth.**

klabär (KLAAR-bah-rr).   Swe. **Amarelles.**

Klaben (KLAH-ben).   Ger. A white bread with **nuts** and dried **fruits.**

klarbär (KLAAR-bahr).   Swe. **Amarelles.**

klejner (KLEIN-ehr).   Dan. **Crullers.**

kletskoppen (KLETS-kawp-puh).   Dut. **Gingersnaps.**

klipfisk (KLEEP-feesk).   Nor. **Cod** that is **salted** and spread out on cliffs to dry, instead of rack-hung as **stokkfisk.**

Klopse (KLOP-ser).   Ger. **Meatballs** of two or three kinds of **ground meat.**

Klösterkäse (KLO-stehr-Kahz-zeh).   Ger. Finger-sized **cheeses** served as snacks with **beer;** formerly made by monks in cloisters; also called *Kloster.*

Klösse (KLUR-skhern).   Ger. **Meatballs; dumplings.**

klyukva (KLYOOK-vah).   Rus. **Cranberries.**

kmaj (kah-MAHJ).   Ara. Round, flat bread with a pocket; used for **sandwiches, dips,** Arabic **pizza.**

Knackwurst (KNAAK-voost).   Ger. Plump **sausages** flavored with **garlic;** means "popping" sausage because the casing makes a popping sound at the first bite. Also called **knockwurst.**

knädlach (KNAHD-lahk).   Jew. **Matzo dumplings** cooked in **chicken broth.**

knafi (kah-NAHF-fee).   Ara. **Dough** that resembles shredded **wheat.** Also referred to as *burma dough.*

knakworst (KNAAK-wurst).   Dut. **Sausage.**

knead (ned).   USA. To work **dough** with heel of hands by folding and stretching for distribution of ingredients, as well as development of **gluten,** and make dough ready for rising.

kneaded butter (NED-ehd BUHT-ehr).   USA. Equal parts **butter** and **flour,** kneaded with the fingers; used to thicken **sauces.**

knish (kah-NEESH).   Jew. **Chopped chicken** livers wrapped in mashed **potatoes** thickened with flour.

Knoblauch (KNOP-lowkh). Ger. **Garlic.**

Knoblauchwurst (KNOP-lowkh-voost). Ger. Garlicky **sausage** with chunks of fat in it.

knockwurst (KNOHCK-wuhrst). USA. A German **sausage** of **smoked** beef and **pork,** used **boiled, grilled,** and **steamed,** often eaten with **sauerkraut.** See **knackwurst.**

Knödel (KNUR-derl). Ger. **Dumpling.**

knoflook (KNAWF-lohk). Dut. **Garlic.**

knol (knaul). Dut. **Turnip.**

Kobe beef (KOH-bee bef). USA. Japanese-raised steer, noted for its tenderness and flavor, attributed to the fact that the cattle are fed **beer** and massaged with **saké.**

Kochenkäse (KO-chen-KAHZ-zeh). Ger. A cooked curd **cheese,** salt-free, firm, and bland.

kød (kurdh). Dan. Meat.

kødboller (KURDH-boal-err). Dan. **Meatballs.**

kødfars (KERTH-fahrs). Dan. **Forcemeat.**

koek (kook). Dut. **Cake.**

koekjes (KOOK-yus). Dut. **Cakes** or **cookies.**

kofe (KO-fyeh). Rus. **Coffee.**

koffie (KAWF-fee). Dut. **Coffee**

koffie verkeerd (KAWF-fee VAH-kehrd). Dut. **Coffee** with more **milk** than coffee.

koffie zonder melk (KAWF-fee ZAWN-dur MEL-uk). Dut. **Coffee** without **milk.**

kofta (KOHF-tah). Ind. **Ground meatballs** simmered in **sauce** with spices.

kogt (koat). Dan. **Boiled.**

kohi (KOH-hee). Jap. **Coffee.**

kohi keki (KOH-hee KEH-kee). Jap. Coffeecake.

kohitsuji (koh-HEE-tsoo-jee). Jap. **Lamb.**

Kohl (koal). Ger. **Cabbage.**

kohlrabi (KOHL-rah-bee). USA. A small, pale green, slightly knobby, slightly sweet, turnip-shaped **vegetable** with collard-like leaves;

tastes like fresh, crunchy **broccoli** stems, with a hint of radish and **cucumber;** usually cooked.

Kohlrouladen (KOAL-roo-laa-dern). Ger. **Stuffed cabbage.**

koi-kuchi shoya (KOO-ee koo-chee SHOH-you). Jap. Dark, thick, heavy **soy sauce.**

kokosnoten (KOH-kah-snoten). Dut. **Coconut.**

kokosnøtt (KOO-koos-noht). Nor. **Coconut.**

kokt (kookt). Nor. **Boiled.**

kola (KOA-lah). Swe. **Toffee; caramel.**

kolache (ko-LAH-chee). Pol. **Kolachy.**

kolachy (ko-LAHCH-ee). Cze. **Fruit**-filled **bun.**

kolbászfélék (KAWL-baas-fay-layk). Hun. **Sausages.**

koldtbord (KOL-brurdh). Dan. Cold table; **buffet;** a great assortment of **salads,** cold meats, and **chesses.**

koldbord (KOLT-boor). Nor. Cold table; varieties of fish, meat, **cheeses, salads.**

koldt kød (kolt kurdh). Dan. Cold cuts.

kolja (KOL-yah). Swe. **Haddock.**

kolje (KOL-ye). Nor. **Haddock.**

Komijnikaas (Ko-meh-nee-Kahs). Dut. A spiced **cheese** containing both **anise** and **cumin** seeds.

kombu (KOHM-boo). Jap. Kelp. See also **konbu.**

kome (koh-MEH). Jap. Uncooked **rice;** cooked rice served on a plate Western style is **raisu;** cooked rice served Japanese style in a bowl is **gohan;** it is the same rice.

komió (KAWM-iaw). Hun. **Hops.**

komkommers (kawm-KAWM-ur). Dut. **Cucumbers.**

Kompott (KOM-pott). Ger. Compote, stewed **fruit.**

konbu (KON-boo). Jap. Dried tangle **seaweed; kelp;** essential to **dashi** and various dishes.

konfeta (kahn-FYEH-ti). Rus. **Candy.**

Königinpastete (KUR-nig-gin-pahs-tay-ter). Ger. Pastry with savory **fillings,** usually meat and **mushrooms.**

Königinsuppe (KUR-nog-gin-zup-per).   Ger. **Soup** thickened with **eggs** and **cream;** very rich.

Königskäse (KUR-nehgs-kahz-zeh). Ger. A semisoft **cheese** similar to **Bel Paese.**

konijn (koh-NEYN). Dut. **Rabbit.**

konnyaku (kohugn-NYA-koo).   Jap. "Devil's tongue jelly"; a dense, gelatinous, dark brown to hazy gray **cake,** neutral flavor, cooked with other foods; has two filament forms: **sinrataki,** used in sukiyaki, and konnyaka, a thicker "string".

konsome (KOHN-soh-meh). Jap. **Consommé.**

kon'yak (kah-NYAHK). Rus. **Cognac.**

kool (kuhl). Dut. **Cabbage.**

koolraap (KUHL-rahp). Dut. **Turnips.**

koosmali (KOHS-ma-lee). Ind. **Relish** made with **raw grated carrots** and **fried** black **mustard** seeds.

Kopfsalatherzen (KOPF-zah-laat-hehrt-zen). Ger. Hearts of **lettuce.**

Kopfsalatsuppe (KOPF-zah-laat-ZUP-per). Ger. **Lettuce soup.**

Koppen (KOPF-fern).   Ger. A goat's sour-milk **cheese** with a sharp, pungent flavor.

korinkake (koo-RIN-kaa-ker). Nor. **Currant cake.**

korma (KOHR-mah). Ind. **Braise** or **stew.**

Korn (kahrn).   Ger. **Cereal** or **grain;** may be **wheat, rye,** or **barley,** not necessarily **corn.**

Körsbär (CHOHSH-bahr). Swe. **Cherries.**

Körte (KURR-teh). Hun. **Pear.**

korv (korv). Swe. **Sausage.**

kosher (KO-shehr). Jew. According to Jewish dietary laws.

kosher salt (KO-shehr sawlt).   USA. A squarish-grained **salt;** very flavorful; used sprinkled over meats, **pretzels,** breads, **rolls.** Also called **coarse salt** or **sea salt.**

koshian (koh-SHE-ah-ung).   Jap. **Dried beans,** usually red ones, already mashed and sweetened for pastry **fillings;** sweet **bean paste** or prepared red **bean flour.**

kosho (koh-SHOH). Jap. **Pepper.**

Kossuth cake (KAUGH-suhth kak). USA. A **sponge cake** filled with **whipped cream** or **ice cream,** then covered with **icing;** usually made in individual servings.

Kotelett (KOT-leht). Ger. **Cutlet.**

koteletter (koa-der-LEHT-terr). Dan. Chops.

kött (khurt). Swe. Meat.

köttbullar (KHURT-bew-larr). Swe. **Meatballs.**

köttfärs (KHURT-fahrs). Swe. **Meatloaf;** minced meat.

koud (kout). Dut. Cold.

koud vlees (kout flaasch). Dut. Assorted cold cuts.

kourabiedes (koor-ahm-bee-EHSS). Gre. **Biscuit; cookie;** usually a crescent shaped, crisp, **almond-** and **anisette-**flavored cookie.

krab (krahb). Rus. **Crab.**

krabba (KRA-ba). Swe. **Crab.**

krabbe (KRAHB-er). Dan. **Crab.**

krabbe (KRAHB-ber). Nor. **Crab.**

Krabben (KRAH-bern). Ger. **Prawns.**

krabbesalat (KRAHB-ber-ssah-latt). Nor. **Crab** salad made with **celery, lettuce,** and **dill** in **mustard dressing.**

krabbetjes (KRAHB-beht-tish). Dut. **Pork spareribs.**

kraemmerhusemed flødeskum (kray-mehr-hoo-see meth FLEHR-the skoam). Dan. Airy, cone-shaped **cakes** filled with **whipped cream** and **jelly.**

kräfta (KREHF-tah). Swe. **Crayfish.**

Kraftbühe (KRAHFT-brew-er). Ger. Beef **consommé.**

Kraftbühe mit Hühnerfleisch (KRAHFT-brew-er mit hoon-er-flighsh). Ger. **Chicken soup.**

Krakauer (KROCK-kaur). Ger. Polish **ham sausage.**

krakelingen (KRACK-leng-en). Dut. **Cracker, pretzel.**

kransekage (KRARN-see-kah-yeh). Dan. **Almond** pastry ring.

Kranzkuchen (krahnts-KOO-kern). Ger. Braided sweet **cake.**

Krapfen (KRAP-fen). Ger. Sweet **fritters; doughnuts.**

Krapfenchen (KRAP-fen-chen). Ger. Special **doughnuts** served at pre-Lenten carnivals.

kråsesuppe (KROA-se-soap-pay). Dan. **Frugtsuppe** with the addition of **chicken giblets** and **apples.**

Kraut (krowt). Ger. **Sauerkraut.**

Kräuterkäse (Kroy-tehr-Kahz-zeh). Ger. An **herb**-flavored **cheese** made of skimmed milk.

Kräuterklösse (KROY-tehr-klur-sser). Ger. Green **dumplings,** made green with **spinach** and **herbs.**

Kraut Fleckerl (kraut FLECK-erl). Ger. **Boiled cabbage** and **noodle** combined in a dish.

Krautkräpfli (KRAWT-kept-flee). Ger. Swiss **spinach turnovers,** similar to **ravioli.**

Kraut mit Eisbein und Erbensuppe (krawt mit IGHS-bighn unt EHRP-zern-zup-per). Ger. The German national dish of **cabbage,** pigs' knuckles, and **pea soup.**

Krautwürsteln (KRAWY-vewrst-erln). Ger. An Austrian dish of **stuffed cabbage,** using minced beef and **onions.**

kreatopita (kreh-ah-TO-ppeetah). Gre. A meat **pie** wrapped in **phyllo** dough.

Krebs (krayps). Ger. **Crab, crayfish.**

krebs (KRAYBSS). Dan. **Crayfish.**

kreeft (krayft). Dut. **Lobster.**

krem (kraym). Nor. **Whipped cream; custard.**

Kren (krays). Ger. **Horseradish.**

Krenfleisch (KRAYN-flighsh). Ger. **Boiled** beef, **sliced,** and served with **horseradish.**

krenten (KREN-ten). Dut. **Currants.**

krentenbrood (KREN-tuh-broht). Dut. **Raisin bread.**

krentenbroodjes (KREN-tuh-broht-yus). Dut. **Raisin** buns.

kreplach (KREHP-lahk). Jew. Small **dough turnovers** with savory **fillings.**

kreps (krehpss). Nor. Tiny, tender **crayfish.**

Krevetten (krau-VET-ten). Ger. **Shrimps.**

Kriek-lambric (kreek-LAHM-brik). Dut. A Belgium **cherry**-flavored **beer.**

kringlor (KRING-loor). Swe. Pastry twists; **cracknels.**

kroepoek (KREW-pook). Dut. Indonesian tidbit, like a huge, crunchy **potato** chip, but made of pulverized **shrimp.**

Krokette (kroh-KEH-teh). Ger. **Croquette.**

krona (KROA-nah). Mex. A mild red **pepper.**

kronärtskocka (KROO-nahrts-KO-ka). Swe. **Artichoke.**

Kronsbeer (KOHNS-beer). Ger. **Cranberry.**

kroppkaker (KROP-KA-koor). Swe. **Pork** and **potato dumplings.**

kropsla (KRAHP-slah). Dut. Head **lettuce.**

krusbär (KREWSS-baer). Swe. **Gooseberry.**

kruiden (KROHW-dehn). Dut. **Herbs.**

kruiden azÿn (KROHW-dehn ah-ZAYN). Dut. **Herb vinegar.**

kruidenagelen (KROHWT-nahg-ah-len). Dut. **Cloves.**

kruisbes (KROHWT-bess). Dut. **Gooseberry.**

krusbär (KRUS-bahr). Swe. **Gooseberries.**

krydder (KREW-ther). Dan. Bun cut in half and baked.

kryddersild (KREW-dehr-sil). Nor. Spiced **herring.**

kryddor (KRU-door). Swe. **Condiments.**

Kryddost (KREW-dah-oost). Swe. **Anise**-flavored **cheese.**

kryddpeppar (KREW-dah-pay-pahr). Swe. **Pimento; allspice.**

kuàngquán shui (KWANG-chuan shui). Chi. **Mineral water.**

kuchen (KOOK-hern). Ger. A pastry or **cake.**

kudamono (koo-DAH-moh-noh). Jap. **Fruit.**

kufta (KUF-ta). Ara. **Minced grilled** meat.

kugel (KOO-ghel). Jew. Baked **casserole** or **pudding.**

Kugelhopf (KOO-ghel-hopf). Ger. A **yeast cake** with **currants** steeped in **brandy,** baked in a special mold strewn with **almonds.**

Kugelhoph (KOO-ghel hoff). Swi. Puffy Swiss buns filled with **whipped cream.**

ku gua (koo gwah). Chi. **Bitter melon.**

kuha (KOO-hah). Fin. **Perch-pike.**

Kühbacher (KEW-bah-kehr). Ger. A soft, ripened **cheese** made from whole or partly skimmed cow's milk.

kuiken (KIR-kuh). Dut. **Squab.**

kukki (KOOK-kee). Jap. **Cookies.**

kukorica (KOO-kaw-ree-tso). Hun. Sweet **corn.**

kukuruza (koo-koo-ROO-zah). Rus. **Maize; corn.**

kulcha (KULL-cha). Ind. Leavened white-flour **dough** shaped into rounds and **baked.**

kulfi (KULL-fee). Ind. Indian **ice cream** made with cooked-down **milk,** frozen in special conical molds.

Kulibyaka (KOO-lee-byah-kah). Rus. A hot fish **pie** filled with layers of **salmon** or fish, **rice, mushrooms, herbs, onions.**

Kuminost (KOO-men-oost). Nor. A **cumin**-flavored **cheese.** *Kumminost* is the Swedish version.

kumiss (kuh-MEHS). USA. A drink of fermented **milk,** thought to have some digestive benefits; originated with the Mongols; similar to **laban.**

kumler (KHEWM-lehr). Nor. **Potato dumplings.**

kummel (KU-mehl). Swe. **Hake.**

Kümmel (KEW-merl). Ger. **Caraway** seeds; also a liqueur flavored with caraway seeds.

Kümmelkäse (KEW-merl-kahz-zeh). Ger. A good snack **cheese** with **beer;** flavored with **Kümmel** and **caraway.** A cheese by this name is also made in Wisconsin.

Kümmelsuppe (KEW-merl-zup-per). Ger. An Austrian **soup** flavored with **caraway** seeds.

kumquat (KUHM-kwaht). Chi. A small oblong **fruit,** resembling an **orange,** but is not a **citrus;** has a rind that is deliciously sweet and pulp that is sour; used in **stuffings, cakes, muffins, sauces, syrups, preserves,** and **jellies.**

kunafa (ku-NEH-fa). Ara. Fine-spun pastry stuffed with **nuts.**

Kurbis (KEWR-biss). Ger. **Squash, pumpkin.**

kuri (koo-REE). Jap. **Chestnuts;** Tamba chestnuts are large and pleasantly mealy; Shiba chestnuts are small, firm, sweet.

kurista (KOO-ree-tsash). Rus. **Boiling chicken; hen.**

kuro goma (KOO-roh GAH-mee). Jap. Black **sesame** seeds that have a pungent flavor.

kusa (KOO-sah). Ara. **Summer squash.**

kushary (KU-sha-ree). Ara. **Macaroni** or **rice** with **noodles,** lentils, **fried onion,** and a hot **tomato sauce.**

kushikatsu (koo-SHEE-kah-tsoo). Jap. **Pork, chicken, seafood,** and **vegetables skewered** on bamboo sticks, **breaded,** and **deep-fried,** then eaten with **salt,** hot **mustard,** and **sauces.**

Kutteln (KUT-terln). Ger. **Tripe.**

kuzu (KOO-zoo). Jap. An excellent thickening agent; produces a sparkling, translucent **sauce;** adds shiny gloss to **soups;** has pleasant gentle aroma.

kvaeder (KVAIDH-err). Dan. **Quinces.**

kvass (KBAH-ssoo). Rus. A **beer**-like drink, made from **barley, rye,** and **yeast;** used to flavor **borsch, chlodnik;** usually a grocery item as restaurants consider it inelegant.

kveite (KVAY-ter). Nor. **Halibut.**

Kwark (kwark). Dut. A skimmed milk **cheese** similar to **cottage cheese.**

kyabetsu (KYAH-beh-tsoo). Jap. **Cabbage.**

kyckling (TYEWK-ling). Swe. **Chicken.**

kylling (KEWL-ling). Nor. **Chicken.**

kylling (KEW-leeng). Dan. **Chicken.**

kyllingesalet (KEW-leen-ger-sah-laat). Dan. **Chicken salad** with chicken meat, **macaroni, tomato slices, green peppers, olives, green peas, lettuce,** and **mushrooms,** covered with **tomato dressing.**

kyllingsuppe (KEWL-ling-ssewpper). Nor. **Chicken soup.**

kyodo ryori (KYOH-doh ryoh-ree). Jap. Local or regional specialities; may consist of one dish or an entire meal that typifies the cooking of a particular area.

kyuri (KYOO-ree). Jap. Thin-skinned cucumber, about one inch in diameter and about eight inches long.

L

là (lah). Chi. Hot, peppery.

là báicàl (lah bai-tsai). Chi. Hot pickled **cabbage.**

laban (LA-ban). Ara. **Yogurt;** a soured **milk** similar to **buttermilk.**

Labneh (lahb-ne). Syr. A sour-milk **cheese.**

labni (LAB-ne). Ara. **Yogurt cheese paste.**

Labskaus (LAAPS-kowss). Ger. A **stew** of pickled **pork** or beef cooked with **potatoes** and **onions,** and sometimes **pickled** fish, **beets,** or **gherkins** as **garnish.**

là cháng (lah chaang). Chi. Spicy **pork sausages.**

Lachs (lanks). Ger. **Salmon.**

Läckerli (LEH-kerrli). Ger. Swiss **sugar cookies** with chopped **nuts** and bits of **orange** peel in the **dough.**

Lacksforelle (LAHKS-fo-reh-ler). Ger. **Salmon trout.**

lacón con grelos (lay-CHON kon greh-loas). Spa. **Cured port** shoulder with **turnip** tops.

lactic acid (LAHK-tahk AHSS-ehd). USA. The bacteria-producing acid that breaks down **lactose** (milk sugar) causing the coagulation of **milk** and is the first step in the **cheese**-making process; it is also found naturally in muscle tissue and acts as a natural preservative in slaughtered meat.

lactose (LAHK-tos). USA. **Milk sugar.**

la cuite (lah kwet). USA. Cooked **sugar syrup** in the last stage before it blackens and turns bitter; final stage of the **sugar crystallization** process.

låda (LOA-dah). Swe. **Casserole.**

là de (lah de). Chi. Spicy.

lady apple (LA-de AHP-pul). USA. A light green, mini **apple** with a red blush and a mild-sweet flavor; eaten fresh.

Lady Baltimore cake (LA-de BAHL-te-mohr kahk). USA. A white **cake** filled with **raisins** and **nuts** in a **frosting** of egg whites and flavored with **vanilla.**

lady finger (LA-de FENG-gehr). USA. A pastry made from a **sponge cake batter,** shaped about 3 inches long using a plain pastry tip; used filled by pressing two together around a filling, or singularly to line a springform pan or mold.

Lafayette gingerbread (lah-fehy-ette JEHN-juhr-brehd). USA. A **cake**-like **ginger** and spice bread made with the juice and rind of an **orange** added.

lagerblad (LAA-gerr-blaad). Swe. **Bay leaf.**

lagerøl (LAA-err-url). Dan. Dark **beer.**

lagkage (LAHG-kaaer). Dan. A towering layer **cake** filled with **whipped cream.**

lagmi (LAHG-me). Ara. **Palm** wine; made from the sap when the palm is dying.

lagôsta (la-GAW-shta). Por. **Lobster.**

lagôstim (lah-goush-TEM). Por. **Praw.**

Laguiole (LUHK-yohl). Fre. A hard **cheese** made of whole or partly skimmed milk.

lahm (LAH-ma). Ara. Meat, usually **lamb** or **mutton.**

lahm bagar (LAH-ma BA-a-re). Ara. Beef.

lait (leh). Fre. **Milk.**

laitance (lay-tounce). Fre. Soft fish **roe.**

laitances d'alsoe (lay-tounce d'al-soh). Fre. **Shad roe.**

laitue (lay-tew). Fre. **Lettuce.**

làjiao fen (lah-jiao fen). Chi. **Chili pepper.**

là jiao jiàng (lah jiao jiang). Chi. Hot chili **sauce;** red in color, red-hot in taste; made from **chili peppers, vinegar,** and seasonings.

làjiao yóu (la-jiao yoh). Chi. Pepper oil.

lakka (LAHK-kah). Fin. **Cloudberry; used on ice cream** and in making **liqueur.**

laks (lahks). Nor, Dan. **Salmon.**

laks øg-røraeg (lahks oa RURR-ehg). Dan. **Salmon** in scrambled **eggs.**

lal mirch (lahl merch). Ind. Red **pepper.**

lam (lahm) Dut. **Lamb.**

lamb fries (lahm friz). USA. Testicles of a bull, pig, or lamb; breaded and fried. Also called **animelles, frivolitées, mountain oyster, prairie oyster, Rocky Mountain oyster.**

Lambic (LAHM-brik). Ger. Austrian Gueuze on tap; a very special wheat and barley **beer.**

lamb's lettuce (lahmz LEHT-uhs). USA. A European plant with dark green, nutty-flavored leaves that are used for winter salads; prized by the French. Also called **corn salad** and **mache.**

Lamm (lahm). Ger, Swe. **Lamb.**

lammas (LAIIM-mahss). Fin. **Lamb, mutton.**

lammesteg (LAHM-stayg). Dan. **Roast lamb.**

lammkotlett (lahm-KOT-leht). Swe. **Lamb** chop.

lammstek (LAHM-stay). Swe. **Roast lamb.**

lampaankyljys (LAHM-paan-KEWL-yewss). Fin. **Mutton** or **lamb** chop.

lampaanpaisti (LAHM-paan-PAHS-ti). Fin. **Roast** leg of **lamb** or **mutton.**

lamponi (lahm-POA-ne). Ita. **Raspberries.**

lamprede (lahm-PRAY-day). Ita. A salt-or freshwater fish resembling the **eel** whose fatty flesh is usually stewed.

lamsbout (LAHMZ-bout). Dut. Leg of **lamb.**

lamsvlees (LAHMZ-vlays). Dut. **Lamb.** Also called **lam.**

Lancashire (LANK-kah-shur). Bri. A full-flavored, creamy white cow's-milk **cheese** from England, cooked and pressed, yet soft and crumbly. Used for **Welsh rarebit.**

Landjäger (LAUND-yea-ger). Ger. A **smoked sausage.**

ländstycke (LAHND-stayk). Swe. **Sirloin steak.**

Lane cake (lan kak).   USA. A layer **cake** with a fluffy frosting containing **coconut,** chopped **fruits,** and **nuts.**

lángos (LAAN-gawsh).   Hun. Fried **doughnuts.**

langoustines (lahn-ggoo-sten).   Fre. **Prawns.**

Langres (lowng-rehn).   Fre. A soft **cheese,** similar to **Livarot.**

langue (lahngg).   Fre. Tongue.

languedocienne (lohn-ger-do-ce-en).   Fre. A meat or poultry dish garnished with a mixture of **sautéed eggplant, tomatoes, mushrooms,** and **chopped parsley.**

langues-de-chat (lahngg-der sha).   Fre. Cat's tongue; a long, thin, light, dry **cookie** whose shape resembles a cat's tongue. Often accompanys simple **desserts** and sweet wine.

Languste (lahng-GOOS-ter).   Ger. Clawless variety of **lobster.**

lanttu (LAHNT-too).   Fin. **Rutabaga.**

laos (lohsc).   Ind. A root of the **ginger** family much used in Middle Eastern and Oriental cooking for seasoning.

lapereau (lah-peh-roa).   Fre. Young **rabbit.**

lapin (lah-pang).   Fre. **Rabbit.**

lapin de garenne (lah-pang der gahr-r).   Fre. Wild **rabbit.**

lapin en gibelotte (lah-pang uhn zje-ber-loht).   Fre. **Rabbit stew.**

Lapj (LAHP-yuhs).   Dut. **Scallops,** small slices of meat.

Lapland (LAHP-lahnd).   USA. A very hard **Swiss**-type **cheese** made by Laplanders from reindeer milk.

lapocka (LOP-paw-tsko).   Hun. Shoulder cut of meat.

lapskojs (LOBS-couse).   Swe. A corned beef **hash.**

laqtin (lak-TEN).   Ara. A vegetable similar to **pumpkin.**

laranjada (lah-rahn-ZHAM-dah).   Por. **Orangeade.**

laranjas (lah-RAHN-zhah).   Por. **Oranges.**

lard (lahrd).   USA. Rendered **pork** fat, softer, oilier than other **shortenings;** used in making flaky pastry and for **deep-frying.**

lard (lahr).   Fre. **Bacon.**

larding (LAHR-deng).   USA. The insertion of strips of **pork** fat **(lardoons)** into lean cuts of meat, giving the meat juiciness and flavor.

lardo (LAHR-doa).   Ita. **Salt pork.**

lardo affumicato (LAHR-doa AHFF-oom-e-KAA-toa).   Ita. **Bacon.**

lardoon (lahr-doon).   Fre. A strip of fat with which meat is larded; that is, threaded through with a needle in order to moisten the meat as it cooks.

largo (LAHR-goh).   Mex. A long, thin, yellow-green, fairly hot **chili pepper.**

lasagne (lah-ZAAN-ynah).   Ita. A **casserole** of lasagna **noodles** layered with **sauce,** meat, **cheese,** and other fillings.

lasagna (lah-ZAAN-yah).   Ita. Wide flat strips of **pasta** with rufflled edges; used to make a **casserole** known as **lasagne.**

lassan (LAH-sahn).   Ind. **Garlic.**

lassi (LAH-se).   Ind. **Yogurt** flavored with **rosewater** and **sugar.**

latkes (LAHT-kehs).   Jew. **Potatoes grated** and **fried** in **pancakes.**

letspraengt oksebryst (let-sprayngt OAK-se-brurst).   Dan. **Corned beef.**

latte (LAHT-tay).   Ita. **Milk.**

Lattich (LAH-tikn).   Ger. **Lettuce.**

lattuga (laht-TOO-gah).   Ita. **Lettuce.**

lauch (lowkh).   Ger. **Leeks.**

laugenbrezel (LAU-ken-pret-zehl).   Ger. A special type of **pretzel.**

laung (longh).   Ind. **Clove.**

lauro (LAH-ooroa).   Ita. **Bay leaf.**

lavender (LAH-vehn-dehr).   USA. An **herb** with highly aromatic leaves and flowers that give a bitter pungency to salads.

lavender gem (LAH-ven-dehr gehm).   USA. A delicate, sweet, pink, mini **grapefruit.**

laver (LAH-vehr).   Ind. Thin black **seaweed,** called **sea lettuce.** Called **nori** in Japan.

lax (lahks).   Swe. **Salmon.**

laxforell (LANKS-fo-rayl).   Swe. River **trout.**

laymun bussfayr (lay-MOON BOOC-fair).   Ara. A **citris** fruit found in hot climates; flavor is of **lemon** and **grapefruit.**

Leather cheese (LEH-thehr chez). Ger. A **cheese** made of skim-milk; also known as *Leder.*

leather (LEH-thuhr). USA. A **confection** from early America made of dried-fruit **purées** mixed with **brown sugar** or **honey,** then spread on a baking sheet and thoroughly **dried** in a slow oven; cut in strips and usually rolled and dusted with **sugar.**

leavening (LEAH-vehn-eng). USA. A substance such as **yeast, baking powder, baking soda,** or **egg** white used to produce gas in **dough** or **batter** to lighten and raise it.

Leber (LAY-ber). Ger. Liver.

Leberkäs (LAY-berr-kaizer). Ger. A loaf of mixed **ground meats.**

Leberklösse (LAY-berr-klur-zeh). Ger. Liver **dumplings.**

Leberknödelsuppe (LAY-berr-knur-derl-zup-per). Ger. A **soup** of clear meat **broth** with liver **dumplings.**

Leberspiessli (LAY-ber-spess-le). Ger. A Swiss **shish-kabob** made of bits of liver flavored with **sage** and **bacon,** grilled on a **skewer.**

Leberwurst (LAY-berr-voorst). Ger. A **smoked sausage** made of **ground pork** liver and usually combined with ground pork or **veal.**

Lebkuchen (lab-KOO-ckhen). Ger. Spiced **honey cake.**

lebre (LEH-bruh). Por. **Hare.**

leche (LEH-cheh). Spa. **Milk.**

lechechillas (lay-chay-THE-liahs). Spa. **Sweetbreads.**

lechoncillo asado (loa-che-NE-lyoa ah-SSAH-dhoa). Spa. **Roast** suckling pig.

lechuga (leh-CHOO-gah). Spa. **Lettuce.**

lecithin (LEHS-eh-thehn). USA. An emulsifier used in confectionery goods; keeps oil and water from separating.

Leckerli (LEH-kerr-li). Ger. A rectangular **cinnamon**-flavored Swiss **biscuit** made with **honey,** dried **citrus** peel, **almonds.**

Lee cake (le cak). USA. A white **cake** flavored with **citrus** juice and rind.

leechee (LAY-che). Ind. **Litchi.**

leek (lek). USA. A mild, subtle flavored **onion,** with broader green leaves and white bulb than the **green onion** or **shallot;** lends itself well to **soups, stews;** should be used cooked.

legumbres (leh-GOOM-bres). Spa. **Vegetables.**

legumbres secos (leh-GOOM-bres SEH-kos). Spa. **Dried vegetables.**

legumes (leh-GOOMEZ). USA. **Peas, beans, peanuts;** eaten fresh or **dry, sprouted** or not; high in protein and carbohydrate value.

legumes (lay-GOO-mayss). Por. **Vegetables.**

légumes (lay-gewm). Fre. **Vegetables.**

legumi (lay-GOO-me). Ita. **Vegetables.**

Leicester (LES-tur). Bri. A whole-milk cow's **cheese** made in large cylinders with a hard reddish-brown rind and yellow flaky, moist interior; similar to **Cheddar.**

Leichte Kraftsuppe (LICH-ter krahft-zup-per). Ger. **Chicken** and **veal broth.**

Leidse Kaas (LEYT-ser kahs). Dut. A hard Dutch **cheese** made from partially skimmed cow's milk flavored with **cumin, caraway,** and spices, then molded and pressed.

leipää (LAY-pae). Fin. Bread.

leitão assado (lay-TAWNG ah-SAH-doo). Por. Roast suckling pig.

leite (late). Por. **Milk.**

leite-créme com forófias (LAY-tuh-KREH-muh kohm fou-ROU-feah). Por. **Meringues** in **custard,** similar to **floating island.**

lekash (LE-kasch). Jew. **Honey**-spice **cake,** traditionally served for Rosh Hashanah.

lemon (LEH-muhn). USA. The oblong, acidic, pale yellow fruit of the lemon tree; used for seasoning food and drink.

lemon balm (LEH-muhn bahlm). USA. An **herb** with lemon-scented leaves used fresh in **teas, salads,** and **compotes,** and in making **Chartreuse.**

lemon cucumber (LEH-muhn KU-kom-behr). USA. A burpless **cucumber;** a more delicate flavor than green-skinned varieties; about the size of a tennis ball; turns from lemon to golden-yellow as it matures; use as common cucumber.

lemon curd (LEH-muhn kuhrd). Bri. A pastry **custard** of **lemon** juice, **sugar, butter,** and **egg yolks.**

lemongrass (LEH-muhn-grahss). USA. An **herb** of lemon-scented pampas-grass-type leaves for use in **tea** blends, punches, and **salad**

dressings; a must in Thai and Vietnamese cooking, especially with fish and **poultry.**

lemon verbena (LEH-muhn vehr-BE-nah).   USA. An **herb** of lemony flavored, elongated leaves to be used fresh or dried in **salad dressing,** cold salads, **desserts,** drinks, **teas.**

lencse (LEHN-cheh).   Hun. Lentils.

Lendenbraten (LEHN-dern-braa-tern).   Ger. Roast **sirloin** of beef.

Lendenstuk (LEHN-dern-stayk).   Ger. **Loin.**

lengpán (leng-pan).   Chi. Cold platter.

lengua (LEN-guah).   Spa. Tongue.

lengua de ternera (LEN-guah deh tehr-NEH-rah).   Spa. Calf's tongue.

lenguado (len-GWAH-do).   Spa. **Sole.**

lentejas (layn-TAY-khahss).   Spa. Lentils.

lenticchie (layn-TEK-keay).   Ita. Lentils.

lentilhas (lehn-TE-leahs).   Por. Lentils

lentilles (lahng-te).   Fre. Lentils.

lepre (LAI-pray).   Ita. **Hare.**

LeRoi (lure mwah).   USA. A semisoft **cheese** produced in Wisconsin, bright yellow in color, piquant in flavor.

le rouge royal (lay roogz rah-yahl).   USA. an uncharacteristically large, thick-walled **pepper** with a sweet, mild taste and brilliant flame red coloring; use fresh or cooked.

leshch (lyehshch).   Rus. **Bream.**

lesso (LAYS-soa).   Ita. **Boiled,** or boiled meat.

letterbanket (LET-tur BAHNG-ket).   Dut. **Almond paste.**

lettuce (LETT-us).   USA. Succulent **vegetable** whose leaves are used mostly in **salads.** Lettuce is divided into five categories: **crisphead, butterhead, romaine, looseleaf,** and **stem.** See individual names.

lever (LEH-vehr).   Dan. Liver.

lever (LAY-ver).   Swe. Liver.

leverkorv (LAY-ver-korv).   Swe. Liver **sausage.**

leverpostej (LEH-vehr-poa-stai).   Dan. Liver **pâté.**

levest (LEH-vehsht). Hun. **Soup.**

Leyden (lay-DEHN). Dut. A spiced **cheese** with hard outer crust; pale yellow, semifirm interior streaked with green.

liaison (le-yeh-zon). Fre. The mixture of **egg yolks** and **cream,** used for thickening or binding white **soups** and **sauces.**

liángkaishui (LIANG-kai-shui). Chi. Cold water.

liba (LE-bO). Hun. Goose.

libamá pástértom (LE-bom-maa PAASH-tay-tawn). Hun. A hot appetizer of goose live **pâté** mixed with **butter** and **béchamel sauce,** spices and **brandy,** and served in a flaky **pastry shell.**

libamáj rizottó (LE-bomaa RE-zawt-taw). Hun. Goose liver **risotto.**

licorice (LEHCK-ah-rehsh). USA. An **anise**-flavored **herb** used for flavoring **candies,** pastries, cough lozenges, tobacco preparations.

lichee (LE-zhi). Chi. **Litchi.**

licuado (le-KWA-dou). Spa. **Fruit** drink, usually **citrus.**

liebre (LYAH-bray). Spa. **Hare.**

Liederkranz (LE-der-krantz). USA. One of the most world-renowed of American **cheeses;** soft, mild, rectangular, surface-ripened cheese made in Ohio.

liégeoise (lea-zhwah). Fre. **Garnished** with **juniper berries.**

lien jee (lain ze). Chi. **Lotus** seeds.

lien ngow (lian ou). Chi. **Lotus** root.

lier (le-ay). Fre. To blend.

lièvre (ly-ehvr). Fre. **Hare; rabbit.**

lifit (LEF-feht). Ara. **Turnips.**

light cream (lit krem). USA. **Cream** containing 18–30% milk fat. Also called **coffee cream** or **table cream.**

light whipping cream (lit WHEHP-eng kreem). USA. **Whipping cream** containing 30–36% milk fat.

lights (lits). USA. The lungs of an animal combined with other organs and meat in **stews, pâté,** used in countries around the world, but in United States used in pet foods.

lihaliemi (LI-hah-LAY-mi). Fin. **Broth;** clear **soup.**

lihamurekepiiras (LE-hah-moo-reh-keh-PE-rah). Fin. Meat **pie** with **sour cream** crust.

lihapyörykät (LI-hah-PEWUR-rew-kaet). Fin. Meatball.

lihapiirakka (LI-hah-PER-rah-khah). Fin. Meat **pie.**

li jiàng (le jeang). Chi. **Oyster sauce,** used mostly in Cantonese cooking.

lima (LE-mah). Spa. **Lime.**

lima bean (LI-mah ben). USA. An edible, nutritious, flat, cultivated **bean;** light green color; starchy texture; fibrous pod usually not edible.

limade (le-mahngd). Fre. **Lemon sole.**

limão (le-MOW). Por. **Lemon.**

Limburger (LEHM-buhrr-gehr). Ger. A soft, creamy, surface-ripened, dense, yellow pasteurized cow's milk **cheese** that is highly pungent; has a strong flavor and aroma.

limes (limmz). USA. The fruit of the **lime** tree; having thin rinds and green-yellow; acidic flavor; aromatic.

limon (le-MON). Rus. **Lemon.**

limón (le-MON). Spa. **Lemon.**

limonad (lye-mah-NAH-dah). Rus. Lemonade.

limonada (le-moh-NAH-dah). Por. Lemonade.

limonade (lim-o-nah-deh). Fre. Lemonade.

limonmádét (LE-maw-naadayt). Hun. Lemonade.

limoncillo (le-MON-cel-lo). Spa. **Lemongrass.**

limone (le-MOA-nay). Ita. **Lemon.**

limpa (LEHM-pah). Swe. **Rye** bread.

limpet (LEHM-peht). USA. An edible marine **mollusk,** conical shape; eat the foot and discard the visceral hump; tastes much like **oysters.**

Limpin' Suzan (LEHMP-eng Su-zuhn). USA. A dish of **red beans** and **rice;** a corollary to **Hoppin' John.**

Lingon (LING-on). Swe. Lingonberries, the fruit of the mountain **cranberry.**

lingua (LEN-gwah). Por, Ita. Tongue.

lingua di bue (LENG-gwah de boo). Ita. Ox tongue.

linguado (leng-WAH-doo). Por. **Sole.**

lingue di passero (LEN-gwah de pah-SEH-roh). Ita. Eggless **pasta** that is very flat and thin.

linguiça (len-GWE-sa). Por. **Garlic**-flavored **pork sausage.**

linguine (lynn-GWE-kne). Ita. Flat, thin, narrow, oval-shaped, eggless ribbons of **pasta,** about ⅛-inch wide.

Linse (LIN-zern). Ger. Lentil.

Linsensuppe (LIN-zern-zup-per). Ger. Lentil **soup** made with **sausage.**

linser (LIN-sserr). Nor. Lentils.

linser (LIN-sehr). Dan. Cream **tarts.**

Linzertorte (LIN-tser-tor-ter). Ger. An Austrian **tart** of **ground hazelnut** pastry filled with **raspberry jam** and a latticework crust.

lipeäkala (LI-ppayae-KAH-lah). Fin. Highly pungent, lye-soaked **codfish.**

Liptauer (lep-tower). Ger, Hun, Aus. A white, crumbly sheep's-milk **cheese.**

liqueur (leh-keweur). Fre. A usually sweetened alcoholic beverage, usually flavored variously.

litchee (LE-che). Chi. **Litchi.**

litchi (LE-che). Chi. A delicious, round **fruit** with a very sweet flavor similar to **raisins;** red, leathery outer covering; fresh pulp is translucent white to pale cream in color, when **dried** becomes brown; can be eaten alone or combined with other fruits.

Livarot (le-vah-ro). Fre. A soft, even-textured, tangy, disc-shaped, whole cow's-milk **cheese** with a hard, shiny surface, colored yellow-brown or red.

liverwurst (LEH-vahr-worst). USA. A **sausage** of very smooth texture made of chopped liver seasoned with **onions, pistachios,** and other spices; usually **smoked.**

liyí (le-yu). Chi. **Carp.**

liymuwn (la-MOON). Ara. **Lemon.**

lizhi (le-dzi). Chi. **Litchi.** Also spelled **lichee, lichi, litchie, lizin, lychee.**

lízi (le-dze). Chi. **Chestnut.**

lízi (LE-dzi). Chi. Pear.

lizi (leh-dzi). Chi. **Plum.**

loaf sugar (lowf SCHU-gahr). USA. Granulated **sugars** molded into loaf or rectangular shapes; used in hot drinks; crushed it makes a sparkling **garnish** for iced **cakes.**

lobhia (LHOB-he-ah). Ind. **Balck-eyed peas.**

lo bok (luo bo). Chi. **Loh baak.**

lobscouse (LAHB-skaus). USA. A New England beef and **potato stew.**

lobskovs (LAHB-skoo-oss). Dan. A thick **stew** of beef, **diced potatoes, slices** of **carrots** and **onions;** served with **rye** bread.

lobster (LOHB-stuhr). USA. A family of **crustaceans** prized for its delectable, flavorful meat, particularly the claw and tail meat, but also the **coral (roe)** and **tomalley** (liver).

lobster mushroom (LOHB-stuhr MUHSH-room). USA. A **mushroom** with a slight fish taste; ranging from orange to red in color, and looking like papier mache.

lochshen (LAHK-shehn). Jew. **Noodles.**

locust bean (LOH-cuhs ben). USA. **Carob.**

Lodigiano Formaggio (loa-de-je-AHN-oa fohr-MAHG-je-oa). Ita. A hard, grating **cheese.**

lofschotel (LAHF-scho-tel). Dut. **Chicory.**

løg (lurg). Dan. **Onion.**

loganberry (LOW-guhn-behr-re). USA. The red **berry-fruit** that is a hybrid of the Western **dewberry** and the red **raspberry.**

loh baak (luo bo). Chi. A giant white **radish,** squatty, and slightly fibrous; very crisp, tender, mild, and sweet, much like a turnip in flavor. See **lo bok.**

lohi (LOA-hi). Fin. **Salmon.**

lohipiirakka (LOA-hi-PE-rahk-kah). Fin. **Salmon pie.**

loin (lohen). USA. That part of the beef between the rib and the round; contains the tenderest cuts of the **sirloin** and **short loin.**

löjrom (LURJ-room). Swe. **Roe** from tiny freshwater fish served on hard-cooked **egg** halves with **chopped onion.**

lök (lurk). Swe. **Onion.**

løk (lurk). Nor. **Onion.**

lökodlmar (LUHK-dohl-MAR). Swe. **Stuffed onion rolls.**

lok dow (lok dou). Chi. Tiny olive-green **mung beans,** used for sprouting.

löksoppa (LOHK-sop-pa). Swe. **Onion soup.**

lombata (loam-BAA-tah). Ita. **Loin.**

lombardo (lohm-BAHR-doh). Ita. A **Parmesan**-type **cheese** with a sharp, aromatic flavor and granular texture.

lombo (LOAM-boa). Ita. **Loin.**

lombo (LOHN-boh). Por. **Loin.**

lombo de vitela (LOHM-boh day ve-TEH-lah). Por. **Veal loin.**

lo mein (low mian). Chi. Fresh Chinese **egg noodles.**

lomi-lomi salmon (LOH-me-LOH-me SAHM-uhn). USA. A Hawaiian dish of **salted salmon** cooked with chopped **tomatoes, Maui onions,** and **scallions.**

lomo (LOH-moh). Spa. **Loin.**

London broll (LUHN-dohn browl). USA. A boneless cut of beef from the **flank** that is **marinated** and **broiled** and **sliced** on an angle.

longans (lohng-yahn). Chi. "Dragon's eye"; a small, round **fruit** with brown skin, crispy opaque flesh, and a single large seed; similar to **lithci,** but not as sweet; dried or fresh-canned.

longaniza (lohn-gah-NE-thah). Spa. A large **sausage** of **pork, pimento, garlic,** and **majoram.**

long beans (lohng ben). USA. A member of the Chinese **green bean** family, whose flavor is somewhat stronger than ordinary green beans; also called **asparagus beans, yard-long beans.**

longe de veau (lonzhe der voa). Fre. **Loin** of **veal.**

long-grain rice (lohng-gran ris). USA. A basic type of rice that separates into distinct kernels when cooked; grains are four to five times as long as wide; many varieties; **basamati,** bluebonnet, **Carolina,** della, lebonnet, newrex, jojutla are a few.

Longhorn (LOHNG-hohrn). USA. A mild, firm **Cheddar** named after a breed of cow from whose milk the **cheese** is made.

Long Island duck (lohng I-luhnd duhk). USA. A specially raised **duck** for commercial use; commonly seven to eight weeks old and weighs three to five pounds.

lóngxia (loung-siah). Chi. **Lobster.**

lóngxu niú rò (loong she niu row). Chi. Thinly sliced beef served with **sautéed asparagus.**

long white potato (lawng whit pah-TA-toah). USA. One of four main varieties of **potatoes;** best used for **boiling,** good for **baking** and **frying;** other varieties are **round red, round white,** and **russet.**

lonza (LOHN-tzah). Ita. **Cured pork loin.**

looseleaf lettuce (LOOS-lef LEHT-uhs). USA. A fragile, delicious **salad lettuce;** the loose leaves branch from a single stalk, do not bunch, vary in color; used as plate liners and garnishes. Varieties include Matchless (deer's tongue variety), Oakleaf (green and bronze), Prizehead (red-pigmented leaf), and Salad Bowl (looks like a nosegay).

lop cheeng (lah chaoong). Chi. Spicy **pork sausages.**

loquat (LOA-kwaht). USA. The sweet-sour **apricot**-shaped **fruit** of a Japanese evergreen; has yellow-orange skin, deep orange flesh, cherry-like flavor; used cooked in **jams** and **jellies;** eaten fresh in **fruit salads,** or **baked** in **desserts.**

Lorraine (loh-RAIN). Ger. A small, firm, delicate **cheese** often containing **pine nuts** or **pistachio nuts.**

lorraine, a la (lohr-rain). Fre. Served with the **garnish** of red **cabbage** balls and small **potatoes sautéed** in **butter.**

lotte (lot). Fre. **Burbot; monkfish.**

lotus root (LO-tuhs root). USA. Root of the Chinese **lotus** plant, when peeled and sliced is crisp, white, and filled with holes resembling snowflakes; may be eaten **raw** or cooked.

lotus seeds (LO-tuhs seds). USA. Seeds of the Chinese **lotus** plant that when dried are yellow in color, used in **stews** and **desserts** and **roasted** to make a kind of **popcorn.**

loup (loo). Fre. **Sea bass.**

lovage (LOHV-adj). USA. **Celery**-flavored **herb** whose leaves, stems, roots, and seeds are all edible.

love and tangle (lohv and TAHNG-uhl). USA. **Doughnuts** that are twisted and entwined, then **deep-fried.**

love apples (lohv AHP-puhl). USA. A romantic term for **tomatoes** because originally they were thought to have aphodisiacal attributes.

low-fat milk (lo-faht mehlk).   USA. Cow's **milk** that contains not more than 2% milk fat.

low mull (lo-muhl).   USA. A **vegetable** and meat **stew** of varying ingredients; related to **mulligan stew.**

lowza (lahz).   Ara. **Almond.**

lox (lohks).   Jew.   Salt-cured **salmon** soaked in water to remove some of the **salt,** traditionally eaten with **bagels.**

lsanat (LI-SAH-naht).   Ara. **Tongue.**

lubina (loo-BE-nah).   Spa. **Sea bass.**

lubyi (LLOO-be).   Ara. **Green beans.**

lü chá (lu tsah).   Chi. Green **tea.**

lucullus (luh-KEHL-luhs).   Ita. Lavish, luxurious; applies to a subterranean **mushroom**-like fungus used for **garnishing** and flavoring.

luganeaga (loo-gah-neh-AH-gah).   Ita. Fresh **pork sausage,** mildly flavored with **Parmesan cheese** and made in long tubes, not links.

luk (look).   Rus. **Onion.**

lukewarm (LOOK-wahrm).   USA. Moderately warm; approximately 100°F.

lumaca (loo-MAA-kay).   Ita. **Snail.**

lumberjack pie (LUHM-behr-jahk pi).   USA. A meat **pie** made of **vegetables** and deer meat.

lumpfish caviar (LUHMP-fisch KAHV-e-ahr).   USA. A **caviar** substitute; **roe** of the lumpfish salted and sold as caviar.

lump sugar (luhmp SCHU-gahr).   USA. A granulated **sugar** cut into half-inch by half-inch cubes; usually used in hot beverages.

Lüneberg (LOO-neh-behrg).   Aus. A **cheese** made with milk that has been colored with **saffron.**

luó bo gao (luo bo gao).   Chi. **Turnip cake; a dim sum.**

luó hàn zjai (law han dzai).   Chi. "Budda's vegetable dish"; **bamboo shoots, nuts, mushrooms** sautéed in **soy sauce** and **sherry.**

lutefisk (LOO-teh-fesk).   Nor. Dried **cod,** soaked in lye prior to cooking; eaten with **cream sauce** or **pork** drippings.

lutefisk (LOOT-fesk).   Swe. Stockfish, usually **cod,** soaked in lye prior to cooking; a Christmas specialty.

luumut (LOO-moot). Fin. **Plums.**

luzener alleblei (loo-ZEN-ner AHL-le-bly). Ger. A Swiss **vegetable** and **mushroom salad.**

lychee (LE-che). Chi. **Litchi.**

Lymeswold (LIMZ-wohld). Bri. A new **cheese,** essentially a milk blue **Brie** with a delicate white rind and soft creamy **paste** with blue veining.

Lyonerwurst (LEW-oa-nayr-voorst). Ger. **Garlic**-flavored **ham sausage.**

lyonnaise (ly-awng-nehz). Fre. Seasoned with **onions;** generally **chopped** onions **sautéed** in **butter** and reduced with white wine and **vinegar,** then **strained.**

lys saus (lewss sowss). Nor. Any light **sauce:** white wine sauce, **curry** sauce, **horseradish** sauce.

maanz (mahz). Ind. Meat.

maçã (mah-SAH). Por. **Apple.**

macadamia nut (mahk-ah-DAM-e-ah nuht). USA. A round **nut** that is white, sweet, high in fat, and usually roasted before purchase; a fine **dessert nut.**

maçapão (mah-sah-PAHNG). Por. **Marzipan.**

macaron (mah-kah-rohn). Fre. **Macaroon.**

macaroni (mahc-ah-RON-e). Ita. Tube-shaped dried **pasta.**

macaroni and cheese (mahc-ah-RON-e ahnd chez). USA. An original American dish made by layering boiled **macaroni** in a dish, alternating with **grated** or **diced American Cheddar** or **Swiss cheese,** then baking till the cheese melts and the top is lightly browned.

macaroon (MAHK-ah-roon). USA. A small, round **cookie** made of **almond paste, sugar, and egg** whites; in United States usually shredded **coconut** is added.

macarrão (mah-kah-RROW). Por. **Macaroni.**

macarrones (mah-kahr-ROA-nehs). Spa. **Macaroni.**

macarrones con queso (mah-kahr-ROA-nehs kohn KAY-ssoa). Spa. **Macaroni and cheese.**

macãs (ma-SANSH). Por. **Apples.**

maccarello (mahk-chah-REHL-loa). Ita. **Mackerel.**

maccheroni (mahk-keh-ROA-ne). Ita. Large **spaghetti** with a hole in the middle.

mace (mac). USA. A spice made from the net-like covering of the **nutmeg** seed that is dried to an orange-brown color and powdered; tastes like nutmeg with a hint of **cinnamon.**

macédoine (mah-sah-dwan). Fre. A mixture of various **vegetables** or **fruits** set in a galatin mold; also, a **fruit salad** flavored with **liqueurs** and **syrup.**

macédonia (mah-CHAY-doa-ne). Ita. **Fruit compote** flavored with **maraschino liqueur.**

macerate (MAHS-er-rat). USA. To steep in liquid; usually refers to fresh **fruit** steeped in **liqueur.**

macéré (mahs-eh-re). Fre. **Pickled.**

mache (mah-che). Fre. **Lamb's lettuce;** spoon-shaped, rounded green leaves; a sweet **hazelnut** taste; used fresh in **salads** or cooked like **spinach.**

machi (MAH-che). Ind. Fish.

made (MAH-day). Fin. **Burbot.**

madeleine (mad-ah-lynn). Fre. A classic **tea cake** made of **flour, sugar, butter,** and baked in a shell mold.

madère (mah-dehr). Fre. Prepared with the Spanish wine, **Madeira.**

maderise (mah-dres). Fre. Wine that has acquired a brownish color and the aroma of **Madeira** due to spoilage by oxidation.

madras (mahd-rahs). Fre. Flavored with **curry** or **chutney.**

madrilene (mah-dre-len). Fre. **Tomato**-flavored **beef consommé.**

maelk (mehlk). Dan. **Milk.**

mafalde (mah-FAHL-day). Ita. Long strips of narrow or medium width **pasta** with fluted edges.

magdalenas (mahg-dah-LEH-nahs). Spa. **Cornmeal muffins.**

Magerkäse (mah-gehr-Kahz-zeh). Aus. A semifirm, skimmed-milk, sweet, mild, but "thin" **cheese;** low butter fat content.

maggi (MADG-ji). USA. A concentrated seasoning **sauce** used to enhance the flavor of **gravies,** sauces for meats, as well as to make **broth.**

maggiorana (mad-joar-RAA-nah). Ita. **Majoram.**

magliyy (MAHK-le). Ara. **Fried.**

magro (MAH-groa). Ita. Lean; a dish without meat.

mahlab (MAAH-lahb). Ara. A seasoning used in **dough** or pastries; it is a small seed of the stone of a wild **cherry.**

Mahón (MA-hon). Spa. A goat **cheese** from Menorca.

mahonesa (mah-oa-NAY-sah). Spa. **Mayonnaise.**

mah tai (maah te). Chi. **Water chestnuts.**

maiale (maae-AA-lay). Ita. **Pork.**

Maifisch (MAE-fish). Ger. **Shad.**

maigre (meh-gruh). Fre. A dish without meat; applied to Lenten dishes.

Mainauer (MEH-nowr). Ger. A semihard, whole-cream **cheese.**

maionese (mahe-OA-nays). Ita. **Mayonnaise.**

Mais (mighss). Ger. **Corn.**

mais (mays). Fre. Sweet **corn.**

maison (meh-zhon). Fre. Designates a dish of the restaurant's own special recipe.

Maisturta (MIGHSS-tuhr-tah). Ger. **Corn pudding.**

maito (MAH-toaah). Fin. **Milk.**

maitokahvi (MAH-toaah-KAH-vi). Fin. **Coffee** with hot **milk.**

maitre d'hotel sauce (meh-tr doh-tel saus). Fre. A yellow sauce of **butter, lemon** juice, **parsley, egg** yolk, seasonings; served on **grilled** meats; also, food that is quickly and plainly prepared and flavored with **parsley.**

maiz (mah-ES). Spa. **Dried corn.**

maize (maz). USA. An American Indian word for **corn.**

majonnäs (mah-yoo-NAYSS). Swe. **Mayonnaise.**

Majoran (mah-yo-RAAN). Ger. **Marjoram.**

Makaroni (MAH-kah-roa-ne). Ger. **Macaroni.**

makaronilaatikko (MAH-kah-roa-ni-LAA-tik-koa). Fin. **Macaroni** stewed in **milk** and **cream** with **egg yolks.**

makaruni (MAAH-kah-roa-ne). Ara. Refers to **pastas; spaghetti** and **macaroni.**

makbus (mack-BOOC). Ara. **Pickled** or **preserved** in **vinegar** or oil.

makhan (MAH-kehn). Ind. **Butter.**

makkara (MAHK-kah-rah). Fin. **Sausage.**

mako (MA-koh). Jap. **Shark.**

makreel (mah-KRAYL). Dut. **Mackerel.**

Makrele (mah-KRAY-ler). Ger. **Mackerel.**

makrill (MAHK-ril). Swe. **Mackerel.**

Makronen (mah-KROA-nern). Ger. **Macaroons.**

makroner (mah-KRO-nehr). Dan. **Macaroons.**

maksa (MAHK-sah). Fin. Liver.

malaga (mah-LAH-ghah). Spa. A sweet **sherry** that is dark and heavy.

malai (ma-LIE-e). Ind. **Cream** of all kinds: **heavy, light, sour,** and **coconut.**

malanga (mah-LAHNG-gah). Mex. A tuber whose stems are also peeled and cooked like **potatoes;** a somewhat starchier taste than ordinary potatoes; a staple in Central American countries.

malasado (mah-lah-SAH-doo). Por. A **puff pastry** made from an **egg batter, deep-fried,** then rolled in **sugar.**

malay apple (MA-la AHP-pul). USA. A crispy, red, **pear**-shaped **fruit** with a bland flavor.

malet kött (MAH-let choht). Swe. **Ground beef.**

malfatti (mahl-FAHT-te). Ita. **Gnocchi** of **spinach** and **ricotta.**

malfuf (mahl-FUHF). Ara. **Cabbage.**

malfrewfa (MAL-fuf). Ara. **Cabbage.**

malk (mal). Ara. Salt.

malosol (mah-lah-SAWL). Rus. "Prepared with little salt"; All types of **caviar** can be prepared malosol and be considered fresh caviar.

malpoora (mal-POOH-rah). Ind. Sweet whole **wheat crepes** flavored with **crushed fennel.**

malsouka (mahl-SOO-kah). Gre. Phyllo. Also known as **filo, brik, yukka.**

malt (mahlt). USA. **Barley** germinated by softening in water, used in brewing and distilling. Also, **malt** powder can be flavored, such as with **chocolate,** then dissolved in **milk** to make a beverage.

malt-based vinegar (mahlt-basd VEH-neh-gahr). USA. Fermentation of an infusion of **barley malt** or **cereals** whose starch has been converted by malt.

maltagliati (mahl-tahl-YAH-teh). Ita. Flat **pasta,** half-inch thick, cut on the bias; used basically in **bean soups.**

maltaise (mahl-teh). Fre. **Hollandaise sauce** flavored with **grated orange** rind and the juice of a **blood orange.**

Malzbier (MAHLTS-ber). Ger. A dark and sweet low-alcohol **malt beer.**

mamão (mah-MOW). Por. **Papaya.**

mamey sapote (mah-me sah-PO-tay). Mex. The round **fruit** of a Central American tropical tree with coarse, brown skin, smooth orange pulp, eaten fresh or in **ice cream.** Also called *mammee.*

mämmi (MAEM-mi). Fin. A **rye pudding** made with **molasses,** flavored with **bitter orange** and served with **cream;** traditional at Easter.

manapua (mah-nah-POO-ah). USA. A **Hawaiian dough** bun filled with **pork, bean paste,** or other **stuffings,** then steamed.

manche (mensh). Fre. The projecting bone of a chop.

Manchego (mahn-CHAY-goa). Spa. A ewe's-milk **cheese** with a pale, golden curd whose rind is rubbed with **olive oil** after a greenish-black mold is brushed off.

manchette (mensh-ayt). Fre. The paper frill used to cover the projecting bone of a chop.

Mandarine (mahn-dah-RE-ner). Ger. **Tangerine.**

mandarine (mahng-dah-ren). Fre. **Tangerine.**

mandarino (mahn-dah-REE-noa). Ita. **Tangerine.**

mandarin orange (MAHN-dah-rehn AWH-rahnj). USA. The reddish-orange, loose-skinned fruit of the spiny Chinese orange tree.

mandelbiskvier (MAN-dehl-bisk-VE-er). Swe. **Almond cookies.**

Mandeln (MAHN-derln). Ger. **Almonds.**

mandeln (MAHN-dayl). Swe. **Almonds.**

Mandeltorte (MAHN-derl-tor-ter). Ger. An **almond torte** with a **custard filling** and **butter icing.**

mandlar (MAND-lar). Swe. **Almonds.**

mandler (MAHN-dlerr). Nor. **Almonds.**

mandler (MAHN-lerr). Dan. **Almonds.**

mandoo (MAN-du). Kor. Meat-filled **dumplings,** seasoned **with soy sauce, toasted sesame** seed, **garlic, pepper,** and **onion; steamed, fried,** or **boiled** in a **broth;** similar to **won ton.**

mandorla (MAHN-doar-lay). Ita. **Almond.**

mange-tout (monj-too). Fre. A **pea** or **bean** eaten with the shell on; such as **sugar snap** or **snow pea.**

mángguo (mang-guo). Chi. **Mango.**

manglam. (MAHNG-luhm). Iri. **Pie.**

mango (MAHNG-go). USA. A flattish-oval tropical Indian **fruit;** when full-ripened, has deep orange or yellowish-green skin with smooth golden flesh; eaten fresh or when green is cooked in **chutneys** and **preserves.**

mangosteen (MAHN-go-sten). USA. A two- to three-inch **fruit** with an exquisite milky juice; has five or six sections; may be easily scooped out and eaten with a spoon.

mangue (mahn-gah). Fre. **Mango.**

manicotti (mahn-eh-COHT-teh). Ita. A thin, tubular **pasta** stuffed with a **ricotta cheese** mixture and baked in a **sauce.**

manioc (mah-NE-oahk). Spa. **Tapioca.** Also called **cassava,** yuca.

mannagrynspudding (MAH-na-gri-ins-PU-ding). Swe. **Semolina pudding.**

mannitol (MAHN-e-tohl). USA. A sweetening agent.

mano (MAHN-oh). Mex. A stone that is rolled over the surface of a metate to **grind grains** and spices.

manoa (mah-NOH-ah). USA. A Hawaiian **salad lettuce** of the **butterhead lettuce** family; smallish head, slightly loose leaves; darker green on outer leaves, pale green on inner leaves; holds up well in warm weather.

mansikkasoppa (MAHN-sik-kah-soh-pah). Fin. **Strawberries** with **cream** and **sugar.**

mansikkat (MAHN-sik-kaht). Fin. **Strawberries.**

mansikkatorttu (MAHN-sik-kah-TOART-too). Fin. **Strawberry tart** or **pie.**

mántáu (man-toh). Chi. **Steamed** buns.

manteca (mahn-TEH-kah). Mex. **Lard.**

Manteca (mahn-TE-kah). Ita. A cow's-milk **cheese** wrapped around a pat of **butter.**

mantecado (mahn-teh-KAH-dhoa). Spa. A rich vanilla **ice cream** into which **whipped cream** has been folded.

manteenmäti (MAH-tayn-MAE-ti). Fin. **Burbot caviar;** a supreme delicacy.

manteiga (mahn-TAY-gah). Por. **Butter.**

manteli (MAHN-tay-lit). Fin. **Almond.**

mantelikokkare (MAHN-tay-lit-koak-kay-ray). Fin. **Almond custard** served with **fruit sauce.**

mantequilla (mahn-teh-KE-yah). Spa. **Butter.**

mányú (man-yu). Chi. **Eel.**

manzana (mahn-ZAH-nah). Spa. **Apple.**

manzanilla (mahn-zah-NILL-lah). Spa. **Chamomile** tea; also, a Spanish **sherry.**

manzano banana (mahm-ZAHN-noh bah-NAH-nah). Mex. A short, stubby **banana,** with its flavor accented by that of **strawberries** and **apples;** eaten fresh out of hand or in **salads** and **desserts.**

manzo (MAHN-dzoa). Ita. Beef; *manzo arrosto* (MAHN-dzoa ahr-ROA-stoa) **roast** beef; *manzo brasiato* (MAHN-dzoa brah-SAA-toa) **braised** beef; *manzo salato* (MAHN-dzoa sah-LAH-toa) **corned beef;** *manzo stufato* (MAHN-dzoa stoo-FAH-toa) **beef stew;** *manzo uso* (MAHN-dzoa OO-soa) **pot roast.**

maple syrup (MA-puhl seh-ruhp). USA. **Syrup** made from the sap of the sugar maple tree, used for flavoring.

mápó dòufù (MA-po doh-FOO). Chi. **Bean curd** with minced **pork** in **hot sauce.**

maque choux (MAHCK-shoo). USA. A **Cajun corn** dish, sweet and highly seasoned.

maquereau (mah-ker-roa). Fre. **Mackerel.**

maräng (ma-RANG). Swe. **Meringue.**

maraschino (mahr-ah-skee-noh). Fre. A flavoring for beverages and **confectionery** made from oils extracted from the crushed seeds of the Royal Anne **cherry;** a favorite flavoring of the Middle East.

marasquin (mah-rah-sken). Fre. A delicately flavored white liquor, used for flavoring.

marble (MAHR-buhl). USA. A term used to describe the small, white flecks of fat throughout muscle tissue, generally favored in beef for tenderness and taste. In pastry it denotes light and dark **dough** swirled together to resemble marbled stone.

marcassin (mahr-kahs-sang). Fre. Young wild boar.

marchand de vin (mah-shon day vang). Fre. A red wine **sauce** flavored with **chopped shallots, parsley,** and **butter;** similar to **bordelaise;** served on **grilled** meats.

marchpane (mahrch-payn). Fre. **Marzipan.**

marechale (mahr-shahl). Fre. Small cuts of **poultry** or meats, dipped in beaten **egg,** rolled in bread crumbs, **fried** in **butter,** and **garnished** with sliced **truffles, green peas,** or sometimes **asparagus** tips.

maree (mah-rer). Fre. All saltwater fish and **shellfish.**

marennes (mah-rehyn). Fre. A variety of small **oyster.**

margarine (mahr-jah-rehn). Fre. A **butter** substitute (oleomargarine) made from vegetable oils and ripened skim **milk** churned to spreading consistency, usually fortified with vitamin A; also, called oleo.

marguery (mahr-gew-rey). Fre. **Hollandaise** flavored with **oyster** or fish **essence.**

Maribo (MAH-re-boa). Dan. A soft, mild, long, oblong **cheese** of cow's milk with yellow wax coating and a white interior with small holes.

Marie Louise (mah-re loo-ez). Fre. A classic **garnish** of **artichoke** hearts filled with **mushroom purée** and **soubise.**

marignan (mah-re-yawng). Fre. A rich, rum-syrup-soaked **yeast dough** pastry with **apricot glaze** and filled with **chantilly creme.**

marigold (MAHR-e-gold). USA. A plant whose dried centers are sometimes used as a color substitute for **saffron,** and the young leaves used in **salads;** not an **herb,** but used as an herb.

Marille (mah-RIL-lern). Ger. **Apricot.**

marinade (mah-re-nahd). Fre. A preparation of oil, **herbs, vinegar,** or wine in which food is steeped before cooking, or serving, to flavor, moisten, and soften it.

marinara (mahr-ah-NAHR-rah). Ita. A spicy **tomato sauce** that is prepared quickly from few ingredients, but never includes cheese.

marinate (MAH-re-nate). USA. The act of steeping food in a **marinade.**

marinato (mah-re-NAA-toa). Ita. **Pickled; marinated.**

mariné (mah-re-nay). Fre. **Marinated, pickled.**

mariniere (mah-re-nehr). Fre. **Seafood** cooked with **parsley, chopped shallots, butter** in white wine and **garnished** with **mussels.**

Mariniert (mahrin-NERT). Ger. **Pickled.**

Marinierter Hering (mahrin-NERT HAY-ring). Ger. **Pickled herring.**

marionberry (MAH-re-und BEHR-re). USA. A hybrid of two varieties of **blackberries:** ollalie and chehalis.

mariscos (mah-RES-kohs). Spa. **Shellfish; shrimp** or **scallops.**

maritozzo (mah-re-TOHZ-zoh). Ita. Breakfast bun.

marjolaine (mahr-zho-lehn). Fre. Sweet **marjoram.** Also a pastry of **meringue** with **almond** and **filbert** layered with **chocolate, praline,** and **buttercream.**

marjoram (mah-JOR-rum). USA. An **herb** with a warm, sweet fragrance, and delicate **oregano**-like flavor; use with meats, **egg** dishes, **soups, vegetables;** also called **sweet marjoram.**

Mark (mahrk). Ger. **Marrow.**

markklösschen (mahrk-KLURSK-hern). Ger. Bread **dumplings** mixed with beef **marrow;** served with clear **soups.**

Marlborough pie (MAHRRL-burr-rou pi). USA. An **applesauce** and **cream pie,** thickened with **eggs** and **sugar,** flavored with **nutmeg** and **sherry;** baked to a gelled texture.

marmalade (MAHR-mah-lad). Bri, USA. A clear, sweetened, tender **citrus jelly** in which pieces of the **fruit** and rind are suspended.

marmelad (mar-meh-LAHD). Swe. **Marmelade.**

marmelade (mahr-mer-lahd). Fre. A thick, sweetened, **jelly**-like **purée** of **fruit** or **onion.**

Marmelade (mahr-meh-LAA-der). Ger. **Jam.**

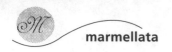

marmellata (mahr-mayl-LAA-tah). Ita. **Marmelade; jam.**

marmite (mahr-met). Fre. A pure **vegetable extract,** used to make a strong, rich **stock** for meat **soups.** Also a cooking pot.

Marmorkuchen (mahr-mor-KOOK-hern). Ger. Marble **cake.**

Maroilles (mahr-wahl). Fre. A square cow's-milk **cheese** with a reddish rind, yellow interior, creamy flavor, rich and tangy, strong aroma.

Maronen (mah-RAH-nehn). Ger. **Chestnut.**

marquise (mahr-quehss). Fre. A fruit ice with **whipped cream** folded in.

marquq (mahr-KOOK). Ara. Very thin, round, flat bread, rolled like Italian **pizza dough.**

marron (mahr-awng). Fre. A cultivated **chestnut** used in **stuffings,** pastries.

marroni (mahr-ROA-ne). Ita. **Chestnuts.**

marrow (MAHR-ro). Bri. A long, large **summer squash.**

marrow (MAHR-ro). USA. The soft connective tissue in the hollow of long bones, used in **osso bucco** and **bordelaise sauce.**

marrow bones (MAHR-ro bonz). USA. The long bones of beef and **veal,** cut in short pieces to **poach** or **braise** to solidify the marrow for use in certain dishes or to eat as a delicacy.

Marsala (mahr-SAH-lah). Ita. A wine similar to **Madeira.**

marsepein (MAHR-seh-pain). Dut. **Marzipan.**

marshmallow (MAHRSH-mahl-lo). USA. A **confection** made from **corn syrup, sugar, egg** whites, and **gelatin** beaten to a light, spongy, creamy consistency.

marzipan (MAHR-ze-pahn). USA. An Arabian confection of **almond paste, sugar, and egg** whites, often colored and shaped into various of fruits, flowers, animals.

masa (MAH-sah). Mex. **Dough** made from **corn flour.**

masa harina (MAH-sah ah-RE-nah) Mex. Dehydrated **corn flour.**

masala (ma-SAH-la). Ind. A blend of seasonings and spices.

masar dal (MA-sahr dahl). Ind. Pink lentils.

Mascarpone (mahz-KAHRR-poan). Ita. A thick, velvety, rich, soft cow's-milk **cheese** that has a delicate sweet flavor and is served with fruit and pastries like **cream;** has the texture of **whipped cream.**

mash (mahsh). USA. To crush food until its original form is entirely lost.

mask (mahsk). USA. A French term meaning to cover food completely; such as a **sauce** over food before serving, or to put **meringue** on a **pie.**

maslina (mahs-LYE-ni). Rus. **Olives.**

maslo (MAH-sloh). Rus. **Butter.**

masquer (mahsk). Fre. To **mask.**

massa (MAH-sah). Por. The word for a number of **spaghetti** products.

massepain (mah-sah-pahng). Fre. **Marzipan.**

Mastgeflugel (MAHST-ger-flew-gerl). Ger. Specially raised grain-fed **poultry** of exceptionally fine quality.

matar (MA-tehr). Ind. **Chickpeas.**

matcha (mah-CHAH). Jap. A powdered **tea** used for the famous Japanese tea ceremony.

maté (MAH-ta). Spa. The leaves and shoots of a South American holly, rich in caffeine, used to make the aromatic beverage, yerba maté. Also referred to as **yerba maté.**

matelote (mah-ter-lot). Fre. A **stew** of freshwater fish usually and red or white wine. Also **pochouse.**

matignon (mah-te-yawng). Fre. A blend of **minced vegetables** used as a base or for seasoning; similar to **mirepoix,** which is **diced.**

Matjesherring (MAHT-yeh-hay-ring). Ger. Young virgin **herring** that has not yet spawned; of high quality.

matjessill (MAAT-yehs-sil). Swe. Marinated **herring fillets,** served with **sour cream** and **chives.**

matsutake (maht-soo-tah-ke). Jap. Pine **mushrooms;** dark brown with thick, meaty stem; scented with the fragrance of pine woods.

mattha (MAH-tah). Ind. **Yogurt** drink flavored with **salt, roasted cumin,** and fresh **mint** leaves.

matzo (MAHT-sah). Jew. Flat, unleavened bread eaten during Passover. Also spelled *matzoh.*

matzo meal (MAHT-sah mel). Jew. Meal made of **matzo** to be used in breading food as well in various dishes served during Passover.

Maui onion (MAWH-we UHN-yuhn). USA. A mild, sweet Hawaiian **onion;** golden brown bulb with white flesh; eaten raw in **salads** or cooked in **soups, stews.**

Maultaschen (MAHUL-teaschen). Ger. A savory dish of **ground pork, veal,** and **spinach** wrapped in **noodle dough** and served in **gravy.**

maward (mahw-wahrd). Ara. **Rose water;** a flavoring used in **confectionery.**

mawzat (mahw-oo-ZEHT). Ara. Meat shanks; the leg portions of beef or **lamb.**

May wine (mai vighn). Ger. A spring punch made of white wine lightly sweetened and flavored with **woodruff,** then chilled and served with **strawberries.**

mayonnaise (may-o-nayz). Fre. A basic cold **sauce** that is an emulsion of **egg yolks** seasoned with **vinegar** and **mustard** with oil gradually added to make a thick sauce.

mayonnaise verte (may-o-nayz vehrt). Fre. **Mayonnaise** flavored with finely **minced spinach, watercress, parsley,** or **tarragon,** which **colors** the sauce green.

Maytag Blue (MA-tahg bloo). USA. A blue-veined, tangy, smooth-textured **cheese** made with the milk of holstein-friesian cows from the farmlands of Newton, Iowa; rarely seen elsewhere.

maza (MAZ-zah). Ara. **Appetizers** or **hors d'oeuvres.**

mazahir (mah-ZAH-hehr). Ara. **Orange** blossom **essence.**

mazat (MAHS-lah). Rus. Oil.

mazzancolle (mats-tsan-KOL-le). Ita. Large **prawns.**

mead (med). Fin. A fermented drink of water, **honey, malt,** and **yeast.**

mealie crenchie (MEL-e KREN-che). Bri. **Oatmeal** flakes fried in **bacon fat;** served with **eggs** and **bacon** at breakfast. Also called *mealie greachie.*

meatballs (MET-bawlz). USA. **Ground meat** shaped into globular shapes, varying in size from half-inch to one inch.

meat birds (met burdz). USA. Very similar to **veal** birds; slices of meat filled with savory **stuffing,** rolled, **skewered** or tied, browned in fat, and **braised.**

meat grades (met gradz).   USA. Grades of beef as designated by the U.S. Department of Agriculture:
Prime: (prym).   From young, specially fed cattle, well marbled; tender fine flavor and texture; usually aged.
Choice: (choys).   High quality, with somewhat less marbling than prime; tender, good flavor.
Good: (guhd).   Still a relatively tender grade, with a higher ratio of lean; less juiciness and flavor.
Standard: (STAHN-dahrd).   From low-quality young animals, virtually no marbling; bland flavor; not tender.
Commercial/Utility: (kom-MEHR-shuhl/u-TEHL-ee-te).   Meat from old animals; better flavor than Standard; tough.

meat loaf (met lohf).   USA. A dish made of **ground beef,** bread crumbs, and seasonings, baked in a deep rectangular pan, turned out on platter and served.

Mecklenburg Skim (MEHK-lehn-burg Skehm).   Ger. A hard, skim-milk **cheese** colored with **saffron.**

medaglioni (may-dah-LYOA-ne).   Ita. **Filet** of beef.

médallion (may-dah-yawng).   Fre. A small circular slice of meat or **poultry.**

medisterpølse (meh-DES-terr-purl-sserr).   Dan. **Pork sausage.**

medium batter (ME-de-uhm BAHT-tehr).   USA. A **flour** mixture that contains one and a half parts flour to one part liquid; such as **thick gravies, pie fillings.**

medium white sauce (ME-de-uhm whit sahus).   USA. A **roux**-liquid mixture that contains a fat-flour ratio of two tablespoons each to one cup liquid; such as used in **soups** and thin **gravies.**

medlar (MEHD-lehr).   Bri. **Loquat.**

meen see jeong (me soh GE-ong).   Chi. Salty yellow or brown **bean sauce.**

Meerrettich (MAYR-reh-tikh).   Ger. **Horseradish.**

meetha (ME-tah).   Ind. Sweet.

Mehlpüt (MAYL-pewt).   Ger. A **dessert** of stewed pears with **dumplings.**

Mehlspeise (MAYL-shpigh-zer).   Ger. A flour-based **pancake** or **dumpling** with which to make a dish, such as **Strudel.**

mehu (MAY-hoon). Fin. Juice.

mein (men). Chi. The general word for **noodles.**

méizi (may dzi). Chi. **Prunes.**

mejillones (may-khe-LYOA-nayss). Spa. **Mussels.**

mejorana (meh-khoa-RAH-nah). Spa. **Marjoram.**

mel (mayl). Por. **Honey.**

mela (MAY-lah). Ita. **Apple.**

melaço (may-LAH-soo). Por. **Molasses.**

melagrana (may-lahg-RAH-nah). Ita. **Pomegranate.**

melancia (meh-lahn-SE-ah). Por. **Watermelon.**

melanger (may-lon-zhay). Fre. To mix or blend; **mélange:** a mixture.

melanzana (may-lahn-TSAA-nay). Ita. **Eggplant.**

melão (mel-OWN). Por. **Melon.**

melba toast (MEHL-bah tost). Bri. Very thin slices of bread, **toasted** very dry.

melboller (mehl-BOAL-er). Dan. **Dumplings.**

Mel Fino (mehl FE-noh). Ita. A blue-veined, creamy, unusual **dessert cheese.**

melidzanes (meh-le-DZAH-nah). Gre. **Eggplant.**

melk (MEL-uk). Dut. **Milk.**

melkbrood (MEL-uk-broht). Dut. **Milk** bread; as opposed to bread made with water.

melkchocolade (MEL-uk-zhoh-ko-lah-duh). Dut. **Chocolate** made with **milk.**

meloen (muh-LOON). Dut. **Melon.**

melon (MEHL-uhn). USA. An edible gourd, such as a **muskmelon** or watermelon; variable in size; vine grown; usually eaten raw and fresh. Well-known varieties are **cantaloupe, casaba, crenshaw, honeydew, juan canary, Persian.**

melón de verano (meh-LOHN day bay-RAH-noa). Spa. **Cantaloupe.**

Melone (may-LOA-ner). Ger. **Melon.**

melt (mehlt). USA. To liquify by heating.

Melton Mowbray pie (MEHL-tuhn MAHW-bre pi). Bri. A double-crust **pork pie,** served cold.

Melun (mehr-lang). Fre. A **cheese** of the **Brie** type, but has a somewhat firmer **curd** and a sharper flavor.

menestra (may-NAYS-trah). Spa. **Stew.**

Menggu kao ròu (MENG-goo kao row). Chi. Mongolian **barbecue;** beef and fresh **vegetables grilled** in barbecue sauce.

Menorcan (Mehn-OHR-cahn). Spa. A semifirm, delicate, natural **cheese** with a distinctive flavor. Can also be processed.

mente (MAYN-tah). Ita. **Mint.**

menthe (mahngt). Fre. **Mint.**

menu (men-you) Fre. The bill of fare.

menudillos (mah-noo-DHEE-lyahss). Spa. **Giblets.**

menudo (meh-NOO-doh). Spa. **Tripe** and **corn stew.**

merga (MEHR-aw). Ara. Stock of **mutton** and/or **chicken,** strongly spiced; drunk when the weather is very cold or when a person is sick.

meringue (mah-RANG). USA. Light pastry, made of **egg** whites and **sugar,** then filled with **cream** or **custard;** also used as a **pie** topping.

merlan (mahr-lahng). Fre. **Whiting.**

merlano (mayr-LAA-noa). Ita. **Whiting.**

merluche (mehr-lusch). Fre. Stock fish, **haddock; dried** or **smoked.**

merluza (mayr-LOO-thah). Spa. **Hake.**

merluzzo (mayr-LOOT-tsoa). Ita. **Cod.**

mero (MEH-roa). Spa. Rock **bass.**

meshimono (me-she-mo-no). Jap. **Rice** with other ingredients.

mesimarja (MAY-ssi-MAHR-yah). Fin. An Artic brambleberry, the honeyberry; used to make a very sweet **liqueur.**

Mesost (MAYSS-oost). Swe. Amber-colored, sweet whey **cheese.**

mesquite (mehs-SKET). Mex, USA. A wild scrub tree of Southwestern United States and Mexico, with distinctively fragrant wood, highly prized for open-fire cooking of meats.

messicani (mes-se-KA-ne). Ita. **Stuffed veal** rollups; **saltimbocca.**

mesticanza (may-ste-KAHN-zah).   Ita. A mixture of small, tender **salad** greens.

metate (meh-TAH-teh).   Mex. A stone with a concave upper surface used for grinding **grains** and **spices** using a **mano.**

methi (MAHT-he).   Ind. **Fenugreek.**

metso (MAYT-soa).   Fin. A game bird. Also called *capercaillie.*

Mettwurst (MEHT-voorst).   Ger. **Smoked pork sausage** of coarse texture with red skin.

meunière (meh-nyair).   Fre. Lightly floured, **sauteed,** and served in **butter** with **lemon** slice.

Mexi-bell pepper (MEHX-e-behl PEHP-pehr).   USA. A mildly hot **bell pepper** that can be red or green or a combination of both.

Mexican saffron (MEHX-e-kahn SAHF-frohn).   Mex. **Safflower.**

mexilhão (meshel-YOwnsh).   Por. **Mussels.**

mezcal (mehs-KAHL).   Mex. Distilled liquor made from **agave** (century plant).

mezzani (medz-DZAHN-ne).   Ita. Long, narrow, tube-shaped **pasta.**

m'habia (mm-hah-lah-BE-ah).   Ara. **Cake** made of **milk, semolina, pistachio nuts, walnuts,** and **pine nuts.**

m'hamsa (mm-HAHM-sah).   Ara. **Soup** with **pasta** and **tomatoes.**

miànbao (mien-bao).   Chi. Bread.

miàntiáo (mien-tiao).   Chi. **Noodles.**

miche (mesh).   Fre. Loaf.

midollo (meh-DOHL-lah).   Ita. **Marrow.**

mie (me).   Fre. The soft interior part of a loaf of bread.

miel (myehl).   Fre. **Honey.**

miele (me-AY-lay).   Ita. **Honey.**

mifàn (me fan).   Chi. **Rice.**

mignon (mehn-yuon).   Fre. A small cut of beef; a **medallion.**

Mignot (men-noh).   Fre. A **cheese** similar to **Maroilles** but smaller; there are two types: white, which is fresh, and passé, which is ripened.

mihli (MOOH-le).   Ara. Assorted sweets made with **phyllo dough.**

mihshi (MEH-she).   Ara. **Stuffed meats** or **vegetables.**

mi jiu (ME choo).   Chi. Yellow **rice** wine.

mijoter (me-zho-tay).   Fre. To simmer.

mikado (meh-kah-doh).   Fre. Japanese style.

mikan (ME-kahn).   Jap. **Tangerine.**

milanaise (me-lahn-ayz).   Fre. A classic **garnish;** implies the use of **pasta** and **cheese** with a suitable **sauce,** often **béchamel.**

Milano (me-LAHN-o).   Ita. A soft, sweet, fast-ripening table **cheese;** yellow color, thin rind, and may be wrapped in muslin.

Milch (milkh).   Ger. **Milk.**

milho (MEL-yoh).   Por. **Corn.**

milk (melk).   USA. The fluid secreted by the mammary glands of cows, ewes, etc, used as a food. See **sweet milk.**

milk chocolate (melk CHOHK-oh-laht).   USA. **Chocolate** with **sugar, milk,** and **vanilla** added; used for **candy, icings, pies,** and **puddings.**

milk punch (melk puhnch).   USA. Any of various low-proof alcoholic drinks of **milk, sugar,** and liquor; streamlined versions of **egg nog.**

milk shake (melk shakah).   USA. A drink of **milk** and **ice cream,** blended to a thick consistency.

mille-feuille (mel-fey).   Fre. **Puff pastry.**

mille foglie (MEL-le FOL-yeh).   Ita. **Puff pastry.**

millet (MEHL-eht).   USA. Tiny, hulled **grain,** high in protein, may be cooked with **rice** or in place of rice; a staple food in many parts of the world.

milt (mihlt).   Dut. Male fish sperm gland when filled; usually prepared like **roe.**

Milzwurst (MELTZ-voorst).   Ger. Bavarian **veal sausage.**

mimosa (meh-MOH-sah).   USA. A **garnish** of finely chopped hard-boiled **egg** or **egg yolk.**

Mimosa (meh-MOH-sah).   USA. A brunch drink of **champagne** and **orange** juice.

mince (mincz).   USA. To chop food into very small pieces; not as fine as grinding, but finer than chopping. See also **cube, chop,** and **dice.**

mince (mincz).   Bri. **Ground beef; hamburger.**

mincemeat (MINCZ-met).   Bri. A finely chopped mixture of fresh or dried **fruits,** mainly **apples,** and **raisins,** spices, **nuts,** rum or **brandy,** and **suet.**

Mineralwasser (min-ner-RAAL-vah-sserr).   Ger. **Mineral water.**

mineral water (MIHN-ehr-uhl WAH-tehr).   USA. Water with naturally occuring, or artifically impregnated, mineral salts or gasses.

minestra (men-ah-STRA-ah).   Ita. A thin **soup** served as the first course.

minestrone (me-nah-STROH-nay).   Ita. A thick, hearty **vegetable soup** in a meat **broth** with **pasta;** a meal in itself.

Minnesota Blue (mehn-neh-SO-tah bloo).   USA. A natural blue-veined **cheese** of America.

mint (mehnt).   USA. An aromatic Mediterranean **herb** divided in two basic groups; spearmint and peppermint; with diverse culinary uses for **sauces,** beverages, **confections, vegetables,** flavoring **liqueurs,** etc.

Mintzitra (Mehn-zith-rah).   Gre. A **cheese** the same as **Mitzithra.**

miqli (MEHC-le).   Ara. **Fried.**

Mirabeau (mer-ah-boa).   Fre. A **garnish** for **grilled** meats of **anchovy fillets,** pitted **olives, tarragon,** and anchovy **butter.**

mirabelle (mer-ah-behl).   Fre. A small, highly aromatic golden plum used in **preserves, tarts,** and a colorless fruit **brandy.**

mirchi (MER-che).   Ind. **Chili peppers.**

mirepoix (mer-pwa).   Fre. A mixture of **diced vegetables, herbs,** and fat, for flavoring brown **soups** and **sauces,** also **braised** meats; similar to **matignon,** which is **minced.**

mirin (MEH-rehm).   Jap. A sweet, syrupy thin, golden-colored **rice** wine used for cooking, not drinking.

mirliton (MER-le-tohn).   USA. **Chayote.**

miroton (mehr-rohl-tawng).   Fre. A **stew** of meat and **onions** in brown **gravy.**

mise en place (mez on plas).   Fre. "The preparation is ready up to the point of cooking."

mish mish (mesh mesh).   Ara. **Apricots.**

mishwi (MASH-we).   Ara. **Grilled.**

miso (me-SOH). Jap. Fermented soy **bean paste;** used as a thickener for many soups, barbecue **sauce,** and in **salad dressing;** comes in two forms: mild white or pungent brick-red; many types.

misoramen (me-SOH -rah-mehn). Jap. A white, curled **noodle** containing **miso bean paste.**

misoshiru (me-SOH-she-roo). Jap. Soup made with **miso bean paste.**

misticanza (me-stee-CAHN-tsa). Ita. Mixed **salad.**

mistki (MEST-kee). Ara. **Arabic gum;** used as emulsifiers and thickeners in certain processed foods such as **ice cream, candy,** commercial **sauces;** mustica.

misto (ME-stoa). Ita. Mixed.

mithai (mit-HIE-e). Ind. Sweets.

mitsuba (me-TSOO-bah). Jap. **Trefoil;** a member of the **parsley** family; flavor between **sorrel** and **celery;** attractive light green color; used to add flavor and color accent; a type of clover.

Mitzithra (Meh-ZETH-thrah). Gre. Made of **whey** left from **Feta;** semisoft, white, lightly salted. A **cheese** of the same name is made in Turkey of goat's milk; also spelled **Mintzithra.**

miúdos (me-OO-dahsh). Por. **Giblets.**

mix (mehx). USA. To combine two or more ingredients by stirring or blending.

mixed grill (mehxd grehl). Bri. Various **grilled** meats, such as beef steak, **lamb** chop, **pork** chop, **kidneys** served with **fried potatoes, grilled mushrooms,** and **tomatoes.**

mizu (me-zoo). Jap. Water.

mjölk (myurlk). Swe. **Milk.**

mjuka småfranska (MYU-ka SMO-FRAN-ska). Swe. Soft **rolls.**

Mjukost (MYEW-kah-oost). Swe. A soft, white, bland **cheese.**

mlabbas (mm-LAB-bahs). Ara. Sugar-coated **almonds.**

mlukhiyyi (mm-loo-HEYE). Ara. Green leafy **vegetable,** similar to **spinach.** Also known as *Jew's mallow.*

mnaqish (man-rah-QUESH). Ara. Flat **tarts.**

mnazli (mm-NAH-zah-le). Ara. **Stew;** refers to dishes made with **eggplants** or other **vegetables** as the basic ingredients.

mocha (MOH-kah).   USA. A flavoring of **coffee** infused with **cocoa** or **chocolate.** Originally, a fine, superior Arabian **coffee.**

mochi (moh-CHE).   Jap. Sweet **rice cakes.**

mochi-gome (moh-CHE goh-MEH).   Jap. A special, sticky, glutinous **rice** used for certain **dumplings, noodles,** in red rice and sweet rice **cakes.**

mochiko (moh-che-KO).   Jap. A **rice flour** made from **mochi-gome,** used as thickening agent.

mochomos (moh-CHOH-mohs).   Mex. Meat that has been cooked, **shredded,** then crisply **fried.**

mock duck (mahk duhk).   Iri. A dish of **pork tenderloin** filled with **poultry stuffing, chopped apple,** and cooked under a topping of **chopped onion** and **rashers** of **bacon.**

Modena (moh-DEN-nah).   USA. A **Parmesan**-type **cheese** made in US during World War II; also called **Monte.**

moelle (mwahl).   Fre. Beef **marrow;** used as a **garnish** or spread.

moh gwah (moh gua).   Chi. The Chinese fuzzy **melon;** sweet-flavored with gray-green, fuzzy skin.

môhlo (MOHL-yoh).   Por. **Gravy; sauce.**

môhlo de maças (MOHL-yoh der mas-ANSH).   Por. **Applesauce.**

Mohn (mon).   Ger. **Poppy seed.**

Mohnbrötchen (mon-BRURT-khern).   Ger. **Poppy seed rolls.**

Mohnkipfel (MON-kip-ferl).   Ger. **Poppy-seed** crescent **rolls.**

Mohrenköpfe (MOA-rern-kopf).   Ger. Moors' heads; a genoise **cake** baked in a special half-round mold, then filled with **chocolate pudding,** then the halves joined together and covered with **whipped cream.**

Mohr Im Hemd (moar em hehmt).   Ger. An Austrian **dessert** of **chocolate pudding** in **whipped cream.**

Mohrrüben (MOAR-rew-bern).   Ger. **Carrots.**

moisten (MOHY-sehn).   USA. To add liquid.

moka (mauka).   Fre. **Mocha.**

molako (mah-lah-KAH).   Rus. **Milk.**

molasses (moh-LASS-ehsz).   USA. The thick dark to light brown syrup remaining after sucrose crystallization.

mold (mohld).   USA. To mix or knead into a required consistency or shape.

mole (MOH-leh).   Mex. An elaborate **sauce,** made of various ingredients depending on the dish with which it is served.

moleas de vitela (MOH-lehss der ve-TEl-a).   Por. **Veal sweetbreads.**

molecche (moh-LEHK-ke).   Ita. Soft-shelled **crabs.**

mòli hua chá (MAW-lee hua tsah).   Chi. Jasmine **tea.**

molinillo (moh-le-NE-yoh).   Mex. Carved wooden beater used to make Mexican **hot chocolate.**

Moliterno (Moh-le-TEHR-noh).   Ita. A plastic-curd **cheese** usually made of ewe's milk.

mollette (moh-LEH-teh) Ita. French roll.

mollusc (moh-lysk).   Fre. **Mollusk.**

mollusk (MAHL-uhsk).   USA. Shellfish, such as **crab, shrimp, lobster, snail, clam, oyster,** or **squid.**

molto cotto (moal-toa KOT-toa).   Ita. Cooked thoroughly; well done.

Moncenisio (Mahw-seh-ne-SE-o).   Ita. A blue-mold, **Gorgonzola**-type **cheese.**

Mondseer Schachtelkäse (Mont-sehr Schah-tehl-kahz-zer).   Ger. A **Münster**-type **cheese,** made from whole or partly skimmed milk, with a somewhat sharp, acid flavor, similar to mild **Limburger.**

monegasque (moh-neh-gahsk).   Fre. A **salad** of **nonats, tomatoes,** and **rice.**

monégasque, a la (moh-neh-gahsk, ah lah).   Fre. In the style of Monoco; with **tomatoes** and **rice.**

mongo-ika (MOHN-goh e-kah).   Jap. Cuttlefish.

mongolian hot pot (mohn-GOA-le-uhn haht paht).   USA. A Chinese one-dish meal composed of various pieces of **seafood, poultry,** and meat cooked individually in simmering **stock** and served with **sauces;** shùan yángròu.

monkey bread (MUHNC-key brehd).   USA. A sweet bread made of separate pieces of bread **dough** randomly piled in a tube pan and baked. **Nuts, currants,** or **cinnamon** and **sugar** are sometimes added.

monkfish (MUNCK-fish).   USA. Goosefish, whose tail section is firm white flesh similar in flavor to **lobster;** can be **sautéed, baked,**

broiled, poached, or cut in fingers and **deep-fat fried.** Also known as frogfish, sea devil, and **angler.**

monosodium glutamate (mow-noh-SO-de-uhm GLU-tah-mat). USA. MSG; a crystalline **salt** used as a taste intensifier and enhancer; widely used in Oriental cooking.

Monsieur Fromage (mohn-seur fro-mahgjz). Fre. A ripened cream **cheese** of Normandy, soft, delicate; packaged in five-ounce wooden boxes.

monstera (mon-STAIR-a). USA. **Ceriman.**

Montasio (mohn-TAH-ze-oa). Ita. A cow's whole-milk **cheese** that is firm and pale yellow with a smooth rind, has scattered holes, and is made in large wheels. When young it is a good table cheese with a mild, nutty flavor; when old it is a good, pungent grating cheese.

Montavoner (mon-tah-VOE-nehr). Aus. A sour-milk **cheese** with dried **herbs** added.

Mont Blanc (mon blon). Fre. A classic **dessert** of **chantilly cream** and **chestnut purée.**

Mont Cenis (mowng sehr-ne). Fre. A hard, blue-mold **cheese** usually made of a mixture of cow's, ewe's, and goat's milk.

Mont d'Or (mohn day-ohr). Fre. A briefly cured soft **cheese** of the Rhone region.

Monte Bianco (moan-teh be-AWHN-ko). Ita. A classic dessert of **chantilly cream, chestnut purée, chocolate,** and rum.

monter (mohn-teh). Fre. To whip **cream** or **egg** whites to give volume.

monter au beurre (mohn-teh oa burr). Fre. To enrich a **sauce** with **butter.**

Monterey Jack (MOHN-tehr-ra Jahk). USA. A cow's whole-milk **cheese** that is pale, soft, creamy, and bland; the skimmed-milk version is harder and stronger.

Monthéry (mowng-tehr-re). Fre. A soft, surface-ripened, cow's-milk **cheese** with a blue mold on the surface with red spots.

Montlénis (mohn-le-knes). Fre. A firm, blue-veined **cheese** of mixed sheep's, goat's, and cow's milk from a region neighboring Roquefort.

montmorency (mo-mo-rahn-ce). Fre. Prepared with **cherries.**

montone (moan-TOA-nay). Ita. **Mutton.**

Montpensier (mo-pahn-ce-a). Fre. A **garnish** of **sliced truffles**, green **asparagus** tips, **artichoke** hearts, and **Madeira sauce.**

montreuil (mohn-hoia). Fre. With **peaches.**

Montreuil (MOHN-treall). Ger. Fish **poached** in white wine, served with large **potato** balls and **shrimp sauce.**

moolee (MO-lee). Ind. In **coconut sauce.**

moorkoppen (MOHR-kop-pen). Dut. Filled **tarts** with **cream.**

Moors' heads (muhrz hehdz). USA. A **genoise cake batter** baked in a special half-round mold, then filled and the halves joined.

moo shu zoh (moo she zoh). Chi. A **rolled pancake** stuffed with **shredded pork stir-fried** with **scallions, egg,** and **cloud ears.**

moqua (MOH-gwah). Chi. **Fuzzy melon.**

morangos (moh-RAHN-gohss). Por. **Strawberries.**

mørbrad (MURR-braa). Dan. **Pork tenderloin.**

mørbradøf (MURR-braa-urf). Dan. **Pork filet.**

Morcheln (MOHR-chaund). Ger. **Morels.**

morcilla blanca (moar-THE-lyah BLAHN-kah). Spa. A **sausage** made of **chicken, bacon,** hard-boiled **eggs,** and **parsley.**

morcilla negra (moar-THE-lyah NAY-grah). Spa. A **sausage** made of **pork,** pig's blood, **garlic,** spices.

more (MO-ray). Ita. **Blackberries.**

morel (moh-REHL). USA. A wild **mushroom** with a honeycomb-like cap that resembles a pine cone; creamy tan to brown to black; used either **dried** or cooked; has a nutty flavor.

morena (mohr-RE-nah). Spa. **Brown bread.**

Morgenrot (MOHR-gahn-roat). Ger. "Red Dawn"; a **chicken broth soup** with **tomato purée** and bits of chicken.

morille (mo-rey). Fre. **Morel.**

morkov (mahr-KOV). Rus. **Carrots.**

mörkt rågbröd (mohrkt ROG-brohd). Swe. **Toast.**

mornay (mohr-nay). Fre. **Béchamel sauce** with **butter,** grated **Parmesan** and **Gruyère cheese,** and **egg yolk;** a classic sauce.

morötter (MOO-ROH-terr). Swe. **Carrots.**

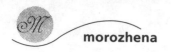

morozhena (mah-RO-zhi-nah-yeh). Rus. **Ice cream.**

mortadela (mohr-tah-DEH-lah). Por. **Bologna.**

mortadella (mohr-tah-DELL-lah). Ita. A **sausage** of **ground pork** with **white** cubes of fat, **coriander, pistachio nuts,** and wine.

morue (mo-rew). Fre. **Salt cod.**

moscada (mos-KAH-dah). Spa. **Nutmeg.**

Moscht (mohst). Ger. Swiss **apple cider.**

moskovitaeg (mo-SKO-vit-egg). Dan. Hard-boiled **egg** with **mayonnaise.**

mosselen (MAWS-suh-luh). Dut. **Clams, mussels.**

Most (must). Ger. **Fruit** juice or **cider.**

mostaccioli (mo-stash-che-OA-le). Ita. Hollow, tubular **pasta** cut obliquely about two and a half inches long.

mostard (MAWS-turt). Dut. **Mustard.**

mostarda (mohss-TAHR-dah). Por. **Mustard.**

mostarda di frutta (mohss-TAHR-dah de FROOT-tah). Ita. A **mustard**-flavored **syrup** with various preserved **fruits,** eaten with bread or cold meat, like **chutney.**

mostaza (moas-TAH-thah). Spa. **Mustard.**

mosterd (MAWS-turt). Dut. **Mustard.**

moulange (moul-ahng). Fre. The act of molding, such as **ice cream** or **butter.**

moule (mool). Fre. Mussel. Also, a mold.

moules à l'Escargot (mool ah l'ehs-kahr-goa). Fre. A Belgian dish of **mussels** stuffed and prepared to look like **snails.**

Mountain Cheese (MAWN-tahn chez). USA. A semisoft, cream-colored **cheese** made in the Alps; mild and delicious; used in making Raclette; also called **Mütschli.**

mountain oyster (MAWN-tahnn ouy-stur). USA. Testicles of a bull, pig, or lamb, breaded and fried. Also called **animelles, frivolitées, lamb fries, prairie oyster, Rocky Mountain oyster.**

moussaka, mousaka (moo-SOCK-kah). Gre. A dish of **eggplant, lamb, tomatoes,** and **white sauce.**

mousse (moos). Fre. A sweet or savory dish lightened with beaten **egg** whites and frothy cream.

mousseline (moos-len). Fre. A sauce, usually **mayonnaise** or **hollandaise,** or a dish with beaten **egg** whites or **whipped cream** folded in.

moutarde de Meaux (moo-tahrd der moa). Fre. **Mustard** from Meaux made with partly crushed seeds.

mouton (moo-ton). Fre. **Mutton.**

mowz (mohz). Ara. **Banana.**

moyashi (mo-YAH-she). Jap. **Bean sprouts** from the tiny, olive-green **mung bean.**

Mozarinelli (Mot-zahr-re-NEHL-le). Ita. A **cheese** made from cow's or buffalo's milk.

Mozzarella (mots-ah-REHL-lah). Ita. A fresh, unsalted, white, moist **cheese** with a delicate flavor, eaten **sliced** or in baked dishes; rindless; sometimes **smoked.**

mqania (mm-AH-nec). Ara. **Sausage.**

mrabba (mm-RAHB-bah). Ara. **Jam.**

MSG (m-s-g). USA. **Monosodium glutamate;** a flavor enhancer.

muffin (MUHF-ehn). Bri. A flat **yeast bread** baked on a griddle.

muffin (MUHF-ehn). USA. A raised, **quick bread** made of various flours, with **fruits** or **nuts, baked** in a mold in an oven.

muffuletta (muhf-feh-LEHT-toh). USA. An indigenous New Orleans **sandwich** with some Italian background; a huge round loaf of bread filled with imported **cheese, ham,** and **salami,** then dressed with an olive **salad dressing** heavy with **garlic.**

muhennettu (MOO-hayn-nayt-too). Fin. Stewed.

muhennos (MOO-hayn-noas). Fin. **Stew.**

muikku (MWEEK-koo). Fin. Tiny freshwater fish related to the **salmon.**

muisjes (MIRS-yus). Dut. Small **anise**-flavored sugar pellets eaten on a **sandwich.**

mulard (mew-lahrd). Fre. A hybrid **duck** bred for its meat and liver.

mulato (moo-LAH-toh). Mex. A large, brown, dried, pungent **chili pepper.**

mulberry (MUHL-behr-re). USA. A purplish-black **berry** that resembles the **raspberry** in appearance, whose flavor is a cross between a raspberry and **boysenberry;** used as a **fruit** in salads and in **jams, jellies, preserves,** and **syrups.**

mull (muhl). USA. To make a hot drink of **cider,** wine, or **ale** by heating and adding **sugar** and spices.

mullet (MUHL-eht). USA. The name of various fish found throughout the world, of which the **red mullet** found in the Mediterranean is the most highly prized, with the **silver mullet** of the Gulf and south Atlantic coasts of the United States also desirable.

Mulligan stew (MUHL-eh-gahn stoo). Iri. A meat-**vegetable stew** thickened with **okra.** Also known as **burgoo.**

mullagatanni (mool-ah-sa-TAH-nee). Ind. **Black pepper** and **broth;** the origin of **mulligatawny soup.**

mulligatawny (mul-e-ga-TAW-ne). USA. A rich soup of **chicken** or **lamb stock** flavored with spices and **curry** and served with **rice,** the diced meat, **lemon,** and **cream.**

multer (MEWL-terr). Nor. **Cloudberry.**

mulukhiyya (moo-loo-KHEE-yah). Ara. **Vegetable soup** with **rice** and meat.

muna (MOO-nah). Fin. **Egg;** *hyydytetyt munat* (HEW-day-tay-tewt MOO-naht) poached egg; *munakokkeli* (MOO-nah-KOAK-kay-li) scrambled eggs; *muna kova* (MOO-nah KOA-vah) hard-boiled eggs; *muna pehmeä* (MOO-nah PAYH-mayea) soft-boiled eggs.

muna ja pekonia (MOO-nah yah PAY-roa-yah). Fin. **Bacon** and **eggs.**

munchies (MUHN-ches). USA. Any snack food such as **popcorn, potato chips, pretzels,** trail mix.

Munchner (MUENCH-nehrn). Ger. Designates the dark, malty **beers** found in Munich, Germany.

mung bean (muhng ben). Ind. Various dried **beans,** rich in protein, and used at virtually every meal in Asia.

mung dal (muhng dahl). Ind. Split **mung beans.**

mun (mewngk). Swe. **Doughnut.**

munkar (MUNG-kar). Swe. **Dumplings.**

Münster (muhn-stur). Fre. A cow's whole-milk **cheese** that is round with a smooth orange rind, pale yellow, soft interior with cracks, and a lightly salty flavor that gets tangy with age.

Murazzano (moo-rahz-ZAHN-noh). Ita. A cylindrical **cheese** with no rind and a dense white interior that ages to pale yellow, made mostly of ewe's milk.

Mürbeteig (MOOR-bay-tike). Ger. A rich, sweet **egg tart dough;** a tender paste for fresh **fruit** and **nut fillings.**

Murcott orange (muhr-kot auh-renj). USA. A hybrid **orange** resulting from an orange and **tangerine** cross.

mure (mewr). Fre. **Blackberry** or **mulberry.**

murgh (moorgh). Ind. **Chicken.**

Murol (mehr-hoyl). Fre. A wheel-shaped cow's milk hard **cheese** with a pinkish rind and a hole in the center.

muscadine (MUHS-kah-din). USA. A white **grape** with a musky flavor used for **raisins** as well as **table grapes.**

muscat (muhs-kaht). Fre. A white or black **grape** with a musky flavor used for wine.

Muscheln (MU-sherln). Ger. **Shellfish,** such as **scallops, clams, mussels.**

muscoli (moos-KOA-le). Ita. **Mussel.**

mush (muhsh). USA. A thick **porridge** made with **cornmeal** boiled in water or **milk** that, when cooled, can be **sliced** and **fried.**

mushimono (moo-SHE-mo-no). Jap. **Steamed** food.

mushroom (MUHSH-room). USA. A complex fleshy fruiting body of an edible fungus that consists typically of a stem bearing a cap; countless varieties throughout the world; many are listed in this volume.

Muskatnuss (mus-KAHT-nuss). Ger. **Nutmeg, mace.**

muskmelon (MUHSK-mehl-uhn). USA. A sweet, musky-odored netted **melon,** also called **canteloupe** and **winter melon.**

muslin bag (MUHS-lehn bahg). USA. A bag of loosely woven muslin in which spices and **herbs** are tied, then placed in cooking liquids to impart flavors, then removed and discarded.

muslinger (MOOS-len-gerr). Dan. **Mussels.**

mussel (MUHS-suhl).   USA. A **mollusk** with a dark blue-black or light brown elongated shell, popular in Europe.

mussla (MEWSS-lah).   Swe. **Mussel, clam.**

Must (moos).   Ger. Juice of **fruit,** especially **grapes,** before and during fermentation.

mustaa kahvia (MOOS-tah KAHHH-viah).   Fin. Black **coffee.**

mustard (MUHS-tuhrd).   USA. A seasoning made from **powdered mustard** seeds and a liquid blended to make a **paste.**

mustard greens (MUHS-tuhrd grehns).   USA. Green leafy **vegetable** for table use.

mustard seeds (MUHS-turd sehds).   USA. Two basic varieties of the **mustard** family are dried for use as seasonings: white or yellow seeds that have a mild flavor, and dark brown or black seeds that have a pungent taste; used whole, **crushed, ground,** and **powdered.**

mustawiy (MISS-tah-we).   Ara. Cooked well-done.

mustikka (MOOS-tik-kah).   Fin. **Blueberry.**

mustikkakeitto (MOOS-tik-kah-KAYT-toa).   Fin. **Blueberry** soup, a **dessert.**

mustikkapiiras (MOOS-tik-kah-PE-rah-kah).   Fin. **Blueberry tart** or **pie.**

mutton (MUH-tuhn).   USA. The flesh of mature sheep, has rich flavor, and is dark red in color.

muttonfish (MUT-tuhn-fisch).   USA. One of the names for the ocean pout fish, whose flesh is sweet, white, and has few bones.

muy hecho (mwe AY-choa).   Spa. Well done, as referring to steak.

myaso (my-AH-ssah).   Rus. Meat.

mylta med grädde (MUL-ta mah GRAHDE).   Swe. **Cloudberry** compote with **cream,** a northern Swedish **dessert.**

myrtilles (mer-tey).   Fre. **Blueberries.**

Mysost (MEWSS-oost).   Nor. A firm, dense cow's-milk **cheese** that is dark brown and sweet.

mystery meat (MYSS-tre met).   USA. A college-cafeteria term for any meat item covered with a **sauce** or **gravy,** rendering it unidentifiable.

Noix de Coco · French · Coconut

naawr mai (noah me). Chi. A special sticky, glutinous **rice** used for certain **dumplings, noodles,** and pastries.

naba (NAH-bah). Spa. **Rutabaga.**

nabos (NAH-bohss). Spa, Por. **Turnips.**

nacho (NAH-choh). Mex. **Tortilla** chips with melted **cheese,** topped with green **chilies, chopped** or **sliced.**

Nachspeise (NAAKH-shpigh-zer). Ger. **Dessert.**

naganegi (nah-GAH-ne-ge). Jap. Long **onion,** 14–16 inches long, of which only the white part is used.

nage (nahj). Fre. Cooked in a **stock** of white wine, **carrots, onions, shallots,** and **herbs.**

nagerechten (nawh-her-RES-ten). Dut. **Desserts.**

Nägles (Na-glez). Dut. A **cheese** made of cow's skim milk with **cumin** and **cloves** mixed in the curd.

naiyóu báicài (nai-YOU BAI-tsai). Chi. **Chinese cabbage** in **cream sauce.**

näkkileipää (NAEK-ki-LAY-pae). Fin. A hard, crisp bread.

namak (NAH-mak). Ind. Teardrop-shaped bread made with leavened **dough** and **baked.**

naméko (nah-ME-koh). Jap. A tiny, delicate, slippery **mushroom** with a button top; usually canned; used in **soups.**

nam pla (nahm pla). Thi. Pungent, salty fish **sauce.**

nam prik (nahm prek). Thi. Pungent salty **fish** sauce with **chilies** served hot as a **dipping** sauce.

nana (nah-NAH). Ara. Green **mint** leaves.

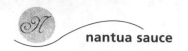

nantua sauce (nahn-tew saus). Fre. **Béchamel sauce** reduced with **cream,** beaten with **crayfish butter,** and garnished with **crayfish tails.**

Napfkuchen (napf-KOOK-hern). Ger. Light **yeast cake** with **raisins.**

Naples biscuit (NA-puls behs-keit). USA. A light **dessert** or tea **biscuit,** resembling a **ladyfinger.**

napoleon (nah-pohl-yuhn). Fre. A **dessert** of **puff paste** spread with pastry **cream,** stacked in layers, sometimes iced.

napoletana (nah-poa-lay-TAA-nah). Ita. Made meatless with **tomatoes, garlic, onion,** and **olive oil.**

napolitain (nah-po-le-tahng). Fre. A **genoise** spread with **jam,** then spread with **Italian meringue,** then more **jam.**

napolitaine (nah-po-le-tahn). Fre. **Scallops** of **veal** dipped in beaten **eggs,** then covered with breadcrumbs mixed with **grated Parmesan, fried,** and served with **spaghetti,** topped with **tomato sauce** sprinkled with **Parmesan.**

naranja (nah-RAHN-jah). Spa. **Orange.**

nargisi kofta (NEHR-geh-se KOF-tah). Ind. **Meatballs** stuffed with whole **eggs, fried,** cut in half to expose the egg, and simmered in onion **gravy.**

narial (NAH-re-el). Ind. **Coconut.**

nasello (nah-SEHL-loa). Ita. Coal fish; a food fish related to **whiting.**

nashi (nah-SHE). Jap. **Pears;** several varieties; apple-like in shape and crispness, light yellow to brown in color, and a tart juiciness.

nasi goreng (NAH-se GOH-reng). Dut. An Indonesian dish of **fried rice** cooked with various spices and ingredients, including **chicken, shrimp,** meat, **onions, garlic, shrimp paste, chilies.**

nasturtium (nahs-TUHR-shuhm). USA. An **herb** whose blossoms and leaves have a peppery flavor that enhances **salads** and **sandwiches.** Its seeds can be **pickled** and are much like **capers.**

nasu (NAH-soo). Jap. **Eggplant.**

natillas (nah-TE-yah). Spa. A soft runny **custard** made from ewe's milk, sweetened and flavored with **cinnamon** and **lemon.**

nattmat (NAHT-awt). Swe. "Night food"; offered just before a party breaks up.

natur (nah-TOOR). Ger. Plain, simple, ungarnished.

naturale (nah-too-RAHL). Ita. Plain, simple, ungarnished.

naturel (nah-tewr-erl). Fre. Plain, simple; plainly and simply prepared.

naturschnitzel (nah-TOOR-schnet-zehl). Ger. Unbreaded **veal cutlet.**

naudanliha (NAH-oo-dahn-LI-haa). Fin. Beef.

nauris (NAH-oo-riss). Fin. **Turnip.**

navarin (nah-veh-rahng). Fre. A **stew** of **turnips** with **lamb** or **mutton, onions,** and **potatoes.**

navel orange (NA-vahl AWH-ranj). USA. A thick-skinned, seedless **orange** with easy-to-peel rind, and a navel-like protrusion on the blossom end; a good table fruit.

navet (nah-veh). Fre. **Turnip.**

navy bean (NA-ve behn). USA. A small, white, common **bean** used dried in such dishes as navy bean **soup, boston baked beans, cassoulet.**

nayyi (nah-HE). Ara. **Raw,** in reference to food.

neapolitan ice cream (ne-oh-POHL-e-tuhn is krem). USA. **Chocolate, vanilla,** and **strawberry ice cream** layered in a mold to display the ribbon of three flavors.

nectarine (NEHK-tehr-ren). USA. Actually a **peach** with smooth, slick skin, and flavor a cross between **peach** and **plum.**

neeps (nehps). Sco. **Turnips.**

négi (NAH-ge). Jap. **Scallion, onion, leek.**

négresse (nay-grehss). Fre. **Chocolate mousse** topped by **whipped cream.**

negrítas (nay-GRE-tahs). Spa. **Chocolate mousse** topped by **whipped cream.**

negus (ne-GAHS). Ara. A warm wine punch with **lemon,** spices, and sweetened with **sugar.**

neige (nehzh). Fre. Snow; white of **eggs** beaten to a froth or snow.

neopolitan parsley (ne-O-POHL-eh-tahn PAHR-sle). USA. **Parsley;** also called **Italian parsley.**

nepaul pepper (NAH-paul PEHP-pehr). USA. A red **pepper** of the same characteristic as **cayenne;** has a sweet, pungent flavor.

neslesuppe (nehs-leh-SEWP-peh). Nor. **Nettle soup;** tastes like **spinach soup.**

Nessel (nehss-sehl). Bri. A soft, cured **cheese** made of cow's whole milk; round and thin.

nesselrode (nehs-sehl-ROHD). USA. A frozen **custard pudding,** topped with **whipped cream,** flavored with **chestnut purée** mixed with candied **fruits.**

nettles (NET-teul). Iri. A coarse **herb** with stinging hairs; when picked young and cooked, the nettles have no sting; similar to **spinach** in taste.

Neufchâtel (neu-cho-tel). Fre. A soft, uncooked, cow's milk **cheese** similar to **cream cheese** with a velvety white crust, which may also be eaten; has been made for centuries in Normandy; an American version contains less fat and is never ripened.

New Bedford pudding (neu BEHD-fohrd PUHD-dehng). USA. A **pudding** made from **cornmeal, flour,** eggs and flavored with **molasses.**

Newburg (NEU-berg). USA. A thick **cream sauce** with **egg yolk** and **sherry** in which **lobster, shrimp,** or various **seafoods** are served.

New England boiled dinner (neu EHNG-land boild DEN-nehr). USA. A one-dish dinner with **corned beef, cabbage, potatoes, carrots,** and other **vegetables** cooked together and served with **horseradish** or **mustard. Chicken** sometimes replaces the corned beef.

New England clambake (neu EHNG-land KLAHM-bak). USA. See **clambake.**

New Zealand spinach (neu ZE-lund SPEHN-nehch). USA. A **vegetable** with a mellow taste when cooked and a flavor similar to garden grass with a tang when raw; leaves are dark green with slight fuzz; best when cooked, but add raw to **salads.**

ng heung fun (ng hung fon). Chi. **Five-spice seasoning;** the Cantonese name for the blend of ground **cloves, fennel, licorice root, cinnamon,** and **star anise.**

niboski (ne-BO-she). Jap. **Dried sardines** for making **stock.**

niçoise (kne-qwau). Fre. **Chopped tomatoes sauteed** in **olive oil** with **garlic, capers, anchovies,** black olives, sliced **lemon.**

Nieheimer Hoppenkäse (Neh-hi-mehr Hohp-pehn-kahz-zeh). Ger. A sour-milk **cheese** similar to **Hop cheese.**

nierbroodje (NER-broht-yuh). Dut. **Kidney** patty.

nievwe haring (NEW-ah HAHR-reng). Dut. Fresh **herring.**

nigauri (ne-GOHW-oo-lee). Jap. **Chinese bitter melon; balsam pear.**

nigiri zushi (ne-GE-lei zoo-she). Jap. A type of **sushi** that consists of **rice balls** topped with various ingredients such as fish or **shrimp.**

niku (NE-koo). Jap. Meat.

nimboo (NIM-boo). Ind. **Lime, limon.**

nimono (ne-MOH-noh). Jap. Simmered or braised food.

ninaa (ni-NEH). Ara. **Mint;** an important seasoning in Middle Eastern cookery.

ningméng (ning-meng). Chi. **Lemon.**

ninjin (NEN-jen). Jap. **Carrot.**

nioi (ne-O-e). USA. A Hawaiian seasoning made with **chili peppers,** water, and salt, used in various dishes.

Niren (NE-rern). Ger. **Kidneys.**

niú ròu (niu row). Chi. Beef.

njure (NYEW-rer). Swe. **Kidney.**

nkhaat (nn-HAH-aht). Ara. **Lamb** or beef brains.

nocchette (noh-KOYT-teh). Ita. Small bow-tie **pasta** used in **soups.**

nocciole (noat-CHO-lay). Ita. **Hazelnut.**

noccioline Americane (noat-CHO-len ah-mahr-E-cahn). Ita. **Peanuts.**

noce moscata (NOA-chay moa-SKAA-tah). Ita. **Nutmeg.**

noci (NOA-che). Ita. **Walnuts.**

Nock (nokh). Ger. **Dumpling.**

Nockerl (NOKH-rehl). Ger. **Dumplings.**

nødder (NURDH-err). Dan. **Nuts.**

Noeuds de Bruges (nuh day broogz). Fre. "Bruges Knots," a delicious, fragile Belgian pastry.

noga (NOH-hah). Dut. **Nougat.**

nogada (noh-GAH-dah). Mex. **Walnut sauce;** usually served with **poblano chilies** stuffed with **shredded pork** and **garnished** with **pomegranate seeds.**

noisette (nooa-zet). Fre. **Hazelnut;** also a cut of meat from the **rib** of a **lamb,** trimmed, rolled, tied in a small round shaped like a hazelnut (about ½ inch in diameter), and served as an individual portion.

noisette potatoes (no-ZEHT po-TA-toz). USA. **Potatoes** shaped like **hazelnuts** and browned in butter; the American version of **pommes noisette.**

noix (nwah). Fre. **Walnut.**

noix de coco (nwah day ko-koa). Fre. **Coconut.**

noix de veau (nwah day voa). Fre. Cut of **veal** from the **tenderloin.**

noix muscade (nwah mew-skahd). Fre. **Nutmeg.**

Nøkkelost (NUR-ker-loost). Nor. A hard **cheese** based on the Dutch **Leyden** and similarly flavored with **caraway** and **cumin;** made from partly skimmed milk; also spelled *Noekkelost.*

nonat (no-naht). Fre. A very small Mediterranean fish, usually **deep-fried.**

nondairy creamer (nohn-DAR-re KREM-mehr). USA. A manufactured creamer containing no **milk** or **cream,** usually using **palm** or **coconut oil** instead.

nonfat milk. (nohn-faht melk). USA. Cow's milk containing less than ½% milk fat. Also called skim milk.

nonpareille (nuhn-pah-reel). Fre. A small flat disk of **chocolate** covered with white **sugar** pellets. Also small sugar pellets of various colors.

noodles (NOO-dlehs). USA. A type of **pasta,** long, flat like a ribbon, and of varying widths and thicknesses.

nopale (no-PAHL). Mex. The fleshy oval parts of a cactus, eaten with scrambled **eggs** or in **salad.**

nopalitos (no-pah-LE-tos). Mex. Cactus leaves used in **salads.**

noques (noa-che). Fre. **Gnocchi.**

noques (nohks). Fre. A light, sweet Austrian **dessert** of egg-shaped **meringues,** poached in **milk,** and served in a **custard sauce.** Also known as **Snow Eggs.**

noquis (NOA-ke). Spa. **Gnocchi.**

nori (NOH-re). Jap. A **seaweed;** thin, black sheets of **sea lettuce,** used lightly toasted as a **cracker,** as a wrapper for **sushi,** or crumbled over **rice** and **noodle** dishes.

norimaki zushi (noh-re-MAH-ke ZHU-she). Jap. A type of sushi that consists of **rice** and an assortment of colorful ingredients rolled pinwheel fashion inside a wrapping such as a sheet of **nori** seaweed or a sheet of cooked **egg.**

normande (nor-muhnd). Fre. A classic **sauce** of fish **veloute** with **oyster** liquor, **mushrooms, egg yolks, cream,** and **butter;** with **oysters, mussels, shrimp,** mushroom caps, and **truffles** added, it becomes a classic **garnish.**

Normande, a la (nor-muhnd). Fre. Implies that the flavor of **apple** has been introduced into the dish.

norvégienne (nor-vayzh-yehn). Fre. A sauce of mashed hard-boiled **eggs,** seasoned with **vinegar** and **mustard** and beaten with oil into a thick **sauce.**

Norway haddock (NOHR-way HAHD-duhk). USA. One of the names for ocean **perch.**

Norway lobster (NOHR-way LOHB-stuhr). USA. A saltwater **crayfish.**

Nostrale (noh-STRAH-le). Ita. The local name for two kinds of cheese made from cow's milk; one is a hard cheese (*Fromaggio Duro*) made in the spring while the herds are still in the valleys; the other is a soft cheese (*Fromaggio Tenero*) that is made in the summer when herds are pastured in the mountains. *Ruschera* is probably the same as Nostrale.

nostrano (noh-STRAH-noh). Ita. Homegrown.

noten (NO-tuh). Dut. **Nuts.**

nötkött (NOHT-chot). Swe. **Beef.**

nøtteterte (NURT-teh-tehr-teh). Nor. **Nut** layer **cake.**

nougat (noo-gah). Fre. A **confection** made of roasted **nuts,** usually **almonds,** and **honey** or **syrup.**

nougatine (noo-gah-ten). Fre. Can be any of several **confections** such as **almond brittle** or **nougat** combined with **chocolate;** a vague term.

nouilles (noo-yuh). Fre. **Noodles.**

nova (NOH-veh). USA. Cold-smoked **salmon,** eaten like **lox** with **cream cheese** and **bagels.**

nouvelle cuisine (noo-vehl-le koo-szen). Fre. The movement toward fresher, lighter foods, served in smaller portions; prepared by classic French techniques.

noyau (nwah-yoh). Fre. The stone of a **fruit; a liqueur** flavored with **peach** or **nectarine** kernels.

noz (nosh). Por. **Walnut.**

Nudeln (NOO-derln). Ger. **Noodles** of a stiff paste made with **flour** and **eggs,** rolled out very thin, cut up in thin strips and boiled, and served as a **garnish,** or **fried** and served as a sweet.

Nudelschöberl (NOO-derl-shor-berl). Ger. Austrian **noodle** pie, usually served with meat.

nudlar (nood-lahr). Swe. **Dumplings.**

nuez (new-ez). Spa. **Walnut** or **nut.**

nuka (noo-KAH). Jap. **Rice bran;** one of the basic **pickling** media in Japan.

nun's toast (nuhnz tohst). USA. Hard-boiled **eggs** with milk **gravy,** served over **toast.**

nuò mi zóngzi (nuo me DZONG-dze). Chi. A dish of **lotus** leaves stuffed with sweet **rice** and meat.

Nur Hier (noor her). Ger. "Only Here"; a solid, black bread sold only in Hamburg.

Nuss (NEW-sser). Ger. **Nut, walnut.**

nut meal (nuht mel). USA. Finely **ground** dry **nuts** used as a **flour** substitute in many **Torten.**

nutmeg (NUHT-mehg). USA. The dried seed found inside the tropical fruit of the **nutmeg** tree, which is **ground** and used to flavor a wide range of sweet and savory dishes.

nuts (nuhtz). USA. A generic term referring to the edible **nut** of a given tree. Varieties listed in this volume are **almonds, Brazil nuts, filberts (hazelnuts), peanuts, pecans, pistachios, walnuts.**

nymphes à l'aurore (nehf ay l'ohr-ohr). Fre. A beautiful, shimmery dish; **frog legs** poached in white wine, covered with pink **chaud-froid sauce, garnished** with chopped **aspic.**

nypon (NEW-poan). Swe. **Rose hips;** used in **jellies, soups.**

nyponsoppa (NU-pon-SOHP-pa). Swe. **Rose-hip soup.**

nyrer (NEW-rerr). Dan, Nor. **Kidney.**

nyrøket laks (NEW-rurkt lahks). Nor. **Smoked salmon.**

oatmeal (OUHT-mel). USA. Coarse ground **oats,** used in baking or as hot **cereal.**

oats, rolled (ouhts, rold). USA. Hulled **oats ground** to a meal, steamed to gelatinize starch, rolled into flakes, then dried, allowing much shorter cooking time.

oboro konbu (o-BOL-o KOHM-boo). Jap. A form of **konbu** that is soaked in **vinegar** and shaved the width of the leaf to form a thin sheet.

O'Brien (oh-BRY-N). USA. A **garnish** of **sautéed bacon, onions,** red and green **peppers** usually served over a **potato** dish.

Obst (oapst). Ger. **Fruit.**

Obstsauce (OAPST-saus). Ger. A sweet-sour **fruit sauce** made to accompany roasted meats.

Obstsuppe (OAPST-zup-per). Ger. **Soup** of **puréed fruits.**

Obsttorte (OAPST-tor-ter). Ger. An open **fruit tart, glazed** and usually **garnished** with **whipped cream** or **meringue** and **almonds.**

oca (OH-kah). Ita. Goose.

ocha (oh-CHAH). Jap. Green **tea.**

Ochs (ahks). Ger. Ox, beef; rindfleisch.

Ochsenbraten (AHK-sern-braa-tern). Ger. **Roast** beef.

Ochsenlende (AHK-sern-lehn-dern). Ger. Beef **filet.**

Ochsenmausalat (AHK-sern-maw-zah-laa-ter). Ger. **Salad** of cold beef, **onions, vinegar.**

Ochsenniere (AHK-sern-ner). Ger. Beef **kidney.**

Ochsenschwanz (AHK-sern-shvnz). Ger. **Oxtail.**

Ochsenzunge (AHK-sern-tsun-ger). Ger. **Ox tongue.**

octopus (OHK-tah-puhs).   USA. A sea **mollusk** of flavorful but tough meat, often **smoked, stewed,** or **marinated;** used mainly by Oriental and Mediterranean cultures.

oeil d'anchois (uhy d'on-shwah).   Fre. An **hors d'oeuvre** of raw **egg yolk** surrounded by **anchovies** and **chopped onion;** literally "eye of anchovy."

oester (OOS-turs).   Dut. **Oyster.**

oeufs (uhfs).   Fre. **Eggs;**
>   **oeufs à la coque** (uhfs ah lah kok mol-leh)   soft-boiled eggs;
>   **oeufs à la coque** (uhfs ah lah kok) boiled eggs;
>   **oeufs au plat** (uhfs oa plah) fried eggs;
>   **oeufs brouillés** (uhfs broo-yay) scrambled eggs;
>   **oeufs bûcheronee** (uhfs boo-cher-rohn) beaten eggs poured over slices of **ham** on **toast** and baked;
>   **oeufs chasser** (uhfs shah-ser) scrambled eggs with **chicken** livers;
>   **oeufs durs** (uhfs dewrz) hard-boiled eggs;
>   **oeufs en cocotte** (uhfs uhng koh-koht) eggs poached in a **casserole;**
>   **oeufs farcis** (uhfs fahr-se) **stuffed** eggs;
>   **oeufs frits** (uhfs fre) fried eggs;
>   **oeufs en gelée** (uhfs uhng zhel-ah) eggs **poached** and chilled in **aspic;**
>   **oeufs justine** (uhfs zjos-sten) hard-cooked eggs stuffed with **mushrooms** in **cream sauce,** coated with breadcrumbs and **fried** in butter;
>   **oeufs pochés** (uhfs poh-shay) **poached** eggs;
>   **oeufs pochés bénédictine** (uhfs poh-shay bay-nay-dehk-ten) eggs **poached** and served on a creamed **salt-cod base,** not **Eggs Benedict;**
>   **oeufs poêles** (uhfs pwahl) eggs sunny side up;
>   **oeufs rossini** (uhfs roh-ze-ne) egg yolks baked on a **meringue** of whites;
>   **oeufs sur le plat** (uhfs syr ler pla) baked eggs.

oeufs à la neige (uhfs ah lah nehzh).   Fre. **Snow eggs,** which are egg-shaped **meringues, poached** in sweetened **milk,** drained, and served with a **custard sauce.**

offal (OWF-fuhl).   USA. Internal organs or trimmings removed from the skeletal meat, such as brains, heart, **sweetbreads,** liver, **kidneys,** pancreas, spleen, **tripe, tongue,** headmeat, tail, blood, skin, feet, horns, intestines; carrion; can mean inedible waste.

ofentori (oh-fehn-TOH-re).   Ita. A Swiss dish of mashed **potatoes** flecked with **diced bacon.**

Ohio pudding (oh-HI-oh PUHD-dehng). USA. Mashed **sweet potatoes, carrots,** and **squash mixed** with **brown sugar,** bread crumbs, and **light cream,** baked until firm; served with sauce of **butter, confectioner's sugar, cream,** and **lemon** juice.

ohraryynipuuro (oah-rah-rew-ne-POO-roa). Fin. Thick **barley porridge** eaten with cream and sugar.

oie (wah). Fre. Goose.

oie á l'instar de visé (wah a'lehn-stahr day veh-say). Fre. A Belgian speciality of roast goose in a rich **cream** and **garlic sauce**; a gastronomic triumph of Visé.

oignon (ohn-nawng). Fre. **Onion.**

oignon cloute (ohn-nawng kloo-teh). Fre. **Onion** studded with **cloves.**

oiseau (wah-zoh) Fre. Bird.

oiseaux sans tête (wah-zoh seh teht). Fre. Meat birds; meat **scallops stuffed,** rolled, and cooked.

oison (wah-zyoh). Fre. Gosling.

Oka (o-KAH). Can. A cheese that is a type of Port du Salat made by Trappist monks in Oka, Canada.

okara (o-KAH-lah). Jap. **Soybean** pulp that is the by-product of **tofu-**making; crumbly, white, high in protein; provides bulk and roughage; use with **vegetables,** in **salads** and **soups.**

okayu (o-KAI-yoo). Jap. **Rice gruel.**

okra (OH-krah). USA. A tropical plant from Africa whose seed pods are used as a **vegetable** or as a thickener for **gumbos** and **soups.**

oksebryst (OAKS-er-stayg). Dan. Beef **brisket.**

oksefilet (OAKSS-er-fil-lay). Nor. **Filet** of beef.

oksekødsuppe (OAKS-er-kurdh-soob-ber). Dan. Beef **soup.**

oksesteg (OAKS-er-stayg). Dan. **Roast beef.**

oksestek (OAKSS-ers-stayk). Nor. **Roast beef.**

oksetunge (OK-seh-toong-eh). Dan. Beef **tongue.**

Öl (url). Ger. Oil.

öl (url). Swe. **Beer.**

øl (url). Dan, Nor. **Beer.**

Old Heidelberg (Old HI-dehl-behrg).   USA. A soft, surface-ripened **cheese** made in Illinois; very much like **Liederkranz.**

olie (O-le).   Dan, Dut. Oil.

oliebollen (O-le-bawl-luh).   Dut. **Doughnuts,** usually filled with **currants** and **raisins.**

olijfolie (oh-LIF-oh-le).   Dut. **Olive oil.**

olijven (oh-LIV-vahn).   Dut. **Olives.**

olio (OL-yoa).   Ita. Oil.

Oliven (o-LE-veh).   Ger. **Olives.**

olive oil (AHL-leev ohul).   USA. Important cooking oil pressed from **olives;** basic oil in Italian cooking; most common grades are:
   Extra virgin: first cold press from superior quality olives; contains no cholesterol; less than 1% acidity; light, delicate taste; clear greenish color.
   Superfine virgin: second cold press from superior quality olives; less than 1.5% acidity; clear greenish color.
   Virgin: third cold press from olives of superior quality olives; contains no cholesterol; 1–3% acidity; light taste.
   Refined: has higher acidity; limpid yellow color; contains no cholesterol. 100% pure: pressed from blended olive varieties; a mixture of refined and 5–10% virgin; contains no cholesterol.
   Pomace (POH-muhs): a hot press after the third press, higher acidity, stronger flavor.
   Sansa (SAHUN-zah): a low grade oil; hot pressed, high acidity, very strong flavor.

oliver (oo-LI-ver).   Swe. **Olives.**

olives (o-LE-vay).   Ita. The fruit of the **olive** tree; used **brined** or preserved in oil.

olives (AHL-levez).   USA, Bri. The fruit of the **olive tree,** used brined or preserved in oil. Also meat birds; a small slice of meat wrapped around a savory **filling.**

Olivet (oh-le-veh).   Fre. A soft, cow's-milk **cheese** similar to **Camembert.** There are three types: Unripened, made from whole milk with cream added; Half-ripened or blue, made with whole or partly skimmed milk (this is the most common type.); Ripened, also made from partly skimmed or whole milk.

Olivet Bleu (oh-le-veh bluhr).   Fre. **Olivet cheese** matured for a month, having a delicate blue rind.

olivette (oh-le-vay).   Fre. Refers to food cut oblong-shaped and about ⅛ inch in diameter.

olivette di vitello (oh-LE-veh de ve-TEHL-loa).   Ita. Veal birds; veal **scallops stuffed,** rolled, and **braised.**

olivetti (oh-le-VE-te).   Ita. Meat birds.

olja (OL-yah).   Swe. Oil.

Olmutzer Quargel (Ole-moot-zehr Quaw-keal).   Ger. A sour-milk, spiced **Hand cheese** containing **caraway** seed.

olla Gitana (ohl-lah je-TAH-nah).   Spa. An all-**vegetable,** no meat **stew;** gypsy stew.

olla podrida (ohl-lah poh-DRE-dah).   Spa. A stew of different meats, mainly **pork,** and **cabbage, chickpeas, tomatoes.**

øllebrød (URL-er-brurdh).   Dan. **Soup** made with black bread and nonalcoholic malt **beer.**

olut (OA-loot).   Fin. **Beer.**

omenalumi (OH-meh-na-LOO-me).   Fin. **Apple snow dessert.**

omelet (OHUM-leht).   USA. Beaten **eggs** cooked in **butter,** in an omelet pan, until set; usually filled with a wide variety of seasonings and **fillings;** can be savory or sweet.

omeletta (OHUM-leh-tay).   Ita. A rolled **omelet.**

omelette (ohum-let).   Fre. **Omelet.**

omelette à la norvégienne (ohum-let ah lah nor-vay-zhyehn).   Fre. **Baked Alaska.**

omena (OA-may-nah).   Fin. **Apple.**

omenasose (OA-may-nah-SOA-ssay).   Fin. **Applesauce.**

omuretsu (oh-MOO-reh-tsoo).   Jap. **Omelet.**

onion (UN-yun).   USA. The generic name for the edible bulbs of the lily family; numerous varieties worldwide. See specific name.

onion rings (UN-yun rengs).   USA. Slices of large **onions,** separated into rings, **dipped** in **batter,** and **deep-fried.**

ontbijtkoek (awnt-BAY-tuh-kook).   Dut. A breakfast spice **cake.**

oolong (OO-lohng).   Chi. An amber-colored, partially fermented **tea.**

operatärta (OO-peh-ra-TOR-ra).   Swe. Creamy layer **cake.**

opgerolde koek (oh-per-ROLD kook).   Dut. Rolled-up **cake.**

orange (AWH-rehnj). USA. The globular fruit of the **orange** tree; peel is a bright orange; pulp is segmented, juicy, sweet, slightly acidic.

orange flower water (AWH-rehnj flawr wah-tuhr). USA. Liquid distilled during the extraction of essential oil from bitter **orange** blossoms and used as a flavoring; principal flavoring extract of the Middle East.

orange pekoe (AWH-rehnj PE-koh). USA. A superior grade of **tea** from India or Ceylon with leaves slightly larger than **pekoe.**

orange roughy (AWH-rehnj RUFF-fe). USA. A fish of the South Pacific found in New Zealand waters; has firm white flesh and a bland taste; is sold in **fillets** and can be **baked, broiled, pan-fried,** or **poached.**

orange sauce (AWH-rehnj saus). Fre. **Demi-glace** with **orange,** and sometimes **lemon,** juice and **julienne** orange zest.

orata (oa-RAA-tah). Ita. Large, fine fish found along the Riviera.

oregano (oh-REHG-guhn-oh). USA. An herb similar to **marjoram,** more pungent; **wild marjoram;** popular in Italian cookery.

Oregon grapes (OHR-re-gohn grapz). USA. **Barberries.**

oreilles (oh-rehy). Fre. Ears of slaughtered animals.

organic (oar-GAHN-iek). USA. Anything grown without artifical or chemical fertilizers or pesticides.

orge (orj). Fre. **Barley.**

orientale (o-ryon-tahl). Fre. Seasoned with **curry** or **saffron,** and sometimes **garnished** with **rice-stuffed tomatoes.**

Oriental garlic (ORE-e-ent-ahl GAR-lick). USA. An exotic name for common **garlic.**

origan (ko-re-gahng). Fre. **Oregano.**

origano (oa-RE-gahg-noa). Ita. **Oregano.**

orly (ohr-le). Fre. A dish of sliced fish or meat dipped in a rich **batter** and **fried** in fat. Also *horly.*

ormer (OHR-mehr). Bri. **Abalone.**

orre (O-rrer). Swe. Black **grouse.**

ørred (URR-erdh). Dan. **Trout.**

ørret (URR-eht). Nor. **Trout.**

ortolan (ort-o-lahng). Fre. A small, nearly extinct bird, prized for its flavor; it is plucked, usually boned, but not drawn, as its entrails are considered delicious.

oscietr (ahs-sye-TRE). Rus. **Roe** of the white **sturgeon;** the world's very best **caviar.**

oseille (oh-zehj). Fre. **Sorrel.**

ossenhaas (AWS-suh-hahs). Dut. **Filet** of beef.

ossestaartsoep (OS-ses-staht soup). Dut. **Oxtail soup.**

osso bucco (O-so BOO-ko). Ita. Veal **shank** or shin boncs slowly braised with **carrots, tomatoes, onions, celery, garlic,** white wine, **stock,** and **garnished** with a mixture of **chopped parsley, garlic,** and grated **lemon** zest called **gremolada.**

ost (oost). Swe, Nor, Dan. **Cheese.**

østers (URSS-tersh). Dan, Nor. **Oysters.**

ostkaka (OOST-kaw-kah). Swe. **Pudding-**like **cheesecake** that is **baked** in a mold.

ostras (OS-trahss). Spa, Por. **Oysters.**

òstriche (O-stre-kay). Ita. **Oysters.**

ostron (OOST-ron). Swe. **Oyster.**

ostronläda (OOST ron LOΛ-dah). Swe. Escalloped **oysters.**

ou (oh). Chi. **Lotus** root.

ouaouaron (ooah-ooah-RROWN). USA. **Cajun** word for frog.

ouzo (OO-zo). Gre. A sweet **anise-**flavored **liqueur.**

ovenfry (UH-vehn-fri). USA. A method of cooking meats by dredging in seasoned flour, rolling in melted fat, placing on sheet pans and baking in a hot oven; results in browning without turning.

ovoli (oa-VAWL-le). Ita. A highly prized **mushroom** that resembles an **egg;** has a bright orange cap; eaten raw as a salad.

ovos (AH-vohss). Por. **Eggs;** *ovos cozidos* (AH-vohss koh-ZEE-dohss) hard-boiled eggs; *ovos estrelados* (AH-vohss ess-tray-LAH-dohss) fried eggs; *ovos mexidos* (AH-vohss meh-SHEE-dohss) scrambled eggs; *ovos pochê* (AH-vohss poh-SHAY) poached eggs; *ovos quentes* (AH-vohss KEN-tayss) soft-boiled eggs.

ovos moles (AH-vohss MOH-layss). Por. **Egg yolks** mixed with **sugar** and used as a **sauce** or **filling;** can be molded, cooked in **rice water,** and sprinkled with **cinnamon.**

ox (ooks). Swe. Beef.

oxbringa (OOKS-bringah). Swe. Beef **brisket.**

oxfilé (OOKS-fil-lay). Swe. Beef **filet.**

Oxford pudding (OHKS-ford puhd-deng). Bri. **Apricot tart** masked with **meringue.**

Oxford sauce (OHKS-ford saus). Bri. **Red currant jelly** dissolved with **port,** flavored with **shallots, orange zest,** and **mustard;** an accompaniment for **game.**

oxidation (OHKS-e-da-shun). USA. Exposure to oxygen, generally causing a darkening of the product, as well as a deterioration of freshness.

oxkött (OOKS-tyurt). Swe. Beef.

oxrulader (OOKS-roo-la-der). Swe. Piquant rolled **beef.**

oxstek (OOKS-stayk). Swe. **Roast beef.**

oxsvanssoppa (OOKS-svans-SO-pa). Swe. **Oxtail soup.**

oxtail (OHKS-tal). Bri. Tail of beef; excellent in **soups** and **stews** because of high percentage of **gelatin.**

oxtunga (OOKS-toong-er). Swe. Beef **tongue.**

oyster (OEHY-stuhr). USA. A bivalve **mollusk** with a rough, irregular shaped shell; eaten **raw** or prepared in numerous ways: **stews, dressings, soups, baked, fried, sautéed.**

oyster crab (OEHY-stur krahb). USA. A tiny, ½-inch, crispy , pink **crab** found living in the shell of a live oyster; may be eaten **raw, sautéed,** or **deep-fried.**

oyster mushroom (OEHY-stuhr mush-rohm). USA. Has an oyster shell shape; is grey-brown with a delicate flavor and texture; tastes peppery when raw; use with **veal, chicken, pork** chop, **hamburger,** or steak; also use in **omelets** and **stews.**

oyster plant (OEHY-stuhr plahnt). USA. **Salsify.**

oyster sauce (OEHY-stuhr saus) USA. A thick paste consisting of **oysters, salt,** and seasonings; **li jiang.**

Oysters Bienville (OEHY-stuhr be-ehn-vell). USA. **Oysters** with **béchamel sauce** of green **peppers, onions, cheese,** and bread crumbs; originated in New Orleans.

Oysters Rockefeller (OEHY-stuhrs ROK-e-fehl-lehr). USA. **Oysters** on the half shell, resting on a bed of **rock salt,** each topped with **puréed,** seasoned **spinach,** then quickly browned.

Paj - Swedish - Pie

P

paalaeg (poh-LAYGH). Dan. "Something laid on"; that which is put on buttered bread, such as cold meats or **salads** to make open-face **sandwiches.**

paan (pahn). Ind. Betel leaves, used as a **vegetable** by stuffing with spices and nuts; used as a digestive agent.

paani (PAH-ne). Ind. Water.

paaskebryg (poah-skeh-BREHRG). Dan. A high alcoholic content dark **beer.**

pachadi (PAH-cha-re). Ind. **Vegetables** and **yogurt** flavored with **mustard** seeds.

paella (pah-AY-lyah). Spa. A **rice** dish cooked with a variety of meats, **sausage, shellfish, game;** assorted **vegetables** including **peas** and **tomatoes;** flavored with **garlic, onions,** and **saffron;** exact ingredients vary widely.

pære (PAER-err). Dan. **Pear.**

pagello (PAH-jahl-loa). Ita. Red snapper.

Paglia (Pahg-LE-ah). Swi. A Swiss blue-veined **cheese** with a soft, mellow body and a pleasing aromatic flavor; similar to **Gorgonzola.**

paglia e fieno (PAL-ya e FYE-noh). Ita. "Straw and hay" **fettucine;** half green, made with **spinach,** and half white, made with **egg** only; served simply with melted **butter** and **Parmesan cheese,** or sometimes with reduced **cream** and Parmesan.

Pago (PAH-goh). Ita. A **cheese** made from ewe's milk.

pähkinäkakku (PAEH-kin-nae-KAHK-koo). Fin. A very rich **cake** made with **ground walnuts,** served covered with **whipped cream.**

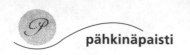

pähkinäpaisti (PAEH-kin-nae-PAH-sti). Fin. A meatless meaty-tasting patty made of ground **nuts** and **rice.**

paillarde de veau (pahy-lahrd der voa). Fre. **Grilled veal scallop.**

paillettes (pahy-leht). Fre. Pastry straws; can also be **potatoes** cut in very thin straw-like shreds.

pain (pang). Fre. Bread, loaf.

pain à la Greque (pang ah lah grehs). Fre. Belgian Greek bread; rich little **cakes.**

pain a l'anglaise (pang ah l'ahng-glehz). Fre. Bread sauce, a **sauce** of **milk** thickened with bread crumbs.

pain bis (pang bez). Fre. **Brown bread.**

pain complet (pang kohm-pleh). Fre. Whole grain bread.

pain de Genes (pang day zheh-nehz). Fre. Genoa **cake,** a rich **almond** pound cake.

pain de mie (pang day my). Fre. **Sandwich** bread.

pain d'epice (pang d'eh-spehs). Fre. **Gingerbread.**

pain de seigle (pang day sehgl). Fre. Rye bread.

pain de veau (pang day vooh). Fre. Wonderfully flavored Belgium **veal** loaf.

pain fourré (pang foo-reh). Fre. Small **rolls,** filled like **sandwiches.**

pain grille (pang grehj). Fre. **Toast.**

pain mollet (pang moh-leh). Fre. Soft bread.

pain noir (pang nwahr). Fre. Black bread made of rye, wheat, and **buckwheat.**

pain perdu (pang per-dru). Fre. **French toast** as made in France from stale bread, usually sweetened, with **cinnamon** added.

pain tôti (pang toa-te). Fre. **Toast.**

pain trouvé (pang truh-veh). Fre. "Found Bread"; A Belgian dish of **French toast** topped with **béchamel sauce, chopped ham,** and **Parmesan cheese.**

paio (pah-E-oo). Por. Meaty **garlic sausage.**

paistettu kana (PAHS-stayt-too KAH-nah). Fin. **Fried chicken.**

paisteutut sienet (PYE-steh-toot SE-yen-ett). Fin. **Fried mushrooms.**

paistinperunat (PAHS-stern-pay-roo-naht). Fin. **Fried potatoes.**

paj (pay). Swe. **Pie.**

pakode (pah-KOOH-ray). Ind. **Fritters.**

pakoras (pah-KOOH-rayz). Ind. A spicy **fritter,** served hot as an **appetizer** or snack.

palacsinta (POL-lo-chen-to). Hun. **Crepe.**

palak (PAH-lek). Ind. **Spinach.**

palate knife (PAHL-laht nif). USA. A wide, flexible spatula used for spreading **butter** or **icing.**

palatschinke (pah-lah-TSHIN-kern). Ger. **Pancakes** with sweet or savory **fillings.**

pale (pael). Nor. A young, very bony fish of the **cod** family.

paleron de boeuf (pah-ler-ron der burf). Fre. **Marinated chuck roast.**

paling (PAH-ling). Dut. **Eel.**

palm (pahlm). USA. A large family of tropical trees and shrubs; many of its parts are edible.

palm butter (pahlm BUHT-ter). USA. Palm oil.

palm cabbage (pahlm CAHB-bahge). USA. The terminal head of a type of the edible palmetto; eaten as a **vegetable.** Also called swamp cabbage.

palm heart (pahlm hahrt). USA. New buds or shoots of the palm tree.

palmier (pahlm-ay). Fre. A pastry made from strips of a **puff pastry,** sprinkled with **sugar, folded, sliced,** and **baked;** looks like a palm leaf.

palm oil (pahlm ouyl). USA. Oil extracted from parts of the palm tree.

palm wine (pahlm wyne). USA. Wine made from the sap of a dying palm tree; called lagmi.

paloise (pahl-wahz). Fre. **Bearnaise** sauce flavored with **mint** instead of **tarragon.**

palombe (pahl-lomb). Fre. Dove; wild **pigeon.**

palourde (pah-loord). Fre. **Clam.**

Pampasgrass (PAHM-pahs-grahs). Arg. A blue-veined grass.

Pampelmuse (PAHM-perl-moo-zwe). Ger. **Grapefruit.**

pamplemousse (pahng-pler-moos). Fre. **Grapefruit.**

pan (pahn). Spa. Bread.

panache (pah-nach). Fre. Used to describe **salad, fruit, ice cream;** means mixed colors.

panade (pah-nahd). Fre. Culinary **paste** of **flour** and water or soaked bread, used for preparing **forcemeat, mousse,** or **stuffing;** can also be a peasant **soup** of water, **stock,** or **milk** thickened with bread.

panais (pah-neh). Fre. Parsnip.

panato (pah-NAH-toa). Ita. Coated in breadcrumbs, then **fried.**

pan broil (pahn-brouyl). USA. A method of cooking meat without added liquid, uncovered, using a very hot heavy iron skillet, **searing** and **browning** the meat on the bottom side, then turning at once to sear and brown the other side.

pancake (PAHN-kak). USA. A batter **cake** cooked on a griddle or pan. Usually served in stacks with melted **butter** and **syrup.**

pancetta (pahn-CHEHT-tah). Ita. Unsmoked **bacon cured** with spices, salt, and pepper; may be rolled or flat.

pancetta affumicata e uova (pahn-CHEHT-tah ahf-foo-me-KAA-tah ay WAW-vah). Ita. **Bacon** and **eggs.**

panchporan (PAHUNCH-por-rahn). Ind. A five-spice seasoning: whole **cumin** seeds, whole black **mustard** seeds, whole **fennel** seeds,whole kalonji, and whole **fenugreek** seeds, mixed in equal portions. See **wu hsiang fun; five-spice seasoning.**

pancit (PAHN-cet). Phi. **Pasta,** usually in shape of **noodles,** often **stir-fried** with **chopped** meats, **seafood, vegetables.** Also **dough** wrappers that are **stuffed** with savory **fillings.**

pancotto (pahn-KOT-toa). Ita. A Milanese **soup** made of stale bread.

panderkager (PAHN-er-kaa-err). Dan. **Pancakes.**

pan di genova (PAA-nay de jayn-oa-vay). Ita. **Almond cake.**

pan di natale (PAA-nay de nah-TAA-lay). Ita. "Christmas bread"; a soft sweet **yeast dough** with candied **fruits, nuts, raisins, pine nuts** added, made into varying shapes and textures.

pan di Spagna (PAA-nay de SPAA-nah). Ita. A **sponge cake** filled with **cream** or **jam** and soaked with **liqueur.**

pandorato (pahn-doh-RAH-toa). Ita. Bread dipped in an **egg-milk batter,** usually **stuffed** with a savory **filling,** and **deep-fried; French toast.**

pandoro (pahn-DOH-roa).   Ita. A **cake** traditionally served at Christmas-time; very light in texture, like a **sponge cake,** and is shaped like an octagonal cone.

pandours (pahn-doers).   Bri. A variety of **oyster** found in the Firth of Forth.

pandowdy (pahn-DOW-de).   USA. A **cobbler** of **sliced apples, cider,** spices, **brown sugar** or **molasses,** and **butter,** covered with **biscuit dough,** then **baked.**

pan drippings (pahn DREHP-pengs).   USA. The browned bits of meat and fat left in the pan after **roasting, frying;** used as basis for **pan gravy,** adding **flour** and liquid.

pan dressed (pahn-drehsd).   USA. Refers to a gutted and scaled fish with head and fins removed, ready for **sautéeing** or **deep-frying.**

pan-fry (pahn-fri).   USA. To cook in a skillet in small amount of fat.

pané (pah-nay).   Fre. Breadcrumbed.

pane (PAA-nay).   Ita. Bread.

pane bianco (PAY-nay be AHNG-koa).   Ita. White bread.

pane bolognese (PAY-nay boa-loa-nays).   Ita. **Corn** bread.

pane di frumento (PAY-nay de froo-MEHN-toa).   Ita. **Whole wheat** bread.

pane di segala (PAY-nay de say-GAH-lah).   Ita. Black **rye** bread.

paneer (pah-NER).   Ind. Chenna, **Indian cheese,** compressed into a **cake** and cut in small pieces; also chhena.

pane grattugiato (PAY-nay graht-too-AH-toa).   Ita. Bread crumbs; **pangrattato.**

pane scuro (PAY-nay SCHOO-roa).   Ita. Dark bread.

pane tostato (PAA-nay to-STAA-toa).   Ita. **Toast.**

panettone (pahn-EHT-tohn).   Ita. A cylindrical-shaped **yeast-dough cake** with **sultana raisins** and candied **lemon** peel, eaten at breakfast; traditional at Christmas.

Panfisch (PAHN-fish).   Ger. Minced fish and **onion** in mashed **potatoes.**

panforte (pahn-FOHR-teh).   Ita. **Fruitcake;** a flat, very rich **cake** containing **walnuts, almonds, hazelnuts, honey,** candied **fruits,** lots of spices.

pangrattato (pahn-grah-TAH-to). Ita. "Grated bread"; breadcrumbs produced by drying stale bread in the oven, then processing in a food processor until the texture of coarse sand.

pángxiè (pong-sieh). Chi. **Crab.**

panino (pah-NE-noa). Ita. A **biscuit; roll.**

panna (PAHN-nah). Ita. **Cream.**

panna montana (PAHN-nah moan-TAH-nah). Ita. **Whipped cream.**

Pannarone (pahn-nay-ROAN-nay). Ita. A fast-ripening **Gorgonzola-**type **cheese** with white curd without blue veining.

pannbiff med lök (PAHN-bif mit lurk). Swe. **Chopped** steak with **onions.**

pannee (pahn-nay). Fre. A method of **frying cutlets** of meat or fish in a pan using a thick crust of seasoned breading with the end result a very hot, oily, delicious tidbit of **chicken, veal,** or steak.

pannekoeken (PAHN-nuh-koo-kuh). Dut. **Pancakes.**

pannequet (pahn-nuhr-kahy). Fre. Small **crepe** filled with sweet or savory **filling** and folded in quarters.

Pannerone (pahn-nay-ROAN-nay). Ita. An unsalted cow's-milk **cheese;** pale yellow, creamy; delicate, slightly tangy, flavor. Also called *White Gorgonzola.*

panning (PAHN-neng). USA. To cook a vegetable in a tightly covered skillet, using a small amount of fat; no water is added.

pannkakor (PAHN-kaa-koor). Swe. **Pancakes.**

pannkakor med sylt (PAN-KAH-koor mah SULT). Swe. Large, thin **pancakes** with **jam.**

pannukakku (PAHN-noo-KAHK-koo). Fin. Oven-baked **pancake** used for **dessert.**

panocha (pah-NOH-chah). Mex. A **candy** made of **brown sugar, milk, butter,** and **nuts.** Also spelled **penuche.**

pan pepato (PAA-nay pay-PAH-toa). Ita. A **cake** made with **nuts, raisins, almonds, chocolate,** and **hazelnuts** and flavored with **nutmeg** and **pepper.**

pantostato (paa-nay-to-STAA-toa). Ita. **Toasted bread.**

panucho (pah-NOO-choh). Mex. A small **tortilla fried** until puffed-up, filled with savory **filling,** then fried until crisp.

panure (pahn-nyr). Fre. Golden breadcrumb crust.

panurette (pahn-oo-rett). Fre. Grated **rusks,** used for crumbs and for lining the inside of molds.

panvis (PAHN-ves). Dut. **Casserole** of **dried codfish, onions, potatoes.**

panzanella (pahn-tsah-NAYL-lah). Ita. A **vegetable** and **anchovy salad,** served with stale bread that has been soaked in water, squeezed dry, fried in **olive oil.**

panzarotti (pahn-tsah-RAWT-te). Ita. **Deep-fried cheese**-stuffed **noodle** crescents.

pão (pan). Por. Bread.

pap (pahp). Dut. **Porridge.**

papa (PAH-pah). Mex. **Potato.**

papad (PAH-per). Ind. Lentil wafers.

papain (pah-PAHI-un). USA. An enzyme from the **papaya,** used for tenderizing meats.

papatzul (pah-paht-SUIIL). Mex. Egg-stuffed tortilla with **pumpkin** seed.

papaw (PAW-paw). USA. **Papaya.**

papaya (pah-PAHY-yah). USA. A large pear-shaped tropical **fruit** with orange flesh, black seeds, skin turns yellow when ripe; unripe, it is cooked as a **vegetable;** ripe, eaten **raw** as a **fruit;** leaves when cooked resemble **spinach.**

papeeta (pa-PE-tah). Ind. **Papaya.**

papillon (pah-pe-yawnh). Fre. A butterfly-shaped **cookie** of flaky pastry.

papillote (pah-pe-joht). Fre. A paper frill used to dress the bone-end of chops or **crown roast.**

papillote, en (pah-pe-joht, ahng). Fre. Baked in a greased paper wrapper.

papos de anjo (PAH-pahsh deh AHN-zhoo). Por. Small **egg cakes** served with **syrup.**

pappa al pomodoro (pah-pah al pohm-oh-DOH-roa). Ita. A Tuscan **soup** made of stale bread.

pappardelle (pahp-pahr-DEHL-leh).   Ita. Long, flat, broad **egg noodles** with crimped edge; traditionally served with **hare** cooked in a rich **wine sauce; fettuccine, tagliatelle.**

paprika (PO-pre-ko).   Hun. Red **pepper;** sweet, brilliant scarlet color, and slight pungent odor.

paprikas (PAH-pre-kahs).   Dut. Green **peppers; capsicum.**

paprikas csirke (PO-pre-ko CHEER-kae).   Hun. A dish of **chicken braised** with **garlic, onions, sour cream,** and **paprika.** Also made with meat or fish.

papu (PAH-poo).   Fin. **Bean.**

paquette (pah-kett).   Fre. Mature **lobster roe,** dark greenish-black in color, about to be laid; Also refers to the female lobster carrying such roe.

paradeiser (pah-rah-DIGH-zerr).   Ger. **Tomato.**

paratha (pa-RAHT-ha).   Ind. Griddle-fried flaky **whole wheat** bread.

parblanch (pahr-blahnch).   USA. Placing food item in large quantity of cold water, bringing it slowly to a boil, uncovered, simmering, then draining of hot water bath, followed by plunging quickly into cold water to firm it and to stop any further cooking; then finished as instructed in the recipe; This process is used to leach excess **salt** from **cured** or **salted** meats, to remove excess blood or strong flavors from variety meats, and to firm proteins in fragile meats such as **sweetbreads.**

parboil (PAHR-boyl).   USA. To boil briefly; a preliminary cooking procedure.

parboiled rice (PAHR-boyld rice).   USA. Rough **rice** soaked in warm water under pressure, steamed, and dried before milling, thus gelatinizing the starch in the **grain,** which ensures a separateness of grain.

parch (pahrch).   USA. To cook in dry heat until slightly brown.

pare (pahcr).   USA. Cut off the outside peeling or covering, usually with a knife.

Parenica (Pah-rhen-ET-sah).   Hun. A **cheese** made of ewe's milk similar to **Caciocavallo.**

pareve (pahrv).   Jew. Kosher; containing no meat or milk, therefore suitable to be eaten with either.

parfait (pahr-FAY).   Fre. A cold or frozen **dessert** of layers of **fruit, syrup, nuts,** and **whipped cream.**

parfait (pahr-FAY).   USA. A **dessert** of **ice cream,** layered with **sauces** and **whipped cream** served in a tall narrow glass.

Paris-Brest (pah-re brehst).   Fre. A **dessert** of creamy **puff pastry** ring filled with **praline creme** topped with **sliced almonds,** or **chantilly cream** topped with fresh **strawberries.**

parisersmørgaas (par-rea-ser-SMEHR-goahs).   Dan. Scraped **raw** beef slightly **grilled** on **toast** with **egg.**

Parisienne (pa-re-zyan).   Fre. "After the fashion of Paris"; elaborately **garnished.**

Parker House Rolls (PAHR-kehr howus rolz).   USA. A **yeast roll** folded in two halves before baking; originated at the Parker House in Boston in nineteenth century.

Parma (PAHR-mah).   Ita. A semifirm to firm **cheese** that takes more than a year to cure; usually served in wedges; flavor is a cross between **Parmesan** and **Provolone.**

parmentier (pahr mahng-tc).   Frc. Containing **potatoes** in some form.

Parmesan (PAR-meh-szan).   Ita. One of the best known Italian **cheeses;** a cow's skim-milk cheese shaped in large, squat cylinders; pale yellow with a golden rind; dense, grainy, sweet, fragrant, mellow; young, it is a table cheese; aged at least two years, a sharp grating cheese; use freshly **grated** over many dishes; has been produced in Italy since 1200 AD.

parmigiana (par-me-ZHAN-ah).   Ita. **Veal, chicken,** or **eggplant** covered with **tomato sauce, mozarella cheese** and **Parmesan cheese;** then browned in an oven or broiler.

Parmigiano (pahr-me-JAA-noa).   Ita. One of the hard Italian **cheeses,** very similar to **Parmesan.**

päron (PAH-ron). Swe. **Pear.**

parrilla (pahr-RE-lyah). Spa. **Grill.**

parrillada di pescado (pahr-RE-lyah-doh de pays-KAH-dhoa).   Spa. Mixed **seafood grill** with **lemon.**

parsa (PAHR-sah). Fin. **Asparagus.**

parsley (PAHRS-le).   USA. A flavorful **herb** whose root, stem, and leaves have a high vitamin A-carrying factor; valuable as an agent for blending the flavors of other herbs and having the power to destroy the scent of **garlic** and **onion;** used **raw** or cooked.

parsley root (PAHRS-le ruht). USA. A **vegetable** similar in shape to a **carrot** topped with green leaves; tastes somewhat like **celery;** eaten fresh or cooked.

parsnips (PAHRS-nehps).   USA. A root **vegetable** of the **carrot** family usually served **boiled** and **buttered.**

parson's nose (PAHR-son's nohz).   USA. The tailpiece of a bird. Also **pope's nose.**

parsteaming (pahr STEM-eng).   USA. Steam-blanching; short duration **steaming;** for foods to be frozen or canned.

partans (PAHR-uns).   Bri. Large, tasty **crabs.**

partridge (PAHRT-trehdg).   USA. A medium-sized game bird with delicate flesh; the American ruffed **grouse,** bobwhite, **quail, pheasant;** a general term.

pasa (PAH-sah).   Mex. **Raisin.**

pasa ciruela (PAH-ssahss the-RWAY-lahss).   Spa. **Prune.**

pasha (PAH-sha).   Fin. **Cheesecake** of Russian origin.

pasilla (pah-SEHL-lah).   Mex. A very hot, long, dark brown **chili pepper.**

pass (pahss).   USA. To cause to go through a sieve or strainer.

passas (PAH-sahss).   Por. **Raisins.**

passata (pah-SAH -tah).   Ita. **Purée.**

passatelli in brodo (pah-sah-TELL-le en BRAW-doa).   Ita. A **pasta** of Parmesan, **eggs,** and breadcrumbs forced through a tool to form strands that are cooked and served in meat broth.

passato (pahs-SAH-toa).   Ita. Creamed.

passer (pah-say).   Fre. "To pass" a **sauce, soup, vegetable** or meat means to run it through a sieve, strainer, or cheesecloth. Also means to slightly **fry** over a quick fire to form a crusty surface on meats or **vegetables** intended to be finished by another method of cooking.

passion fruit (PAH-shun froot).   USA. The purple egg-sized tropical **fruit** whose sweet yellow flesh is eaten **raw** with the small black seeds, or squeezed for juice; has sweet-acid flavor. Also called **purple granadilla.**

pasta (PAHS-tah). Ita. A dough composed chiefly of **flour,** water, and sometimes **eggs,** and made into many shapes and sizes; 66 pastas are listed in this volume.

pasta al uovo (PAHS-tah ahl WAW-voa). Ita. **Egg pasta.**

pasta ascuitta (PAHS-tah a-SHOOT-toa). Ita. Dry or plain **pasta;** can be **stuffed** or in **sauce;** not served in **broth;** general term for cooked pasta.

pasta e fagioli (PAHS-tah ay fah-JOA-le). Ita. A soup of **pasta, white beans,** and **salt pork.**

Pasta Filata (PAHS-tah fe-LAH-toa). Ita. A "plastic curd" **cheese;** characterized by the fact that, after the whey is drained off, the curd is immersed in hot water or hot whey and is worked, stretched, and molded while in a plastic condition.

pasta foglia (PAH-syah FOL-yah). Ita. Puff pastry.

pasta frolla (PAHS-tah FROH-lah). Ita. Short **pasta.**

pasta in brodo (PAHS-tah en BRAW-doa). Ita. **Pasta** cooked in **soup.**

pasta primavera (PAHS-tah prc-mah-VEH-rah). USA. A dish of **pasta** made with a sauce of spring **vegetables.**

paste (past). USA. Soft, smooth mixture made of dry ingredients and a liquid.

paste (paast). Bri. Anything that spreads easily, such as **sandwich paste.**

pastei (PAHS-tay). Dut. Meat **pie; creamed chicken** or meat in **pastry shell.**

pasteijes (PAHS-tay-yers). Dut. **Pastry shells.**

pastéis (pahsh-TAYISH). Por. **Cakes;** used for either sweet cakes or savory such as codfish cakes.

pastej (PAHS-tay). Swe. **Pie.**

pastel (pahs-TAYL). Spa. Pastry, **cake, pie, pâté.**

pastél (pash-TEL). Por. **Pie, tart,** pastry.

pastélinho (pahsh-tay-LE-nyoo). Por. Small **pie.**

pastelitos (pah-stehl-E-tohs). Mex. **Cookies;** little **cakes.**

pastèque (pah-stehk). Fre. **Watermelon.**

Pastete (pas-TAY-teh). Ger. **Pie.**

pasteurize (PAHS-tuhr-riz). USA. Partial sterilization of perishable food products such as meat, fish, or **milk** with gamma ray radiation.

pasteurized process cheese (PAHS-tuhr-rizd PRAH-sess chez). USA. A blend of two or more natural cheeses, ground into fine particles, heated together to 150° F, cooled, poured into packaging, and hermetically sealed.

pasticcini (pahs-tet-CHE-ne). Ita. Savory or sweet **pies;** usually layers of **pasta** with a savory **filling; timbales.**

pastillage (pahst-te-ahz). Fre. A **paste** of **sugar,** water, and **gum tragacanth** used in the past to make various shapes; used for elaborate table decorations.

pastina (pahs-STE-nah). Ita. Small **pasta** used in **soups.**

pastis (pahs-tihs). Fre. An **anise**-flavored **liqueur.**

pastrami (pah-STRAH-me). Jew. A highly seasoned **smoked** beef prepared from shoulder cuts; used very thinly **sliced.**

pastry flour (PA-stre flawr). USA. Milled of soft **wheat; fine** granulation; low **gluten;** excellent for **quick breads** and pastries.

pasty (PA-ste). Bri. A Cornish **turnover** with various **fillings,** usually of meats or **vegetables.**

pata (PAH-toa). Spa. **Duck.**

Patagras (Pah-tah-grahs). Cuba. A hard **cheese** made from pasteurized, whole or slightly skimmed cow's milk; almost identical to **Gouda;** one of Cuba's best cheeses.

patakukko (PAH-tah-kook-ko). Fin. "Pot fowl"; a **casserole** of small freshwater fish and **salt pork** baked under a **rye crust.**

patata (pah-TAH-tah). Spa. **Potato;** *patata fritas* (pah-TAH-tahss FREE-tahss) fried potatoes, french fries.

patata (pah-TAA-tay) Ita. Potato; *patata fritte* (pah-TAA-tay FREET-tay) fried potatoes; french fries; *patata lesso* (pah-TAA-tay LAYS-soa) boiled potatoes; *patata stacciate* (pah-TAA-tay stah-CHA-tay) mashed potatoes.

patate (pah-TAA-tay). Ita. **Sweet potato.**

pâte (paht). Fre. Pastry; **paste, pasta, dough** or **batter.**

pâté (pah-tay). Fre. A rich savory spread or mixture made from food finely ground to **paste** consistency; can be anything from **almonds** to pig's head.

pâte à choux (paht ah sho). Fre. Cream **puff pastry,** made by stirring **flour** into boiling water and **butter,** then the **eggs,** which when cooked, puff up making a cavity that is filled with flavored **cream** or **custard** as in **éclairs, cream puffs,** etc.

pâte à croissant (paht ah cro-sawng). Fre. Pastry **dough** for **croissants.**

pâte d'amandes (paht dah-mahngd). Fre. **Almond paste, marzipan.**

pâte de compagne (paht der kon-pa-nye). Fre. A pastry with a coarse, crumbly texture.

pâte de foie gras (pah-tay d'fwah-grah). Fre. A well-known delicacy prepared from the livers of fat geese.

pâte en terrine (paht en tehr-ren). Fre. "Cooked in an earthenware dish."

pâte feuilletée (paht fuhy-leh-tay). Fre. Puff-paste; many thin layers; "thousand leaves".

pâte levée (paht leh-vay). Fre. Raised or leavened **dough.**

pâte sucrée (paht sew-kra). Fre. Sweet **dough** used for **pie** shell, pastry shells, etc.

patinho (pah-TE-nyoo). Por. Young duckling.

patis (pah-tesc). Phi. Fermented fish **sauce** that is salty and pungent.

patisserie (pah-tess-ree). Fre. A pastry shop, or a piece of pastry.

Patna rice (paht-NAH rics). USA. **Rice** with less hard, less transparent, and less shiny grains; milky white and more cylindrical in form.

pato (PAH-toh). Spa, Por. **Duck.**

pato bravo (PAH-toh BRAH-voh). Por. Wild duck.

patrijs (pah-TRAYS). Dut. **Partridge.**

patty pan (PAH-te pahn). USA. A yellow or white, round **summer squash** with a scalloped edge. Also known as **cymling squash.**

patty shell (PAH-te schehl). USA. A puff paste or pastry shell or case for serving individual portions of creamed mixtures.

paunce bourré (pons boo-RAY). USA. A **Cajun** dish of stuffed **pork** stomach.

paupiettes (po-pe-ett). Fre. **Slices** of meat or fish rolled with **force-meat** or **vegetables.**

pausnaya (PAH-yoos-nah-yah). Rus. Pressed **caviar.**

pavé (pau-va). Fre. Designates a square or rectangular shape; indicates a dish chilled in a square mold and garnished; a **sponge cake** in a square shape, spread with **buttercream** and **garnished.**

pavo (PAH-bhoa). Spa. **Turkey.**

pavot (pah-vo). Fre. **Poppy seed.**

pawpaw (PAU-pau). USA. The edible fruit of a North American tree of the custard-apple family; yellow skin; smoky taste.

payasam (PIE-ya-sahm). Ind. A **pudding** made of **mung beans, coconut milk,** and **peas.**

paysanne, à la (pahy-sahn). Fre. "Peasant style"; with **potatoes, carrots, onions,** and **bacon.**

peach (pech). USA. The mostly round **fruit** of the peach tree; downy, golden skin with reddish blush; an indention from bloom end to stem end on one side; fragrant, juicy, firm flesh; use fresh out of hand or in **salads, stewed, jam, preserves,** juice; two types: freestone and clingstone, which are canned commercially.

peach Melba (pech MEHL-bah). USA. A **dessert** of **peaches** poached in **vanilla**-flavored **syrup,** served over **ice cream,** and topped with **raspberry purée.**

peaman (PE-mahn). Jap. Green **bell peppers.**

peanut (PE-nuht). USA. The seed or seed-containing pod of a South American leguminous **herb;** fibrous hourglass-shape shell, usually containing two nuts; highly nutritious; a staple food in Africa, an important crop in India and China.

peanut butter (PE-nuht BUTT-ehr). USA. The resultant product when **peanuts** are crushed to a **paste** with a mortar and pestle or in a blender; a smooth, creamy, spreadable product.

peanut flour (PE-nuht flawr). USA. Contains 16 times the protein value of **wheat;** used to enrich **flours.**

peanut maki (PE-naht-tsoo mah-ke). Jap. A **sesame**-studded crisp **cracker,** wrapped around a whole **peanut.**

peanut oil (PE-nuht oul). USA. The oil extracted from the **peanut** during processing; very light in texture and color; very mild flavor that does not mask other flavors.

pea pods (pe pohds). USA. **Snow peas; Chinese pea pods.**

pear (paher). USA. The fleshy oblong **fruit** of the pear tree; larger on the bloom end; slick, smooth skin that may be yellow-green, green, red-green, or red; sweet, softly granular aromatic flesh. Some varieties are bartlett, red bartlett, bosc, comice, forelle, and seckel.

pearl barley (pehrl BAHR-le). USA. Hulled and polished **barley;** looks like pearls; used in **soups** or like **rice.**

pearl rice (pehrl ris). USA. **Rice** that is a little shorter than medium grain rice, more tender and clings as it cooks.

peas (pez). USA. The edible seedpod of various leguminous vines; three main types: English peas, which are usually eaten with seeds, or peas, removed from the pods; **snow peas;** and snap peas, which are both eaten pod and all.

peber (PAH-ooerr). Dan. **Pepper.**

pebernødder (PEH-ber-NUEH-dor). Dan. "Pepper nuts"; a variety of Christmas **cookie.**

peberrod (PEH-ooer-roadh). Dan. **Horseradish.**

pecan (pea-KAHN). USA. The oblong, light brown, thin-shelled, oval **nut** of the pecan tree; an important nut in the United States; uncommon elsewhere.

pêche (pehsh). Fre. **Peach.**

pêche Melba (pehsh mehl-bah). Fre. **Peach Melba.**

pecho de ternera (PAY-choo day tehr-NAY-rah). Spa. Breast of **veal.**

pechuga (peh-CHOO-gah). Spa. **Chicken** breast.

Pecorino (pay-koa-RE-noa). Ita. Hard, firm **cheeses** made from ewe's milk; produced in Italy since Roman times; best known variety is **Pecorino Romano.**

Pecorino Romano (peck-oh-RE-noh rah-MAH-noa). Ita. A ewe's whole-milk **cheese** round in shape, white or very pale yellow interior, dense, with a yellow brown rind; sharp, salty, and intense.

Pecorino Siciliano (peck-oh-RE-noh se-sill-e-AHN-oa). Ita. A ewe's milk cheese that is hard and made pungent by the addition of **peppercorns;** good for grating.

pectin (peck-tehn). Fre. Various water-soluble substances that bind plant cells, particularly in **apples, quinces, citrus, currants,** and yield a gel used in jelly-making to "set" the **jelly.**

peda (PEH-ray). Ind. **Milk fudge** molded into small pillows and garnished with **pistachio nuts.**

peel (peal). USA. Strip off, by pulling or cutting, the outside covering of a food.

peertjes (PAYR-tyus). Dut. Cooking **pears.**

peixe (PAY-shay). Por. Fish.

Peking duck (PEA-keng duhk). USA. An elaborate Chinese dish made from specially reared **ducks;** a finger food. **Beijing kao ya.**

pekoe (PE-ko). Ind. A superior grade of black **tea** from India and Ceylon, made from the first three leaves on the spray of the tea bush.

pekonia (PAY-koa-niah). Fin. **Bacon.**

Pellkartoffeln (PEHL-kahr-tof-ferln). Ger. **Potatoes boiled** in their skins.

peltopyy (PAYL-toa-pew). Fin. Grey **partridge.**

pemmican (PEM-eh-kan). USA. A dried meat product made of lean meat pounded fine, mixed with melted fat, and sometimes **berries, flour, molasses,** and **suet,** pressed into **cakes;** used as emergency rations by North American Indians and settlers.

penchenè (pe-ROZH-niyeh). Rus. Tea **cakes; cookies.**

penne (PEHN-neh). Ita. **Pasta** tubes cut on the diagonal.

Pennich (Pehn-nesch). Tur. A sheep's-milk **cheese;** the curd is packed into sheep-or lamb-skin for curing.

Penrod (pahng-ro). Fre. **Anise**-flavored **liqueur.**

penuche (peh-NOO-che). Mex. A **fudge**-like **candy** made with **brown sugar, cream, nuts;** poured into a pan to cool, then cut in squares. Also called **panocha.**

Pepato (Peh-PA-toh). Ita. A **cheese** that is sharp and crumbly; curd is layered with black pepper for spicy flavor; made in Sicily; good **cocktail** cheese.

pepe forte (PAY-pay FOUR-tay). Ita. **Chili pepper.**

pepe nero (PAY-pay ne-roh). Ita. **Black pepper.**

peper (PAY-pur). Dut. **Pepper.**

peperkoek (PAY-pur-kook). Dut. **Gingerbread.**

pepermunt (PAY-pur-moont). Dut. Peppermint.

pepernoten (PAY-pur-no-tuh).   Dut. Tiny, spicy ball-shaped **cakes** served on December 5, the eve of St. Nicholas Day.

peperonata (pay-pay-roa-NAH-tah).   Ita. A dish of sweet **peppers** cooked in **olive oil** with **tomatoes, garlic, onions;** served cold.

peperoncino (pay-pay-rohn-CEE-noa).   Ita. A hot red **chili pepper** used **dried** or fresh.

peperoni (pay-pay-ROA-ne). Ita. Bell **peppers,** red or green.

pepe rosso (PAY-pay ROAS-soa). Ita. Red **pepper.**

pepininhos de conserva (pay-pe-ne-nyoos duh kon-SAYR-vah). Por. **Pickles.**

pepino (pe-PE-noo). Por. **Cucumber.**

pepino (peh-PE-noh).   Spa. A small, oval **fruit** with a delicate, sweet **cucumber-melon** flavor; skin is pale yellow with purple stripes; eaten fresh.

pepita (peh-PE-tah). Spa. **Pumpkin** seed.

peppar (PAH-pahr). Swe. **Pepper.**

pepparkakor (PEH-pahr-kah-koor). Swe. **Gingersnap cakes.**

pepparrot (PEH-pahr-root). Swe. **Horseradish.**

pepper (PEP-per). Ind. **Black pepper** is the dried, unripened fruit of a tropical semiwoody vine; white pepper is exactly the same fruit with the outer black covering removed.

pepperoncini (peh-pehr-rohn-CE-ne). USA. Mild **chili peppers** used in salads; green, two to three inches long.

pepperoni (pep-pehr-ROW-ne).   Ita. A **sausage** of beef and **pork,** highly seasoned with hot red **peppers.**

pepperpot (PAH-pehr-poht). USA. A highly seasoned **stew** or **soup** made from **tripe.**

pepperpot (PEH-pehr-poht). Spa. A highly seasoned West Indies **stew** or **soup** made with meat, **seafood, vegetables,** as well as **cassava juice.**

pepper sauce (PEH-pehr saus).   USA. The traditional **sauce** served with **venison; poivrade.**

pepperrot-saus (PEHPP-ehr-root sows).   Nor, Dut. **Horseradish sauce.**

peppers (PEH-pehrs). USA. A generic term for the seedpods of various pepper bushes; two main types: mild or sweet-fleshed such as the **bell peppers,** and hot or pungent-fleshed such as the various **chili peppers;** colors vary from green to yellow to red to purple to black (when **dried**).

pêra (PAY-rah). Por. **Pear.**

pera (PEH-rah). Spa. **Pear.**

pera (PAY-rah). Ita. **Pear.**

percebes (pehr-THAY-bhayss). Spa. A type of **shellfish;** goose barnacles.

perch (puhrch). USA. Various related and unrelated freshwater and saltwater fish, including the white perch, yellow perch, snappers of coastal West Africa, snook, walleye.

perche (pehrsh). Fre. **Perch;** a fresh- and saltwater fish.

perciatelli (pay-chaa-TEHL-le). Ita. Long, tubular **pasta.**

perdiz (pehr-DETH). Spa. **Partridge.**

perdreau (pehr-droa). Fre. Young **partridge.**

perdrix (pehr-dre). Fre. **Partridge.**

perejil (PEHR-eh-jel). Mex. **Parsley.**

peren (pe-AHR-en). Dut. **Pears.**

périgourdine (pehr-re-go-den). Fre. **Garnished** with **truffles.**

périgueux sauce (pehr-re-goh saus). Fre. **Truffle sauce** made with **Madeira** wine.

Perilla (peh-RE-lyah). Spa. A cow's-milk **cheese** firm in texture and mild in flavor. Also known as *teta.*

periwinkle (pear-e-WEN-kl). Bri. A small **snail**-like **mollusk** eaten uncooked or **roasted** in the shell.

perle (perl). Fre. Pearls; refers to the shape of any vegetable cut and shaped round and small.

perleløge (payr-LER-lurg). Dan. Pearl **onions.**

Perlhuhn (PEHRL-hoon). Ger. **Guinea hen.**

pernice (payr-NE-chay). Ita. **Partridge.**

perry (PAHR-re). USA. **Pear cider.**

Persian melon (PUHR-szhun MELL-un).   USA. A **melon** with a dark green rind with fine brown netting; globular in shape with thick, bright pink-orange flesh.

Persian-style rice (PUHR-szhun-styl ris).   USA. An Arabian dish of plain boiled **rice** with a crust; **kateh.**

persika (PAER-shi-kah).   Swe. **Peach.**

persil (pehr-se).   Fre. **Parsley.**

persilja (POER-silyah).   Swe. **Parsley.**

persillade (payr-se-yad).   Fre. Served with or containing **chopped parsley.**

persille (pear-SILL-eh).   Dan. **Parsley.**

persillé (pehr-ssay).   Fre. Designates beef of the highest quality, well marbled with fat; also, green-veined **cheeses;** sprinkled with **parsley.**

Persille des aravis (pehr-se day Ah-voh-ve).   Fre. A **cheese** made from goat's milk, flavored with **parsley;** molded into a cylindrical roll.

persimmon (puhr-SEHM-mun). USA. A large, orange, globular **fruit** that is edible when fully ripe, but extremely astringent when unripe; **kaki.**

peru (pay-ROO).   Por. **Turkey.**

peruna (PAY-roo-nah).   Fin. **Potato.**

perzik (PEHR-zik).   Dut. **Peach.**

pesca (PEH-skah).   Ita. **Peach.**

pescada (paysh-KAH-dah).   Por. **Haddock.**

pescadilla (pay-skah-DHEL-yah).   Spa. **Whiting.**

pescado (pays-KAH-dhoa).   Spa. Fish.

pescado a la sal (pays-KAH-dhoa ah lah sahl).   Spa. Whole fish baked in **rock salt.**

pesca noce (PEH-skah NOA-chay).   Ita. **Nectarine.**

pesce (PAY-shay).   Ita. Fish.

pesce persico (PAY-shay PEHR-se-koa).   Ita. **Perch.**

pesce San Pietro (PAY-shay saun pe-EHT-troa).   Ita. **John Dory.**

pesce spada (PAY-shay SPAA-dah).   Ita. **Swordfish.**

pêssego (PAY-say-goh).   Por. **Peach.**

pesto (PEHS-to).   Ita. A sauce of **basil, garlic, parsley, pine nuts,** or **walnuts** and **Romano** or **Parmesan cheeses** mixed together in virgin **olive oil.**

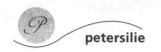
petersilie (pay-terr-ZE-lier). Ger. **Parsley.**

petite marmite (peh-te mahr-met). Fre. A clear **consommé** in which is cooked lean meat, a whole **chicken, marrow** bones and **vegetables** for flavor; served with **croutes** spread with **marrow** and sprinkled with **grated cheese.**

petite sèches (peh-te say-shay). Fre. Little **cream biscuits.**

petit four (pe-te foor). Fre. Small fancy **cake** covered with **icing** and highly decorated.

petit lait (pe-te lot). Fre. **Whey.**

petit pain (pe-te pahn). Fre. Very small **roll** scooped out and stuffed with various savory purées, served as side dish or **appetizer.**

petits pois (per-te pwah). Fre. **Spring peas;** fine, very small **peas** with a delicate flavor.

petits pois princesse (per-te pwah pran-ses). Fre. **Snow peas.**

Petit Suisse (per-te swess). Fre. A cow's-milk **cheese,** mild in flavor, shaped in small cylinders; a double crème cheese; highly perishable, superb with **strawberries** and is sometimes stirred with **honey** as a **dessert.**

petticoat tails (PEHT-te-koat tails). USA. Thin **shortbread cakes,** with scalloped edge to resemble petticoats.

petti di pollo (PEHT-te de POAL-loa). Ita. **Chicken** breasts.

petto (PEHT-toa). Ita. Breast, **brisket,** chest.

peultjes (PERLT-yers). Dut. A **vegetable** similar to **snow peas;** podded **peas;** young early peas.

pez espada (payth ays-PAH-dhah). Spa. **Swordfish.**

pezzo (PEHT-soa). Ita. Chunk, piece.

Pfannkuchen (PFAN-eh-kook-hern). Ger. **Pancake.**

Pfeffer (PFEH-ferr). Ger. **Pepper.**

Pfefferkuchen (PFEH-ferr-kook-hern). Ger. Spice **cake,** similar to **gingerbread,** traditional at Christmas time.

Pfefferminz (PFEH-ferr-mints). Ger. Peppermint.

Pfeffernüsse (pfeh-ferr-NEW-sser). Ger. Spicy **ginger cookies.**

Pfefferpothast (pfeh-ferr-PO-tahast). Ger. A **stew** of beef **ribs** and **onions,** seasoned with **pepper** and **lemon.**

Pfifferlinge (PFIF-ferr-ling-er). Ger. **Chanterelle.**

pfirsich (PFER-zikh). Ger. **Peach.**

Pfister (FEHS-tehr) Swi. A cow's fresh, skimmed milk **cheese.**

pflaume (PFLOW-mern). Ger. **Plum.**

pfnutli (FRU-dle). Ger. Swiss **apple fritters.**

pheasant (PHEH-szehnt). USA. Any of a variety of **game** birds with colorful plumage and characteristic long tail feathers.

Philadelphia cheesesteak (phehl-ah-DEHL-phe-ah CHEZ-stehk). USA. A crisp Italian-style **roll** covered with thin slices of beef, **cheeses,** and other condiments, including **sautéed onions.**

Philadelphia Cream (phehl-ah-DEHL-phe-ah Krem). USA. Brand name for Kraft's fresh **cream cheese.**

Philadelphia eggs (phehl-ah-DEHL-phe-ah ehgs). USA. Two split **muffins** topped with cooked white **chicken** meat, **poached eggs,** and **hollandaise sauce.**

philpy (PHEHL-pe). USA. A **rice bread** with origins in South Carolina.

phool gobhi (POOL GO-bhe). Ind. **Cauliflower.**

phosphated flour (PHAHS-fa-ted flowr). USA. A **wheat flour** with **salt** and leavens added; has short storage life because the leavens lose their potency.

phyllo (PHE-loh). Gre. Leaf-thin sheets of **dough,** made from flour and water; used for sweet and savory dishes by layering with **fillings;** similar to the French **mille-feuille.** Also called **brik, filo, malsouka, yukka.**

physalis (PHYS-sah-lihst). USA. A **fruit** about the size of a large **grape;** smooth-skinned and golden-yellow; encased in a thin, papery husk; sweet flavor; called *ground-cherry;* use in **sauces** and **dessert** toppings.

piadina (pe-ah-DE-nah). Ita. A soft type of flat bread, usually eaten with **salami** or **prosciutto;** also may be filled with **sautéed spinach** or with **ricotta.**

piaz (pih-YAZ). Ind. **Onion.**

picada (peh-CAH-dah). Mex. A small round of **tortilla dough** filled with a savory **stuffing** and cooked; an **appetizer** or **entree; garnacha.**

picada (peh-CAH-dah). Spa. **Minced, shredded,** or **ground meat; hash.**

picadillo (peh-kah-DEHL-loa). Spa. A **salad** of **orange, onion, green pepper,** and shredded salt **codfish.**

picadillo (pe-kah-DE-yoh). Mex. Mixture of meat and other ingredients used as **filling** or **stuffing.**

picado (pe-KAH-doh). Por. **Hash.**

picante (pe-KAHN-ta). Ita, Spa. Piquant; hot, spicy, sharp.

picatostes (pe-kah-TOAS-tehz). Spa. **Deep-fried slices** of bread.

piccata (pek-KAA-tah). Ita. **Veal scallop.**

piccioni (pet-CHOA-nay). Ita. **Squab.**

Pichelsteiner (PIK-herl-shtigh-nerr). Ger. A hearty meat and **vegetable stew.**

pichón (pe-CHON). Spa. **Pigeon; squab.**

pickerel (PEHK-eh-rehl). USA. A long, slender fish of the **pike** family; has soft flesh and a needle-like bone structure. Erroneously called **walleye.**

pickert (PEH-kert). Ger. Peasant bread, made of **potato** or **wheat flour.**

pickle (PEH-kehl). USA. Any food preserved in **brine** or **syrup** and **vinegar.**

pickled cheese (PEHK-elld chez). USA. A term used to describe a group of **cheeses** to which considerable amounts of **salt** are added to prolong their keeping qualities.

pickling cucumbers (PEHK-leng QU-kom-bers). USA. A short, small, hard and spiny cucumber with a tart flavor, especially good for making **dill pickles.**

pickling salt (PEHK-leng sawlt). USA. A pure **salt** that is free from additives that cloud pickling liquid, available in granulated and flake forms.

picnic ham (PEHK-nik haum). USA. A front leg of **pork, cured** and **smoked;** sometimes mistaken for **ham** because of similar flavors.

picón (pe-KOHN). Por. A pungent, blue-veined **cheese** made of goat's milk; same as the Spanish **Cabrales.**

pí dàn (pe dahn). Chi. Thousand-year-old **eggs; duck eggs** preserved in a clay casing made of ashes, **lime, salt,** and strong **tea,** rolled in **rice husks,** and buried for three months; the yolks turn greenish-brown, the whites black-purple. Also known as *hundred-year-old eggs.*

Pie (pi). USA. Any **cheese,** such as **bakers'** or **cottage cheese,** which is used in making cheese **pie, cheese cake,** or other bakery goods.

pie (pi). USA. A sweet or savory dish baked in a pastry crust, with a **filling;** with or without a crust top; may have a crumb, pastry, or **meringue** topping; may also have a top, but no bottom crust.

Piedmont rice (PED-mohnt ris). USA. A short-grain rice, high in starch, wetter and stickier than medium grain rices.

piémontaise, à la (pe-a-mohng-tez). Fre. A **garnish** for meats of **rice, timbales** or mounds, mixed with **grated white truffles.**

pierna de cordero (PYEHR-nah day koar-DAY-roa). Spa. Leg of **lamb.**

pieterman (PET-ur-mahn). Dut. Stingfish.

pigeonneau (pe-zhon-noa). Fre. A young **squab** bred for the table.

piggvar (PIG-varr). Swe. **Turbot.**

piggvar (PIG-vahr). Nor. **Turbot.**

pig-in-a-blanket (pehg-en-a-blanh-keht). USA. **Sausage** wrapped in **dough** and **baked.**

pignola (pihg-NOH-loa). Ita. **Pine nut.**

pihvi (PIH-vi). Fin. **Beefsteak.**

piimä (PE-mae). Fin. **Buttermilk;** a very popular drink in Finland.

piirakka (PE-rah-kkah). Fin. A dish of meat or fish and **rice** cooked in pastry.

píjiu (PE-jiu). Chi. **Beer.**

Pikante sosse (pe-KAHN-tah ZO-seh). Ger. A spicy, piquant **sauce.**

pike (pik). USA. A large, elongated, long-snouted fish, whose sweet, white flesh is used in many fine dishes; found in cooler northern waters.

pilaf (pih-LAHF). Tur. A dish made of seasoned **rice,** served with meat, **pountry,** or **shellfish.** Also **pilauf, pilau, pilaw.**

pilchard (PIHL-chahrd). USA. A small fish of the **herring** family found along European coasts; a **sardine.**

pili-pili (PEHL-e PEHL-e). Afr. **Powdered dried chilies.**

pilot biscuit (PI-loht BISC-kit). USA. **Hardtack.**

pilot bread (PI-loht brehd). USA. **Hardtack.**

pilsner (PEHLZ-nuhr). USA. A high quality lager **beer;** pale golden, lower in alcohol and calories than American beer.

pilsner (PILS-nerr). Dan. Light lager **beer.**

Pilze (PILT-ser). Ger. **Mushroom.**

pilzschnitzel (PILT-ser-shnit-serl). Ger. An Austrian non-meat **cutlet** made with **mushrooms, carrots,** and **peas.**

piman (PE-mahn). Jap. **Bell pepper;** used in nontraditional cooking; used in **grilled** foods and **deep-fried** foods.

pimenta (pe-MEN-tah). Por. **Pepper.**

pimenta (pe-MYAYN-tah). Spa. **Pepper.**

piment doux (pe-mahng doo). Fre. **Sweet pepper.**

pimentos (pe-MYAYN-toass). Spa. Sweet red **peppers;** the seed pod from which **allspice** comes; a sweet red pepper pod used in **salads, vegetable** dishes, as **garnish.**

pimento cheese (pe-MEHN-to chez). USA. A sandwich spread, or filling, made of **cheese,** usually **Cheddar, American,** or **cream cheese,** to which **ground pimentos** have been added.

pimentón (pe-mayn-TON). Spa. **Paprika.**

piments verts (pe-mahngs vehr). Fre. Green **peppers.**

pimienta (pe-MYEHN-tah). Spa. **Black pepper.**

pimiento dulce (pe-MYAYN-toa DOOL-thay). Spa. Hot red **pepper.**

Pimm's Cup (pehmz kup). Bri. The brand name of a starter for various highballs; Pimm's #1 has gin and **bitters,** #2 has whisky, #3 has **brandy,** and #4 has rum.

piña (PE-nyah). Spa. **Pineapple.**

pinaattiohukaiset (PE-natt-te-yo-hoo-KYE-sett). Fin. **Spinach pancakes.**

pinch (pehnch). USA. As much as you can hold between the thumb and first finger, e.g., a pinch of **salt.**

pinda (PEHN-daas). Dut. **Peanuts.**

pindakaas (PEHN-dah-kaas). Dut. **Peanut butter.**

pineapple (PINH-ahp-puhl). USA. The multiple **fruit** of the pineapple plant; has rich, succulent flesh with a slightly acid taste; must be peeled; use **raw** or cooked.

pineapple cheese (PINH-ahp-puhl Chez). USA. A **Cheddar** molded in **pineapple** shape.

pineapple guava (PINH-ahp-puhl GWUA-vah). USA. A slightly bumpy, thin skinned, green South American fruit with a cream colored, slightly soft flesh, like a pear; tart and perfumy; use fresh in salads or make into preserves. Also known as feijoa.

pine nut (pin nuht). USA. The edible seed of the pine cone from the pine tree; also known as **chinquapin, crenata, Indian nut, pignola,** piñon.

píngguo (PING guo). Chi. **Apple.**

pinkel (PIH-kehrl). Ger. A **smoked sausage** of **groats, onions,** and **bacon.**

pink sauce (pehnk saus). USA. A **mayonnaise**-based sauce colored pink with catsup and served with **shrimp.**

pinnekjøtt (Pe-neh-SHUTT). Nor. Salt-cured mutton chops steamed on peeled birch twigs.

pinole (pah-NOH-lah). USA. Sweetened **corn** that has been **dried, ground,** and spiced; sometimes used to make a **chocolate** drink.

pinoli (pe-NO-le). Ita. **Pine nuts.**

piñon (PEN-yohn). Spa. **Pine nut.**

pintada (pen-TAH-dah). Spa. **Guinea hen.**

pintade (pang-tahd). Fre. **Guinea hen.**

pintadeau (pang-tah-doa). Fre. Young **guinea cock.**

pinto bean (PEHN-to ben). USA. A common dried **bean,** mottled reddish color, used alone or as an ingredient in many stewed dishes.

Piora (Pe-ohl-ah). Swi. A **cheese** similar to **Tilsiter;** made of whole cow's milk or a mixture of cow's and goat's milk; made in Italian part of Switzerland.

piperade (pe-pehr-rohd). Fre. **Tomatoes,** green **bell peppers,** and **onions** cooked in **olive oil,** with beaten **egg** and **ham** or **bacon** added.

pipian (pe-PYAHN). Mex. A red sauce of **sesame** and **pumpkin** seeds **ground** with spices and **peanuts** or **almonds;** served on **chicken.**

pipikaula (PE-pe-kah-OO-lah).   USA. A dish of beef **jerky** and **soy sauce,** of Hawaiian origins.

piquant (pe-kahnt).   Fre. Highly seasoned; sharp.

piquante (pe-kahnt).   Fre. "Agreeably stimulating to the palate"; a classic **sauce** of **chopped shallots** reduced with white wine and **vinegar, demi-glace** added, **strained,** then **garnished** with **gherkins, parsley, chervil,** and **tarragon.**

piquin (pe-KEN).   Mex. A very small, very hot, dark green **chili pepper.**

piri-piri (pe-re-pe-re).   Por. A **sauce** made from hot red **chili peppers** and **olive oil.**

pirog (pe-roh).   Fre. Canoe-shaped.

piroy c limon (per-ROHG s lye-MO-nahm).   Rus. **Lemon tart.**

pirogi (per-ROHG-ghey).   Rus. Large pastries cut into servings.

piroshk (per-ROSH-key).   Rus. Small **turnovers** or **dumplings** filled with a savory or sweet **stuffing.**

pisang goreng (PE-sang HOH-reng).   Dut. **Fried** or **baked bananas,** Indonesian-style.

pischingertorte (PESH-eng-er-tor-ter).   Ger. An Austrian **torte** made of round wafers filled with **chocolate hazelnut cream,** covered with **chocolate icing.**

piselli (pe-SEHL-le).   Ita. **Peas.**

piselli alla romana (pe-SEHL-le AHL-lah roa-MAA-nah).   Ita. **Peas** cooked with **butter, onion,** and **ham.**

pissaladiere (pe-sah-lah-daere).   Fre. A **pizza**-like **tart** made with **onions,** black **olives, anchovies,** and **tomatoes** arranged decoratively.

pissenlit (pe-sehn-le).   Fre. **Dandelion greens;** best eaten before flowering or after frost.

pista (PIH-stah).   Ind. **Pistachio.**

pistache (pe-stash).   Fre. **Pistachio nut.**

pistacchio (pe-STACH-cheo).   Ita. **Pistachio nut.**

pistachio (peh-STASCH-ee-oh).   USA. Kernel of the **nut** of the turpentine tree, green in color and delicate in flavor; shells are naturally tan, but sometimes dyed pink-red or green; used as flavoring and **garnishing.**

pisto (PES-toa). Spa. A **vegetable** dish of **chopped tomatoes,** zucchini, **onion,** red or green **peppers** stewed together. Also called samfaina and frito de verduras.

pistolets (pes-sto-la). Fre. Crusty **rolls;** popularly used for **sandwiches.**

pistou (pes-too). Fre. A rich, **garlic**-flavored **vegetable soup** made of **green beans, potatoes, tomatoes,** and **vermicelli.**

pit (peht). USA. To remove pits from **fruits.**

pita (PE-tah). USA. A Middle Eastern round, flat bread slit open to form a pocket; used with endless varieties of **fillings.**

pitepalt (PE-teh-palt). Swe. **Potato dumplings** stuffed with **pork.**

Pithiviers (pe-te-ve-a). Fre. An **almond cake,** a large round of **puff pastry** with **almond paste filling,** decorated in pinwheel or rosette pattern.

pito-ja-joulupuuro (PE-to-ya-YO-loo-poo-roh). Fin. Whole-grain **barley pudding** cooked in **milk** and served with **rose-hip** or **raisin** purée.

piviere (pe-ve-EH-ray). Ita. **Plover.**

pivo (PE-voh). Rus. **Beer.**

pizelle (pets-TSEH-leh). Ita. Deep-fried **pizza dough;** eaten plain, with **tomato sauce, sautéed vegetables,** or **cheese;** also a **cookie** baked on an intricately patterned iron called a pizelle iron. Cookie can be rolled conically for filling with pastry cream or **ice cream.**

pizza (PEAT-zah). Ita. An open-faced **pie** spread with all manner of savory foods.

pizza di ricotta (PEAT-zah de re-KOAT-tah). Ita. **Cheesecake.**

pizzaiola (peat-ze-OHL-ah). Ita. A **pizza sauce** of fresh **tomatoes, herbs,** and **garlic;** served with steak, fish, or leftover boiled meat dishes.

pizz figliata (petz fel-YAH-tah). Ita. A sweet with **honey** and **nuts.**

plaice (plas). Bri. A fish with fine-textured, delicate, white flesh; eaten fresh or **smoked;** a member of the **flounder** family.

plank (plahnk). USA. To bake or broil, meat or fish, on a board of hard wood that seasons the food on it.

plantain (plahn-TAYNE). Spa. A **fruit** similar to the **banana,** with a high starch and low **sugar** content, making it suitable for savory cooking; when cooked, a staple food in Central and South America.

plantano (PLAH-tah-noh). Spa. **Banana.**

plantation shortcake (plahn-TAY-shun SHORT-kak). USA. Hot **cornbread** square served with a rich, **creamy chicken** or **ham sauce** on top.

plättar (PLAH-tar). Swe. Small, thin **pancakes.**

Plättchen (PLETCH-chen). Ger. **Pretzel.**

pletzlach (plehtz-lohk). Jew. Pastry squares with **apricot** or **plum** filling; traditional for Passover.

pleurotus mushroom (PLU-roh-tuhs MUHSH-room). USA. Oyster **mushroom.**

plie (ple). Fre. **Plaice;** a **flatfish** similar to **sole** and **flounder.**

plinz (plenz). Ger. **Fritter, pancake.**

plommegrøt med fløtemelk (PLWM-meh-grurt may FLUR-ter-mehlk). Nor. **Pudding** made of **groats, plums,** and **cream.**

plommon (PLOO-mon). Swe. **Plum.**

plommonkompott (PLOO-mon-kom-POT). Swe. **Plum compote.**

plommonpudding (PLOO-mon-PU-ding). Swe. **Plum pudding.**

plommonspäckad fläskkarré (PLOO-mon-SPAH-kad FLASK-ka-RE). Swe. **Loin** of **pork** with **prunes.**

plover (PLO-vehr). USA. A European shore bird whose **eggs** are highly prized for their delicious taste.

pluck (pluk). USA. The heart, liver, lungs, and windpipe of an animal.

plum (pluhm). USA. The edible **fruit** of a plum tree; round to oval smooth-skinned fruit with oblong seed; flesh is softly-firm and juicy; color ranges from yellow to a blackish-purple or blue; eat **raw** or cooked.

plum duff (pluhm duhf). Bri. A less fancy version of **plum pudding** made with **raisins** or **currants.**

plum pudding (pluhm PUHD-deng). Bri. A steamed dessert of various dried **fruits** and **suet,** often flamed with **brandy.** Traditional at Christmas, and not a plum in it.

plum sauce (pluhm saus). USA. A thick Chinese sweet-sour **sauce** made of **plums, apricots, vinegar** and **sugar; Suan mei jiang; duck sauce.**

plum tomato (pluhm toh-MAH-to). Ita. Shaped like a **plum,** slightly stronger flavored than ordinary **tomatoes;** widely used in Italian cooking.

pluvier (ploo-vay). Fre. **Plover.**

poach (poch). USA. To cook in an open pan at simmering point, with sufficiently seasoned liquid to cover.

poblano (poh-BLAH-noh). Mex. A large, dark green, mild tasting **chili pepper.**

po boy (poh boy). USA. **Hoagie.**

poche (po-shay). Fre. **Poached.**

pochouse (po-shooz). Fre. A freshwater fish **stew** made with wine; **matelote.**

poco hecho (POA-koa AY-choa). Spa. Cooked rare; undercooked.

podina (poh-DE-nah). Ind. **Mint.**

poffertjes (PUF-fer-jes). Dut. Puffy **fritters.**

poi (POH-e). USA. A Hawaiian **paste** preparation made of **breadfruit, banana, sweet potato,** or **taro;** a staple of the native Hawaiian diet.

point, a (pwan, ah). Fre. "To the perfect point"; rare for steak; peak of ripeness for **fruit** and **cheese.**

poire (pwahr). Fre. **Pear.**

poireau (pwah-roa). Fre. **Leek.**

pois (pwah). Fre. **Peas.**

pois a la francaise (pwah ah lah fron-sehz). Fre. **Peas** braised with **lettuce, spring onions, parsley, butter,** a pinch of **sugar,** and a little water.

pois casses (pwah kahs). Fre. **Split peas.**

pois chiches (pwah che-ches). Fre. **Chick peas.**

poisson (pwahs-sawng). Fre. Fish.

poisson brun (pwahs-sawng brang). Fre. "Brown fish," seasoned with many herbs and wine; a Belgian dish.

poitrine (pwah-tren). Fre. Chest, breast, **brisket.**

poitrine de porc (pwah-tren der por). Fre. **Pork** belly.

poivrade (pwahv-rahd). Fre. **Pepper sauce;** the traditional sauce served with **venison.**

poivre (pwahvr). Fre. **Pepper;** spicy, pungent.

poivron (pwahv-rawng). Fre. **Allspice; pimento.**

poke (pok). USA. A Hawaiian dish of marinated fish in various **sauces** such as **chopped seaweed, Maui onions, chili.**

pokel (PUR-kerl). Ger. **Pickle.**

pokeweed (POK-wed). USA. A wild, leafy plant whose young leaves and shoots are edible and are cooked like **spinach** and **asparagus.**

polenta (poa-LEHN-tah). Ita. A **cornmeal pudding** that is cooled, **sliced** and **fried, grilled** or **baked** with other foods, especially **cheese;** an Italian specialty.

polentagrøt (poo-LEHN-tah-grurt). Nor. **Cornmeal pudding.**

polished rice (PAWL-eshed ris). USA. Any **rice** that has had the outer aleurone layer removed.

pollame (poal-LAA-may). Ita. **Poultry.**

pollastrino (poal-lah-STRE-noa). Ita. Spring **chicken.**

pollo (POH-yoh). Ita, Spa. **Chicken.**

pollock (POHL-luhk). USA. A fish of the **cod** family.

polonaise (poh-loh-neh). Fre. A **garnish** of hard-boiled **eggs,** bread-crumbs, and **parlsey,** mixed in melted **butter.**

polpetta (poal-PAYT-tay). Ita. Meat patty, **croquette, meatball.**

polpettine di spinaci (poal-payt-TE-nay de spe-NAA-che). Ita. **Spinach dumplings.**

polpettone (poal-payt-TOA-nay). Ita. **Meat loaf.**

polpo (POAL-poa). Ita. **Squid** or **octopus.**

pølse (PURLSS-err). Nor. **Sausage.**

pølser (PURL-sserr). Dan. **Sausages.**

polsterzipfel (pohstl-ZEF-fehl).   Ger. An Austrian **jam**-filled **turnover.**

pomace (POHM-asc).   USA. The dry or pulpy residue remaining after the liquid has been extracted during the **cider-** or wine-making process.

pomegranate (PAHM-ah-grahn-aht).   USA. An ancient **fruit** with leathery skin and red fibrous pulp in which many red, glistening, refreshingly acid seeds are embedded, that when removed are used in various savory and sweet dishes. The juice of the seeds is used to make **grenadine,** a syrup used in mixed drinks.

pomelo (POHM-eh-loh).   USA. The largest of the **citrus** fruits; native to Southeast Asia; similar to the **grapefruit,** but slightly pointed at one end; sweeter than grapefruit; skin is yellow and slightly bumpy; flesh ranges from pink to rose.

pomfret (POHM-freht).   Ind. Non-oily firm-fleshed fish similar to **flounder.**

pomme (pom).   Fre. **Apple.**

pommes de terre (pomz der tehr).   Fre. **Potatoes;** prepared countless ways in France, including:

> **Anna** (pomz ahn-nah) potatoes Anna; a dish of layered potato **slices,** seasoned with **salt** and **pepper,** dotted with **butter,** baked in a **casserole** until brown and crisp on the outside, soft on the inside; **au lait** (pomz oa leh) creamed potatoes; *bouilli* (boo-ye) boiled potatoes; *farcies* (fahr-se) **stuffed** potatoes;
>
> **frites** (frec) french **fried** potatoes; *paille* (pye) potato "straws", **deep-fried,** match-stick-sized potatoes; *parisienne* (pomz der pah-re-zyang) small oval-shaped potatoes **sautéed** in **butter;** *pommes novelles* (noo-vehl) new potatoes; *purée* (py-reh) mashed potatoes.

pomodoro (poam-oa-DAW-roa).   Ita. Yellow **tomato.**

pompano (POHM-pah-noh).   USA. A silvery fish whose rich white meat is a delicacy cooked many ways.

pompelmo (poam-PAYL-moa).   Ita. **Grapefruit.**

pompelmoes (PAWM-pul-moos).   Dut. **Grapefruit.**

Pont-l'Eveque (pon l'ay-vek).   Fre. A cow's-milk **cheese** with a square golden rind, a full aroma, and a rich creamy texture; has a peculiar taste caused by a unique fungoid mold peculiar to Normandy. This cheese was already renowned in 1230, when it was called "Angelot." Excellent with **tawny port.**

Poona (POO-nah). USA. A soft, ripened **cheese;** round, flat with a reddish surface; sometimes called a "mild **Limberger.**"

poori (POOH-re). Ind. Puffy **deep-fried** bread, made from various combinations of **flours, semolina,** and mashed **potatoes.**

poor boy (poor boy). USA. **Hoagie.**

poor knights of Windsor (poor nits of WEHND-suhr). Bri. Sliced bread soaked in **sherry, dipped** in **egg batter, fried** in **butter,** and served with **cinnamon** and **sugar;** a British version of **French toast.**

popcorn (POHP-korn). USA. An Indian **corn** whose kernels on exposure to dry heat burst open to form a light, crispy, white starchy mass.

pope's nose (pops nohz). Bri. The rump, or tail piece, of a bird. Also called **parson's nose.**

popover (PAHP-ov-ehr). USA. A hollow **quick bread** shaped like a **muffin** and made from a light batter of **eggs, flour,** and **milk;** texture resembles **Yorkshire pudding.**

poppy seed (PAHP-pe sed). USA. The tiny, black, dried seed of the Mediterranean poppy plant, used in pastries, breads, **salad dressing.**

pop tart (pahp tahrt). USA. A commercially made pastry, similar to a **turnover,** but thinner, having various **fillings;** usually heated in a toaster that "pops" up, hence the name; can be heated in an oven or microwave.

porc (por). Fre. **Pork.**

porcella (poar-CHAYL-lah). Spa. Suckling pig.

porchetta (poar-KAYT-tah). Ita. Suckling pig.

porcini. (poar-CHE-ne). Ita. A wild **mushroom** with a thick fleshy cap and stem; **boletus.**

porco (POHR-koh). Por. **Pork.**

porgy (POR-ge). USA. A saltwater fish related to the **bream,** found throughout the world; has delicate, moist, sweet flesh and has many sharp bones.

pork (pohrk). USA. The flesh of swine when dressed for food; can be red or white meat, depending on how the swine is slaughtered.

porkkana (POARK-kah-nah). Fin. **Carrot.**

pörkölt (PURR-kurlt). Hun. Goulash made with **pork** or **lamb.**

poron (POA-roan).   Fin. Reindeer.

poronkäristys (POA-roan-KAE-ris-tewss).   Fin. Paper-thin **slices** of **braised** reindeer meat.

poronkieli (POA-roan-KAY-li).   Fin. Reindeer **tongue.**

porridge (POHR-rehj).   USA. A term used worldwide for a soft food made by boiling **cereal** or **grain,** usually **oatmeal,** in **milk** or water until thickened; may or may not be flavored with **sugar, salt, butter, raisins,** and various other ingredients.

porro (POA-roa).   Ita. **Leek.**

porsaankyljys (POAR-saan-KEWL-yewss).   Fin. **Pork** chops.

porter (POR-tehr).   Iri. Dark **beer,** not as strong or dark as **stout.**

porterhouse (POR-tehr haus).   USA. A large, superior, beef steak cut from the thick end of the short **loin** to contain a T-shaped bone and a large piece of **tenderloin** as the tail.

porto, au (por-toa).   Fre. A sauce of **veal stock, port, orange** juice, **lemon** juice, **shallots, orange** zest, lemon zest, and **thyme.**

Port du Salut or Port Salut (port duh sah-laht).   Fre. A cow's whole-milk **cheese;** mellow to robust flavor similar to **Gouda;** semisoft, smooth elastic texture; creamy white to yellow.

portugaise (pohr-tay-geh).   Fre. A sauce of **chopped onions,** chopped **tomatoes, tomato sauce,** meat **glaze,** chopped **parsley,** and **garlic.**

portugaise, a la (ah lah pohr-tay-geh).   Fre. **Stuffed tomatoes** with chateau potatoes and **portugaise sauce.**

posset (PUH-seht).   Bri. A punch dating to the Middle Ages made of **milk, eggs,** wine or **ale, lemon** juice, spices, and **sugar;** with **whipped cream** folded in, today it is **eggnog.**

posta de carne (POUSH-tah duh KAHR-nuh).   Por. **Slice** of beef, not a steak.

postej (poh-STY).   Dan. **Pâté** or **paste.**

postre (POHS-treh).   Spa. **Dessert.**

potage (pot-ahzh).   Fre. **Soup;** a few of the many French soups are listed here: *bonne-femme* (bon fahm) **leek** and **potato** soup; *condé* (kawng-day) **kidney-bean** soup; *julienne* (zhew-lyehn) **shredded vegetables** soup; *parmientier* (pahr-mahng-tyay) **potato** soup; *pistou* (pee-stoo) provencal **vegetable** soup; *printanier* (prahn-

tahng-yea) **vegetable** soup; *Saint-Cloud* (sahn klood) **puréed green peas** and **lettuce,** served with **croutons;** *velouté* (ver-loo-tay) **cream** soup: *de tomates* (der to-maht) **tomato,** *de volaille* (der vo-lahy) **chicken.**

potaje (poh-tah-hay).   Spa. A thick **soup** or **stew.**

potatis (po-TAA-tiss).   Swe. **Potatoes;** *kokt* (kookt) **boiled** potatoes; *stekt* (staykt) **fried** potatoes; *sturvad* (STEW-vahd) creamed potatoes; *-mos* (-MOOS) mashed potatoes.

Potato (Poh-tah-to).   Ger. A **cheese** usually made from cow's milk, but at times from ewe's or goat's milk; **boiled** and **seived potatoes** are added to the curd and mixed; sometimes **caraway** seeds are added.

potato (pah-TA-to).   USA. The edible, starchy tuber of the potato plant; four types classified as: **russet, long white, round white, round red.**

potato chips (pah-TA-to chehps).   USA. Very thin slices of raw **potatoes** that are **fried,** either homemade or commercially prepared.

potato flour (pah-TA-to flawr).   USA. Made from **potatoes** that have been cooked, **dried,** and **ground;** used in bread making to keep bread moist; used to thicken **soups** and **gravies;** good in **cakes,** particularly **sponge cakes.** Also called **potato starch.**

potato skins (pah-TA-to skenz).   USA. The skin and adhering portion of a cooked **potato** after the pulp has been scooped out.

potato snow (pah-TA-to sno).   USA. Potatoes that have been **boiled, dried,** then **sieved,** and not mixed in any way.

potato starch (pah-TA-to starch). USA. **Potato flour.**

pot-au-feu (po-toa-fur).   Fre. An economical and wholesome **broth** made by cooking vegetables and meat together in water, then serving the meat and vegetables as the main course while using the resulting **broth** as **soup.**

pot cheese (Paht Chez).   USA. Unripened, fresh curd **cheese.**

pot de creme (poa der krehm).   Fre. Individual covered cups filled with **custard** or **mousse.**

potée (po-tay).   Fre. A thick **soup** of **pork, potatoes,** and **cabbage.**

poteter (poo-TAY-terr).   Nor. **Potatoes.**

poteter salat (poo-TAY-terr sah-LAAT). Nor. **Potato salad.**

potetkaker (poo-TAY-terr-kaa-kerr). Nor. **Potato pancakes.**

potiron (po-teer-awng). Fre. **Pumpkin.**

potlikker, pot liquor (POHT-lick-ker). USA. The **broth** in which greens and **vegetables** have been cooked.

potpie (POHT-pie). USA. A savory dish of meat or **poultry** with **vegetables** in **gravy, baked** in a deep dish covered with pie crust.

potpourri (poo-purr-reh). Fre. A **stew** of various kinds of meats and spices.

pot roast (poht rohst). USA. A large cut of meat used for **braising.**

pot roasting (poht ROHST-eng). USA. A method of slowly **braising** large cuts of meat in a tightly covered pot.

potted meat (POHT-ted met). Bri. The English equivalent of French **pâté.**

potted shrimps (POHT-ted shrehmps). Bri. An **hors d'oeuvre** of small shelled **shrimp,** seasoned with **nutmeg,** warmed, and preserved in **clarified butter** a few days.

pouding (poo-deng). Fre. **Pudding.**

poularde (pool-ahrd). Fre. A fattened **hen.**

poule (pool). Fre. A **stewing chicken,** one too old for other cooking methods.

poule-au-pot (pool-oa-po). Fre. Stewed **chicken** served with reduced **pot liquor** and **vegetables.**

poulet (poo-leh). Fre. A young spring **chicken,** used for **frying** or **broiling,** weighing up to four pounds.

poulpe (poolp). Fre. **Squid** or **octopus.**

poultry (POL-tre). USA. All domestic **fowl** kept for **eggs** or meat.

pound cake (pownd kak). USA. A rich **cake** originally made using one pound each of **sugar, butter, eggs, flour.**

pour batter (pohr BAHT-ter). USA. A **batter** that contains one part flour to one part liquid; such as used for **cream puffs, timbale** cases, **crepes, popovers, dip batters.** Also called **thin batter.**

pousser (poo-sayr). Fre. To rise, as in **yeast dough.**

poussin (poos-sang). Fre. A very young **chicken;** spring chicken; a **fryer.**

powdered eggs (PAHW-dehrd ehgs). USA. Beaten **eggs** which have been **dried** and pulverized into **powder** form; used basically in commercial food manufacturing.

powdered sugar (PAHW-dehrd SHU-gahr). USA. Very finely ground **sugar** with **cornstarch** added; quick dissolving. Also known as **confectioners' sugar,** and in England and France, as **icing sugar.**

powsowdie (puh-SUH-de). Sco. Sheep's head **broth.**

pozole (poh-SOH-leh). Mex. A thick **soup** laced with chunks of **ham** and **hominy,** topped with **shredded lettuce** and **fried tortilla** strips, served with **salsa.**

praire (prehr). Fre. Thick-shelled **clam; quahog.**

prairie chicken (PREH-re CHEH-kehn). USA. **Grouse** of the open plains of the West.

prairie oyster (PREH-re OEHY-stuhrs). USA. Testicles of a bull, pig, or lamb; **breaded** and **fried.** Also called **animelles, frivolitées, lamb fries, mountain oyster, Rocky mountain oyster.**

praline (prah-len). Fre. The flavoring of burnt **almonds** in **caramel syrup.**

praline (PRAY-len). USA. A **fudge**-type **candy** made of **brown sugar, cream,** and **pecans;** made in three- to four-inch patties.

praties (PRAHT-tez). Iri. **Potatoes.**

Prato (PRAH-toh). Bra. A **cheese** made of pasteurized milk, semi-cooked, pressed, small-eyed; similar to **Patagras.**

pratos de carne (PRAH-too day karn). Por. Meat dishes.

pratos frios (PRAH-too FRE-oo). Por. Cold dishes; **buffet.**

Prätost (PREHS-toost). Swe. A firm cow's-milk **cheese** cured with whiskey. Also spelled **Prestost.**

prawn (praun). USA. A very large **shrimp.**

precooked rice (pre-KOOKD ris). USA. **Rice** that is milled, enriched, completely cooked and then dehydrated. Also called **quick cooking** and **instant rice.**

pre-formed (PRE-formd). USA. To bring to approximate form or shape.

prei (pry). Dut. **Leek.**

Preiselbeeren (PRIGH-zerl-bay-rern). Ger. **Cranberry**-like **berries.**

preserves (pre-SEHRVZ). USA. Whole or large pieces of **fruit** in a thick **syrup** that sometimes is slightly jellied.

presifted flours (pre-SEHFTD flawrs). USA. **Wheat flours ground** to pulverization and sifted; gives different texture to baking.

Pressburger beugel (prres-buhr-gehr BOY-gerl). Ger. A rich Austrian pastry filled with **ground walnuts.**

pressgurka (PRAYSS-gewr-kah). Swe. **Cucumber salad** or **relish.**

Presskopf (PRRES-kopf). Ger. **Head cheese.**

pressure cookery (PREH-shur KOOK-re). USA. Cooking by steam under pressure, to increase the temperature and shorten the cooking period; done in a special pot called a pressure cooker.

Prestost (PREH-toost) Swi. A cheese the same as **Prätost.**

presunto (pray-ZOON-toh). Por. **Smoked ham.**

pretzel (PRET-zehl). USA. A brittle, glazed kind of **cracker,** tied in a loose knot like a rope, and sprinkled with coarse **salt.**

prezzemolo (preht-TSAY-moa-loa). Ita. **Parlsey.**

prickly pear (PREHK-le pahr). USA. A general term for the edible fruit of certain cactus, whose interior flesh is sweet and mild; used mainly for **dessert** and **candy.**

primavera (pre-mah-VAY-rah). Ita. A garnish of **raw** or **blanched** spring **vegetables.**

prime meat (prim met). USA. The top grade of beef. See **meat grades.**

primeurs (prem-oor). Fre. Early **fruit** or **vegetables.**

princesse (pran-ses). Fre. A garnish of **asparagus** tips and sliced **truffles** in **cream sauce.** Also, asparagus tips stuffed in **artichoke** bottoms.

prinskorv (PRENS-korv). Swe. Small **sausages.**

printanier (prahn-tahng-yea). Fre. Spring **vegetable soup.**

printanière (prin-tan-yey). Fre. **Garnished** with spring **vegetables.**

process cheese (PRO-cess chez). USA. **Cheese** made by blending several batches of different cheeses using emulsifiers, then packaging in plastic while still hot.

profiterolles (pro-fe-ter-rol). Fre. Small puffs of **choux paste** filled with **cream** or **custards; **can be a sweet or a savory.

prosciutto (pro-SHOOT-to). Ita. Dry-cured spiced **ham, **not **smoked.**

protose steak (PRO-tohs stehk). USA. A **vegetable** protein substitute for steak; eaten at certain times when meat is prohibited by kosher dietary laws.

Provatura (pro-vah-TUH-rah). Ita. A soft **cheese** of the plastic-curd type made originally from buffalo's milk, but now made from cow's milk.

provençale (pro-van-syahl). Fre. Cooked with **garlic, parsley, **and **tomatoes** in **olive oil.**

Providence (Pro-ve-daons). Fre. A **cheese** very similar to **Port du Salut**.

Provole (Pro-voh-leh). Ita. A round, plastic-curd **cheese** made from buffalo's milk.

Provoletti (pro-vah-LEHT-te). Ita. A cheese the same as **Provolone.**

Provolone (pro-vah-LOH-ne). Ita. A cows' milk **cheese** with a buttery color, a buttery, mellow to sharp, smoky and salty taste; molded in various shapes and sizes to hang from rafters as it cures.

prugna (PROO-nyah). Ita. **Plum.**

pruim (prirm). Dut. **Plum.**

pruna (PROO-nah). Ita. **Prune.**

prune (prewn). Fre. **Plum.**

prune (proon). USA. A **dried plum.**

pruneau (prew-noa). Fre. **Prune.**

psito arni (pse-TOSS ahr-NE). Gre. **Roast lamb.**

ptarmigan (TAHR-meh-gehn). USA. A Scandinavian **grouse** with feathered feet.

puchero (poo-CHEH-roa). Spa. Meat **boiled** in an earthenware pot.

pudding (POOD-ding). Dut. **Pudding.**

pudding (PUHD-deng). USA. A **dessert** of a soft, thick, creamy consistency.

pudim de ovos (poo-DE day AW-vohss). Por. **Egg pudding.**

pudim flan (poo-DE flahn). Por. **Caramel custard.**

pudin (poo-DEN). Spa. **Pudding.**

puerco (PWEHR-koh). Spa. Pig; **pork.**

puerros (PWAYR-roass). Spa. **Leeks.**

Puffer (POO-fehr). Ger. **Pancake; fritter.**

puff pastry (puhf PA-stre). USA. Flaky, rich pastry, made by enclosing **butter** in the **dough,** rolling thin, folding, rolling, turning many times to produce many leafy thin layers.

puit d'amour (pwe d'ah-moor). Fre. A small round pastry usually filled with **cream** or **jelly; fruit** is also used.

pulla (POOL-lah). Fin. Braided **yeast cake.**

pullao (poo-LAW-oo). Ind. **Pilaf.**

pullet (PUHL-eht). USA. A young **chicken hen,** weighing up to four pounds, used for **frying** or **broiling.**

pulpo (POOL-poa). Spa. **Squid** or **octopus.**

pulque (POOL-keh). Mex. Distilled sap of **agave (century plant).**

pulse (puhls). USA. **Dried,** edible seeds of **legumes,** such as **peas,** lentils, **chickpeas, beans.**

Pultost (PEWLT-oost). Nor. A rindless cow's milk-**cheese,** soft, sweet, and **caraway** flavored; made of whey, and **caramelized.**

pummelos (PUHM-mehl-lohz). USA. **Chinese grapefruit.**

pumpa (PEWM-pah). Swe. **Pumpkin.**

pumpernickel (POOM-pehr-neh-kehl). Ger. A dark, slightly sour, coarse texture **rye** bread.

pumpkin (PUHM-kehn). USA. A usually large, round, yellow-orange **fruit** of the gourd family that is cultivated as a food.

punajuuri (POO-nah-YOO-ri). Fin. **Beetroot.**

punajuurikeitto (POO-nah-YOO-ri-KAYT-toa). Fin. **Borscht; beet soup.**

punajuuri salaati (POO-nah-YOO-ri SAH-laa-ti). Fin. **Beet salad.**

punch (puhnch). USA. A beverage mixture, alcoholic or nonalcoholic, made from a variety of ingredients, usually **fruit** based.

punchero (puhn-CHER-oh). Mex. A one-pot dish of meats, **vegetables, legumes,** served **broth** first, then meats and **vegetables.**

Punschtorte (PUNSH-tor-ter). Ger. Rum **cake.**

puntarelle (poon-tah-REHL-lea). Ita. A special Roman **salad** green, served only in winter; very long stalks with needle-like serrated leaves that curl when cut; served with oil, **vinegar, salt, anchovy,** and **crushed garlic.**

puppadam (PA-pa-rahm). Ind. Puffy lentil wafers.

purée (pur-ray). Fre. Food that is passed through a sieve to achieve a smooth consistency.

puri (POOH-re). Ind. Another spelling for **poori.**

purjo (PEWR-yoo). Swe. **Leeks.**

purple granadilla (PUHR-puhl grahn-nah-DEHL-lah). USA. The purple egg-sized tropical **fruit** whose sweet yellow flesh is eaten **raw** with the small black seeds or squeezed for juice; has sweet-acid flavor. Also called **passion fruit.**

purslane (PURSC-len). USA. An **herb** with succulent, fleshy leaves that have a tart, vinegary taste; good in **sandwich** spreads and in **soups.**

puss pass (POOSS-pass). Nor. **Stew** of **mutton, carrots, potatoes,** and **cabbage.**

pútáo (poo-tao). Chi. **Grapes.**

pútaogan (poo-tao-GAN). Chi. **Raisins.**

pútáojiu (poo-tao-JIU). Chi. Wine.

putt i panna (pewt e PAHN-nah). Swe. "Tidbits in a pan"; chunks of meat, **sausages,** and **fried potatoes** topped with a **fried egg.**

puuro (POO-roa). Fin. **Porridge;** used as main dish or **dessert;** may be **oats, rice,** or **rye.**

Pyramide (pe-ra-med). Fre. A generic name for goat's-milk **cheese;** is very white, soft, crumbly, delicately flavored.

pyy (pew). Fin. Hazel **hen.**

qarnabit (ar-na-BET). Ara. **Cauliflower.**

qasbi (AHUS-be). Ara. Liver.

qatayif (a-TAA-yif). Ara. Tiny **pancakes,** layered with **nuts, syrup,** and **cream.**

qdemi (DAH-me). Ara. Roasted and unsalted **garbanzo beans.**

qiaokeli (chiao-ke-le). Chi. **Chocolate.**

qiézi (chieh-dzi). Chi. **Eggplant.**

qíncài (ching-tsai). Chi. **Celery.**

qingcài dòufù tang (ching-tsai doh-foo tong). Chi. **Vegetable soup** with **bean curd.**

qingjiao niúròu (ching-jiao niu-row). Chi. **Shredded** beef with **green peppers.**

qingyú (ching-yu). Chi. **Mackerel.**

qingzheng (ching-dzeng). Chi. To **steam** food.

qing jiao (ching jiao). Chi. **Green pepper.**

qing-zheng quán yú (ching-dzeng chuan yu). Chi. Whole fish **steamed.**

qìshui (chi-shui). Chi. Soft drink.

quaglia (KWAH-lyah). Ita. **Quail.**

quahog (KO-hahg). USA. A thick-shelled **clam** found in the New England coastal waters.

quail (kwal). USA. A small migratory **game** bird found the world over and prized for its delicious flavor; bobwhite.

quaking custard (KWAK-eng KUHS-tahrd). USA. A shivering, quivering **cream custard,** usually **garnished** with **egg** whites; native to New England.

Quargel (Quay-zgell). Aus. A **cumin**-flavored skim-milk **cheese.**

Quark (kwark). Ger. A cow's skim-milk **cheese,** soft, runny; a type of **cottage cheese** eaten with **fruit, salads,** or used in cooking.

Quarkklösse (KVAHRK-klurs-ser). Ger. Sweet **cottage cheese dumplings.**

Quartirolo (Kwar-te-ROH-loh). Ita. A soft, cow's-milk **cheese** made from September through November.

quartre-épices (ka-truh ay-pe-say). Fre. A spice mixture of **ground ginger, nutmeg, cloves,** and **cinnamon** when used with sweet, or white **pepper** when used with savory dishes. Also called **four spices.**

quartre-quarts (ka-truh kar). Fre. A **pound cake** made of four ingredients in equal parts: **sugar, butter, eggs,** and **flour.**

quasi de veau bourgeoise (kwa-zi da voo boars-zwah). Fre. A **casserole** of **veal rump** braised with **pork,** calf's foot, and **vegetables.**

quassia-amara (kahs-se-ah-ah-mah-rah). Fre. An **aperitif** made by the decoction of the bark, wood, or root of the Surinam tree, native to South America.

queen of puddings (kwen of PUHD-engs). Bri. A **pudding** of **custard** and breadcrumbs, spread with **strawberry jam,** covered with **meringue,** then lightly browned.

Queensland nut (KWENZ-lund nuht). Aus. **Macadamia nut,** a native of Australia, now grown in Hawaii.

queijadas de sintra (kaye-SHAH-dahsh duh SEN-trah). Por. Rich **cakes** made with **cheese, almonds, eggs.**

Queijo (kaye-ZHOO). Por. The Portuguese word for **cheese,** used with the names of towns and provinces where the cheeses are made in Portugal and Brazil.

Queijo de Azeitão (kaye-ZHOO duh AH-layn-tawng). Por. A strong-tasting, but delicious **cheese;** very creamy when fresh.

Queijo do Alentejo (kaye-ZHOO doo-AH-layn-tay-zhoo). Por. A ewe's and goat's milk **cheese;** savory, salty.

Queijo Flamengo (kayee-ZHOO flah-MAYN-goo). Por. Portugese version of **Edam cheese.**

Queijo Prato (kaye-ZHOO PRAY-do). Bra. A small-holed, smoky, firm **cheese.**

quemada (keh-MAH-tha). Mex. Burnt **milk; caramel**-colored.

quenelles (kern-ehl). Fre. A light **dumpling** made of various **force-meats,** bound with **eggs,** shaped variously, **poached** in **broth,** and served as an **entree** with a **butter sauce** or as a **garnish** to **soup.**

quente (kent). Por. Warm; hot.

quesadilla (keh-sah-DE-yah). Mex. A **turnover** made by **stuffing** a **tortilla** with a savory **filling** and **frying** or **broiling.**

Queso (KEH-so). Spa. The Spanish word for **cheese,** and like **queijo, fromage,** and **käse,** used along with names of regions to designate varieties.

Queso Anejo (KEH-so Ah-NAY-ho). Mex. A white, rather dry, skim-milk **cheese** with a crumbly texture.

Queso Blanco (KEH-so BLAHN-ko). Spa. A cow's-milk **cheese** that is smooth, rindless, and eaten fresh with **fruit** or matured.

Queso de Bola (KEH-so day BO-lah). Mex. A whole-milk **cheese** similar to **Edam.**

Queso de Cavallo (KEH-so day Kah-VAHL-lo). Ven. A pear-shaped cheese made in Venezuela.

queso de cerdo (KEH-soh day THEHR-do). Spa. **Head cheese.**

Queso de Cincho (KEH-so day SENK-ko). Mex. A sour-milk **cheese,** also called *Queso de Palma Metida.*

Queso de Crema (KEH-so day KRE-mah). Spa. A soft, whole-milk **cheese** that resembles **Brick cheese;** made in Costa Rico.

Queso de Hoja (KEH-so day HO-yah). Spa. A cow's-milk **cheese** made in Puerto Rico.

Queso del País (KEH-so dehl PIE-es). Spa. A white, pressed, semisoft, perishable **cheese** made in Puerto Rico.

Queso de Prensa (KEH-so day PRAHN-zah). Spa. A type of **cottage cheese** that is molded in forms.

Queso Fresco (KEH-so FREHS-ko). Spa. A rather dry **cottage cheese** that is made of skim milk in El Salvador.

Queso Enchilado (KEH-so EN-chah-LAH-doh). Mex. A firm, aged **cheese** with rind covered with hot red **chili powder.**

Queso Manchego (KEH-so Mon-che-gehr).   Spa. Another name for the **cheese Manchego.**

quetsch (ketch).   Fre. A **plum** used to make **tarts** and other **confections;** the juice is distilled into a colorless **liqueur** used to make **brandies.**

queue (kuh).   Fre. Tail.

queue de boeuf (kuh day buhf).   Fre. **Oxtail.**

queue d'écrevisses (kuh d'ay-kruh-vee).   Fre. **Crayfish** tails.

quiche (kesh).   Fre. An open, savory **custard tart** using a base of **egg custard** and **cheeses** with infinite variations.

quiche Lorraine (kesh lo-rehn).   Fre. **Quiche** with **bacon** or **ham** added to the **custard.**

quick bread (kwihk brehd).   USA. Breads made with a quick-acting leavening agent, such as **baking soda** or **baking powder,** that permit immediate baking, such as **biscuits, muffins.**

quince (kwehnc).   USA. A **fruit** of the rose family that resembles a hard-fleshed yellow **apple** and is used in **jelly, marmalades,** and **preserves.**

quinoa (KEN-wah).   Spa. A nutritious **grain** that is the seed of the pigweed, native to the Andes; used same as **barley, rice, oats.**

quitte (KVIT-ter).   Ger. **Quince.**

quittengelee (KVIT-ter-zher-LAY).   Ger. **Quince marmalade.**

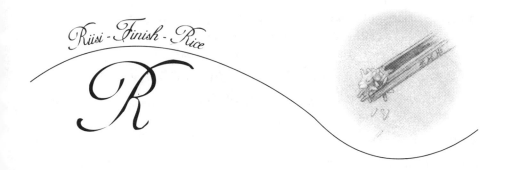

Rabaçal (Rah-bah-SAHL). Por. A Pombal **cheese.**

rabadi (RA-bhre). Ind. **Milk** thickened by reduction.

rabanadas (rah-bah-NAY-dahs). Por. A fried bread **dessert.**

rabanetes (rah-bah-NAY-tay). Por. **Radishes.**

rábano (RAH-bah-noh). Spa. **Radish.**

rábano picante (RAH-bhah-noa pe-KAIIN-tc). Spa. **Horseradish.**

rabarber (rah-BAHR-berr). Dan, Swe. **Rhubarb.**

rabarbergrød (rah-BAHR-berr-grurdh). Dan. **Rhubarb pudding** or **sauce.**

rabarbra (rah-BAHR-brah). Nor. **Rhubarb.**

rabbit (RAH-beht). USA. Small member of the **hare** family; both domesticated and wild; has white flesh, less fat and sweeter taste than **chicken;** prepared similar to chicken. Also called **hare.**

råbiff (raw-BIFF). Swe. **Raw** beef; steak tartar.

Rachel (rah-shell). Fre. A **garnish** for **tournedos:** bone **marrow** and **bordelaise sauce.**

racine (ra-sen). Fre. Root **vegetable.**

rack (rahk). USA. A cut of **lamb** or **veal** from the **rib** section; served whole, in seven rib chops, or as **crown roast.**

Râclette (rahk-leht). Fre. A variety of **Swiss cheese fondue** made by melting a big piece of cheese by the fire and scraping off the softened cheese onto a plate of **potatoes** cooked in their jackets, accompanied by a glass of very heavy white wine.

radicchio (rah-DEK-ke-oa). Ita. Red **chicory;** looks like a miniature head of red **cabbage** with white stalks and veins; bittersweet, satiny, crisp; used as a **salad** green or cooked **vegetable.**

radici (rah-DE-ce). Ita. **Radishes.** Sometimes called **ravanélli.**

Radieschen (rah-DES-khern). Ger. **Radishes;** red, white, purple, black; mild to very hot.

radijis (rah-DEYS). Dut. **Radish.**

radis (rah-de). Fre. **Radish.**

radish (RAH-dehsh). USA. A root **vegetable;** small, round with red outer peel and white interior; ranges from slightly to fiery hot taste; eaten **raw;** seeds used for **sprouts.**

rädisor (REH-dis-soor). Swe. **Radishes.**

rådjurssadel (REH-dis-soor-saa-dayl). Swe. **Saddle** of **venison roasted.**

rådjursstek (RO-yuussh-STEK-kah). Swe. **Venison** steak. Also called **hjortstek.**

Radener (Thah-dah-nah). Ger. A hard **cheese** made from cow's skim milk; also known as skim-milk *Rundkäse* and in Switzerland as *Magere Schweizerkäse.*

Radolfzeller Cream (Rhar-dolf-zehl-lehr Kreh-mah). Ger. A fresh, whole-milk **cheese** much like **Mainauer** and similar to **Münster.**

rädyr (RAW-dewr). Nor. **Venison.**

rafano (rah-FAH-noh). Ita. **Horseradish.**

raffinade (ra-fe-nahd). Fre. Refined **sugar.**

raggmunkar (RAG-MUNG-kahr). Swe. **Potato pancakes.**

ragout (ra-goo). Fre. A rich, highly seasoned **stew** of meats, **poultry,** or fish, browned or not browned, with or without **vegetables.**

Ragoût fin (rah-GU fehn). Ger. A delicate combination of organ meats such as **sweetbreads** and brains, cooked with **mushrooms** in a **wine cream sauce,** often served in a **puff pastry shell.**

ragù (rah-GOO). Ita. A sauce made of **olive oil, butter,** meat, and **garlic.**

ragù Bolognese (rah-GOO boa-loa-NAY-zay). Ita. A meat sauce of **ground beef, pork,** and **ham sautéed** in **butter** and oil with **chopped vegetables,** and simmered with **milk,** white wine, and **tomatoes;** often used for **pasta.**

Ragusano (rah-goo-SAHN-oa).   Ita. A rectangular, cow's-milk **cheese;** delicate and sliceable when young, firm and sharp when aged; sometimes **smoked.**

Rahm (rahm).   Ger. **Cream.**

Rahmschnitzel (RAHM-shnit-serl).   Ger. A Swiss dish of **veal scallops** in **cream.**

rai (RAH-e).   Ind. **Mustard.**

raie (reh).   Fre. **Skate,** a fish of the ray family; the edible portions are the "wings," which have a firm white meat so similar to sea **scallops** in texture and flavor that it has been used as a substitute for many years.

raifort (ray-for).   Fre. **Horseradish.**

raisin (reh-zang).   Fre. **Grape.**

raisin (RA-zehn).   USA. **Dried grapes;** eaten as **dessert;** used in breads, **cakes, cookies, confections,** as well as in savory dishes.

raisin de Corinthe (reh-zang day kor-enth).   Fre. **Currants;** used in baked goods, **puddings.**

raisin sec (reh-zang sehk).   Fre. **Dried grapes;** same as **raisin.**

raisu (RAH-e-soo).   Jap. Cooked **rice** served in a bowl Japanese style. See **kome, gohan.**

rajas (RAH-khahs).   Mex. Strips of **poblano chili** pods **fried** with **onions** and **potatoes** or **tomatoes.**

rajma (RA-jeh-mah).   Ind. **Red kidney beans.**

räkor (RAI-kor).   Swe. **Prawns; shrimp.**

rakørret (RAH-ker-ret).   Nor. **Trout** that has been salted down and **cured,** a Norwegian speciality.

ramekin (RAHM-eh-kehn).   Bri. A small **cheese tart.** Also a small flameproof dish.

ramen (RAH-mehn).   Jap. White curled **noodles** used in **soups.**

ramequin (ram-e-kihn).   Fre. A small flameproof dish.

ramequins (rah-mer-kang).   Fre. Tiny **cheese pies.**

ramp (rahmp).   USA. A wild **leek;** member of the **onion** family; looks like a **scallion;** has a strong flavor.

rampion (RAHM-pe-yon).   USA. A plant whose tuberous root is eaten **raw** or cooked and whose leaves are eaten like **spinach.**

ram tulsi (rahm TOOL-se).   Ind. White **basil.**

ranchero (rahn-CHEH-roh).   Spa. Country style.

rane fritte (RAH-neh FRE-teh).   Ita. **Fried frog legs.**

Rangiport (Rhawng-ge-pohrt).   Fre. A **cheese** that is practically the same as **Port du Salut.**

rankins (RAHN-kens).   USA. A **cheese pudding** that is a type of **souf-flé** because beaten **egg** whites are incorporated in the dish.

rapa (RRA-pah).   Ita. **Turnip.**

raparperi (RAH-pahr-payri).   Fin. **Rhubarb.**

rape (rapeh).   USA. A European **herb** of the **mustard** family whose seeds yield an oil used in the Mediterranean and Middle East countries for **salads** and **frying.**

rapé (RAH-pay).   Spa. An ugly-looking fish whose tail section is a delicacy; white, firm flesh; known as **monkfish** or **goosefish.**

râpé (rah-pay).   Fre. **Grated cheese;** commonly used abbreviation for *fromage râpé.*

râper (rah-pay).   Fre. To **grate,** especially **cheese.**

rapini (rah-PE-ne).   USA. A **vegetable** with dark green chard-like leaves on a stalk; a slightly bitter flavor; served as vegetable by **steaming,** or added **raw** to **salads.** Also known as **broccoli rabe** and **choysum.**

rapphøne (RAHP-hur-ner).   Nor. **Partridge.**

rårakor (rROHrah-koor).   Swe. Lacy **potato pancakes.**

rarebit (RAHB-biet).   Bri. Hard **Cheddar**-type **cheese** melted with **beer** or **milk** and seasonings, served over **toast; Welsh rarebit.**

rasam (REH-sahm).   Ind. Spicy lentil **broth:** tart, **tamarind**-flavored; either drunk at the start of a **meal** or eaten with **rice.**

rasedar (reh-seh-DAHR).   Ind. **Vegetables** in thin **gravy.**

rasher (RAH-shehr).   Bri. A single thin slice of **bacon** or **ham.**

ras malai (RAHS ma-LIE-e).   Ind. **Dessert** of **cheese dumplings** in **pis-tachio**-flecked **cream sauce.**

raspberries (RAHZ-behr-rez).   USA. A fleshy, dark-purple or red **berry** grown on various bramble-like plants.

raspings (RAHSP-ehngs).   USA. Bread crumbs prepared from oven-dried crusts.

ratafia (raht-ah-FE-ah).   USA. The **essence** of **bitter almonds; a macaroon;** a small airy **biscuit** made of beaten **egg** whites, **sugar, butter,** and **ground almonds.**

ratafia (rah-tahf-FE-ah).   Ita. A sweet **liqueur** made by **marinating** black **cherries** in **sugar.**

ratatouille (rat-ah-too-e).   Fre. A **stew** of **diced eggplant, tomatoes, green peppers, zucchini, onions,** and **garlic,** cooked in **olive oil.**

Rat cheese (Raht Chez).   USA. A popular name for any well-aged firm textured **Cheddar.**

raton (reh-toyn).   Fre. A kind of **cheesecake.**

Räucherall (ROY-kher-raal).   Ger. **Smoked eel.**

ravanélli (rah-vah-NAHL-le).   Ita. **Radishes.** Also called **radici.**

Raviggiolo (Rah-veg-jge-oh-loh).   Ita. A **cheese** of ewe's milk that is uncooked, sweet, soft, creamy, and fast curing.

ravigote (rah-ve-goht).   Fre. A classic richly flavored, cold green **herb sauce** made with **capers, chopped onions,** and **herbs;** as a classic sauce served hot, it is **veloute** with white wine, **shallot butter,** and **herbs.**

ravioli (rav-ve-OH-le).   Ita. Small **pasta** squares stuffed with **forcemeats, spinach,** or **cheeses.**

raw (raugh).   USA. Uncooked, fresh.

rawbi (RAH-be).   Ara. A starter or culture for making **yogurt.**

raw pack (raugh pahk).   USA. A term used in canning of foods; boiling **syrup,** juice, or water added to **raw** foods in the canning jars or cans, then processed in a boiling-water bath.

raw sugar (raugh SCHU-guhr).   USA. Processed from cane; U.S. Department of Agriculture notes that it is "unfit for direct use as a food ingredient because of the impurities it ordinarily contains."

Rayon (rha-yowng).   Fre. A special type of **Swiss cheese;** made of partly skimmed milk; very dry, hard with no eyes.

razza (RAHT-tsah).   Ita. Skate; of the **flatfish** family.

Rebhuhn (REHP-hoon).   Ger. **Partridge.**

Reblochon (roh-blo-shahng).   Fre. A **cow's**-milk **cheese** that is rich, soft, and has a delicately fruity flavor; pale-yellow interior; disc shape; gold rind.

recette (ruh-set). Fre. Recipe.

rechauffé (ray-sho-fay). Fre. Leftover food that is recooked or remade.

recheio (ray-SHAY-yoh). Por. **Stuffing.**

reconstitute (re-KON-ste-toot).   USA. To restore concentrated foods to their original state, usually by adding a liquid.

red banana (rehd bah-NAN-nah).   USA. A short, squat **banana** with a sweeter taste than a yellow banana; peel is purple-red when ripe; flesh is creamy white with a tinge of light pink.

red bartlett pear (rehd BAHRT-lett pair).   USA. A bell-shaped, sweet tasting **pear** with red or red-over-green skin and white flesh; eaten fresh out of hand.

red beans and rice (rehd benz ahnd ris).   USA. A specilaty of southern Louisiana where red **kidney beans** are cooked with **ham** hock and served over **rice.**

red currants (rehd KUHR-rahnts).   USA. Small red, semitransparent **berries;** pleasant, sour flavor; use for **jellies, preserves, syrups, sauces;** add to baked goods such as **muffins, breads.**

redeye gravy (REHD-ey GRAV-e).   USA. **Ham gravy** made by **deglazing** the utensil in which the ham was cooked, using ice water or **coffee** with a little **brown sugar** as the liquid.

redfish (REHD-fesch).   USA. One of the names for ocean **perch.**

red flannel hash (rehd FLAHN-nul haesh).   USA. Made from leftovers of a New England boiled dinner, by chopping the **beets, potatoes, turnips, cabbage, corned beef,** then browning together in a skillet.

red-leaved chicory (rehd-levd CHEHCK-er-rey).   USA. A **lettuce**-like plant used in **salads;** spectacular crimson color; livens up salad taste; much used in northern Italy.

red herring (rehd HEHR-eng).   USA. **Herring** left whole and ungutted, then heavily **salted,** and cold-**smoked** for three weeks until it becomes deep red in color and hard.

redikker (REHD-di-kerr). Nor. **Radishes.**

red mullet (rehd MUHL-leht).   USA. **Rouget;** a very desirable Mediterranean fish; white, sweet, delicate flesh.

red onion (rehd UN-yuhn).   USA. A fancy edible bulb of the lily fami- ly whose flesh is a light pinkish-white with the outer layer of each ring a maroon color; used widely in **salads** and as **garnishes.**

red perch (rehd purch).   USA. One of the names for ocean **perch.**

red potatoes (rehd poh-TA-toas).   USA. A round **potato** with white flesh and a pinkish-red skin.

red sauce (rehd saus).   USA. Any Italian-style **tomato sauce** or toma- to-flavored **clam sauce.**

red seedless watermelon (rehd SED-lehss WAH-tehr-mehl-lohn). USA. A **melon** about the size of a basketball that has all the charac- teristics of a **watermelon** but contains no seeds.

red snapper (rehd SNAHP-pehr).   USA. A saltwater fish, abundant around Florida and the Gulf of Mexico; best known of the species; rose-red in color, carmine fins; white, succulent, sweet flesh.

red stew (rehd steu).   Chi. Meat cooked without browning in liquid that is half **soy sauce** and half water, seasoned with **ginger, scal- lions,** and **curry;** meat is colored during cooking.

reduce (re-DUCS).   USA. To **boil** down, evaporating liquid from a cooked dish to thicken its consistency and concentrate its flavor.

reduction sauce (re-DUHK-shun saus).   USA. A **sauce** that is thick- ened by the evaporation of liquid during very slow simmering to achieve more richness and subtely of taste and flavor.

réduire (ray-dwer).   Fre. To **reduce** a liquid.

ree (reh).   Dut. **Venison.**

Réforme, à la (reh-fohr-ma, ah lah).   Fre. A **garnish** of **julienne** strips of **ham, truffles, carrots,** hard-boiled **egg** whites in **poivrade sauce;** usually served with **breaded** and **fried lamb** chops.

refresh (re-FREHSH).   USA. To make cold under running water.

refried beans (RE-frid bens).   Spa. **Frijoles refritos;** dried pinto or pink **beans** cooked, mashed, and added to **bacon** drippings, then cooked until thickened and drippings are absorbed.

refrigerator cookies (re-FREHG-ehr-a-tor KOOK-es).   USA. **Cookie dough** that is prepared, rolled, and wrapped, then stored in the refrigerator to chill until ready to bake; facilitates very thin slicing.

Regensburgerwurst (RAY-gerns-bur-gerr-voorst).   Ger. A short, fat **pork** and beef **sausage.**

Reggiano (Reh-ge-AHN-noh). Ita. A hard **cheese** used for **grating;** one of the sub-varieties of **Grana;** nearly the same as **Parmesan** and **Emiliano.**

réglisse (ray-gles). Fre. **Licorice.**

Reh (ray). Ger. **Venison.**

Rehrücken (RAY-rew-kern). Ger. **Saddle** of **venison.**

rehydrate (re-HI-drat). USA. To restore water lost during drying process, usually by cooking or soaking.

Reichkäse (RIKSCH-kahz-zeh). Ger. A cheese similar to **Gouda,** but **hickory-smoked.**

reine, à la (rehn, ah lah). Fre. **Garnished** with **chicken** in some form.

reinette (reh-neh). Fre. Russet **apple.**

reinsdyr (RAYNSS-dewr). Nor. Reindeer.

reinsdyrstek (RAYNSS-dewr-sstayk). Nor. Reindeer steak.

Reis (righss). Ger. **Rice.**

Reisauflauf (righss-OWF-lowf). Ger. **Rice pudding.**

rejemad (RIGH-er-mahdh). Dan. **Smørrebrød** delicacy of mounds of tiny pink **shrimps.**

rejer (RIGH-err). Dan. **Shrimps.**

reker (RAY-kerr). Nor. **Shrimps.**

relish (REHL-esh). USA. A spicy, often **pickle**-based **condiment** used as a spread or as a side dish.

rellenos (rreh-YEH-nohs). Spa. **Stuffed, stuffing.**

remolacha (ray-moa-LAH-chah). Spa. **Beet.**

remoulade (ray-moo-lahd). Fre. A classic **sauce** of **mayonnaise** to which **chopped gherkins, capers, parsley, spring onions, chervil,** chopped **tarragon,** and **anchovy essence** are added; served with a cold dish or used as **salad dressing.**

Renaissance, à la (reh-ne-zsahnce, ah lah). Fre. With spring **vegetables.**

render (WREHN-der). USA. To melt down, or free fat from connective tissue, at low heat.

renkon (LEHNG-kong). Jap. Fresh **lotus** root.

rennet (WREN-neht).   USA. An enzyme from the stomach lining of calves, kid, or lamb that coagulates the casein of **milk; vegetable** rennets have the same property.

rensdyrstek (RAYNSS-dewr-stayk).   Nor. **Roast** reindeer.

renstek (RAYN-syayk).   Swe. **Roast** reindeer.

renverser (ron-vehr-say).   Fre. To unmold on a plate.

repollo (ray-POAL-yoa).   Spa. **Cabbage.**

Rettich (REH-tikh).   Ger. **Radish.**

reuben (ROO-behn).   USA. A **sandwich** of sliced **corned beef** and **Swiss cheese** on **rye** bread that has been spread with Russian dressing, then topped with **sauerkraut** and **grilled.**

revbensspjäll (RAYV-bayns-spyehl).   Swe. **Roast spareribs.**

revenir (ruh-vuh-ner).   Fre. To **brown.**

Rhabarber (rah-BAHR-berr).   Ger. **Rhubarb.**

Rheinlachs (RIN-lahks).   Ger. Rhine **salmon,** a real delicacy. Also called **Rheinsalm.**

Rheinsalm (RIN-zahlm).   Ger. Rhine salmon. Also called **Rheinlachs.**

rhubarb (RU-barb).   USA. A plant with thick reddish stalks used in **pies, tarts, compotes,** and **jams;** only the stalks are edible.

rib (rehb).   USA. On a beef carcass, that part of the forequarter between the **chuck** and the **loin;** used whole as a standing rib roast or cut into individual rib chops.

ribbe (REB-beh).   Nor. **Rib pork** chops.

ribes (RE-bays).   Ita. **Currants.**

ribollita (re-bohl-LE-tah).   Ita. A famous **bean soup** made with black **cabbage,** a very dark-colored vegetable with elongated leaves.

ricci (RE-che).   Ita. **Sea urchins; a shellfish.**

ricciarelli (rech-chah-REHL-le).   Ita. **Almond cookies; biscuits.**

rice (ris).   USA. A semiaquatic member of the grass family; its edible seed is the staple **grain** for over half the world's population; basically divided into long-grain, medium-grain, and short-grain; very low in fat, high in **gluten,** but does not give an elastic paste. See also the following varieties of rice: **arwa chawal, basmati, brown, Carolina, converted, glutinous, Indo-Chinese, instant, Japanese, Java,**

Patna, Persian-style, Piedmont, **polished, Roman, unpolished,** and **wild.**

rice (ris). USA. To force **potatoes** and other **vegetables** and **fruits** through a tool that has small holes called a ricer, so that the food resembles grains of **rice.**

rice flour (ris flowr). USA. Makes a close but delicately textured **cake** in recipes heavy in **eggs;** not to be confused with the waxy rice flours known as *sweet flour* or **mochika.**

Richelieu (risch-eh-lou). Fre. A large sweet pastry made in **cake** layers spread with **apricot jam** and **frangipane cream,** then iced with white fondant flavored with **maraschino** and decorated with **angelica.**

Richelieu, à la (risch-eh-lou, ah lah). Fre. A classic **garnish** for meat; **stuffed tomatoes** and **mushrooms, braised lettuce** and **potatoes** lightly **roasted** in **butter.**

Ricotta (Re-COHT-toh). Ita. A **cheese** made from skimmed sheep's **buttermilk** or the whey left from **Pecorino Romano;** sometimes enriched with **cream;** bland, sweet, soft, and dry; eaten fresh or cooked: American Ricotta is made from whole or skimmed cow's milk and is much like **cottage cheese.**

Ricotta Romana (Re-COHT-toh Roh-MAH-nah). Ita. An aged **cheese;** firm, hard enough to **grate.**

Ricotta Salata (Re-COHT-toh Sah-LAH-tah). Ita. **Ricotta** with more of the liquid drained off, giving the texture of **Feta.**

riekko (RAYK-koa). Fin. **Ptarmigan;** Scandinavian **grouse.**

Riesengebirge (Re-zen-geh-ber-gah). Ger. A soft **cheese** made from goat's milk.

rigaglie (rah-GAHG-le). Ita. **Giblets.**

rigatoni (rehg-ah-TON-e). Ita. **Macaroni** with fat ribs.

rigodon (reh-gah-dohn). Fre. A **custard tart** served either warm or cold, either savory with **ham** or **bacon** or sweet with **fruit purée.**

riisi (RE-ssi). Fin. **Rice.**

rijst (rayst). Dut. **Rice.**

rijstaffel (RAYS-tah-ful). Dut. **Javanese rice** table; an elaborate feast with **rice** as the focal point and dozens of side dishes including meat and **seafood** dishes, **fried, steamed** savory foods, **vegetables, fruit, chili** dishes, **sauces** and **marinades;** hot, cool, spicy, bland.

rillauds (re-yo). Fre. A preparation of **pork,** cut into very small pieces, gently cooked in **lard** with seasonings, cooled; not pounded.

rillettes (re-yeht). Fre. A preparation of **pork,** cut into very small pieces, gently cooked in **lard** with seasonings, cooled and pounded in a mortar.

rillons (re-yahng). Fre. A preparation of **pork,** finely chopped, cooked in fat and seasoned with **salt** and **pepper;** served hot or cold.

rillots (re-yo). Fre. **Rillauds.**

rimmad skinka (RI-mad SHING-KAH). Swe. **Salted ham.**

rimmat kött (RI-mat choht). Swe. **Salt meat.**

Rind (rint). Ger. Beef.

Rinderbraten (RINT-err-braa-tern). Ger. **Roast beef.**

Rinderbrust (RINT-err-brust). Ger. Beef **brisket.**

Rinderleber (RINT-err-lay-berr). Ger. Beef liver.

Rinder Rouladen (RINT-err roo-LAA-dern). Ger. Beef rolls, **stuffed** and **braised.**

Rinderwurst (RINT-err-voorst). Ger. A type of beef **sausage,** pressed into a block, **fried** with **apples,** and eaten with **toast.**

Rindswurst (RINTS-voorst). Ger. Beef **sausage.**

riñones (re-YNOS-nayss). Spa. **Kidneys.**

rins (ress). Por. **Kidney.**

ripiéno (rip-YEN-noa). Ita. **Stuffing.**

Ripp (rip). Ger. **Rib.**

Rippchen (RIP-chern). Ger. **Pork** chops, but can be any chops.

Rippenbraten (RIP-pern-braa-tern). Ger. **Roast loin.**

Rippenspeer (RIP-pern-shpayr). Ger. **Pork ribs; spareribs.**

Rippenstück (RIP-pern-shtewk). Ger. Beef **ribs.**

ris (ress). Dan, Nor, Swe. **Rice.**

ris à l'amande (RE ah-lah-mahnd). Dan. **Rice pudding** with **whipped cream** and **chopped almonds** served with **cherry sauce.**

ris d'agneau (re dah-noa). Fre. **Lamb sweetbreads.**

ris de veau (re der vo). Fre. **Veal sweetbreads.**

risengrød (REA-sen-grehrth).   Dan. **Porridge** or **soup** made with **rice.**

risengrynsklatter (rea-sen-grewns-KLAT-ter).   Dan. **Rice fritters.**

risengrynslapper (rea-sen-grewns-SLAHP-per).   Nor. **Pancakes.**

risgrøt (RESS-grurt).   Nor. **Rice pudding.**

risgryn (RESS-gruhn).   Swe. **Rice;** also **ris.**

risgrynsgröt (RESS-gruhns-groht).   Swe. **Rice pudding.**

risi e bisi (RE-se eh BE-se).   Ita. **Rice** and **peas** cooked in **broth** with **onion, parsley,** and **Parmesan.** Also called risi bisi.

riso (RE-sos).   Ita. **Rice.**

risoles (re-SOH-lehs).   Mex. **Fritters.**

risotto (re-SOT-toa).   Ita. **Rice** cooked in **butter** with **chopped onions** to which **stock** is added until absorbed; then various savory foods are added.

rissole (re-sall).   Fre. A mixture of minced fish or meat, enclosed in pastry, half-moon shaped, and **fried;** a puff-pastry **fritter** or **turnover.**

rissolé (re-sohl).   Fre. Food such as **potatoes** that has been fried.

ristet (RIS-teht).   Nor. **Roasted, grilled, fried.**

ristet brød (RIS-teht brut).   Nor. **Toast.**

ristet brød (RES-tert brurdh).   Dan. **Toast.**

ristet torskerogn (RES-tert TOARS-ker-roan).   Dan. **Fried roe.**

rivierkreeft (re-VE-krehft).   Dut. **Crayfish.**

riz (ruzz).   Ara. **Rice.**

riz (re).   Fre. **Rice.**

riz à l'impératrice (re ah l'eim-peh-rah-tres).   Fre. A **vanilla**-flavored **rice pudding** with candied **fruits** and **custard cream.**

rizards (REH-zahrds).   Sco. Currants. Also *rizzerberries.*

riz sauvage (re so-vazh).   Fre. **Wild rice.**

roast (rost).   USA. To cook uncovered by exposing to dry heat; in an oven, on a spit, on or near hot embers or stones.

roast (rost).   USA. A cut of meat suitable for roasting.

roast beef (rost bef).   USA. A cut of beef from the **chuck,** or the hindquarter cuts of **rump, round,** or **tip** that has been **roasted.**

roaster (ROST-tehr). USA. As a food, refers to a **chicken** of either sex, under eight months old and weighing three and a half to five pounds. Also see **broiler, fryer, stewing chicken, capon, stag chicken,** and **cock.**

Robiola (Ro-be-O-lah). Ita. A soft cow's- or ewe's-milk **cheese,** rectangular or disc shaped, reddish thin rind, smooth and even paste, piquant in flavor; also called *Robiolini.*

robusta (ro-BUS-tah). USA. A **coffee bean** used mostly in commercial blends of coffee and in **instant coffee,** high in caffeine, inferior in taste to **Arabica.**

Rocamadur (Roh-kah-mah-dooer). Gre. A soft **cheese** made from ewe's milk.

Rochen (RO-khehn). Ger. **Skate,** a saltwater fish.

Rock Cornish game hen (rahk KORN-esh gahm hehn). USA. A crossbreed **chicken** with succulent flesh.

rock crab (rahk krahb). USA. A cousin of the **Dungeness crab.**

Rockefeller (RAHK-ah-fell-eh) USA. A **garnish,** usually for **oysters,** of **creamed spinach** with breadcrumbs, **chopped bacon,** seasonings, **herbs.**

rocket (RAH-kett). Ita. A peppery, piquant tasting aromatic **herb** used in **salads;** not to be confused with the poisonous weed also called *rocket.* Also known as **arugula, misticanza; rugola.**

rockfish (RAHK-fehsh). USA. A fish of the Pacific, sometimes mistakenly called **red snapper;** has firm, delicate flesh that is lean and used extensively by the Chinese.

rock salt (rahk sawlt). USA. A nonedible, unrefined salt used as a base for baking **potatoes,** heating **oysters** on the half shell, freezing **ice cream;** use is based on its ability to retain heat or cold.

Rocky mountain oyster (RAH-ke moun-tahn OYU-stuhr). USA. Testicles of a bull, pig, or **lamb; breaded** and **fried.** Also known as **animelles, frivolitées, lamb fries, mountain oyster, prairie oyster.**

rocky road (RAH-ke rod). USA. A **confection,** can be **candy, ice cream, cake, pie,** made of **milk** or **dark chocolate** mixed with **marshmallows** and **nuts.**

rodaballo (roa-dhah-BHAH-lyoa). Spa. **Turbot.**

rödbetor (RUR-bay-toor). Swe. **Beets.**

rode kool (RO-yuh kohl). Dut. **Red cabbage.**

rødgrød med fløde (rohth-GROH meh FLUH-theh). Dan. "Red gruel" with **cream; pudding** of thickened **raspberry** and **currant juices** eaten with sweet **cream.**

rødgrot (RUR-grot). Nor. **Pudding** made of **currants** and **raspberries.**

rødkaal (RURTH-kohl). Dan. Red **cabbage.**

rødkål (RUR-kawl). Nor. Red **cabbage.**

rödkål (RURD-koal). Swe. Red **cabbage.**

rødspaette (RUR-spaider). Dan. **Plaice.**

rödspätta (RUR-speh-tah). Swe. **Plaice.**

roe (ro). USA. **Eggs** of fish and **shellfish.**

roebuck (ro-buhk). USA. Male roe deer; **venison.**

rogani gosht (RO-gah-ne gohsht). Ind. Rich meat dish made with **cream, usli ghee,** and spices.

rogan josh (RO-gahn joosh). Ind. Lamb braised in **yogurt** and **cream** with Moghul spices.

Rogen (RO-gehn). Ger. Fish **roe.**

røget (ROI-ert). Dan. **Smoked.**

røget sild (ROI-ert sel). Dan. **Smoked herring.**

Roggenbrot (RO-gehn-brot). Ger. **Rye** bread.

roggerbrood (RAWKH-uh-broht). Dut. **Rye** bread.

rognoni (roa-NYOA-ne). Ita. **Kidneys.**

rognons (ro-nyawng). Fre. **Kidneys.**

roh (ro). Ger. **Raw.**

Rohkost (RO-kohst). Ger. **Raw vegetables; crudités.**

Rohkost tomaten (RO-kohst tom-MAA-tern). Ger. Savory **stuffed tomatoes.**

roi (RO-e). Ind. A local Calcutta fish.

rojões (ROU-zehngsh). Por. **Pork** prepared with white wine, **paprika,** and **potatoes.**

røket fisk (RUR-ket-fisk). Nor. **Smoked** fish.

rökt (rurkt). Swe. **Smoked.**

roll (rohl). USA. A small piece of variously shaped baked **yeast dough;** a bread product.

rollatini (rohl-lah-TE-ne). Ita. Small slices of meat **stuffed** and rolled; **saltimbocca.**

rollè (rol-LEH). Ita. **Slices** of meat **stuffed** and rolled.

rolled oats (rold ouhts). USA. Separate flakes formed by rolling the **groats** with hulls removed and steaming them; thinness of flake determines regular or quick-cooking; popular for adding flavor to **cookies;** also used as a hot breakfast **cereal.**

rollmop (rohl-mohp). Fre. An **hors d'oeuvre** of **fillet** of **herring** rolled around a **gherkin** and **skewered.**

Rollmop (ROL-mops). Ger. A **pickled herring** rolled around a tiny sour **onion.**

rollo (ROHL-loh). Spa. A **slice** of meat **stuffed** and rolled.

roly-poly pudding (ROH-le POH-le PUHD-deng). Bri. **Suet** pastry spread with **jam,** rolled in shape of **sausage, steamed** or **baked.**

rom (rom). Swe. **Roe.**

Romadurkäse (Roh-mah-durah-kazh-zeh). Ger. A soft **cheese;** similar to **Limburger,** with less assertive aroma.

romaine (ro-MAN). USA. . A **salad lettuce** with firm, thick, narrow leaves; **cos** lettuce, *romaine lettuce.*

Roman rice (RO-mahn ris). USA. A variety of **rice** that has dull, greyish-white grains.

Romano (Ro-MAHN-o). Ita. A round ewe's whole-milk **cheese,** white or very pale yellow paste, dense, with a yellow brown rind; sharp, salty and intense. Same as **Pecorino Romano.**

romarin (roa-mah-rang). Fre. **Rosemary.**

romaavaya baba (RO-mah-vah-yah BAH-bah). Rus. Rum **cake.**

rombo (ROAM-boa). Ita. **Turbot.**

romfrommage (ROM-froa-maa-sher). Dan. Creamy rum-flavored **dessert.**

rømmegrøt (ROHM-meh-greht). Nor. **Sour cream porridge.**

rømmekolle (rohm-meh-KOHL-le). Nor. **Yogurt**-like **dessert** of **clabbered cream** and **zwieback** crumbs.

rømmesalat (rohm-meh-sah-LAHT). Nor. **Lettuce** with dressing of **sour cream.**

Roncal (ron-KAHL). Spa. A hard, close-grained, pungent, sharp-flavored, cow's-milk **cheese.**

rookspek (ROHK-spek). Dut. **Bacon.**

rookvlees (ROHK-vlays). Dut. **Smoked chipped beef.**

rookwurst (ROHK-voorst). Dut. **Smoked sausage.**

room (rohm). Dut. **Cream.**

roomeiersaus (rohm-AY-uh-sows). Dut. **Sour cream sauce** with **eggs,** served on fish.

roomijs (ROHM-ays). Dut. **Ice cream.**

roomkaas (ROHM-kahs). Dut. **Cream cheese.**

rooster (ROO-stuhr). USA. An adult male domestic foul; cock.

Roos (Rooz). Iraq. A round sheep's-milk **cheese** the size of an orange; molded by hand and ripened in sheepskin bags for six months.

Roquefort (rowk-fort). Fre. A celebrated **cheese** of ewe's milk, with thin orange rind, ivory interior, blue-green veining; salty, sharp, creamy taste; a unique cheese in that powder-fine breadcrumbs containing a special greenish mold are mixed with the curds. One of the world's great blue-veined cheeses, the only one made of whole ewe's milk during the lambing season. Truly a gastronomic jewel.

roquette (roh-kay). Fre. **Rocket,** a **salad herb.**

rosbif (ros-bef). Fre. **Roast beef.**

rosbif (ROS-bef). Ita. **Roast beef.**

rosbife (rohz-BE-fay). Por. **Roast beef.**

rose hips (rohz hehps). USA. The **fruit** of certain rose plants, high in vitamin C, used in making **jellies** and **syrup.**

rosefish (ROHZ-fesch). USA. One of the names for ocean **perch.**

rosemary (ROHZ-mahr-ee). USA. An **herb** with narrow, glossy dark green needle-like leaves that are grayish white underneath; enhances the flavor of **pork** and **lamb.**

Rosenkohl (ROA-zern-koal). Ger. **Brussels sprouts.**

rosenkohl (ROASS-ern-kawl). Dan. **Brussels sprouts.**

rosette (roh-zet).   Fre. Thin, rich **batter** made into fancy shapes using a special iron and **fried** in deep fat.

rose water (ROZ-wah-tehr).   USA. An oil extracted from the petals of roses, used as a flavoring.

Rosinen (ro-ZRR-nern).   Ger. **Raisins.**

rosmarino (roaz-mah-RE-noa).   Ita. **Rosemary.**

rosolio (roz-soh-LE-oa).   Ita. A very sweet traditional **liqueur;** delicate taste.

Rossini (roh-se-ne).   Fre. A classic **garnish** for small cuts of meat; **slices of foie gras sautéed** in **butter,** thick **slices** of **truffles,** and **stock** blended with **Madeira.**

rostat bröd (ROS-taht brurd).   Swe. **Toast.**

Rostbraten (ROAST-braa-tern).   Ger. **Roast beef.**

Rostbratwurst (ROAST-braat-voorst).   Ger. **Roasted ham sausage.**

Rösti (RUR-shte).   Ger. A Swiss dish of **shredded potatoes fried** in a **pancake.**

Röstkartoffeln (RURST-kahr-tof-ferln).   Ger. Home-fried **potatoes.**

Rotbarbe (ROAT-bahrb).   Ger. **Red mullet.**

Rote Grütze (RO-dah GRUT-zeh).   Ger. A **fruit pudding** made with **farina, heavy cream, fruit** juice and **sugar; tapioca** may be used in place of **farina.**

Roterübe (ROA-ter-rewb).   Ger. **Beet.**

roti (RO-te).   Ind. Flat bread.

rôti (roa-te).   Fre. **Roasted.**

rôtir (ro-ter).   Fre. **Toast;** a toasted slice of bread.

rotkohl (ROAT-koal).   Ger. Red **cabbage.**

rotkraut (ROAT-krowt).   Ger. Red **cabbage** with **apples** and **vinegar.**

rotmos (ROOT-mooss).   Swe. Mashed **turnips.**

Rotwein (ROAT-vighn).   Ger. Red wine.

ròu (row).   Chi. Meat.

rouelle (rwehl).   Fre. A fairly thick **slice** of **veal,** across the leg.

rouennaise (rwah-nayz).   Fre. A red wine reduced **bordelaise sauce** with **shallots** and **puréed raw duck** livers.

rougail (ROO-guye). USA. A highly spiced **Creole condiment** that accompanies Creole dishes served with **rice.**

rouget (roo-heh). Fre. **Red mullet;** a very desirable fish found in the Mediterranean; white, sweet, delicate flesh.

rouille (roo-yuh). Fre. A spicy **mayonnaise** with red **pepper** and **garlic;** served with fish.

roulade (roo-lahd). Fre. **Slices** of meat rolled around a **filling,** then **browned,** and slowly **braised.**

Rouladen (roo-LAA-dern). Ger. Beef rolls.

round (rownd). USA. The part of the beef hindquarter between the **rump** and the **tip;** used in various cuts, such as top **round,** bottom round, top **sirloin,** or left whole to **braise** or **roast.**

round red potato (rownd rehd pah-TA-to). USA. One of four main varieties of **potatoes;** has white flesh with paper-thin red skin; used for **boiling;** other varieties are **long white, round white,** and **russet.**

round white potato (rownd whit pah-TA-to). USA. One of four main varieties of **potatoes,** white flesh with thin light tan skin; used for **boiling, baking,** and **french fries;** other varieties are **long white, round red,** and **russet.**

roux (roo). Fre. A thickener for **sauces;** a mixture of **butter** or fat and **flour,** cooked for varying lengths of time depending on its use; white roux, blond roux, and brown roux.

rova (ROO-vah). Swe. **Turnip.**

rowanberry (roa-uhn-behr-re). Fre. **Fruit** of the rowan tree; makes a bright red, tart **jelly** served with **venison, game, lamb.**

Royal Brabant (Roh-yahl Brah-haa-bourgh). Bel. A small **Limburger**-type **cheese** made from cow's milk.

royale (rwah-yal). Fre. Molded **custard,** flavored but not sweetened, used as **garnishes** in clear **soups.**

royal icing (ROHY-yahl I-seng). USA. A glazing icing made of **confectioners' sugar, egg** white, and **lemon** juice; used for wedding cakes, special cakes, pastry writing; dries hard. Sometimes called *royal glaze* and **Swiss meringue.**

royan (wah-yahng). Fre. A large **sardine.**

rozijnen (roh-ZI-en). Dut. **Raisins.**

Rübe (rewb). Ger. **Turnip.**

rubyaana (rihbb-YAHN). Ara. Persian Gulf **shrimp.**

ruchetta (ru-KET-tah). Ita. **Rocket, a salad herb.**

rucola (roo-CHOA-lah). Ita. **Rocket, a salad herb.** Also **ruchetta.**

rue (roo). Ita. An **herb** used for flavoring some **brandies.**

rugbrød (ROO-brurdh). Dan. Dark **rye** bread.

rugde (REWG-der). Nor. **Woodcock.**

rugola (roo-GOA-lah). Ita. **Rocket, a salad herb.** Also **roquette, ruco-la, ruchetta.**

ruh (rooh). Ind. **Essence.**

ruibarbo (rwe-BHAHR-boa). Spa. **Rhubarb.**

rulader (REW-lah-derr). Swe. Beef roll.

rull (rooll). Nor. Spiced beef roll.

rullepølse (ROO-luh-PUL-seh). Dan. Spiced and **larded** meat roll of **veal,** beef, or **lamb.**

rullesild (REWL-leh-sill). Nor. Rolled **herring.**

rumaki (roo-MAH-ke). Jap. An **appetizer** of **chicken** livers and **water chestnuts** wrapped in **bacon,** then **broiled.**

rump (ruhmp). USA. The cut of beef above the **round,** from the hindquarter.

rundergehak (RHUN-der-her-HAHK). Dut. **Chopped** or **ground beef.**

rundstykker (ROONN-stewk-kewh). Nor. Roll.

rundvlees (ROONT-vlays). Dut. Beef.

ruote (RWO-tah). Ita. Pasta, wheel-shaped.

rusinat (ROO-ssin-naht). Fin. **Raisins, sultanas.**

rusk (ruhsk). USA. Slices of a special bread, rebaked, used for bread-crumbs, **appetizers,** as hard **toast.**

russe (roos). Fre. "With strawberries," as in **charlotte russe.**

russe, à la (roos ah lah). Fre. Served with **sour cream.**

russet potato (RUH-seht pah-TA-tah). USA. One of four main vari-eties of **potatoes;** has creamy white flesh with brown skin; best used

for **baking,** but also good for **boiling, frying, grilling;** other varieties are **long white, round white,** and **round red.**

russin (ru-sin). Swe. **Raisin.**

rustica, alla (roor-STE-kah). Ita. **Anchovies, cheese, garlic, oregano** in a sauce served with **spaghetti.**

rutabaga (roo-tah-BAHG-gah). USA. A yellow **turnip.**

ryba (RI-boo). Rus. Fish.

rye flour (ryi flowr). USA. Fine granulation; usually combined with **wheat flour** because **rye** flour **gluten** provides stickiness but lacks elasticity; breads made largely from rye flour are moist, compact, made with **sourdough** leavener.

rye meal (ryi meal). USA. Coarsely ground whole-**rye flour.**

rygeost (REW-eh-oast). Dan. **Smoked cream cheese.**

rype (REW-ber). Dan. **Grouse, ptarmigan.**

rype (REW-per). Nor. **Grouse, ptarmigan.**

rype i fløtesaus (REW-per e FLUR-ter-ssowss). Nor. **Ptarmigan** in **cream sauce;** a Norwegian delicacy.

Salsa - Portugal - Parsley

saag (sahng). Ind. Greens: **spinach, collard** greens, **beet** greens, **escarole, mustard** greens, **fenugreek** greens.

Saanen (zahn-nahn). Swi. A cow's-milk **cheese** with a mellow fragrant flavor; hard, large orange discs; **dessert** or grating **cheese.**

Saankäse (zahn-KAHZ-zer). Ger. A **cheese** the same as **Saanen.**

saba (sah-BAH). Jap. **Mackerel.**

sabayon (sa-by-on). Fre. A cream **mousse** made of **egg** yolks, **flour, sugar,** wine or other alcoholic flavorings, beaten over heat while thickening; **zabaglione.**

sablé (sab-leh). Fre. A **shortbread;** a delicate small **biscuit** or **cake.**

sabzi (SAHB-ze). Ind. **Vegetables.**

saccharin (SAH-kehr-rehn). USA. A noncaloric **sugar** substitute; an artificial sweetener 350 times sweeter than sugar.

Sachertorte (ZA-kher-tor-teh). Ger. A very rich, world-famous Austrian **chocolate cake** layered with **apricot jam** and covered with **chocolate icing.**

sacristain (sahc-chres-stahng). Fre. A spiral-shaped **puff pastry,** flavored with **cheese** or **almonds** and **sugar.**

sadaf (sah-DOHF). Ara. **Oyster.**

saddle (SAH-duhl). USA. The cut from the whole carcass of meat from the end of the **rib** section and to the legs on both sides.

safflower oil (SAHF-flawr oyl). USA. Oil from the seeds of the safflower plant; light in flavor, high in polyunsaturates.

saffron (SAHF-fron). Ita. An **herb** of an autumn-blooming crocus whose orange-red stigmas are harvested by hand and dried; used for delicately coloring dishes, as well as seasoning.

safran (sahf-rahng). Fre. **Saffron.**

Safran (zah-FRAAN). Ger. **Saffron.**

Saft (zahft). Ger. Juice, **gravy.**

Saftbraten (zaft-bra-ton) Ger. Beef **stew.**

sage (saj). USA. An **herb** of the **mint** family with a delicate flavor used to season dressings, **pork**, goose, **cheese, chowder.**

Sage Cheddar (Saj Cheh-dehr). USA. A natural **Cheddar,** flavored with **sage.**

Sage Cream (Saj Krem). Bri. An unripened **cream cheese,** to which bruised **sage** leaves and **spinach** juice is added, giving a delicate green color.

Sage Derby (saj DAHR-be). Bri. A **sage**-flavored **cheese;** flaky, mild, marbled with sage; this cheese is a traditional food at Christmas in Britain.

Sage Lancashire (Saj LAHNK-kah-shuhr). Bri. A variety of **Lancashire cheese** with chopped **sage** leaves added.

sago (SAY-go). USA. A starch made from the trunk of Indian palms, used as a thickening agent; pearl-like beads, similar to **tapioca.**

sahlab (SAH-bab). Ara. A starch extracted from tubers of any of various orchids and used like **tapioca; cornstarch** may be substituted; also a hot milky drink topped with **chopped nuts** and **shredded coconut.**

Sahne (ZAH-neh). Ger. **Cream.**

Sahnenkuchen (ZAH-neh-koo-kern). Ger. **Cheesecake.**

Sahnequark (ZAH-neh-kvark). Ger. **Cream cheese.**

saignant (seh-nyahng). Fre. Rare, as for meat.

saigneux (say-noo). Fre. Neck of **veal** or **lamb.**

Saingorlon (sawng-gor-lawhn). Fre. A cow's-milk **cheese,** semisoft, ripened, blue-veined, very rich, and delicate in flavor.

Saint-Benoit (sawng behn-nwah). Fre. A soft **cheese** that is rubbed with **salt** and charcoal before ripening.

Sainte-Maure (san-mo-reh). Fre. A log-shaped ewe's-milk **cheese** with soft white interior, white rind.

St. Ivel (Sahnt I-vehl). Bri. A ripened, soft **cheese** that develops a flavor like that of **Camembert** after innoculation with the same culture that is used for making **yogurt.**

Saint-Marcellin (sawng-mah-ceh-lawn). Fre. A soft goat's-milk **cheese** made in the Alps.

Saint-Nectaire (sawng nech-tehr). Fre. An aged, sharp, firm goat **cheese**.

Saint-Paulin (sawng poo-lawng). Fre. A variation of **Port du Salut,** created by Trappist monks of Notre Dame in 1816; young, it is semi-soft and will so remain in cold countries, but in hot climates it ages to semifirm consistency.

Saint-Pierre (san-pyehr). Fre. **John Dory,** a very tasty, ugly-looking fish.

saisir (seh-zer). Fre. To **sear.**

saiten (zye-ten). Ger. One of many varieties of **sausages.**

saj (sahjg). Ara. Paper-thin bread baked over a metal dome on an open fire.

sakana (sah-KE-nah). Jap. Fish.

sake (SAH-keh). Jap. **Salmon.**

saké (sah-KAH). Jap. Sweet or dry white **rice wine.**

sal (sahl). Spa, Por. **Salt.**

salad (SAHL-ehd). USA. A dish of mixed **raw,** fresh **vegetables** or **fruits,** usually served with a dressing; can also be made of meats, fish, **poultry,** or **seafood.**

salada (sa-LAH-da). Por. **Salad.**

salad dressing (SAHL-ehd DREHS-eng). USA. A liquid mixture, either cooked or uncooked, normally containing either **vinegar** or **mayonnaise,** with seasonings.

salade de pissenlit (sah-lahd duh pe-sehn-le). Fre. Wilted dandelion greens **salad.**

salade verte (sah-lahd vehrt). Fre. Green **salad.**

salado (SAH-doh). **Spa.** Salty, **salted.**

salambo (sahl-lahm-bo). Fre. A small pastry filled with **kirsch-**flavored **cream filling** and iced with **caramel.**

salame di fegato (sah-LAA-may de fay-GAH-toa). Ita. **Liverwurst.**

salami (sah-LAHM-me). Ita. A highly spiced **sausage,** often **smoked;** used as a **sandwich** meat or cold cut.

Salat (za-LAHT). Ger. **Salad.**

salata (sah-LAH-tehss). Gre. **Salad** of **raw** fresh **vegetables.**

salatagurker (sah-LAA-tah-GEWR-kehr). Nor. **Dill pickles.**

Salbei (ZAL-bye). Ger. **Sage.**

salchichas (sahl-CHE-chahs). Spa. **Sausages.**

sale (SAA-lay). Ita. **Salt.**

salé (sa-lay). Fre. **Salted.**

salées au fromage (sah-layz o fro-mazh). Fre. **Cheesecake.**

salgado (sahl-GAH-doo). Por. **Salted.**

Salisbury steak (SAHLS-buhr-re stehk). USA. A seasoned beef patty, **broiled.**

salladsås (SAH-lahd-soass). Swe. **Salad dressing.**

Sally Lunn (SAHL-e Luhn). Bri. A kind of **tea cake,** slightly sweet and raised with **yeast.**

Salm (zahlm). Ger. **Salmon.**

salmagundi (sal-mah-GUN-de). Bri. A carefully arranged **salad;** greens, **pickles,** hard-boiled **eggs, anchovy,** chopped meats, **onions.**

salmão (sal-MEOWN). Por. **Salmon.**

salmon (SAHM-uhn). USA. A salt- and freshwater fish; firm, rich, flavorful meat; very pale to deep orange-red colored flesh; many species, but **chinook, sockeye,** coho, and Atlantic are best; **lox** is a salmon product.

salmone (sahl-MOA-nay). Ita. **Salmon.**

salmone affumicato (sahl-MOA-nay ahf-foo-me-KAA-toa). Ita. **Smoked salmon.**

salmonette (sahl-moa-NAY-tayss). Spa. **Red mullet.**

salpicão (SAHL-pe-kahng). Por. **Smoked ham roll.**

salpicon (sal-pe-con). Fre. A **mince** of **poultry, game,** or **vegetables,** bound with a **sauce;** used as a **stuffing** or **filling.**

salsa (SAHL-sah). Ara. **Sauce.**

salsa (SAHL-sah). Por. **Parsley.**

salsa (SAHL-sah). Spa. Seasoned **sauce;** used for **dipping** or as a **condiment.**

salsa borracha (SAL-sah bow-RAA-cah). Mex. "Drunken sauce"; made with tequila, **orange** juice, **onion, pasilla chilies.**

salsa de tomate (SAHL-sah day toh-MAH-tay). Spa. Catsup.

salsa francesa (SAHL-sah FRAHN-theh-sah).   Spa. French dressing.

salsa inglesa (SAHL-sah en-GLAY-sah).   Spa. **Worcestershire sauce.**

salsicce (sahl-SET-chay).   Ita. **Sausages.**

salsicha (sahl-SE-shash).   Por. **Sausage.**

salsifis (sahl-suh-fe).   Fre. Salsify; **oyster plant**

salsify (SAHL-sah-fe).   USA. A plant whose root is eaten boiled or sauteed; called **oyster plant.**

salt (sawlt).   USA. Sodium chloride; an edible crystalline compound, abundant in nature, and used for seasoning or preserving food. See also **coarse salt, cooking salt, flake salt, iodized salt, kosher salt, pickling salt, rock salt, sea salt, table salt.**

saltfiskballer (sahlt-fisk-BOOL-lehr).   Nor. **Dumplings** of **potatoes** and fish.

saltimbocca (sahl-tem-BOAK-kah).   Ita. **Veal scallop** with **prosciutto braised** in **butter** and **Marsala.**

saltpeter (SAWLT-pe-tehr).   USA. Potassium nitrate; gives flavor and red color to meat.

salt potato (sawlt po-TA-to).   USA. A small new **potato** that has been soaked or boiled in brine; a specialty of Syracuse, New York.

salva (SAL-vah).   Por. **Sage.**

salvia (SAHL-veah).   Ita. **Sage.**

Salz (zahlts).   Ger. **Salt.**

Salzburger Nockerl (zaltz-BOOR-gehr nokh-rehl).   Ger. Light, airy **dessert dumplings.**

Salzgebäck (zahlts-ger-BAHK).   Ger. Salty **cracker; pretzel.**

Salzgurken (zahlts-GOOR-kern).   Ger. **Dill pickles.**

Salzkartoffeln (ZAHLTS-kahr-tof-ferln).   Ger. Plain **boiled potatoes.**

samak (SAH-mak).   Ara. Fish.

sambaar (SAHM-bahr).   Ind. A very, very **chili**-hot stew of large split peas (dals) and vegetables served with rice.

sambusik (sahm-BOO-sek).   Ara. A **nut**-filled **cookie;** nut moons.

samni (SAHM-ne).   Ara. The equivalent of **butter.**

samosa (sa-MO-sah).   Ind. A **stuffed,** savory **deep-fried** pastry cone.

samphire (sahm-FEHR).   USA. A **salad** green, grown wild or under cultivation; bacile.

Samsø (SAHM-sur).   Dan. One of the finest of Danish **cheeses;** made of cow's whole-milk, large round, golden yellow; scattered holes; nutty, mild flavor; produced on the island of Samsø.

sanamura (sah-nah-MOOR-rah).   Ara. **Herring.**

sanbusak (sahn-BOO-sahk).   Tur. A thin **yeast dough turnover** filled with **minced** meat, **pine nuts, onions,** and **cinnamon.**

sandia (sahn-DE-ah).   Spa. **Watermelon.**

sandkage (sahnd-KAH-gheh).   Dan. Sand **cake,** rich with **eggs, butter, sugar.**

sandre (sahn-drah).   Fre. Large **perch.**

sandwich (SAHN-wehch).   USA. Two slices of bread, usually, filled with any variety of meats, **cheeses, fillings, relishes, jellies, butters, vegetables, lettuce.**

sang chow (sehn tso).   Chi. A light colored **soy sauce.**

sanglier (sahng-glyay).   Fre. Wild boar.

sangria (sahn-GRE-ah).   Spa. A punch made of mostly wine, flavored with **brandy, Cointreau,** and fruits; best chilled.

sangue (SAHNG-gooay).   Ita. Rare, as for meat.

San Pedro (sahn PEH-droh).   Spa. Better known as St. Peter's fish; the classic ingredient of **bouillabaisse;** flesh is white, firm, and finely flaked.

sansho (SAHN-sho).   Jap. A greenish-brown ground spice called "Japanese pepper"; tangy but not hot.

San Simon (sahn se-MOHN).   Spa. A semihard cow's-milk **cheese** that is pear-shaped and bland; sometimes **smoked.**

Santa Claus melon (SAN-tah klaus MELL-uhn).   USA. A **melon** that resembles a small **watermelon** with a mottled yellow and green rind; has pale green flesh that tastes similar to **honeydew.** Also known as *Christmas melon.*

santola (san-TOL-ah).   Por. **Crab.**

santola gratinada (san-TOL-ah grah-te-NAH-dah).   Por. Deviled **crab.**

sap (sahp).   Dut. Juice.

sapodilla (sahp-o-DEHL-lah). USA. A round **fruit** with thin, brown leathery skin and flesh from honey-blonde to deep red-brown and tastes similar to **maple** sugar; eat out of hand or in **salads** and **ices.**

saporoso (sa-poh-ROA-soa). Ita. **Relish.**

Sapsago (Sahp-SAH-go). Swi. A **cheese** made from slightly sour, skim milk; the cured cheeses are cone shaped; used for **grating.**

sapsis (SAHP-sehs). USA. A **bean porridge.**

saracen corn (SAH-rah-cen korn). USA. **Buckwheat.**

Sarah Bernhardt (sa-rah burn-hahrt). Fre. Served with **purée** of **foie gras.**

sarapatel (sah-rah-pah-TELL). Por. Liver and **bacon.**

Saratoga potatoes (sah-rah-TOH-gah po-TA-tos). USA. **Potato chips.** Also called *Saratoga chips* because they originated in Saratoga, New York.

sarcelle (sahr-sehl). Fre. Wild **duck.**

sarde (sahr-DEH). Ita. **Sardines.** Also **sardelle, sardine.**

sardelle (sahr-DEH-leh). Ita. Sardines. Also **sarde, sardine.**

Sardelle (zar-DE-leh). Ger. **Anchovy.**

sardin (sar-DIN). Swe. **Sardine.**

sardine (sahr-DE-neh). Ita. **Sardelle, sarde.**

Sardinen (zar-DE-ne-en). Ger. **Sardines.**

sardines (sahr-DENZ). USA. Very young **herring.**

sardinha (sar-DEN-yash). Por. **Sardine.**

Sardo (SAHR-do). Ita. A hard, grating **cheese** of the **Romano** type, made of cow's and ewe's milk.

sarsoon (sahr-SOHN). Ind. **Mustard** greens.

sås (soass). Swe. **Sauce.**

sasage (sah-SAH-geht). Jap. Very thin, very **long green beans;** taste is stronger than ordinary green beans; also known as **asparagus beans, dow ghok, long beans, yard-long beans.**

sashimi (sah-SHE-me). Jap. Sliced **raw** fish.

sassafras (SAHS-sah-frahs). USA. An aromatic tree of the laurel family whose bark is dried and used as a flavoring for root beer; the bark is

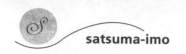

also pounded to make **filé powder,** an essential ingredient in **gumbos.**

satsuma-imo (sah-TSOO-mah-e-moh). Jap. **Sweet potato.**

sato imo (sah-TO e-moh). Jap. Field **yams.**

Saubohnen (zow-BOA-nern). Ger. **Broad beans.**

sauce (saus). USA. A liquid **dressing** or **topping** for food; can be very simple, such as melted butter, or very complicated with many ingredients. There are several basic sauces from which all others are made:

béchamel (bay-shah-mehl). basic white sauce: white **roux** and **milk.**

espagnole (ehs-spon-yole). basic brown sauce: brown **roux** and a brown **stock.**

mayonnaise (mah-ohn-aiz). basic yellow sauce: raw **egg yolks,** oil, and **lemon** juice or **vinegar;** for cold sauces.

tomato (to-may-to). basic red sauce: blond **roux** and **tomato purée.**

vinaigrette (ve-nay-greht). basic clear sauce: oil and **vinegar.**

volouté (ve-loo-tay). basic blond sauce: white **roux** and light stock (**chicken,** fish, or **veal**).

Any combination of two or more basic sauces creates one of a countless number of compound sauces. Listed here are a few well-known sauces (simple and compound) with a hint as to their contents:

aïoli (ah-oa-le). **garlic mayonnaise.**

allemande (ahl-mange). **veloutée** base thickened with **egg yolks.**

américaine (ah-may-re-kehn). white wine, **brandy, garlic, shallots, tomatoes, shrimp** or **lobster** flavoring.

béarnaise (bayr-naiz). a creamy sauce flavored with **vinegar,** white wine, **tarragon, shallots,** and **egg yolks.**

bercy (burr-ce). **velouté** based on fish **stock** with **shallots,** white wine, **butter.**

beurre blanc (berr blank). **butter, shallots,** white wine, **vinegar.**

beurre noir (berr nohr). browned **butter, lemon** juice and/or **vinegar.**

bordelaise (boar-deh-laiz). **boletus mushrooms, shallots,** red wine, and beef **marrow.**

bourguignone (boor-gee-nyawng). red wine and **herbs.**

bread sauce (brehd saus). **consommé, shallots,** finely **diced ham,** breadcrumbs fried in **butter** as the **roux.**

brown gravy (brahwn gra-ve). **beurre noir,** au jus, **Harvey** or **Worcestershire sauce,** and catsup.

chasseur (sha-sehr). **mushrooms, onions, shallots, herbs,** wine.

chaud-froid (sho-fro). **dressing** containing **gelatin.**

diable (de-ahbl). white wine, **shallots, thyme, demi-glace,** parsley, **hot peppers.**

duxelles (dews-sehl). with **mushrooms.**

financière (fe-non-syehr). **Madeira** wine, **truffles, olives, mushrooms.**

fines herbes (fen zehrb). with **herbs.**

florentine (flor-en-ten). with **spinach.**

hollandaise (hah-lohn-daiz). raw **egg yolks, butter,** and **lemon** juice.

indienne (ahn-dyen). **curry** sauce.

lyonnaise (lyi-ohn-naiz). with **onions.**

madère (mah-dehr). with **Madeira** wine.

marinière (mah-rahn-yeh). white wine, **mussel broth** thickened with **egg yolks.**

Mornay (mohr-nay). **cheese** sauce.

mousseline (moos-ser-len). **mayonnaise** with **cream.**

moutarde (moo-thard). **mustard** sauce.

normande (nohr-mond). with **mushrooms, eggs,** and **cream.**

Périgueux (pay-re-go). with **goose-** or **duck-** liver **purée** and **truffles.**

poivrade (pwah-vrahd). **pepper sauce.**

porto (por-toh). with **port wine.**

provençale (por-van-syahl). with **onions, tomatoes, garlic.**

ravigote (rah-ve-goht). a classic sauce used hot or cold of chopped **capers, chives, parsley, tarragon, chervil.**

rémoulade (rue-mah-lahd). sauce flavored with **mustard** and **herbs.**

Robert (rah-burt). **espagnole** base with **sautéed** finely **diced onions, consommé, vinegar,** and fine **mustard.**

Russian (RUHSH-uhn). mayonnaise with puree of caviar and lobster, mustard.

Soubise (su-besc). **onion-cream** sauce.

suprême (sew-prehm). rich, delicately flavored thickened **chicken broth** made with **heavy cream.**

Swedish (swe-desh). **mayonnaise** with **apple purée, grated horseradish** or **mustard.**

tartare (tahr-ter). **mayonnaise** flavored with **mustard** and **herbs.**

verte (vehrt). **mayonnaise** with **spinach, watercress,** and **herbs.**

Vincent (vehn-sawng). **mayonnaise** with **purée** of green **herbs,** chopped hard-boiled **egg yolks.**

Yorkshire (york-shur). **espagnole** base with **red currant jelly, port, cinnamon, orange juice** and peel.

saucijsjes (so-SAY-shus). Dut. **Sausages.**

saucisse (so-ses). Fre. Fresh, small **sausage.**

saucisson (so-se-son). Fre. Large cured **sausage.**

Sauerbraten (zow-er-BRAH-ten). Ger. Beef marinated in spicy **vinegar,** pot-roasted, and served with **gingersnap gravy.**

Sauerkraut (SOUR-kraut). Ger. A kind of **pickled cabbage,** made by chopping cabbage that is salted, then fermented in its own juice.

sauerkrout (SOUR-krot). Eng. **Sauerkraut.**

sauge (soazh). Fre. **Sage.**

saumon (soa-mawng). Fre. **Salmon.**

saunf (sohnf). Ind. **Anise; fennel.**

Saure Rahmsauce (ZOY-re RAHM-sous). Ger. **Sour cream dressing** used for **salads** and **vegetables.**

Saure Sahne (ZOY-re ZAH-neh). Ger. **Sour cream.**

saus (sows). Dut. **Sauce.**

sausage (SAW-sahg). USA. A highly seasoned **minced** or **ground meat filling** stuffed into a casing.

sauté (saw-TAY). USA, Fre. Cook in an open pan in a small amount of fat to tenderize and sear in flavor.

sauté pan (saw-tay). Fre. A shallow, thin-bottomed cooking pan, traditionally made of copper.

sauter (so-tay). Fre. Toss over the fire, in a **sauté pan** or frying pan using little butter or fat.

sauvage (so-vazh). Fre. Wild, undomesticated.

sával (SAH-vahl). Por. Shad.

savarin (sah-vah-rahng). Fre. A ring-shaped **yeast dough cake** soaked in flavored **syrup,** with rum or **kirsch** added, and filled variously.

savoiardi (sahr-WAHR-de). Ita. **Lady fingers.**

savories (SAY-vor-es). Bri. A course presented before the **fruit** and after the sweet to cut the sugar taste before the **port is** served; similar to **hors d'oeuvres,** but a little larger.

savory (SAY-vor-re). USA. Food that is not sweet.

savory (SAY-vor-re).   USA. An **herb** of the **mint** family; combines well with other herbs, especially those used with **poultry;** indispensable for **vegetable** cookery; has a particular affinity for **beans** of every sort.

savoyarde (sahv-wah-yahd).   Fre. With **cheese** and **potatoes.**

savoy cabbage (sah-vohy KAHB-ahgj).   USA. A hardy **cabbage,** in season throughout the winter; a milder flavor than common cabbage, improved by frost; has large, wrinkled leaves that are either purple or cream-colored laced with green trim. Also called salad savoy.

savu (SAH-voo).   Fin. **Smoked.**

saya éndo (SAH-yah ehn-DOE).   Jap. Edible-pod **peas.** Known as **sugar snap peas, snow peas,** or **Chinese pea pods.**

sbanikh (sa-BEH-nikh).   Ara. **Spinach.**

Sbrinz (Shbrehnz).   Swi. Made since ancient times, this **cheese** is aged, hard, of even texture without eyes; excellent for **grating** and preferable to **Parmesan** due to its high-fat content and richer flavor. The Swiss slice the not-yet-hard cheese in very thin slices and eat it with bread.

sbrisolona (sbree-suh-LOH-nah).   Ita. A famous flat and crisp **cake,** made with a combination of white **flour, cornmeal,** and **chopped almonds.**

scald (skahld).   USA. Heat liquid to just below boiling, about 185° F, and either pour over food or dip food into.

scallion (SKAHL-yun).   USA. Young **onion** pulled while the tops are green and tender and the bulb undeveloped; **green onion.**

scallop (SKAH-lop).   USA. To cover with **sauce** or **milk** and bread crumbs and bake in a **casserole.** Also called **escallope.**

scallopine (skol-a-PE-ne).   Ita. Small flat pieces of **veal, sautéed** and served in **sauce.**

scallops (SKAH-lohps).   USA. Marine **mollusks** whose edible part is the adductor muscle; has a radially ribbed hinged shell.

Scamorza (skah-MOR-dzah).   Ita. A salty, white **cheese** made of cow's whole milk; pear-shaped and netted to hang from rafters for ripening; has a smooth, thin rind that is repeatedly rubbed with oil while ripening.

scampi (SCAM-pe).   Ita. Saltwater **crayfish,** pale in color, quite large. Also called **Dublin Bay prawn, langoustine,** and **Norway lobster.**

scarola (skah-ROH-lah).   Ita. **Escarole.**

Schabzieger (SHARB-zeh-ger).   Ger. A pungent cow's skimmed-milk **cheese** from Switzerland; hard, green, cone shaped, flavored with blue melilot clover; made exactly the same way since the fifteenth century.

Schalotten (sha-LO-tern).   Ger. **Shallots.**

Schaltiere (SHAHL-te-reh).   Ger. **Shellfish.**

Schaum (showm).   Ger. **Mousse,** froth, foam.

Schaumrollen (SHOWM-eo-lehn).   Ger. **Puff-pastry rolls** filled with **whipped cream.**

Schaumwein (SHOWM-vighn).   Ger. Sparkling wine, **champagne.**

Schellfisch (SHEL-fish).   Ger. **Haddock.**

schelvis (SKHEL-vis).   Dut. **Haddock.**

schiacciata (skya-CHAH-tah).   Ita. A bread, rolled out thin like **pizza dough,** seasoned only with oil and **salt,** sometimes **rosemary , sage, sliced onions** or small pieces of **olives.**

Schildrötensuppe (SHILT-krur-ten-zoo-peh).   Ger. **Turtle soup.**

Schimmelkäse (SKEM-mehl-kahz-zer).   Ger. A soft **cheese** with a white crust; often added to scrambled **eggs.**

Schinken (SHING-kehn).   Ger. **Ham.**

Schlachtplatte (SHLAKHT-plah-ter).   Ger. Plate of cold meats and **sausages.**

Schlag (shlahk).   Ger. With **cream.**

Schlagsahne (SHLAHK-zah-neh).   Ger. **Whipped cream.**

Schlegel (SHLAY-gehl).   Ger. Drumstick.

Schlosskäse Bismarck (SCHLOWSS-kahz-zeh BEHZ-mahrk).   Ger. This **cheese** is the one Emil Frey was trying to copy when he created **Liederkranz;** he named it after the famous German Prime Minister.

Schmalz (shmahltz).   Ger. Melted fat, **lard,** grease.

Schmalzgebackenes (SHMAHLTZ-ger-braa-tern).   Ger. **Fried food.**

Schmand (shmahnd).   Ger. **Sour cream.**

Schmierkäse (SHMEER-kahz-zeh).   Ger. A soft, odorous, yellow **cottage cheese** so named by the Pennsylvania Dutch; it may be flavored with **onion.**

Schmorfleisch (SHMOR-flighsh).   Ger. Spiced meat.

Schnapps (shnahps). Ger. A liquor distilled from **grain** or **potatoes** and flavored variously; served very cold.

Schnitte (shnit). Ger. A chop or steak.

Schnittlauch (SHNIT-lowkh). Ger. **Chives.**

Schnitzel (SHNIT-sehl). Ger. A **cutlet** or **scallop.**

Schöbrunner Lunch (SHUR-broo-nehr). Ger. **Ham** and **vegetable pie.**

Schokolade (sho-ko-LAH-deh). Ger. **Chocolate.**

Schokoladeneis (shok-kol-LAA-dern-ighss). Ger. **Chocolate ice cream.**

schol (skhawl). Dut. **Plaice, flounder,** a **flatfish.**

Schöpsenschlegel (SHURP-zehn-shlay-gerl). Ger. **Roast** leg of **lamb.**

schorseneren (scors-seh-NAH-en). Dut. A slim, black root **vegetable.**

Schotensuppe (SHO-ten-zup-per). Ger. Fresh **green pea soup.**

schrod (skrahd). USA. The commercial name used to market **codfish** that weigh less than three pounds; also applies to **haddock.**

Schrotbrot (SHROAT-broat). Ger. **Whole wheat bread.**

schüblig (SHOOB-lerg). Ger. A Swiss **sausage** made in St. Gallen.

Schulter (SHOOL-ter). Ger. Shoulder.

Schupfnudeln (SHOOPF-noo-dehln). Ger. Thick, heavy **noodles.**

Schwamm (shvam). Ger. **Mushroom.**

Schwärtelbraten (SHVART-ehl-braa-tern). Ger. **Roast** leg of **pork,** cooked with **sauerkraut** and **dumplings,** served with **sour cream.**

Schwartzbrot (SHVART-broat). Ger. The famous black bread; gets its color from black **molasses.**

Schwartzwälder Kirschtorte (SHVARTS-vehl-derr KERSH-tor-ter). Ger. **Rich chocolate cake** with **cherry filling** between the layers and on top of icing; from the Black Forest.

Schwarzenberger (SHVART-zehn-behr-gehr). Ger. A **Limburger**-type **cheese** made from cow's milk.

Schwarzer Kaffee (SHVART-ser KAH-fay). Ger. Black **coffee.**

Schwarzfisch (SHVARTS-fish). Ger. **Carp.**

Schwarzsauer (SHVARTS-zoe-ehr). Ger. A **stew** of **goose giblets** and blood with **dried apples, prunes,** and **pears.**

Schwarzwürste (SHVARTS-voorst).   Ger. **Pork sausage** black with pig's blood.

Schwarzwurzeln (SHVARTS-voor-tseln).   Ger. **Salsify; oyster plant.**

Schwein (shvine).   Ger. **Pork.**

Schweinebauch (SHVINE-eh-baux).   Ger. **Pork** belly.

Schweinebraten (SHVINE-braa-tern).   Ger. **Roast pork.**

Schweinekeule (SHVINE-eh-koy-leh).   Ger. Leg of **pork.**

Schweinekotelett (SHVINE-eh-kot-let).   Ger. **Pork** chop.

Schweineohren (SHVINE-eh-o-rehn).   Ger. Crisp, sweet, very thin pastry.

Schweinepfeffer (SHVINE-eh-pfe-fehr).   Ger. Highly seasoned **pork.**

Schweinerippchen (SHVINE-eh-rip-khern).   Ger. **Spareribs.**

Schweinerucken (SHVINE-eh-roo-kern).   Ger. **Pork tenderloin.**

Schweineschenkel (SHVINE-eh-sheng-kerl).   Ger. **Roast pork** leg.

Schweinsjungfernbraten (shvines-yoong-fern-BRAA-tern).   Aus. A very tasty strip of **pork** roasted until skin is crunchy.

Schweinskarre (SHVINES-kah-re).   Ger. **Smoked pork** chops.

Schweinssulz (SHVINES-zoolz).   Ger. Jellied **pork.**

Schweizerkase (SHVITES-ehr-kay-ze).   Ger. **Swiss cheese.**

sciroppo (shee-ROAP-poh).   Ita. **Syrup.**

scone (scahn).   Sco. Quick bread usually containing **currants.**

score (skohr).   USA. Make shallow slits on the surface of meat, lengthwise and crosswise.

scorzonera (skor-tho-NAY-rah).   Spa. Black-skinned **salsify** that is peeled immediately after cooking to preserve its color.

Scotch broth (skotch brawth).   Sco. A soup of **vegetables, barley,** and **lamb.**

scotch egg (skotch ehg).   Sco. Hard-cooked **egg,** encased in **sausage,** and **fried.**

Scotch woodcock (skotch WOOD-kock).   Bri. Creamy scrambled **eggs** on **toast** with **anchovies.**

scottadito (skoa-tah-DE-toa).   Ita. "Burning fingers"; small **cutlets** on the bone; eaten with the fingers while very hot, hence the name.

scramble (SKRAHM-buhl).   USA. To prepare **eggs** or mixture containing eggs by stirring while cooking until mixture sets.

scrapple (SKRAHP-ehl). Ger. **Pork** scraps, including heart, liver, and tongue, boiled together, chopped, seasoned with **pepper, sage, salt;** thickened with **cornmeal; serve sliced** and **fried.** If made with oats it is called *geotta.*

scratchins (SKRAHT-chens). Bri. **Cracklings.**

scrod (skrohd). USA. A marketing term for young **cod** under two and one-half pounds; **schrod** (spelled with an h), indicates that the fish is a young haddock.

scungilli (skoon-JEL-le). Ita. Conches; flavor similar to **scallops.**

scuppernong (SKUHP-pehr-nong). USA. A table **grape** of the muscadine class.

sea bass (se bahss). USA. An edible fish of the **bass** family, with firm white meat and a delicate flavor derived from feeding chiefly on **crabs, shrimp,** and **mollusks.** Also called **black sea bass.**

sea biscuit (se behs-keht). USA. **Hardtack.**

sea bread (se-brehd). USA. **Hardtack.**

Seabutt (ZAY-but). Ger. A tasty European flatfish of the flounder family. Also known as **barbue, brill.**

sea cucumber (se QU-kum-ber). USA. **Hai shen;** a sea creature that looks like a large fat slug; when gutted, boiled, and dried, it shrinks and becomes firm, resembling a cigar butt; must be soaked in water for several days before using; mostly used in Oriental cooking.

sea fennel (se FEHN-nul). USA. **Samphire;** an edible **seaweed** with the taste of **fennel.**

seafood (se food). USA. Edible **shellfish** or saltwater fish.

sea kale (se kale). USA. A plant that grows wild and under cultivation; has thick, glaucous basal leaves; nutty flavor; use as **salad** green.

sea moss (se mohss). USA. An edible **seaweed,** principally used in Oriental cooking.

sea pie (se pi). USA. A **stew** of New England origins made of **pork, veal,** or **fowl** mixed with sweet **dried apples, molasses,** and **dumplings.**

sear (ser). USA. Brown meat quickly at a very high temperature until it is cooked.

sea salt (se sawlt). USA. A squarish-grained **salt;** very flavorful, used sprinkled over meats, **rolls, pretzels,** breads. Also called **kosher salt** and **coarse salt.**

sea slug (se sluhgh). USA. **Sea cucumber.**

seasoned salts (SE-szond sawltz). USA. A compound of **vegetable salts,** spices, and usually **monosodium glutamate.**

seatrout (SE-traut). USA. **Weakfish.**

sea trout (se trauwt). USA. A brown trout from the Atlantic waters, succulent pink flesh. Also called *salmon trout.*

sea urchin (se UHR-chen). USA. A spiny marine animal that looks like a large pin cushion; the cream to orange-colored **roe** is a delicacy.

seaweed (SE-wed). USA. Vegetation of the ocean waters. See **carrageen, dulse, faht choy, gee choy, hijiki, Irish moss, kelp, konbu, laver, nori, wakame.**

séco (SAY-koo). Por. **Dried.**

sedano (SEH-dah-noa). Ita. **Celery.**

Seekrabben (ZAY-kra-bern). Ger. **Crabs.**

Seezunge (ZAY-tsun-ger). Ger. **Sole.**

sel (sehl). Fre. **Salt.**

sel'd (syehld). Rus. **Herring.**

selderie (SEL-duh-re). Dut. **Celery.**

self-rising flour (sehlf-RI-zeng flawr). USA. An all-purpose **flour** with **salt** and a leavening agent added; if used for pastry, texture will be spongy, rather than flaky.

selha chawal (SEHL-ha CHAH-vel). Ind. **Converted rice.**

selleri (SAH-lea-RE). Swe. **Celery.**

selleri (SEHL-er-re). Dan. **Celery.**

Sellerie (ZE-leh-re). Ger. **Celery.**

Selles-sur-Cher (sell-sue-cher). Fre. A semifirm, salty goat **cheese.**

selters (SEHL-tehrs). Nor. **Mineral water.**

seltzer (SEHL-szuhr). USA. Plain, natural or man-made effervescent **mineral water.**

selvaggina (say-lvahd-JE-nah). Ita. **Venison; game.**

sem (saym). Ind. **Green beans.**

sembei (sem-bay). Jap. A small, crispy **rice cracker.**

semifreddo (se-me-FRAYD-doh). Ita. A chilled or frozen **mousse**-like **dessert,** including **cream, custard, cake,** and **fruit.**

semifrío (se-me-FRE-oa). Spa. **Semifreddo.**

semisweet chocolate (SEHM-e-swet CHOHK-o-laht). USA. A slightly sweetened **chocolate** used in **candy** making because of its sheen when melted; also used for **icings, sauces,** and **fillings.**

semlor (SAHM-loor). Swe. Buns eaten during Lent.

semmel (ZEH-merl). USA. Breakfast **yeast roll** from the Pennsylvania Dutch.

Semmelkloss (ZEH-merl-klos). Ger. Bread **dumpling.**

semolina (sehm-o-LE-nah). USA. A creamy-colored, granular, protein-rich **durum wheat flour** used commercially for all types of pasta.

senap (SAY-nahp). Swe. **Mustard.**

senape (SAY-nah-pay). Ita. **Mustard.**

Senf (zehnf). Ger. **Mustard.**

senf kartoffeln (zehnf kahr-TOF-terln). Ger. The Austrian version of **escalloped potatoes** in **mustard** sauce.

sennep (SEHN-erp). Dan. **Mustard.**

seppie (SAYP-pe-ah). Ita. **Cuttlefish.**

Septmoncel (seht-mo-cehll). Fre. A blue-veined Alpine **cheese** of mixed cow's, goat's, and sheep's milk; sometimes called *Jura Bleu.*

serendipity berry (sehr-ehn-DIHP-pe-te BEHR-re). USA. A small edible red **berry,** native to Africa, that contains the sweetest substance known to man; 1,000 times sweeter than sucrose.

seroendeng (scah-ROON-dang). Dut. Indonesian **fried coconut** with **peanuts.**

Serra de Estrella (SEHR-rah dur Eh-strahl-lah). Por. A ewe's milk **cheese;** yellow rind; creamy white with a runny interior when young; pungent, hard, and crumbly when aged. Also called *Serra.*

serrano chili (sehr-RAHN-no). Mex. A very hot green **chili pepper;** used fresh, canned, and pickled; the tiniest and hottest of chilis.

Serviettenklösse (zar-ve-E-tern-klur-skhern). Ger. "Napkin dumpling"; a bread **dumpling** cooked in a tied napkin to hold its shape; when served it is surrounded with cooked **pears, string beans,** and **bacon** in a sweet-sour **sauce.**

sesame (SEHS-eh-me). USA. The small, somewhat flat seeds of the sesame plant; a mild nutty flavor that is strongest when toasted; used as a flavoring agent and a source of oil. Also called *benne seeds;* when crushed, called **tahini.**

sesame oil (SEHS-eh-me ohul). USA. Oil extracted from **sesame** seeds; bland nutty flavor; clear, pale yellow color.

sesos (SAY-sohs). Spa. Brains.

set (seht). USA. To allow to stand until congealed. Also, to seal the outside surface.

setas (SAY-tahss). Spa. **Mushrooms.**

seven-minute icing (SEHV-ehn MEHN-ute I-ceng). USA. A very fluffy icing made of cooking **egg** whites, **sugar, corn syrup,** and **cream of tartar** in the top of a double boiler; this is a never-fail icing.

seviche (sah-VESH). Spa. **Raw** fish "cooked" by chemical reaction when **marinated** in **lime** juice.

Seville orange (seh-VEL AWH-ranj). USA. A bitter **orange** with a thin skin that is much used in the making of **marmalade,** and used to lend piquancy to meat, fish dishes, and various drinks.

servuga (se-VROO-gah). Rus. The smallest, yet most prolific of the **sturgeons,** which produce small, dark gray to black **caviar** of exceptionally fine flavor.

sfarjal (SFAFR-jahl). Ara. Quince.

sfogliata (sfog-le-AHT-tah). Ita. **Puff pastry.**

sformato (sfor-MAH-toa). Ita. **Pie, pudding.**

sgombro (ZGOAM-broa). Ita. **Mackerel.**

shaay (shayy). Ara. **Tea.**

shabu-shabu (shah-BOO-shah-bOO). Jap. Meat and **vegetables** cooked at table in **stock,** served with seasoned **sesame sauce;** one-pot cooking; similar to **sukiyaki.**

shad (shahd). USA. A fish of the **herring** family; flesh has a distinctive, rich, sweet flavor; **roe** is **poached, broiled,** or **sautéed,** has nutty flavor and served with **bacon** and **lemon.**

shaddock (SHAHD-dohck). USA. The largest of the **citrus** family; has thick, coarse skin and fibrous, dry, sweet pulp. Also known as *pomelo* and *pummelo.*

shagou dòufù (shah-guo doh-foo).   Chi. **Bean curd,** or **tofu,** in **casserole.**

shakuwlaata (sho-ko-LAA-tah).   Ara. **Chocolate.**

shallot (SHALL-lawt).   USA. A small onionlike bulb with a papery brown covering; has mild, **onion-garlic** flavor; use **sautéed, braised,** or **steamed** with **vegetables, chicken,** or fish.

shamme kabab (SHAH-me ka-BOHB).   Ind. **Ground meat** and yellow split **peas,** flavored with **mint, gingerroot,** and spices, shaped into small patties and **fried.**

shammoama (sham-MEHM).   Ara. **Melon.**

shamouti (sha-MOO-te).   USA. An **orange** that is fragrant, sweet, and juicy; easy to peel, no navel. Also known as **Jaffa.**

shandy (SHAHN-de).   Bri. **Beer** mixed with lemonade.

shandygaff (SHAHN-de-gahf).   Bri. **Beer** mixed with gingerbeer.

shank (shahnk).   USA. That part of the leg between the knee and ankle.

shao (shao).   Chi. **Braising.**

shao mài (shao my).   Chi. **Steamed pork dumpling.**

sharbat (shahr-BAHT).   Ara. Beverages.

shark (shahrk).   USA. An ocean fish whose edible dense, delicate flesh is not popular in the United States but is used throughout the world.

shark fin (shahrk fehn).   USA. **Yú chì;** savored for its gelatinous texture; used for special occasions and banquets in China.

sharon fruit (SHA-rohn froot).   USA. A sweet-tasting **fruit** resembling the **persimmon;** seedless; eaten like a **apple** or **peach.**

shawirma (sha-WIR-mah).   Ara. Spiced **lamb** or **veal grilled** on a vertical spit; **gyros.**

she-crab soup (SHE krahb soop).   USA. A **soup** of South Carolina origin, made with the **roe** and meat of the female blue **crab;** flavored with **cream, Worcestershire sauce,** and **sherry.**

shellfish (SHEHL-fesch).   USA. Any kind of **seafood** with a shell, such as **shrimp, crab, scallop.**

shell steak (shehl stak).   USA. A boneless, tender steak, cut from the strip **loin** of beef.

sheng cài (sheng tsai).   Chi. **Lettuce.**

shepherd's pie (SHEH-pard's pi).   USA. A **pie** of **cubed** or **ground meat,** covered with mashed **potatoes.**

shepherd's purse (SHEH-pahrd's puhrs).   USA. A European wild **green** of the **mustard** family.

sherbet (SCHUR-beht).   USA. A frozen dessert made of **sugar** and water, **fruit** juice or **purée,** flavoring such as **coffee, liqueurs;** may have added beaten **egg** white, **milk,** or **cream.**

shichimi (SHECHE-me).   Jap. Seven-spice mixture; red **pepper** (togarashi) flakes, sansho pepper pods, flakes of dried **mandarin orange** peel, black kelp seeds, dark green **nori seaweed** bits, white **sesame** seeds, and white **poppy seeds.**

shiitake (SHE-tah-keh).   Jap. **Mushroom;** has woodsy-fruity flavor; dark brown, thick, smooth velvety caps, flesh is firm, cap edges curl under; inner meat is light pinky beige.

shio (she-O). Jap. **Salt.**

ship biscuit (shehp BEHS-keht). USA. **Hardtack.**

ship caviar (shehp KAHV-e-ahr). USA. The **roe** or **eggs** of a hybrid **sturgeon** resulting from a cross between the osietr and the sevruga; is particularly firm, and produces an excellent **caviar;** in short supply.

shiraita konbu (she-LAH-e-tak KONG-uh-boo).   Jap. The remaining core of the konbu leaf after shaving for **oboro** and **tororo;** looks like a very fine square of ecru-colored silk; is moistened with **vinegar** and used as an edible wrapper; has a unique, delicate, sweet ocean taste.

shirataki (she-RAH-tah-ke).   Jap. Translucent **noodles** made using **arum root.**

shiratamako (she-RAH-tah-mah-ko).   Jap. A **flour** made from raw glutinous **rice,** used in making refined sweet **confections.**

shiriyyi (shah-RE-ye). Ara. **Vermicelli.**

shirona (SHE-rohn-nah).   Jap. Chard **cabbage;** consists of a clump of snow-white stalks ending in wide, dark-green leaves.

shirred eggs (sherd eggs). USA. **Eggs** broken into a cup, covered with **cream** and crumbs, and **baked.**

shiru (she-rou). Jap. **Soup** of all kinds.

shirumono (she-rou-moh-noh). Jap. **Soup.**

shish kabob (shish kah-BAHB).   USA. Cubes of meat and **vegetables** cooked on a **skewer.**

shiso (she-SO).   Jap. A **pepper** leaf used fresh, **dried,** or **powdered;** beefsteak plant; member of the **mint** family.

shízi (shi-dzi).   Chi. **Persimmon.**

shi zi tóu (shi dzi toh).   Chi. Large **minced pork meatballs.**

shizuoka no ume shiso zuke (she-ZOO-o-kah no OO-meh she-SO ZOO-ke).   Jap. Tiny **pickled plums** with **shredded** magenta-colored **ginger** and **pepper** leaves.

shoga (shoh-gah).   Jap. Fresh **gingerroot.**

shoga sembei (SHOH-gah SEM-bey).   Jap. A small, crispy **rice cracker** coated with **ginger**-flavored **sugar.**

shoofly pie (shoo-fli pi).   USA. A very sweet **pie** of Pennsylvania Dutch origin made of **molasses** and **brown sugar.**

shore dinner (shor DEHN-ner).   USA. A dinner consisting mainly of **seafoods.**

shortbread (SHOHRT-brehd).   Sco. A rich pastry of **butter, flour,** and **sugar;** cut in round shape and **baked** to a golden brown.

short cake (shohrt kak).   USA. A **cake** of **biscuit-** like **dough,** spread with sliced or crushed **fruit,** and topped with **whipped cream.**

shortening (SHOHRT-ehn-eng).   USA. Fat suitable for **frying** and **baking.**

short-grain rice (SHOHRT-gran ris).   USA. A type of **rice** that is higher in starch, wetter, and stickier than medium or long-grain rices when cooked; some varieties are **Japanese, Indo-Chinese, Piedmont.**

short loin (shohrt loin).   USA. The cut of beef from which the **porterhouse, T-bone,** and club steaks are cut.

shortnin' bread (SHOHRT-nehn brehd).   USA. A **quick bread** made with **butter** or **lard;** of Southern origins.

shorva (SHOOR-wah).   Ind. **Soup.**

shòu de (shou de).   Chi. Lean, as in meat; lacking fat.

shoyu (SHOH-yoo).   Jap. A lightly salty and sweet **soy sauce** made from toasted **wheat;** bright taste and aroma.

shproti (SHPRO-ti).   Rus. **Sprats.**

shred (shrehd).   USA. Cut into thin pieces using the large holes of a grater.

shrimp (shrehmp).   USA. An edible **crustacean** of many species and varying sizes found throughout the world; flesh has crisp texture and sweet taste; preparation varies widely.

shrub (shrub).   Bri. An old-fashioned homemade **fruit** cordial, some-times alcholic.

shuàn yángròu (shwan YANG-row).   Chi. **Mongolian hot pot;** various pieces of **seafood, poultry,** and **lamb** cooked individually in a communal pot of simmering stock that is placed in the middle of the table; it is served with **sauces,** and the rich **stock** is consumed after-ward; a kind of Chinese **fondue.**

shuck (shuhk).   USA. To remove the outer shell or **husk** of a food, such as oyster shell or corn husk.

shuiguo (shui guo).   Chi. **Fruit.**

shuiguo zhi (shui-guo dzih).   Chi. Juice.

shui jiao (shui jiao).   Chi. **Boiled dumpling.**

shungiku (SHURNG-ge-kaok).   Jap. A **vegetable,** garland chrysanthe-mum, having notched leaves; used like spinach; kikuna.

shurba (SHUR-ba).   Ara. **Soup.**

sianliha (SI-ahn-LI-haa).   Fin. **Pork.**

sienet (SIAY-nayt).   Fin. **Mushrooms.**

sienisalaatti (SE-yen-e-sa-LAAT-te).   Fin. **Mushroom salad.**

sieve (cehv).   USA. Rub or press food through a sieve with a spoon.

sift (cehft).   USA. Shake a dry ingredient through a sieve to remove lumps and aerate dry ingredients.

sigtebrød (SIG-teh-brehrth).   Dan. Light **rye** bread.

sik (sehk).   Swe. **Whitefish.**

sikkar (SUK-kar).   Ara. **Sugar.**

silakka (SE-llahk-kah).   Fin. Baltic **herring.**

sild (sel).   Nor. **Herring.**

sild (sel).   Dan. Baltic **herring.**

sildeboller (SEL-er-boa-lerr).   Nor. **Herring** balls.

sildegryn (SEL-er-grewn).   Nor. **Herring soup.**

sildesalat (SEL-er-sah-laat).   Nor. **Herring salad.**

sill (sel).   Swe. **Herring** other than that from the Baltic.

sillgratäng (SEL-grah-TANG).   Swe. **Herring casserole** with **potatoes, onions,** and **cream.**

silli (SEL-li). Fin. **Herring.**

sillsalat (SEL-sa-LAHT). Swe. **Herring salad** with **fruit** and **vegetables.**

silq (silk). Ara. **Swiss chard.**

silvano (sel-VAH-noa). Ita. **Chocolate meringue tart.**

silverside (SIHL-vehr-sid). Bri. A cut of beef from the **crown** of the **rump.**

silversides (SIHL-vehr-sids). USA. A term for many species of little fish such as tiny **herring, anchovies, whitebait;** any tiny silver fish.

silver threads (SIHL-vehr threds). USA. A name for Japanese translucent **noodles.**

sima (SE-ma). Fin. **Lemon**-flavored **mead.**

simmaq (sehm-MAHK). Ara. Tart, ground seasoning from seed of sumac tree.

simmer (SIM-ehr). USA. To cook in a liquid just below the boiling point when bubbles form and slowly break just below the surface.

simnel (SEHM-nul). Bri. Spice **cake** filled with dried **fruits,** candied fruit peel, spread with **apricot jam, almond paste;** lavishly decorated.

simsim (SEHM-sehm). Ara. **Sesame** seeds.

sinaasappelen (SE-nahs-ahp-pul). Dut. **Oranges.**

singe (sehnj). USA. To brown or color. Also to finish cleaning a plucked bird by passing bird over a flame to remove any downy feathers remaining.

Single Gloucester (sehn-gull GLOUGH-stehr). Bri. A **cheese** of part-skim, part-whole cow's milk; half as large as Double Gloucester; mild taste.

sippet (SEHP-peht). USA. A **crouton; croûte,** a small piece of bread used for dipping in **soup.**

sipuli (SI-ppooli). Fin. **Onion.**

sipulipihvi (SI-ppooli-PIH-vi). Fin. Beefsteak with **onions.**

sirloin (SUR-lohn). USA. A cut of beef from between the **short loin** and the **round,** from the hindquarter.

sirloin tip (SUR-lohn tehp). USA. The top part of the **sirloin.**

sirop (se-ro). Fre. **Syrup.**

sitron (si-TROON). Nor. **Lemon.**

sitronfromasje (si-TROON-froo-MAH-ski). Nor. **Lemon pudding.**

sitruuna (SIT-roo-nah). Fin. **Lemon.**

sitruunakohokas (SIT-roo-nah-KOA-hoa-kahss). Fin. **Lemon soufflé.**

siu choy (saoh che). Chi. **Celery cabbage;** consists of a solid, oblong head of wide, **celery**-like stalks ending in frilly, pale-green leaves; has a delicate **celery-cabbage** taste.

siyami (se-YAHM-me). Ara. Refers to Lenten foods, or dishes without meat; vegetarian.

sjömansbiff (SHUR-mahns-bif). Swe. Beef **stew;** beef **baked** with **potatoes** and **onions.**

sjø-ørret (SHUR-ur-reht). Nor. **Sea trout.**

sjötunga (SHUR-tewng-ah). Swe. **Sole.**

sjøtunge (SHUR-tewn-ger). Nor. **Sole.**

skaldjur (SKAAL-yewr). Swe. **Shellfish.**

skärbönor (skahr-BUR-noor). Swe. French **beans.**

skarpsås (SKAHRP-soass). Swe. Piquant **mustard** sauce.

skate (skat). USA. A flatbodied, diamond-shaped relative of the **shark,** whose "wings" are edible after being skinned; best **poached;** highly prized in France, Italy, Japan, and China. Also called **ray.**

skewer (SKU-ehr). USA. To thread food on a long pin for **broiling** or **roasting.**

skim (skehm). USA. To remove surface fat or foam from a liquid mixture.

skim milk (skehm mehlk). USA. Cow's milk that contains less than ½% milk fat. Also called **nonfat milk.**

skinka (SKIN-kah). Swe. **Ham.**

skinkbullar (SKINK-bul-lahr). Swe. **Ham** and **potato balls.**

skinke (SKEN-ker). Dan. **Ham.**

skinkestek (SKEN-ker-stayk). Nor. **Roasted** fresh **ham.**

skinkfärs (SKINK-fehrs). Swe. **Ham mousse.**

skinklåda. (SKINK-loa-dah). Swe. **Ham omelet.**

skirlies (SKUR-lez). Sco. **Oatmeal** slightly stirred around with **suet** and **onions.**

skirret (SKEHR-eht). USA. A **vegetable;** similar to a **carrot;** always peel after boiling to retain flavor; remove the inner hard core before serving.

skirt steak (skehrt stak).   USA. The boneless part of the lower forequarter covering the diaphram from which the short plate is removed.

sköldpadda (SHURLD-pahd-ah).   Swe. **Turtle.**

sköldpaddssoppa (SHOHLD-pads-SO-pah).   Swe. **Turtle soup.**

skorpor (SKOR-purr).   Swe. **Rusks.**

skyr (sker).   Ice. Curdled **milk,** formerly known by that name over most of Scandinavia, now found only in Iceland.

sla (slah).   Dut. **Salad; lettuce.**

slagroom (SLAH-room).   Dut. **Whipped cream.**

slaked lime (SLAKD lim).   USA. Calcium hydroxide; a firming agent used in making **pickles;** not to be confused with rock lime, which is not edible.

släpärter (slah-PAER-turr).   Swe. **Peas** in pod.

slapjack (SLAHP-jahk).   USA. A kind of broad, flat **pancake.**

slata (SAH-lah-tah).   Ara. **Salad.**

slätvar (SLAIT-vaar).   Swe. **Brill.**

slice (slis).   USA. To cut food into broad, thin pieces.

sliver (SLEH-vehr).   USA. To cut into long, slender pieces.

Slipcote (SLEHP-coht).   Bri. A soft, fresh, white **cheese** made of cow's whole-milk; rich as **butter;** ripened between **cabbage** leaves; made since the middle of the eighteenth century.

sloe (slo).   USA. A wild European **plum,** small, dark, and astringent; from the blackthorn tree; used for flavoring sloe gin and making **preserves.**

sloke (slok).   Bri. **Laver;** a purplish-brown **seaweed** with semitransparent leaves; used to make **jelly.**

sloppy joe (SLAH-pe jo).   USA. A **sandwich** with a **filling** made of **ground beef,** seasonings, **tomato sauce,** served on a split bun.

slottsstek (SLOHTS-steyk).   Swe. **Pot roast.**

slumgullion (sluhm-GUHL-yuohn).   USA. A term for disgusting or makeshift food or drink.

slump (sluhmp).   USA. A **dessert** of cooked **fruit** with a **dumpling**-like top and served with **cream.**

småbröd (SMOA-brurd).   Swe. Little **cakes, cookies.**

småkage (SMAW-kaaer). Dan. **Biscuits** to the world, **cookies** to United States.

små köttbullar (smo SHIRT-bool-lahr). Swe. Small **meatballs.**

småländsk ostkaka (SMO-lahndsk OOST-KAH-ka). Swe. **Curd cake** from Småland province.

smältost (SMEHLT-oost). Swe. A very mild, runny **cheese,** mostly used in cooking.

småltsill (SMOHLT-sel). Swe. "Melted" sill **herring.**

smasill (SMAA-sil). Swe. **Pilchard;** a small fish of the **herring** family; a **sardine.**

småvarmt (smo-VAHRMT). Swe. The hot part of the **smörgåsbord.**

smelt (smlt). USA. A small silvery fish eaten whole or gutted, floured and **fried.**

smetana (smye-TAH-nye). Rus. **Sour cream.**

smid (smed). Ara. **Grain** similar to **semolina** or **farina;** used for **cake** and filled-**cookie dough.**

smitane (smee-tahn). Fre. **Chopped onions sautéed** in **butter, sour cream added;** cooked, strained, and flavored with **lemon;** a classic **sauce.**

Smithfield ham (SMEHTH-feld hahm). USA. **Ham** from hogs in Virginia that have been fattened on **peanuts; cured, salted, smoked,** and **aged;** uncooked.

smoked (smokd). USA. Meat cured by hanging over a low, steady heat, using wood chips and chemical components to add flavoring.

smoothie (SMOO-the). USA. A thick beverage made of **fruit** pulp, juice, and ice, blended until smooth in a blender.

smör (smurr). Swe. **Butter.**

smør (smurr). Dan. **Butter;** Denmark makes the finest butter in the world.

smørbrød (SMURR-brur). Nor. Open-face **sandwiches** with meat, fish, **cheese** spread.

smörgås (SMURR-goass). Swe. **Sandwich.**

smörgåsbord (smur-gohs-BOARD). Swe. "Bread and butter table"; arrangement of many hot and cold foods on a table in an attractive fashion, traditionally accompanied by **aquavit.**

smørrebrød (SMURR-er-brurdh).   Dan. An open-face **sandwich** with all kinds of fish, meat, and vegetable fillings and sauces.

smothered (SMUH-thehrd).   USA. **Braised;** cooked in **gravy** or **sauce** in a covered pot.

smultringer (SMEWLT-ring-ehr).   Nor. **Doughnuts.**

smultron (SMEWL-tron).   Swe. Wild **strawberry.**

snack (snahk).   USA. Food item eaten in a hurry, or between meals, such as **candy, potato chips, pretzels.**

snail (snal).   USA. A land-dwelling gastropod **mollusk;** a delicacy; usually canned already prepared for the table; **escargot.**

snap beans (snahp ben).   USA. **String beans;** a bean grown primarily for its green pods; used as a vegetable when young and tender.

snaps (snahps).   Swe. A clear, potent (40% alcohol) **brandy,** served icy cold; drunk with **smørrebrød.** Same as **Akvavit.**

sneeuwballen (SNE-uh-bahl-lehn).   Dut. A cream **puff pastry** often filled with **raisins** or **currants.**

snickerdoodle (SNEHK chr-doo-dle).   USA. A **cookie** of New England origins originally made of **flour, dried fruits, nuts;** flavored with **cinnamon** and **sugar.**

snijbonen (SNAY-bo-nuh).   Dut. **Haricot** or **kidney beans.**

snip (snehp).   USA. Cut into very small pieces with scissors.

snitbønner (snit-BEHRN-nehr).   Dan. French **green beans.**

snöripa (SNORI-pa).   Swe. **Ptarmigan;** Scandinavian **grouse.**

snow cone (sno kon).   USA. A confection of scraped ice or freshly fallen snow, drizzled with flavored **syrups;** usually served in a cone-shaped paper cup.

snow eggs (sno eggs).   USA. **Meringue** shaped with a spoon to resemble **eggs,** poached in sweetened **milk,** served with **custard sauce;** the classic French dessert, **oeufs à la neige.**

snow peas (sno pez).   USA. **Peas** cultivated to have thin, flat pods with underdeveloped peas to be eaten whole; **mange-tout** in French, meaning "eat-all."

soba (so-BAH).   Jap. A **noodle** made of **buckwheat flour.**

sobremesas (sawbr-MEZA).   Por. **Desserts.**

socker (SOK-kerr). Swe. **Sugar.**

sockerdricka (sok-kerr-DRI-kah). Swe. Sweet lemonade.

sockerkaka (sok-kerr-KAA-kah). Swe. **Sponge cake.**

sockeye salmon (SOHK-i SAHM-mohn). USA. A delicately flavored, red fleshed fish of the salmon family; firm, tasty; used for everything from sandwiches to cooked dishes.

socles (sou-kleh). Fre. Stands of fat or **rice** used to raise **entrees;** lending height.

soda (SO-dah). USA. A leavening agent; **bicarbonate of soda;** when moistened it produces carbon dioxide to aerate and lighten **dough.**

soda (SO-dah). USA. Flavored, colored carbonated water; root beers, cola drinks, cream sodas; endless varieties.

sød frugtsuppe (surdh FROOGY-soob-ber). Dan. Sweet **fruit soup.**

sodium bicarbonate (SO-de-um bi-KAHR-boh-nat). USA. **Baking powder; soda;** a leavening agent for **doughs** and **batters.**

soep (soop). Dut. **Soup.**

soezen (SU-szehn). Dut. Large **cream puffs.**

soffritto (so-FRE-to). Ita, Spa. A mixture of **chopped carrots, onions, celery,** and **parsley, fried** in oil or **butter;** used to flavor **soups, sauces,** and meat dishes. Also **sofritto, battuto.**

soft-ball stage (sawft-bahl staj). USA. The second stage of the **crystallization** process: begins at 234º F, a small quantity of **syrup** dropped into chilled water forms a ball that does not disintegrate, but flattens out of its own accord when picked up with the fingers.

soft-crack stage (sawft-krahk staj). USA. The fifth stage of the **crystallization** process: begins at 270º F, a small quantity of **syrup** dropped into chilled water will separate into hard threads, which, when removed from the water, will bend.

soft dough (sawft do). USA. A flour mixture that contains 3 parts flour to 1 part liquid; just stiff enough to be rolled on a lightly floured board, such as used for biscuits, drop cookies, yeast breads.

soft drop batter (sawft drahp BAHT-tehr). USA. A **flour** mixture that contains two parts flour to one part liquid, such as used for **muffins** or **cakes.**

Soft Jack (Sawft Jahk). USA. A young, whole-milk **Monterery Jack cheese.**

soft-shell crab (sawft-shehl krahb). USA. A blue **crab,** while molting, has a new shell so soft and thin that it is edible.

sògliola (SAW-lyoa-lah). Ita. **Sole.**

soh mui jeong (su maae GE-ong). Chi. Canned **plum sauce;** a spicy accompaniment to roast duck. Also called **duck sauce.**

sole (sohl). Fre. A fish of the **flatfish** family whose flesh is firm, white and delicate; related to the flounder.

solho (SOU-lyoo). Por. **Plaice.**

solomillo (soh-loh-ME-yoh). Spa. **Pork tenderloin** steak.

sølvkake (SURLL-kar-ki).Nor. "Silver cake"; a **coconut** and **lemon** flavored light **cake.**

solyanka (sol-YAHN-kah). Rus. Freshwater fish boiled with **onions, olives, cucumbers, vinegar, dill,** and **sour cream.**

somen (SO-mehn). Jap. Thin, round, fine, hair-like **wheat noodles.**

songhua dàn (soong-hwa dan). Chi. Preserved **duck eggs;** actually preserved for 100 days. Also known as **thousand-year-old eggs, hundred-year-old eggs.**

songzi huángyú (soong-dzi huang-yu). Chi. Yellow **croaker** garnished with **pine nuts.**

sonth (sawnt). Ind. Ground dried **ginger.**

sooji (SOO-je). Ind. Farina; **semolina.**

sookha dhania (SOO-kah TAH-ne-yah). Ind. **Coriander** seeds.

soon geung (sehn GE-ong). Chi. **Pickled gingerroot.**

sôpa (SOH-pah). Por. **Soup.**

sopa coada (SOP-pah KOAH-dah). Ita. A famous **soup** made of bread and boned **roast pigeon.**

sôpa de feijão (SOH-pah der fay-ZHOW). Por. **Bean soup.**

sopa de legumbres (SOA-pah day lay-GOOM-brayss). Spa. **Vegetable soup.**

sopa de pescado (SOA-pah day pays-KAH-dhoa). Spa. Fish **soup.**

sopaipilla (soh-pahy-PE-yah). Mex. A puffy **fried bread.**

sopari (soo-PAH-re). Ind. Betel nut.

sopa seca (SOH-pah SEH-kah). Mex. A starchy **casserole** dish.

sope (SOH-peh). Mex. Round **antojito** of **tortilla** dough cooked and **filled** with a savory **stuffing; garnacha; picada.**

soppa (SO-ppah). Swe. **Soup.**

sorbet (sor-BAY). Fre. A water **ice** with **fruit** or **liqueur** flavor. Also, an iced Turkish drink.

sorbetto (sohr-BEHT-toa). Ita. **Sherbet.**

Sorbais (So-Ba). Fre. A **cheese;** pungent, bright yellow with reddish-brown rind; a variety of **Maroilles.**

sorghum (SOHR-guhm). USA. A **syrup** made from the sweet juice of the stem of the sorgo plant; thinner and more sour than cane **molasses;** can be substituted for molasses.

sorghum flour (SOHR-guhm flawr). USA. Used to thicken **soups;** contains no **gluten.** Also called **milo maize.**

sorrel (SAU-rul). USA. A leafy green, lemony-tasting plant similar to **spinach,** used in **salads, purées, soups, sauces.**

sorsapaisti (SOAR-sah-PAH-e-sti). Fin. **Roasted** wild **duck.**

sorvête (sohr-VAY-tay). Por. **Sherbet, ice cream.**

Sosse (ZOH-sah). Ger. **Sauce.**

søtsuppe (SURT-sewp-peh). Nor. Sweet **fruit soup.**

sottaceri (soat-tah-CHAY-te). Ita. **Pickled vegetables.**

sottaceto (soat-tah-CHAY-toa). Ita. **Pickled.**

søtunge (SUR-toon-ger). Dan. **Sole.**

sötvattenfisk (SURT-vah-tern-fisk). Swe. Freshwater fish.

soubise (soo-bes). Fre. A white **sauce** containing **onions;** served with meat **entrees;** implies **onions** are a main ingredient in the composition of a dish.

souchets (soo-shay). Fre. **Flatfish,** as **flounder** or **sole, sliced,** and **boiled** in seasoned water.

soufflé (soo-flay). Fre. A light fluffy baked dish with beaten egg white; may be savory or sweet.

soup (soop). USA. A liquid food made with a meat, vegetable, or fish **stock** as base and usually having pieces of solid food such as meats, **vegetables,** or **pastas.**

soupe (soop). Fre. A hearty, robust peasant **vegetable soup,** usually served with bread.

sour cream (sahur krem). USA. Cow's **cream** allowed to sour, either naturally or with the introduction of bacteria; very heavy and thick.

sourdough (SAHUR-do). USA. **Dough** leavened with a fermented starter culture.

soused (sahusd). USA. **Pickled** in **brine** or **vinegar.**

souvlakia (sohv-LAH-ke-ah). Gre. Meat **marinated** in **olive oil, lemon** juice, and **herbs,** then **grilled.**

sowans (SU-ehnz). Bri. Nutritious smooth **gruel** made of the inner **husks** of **oat grain.**

soybean (SOWE-ben). USA. A very nutritious **legume,** extremely important in Asia; used fresh, **dry,** sprouted, and processed in innumerable ways.

soybean curd (SOWE-ben kuhrd). USA. **Tofu.**

soybean flour (SOWE-ben flawr). USA. Made from very lightly **toasted soybeans** or raw beans; is nutty tasting and fragrant; retains the fat in the beans; sweetened with **sugar,** it is used in many Oriental sweets.

soybean low-fat flour (SOWE-ben lo-faht flawr). USA. Made from **soybeans** from which the fat has been largely removed.

soybean oil (SOWE-ben oyl). USA. A pale yellow oil extracted from the **soybean,** usually a liquid.

soy flour (sowe flawr). USA. There are two types of soy flour— **soybean low-fat flour** and **soybean flour,** q.v.; causes heavy browning of the crust.

soy meal (sowe mel). USA. Coarse ground **soybeans,** used as extender for meats.

soy milk (sowe mehlk). USA. A product made from dried **soybeans** soaked in water, crushed, and **boiled.**

soy sauce (sowe saus). USA. A **condiment** made of fermented **soybeans** and **flour** used extensively in Japanese and Chinese cooking.

spaetzle (SPET-zel). Ger. Fine **noodles** made when **batter** is pressed through a colander into boiling broth or water.

spagetti (spa-GAH-te). Swe. **Spaghetti.**

spaghetti (spah-GEHT-te). Ita. The world-reknowned cord-like Italian **pasta,** intermediate in size between **macaroni** and **vermicelli,** that comes with a bewildering variety of sauces. Some well-known sauces include:

al aglio e olio (ahl AH-lyoa ay O-lyoa). with **olive oil** and **garlic;**

amatriciana (ah-mah-tre-CHAAN-nah). with **bacon,** fresh **tomato sauce,** and **onion;**

bolognese (boa-loa-NYAY-zay). in **tomato** and meat **sauce;**

buro, al (ahl BOOR-roa). with **butter;**

carbonara (kah-boa-NAA-rah). with **raw egg,** grated goats' milk **cheese,** bits of **ham** or **salt pork;**

con carne (kon KAHR-ne). with meat;

carrettiera (kahr-rayt-te-AY-rah). with **tuna, mushrooms, tomato purée,** freshly ground **pepper;**

marinara (mah-re-NAA-rah). with **tomatoes, olives, garlic, clams** and **mussels;**

pesto (PAY-stoa). with **basil leaves, garlic, cheese,** and sometimes **pine kernels** and **marjoram;**

pommarola (poam-mah-RAW-lah). with **tomatoes, garlic, basil;**

puttanesca (poot-tah-NAY-skah). with **capers, black olives, parsley, garlic, olive oil, black pepper;**

ragú (rah-GOO). similar to **bolognese;**

con le vongole (kon lay VOAN-goa-lay). with **clams** and **parsley sauce.**

spaghettini (spagh-eht-TE-ne). Ita. Thin **spaghetti.**

spalla di vitella (SPAHL-lah de ve-TEHL-lah). Ita. **Veal shoulder.**

spanakopita (spah-nah-KOP-pe-tah). Gre. **Spinach cheese pie.**

spandauer (spun-DOW-er). Dan. "Envelope"; a pastry in the shape of a square envelope.

Spanferkel (SHPAAN-fehr-kerl). Ger. Suckling pig.

Spanische Windtorte (shpaa-NISCH wehnd-TOR-ter). Ger. A **meringue** shell, elaborately decorated with swirls, filled with **berries,** and covered with **whipped cream;** Spanish Windtorte.

Spanish lime (SPAHN-nish lim). USA. A fruit similar to a **lychee** or **longan;** has tough, green-brown skin and milky-colored pulp; eaten by removing skin and sucking the sweet-acid pulp away from the seed.

Spanish onion (SPAHN-nish UN-yun). USA. A sweet, yellow globe **onion;** used **raw** or cooked.

spareribs (SPAR-rehbs). USA. A cut of **pork** from the rib section; usually **broiled** or **barbequed.**

Spargel (SHPAAR-gerl). Ger. **Asparagus;** usually white, which is much favored.

sparling (SPAHR-leng). USA. **Smelt.**

sparris (SPAH-riss). Swe. **Asparagus.**

Spätzle (SHPEHTS-ler). Ger. Small, handmade **noodle** or **dumpling;** usually pressed through a colander.

Speck (shpehk). Ger. **Bacon; lard.**

spegepølse (SPIGH-er-purl-sser). Dan. **Salami.**

Speiseeis (SCHPAI-zeh-ighss). Ger. **Ices.**

spekemat (SPEH-keh-MAHT). Nor. **Salt-cured** meats.

spekeskinke (SPAYK-shin-ker). Nor. **Cured ham;** a kind of **prosciutto.**

Spekulatius (shpehk-oo-LAAT-siuss). Ger. Sweet **almond cookie.**

spelt (spelt). Ita. A hard **wheat** with the **husk;** used for **soups,** both thick and thin.

spenat (speh-NAAT). Swe. **Spinach.**

Spencer steak (SPEHN-suhr stayk). USA. A steak cut from the rib section of beef. Also called **Delmonico steak.**

spettekaka (SPA-te-KAH-ka). Swe. A towering **cake** of **eggs** and **sugar** specially baked on a spit; a specialty of southern Sweden.

spèzie (SPE-tsye). Ita. Spices.

spezzatino (spay-tsah-TE-noa). Ita. **Stew.**

spice Parisienne (spics pahr-RE-se-ahn). USA. **Épices composes;** a classic French combination of herbs and spices for seasoning, consisting of dried **thyme, bay leaves, basil, sage, coriander, mace, black pepper.**

Spickgans (SPEK-gahns). Ger. **Smoked** breast of goose.

spiedino (spe-ay-DE-noa). Ita. **Skewered** meat or **prawns.**

Spiessbraten (SHPES-braa-tern). Ger. Meat **roasted** on a spit.

spigola (SPE-goa-lah). Ita. **Sea bass.**

spinach (SPEHN-ehch). USA. A dark green plant with edible leaves, used in **salads,** and cooked as a **vegetable.**

spinaci (spe-NAA-che). Ita. **Spinach.**

spinat (shpe-NAAT). Ger. **Spinach.**

spinazie (spe-NAH-ze). Dut. **Spinach.**

spiny rock lobster (SPI-ne rohk LOHB-stuhr). USA. A **lobster,** smaller than the Northern lobster, found in Australia and New Zealand where it is called **crayfish.**

spitskool (SPETZ-kohl). Dut. **Chinese cabbage.**

split peas (spleht pez). USA. Dried, hulled **peas** that are split apart; used mostly in **soups.**

sponge (spuhng). USA. A **batter** that has **yeast** added.

sponge cake (spuhng kak). USA. A light textured **cake** whose leavening is **eggs** only; contains very little or no **shortening.**

spoom (spoom). Fre. An **ice** or **sherbet,** made of **fruit** juice or wine such as **champagne, muscatel, sherry,** or **port,** when frozen has **Italian meringue** added to the mixture; served in sherbet glasses.

spoon bread (spoon brehd). USA. **Cornbread** baked in a **casserole** and served with a spoon.

spotted dog (SPOHT-tehd dohg). Bri. A steamed **suet pudding** containing **raisins.** Also **spotted dick.**

spraengt oksekød (sprehngt OAKS-ser-kurdh). Dan. **Corned beef.**

sprag (sprahg). USA. A large **cod.**

spränged (spraing'd). Swe, Dan. "Burst" or cured; refers to meat that has been set in **brine** prior to cooking.

sprats (sprahtz). USA. Small fish similar to **herring.**

Springerle (SPRING-ehr-le). Ger. **Anise cookie dough** rolled out, stamped with wooden mold or roller into quaint little designs, and baked; a Christmas tradition.

spring onion (sprehng UN-yun). USA. **Scallion.**

spring roll (sprehng rol). USA. **Chun juan;** a thin pastry wrapper stuffed with various **fillings,** rolled up, **deep-fried.**

spritärter (spre-TAER-terr). Swe. **Green peas.**

spritsar (SPRET-sahr). Swe. **Almond butter cookies.**

spritzwasser (SPRETZ-vahs-serr). Ger. **Soda water.**

Sprotten (SHPROT-tern). Ger. **Sprats.**

sprout (sprowt). USA. A dried **bean** that has germinated; used by removing the hulls and using the new growth as a **vegetable,** either **raw** or lightly cooked.

spruce beer (sprus ber). USA. A beverage made from spruce twigs and leaves boiled with **molasses** or **sugar,** and fermented with **yeast.**

spruiten (SPRIR-tyus). Dut. **Brussels sprouts.**

spud (spuhd). USA. **Potato.**

spuma (SPOO-mah). Ita. A **dessert ice** with **Italian meringue** folded in; frothy; **mousse.**

spumoni (spoo-MOH-ne). Ita. A rich **ice cream** containing candied **fruits** and **nuts,** of different colors and in layers, usually flavored with **brandy.**

squab (squahb). USA. A young **pigeon;** flesh is tender, dark, not gamy.

squash (squahsh). USA. The fruit of plants of the gourd family; several types: soft-shelled summer type such as **zucchini** and yellow **summer squash,** hard-shelled small winter type such as **turban** and **butternut,** and hard-shelled large winter type such as **calabaza, hubbard,** and **spaghetti squash.**

squid (squehd). USA. A **mollusk** with a long body and ten arms; popular in Orient and Mediterranean countries.

srikhand (shre-KAHND). Ind. **Dessert** made with drained **yogurt, sugar, nuts,** and **saffron.**

Stachelbeere (STAH-kherl-bay-rern). Ger. **Gooseberry.**

stag chicken (stahg CHEH-kehn). USA. A male **chicken** that is too old to roast but makes a well-flavored addition to the **stock** pot. Also see **broilers, capon, cock, fryers, roasters, stewing chicken.**

stamppot (STAHM-poht). Dut. Mashed **potatoes** and meat mixed into **vegetables.**

Stangen (STAHN-gehn). Ger. Stick-shaped pastries, sweet or savory. Also **Stangerl.**

star anise (stahr ah-NESC). USA. An Oriental shrub that forms a star-shaped pod holding dark, shiny brown seeds; sweet and extremely aromatic; used in many oriental foods, meats, **curries, confections, pickles; ba jiao.**

starfruit (STAHR-froot). USA. A Malaysian **fruit,** pale yellow with five pointed ridges forming a star when sliced across; **carambola.**

stark senap (stark SAY-nah). Swe. Hot **mustard.**

steack (stehk). Fre. Steak.

steak and kidney pie (stak and KEHD-ne pi). Bri. Pieces of beef and **kidney** flavored with **onion, mushroom, oysters;** baked in a **suet** crust.

steack au poivre (stehk oa pwahvr). Fre. **Sautéed** beef steak seasoned liberally with **peppercorns.**

steam (stem). USA. To cook food by the heat and vapor given off by **boiling** water, with or without pressure.

steam-blanching (stem BLAHN-ching). USA. Par-steaming; short duration steaming; for foods to be frozen or canned.

steamed pudding (stemd PUHD-eng). USA. A mixture of bread crumbs, **sugars, milk, shortening, eggs, raisins,** spices placed in a mold with a tight-fitting lid; then **baked** in a pan with boiling water to create steam, which give this cake a **pudding**-like texture.

steep (step). USA. Cover with boiling liquid and let stand to extract flavors and colors.

steg (staig). Dan. Joint of meat. Also, **roasted.**

stegt kylling (stehkt SHEWL-leng). Dan. **Braised chicken.**

Steinbutt (SHTIGHN-but). Ger. **Turbot.**

Steinpilz (SHTIGHN-pilz). Ger. **Boletus mushroom; cèpe.**

stekt (staykt). Swe. **Fried.**

stem lettuce (stehm LETT-us). USA. A Chinese variety of **lettuce** in which the stem or seedstalk is the edible part, use like a **water chestnut** to give crunch to a dish. Also called **celtuce.**

sterlet (STEHR-leht). USA. The Russian sterlyad (stehr-lyahd), an almost extinct species of **sturgeon,** relatively small, but highly esteemed for its **roe;** the legendary "gold" caviar of the Czars, rarely seen outside the Soviet Union.

stew (stu). USA. To cook in just enough liquid to cover.

stewing chicken (STU-eng CHEH-kehn). USA. A **chicken** usually over ten months old that profits by an extended moist cooking method. Also see **broiler, capon, cock, roaster,** and **stag chicken.**

St. Honoré (sahn on-oh-ra). Ita. A delicious **dessert** which artfully combines puff pastry, sweet **biscuits, whipped cream, chocolate whipped cream,** and **powdered pistachio nuts.**

sticky buns (STEH-ke buhnz). USA. A sweet **roll** flavored with **cinnamon** and **brown sugar;** allowed to rise in a pan lined with brown sugar and **melted butter,** then **baked.**

stiff but not dry (stehf buht noht dri).   USA. Refers to **egg** whites beaten just until they stand in peaks, still glossy and moist-looking, and not too fine-grained.

stiff dough (stehf do).   USA. A **flour** mixture that contains four parts flour to one part liquid; just stiff enough to be kneaded without sticking to a lightly floured board, such as **pie** crust, rolled **cookies.**

stiffen (STEHF-fehn).   USA. To cook meat, poultry, or fish by briefly heating in **butter** or liquid without color, until just cooked.

stifle (STI-fuhl).   USA. A New England **stew** of **salt pork** and **seafood** or **vegetables.**

Stilton (STILT-uhn).   Bri. One of the world's great blue **cheeses;** made of uncooked cow's milk injected with Penicillium roqueforti mold causing the blue veining; creamy paste, brownish crust, moist, slightly crumbly; not dry or salty.

Stint (shtint).   Ger. **Smelt;** a tasty, tiny fish.

stir (stehr).   USA. To mix food using a circular motion.

stirabout (STUHR-ah-bout).   Iri. Name of an Irish dish similar to **Scotch porridge.**

stir-fry (STEHR-fri).   USA. To cook quickly over medium-high heat, using a tossing-stirring motion.

stirrup cup (STUHR-uhp kuhp).   Bri. Same as "one for the road" or "nightcap'; a host's signal that this is the last drink.

stoccafisso (stoak-kah-FES-soa).   Ita. Dried **fillets** of **cod;** stockfish.

stock (stahk).   USA. Liquid in which meats or **vegetables** are cooked.

stoemp mé spek (stump meh spehk).   Ger. **Cabbage** and **potatoes** mashed together and sprinkled with **fried diced bacon.**

stokkfisk (STOHK-fesk).   Nor. Unsalted, rack-dried **cod.** Also called **tørrfisk;** when salted and spread out on a cliff to dry it is called **klip-fisk.**

Stollen (SCHTOL-lehrn).   Ger. A long-shaped **yeast bread** filled with various dried **fruits,** sprinkled with **confectioners' sugar;** traditional at Christmas.

stone crab (stohn krahb).   USA. A coastal Atlantic **crab,** especially from Florida, with large claws that have very fine white meat.

Stor (shturr).   Ger. **Sturgeon.**

stör (stur).   Swe. **Sturgeon.**

stout (stohwt).   Bri. A dark, strong, very alcoholic **ale** brewed from toasted **malt;** the sweetest of all **beers.**

stoved (stohvd).   Sco. Simmered on top of the stove.

stovies (stoh-vez).   Sco. **Boiled potatoes.**

Stracchino (strah-KE-no).   Ita. The generic name for fresh, rindless, uncooked cow's-milk **cheese,** of which **Gorgonzola** is one; the paste is buttery, smooth, and delicate.

stracciatella (strah-che-ah-TEL-lah).   Ita. **Stock** thickened with a **paste** of **egg, cheese,** and **semolina.**

stracotto (strah-KOT-toa).   Ita. Meat **stew** slowly cooked for several hours; a **pot roast.**

strain (stran).   USA. To separate liquids and solids by passing through a strainer.

strasbourgeoise (strahs-buhrzh-wah).   Fre. A garnish of **sauerkraut, chopped bacon,** and **sautéed slices** of goose liver.

strawberries Romanoff (STRAHW-behr-rez RO-mahn-nohff).   USA. **Strawberries** flavored with **orange**-flavored **liqueur** and served with **Creme Chantilly.**

strawberry (STRAHW-behr-re).   USA. The fruit of the strawberry plant; conical shape; red flesh; tiny seeds sprinkled on skin; **berry** topped with green leafy cap.

strawberry shortcake (STRAHW-behr-re SHORT-kak).   USA. A **dessert** made of **biscuit dough** with sliced **strawberries** and **whipped cream.**

straw mushroom (strahw MUHSH-room).   USA. Oriental **mushrooms** cultivated on **rice** straw; have very fleshy conical caps that enclose long, thin stems; among the world's tastiest mushrooms.

streusel (STRU-sehl).   USA. A sprinkling for baked goods; usually of a mixture of **flour** or breadcrumbs, **sugar, butter,** and **spices.**

Streuselkuchen (stru-sehl-KOO-kern).   Ger. A **yeast cake** topped with **cinnamon-sugar** crumbles.

string beans (strehng benz).   USA. A vine cultivated for its long, slender, edible **green bean** pods; used as a **vegetable.**

striped bass (stripd bahss).   USA. A fish of the Western Atlantic that lives in the sea, then migrates to freshwater to spawn; white flesh, flaky, firm, with a delicate flavor; a popular table fish.

strip loin (strehp lowen). USA. A cut from the top of the beef **short loin** that is tender and boneless; usually cut in steaks.

stroganoff (STRO-gan-off). Rus. Sautéed beef strips served in a **sour cream sauce** with **mushrooms** and **onions.**

strömming (STRUR-ming). Swe. Small Baltic **herring.**

stroop (strohp). Dut. **Molasses; syrup.**

struccoli (strook-KOH-le). Ita. **Rolls** of sweet pastry wrapped around **fruit** and **cream cheese.**

Strudel (STROO-duhl). Ger. Flaky, paper-thin **pastry dough** filled with **fruit filling,** rolled, and **baked.**

struffoli (stroof-FOH-le). Ita. **Fried** pastry pocket containing sliced onion.

stuet (stewt). Nor. Creamed.

stufato (stu-FAH-toa). Ita. **Braised** or **stewed.** Also **brasato, stracotto.**

stuffing (STUHF-eng). USA. A seasoned mixture, usually based on bread products such as crumbled **cornbread** or bread cubes, used to stuff foods such as meats, **vegetables, eggs.**

sturgeon (STUHR-juhn). USA. A large migratory fish, that lives in the sea and goes up rivers to spawn; flesh is white, rich, firm, and tight in texture; used **smoked** and **pickled,** as well as fresh; sturgeon **roe** is a delicacy.

stuvad (STEW-vahd). Swe. Creamed.

stuvede (STOO-er-der). Dan. Creamed.

stuvet oksekød (STOO-ert). Dan. Beef **stew.**

su (soo). Jap. White **rice vinegar,** sweeter and milder than American vinegar.

suàn (swen). Chi. **Garlic.**

suan là tang (suan la tang). Chi. Hot-and-sour **soup.**

suan mei jiang (swen may jiang). Chi. **Duck sauce;** served with **duck** or goose; literally, **plum sauce;** made of **plums, apricots, vinegar,** and **sugar.**

suan niúnai (suan niu-nai). Chi. **Yogurt.**

suave (SWAH-veh). Mex. Mild, subtle; as with seasonings, flavorings.

sub (suhb). USA. **Hoagie.**

submarine (SUHB-mah-ren). USA. **Hoagie.**

subric (soo-brek). Fre. A variety of **croquette,** without the **egg wash** and bread crumbs; **sautéed** instead of **fried.**

succo (SOOC-co). Ita. Juice.

succotash (SUHCK-uh-tahsh). USA. A dish made of **corn** and **lima beans.**

sucker (suck-ehr). USA. An abundant freshwater fish in America; important edible species are the fine-scale sucker, the redhorse sucker, and the larger buffalo; when taken from cold deep lakes or clear running streams, this fish has firm, sweet white meat.

suco (SOO-koh). Por. Juice.

suco de laranja (SOO-koh der lah-RAHN-jash). Por. **Orange** juice.

sucre (sewkr). Fre. **Sugar.**

sucre filé (sewkr fe-LAY). Fre. **Spun sugar.**

sudako (soo-DAH-ko). Jap. **Octopus pickled** in **vinegar.**

sudare (soo-dah-leh). Jap. The bamboo mat made for rolling **sushi.**

suédoise (sway-dwah). Fre. A cold **sauce** of **mayonnaise** flavored with **apple purée** and **grated horseradish,** a classic Swedish sauce.

suehn (suen). Chi. **Bamboo shoots;** fresh whole, cut shoots, or canned.

suet (SOO-eht). USA. The hard fat about the **kidneys** and **loins** in beef and **mutton,** used in making pastry, **puddings,** and tallow.

sugar (SCHOO-gahr). USA. A sweet crystalline substance, wholly or essentially sucrose, with color ranging from white to brown depending on purity; used as a sweetener and preservative of food; water soluble. See also **Barbados sugar, beet sugar, berry sugar, brown sugar, carmelized sugar, castor sugar, confectioners' sugar, corn sugar, demerara sugar, dextrose, fructose, icing sugar, invert sugar, loaf sugar, lump sugar, powdered sugar, raw sugar,** and **superfine sugar.**

sugarcane (SCHOO-gahr-kan). USA. A tall grass grown in warm climates from which sucrose is extracted to make **sugar.**

sugar crystallization (SCHOO-gahr krys-tah-lah-ZA-shun). USA. The different stages through which **sugar** passes during various candy-making processes: **thread, soft ball, firm ball, hard ball, soft crack, hard crack, caramelized sugar,** and, finally, **la cuite.**

Sugar Loaf (SCHOO-gahr lof). USA. Squatty, cylindrical pear-shaped **squash** with dark tan grooved exterior and yellow flesh.

sugar snap peas (SCHOO-gahr snahp pes).   USA. A variety of **snap peas** with edible pods; the whole pod may be cooked or eaten fresh.

sugo (SOO-goa).   Ita. **Sauce.**

sugo de carne (SOO-goa day KAHR-neh).   Ita. **Gravy.**

suiker. (SIR-kur).   Dut. **Sugar.**

suimono (soo-E-moh-noh).   Jap. Clear **soup.**

Suiza (soo-E-sah).   Mex. Swiss or Swiss-style.

Suizenji nori (soo-e-ZEN-jge no-re).   Jap. A **sashimi garnish** for vinegared **salads** or clear **soups.**

sukiyaki (soo-ke-YAH-ke).   Jap. A one-pot cooking method using thinly sliced beef and a variety of **vegetables** cooked in **suet** at the table.

sukker (SOOK-kerr).   Nor. **Sugar.**

suklaa (SOOK-laa).   Fin. **Chocolate.**

sultana (suhl-TAHN-nah).   USA. A golden **raisin,** made from dried white, seedless **grapes.**

Sülz (ZEWL-tser).   Ger. **Aspic** with meat, as **head cheese.**

summer pudding (SUHM-ehr PUHD-dehng).   Bri. Fresh **raspberries** and red **currants stewed,** sweetened, then sieved into a bread-lined bowl, left to stand overnight, turned out, and served with **cream.**

summer squash (SUHM-mehr squash).   USA. A variety of **squash** with a yellow rind and, usually, a crooked neck; harvested before rind and seeds harden.

sun (suen).   Chi. **Bamboo shoots.**

sunchoke (SUHN-chock).   USA. A vegetable that looks like a **potato** with small knobs; thin, brown skin, white flesh; has nutty flavor when **raw** and slight **artichoke** flavor when cooked; best when cooked, but used **raw** in **salads.**

sunflower seeds (SUHN-flawr seds).   USA. Seeds of the **sunflower** plant; used **roasted** and eaten like **nuts.** Also seeds yields a light oil.

sunomono (SOO-no-mo-no).   Jap. Vinegared foods.

suomalainen lammasmuhennos (soooa-mah-lahe-nehn LAHM-mahss-MOO-hayn-nohs).   Fin. Finnish version of **Irish stew;** made with **mutton, onions, potatoes, carrots,** and **turnips.**

suomalaisleipä (SOO-wo-ma-lice-rooeys-LAY-pa).   Fin. **Yeast bread.**

superfine sugar (SOO-purr-fin SCHU-gur). USA. **Sugar** of very fine crystals; quickly dissolves in liquid.

Suppe (ZUP-per). Ger. **Soup.**

suppe (SOO-bber). Dan. **Soup.**

suppli (SOO-ple). Ita. **Croquettes.**

suprème de volaille (su-pre-meh day vo-lye). Fre. Breast of **chicken** in a luxurious **sauce.**

Surati (Su-rah-te). Ind. A **cheese** made of buffalo's milk; the best known variety of the few varieties of cheese made in India.

surf 'n' turf (suhrf n tuhrf). USA. **Seafood** and meat served on the same plate.

sur grädde (SUR GRAH-dea). Swe. **Sour cream.**

surimi (soo-RE-me). Jap. Imitation **crabmeat** made from **pollock** and other fish, then colored to resemble **crab legs.**

surkål (SEWR-kawl). Nor. **Sauerkraut.**

surkål (SEWR-koal). Swe. **Sauerkraut.**

sursild (soor-sel). Dan. Sour **herring.**

surströmming (sewr-STRUR-ming). Swe. Fermented Baltic **herring,** a tradition in northern Sweden.

surume-ika (soo-roo-MAAH-e-koht). Jap. A type of **squid.**

sushi (SZU-she). Jap. **Zushi;** seasoned cold **rice** with various other ingredients. See **chirashi zushi, nigiri zushi,** and **norimaki zushi.**

susine (soo-ZE-ne). Ita. **Plums.**

süsse (zewss). Ger. Sweet.

Süssespetsen (zewss-SHPIGH-zern). Ger. Sweet **desserts.** Also called **Süssigkeiten.**

Süssigkeiten (sue-se-KIT-tehrn). Ger. Sweet **desserts.** Also called **Süssespeisen.**

suzuki (soo-ZOO-ke). Jap. **Sea bass.**

svamp (svahmp). Swe. **Mushrooms.**

svarta vinbär (SVAHR-tah VEN-baer). Swe. **Black currant.**

svartsoppa (SVAHRT-SOHP-pah). Swe. Black **soup;** a famous dish prepared from goose and pig's blood, spices, and other seasonings.

Sveciaost (SVAY-ssiah-oost).　Swe. A semihard **cheese** with small holes; often spiced; most popular Swedish cheese.

svine (sven).　Dan. **Pork.**

svinekoteleter (SVEN-koa-der-leh-ter).　Dan. **Pork** chops.

svinemørbrad (SVEN-murr-braa).　Dan. **Pork tenderloin.**

svinestey (SVEN-stayg).　Dan. **Roast pork loin.**

svinestek (SVEN-stayk).　Nor. **Roast pork.**

svisker (SVISS-kerr).　Nor. **Prunes.**

swamp cabbage (swahmp KAH-bahg).　USA. Palm cabbage.

sweat (sweht).　USA. To cook in a little fat under a lid without browning.

Swedish meatballs (SWE-dehsh MET-bahlz).　USA. A small **meatball** covered with a savory brown **sauce.**

sweetbreads (SWET-brehds).　USA. Thymus gland of a young calf, sheep, or pig; highly perishable.

sweet cicely (swet SEHS-e-le).　USA. An **herb** of the **parsley** family; **anise**-flavored leaves, stems, and seeds used in **salads** and **boquet garnis; cicely.**

sweet cream butter (swet krem BUHT-tehr).　USA. **Butter** made from cow's **cream** with little or no salt; must contain 80% milk fat.

Sweet Curd (swet kuhrd).　USA. **Cheeses** made by the usual **Cheddar** process with unripened milk such as **Brick, Edam, Gouda,** and **Munster.**

Sweet Dumpling (swet DUHMP-ling).　USA. Scalloped, pumpkin-shaped **squash** with creamy white and green striped exterior and pale yellow interior.

sweetened condensed milk (SWET-end kon-DENSD mehlk).　USA. **Milk** with its water content reduced by one-half and **sugar** added in ratio of 18 pounds to 100 pounds of milk; often confused with **evaporated milk.**

sweet majoram (swet mah-JOHR-ruhm).　USA. An **herb** of Mediterranean origins; of the **mint** family; warm, sweet fragrance and delicate **oregano**-like flavor; used in savory dishes; **marjoram.**

sweet milk (swet mehlk).　USA. Cow's **milk.**

sweet potato (swet po-TA-to).　USA. A root **vegetable** with a reddish skin, sweetish taste, and texture like the regular **potato;** often confused with the **yam.**

sweet sop (swet sohp).   USA. The yellow-green **fruit** of a tropical American tree; has sweet yellow pulp.

sweet woodruff (swet WUHD-rouf).   USA. An **herb** of dark green star-like whorled leaves; used in cold punches and **May Wine.**

Swiss chard (swehss chard).   USA. An ancient **vegetable** of the **beet** family, with white stalks and dark green leaves; other varieties are red and yellow.

Swiss cheese (swehss chez).   USA. A **cheese** that is American-made **Emmentaler.**

Swiss meringue (swess mehr-RAHNG).   USA. A glazing **icing** made of **confectioners' sugar, egg** white, and **lemon** juice; used for wedding cakes, special cakes, pastry writing; dries hard. Also called *royal icing* and *royal glaze.*

Swiss roll (swehss rohl).   Bri. **Jelly roll.**

swiss steak (swehss stak).   USA. **Rump** or **round** steak baked with **tomatoes, onions, peppers,** and seasoned with **herbs** and spices.

swordfish (SOARD-fesch).   USA. A very large fish, found worldwide, with dense white meat; marketed as steaks or chunks; excellent for **baking** or **broiling.**

syboes (se-BOWS).   Sco. **Spring onions;** young, tender **green onions.**

syllabub (SILL-ah-bub).   Bri. A punch made with **milk** and **cream,** flavored with **liqueurs** and spices.

sylt (sewlt).   Swe. **Jam.**

syltede rødbeder (SEWL-te-the ROHTH-beh-thor).   Dan. **Pickled beets.**

syltetøj (SEWL-ter-toi).   Dan. **Jam.**

syltlök (SEWLT-lurk).   Swe. Pearl **onion.**

syr (syr).   Nor, Swe. **Milk** that has been kept for months before eating.

syr (SI-roo).   Rus. **Cheese.**

syrup (SEHR-up).   USA. A thick, sticky sweet liquid made of **sugar** and any of various liquids, usually water, and flavoring; used on **pancakes, waffles, ice cream.**

Szekeley (SAHZ-kah-lay).   Hun. A soft sheep's-milk **cheese** packed in sheep bladders; look like fat **sausages;** sometimes **smoked.**

Tako - Japanese - Octopus

taart (tahrt). Dut. Layer **cake.**

tabasco (tah-BAHS-koh). USA. Very hot red **pepper sauce.**

tabbuli (tah-BUHL-le). Ara. An Arabic **salad** made with **burghul** (crushed wheat), chopped **tomatoes, onion, mint, parsley, lemon juice, olive oil, cinnamon, pepper;** scoop with **grape leaves, romaine,** or **lettuce.** Also spelled **tabouleh, tabbouleh.**

table cream (TAL-buhl krcm). USA. **Cream** containing 18–30% milk fat. Also called **coffee** or **light cream.**

table d'hote (tahl-buhl dot). Fre. General title for a meal of several courses at a fixed price.

table grapes (TA-buhl grapz). USA. Any of numerous varieties eaten fresh out of hand.

table salt (TA-buhl sawlt). USA. A finely ground free-flowing **salt** used in food preparation. Also known as **cooking salt.**

tacchino (tahk-KE-no). Ita. **Turkey.**

taco (TAH-ko). Mex. A **tortilla** folded or wrapped around a **filling,** may be crisp or soft.

tadjin helou (TAH-jean hehl-LO). Ara. A very delicate **stew** made of beef and **mutton, vegetables, dried prunes** or **raisins,** and **quinces,** covered with **pie** pastry and **baked** in an oven.

tadka (TAHR-ka). Ind. Spice-perfumed **butter** used for flavoring **yogurt, dal, relishes, vegetables,** some meats.

Tafelspitz (TAHF-fehl-spihtz). Ger. A kind of **pot roast** with top **round** of beef **boiled** and served with root **vegetables, horseradish,** and **sauces.**

Taffelost (Tahlf-foh-lohst). Nor, Dan. A creamy, semisoft **dessert cheese** with a red rind; square loaves.

taffy (TAHF-fe). USA. A soft, chewy **candy** made from **sugar, molasses, butter,** and **nuts** and flavorings. Also called *saltwater taffy.*

taffy (TOF-fe). Bri. **Toffee;** a brittle, crunchy **candy** made from **sugar, butter, nuts,** and flavorings.

tagliarini (tahl-yah-RE-ne). Ita. Very thin **noodles,** used in **soups.** Also *tagliolini.*

tagliatelle (tahl-yah-TEHL-la). Ita. A thin handmade **pasta** ⅜ inch wide; **fettuccine, pappardelle.**

tahari (TEH-ha-re). Ind. Spicy **rice** and **peas** dish with **turmeric** and **herbs.**

tahini (teh-HE-nah). Ara. **Puréed chickpeas** mixed with **sesame paste.**

tahini (tah-HE-ne). Ara. Heavy **sesame** oil, almost a **paste;** made by crushing raw sesame seeds; not the type of oil used in Oriental cooking.

tahiyn (tah-HEN). Ara. **Flour.**

tai tempura (TAH-e TEHM-poo-rah). Jap. **Fried fish cakes.**

tako (TAH-koh). Jap. **Octopus.**

tako kushisashi (TOH-koh koo-SHE-sah-she). Jap. **Broiled octopus** on **skewers.**

takenoko (tah-KAY-no-ko). Jap. **Bamboo shoots;** fresh whole, cut shoots, canned shoots; mild, unpretentious taste, crunchy texture.

takuan (TAH-koo-ahn). Jap. A popular **pickle** made from **daikon,** the large white **radish;** often tinted yellow; fresh, canned, bottled.

tala (TEH-lah). Ind. **Deep-fried.**

Taleggio (Tahl-LE-gjeu). Ita. A smooth, pale, aromatic **dessert cheese** with a rosey-hued crust; of the **Stracchino** family.

Telemi (TAHL-eh-me). Rum, USA. Of Rumanian origin, cheese made of sheep's-milk; the **American cheese** of the same name is made of cow's milk, semisoft, much like American **Mozzarella.**

tallarines (tahl-lah-RE-nez). Spa. **Noodles.**

Tallyrand (TAHL-le-rahnd). Fre. A **garnish** for **sweetbreads** and **poultry** consisting of **macaroni** mixed with **butter** and **cheese,** tossed with **julienne truffle** and **diced foie gras.**

talmouse (tahl-moos). Fre. **Cheesecake.**

tamaatim (ta-MAA-tim). Ara. **Tomatoes.**

tamago (tah-MAH-goh).   Jap. **Egg;** *hahjuku* (HAHN-joo-koo) soft-boiled; *medamayaki* (meh-DAN-mah-yah-koe) fried eggs; *pochi* (POH-che) poached; *yyude* (yoo-DEH) hard-boiled.

tamal (tah-MAHL).   Mex. **Tamale.**

tamale (tah-MAH-le).   USA. Highly seasoned meat **filling** rolled in **corn-meal** mush, wrapped in corn **husks,** and steamed. Also spelled **tamal.**

tamale pie (tah-MAH-le pi).   USA. A dish of **cornmeal** mush with a filling of chopped meats and hot **chili sauce.**

tamaras (TAH-mah-rahss).   Por. **Dates.**

tamari (TAH-mah-re).   Jap. A dark, thick, **dipping** and **basting sauce** made from **soybeans.**

tamarind (TAHM-ah-rend).   Ind. Brown pods of a tropical tree whose soft brown, sour pulp is used in Asia as a souring agent the way lemon juice is used; flavor is cross between **apricots** and **dates** with a tinge of **lemon.**

tamatar (ta-MAH-tehr).   Ind. **Tomato.**

tamis (tah-me).   Fre.   *Tammy cloth;* woolen canvas cloth used for straining **soups** and **sauces.**

tammy (TAHM-me).   USA. A fine gauze used for straining food. Also *tammy cloth.*

tampala (thahm-PAH-lah).   Ind. Chinese **spinach.**

tandoori (tan-DOO-re).   Ind. Food marinated in **yogurt** with spices, then **roasted** at a high temperature.

tang (tang).   Chi. **Soup.**

tángcù liji (tang-chu le-je).   Chi. Sweet-sour boneless **pork.**

tangelo (TAHN-geh-lo).   USA. A hybrid **citrus** fruit; cross of a **tanger-ine** and **grapefruit.**

tangerine (tahn-jehr-ren).   USA. A variety of **mandarin orange** with deep rose-orange skin and flesh.

tangmiàn (tang mien).   Chi. **Noodles** in **soup.**

tanmen (TAHNN-mahnn).   Jap. A type of white instant **soup noodle.**

tansy (TAHN-ze).   Bri. An **herb** with strong, bitter, aromatic flavor used to flavor **puddings;** now largely ignored.

tanuki soba (tah-NOO-ke SOH-bah).   Jap. A type of brown **buckwheat noodle.**

taozi (tao-dzi).   Chi. **Peach.**

tapas (TAH-pahs). Spa. **Appetizers** served in Spanish bars with cocktails, in great variety and profusion.

tapenade (tah-pah-nahd). Fre. A **purée** of **anchovies,** black **olives, garlic, capers,** with **olive oil** added to form a **paste; tuna** is sometimes added.

tapioca (tah-pe-O-kah). USA. Processed from the Brazilian **cassava** root, which is poisonous until heated during processing to release the hydrocyanic acid; popular use in **sauces** and **fruit fillings** that are to be frozen; does not become watery on reconstitution; makes clear **sauces.**

tapioca flour (tah-pe-O-kah flowr). USA. Made from finely ground **tapioca;** makes very clear **glazes** and **sauces;** same properties as **tapioca.**

taquitos (tah-KE-tohs). Mex. Small **tortillas** with a small amount of **filling,** either rolled or folded, then **fried** until slightly crisp.

Taramasalata (TAHR-ma-sahl-LAHT-tah). Ger. Pink fish **roe,** bread, **milk, olive oil, lemon** juice, and **garlic puréed,** then served with crusty bread.

taratur (tahr-rah-TOR). Ara. **Tahini sauce.**

tari (TEH-fe). Ind. **Gravy.**

taro (TAH-roa). USA. A Tahitian plant grown throughout the tropics for its rootstock, which is high in starch and **potato**-like texture; its **spinach**-like leaves and **asparagus**-like stems are also eaten; an important staple in Polynesia, Central and South America, Africa, and Asia. Also known as **dasheen.**

tarragon (TAHR-ah-gahn). USA. An **herb** with a delicate **anise**-like flavor; essential in **bouquet garni,** in **bearnaise sauce,** and **chicken** *a l'estragon;* one of the **fines herbs.**

tart (tahrt). USA. **Pie** or pastry, sweet or savory; size varies from two inches to full size pie.

tarta (TAHR-tah). Spa. **Tart;** small **pie** or pastry, sweet or savory. Also called *tartaleta.*

tårta. (TOAR-tah). Swe. Layer **cake.**

tartar med aeg (TAH-tahr maydh ehg). Dan. A favorite **smørrebrød:** scraped **raw** beef, **raw onions,** and **raw egg.**

tartar sauce (TAHR-tahr saus). USA. See **tartare.**

tartare (tahr-tahr). Fre. A cold **sauce** made of **mayonnaise,** hard boiled **egg yolks,** very finely **cnopped onions, capers, gherkins,** served with fried fish or cold meats.

tarte (tahrt). Fre. **Tart;** tartlet; a small pie or pastry, sweet or savory. Also called **tartelette, taurte.**

tarte à l'oignon (tahrt ah l'yon-awng). Fre. Rich, creamy **onion pie;** served as an accompaniment to meats.

tarte des demoiselles Tatin (tart deh dehm-wah-zehl tah-ten). Fre. An **apple tart** baked upside down; devised by the Tatin sisters of Orléans, France; a layer of **sugar** is placed on the tart pan, the apples sliced covering the sugar, **butter** is put on top of the apples, then covered with crust and baked until the sugar **caramelizes** to a hard crust. It is turned out, upside down on plate to serve.

tarte liègeoise (tahrt le-zhwah). Fre. The famous Belgian **dessert;** a cross between the American **fruit pie** and an English **trifle.**

tartina (tahr-TE-nah). Ita. **Tart.**

tartine (tar-ten). Fre. Slice of bread.

tartufi (tahr-TOO-fe). Ita. **Truffle.**

tarwebrood (TAHR-vuh-broht). Dut. **Wheat bread.**

Tascherln (TAHS-shuhr-rehn). Ger. Little pockets of **dough,** like **ravioli,** filled with savory **fillings** or **jam;** Austrian.

tatties (TAH-tes). Sco. **Potatoes.**

Taube (TAW-berr). Ger. **Pigeon.**

T-bone steak (T-bon stayk). USA. A steak cut from the **loin** of beef with the bone resembling a T.

te (teh). Mex. **Tea.**

té (tai). Ita. **Tea.**

té (tay). Spa. **Tea.**

te (teh). Dan, Nor. **Tea.**

te (tay). Swe. **Tea.**

tea (te). USA. A aromatic beverage prepared from tea leaves by infusion with boiling water, using the leaves, leaf buds, and internodes of the tea plant prepared and cured for market, classed according to the method of manufacture such as **green tea, black tea,** or **oolong,** and graded according to leaf size, such as **congou, orange pekoe, pekoe,** or **souchong.**

tebrød (TAY-brur). Nor. **Tea cake.**

Tee (tay). Ger. **Tea.**

teeri (TAY-ri). Fin. Black **grouse.**

teetä (TAY-tae). Fin. **Tea.**

Teewürst (TAY-voorst). Ger. **Sausage** of very finely ground **pork tenderloin.**

Téiggemüse (TIGHG-ger-mewser). Ger. **Macaroni** dishes.

tej patta (tayj PAH-tah). Ind. **Bay leaf.**

tekaka (TAY-kah-kah). Swe. **Tea cake; crumpet.**

tel (tayl). Ind. Oil.

Teleme (TAHL-ah-me). Rum. A pickled **cheese** made of goat's or ewe's milk; much like Greek **Feta;** also spelled *Telemi.*

temper (TEHM-puhr). USA. To bring to a suitable state by mixing in or adding a liquid ingredient, then kneading to a uniform texture.

Temple orange (TEHM-puhl AWH-ranj). USA. A hybrid **orange;** the result of a **tangerine** and **orange** cross.

tempura (TEHM-poo-rah). Jap. **Batter-fried** foods.

tenderloin (TEHN-dehr-loyn). USA. The long, slender, tender muscle that runs through the **loin** of beef and ends at the **ribs;** is divided into **filet mignon, chateaubriand, tournedos;** the tenderest muscle of the carcass.

tentsuyu (TEHN-tsoo-yoo). Jap. **Dipping sauce** for **tempura.**

tepid (TAH-pehd). USA. Lukewarm.

tequila (teh-KE-yah). Mex. Distilled liquor made from **agave** in specific growing areas.

teri (tah-DRE). Jap. **Glaze.**

teriyaki (TEHR-re-yah-ke). Jap. **Glaze-broiled;** meat **marinated** in a sweet **soy sauce** mixture and **grilled** over charcoal so that a glaze is formed.

ternero (tehr-NEH-roh). Spa. **Veal.**

terrapin (TEHR-ah-pen). USA. An edible freshwater or tidal water **turtle.**

terrine (tay-ren). Fre. An earthenware pot similar to a **casserole** in which food is served and sometime prepared.

tetrazzini (teht-trahz-ZE-ne). Ita. A rich **pasta** dish with a creamy **cheese sauce** and **seafood** or **poultry.**

tette melk (TEH-teh MELK). Nor. **Milk** in which tette leaves have been placed to preserve the milk and start a specially flavored culture.

thalj (talg). Ara. **Ice.**

thandai (than-DA-e). Ind. Summer punch made with ground seeds, **almonds,** spices, **sugar,** and whole **milk.**

thé (tay). Fre. **Tea.**

thee (tay). Dut. **Tea.**

thee complet (tay kohm-PLAH). Dut. **Tea** served with food such as **cookies, biscuits,** or **tarts.**

thermidor (THERM-e-dohr). USA. A method of preparing **lobster** using **Mornay sauce** as a base, but substituting **mustard** for the **cheese.** Adding sieved **tomalley** and **coral** and a little **sherry,** mix with chunked lobster tail meat, and **stuff** the lobster tail; sprinkle with **grated Parmesan,** and **broil.**

thick batter (thehk BAHT-tehr). USA. A **batter** that contains two parts flour to one part liquid; such as used for **muffins** and **cakes.** Also called a **soft drop batter.**

thick white sauce (thehk whit saus). USA. A **roux**-liquid mixture that contains a fat-flour ratio of three tablespoons of each to one cup of liquid; such as used for **puddings.**

thicken (THEHK-ehn). USA. Give body to **sauces, gravies,** or **soups** by adding **flour, cornstarch,** or **arrowroot.**

thin batter (thehn BAHT-tehr). USA. A **batter** that contains one part flour to one part liquid, such as used for **cream puffs, timbale** cases, **crepes, popovers,** dip **batters.** Also known as **pour batter.**

thin white sauce (thehn whit saus). USA. A **roux**-liquid mixture that contains a fat-flour ratio of one tablespoon of each to one cup liquid, such as used for **soups** or thin **gravies.**

thon (tawng). Fre. **Tuna.**

Thousand Island dressing (thou-sund EY-lund drehs-seng). USA. A **salad dressing** with a **Russian dressing** base and **chopped pickles, green pepper, cream,** and seasonings added.

thousand-year-old-eggs (THOU-sund-yer-old-ehgs). USA. **Pí dàn;** Chinese duck eggs preserved in a clay casing made of ashes, lime, **salt,** and strong **tea;** rolled in **rice husks,** and buried for three months; the yolks turn greenish-brown, the whites turn black-purple. Also called **hundred-year-old eggs.** Has a cheesy texture.

thread (threhd). USA. The first stage of **sugar crystallization:** begins at 230° F, the syrup makes a two-inch coarse thread when dropped from a spoon.

Thunfisch. (TOON-fish). Ger. **Tuna** fish.

thym (tang). Fre. **Thyme.**

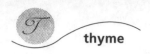

thyme (tim). USA. A pungent, aromatic **herb** used in seasoning and **soups.**

Tia Maria (TE-ah Mah-RE-ah). Spa. A Jamaican **coffee-** and spice-flavored **liqueur.**

tidbid (TED-bed). Dan. Light snack.

tien mien jiàng (ten men GE-ong). Chi. A thick, sweet, salty **paste** made from fermented **red beans;** used to flavor **marinades** and **sauces** and as a **dipping sauce.**

tiges (tezh). Fre. A type of Swiss **sausage.**

Tignard (tehn-yah). Fre. A firm, blue-veined goat's-milk **cheese.**

Tijuana (Te-ah-WAHN-nah). Mex. A firm, pale, fiery provacative **cheese** with bits of hot **red peppers** added to the curd before aging; melts evenly and smoothly.

tikka (TIH-ka). Ind. **Cutlet.**

til (thel). Ind. **Sesame** seeds.

tilefish (TIL-fisch). USA. A western Atlantic food fish, with unusually firm, but tender flesh, which is best compared to **lobster** meat or **scallops.**

Tillamook (TEHL-ah-mouk). USA. An Oregan **Cheddar;** bright yellow, firm, not flaky.

Tilsit (TIHL-siht). Ger. A cooked **cheese** from raw cow's-milk, with a thin yellow rind, straw-colored interior with holes, acidic taste, and sometimes flavored with **caraway.**

timbale (tim-bull). Fre. Thin, **fried** case for holding creamed mixtures; or unsweetened baked **custard** with meat, **poultry,** or **vegetables.**

timo (TE-moa). Ita. **Thyme.**

tin (ten). Ara. **Figs.**

tinda (TIN-dah). Ind. A round **gourd;** a vegetable belonging to the **cucumber** family.

tippaleivät (TEP-pah-leh-vat). Fin. May Day **crullers;** bird's nests; spiral shape, similar to **pretzels.**

tipsy pudding (tehp-se puhd-dehng). Bri. A **dessert pudding** of **sponge cake** soaked with liquor, covered with **custard** or **whipped cream;** similar to **trifle.**

tirolen eierspeise (te-ROAL-ern IGH-err-shpigh-zer). Ger. Hard-boiled **eggs, potatoes, anchovies** in an Austrian **casserole.**

tiropita (te-rop-PE-tah). Gre. A **cheese pie** made with **phyllo dough.**

tisane (teh-ZAHN). USA. Herbal **tea.**

tlami (tah-AH-me). Ara. Round, flat, soft-textured bread without pocket; used for mnaqish and as regular bread.

toad-in-the-hole (tod-en-thuh-hol). Bri. **Sausage** cooked in a **batter.**

toast (tost). USA. **Browning** the surface of a food by direct heat.

tocino (toa-THE-noas). Spa. **Bacon.**

tocino de cielo (toa-THE-noas day the-AY-loa). Spa. A thick **caramel custard dessert;** not made with **bacon.**

toddy (TODD-de). Bri. A punch made of a mixture of whiskey, **sugar,** and hot water.

toffee (TOFF-fe). USA. A hard, brittle, crunchy **candy** made with **sugar** and **molasses, butter, nuts,** flavorings; same as the British **taffy.**

tofu (TOA-foo). Jap. Fresh **bean curd cake;** white with a texture of well-baked custard, easily digestible; many types, each for a different use.

togan (TO-gahn). Jap. **Winter melon;** resembles a **watermelon,** but has white, firm flesh.

togarashi (to-GAHR-dah-she). Jap. Red hot **chili peppers;** also, a seasoning that contains **sesame** seed, **orange** peel, and red hot **chili peppers.**

tokay grapes (to-KA grapz). USA. A purplish-red **table grape** with firm flesh, sweet taste, and either seedless or with seeds.

Toll House cookie (tol hahus KUHK-ke). USA. A **cookie** made with **brown sugar, nuts,** and **chocolate** chips in the **batter;** originated at the Toll House Inn in Massachusetts.

tomalley (toh-MAHL-le). USA. The olive-green liver of the **lobster**— a delicacy.

tomat (toa-MAAD). Dan. **Tomato.**

tomate (to-maht). Frc. **Tomato.**

tomate (toh-MAH-tay). Por. **Tomato.**

Tomaten (tom-MAA-tern). Ger. **Tomatoes.**

tomaten (toh-MAH-tuh). Dut. **Tomatoes.**

tomater (too-MAH-tehr). Swe. **Tomatoes.**

tomates (toa-MAH-tayss). Spa. **Tomatoes.**

tomatillo (toh-mah-TEHL-loh). Mex. A green **tomato,** small and pungent (not an unripe tomato); used in **salsa;** also called *tomato verde.*

tomato (toh-MAY-to). USA. The **fruit** of a plant cultivated for its usually large red or yellow fruit; used extensively in cooking, in **salads,** even in **preserves;** many varieties worldwide. See **cherry tomatoes.**

tomatsaft (toom-MAAT-sahft). Nor. **Tomato** juice.

tomatsoppa (too-MAT-SO-pah). Swe. **Tomato** soup.

tomber a glace (ton-bay au gla-say). Fre. To reduce a liquid until it has the appearance of a thick **syrup.**

Tomino (toh-ME-noh). Ita. An excellent **dessert cheese** made of cow's-milk with a delicate, fresh flavor, and a soft, smooth paste.

Tomme (tuhm). Fre. A **cheese** made of skimmed milk, and usually flavored with **fennel, raisins,** or sweet wine.

Tomme de Chèvre (Tuhm dur Her-veh). Fre. A small **cheese** made of goat's milk.

tonfisk (TOON-fisk). Swe. **Tuna.**

tong (tawng). Dut. Sole; the **flatfish.**

tongue (tuhngah). USA. The flesh of the beef tongue used as food.

tonija (tyoh-NEYN). Dut. **Tuna.**

tonkatsu (tong-KAHT-soo). Jap. Spicy, marinated **pork,** dipped in **egg** and breadcrumbs, then **fried.**

tonno (TOAN-no). Ita. **Tuna.**

Topfen (TOHP-fehrn). Ger. An Austrian cow's skim-milk **cheese** similar to **cottage cheese;** widely used in pastries. Also known as **Quark.**

top round (tohp rownd). USA. A cut from the inner part of a **round** of beef.

top sirloin (tohp SUHR-lown). USA. A cut from the top portion of the **loin** section of beef.

torkad frukt (TOR-kahd frewkt). Swe. **Dried fruits.**

tørkage (TURR-kaaer). Dan. Plain **cake.**

tordo (TOAR-do). Ita. Small thrush.

torigai (toh-REE-gah-e). Jap. A cockle whose edible parts are tender and tasty; a **mollusk** of the **clam** family.

toriniku (toh-RE-NE-koo). Jap. **Chicken** meat.

tororo konbu (to-LOW-low KOHNG-boo). Jap. **Konbu** leaves that have been soaked in **vinegar** and shaved along the length of the leaf, then cut into thread form.

torpedo (tohr-PE-do). USA. **Hoagie.**

torrada (toh-RRAH-dah). Por. **Toast.**

tørret frugtsuppe (TURR-reht FREWKT-ssew-pper). Nor. **Fruit soup** made of dried **fruits;** served hot or cold.

tørrfisk (TORR-fesk). Swe, Nor, Dan. Stockfish.

torrón (too-RON). Ita. A sweet **nougat** based on **honey** and **almonds;** may have **figs** or **chocolate.**

torsk (torshk). Nor. **Cod.**

torsk (toarsk). Dan. **Cod.**

torsk (torsk). Swe. **Codfish.**

torta (TOHR-tah). Mex. A **cake;** loaf.

torta (TOAR-tah). Ita. **Tart, pie,** or **cake.**

torta (TOR-tah). Por. A rolled and **filled cake.**

Törtchen (TUHR-chehn). Ger. Small **tarts.**

Torte (TOR-te). Ger. A rich **cake** made from **eggs, nuts,** and bread-crumbs; or **meringue** shaped like a cake.

tortellini (tor-te-LEN-ne). Ita. Small rounds of egg **pasta stuffed,** folded, and wrapped with ends pinched together in a ring.

Torten (TOR-tern). Ger. A class of **cakes,** made of many **eggs, ground nuts** or dry bread crumbs, various and multiple **fillings,** covered with a rich **frosting,** and in numerous varieties.

tortiglione (tor-TEHG-le-ohn). Ita. **Almond cake.**

tortilha de mariscos (tor-TE-lya duh mah-RESH-koosh). Por. **Omelet** filled with chopped **shellfish.**

tortilla (tohr-TE-yah). Mex. A thin, unleavened **pancake** of ground, dried **maize, baked** on a griddle.

tortilla (toar-TE-lyah). Spa. **Omelet.**

tortilla de huevos (toar-TE-lyah day WAY-bhoass). Mex. **Omelet.**

tortina (toar-TE-nah). Ita. A **tartlet.**

tortino (toar-TE-noa). Ita. A **frittata** that is cooked in an oven, therefore drier in the center than one cooked on a stove top.

tortoni (toar-TOHN-ne). Ita. **Ice cream** topped with **chopped almonds** or **macaroons.** Also **biscuit tortoni.**

tortue (tor-too). Fre. **Turtle.**

Toscanello (tohs-cah-NELL-loa). Ita. A ewe's-milk **cheese** with a brownish yellow rind; pale, dense interior; mild, piquant taste; also called **Toscano.**

toscatårta (TOH-ska-TOR-ta). Swe. An **almond**-topped **cake.**

toss (tohss). USA. To mix ingredients lightly without crushing.

tostada (tohs-TAH-dah). Mex. A crisp-fried **tortilla** that is served with **guacamole, salsa,** and assorted **dips.**

tostaditas (toh-tah-THE-tahs). Mex. **Totopas;** little triangular pieces of crisp-fried **tortillas.**

tostato (to-STAA-toa). Ita. **Toast.**

totani (toa-TAH-ne). Ita. Small **squids.**

totopos (toh-TOH-pohs). Mex. **Tostaditas;** little triangular pieces of crisp-fried **tortillas.**

toucinho (toh-SE-nyoh). Por. **Smoked slab bacon.**

toulouse, a la (too-looz). Fre. A garnish of white meats, **mushrooms, truffles,** in **allemande sauce;** a classic **garnish.**

tourin (too-rahng). Fre. **Onion soup** made with **milk, cream, egg yolks;** served with **grated cheese.**

tourné (toor-nay). Fre. A **vegetable** that is turned or shaped with a knife, as a **mushroom** cap.

tournedos (toor-ner-doaz). Fre. Slices of beef **tenderloin,** the most tender cut of beef.

Tournedos de Boeuf a la Oskar (Toor-NAH-doaz day Boof ah lah OHS-kahr). USA. Thick slices of **sautéed** beef **tenderloin** (or **veal round** steak) served with **crabmeat** and **asparagus** or **artichoke** hearts; topped with a rich creamy **béarnaise sauce.**

Tournedos Rossini (toor-ner-doaz ros-se-ne). Fre. **Sautéed** slices of **beef fillet** on **croutons** or **artichoke** bottoms, topped with goose or duck liver **slices, truffle slices,** and **Madeira wine sauce.**

tourte (toor-teh). Fre. An open **tart,** or **pie,** ususally round and savory; **tart.**

tourtelettes (toor-let). Fre. Small **tartlets.**

toute-épice (toot-ay-pes). Fre. **Allspice.**

tragacanth (TRAHG-ah-kahnth). USA. **Vegetable gum** used as an emulsifier and thickener in commercially made **sauces, candies, ice cream.** Also called **gum.**

Trappiste (trahp-pehst).   Fre. A round, semihard **cheese,** with a soft rind and a dense smooth paste with small holes; made all over the world by Trappist monks. **Port-Salut** is the best known.

Trasch (trash).   Ger. A Swiss **liqueur** made of **pears** and **apples.**

Traube (TROW-ber).   Ger. **Grapes.**

travailler (tra-vye-yay).   Fre. To beat or stir for blending or smoothing ingredients.

Travnik (THRAHV-nek).   Yug. A soft **cheese** made from ewe's milk with a small proportion of goat's milk added.

treacle (TRE-kehl).   Bri. A very sweet, heavy **syrup,** golden or black, similar to **molasses,** used in making **desserts** such as **puddings** and **tarts.**

Trecce (Tra-cha).   Ita. A braided, semisoft **cheese.**

tree ear (tre eher).   USA. **Yún er;** a Chinese fungus used in cooking for its interesting texture. Also called **cloud ear.**

trefoil (TRE-foyil).   USA. **Mitsuba;** a member of a Japanese **parsley** family; flavor between **sorrel** and **celery;** attractive light green color; used to add flavor and color accent; a type of clover.

trenette (treh-NEHT-tay).   Ita. A **pasta similar** to **fettucine** that is flat; the traditional **pasta** for **pesto.**

Trenton cracker (TREHN-tuhn KRAHK-ker).   USA. A light, round, puffy **cracker** made of **wheat flour;** served with **oyster stews.**

trifle (TRI-ful).   Bri. A layered **dessert** made of **sponge cake** soaked in **fruit** juice or liquor, covered with **jam, custard, almonds,** and **whipped cream.**

triglie (TRE-lyay).   Ita. **Red mullet.**

trigo (TRE-goh).   Mex. **Wheat.**

tripa (TRE-pah).   Por. **Tripe.**

tripe (tryip).   USA. The first and second stomachs of ruminants used as foodstuff.

tripe (TREP-pay).   Ita. **Tripe.**

tripes à la mode de Caen (trep ah lah mod der kahng).   Fre. Tripe baked with calf's feet, **vegetables, apple brandy** or **cider.**

Triple-Crème (tre-ple kreh-ma).   Fre. A **dessert cheese** containing more than 75% butterfat; soft, ripened.

Triple-Crème Chèvre (tree-ple kreh-mah ehr-veh). Fre. A soft, ripened, fat **cheese** made of goat's milk; white crust as well as interior may be eaten.

triple sec (TREP-pul sehk). USA. An **orange**-flavored, clear, colorless French **liqueur**. Also called **Cointreau, Curaçao.**

triticale flour (treht-ah-KAL-e flowr). USA. A nutritious sweet-tasting **flour** obtained from intergenetic hybridization by crossing **durum wheat, hard red wheat,** and **rye;** very high in protein and low in gluten; good bread flour when mixed with higher **gluten** flours.

trota (TRAW-tah). Ita. **Trout.**

trota salmonata (TRAW-tah sahl-moa-NAH-tay). Ita. Salmon **trout.**

trout (trowt). USA. A highly prized **game** fish found mostly in freshwater; flesh is firm, succulent, and ranges from white to brilliant reds; very simple bone structure; many varieties worldwide.

trouvillaise (troo-ve-lay). Fre. A garnish of **shrimp, mussels, mushroom** caps in **shrimp sauce.**

trucha (TROO-chah). Spa. **River trout.**

trufa (TROO-fah). Por. **Truffle.**

Trüffel (TREWF-fehl). Ger. **Truffle.**

truffle (truff-uhl). Fre. A subterranean **mushroom**-like fungus used for **garnishing** and flavoring.

truite (trwet). Fre. **Trout.**

truite saumonée (tre-wet soa-mawng-ngay). Fre. Salmon **trout.**

truss (truhs). Fre. To secure with string or **skewer,** the wings and legs of any fowl, in order to hold its shape during cooking.

truta (TROO-tah). Por. **Trout.**

Truthahn (TROOT-haan). Ger. Tom **turkey; gobbler.**

Trut-henne (TROOT-he-neh). Ger. **Turkey hen.**

Tschil (Chill). Arm. A **cheese** made from either cow's or ewe's sour skim milk.

tsukemono (TSKEH-moh-noh). Jap. **Pickles.**

Tuareg (twah-rehg). Afr. A skimmed-milk **cheese,** unsalted; made by the Berber tribes.

tubettini (too-beht-TE-ne). Ita. **Macaroni** in shape of small tubes.

tuffaaha (tuf-FEHH). Ara. **Apple.**

tuile (twel). Fre. A curved, crisp **cookie** made with crushed **almonds;** made curved by placing warm cookie on rolling pin.

tulipe (too-lep). Fre. A pastry shell made of a crisp **cookie** that is ruffled, while still warm, to make a cup to hold **berries** or **ices.**

tum (toom). Ara. **Garlic.**

tuna (TOO-nah). USA. A saltwater fish of varying size, from 300–400 pounds to 1,000–1,200 pounds, sought for its rich meat, which varies in color and oiliness depending on species; albacore is highest quality with its white meat; bonito has darkest meat and much sought-after by Japanese to dry for use in **sashimi;** used **brined,** canned, **flaked, dried,** fresh; an important worldwide food fish.

tuna (TOO-nah). Mex. Prickly **pear.**

tunge (TOONG-er). Dan. **Tongue.**

Tunke (TUHNG-keh). Ger. **Gravy** or **sauce.**

tunny (TOO-ne). Bri. **Tuna.**

turbinado sugar (tuhr-be-NAHD-o SHUH-gahr). USA. A partially refined, coarse-grained, beige-colored crystal containing the **molasses** portion of the **sugar.**

turbot (TUHR-boht). USA. A **flatfish** of the **flounder** family; found in both the Pacific and the Atlantic, but different; has delicate flavor and firm white meat; also known as *Steinbutte* (German), *Rombo chiodato* (Italian), *Piggvar* (Scandinavian), *Plat* (Yugoslavia), *Turbot* (French).

turkey (TUHR-ke). USA. A **game** bird, as well as domesticated for commercial use; a truly original North American native; both toms and hens are used for food; traditionally **roasted** and served for Thanksgiving and Christmas meals.

turkey roll (TUHR-ke rohl). USA. Boned turkey meat, pressed in roll form; usually commercially prepared.

Turkish delight (TUHR-kesh de-LIT). USA. A Turkish **confection** of **fruit paste,** served with afternoon **coffee;** *rahat loukoum.*

turmeric (tehr-MEHR-rik). USA. A root spice of India, when dried yields a vivid yellow color used in **curry** powders and American **mustard;** may be substituted for **saffron** for color, but does not have flavor of saffron; basic spice in bread-and-butter **pickles.**

turn (tuhrn). USA. To shape **fruit** or **vegetable** with a paring knife.

turnip (TUHR-nehp). USA. A cultivated root **vegetable** of the **mustard** family; usually white with purplish top; its green leaves are also used as a vegetable.

turnip greens (TUHR-nehp grehns). USA. The tops of the cultivated root **vegetable** of the **mustard** family.

turnover (TUHRN-ov-ehr). USA. Food encased in pastry and **fried** or **baked.**

turrón (toor-RON). Spa. A traditional Christmas chewy **candy** made of **egg** white, **honey,** and **toasted almonds.**

turtle (TURR-tuhl). USA. A marine reptile that lives both on land and in water; the female terrapin has the choicest of all turtle meat; the green meat from the top shell is considered best, meat taken from the bottom shell is white.

tutti-frutti (TOO-te FROO-te). USA. Mixed **fruits, chopped** and **preserved** in **brandy.**

Tvorog (TVO-rog). Rus. A sour-milk **cheese** of the **cottage cheese** type; also spelled **Tworog.**

twaalfuurtje (TWAHL-few-el-twae). Dut. Cold luncheon.

twelfth-night cake (TWELFTH-nit kak). Bri. Very rich spice cake made with candied **fruits,** dried fruits, **almonds** with almond **paste filling** and topping; a traditional cake.

Tworog (TVO-rog). Rus. A sour-milk **cheese** of the cottage cheese type; also spelled **Tvorog.**

Tybo (TEW-boh). Dan. A cooked cow's milk **cheese,** brick-shaped with large holes and yellow rind, straw-colored interior.

tykmaelk (TEWK-mehlk). Dan. A **junket**-like **dessert** made from **clabbered milk.**

tyrolienne (te-rohl-yehn). Fre. A **garnish** of **fried onion rings** and **chopped tomatoes.**

tyttebaer (TEWD-er-baer). Dan. **Lingonberry.**

tzimmes (TSEHM-mehs). Jew. A **brisket casserole** with **carrots,** dried **fruits, syrup,** and topped with **dumplings** and **potatoes;** traditional for Rosh Hashanah.

Uvas - Portugal - Grapes

uccèlli (oot-CHEHL-le). Ita. Birds.

uchepos (oo-CHEH-pohs). Mex. Special fresh **corn tamales** made in Michoacán, Mexico.

udo (OO-do). Jap. A stalk **vegetable** with a delicate aroma, a **fennel** flavor, and an appealing fresh crispness, used **raw** or barely cooked in **salads.**

udon (oo-dohn). Jap. Wide, flat **rice noodles.**

ugli fruit (OO-gli froot). USA. A Jamaican **citrus fruit** resembling a pear-shaped **grapefruit,** with lime-green to light orange skin, yellow-orange pulp; brightly acid-sweet with a zesty pungency.

ugnspannkaka (UNGNS-pan-KA-kah). Swe. Thick **pancake baked** in the oven.

ugnstekt (EWNGN-staykt). Swe. **Baked** or **roasted.**

uien (IR-uh). Dut. **Onions.**

uitsmijter (OUT-smi-ter). Dut. A substantial snack of bread piled with cold meats and topped with two **fried eggs.**

umé (oo-MEH). Jap. **Plum.**

umeboshi (oo-MEH boh-she). Jap. Tiny red or green **pickled plums;** eaten at breakfast with **rice** and **miso soup.**

umeshu (oo-MEH-shoo). Jap. **Plum wine.**

umido (OO-me-doa). Ita. **Stew.**

unagi (oo-NAH-ge). Jap. **Eel.**

ungarische art (UHNG-gehr-ish ahrt). Ger. Hungarian style, usually meaning "with **paprika.**"

unpolished rice (uhn-POHL-eshed ris).   USA. **Rice grains** that have had the **bran** layer and most of the germ removed; not to be confused with **brown rice.**

unsweetened chocolate (uhn-SWET-hend CHOK-o-laht).   USA. A bitter-tasting **chocolate** used in **baking;** no **sugar** added.

uovo (WAW-vah).   Ita. **Egg; egg yolk** is *tuorlo d'uovo;* **egg** white is *bianco d'uovo.*

> **uovo affogato** (WAW-vah ahf-foa-GAA-toa). **Poached egg.**
>
> **uovo al burro** (WAW-vahahl BOOR-roa). **Fried egg.**
>
> **uovo molle** (WAW-vah MOL-lay). Soft-boiled **egg.**
>
> **uovo piccante** (WAW-vah pe-KAHN-teh). **Deviled egg.**
>
> **uovo sode** (WAW-vah SO-doa). Hard-boiled **egg.**
>
> **uovo strapazzate** (WAW-vah strah-pah-TSAA-tay).   Scrambled **egg.**

upside-down cake (UHP-sid-dohwn kak).   USA. A **batter cake** baked in a pan with the topping for the cake lining the bottom of the baking pan; when baked, cake is turned out upside down on a platter.

Uri (Woo-re).   Swi. A hard, cow's-milk **cheese.**

Urseren (Woo-sahy-rehn).   Ita. A mild-flavored **cheese** made in Switzerland.

usli ghee (USE-le khe).   Ind. Indian **clarified butter.**

usu-kuchi shoya (oo-soo-KOO-che SHOH-yoo).   Jap. A light, clear, thin, salty **soy sauce.**

uunipuuro (OO-ni-poo-roa).   Fin. Baked **barley** or **rice porridge.**

uunissa paistettu hauki (OO-nes-sah PYE-stet-too HOW-ke).   Fin. **Baked, stuffed pike.**

uva (OO-bhahss).   Spa. **Grape.**

uva passa (OO-vah PAHS-sah).   Ita. **Raisin.** Also *uva secca.*

uvas (OO-vahss).   Por. **Grapes.**

uva spina (OO-vah SPRR-nah).   Ita. **Gooseberries.**

uzura no tamago (oo-ZOO-rah tah-MAH-goh).   Jap. **Quail eggs,** speckled brown, one inch long, flavor of **chicken eggs.**

Viini - Finish - Wine

vaca (VAHC-ah). Por. Beef.

vaca cozida (VAHC-ah coo-ZE-dah). Por. **Boiled** beef.

vaca guisada (VAHC-ah ghe-ZAH-doh). Por. **Beef stew.**

vacherin (vah-sher-rang). Fre. A **dessert** ring made of a flat coil of **meringue** with a piped edge to hold a **filling** of **chantilly cream;** the sides and open crown are decorated with large dots of **meringue,** then **baked.**

Vacherin Mont d'Or (Vah-sher-reng Mont Dorr). Fre. A disc-shaped cow's whole-milk **cheese** of Switzerland with a soft, creamy, rich texture with small holes and delicate, buttery, sweet flavor.

vadelmat (VAH-dayl-maht). Fin. **Raspberries.**

våfflor (VOF-loor). Swe. **Waffles.**

vafler (VAHF-fehl). Nor. **Waffles.**

vaktel (VAHK-tayl). Swe. **Quail.**

Valencia orange (vah-LYNN-ce-ah AWH-ranj). USA. A sweet, thin-skinned, nearly seedless orange that produces an excellent juice.

valenciano (vahl-lyn-ce-AHN-noh). Mex. A chili **pepper.**

valencienne (vah-lehn-ceyen). Fre. A **garnish** of rice **pilaf** with chopped sweet **peppers** in a **tomato**-flavored **sauce.**

välikyljys (vae-li-KEW-lyewss). Fin. **Entrecôte** of beef.

valkokaalisalaatti (VAHL-joa-KAA-li-SAH-laat-ti). Fin. **Cabbage salad.**

valnødkage (VAHL-nurd-kaaer). Dan. **Walnut cake.**

valnødromkager (VAHL-nurd-ROHM-kaaer). Dan. **Walnut** rum **cookies.**

vanaspati ghee (va-NAHS-pa-te khe). Ind. **Vegetable shortening.**

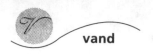

vand (vahn). Dan. Water.

vandreuil (vahnd-rury). Fre. A popular fish found off the coast of Provence.

vaniglia (bigh-NE-lyah). Ita. **Vanilla.**

vanilje (vah-NEL-yer). Nor. **Vanilla.**

vaniljglass (va-NILY-GLAS). Swe. **Vanilla ice cream.**

vaniljsås (va-NEL-SOHS). Swe. **Custard.**

vanilla (vah-NILL-lah). USA. The pod of a vine native to Mexico, picked immature, cured in a long process; used to flavor **desserts, sugars, liqueurs.**

vanille (vah-ney). Fre. **Vanilla.**

Vanille (Vah-NIL-ler). Ger. **Vanilla.**

vanilleijs (vah-NIL-leh-ICS). Dut. **Vanilla ice cream.**

Vanille Rahmeis (Vah-NIL-ler Rahm-ighss). Ger. **Vanilla ice cream.**

vanillin (vah-NIHLL-lahn). USA. A synthetic **vanilla,** chemically created.

vann (vahn). Nor. Water.

vanukas (vah-NUSS-kohr). Fin. **Pudding.**

vapeur (vah-purr). Fre. **Steam.**

variety meat (vah-RI-eh-te met). USA. Internal organs, such as heart, liver, kidneys, **sweetbreads; offal.**

varkenskarbonaden (VAR-kens-kar-boh-nah-den). Dut. **Fried pork** chops.

varkensvlees (VAHR-kuns-vlays). Dut. **Pork.**

varm choklad (varm shook-LAD). Swe. **Hot chocolate.**

varmrätt (VAHRMT-reht). Swe. Hot dish.

vasikanlihaa (VAH-sik-kahn-LI-haa). Fin. **Veal.**

vasikanpaisti (VAH-sik-kahn-PAHI-sti). Fin. **Roast veal.**

Västerbottenost (VEHS-terr-bot-term-oost). Swe. A cow's-milk **cheese** with a firm interior with small holes; a hard rind, covered with wax; pungent taste.

Västgötaost (VEH-shyur-tah-oost). Swe. A Swiss-type cheese.

vatten (VAH-tern). Swe. Water.

vattenglass (VA-tehn-GLAS). Swe. **Sherbet.**

vaxbönor (VAKS-boh-nor). Swe. **Wax beans.**

veado, carne de (vay-AH-doo, KAHR-nay day). Por. **Venison.**

veal (veahl). USA. Young beef, three to five months of age; when milk-fed, flesh is pale pink to white; when grass-fed, flesh is rosy pink.

Veal Cordon Bleu (veahl KOR-dohn blu). USA. Paper-thin **veal slices** rolled around **ham** and **Gruyere cheese**, then **breaded** and **sautéed** until golden and crisp.

veal Orloff (veahl ORR-lohf). USA. **Saddle** of **veal** or **lamb** prepared in the classic haute cuisine manner, with **truffles, Soubise, duxelles,** covered with **béchamel,** and garnished with **asparagus** tips.

veal Oscar (veahl OS-kahr). USA. **Sautéed veal cutlets** served with **béarnaise,** and garnished with **asparagus** tips, and **crab legs** or **crayfish tails.**

veau (voa). Fre. **Veal.**

vegetable (VEHGJ-tah-bul). USA. A herbaceous plant, such as **potato, cabbage, bean, carrot,** grown for an edible part, which is eaten with the principal part of a meal.

vegetable salt (VEGJ-tah-bul sawlt). USA. Pure **salt,** sodium chloride, with added **vegetable extracts,** such as **celery, garlic.**

veggies (VEHG-gez). USA. **Vegetables.**

vellutata (vel-loo-TAH-toa). Ita. A **soup** thickened with **egg yolk.**

velouté (ve-loo-tay). Fre. Velvet; a rich, white **sauce** made with a white **stock, chicken or veal;** similar to **béchamel,** which is made with **milk.**

Vendôme (vahn-dahm). Fre. A soft **cheese,** ripened in charcoal or sometimes buried in ashes.

Vendôme de Chèvre (vahn-dahm dur hehr-vah). Fre. A soft, ripened goat's-milk **cheese.**

venison (VEHN-eh-suhn). USA. Deer meat.

vénitienne (veh-ne-ce-ehn). Fre. Fish **fillets** poached in white wine; served with a reduction **sauce.**

venkel (FEHN-kehl). Dut. **Fennel.**

venudo (veh-NOO-doh). Mex. Deer; **venison.**

verbena (vehr-BE-nah). USA. An **herb** with an exquisitely pungent, sweet lemony aroma; use in **tea,** add to wine punch, perk up frozen **peas,** refresh the flavor of icy-cold white wine. Also called the *Scarlett O'Hara herb.*

verde (BEHR-theh). Mex. Green.

verdura (vah-DOO-ray). Ita. **Vegetable.**

verjuice (VEHR-juic).   USA. The juice of unripened **grapes,** used as sour flavoring in cooking.

vermicelli (ver-me-CHEL-le).   Ita. Very thin **pasta,** often used in **soups** and **puddings.**

Vermont Cheddar (Vehr-MOHNT CHEH-dahr).   USA. One of the finest aged American **Cheddars.**

Vermont Sage (Vehr-MOHNT Saj).   USA. **Vermont Cheddar** with **chopped** or **dried sage** added before **curing.**

Véronique (veh-rohn-nek).   Fre. **Garnished** with white **grapes.**

vert-pré (vehr-preh).   Fre. A **garnish** for **grilled** meats of straw **potatoes, watercress,** and **butter.**

very thick white sauce (VEH-re thehk whit saus).   USA. A **roux**-liquid mixture that contains a fat-flour ratio of four tablespoons of each to one cup liquid, such as **blancmange.**

verza (VEHR-dzah).   Ita. Green **cabbage.**

vetchina (ve-chye-NAH).   Rus. **Ham.**

Vezzena (vez-ZEH-nah).   Ita. A cow's partially skimmed milk hard **cheese;** used for **grating** or as a table cheese.

viande (vyahngd).   Fre. Meat.

viande froides (vyahngd frwah).   Fre. Cold meats.

Vichy water (VE-she WAH-tehr).   USA. Water from the town of Vichy, France, thought to have curative qualities, especially for the liver.

vichyssoise (VE-che-swoy).   USA. **Cream** of **potato** and **leek soup,** garnished with **chopped chives.**

Victoria sauce (vehk-torr-re-ah).   Fre. A **garnish** for fish of **lobster sauce** with **diced lobster** and **truffles.**

Victoria, a la (vehk-torr-re-ah).   Fre. A **garnish** of small **tomatoes** stuffed with **purée** of **mushrooms,** quartered **artichoke** simmered in **butter,** and served with meat juices reduced with **port** or **Madeira.**

viennoise (ven-wahs).   Fre. In the Viennese style; coated with **egg** and breadcrumbs, **fried;** served with a classic **garnish.**

Vierfrucht Marmalade (fer-FRUKHT mahr-meh-LAA-der).   Ger. "Four Fruit **Jam**"; made of **cherries, currants, gooseberries, raspberries.**

viili (VE-le).   Fin. **Clabbered milk,** similar to **yogurt.**

viini (VE-ne).   Fin. Wine.

viinirypäle (VE-ne-REW-pael).   Fin. **Grape.**

viinimarjakiisseli (VE-ne-MAHR-yah-KES-say-li). Fin. **Red currant sauce.**

viipurin rinkilä (VE-poo-rin ren-KE-lah). Fin. A famous coffeecake ring.

vijgen (VAY-khuh). Dut. **Figs.**

Villalón (be-lyah-LON). Spa. A ewe's-milk **cheese;** cylindrical, white, sharp, and salty.

villeroi (ve-lo-wah). Fre. A sauce of **velouté, truffle,** and **ham essence,** used to coat foodstuff before **dipping** in **egg** and breadcrumbs, then **frying.**

viltsuppe (vilt-SSEW-pper). Nor. **Game** or **venison soup.**

vinäger (vi-NAH-gehr). Swe. **Vinegar.**

vinagre (ve-NAH-greh). Spa. **Vinegar.**

vinagre (ve-NAH-gray). Por. **Vinegar.**

vinaigrette (ve-nay-groit). Fre. A mixture of oil and **vinegar** with **herbs, salt,** and **pepper.**

vinbär (VEN-baer). Swe. **Currant.**

vindaloo (VEN-deh-loo). Ind. A dish highly seasoned with **vinegar, garlic,** and **curry,** and rich meat; a hot and pungent **curry.**

vindruvor (VEN-drew-voor). Swe. **Grapes.**

vine leaves (vin levez). USA. Young Mediterranean **grape leaves** blanched and used to wrap **savories.**

vinegar (VEHN-eh-guhr). USA. A sour liquid obtained by **fermentation** of certain liquids from **fruits,** usually, and used as a **condiment** or **preservative.** Types include **white, cider, malt-based, wine,** and **herb.**

vinsuppe (VEN-ssew-pper). Nor. **Wine soup.**

violet (VI-oa-leht). USA. A crystallized flower used as a **dessert garnish.**

virgin olive oil (VEHR-gehn OHL-ehv oyl). USA. Oil from the second cold press of superior quality **olives.** See **olive oil.**

Virginia ham (vehr-GEHN-yah hahm). USA. **Smithfield ham.**

viroflay (ve-roh-fla). Fre. Indicates the use of **spinach** in the dish; usually spinach balls used as a **garnish** accompaniment.

vis (vis). Dut. Fish.

viskoekjes (fisch-KOOK-yus). Dut. Fish cakes.

vispgrädde (VISP-greh-der). Swe. **Whipped cream.**

vitela (ve-TEL). Por. **Veal.**

vitello (ve-TEHL-loa). Ita. **Veal.**

vitello tonnato (ve-TAHL-loa toan-NAA-toa). Ita. The classic dish of cold **veal marinated** in **tuna sauce.**

vitkålsoppa med kroppkakor (vit-KOAL-sop-pah mayd KROP-kah-kor). Swe. **Cabbage soup** with **dumplings.**

vitling (VIT-ling). Swe. **Whiting,** a fish.

vitlök (vit-lok). Swe. **Garlic.**

vitsås (VIT-soass). Swe. **White sauce.**

vitt bröd (vit brohd). Swe. White bread.

vla (vlah). Dut. **Custard.**

vlees (vlays). Dut. Meats.

voi (voa). Fin. **Butter.**

voileipäpöytä (VOY-LAY-pa-PUH-ew-tah). Fin. Cold table; an assortment of foods in the Scandinavian tradition. Same as **smörgåsbord.**

voileivät (VOY-LAY-voa). Fin. **Sandwiches.**

voileivät lämpimät. (VOY-LAY-voa lahm-pe-moa). Fin. Hot **sandwiches.**

voileivät kylmät. (VOY-LAY-voa kel-moa). Fin. Cold **sandwiches.**

vol-au-vent (vohl-o-vahn). Fre. **Baked** pastry filled with various **sauced** meat, fish, or **poultry** mixtures.

volaille (vo-lahy). Fre. **Fowl, chicken, poultry.**

volière, à la (vohl-yahr, ah lah). Fre. **Game** birds served decorated with their plumage.

vongola (VONG-goa-lay). Ita. **Clam.**

voorgerechten (VOR-her-rekten). Dut. **Canapés; appetizers.**

voorjaarssla (FOAH-yah-slah). Dut. Spring **salad.**

vorshmack (VOR-shmahk). Fin. A dish of **ground mutton, beef,** and **salt herring** cooked with **garlic** and **onions.**

Vorspeisen (FOAR-shpigh-zern). Ger. **Hors d'oeuvre;** first course.

vörtbröd (VURT-brewd). Swe. Maltbread.

vørterkake (VURR-ter-KAA-ker). Nor. Spice **cake.**

vørterøl (VURR-ter-url). Nor. A nonalcoholic **beer.**

vrucht (vrookh). Dut. **Fruit.**

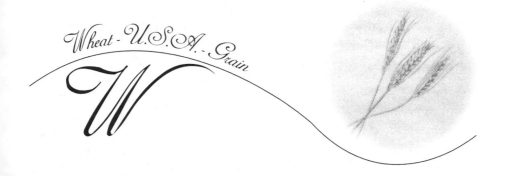

Wachsbohnen (VAHKS-boa-nern). Ger. Yellow, or **wax, beans.**

Wachtel (VAHKH-terl). Ger. **Quail.**

Waffeln (VAH-fehln). Ger. **Waffles.**

waffle (WAH-fuhl). USA. A crisp **cake** of a thin **batter,** baked between two special heated plates giving a honeycomb surface; eaten with sweet or savory toppings.

Wähen (VAY-en). Ger. Swiss open-faced **tarts** filled with **fruit, vegetables** or **cheese;** usually large.

wakame (WAH-kah-meh). Jap. A lobe-leafed **seaweed,** prized for its flavor and texture; available dried or fresh; used as **salad** ingredient and in **soups;** high in nutrition, no calories.

wakegi (wah-KAHY-ghe). Jap. Young, very mild **green onions.**

Waldorf salad (WAHL-dorf SAH-lahd). USA. A **salad** of **chopped apples, celery,** and **walnuts,** mixed together with **mayonnaise.**

Waldmeister (VALT-mye-stehr). Ger. The herb **woodruff.**

walleye pike (WAHL-i pik). USA. A freshwater fish of the **perch** family, with firm, white, fine-textured flesh; native of North American lakes.

Walnuss (VAL-noos). Ger. **Walnut.**

walnut (WAHL-nuht). USA. The edible cream-white **nut** of a tree indigenous to Asia, Europe, and North America; eaten plain, **pickled;** in sweet or savory dishes; an oil is extracted from the nutmeats; a **liqueur** called brou is made from the **husks.** Varieties are black walnut, butternut, English walnut, hickory nut.

wan dòu (wan doh). Chi. **Peas.**

waraq (WAH-rah). Ara. Leaves used in **mihshi,** such as **grape, Swiss chard,** and **cabbage.**

Warmbier (VERM-ber). Ger. Hot **beer soup.**

Warshawski's Syr (Vahr-shahw-skee'z sehr). Pol. A cow's-milk **cheese,** semifirm, pure white, has a wine-like flavor.

wasabi (wah-SAH-be). Jap. Green **horseradish;** used to make a seasoning **sauce;** one of the strongest spices and unique to Japan; has a biting, fresh, cleansing taste; accompanies sushi and other raw fish dishes.

Washington (wahsh-eng-tohn). Fre. A **garnish** of **corn** with **cream sauce.**

Wasser (VAH-sserr). Ger. Water.

wassil (WAH-suhll). Bri. A hot, spiced punch, usually served at Christmas time.

water chestnut (WAH-tehr CHEHS-nuht). USA. The fruit of a long-stemmed water plant, whose starchy fruit has a crisp texture and delicate taste; used many ways.

water ice (WAH-tehr is). USA. A **frozen dessert** of **fruit purée** or juice and flavoring; is smooth without addition of **egg** white; **sherbet, granita, spuma.**

watercress (WAH-tehr-crehss). USA. A peppery, slightly pungent plant with dime-sized dark green glossy leaves that grows in shallow streams; used as **herb,** in **salads,** and as **garnish.**

waterless cooking (WAH-tehr-lehss KOOK-eng). USA. Cooking slowly in a pot with a very tightly fitting lid, with about one table-spoon of water of liquid.

watermelon (WAH-tehr-mehl-luhn). USA. The large, oblong, roundish **fruit** of an African vine; has a hard green rind, plain or striped; pinkish-red or yellow pulp with black seeds.

wax beans (wahx bens). USA. A **kidney bean** whose pods turn creamy yellow when ready to use as **snap beans.**

weakfish (WEK-fesch). USA. A fish of the **drum** family, often mistaken for **trout;** has lean, sweet, delicate flesh.

Weinkraut (VINE-krowt). Ger. **Sauerkraut** and **apples** simmered in white wine.

Weisse Bohnen (vighs BOA-nern). Ger. **Butter beans.**

Weisse Rüben (vighs REW-bern). Ger. **Turnips.**

Weissbier (VIGHS-ber). Ger. White **beer** from Bavaria.

Weissbrot (VIGHS-broat). Ger. White bread.

Weisserübe (VIGHS-roo-be). Ger. **Turnip.**

Weissfisch (VIGHS-fiah). Ger. **Whiting.**

Weisskäse (VIGHS-kay-zeh). Ger. A soft **cottage cheese.**

Weisslacker (VIESS-slah-kehr). Ger. A **cheese,** pungent, soft or semi-soft, similar to **Limburger** but much milder; lustrous white crust.

Weissrüben (VIGHS-roo-behn). Ger. **Parsnips.**

Weisswurst (VIGHS-voorst). Ger. Delicate white **sausage** customarily eaten between midnight and midday in Munich; made of white **pork** and **veal,** flavored with wine and **parsley.**

Weizen (VYE-tsehn). Ger. **Wheat.**

well (wehl). USA. To make a well in flour is to make a hole in the middle of the mound to hold the liquid added.

Welsh cawl (wehlsh call). Bri. A Welsh dish similar to a **New England boiled dinner,** but with **mutton;** has **potatoes, cabbage, meat,** possibly **carrots.**

Welsh rabbit (Welsh RAR-beht). Bri. Melted **cheese,** usually mixed with **milk, ale,** or **beer,** and served over **toast** or **crackers.**

Wensleydale (WEHNS-sle-dal). Bri. A cow's-milk **cheese** in both white and blue; the white is aged three to four weeks, flaky, moist, and mellow; the blue is aged four to six months, smooth, sweet, nutty, moderate veining.

Wentelteefjes (VEN-tul-tayf-yus). Dut. **French toast.**

Werder (Vehr-dehr). Ger. A semi-soft, cow's-milk **cheese,** shaped like **Gouda;** has a mildly acid flavor, softer and not so sharp as **Tilsiter.**

western (WEHS-tehrn). USA. A sandwich of white bread or toast, whose filling is an omelet made with **chopped ham, green pepper,** and **chopped onions.**

Westfälischer Schinken (west-FAIL-ish-churl SHIN-kern). Ger. **Ham** made from acorn-fed pigs; lightly **smoked, cured,** uncooked, and served in paper thin slices with pumpernickel; rivals **prosciutto, Bayonne,** and **Smithfield hams** in quality.

Westminister (wehst-MEN-es-stuhr). Bri. **Lymeswold cheese;** the name used for export.

Westphalian ham (wehst-fal-e-uhn hahm). USA. The famous German **ham Westfälischer Schinken.**

wheat (whet). USA. A **cereal grain** used throughout the world in making **flours.** Major USA varieties and forms are:

bran (brahn). outer covering of the kernel, used to make **cereals;**

bulgur (BUHL-gehr). ground whole **kernel,** called **wheat pilaf;**

cracked wheat (krahkd whet). crushed **whole wheat kernels;**

durum wheat flour (DUH-rum whet flowr): high in **gluten,** ground to make **semolina** for **pasta;**

hard red spring wheat flour (hahrd rehd sprehng whet flowr): high in protein and **gluten,** excellent bread flour;

hard red winter wheat flour (hahrd rehd WEHN-tehr whet flowr): thinner **kernel** than **hard red spring,** flaky, moist, and good bread flour;

soft red winter wheat flour (sawft rehd WEHN-tehr whet flowr): starchier than **hard wheat;** good pastry flour;

wheat-germ flour (whet-jehrm flowr): made by pulverizing **wheat germ** to the **powder** stage; toast slightly before using.

wheat germ (whet jehrm). USA. The embryo of the **wheat kernel,** separated in milling process; rich in vitamins.

whelk (wellk). USA. A **mollusk,** distantly related to the **conch** and **abalone;** delicious meat.

whip (whehp). USA. Beat rapidly to incorporate air and expand the ingredients.

whip topping (whehp TOHP-eng). USA. A commercial product containing mostly vegetable oils that are used as a substitute for **whipping cream.**

whipped cream (whehpd krem). USA. Cow's **milk cream** that has been beaten rapidly until it stands in stiff peaks.

whipping cream (WHEHP-eng krem). USA. Cow's **milk cream:** two types—light, which has 30–36% milk fat; and heavy, which has 36–40% milk fat.

white asparagus (whit ahs-SPAH-ah-guhs). USA. Similar to green **asparagus,** but stalks are white because they have not been exposed to sunlight during cultivation.

whitebait (WHIT-bat). USA. Very small **herring** and **sprat fry;** usually **dipped** in **batter** and **deep-fried** without being cleaned.

white butter sauce (whit BUHT-tuhr saus). USA. **Beurre blanc.**

white cake (whit kak). USA. **Cake batter** in which all ingredients are white and uses only the whites of **eggs.**

white chocolate (whit CHO-ko-layt). USA. Tastes like **chocolate,** but is not a chocolate because it contains no **cocoa;** made of **cocoa butter, milk** solids, and **sugar;** used in **confectionery.**

whitefish (WHIT-fisch). USA. A small freshwater fish related to the **salmon** and **trout;** has delicate white meat, and is often **smoked;** its **roe** is used as a **caviar** substitute.

white meat (whit met). USA. **White pork.**

white mustard (whit MUSS-sturd). USA. A European **salad** green, with small tender green leaves; used in **salad** or as a **garnish.**

white onion (whit UN-yun). USA. Any of several varieties of globe **onions** with white flesh and translucent papery covering.

white pork (whit pohrk) USA. The flesh of swine that are killed by complete bleeding; also called **white meat.**

white sapote (whit sah-PO-te). USA. A **fruit** that looks like a misshapen baseball with edible green skin that has a yellow blush when mature; flesh is white or yellow; texture is that of soft **pear custard.** Also called **custard apple** and **cherimoya.**

white sauce (whit saus). USA. A **sauce** made from a **white roux** with **milk; béchamel, velouté,** also thin, medium, thick, and very thick white sauces.

white vinegar (whit VEHN-eh-gahr). USA. Dilute distilled alcohol fermented to a 4% acetic acid count; used in cooking and **pickling;** maintains the color of the **vegetable** or **fruit.**

whiting (WHIT-eng). USA. A **hake** of the **codfish** family; most often referring to the **silver hake.**

whole milk (hol melk). USA. Cow's **milk** that contains at least 3.25% milk fat, and at least 8.25% protein, lactose, and minerals; will form a **cream** line as the cream rises to the top; not homogenized.

whole-grain flour (hol-gran flowr). USA. Ground and pulverized **cereal grains,** such as **wheat, oats, barley,** or **rye,** using the entire, complete grains.

whole wheat flour (hol-whet flowr). USA. Ground and pulverized **wheat grains,** using the entire, complete grain.

whortleberry (HWEHRT-ehl-beh-re). Bri. European **blueberry.**

Wiener Backhendl (VE-ner BAHK-heng-dehl). Ger. **Chicken** breaded and **deep-fried,** Vienna-style.

Wiener Schnitzel (VE-ner Schnit-sel). Ger. **Veal scallop** dipped in **flour,** beaten **egg,** breadcrumbs, then **fried** in fat; served without a **sauce;** *Wienerschnitzel.*

wienerbrød (VE-nerr-brurdh). Dan. "Vienna Bread', which the Danes call their own Danish pastry.

Wienerschnitzel (VE-nehr-shnit-serl). Ger. Same as **Wiener Schnitzel.**

Wienerwurst (VE-nehr-voorst). Ger. **Frankfurter sausage.**

wijn (vayn). Dut. Wine.

Wild (vilt). Ger. **Game.**

wild rice. (wiyld ris). USA. Not a true **rice;** a **grain** native to North America; a distant cousin of common rice; high in protein and carbohydrate; parched, hulled and polished during milling.

Wildbrettpastete (VILT-bret-pah-stay-ter). Ger. **Venison pie.**

wilde eend (vilt aynt). Dut. Wild **duck.**

Wildgeflügel (vilt-geh-FLOO-gerl). Ger. Feathered **game.**

Wiltshire (Wehlt-shur). Bri. A **Cheddar**-type **cheese,** very sharp, crumbly.

Wilstwermarsch (Vel-stehr-masch). Ger. A **cheese** made of cow's milk with a mildly acid flavor; similar to **Tilsiter.**

Windbeutel (VINT-boy-terl). Ger. **Cream puff.**

wine vinegar (wiyn VEHN-e-gahr). USA. Sharp **vinegars** diluted with red or white wine; usually has a 5% acetic acid content.

wineberry (WIYN-beh-re). USA. A small acid-tasting red **raspberry** of Oriental origin.

winkle (WEN-kl). Bri. **Periwinkle;** a small, snail-like freshwater **mollusk; roasted** or **boiled** in shells; known as *bigorneau* (French), *tamakibi* (Japan), *burrie* (Portugal), *bígaro* (Spain).

wintergreen (WEHN-tehr-gren). USA. An evergreen native to North America whose deep green, round aromatic leaves are used as a flavoring.

winter melon (WEHN-tehr MEHL-uhn). USA. Usually smooth-skinned, striated, little or no netting; little or no aroma; best known varieties are **Casaba, Crenshaw, honeydew, Persian.**

Wisconsin Longhorn (Wehs-KOHN-sehn LOHNG-horn). USA. A **Cheddar cheese** that is medium-sharp in flavor, excellent for cooking.

witlof (WIT-lof). Dut. **Belgian endive; chicory;** used **braised, au gratin,** in **salads.**

witte bonen (VIT-tuh BOH-nuh). Dut. White **lima beans.**

wohn yee (won ye). Chi. A crinkly dried black fungus; same as Japanese **kikurage.**

won ton (wahn tahn). USA. **Hún tún;** a Chinese **noodle** wrapper with a savory **stuffing,** folded in a small triangular shape, then fried for use as **entree,** or simmered in **broth** for **soup;** also spelled **wonton.**

wong nga bok (wong yoh by). Chi. **Celery cabbage;** a solid, oblong head of wide, celery-like stalks ending in frilly, pale-green leaves; has a delicate celery-cabbage taste.

wood ear (wuhd eehur). USA. **Yún er;** an irregularly-shaped Chinese fungus used in Chinese cooking for its interesting texture. Also known as **tree ear, cloud ear.**

woodruff (WUHD-ruff). USA. An **herb** whose leaves are used dried or fresh to flavor teas, drinks and punches; its delicate flowers flavor **May wine.**

wop salad (wohp SAH-lahd). USA. A salad of **lettuce** with **olives, anchovies, oregano, capers, garlic,** and **olive oil.**

worcestershire (WUS-tehr-sher). Bri. An **anchovy**-based **sauce** to use on meats; usually bottled; similar to the Italian **garum.**

wormwood (WUHRM-wuhd). USA. An **herb** whose toxic leaves give **absinthe** its potency and **anise** its flavor; its delicate flowers give **vermouth** its taste.

worst (worst). Dut. **Sausage.**

worteles (VAWR-tuls). Dut. **Carrots.**

wu hsiang fun (oo SHEONG fen). Chi. A **five-spice** seasoning; a variable mixture of **star anise, fennel** seeds, **clove, cinnamon,** and Sichuan **peppercorns** or **licorice** root; very spicy.

Wurst (voorst). Ger. **Sausage.**

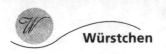
Würstchen (VOORST-khern).   Ger. Little **sausage.**

Würstelbraten (voorst-terl-BRAA-tern).   Ger. **Roast beef larded** with **frankfurters.**

Würz (voorts) Ger. Seasoning; spice.

Würzfleisch (VOORTS-flighsh).   Ger. A beef **stew** with **sour cream sauce,** served with **dumplings** or **potatoes.**

Xiangjiao - Chinese - Banana

xarope (shah-ROU-puh).   Por. **Syrup.**

xató (ZA-toh).   Spa. A winter **salad** of **endive**, red chili **peppers, garlic, almonds,** oil, and **vinegar.**

xérèz (she-REHS).   Por. **Sherry.**

xia (sia).   Chi. **Shrimp.**

xiang cài (sian tsai).   Chi. **Coriander.**

xiangjiao (siang-jiao).   Chi. **Banana.**

xiangsxu ya (siang-soo ya).   Chi. Crispy **duck.**

xiangyóu (siang-yoh).   Chi. **Sesame** oil.

xiao lóng bao (shiao loong bao).   Chi. Small **steamed** buns.

xié (sieh).   Chi. **Crab.**

xiè ròu dòufù (sieh row doh-foo).   Chi. Fresh **crabmeat** mixed with **soy paste.**

xigua (ssi-gwah).   Chi. **Watermelon.**

xihóngshì (ssi-hung-shi).   Chi. **Tomatoes.**

Xihu cuì yú (ssi-hoo tsui yu).   Chi. West Lake crispy fish.

xin xian de (sing sian de).   Chi. Fresh.

xìngrén dòufù (sing-ren doh-foo).   Chi. **Almond gelatin.**

xingzi (sing-dze).   Chi. **Apricot.**

xiz jiao (sia jiao).   Chi. **Shrimp dumplings.**

xoconostle (soh-koh-NOHS-tleh).   Mex. Green prickly **pear.**

Ying-táo - Chinese - Cherries

ya (yah). Chi. **Duck.**

yablochnyi (YAHB-lah-ku). Rus. **Apple.**

yakhni (YAHF-ne). Ara. **Stew;** refers to dishes made with **potatoes** as the main ingredient.

yakhni (YAHK-ne). Ind. Meat **broth.**

yaki hamaguri kushisashi (yah-KE hah-MAH-goo-re koo-she-sah-SHE). Jap. **Baked** white **clams** on **skewers;** a canned product.

yaki soba (yah-KE soh-bah). Jap. A type of instant **soup noodle.**

yakimono (yah-KE-moh-noh). Jap. **Broiled foods.**

yakitori (yah-KE-toh-re). Jap. **Grilled chicken** and **vegetables** on small **skewers.**

yam (yahm). USA. A root **vegetable** whose high starch content makes it a valuable food source throughout the world; has yellow or white flesh, brown skin, and is often mistakenly called **sweet potato.**

yama no imo (yah-MAH no E-mo). Jap. Mountain **yams;** long, beige in color, hairy; mild, pleasant flavor.

yàn cài (yan tsai). Chi. **Bird's nest;** dried nests, either black or white, are soaked in water to restore their gelatinous texture and used to **garnish soups** at banquets and special occasions; very expensive.

yángrou (YANG-row). Chi. **Mutton.**

yao dòu (yao doh). Chi. **Kidney beans.**

yaoguo jiding (yao-guo je-ding). Chi. **Diced chicken garnished** with **cashew nuts.**

yaourt (yah-oort). Fre. **Yogurt.**

yard-long-beans (yahrd-lohng-bens). USA. Bright **Chinese green beans,** about a foot long; flavor stronger than ordinary green beans. Also called **long beans, dow ghok, asparagus beans, sassage.**

yari-ika (yah-ke-e-KAH). Jap. **Grilled squid.**

yarrow (YAH-row). Bri. Fine lacy leaves used as an **herb** or for **tea.**

yasai (yah-sah-e). Jap. **Vegetables.**

yeast (yest). USA. A microscopic fungus that induces **fermentation,** releasing carbon dioxide, important in making bread, **cheese, beer, wine;** a leavening agent; two types: compressed and active dry.

yellow cake (YEHL-o kak). USA. **Cake** made from **batter** in which **egg yolks** are used.

yellow eel (yehl-o el). USA. One name for ocean **pout,** a fish of the eelpout family whose flesh is sweet, white, and has few bones.

yemas de San Leandro (YEM-ah deh sahn le-AHN-dro). Spa. **Egg-yolk** threads poured into hot **syrup** and twisted into sweets.

yemitas de mi bisabuela (yeh-MAH-tahs day me be-sah-BOH-lah). Mex. **Egg yolks, sherry,** and **syrup** formed into balls and rolled in **cinnamon sugar.**

yen wo (yehn woh). Chi. **Yàn cài; birds' nest.**

yerba maté (yehr-bah MAH-ta). Spa. **Maté;** an aromatic beverage made from the leaves and shoots of a South American holly rich in caffeine.

yezi (yeh-dze). Chi. **Coconut.**

ying-táo (ying-tao). Chi. **Cherries.**

yoghourt (YOGH-ourt). Swe. **Yogurt.**

yoghurt (YAH-hurt). Dut. **Yogurt.**

yoghurt (YOGH-oort). Dan. **Yogurt.**

yogur (YOA-goor). Spa. **Yogurt.**

yogurt (YO-guhrt). USA. Ewe's or cow's milk fermented with lactic culture, turning it slightly acidic and custard-like.

yogurt (e-OA-goort). Ita. **Yogurt.**

Yorkshire (YORK-shur). Bri. A **cheese** much like **Neufchâtel** when young—soft, creamy, bland; when aged it becomes sharp and zesty; excellent with **amontillado sherry.**

Yorkshire pudding (YORK-shur PUHD-deng). Bri. A popover **batter** mixture baked in drippings of the **roast;** traditional accompaniment for **roast beef.**

Yorkshire sauce (YORK-shur saus). Bri. **Red currant jelly** thinned with **port wine** and **grated orange** zest added.

youghurt (YOOG-ewt). Nor. **Yogurt.**

yóumèn sun (yoh-men sun). Chi. **Braised bamboo shoots.**

yuán báicài (yuan bai-tsai). Chi. **Cabbage.**

yóuyú (yoh-yu). Chi. **Cuttlefish.**

yú (yoo). Chi. Fish.

yucca root (YUHK-kah root). USA. A root **vegetable,** shaped like an elongated **sweet potato** with pink to brown skin and white flesh; has a starchy taste; use peeled in **soups, stews,** or **boiled** and served like **potatoes.**

yú chì (yu tsi). Chi. **Shark fin;** a delicacy, savored for its gelatinous texture.

yúchì tang (yu-tsi tan). Chi. **Shark fin soup.**

yukka (yuhk-kah). Tur. **Phyllo;** leaf-thin sheets of **dough,** made from **flour** and water; used for sweet and savory dishes by layering with **fillings.** Also known as **filo, brik, malsouka.**

Yule log (yul lohg). Bri. **Büche de Noël; genoise** or **sponge cake** decorated with **buttercream** to resemble a log.

yún er (yuhn ehr). Chi. **Cloud ear;** a fungus used for its interesting texture and colors. Also called **tree ear, wood ear.**

yúxiang ròusi (yu-siang row-sse). Chi. **Shredded** spicy-flavored **pork.**

yuzu (YOO-zoo). Jap. **Citron;** used almost entirely for its aromatic rind to flavor **soups,** simmered dishes, **pickles, relishes,** and sweet **confections.**

.

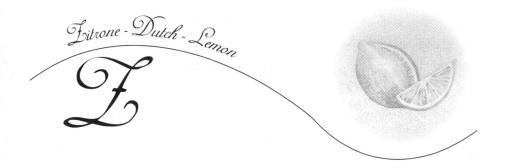

Zitrone - Dutch - Lemon

zabaglione (dzah-bah-LYOA-nay).   Ita. A frothy **dessert custard** flavored with **Marsala.**

zafferone (dzahf-feh-RAA-noa). Ita. **Saffron.**

zaffran (ZAH-frohn). Ind. **Saffron;** same as **kesar.**

zafra (ZAHF-frah).   Ara. Meat curds appearing when cooking meat in water.

zakuski (zah-KOOS-ke). Rus. **Hors d'oeuvres,** always accompanied by vodka.

zalm (zahlum). Dut. **Salmon.**

zampone (tsahm-POA-nay).   Ita. A highly seasoned **pork sausage** encased in the skin of a pig's foot; served **sliced.**

zanahorias (thah-nah-OA-ryahss). Spa. **Carrots.**

zanjabiyl (zahn-jah-BEL). Ara. **Ginger.**

zankha (ZAHN-kah).   Ara. A special "meaty" smell or feel associated with uncooked meat.

zaozi (dzao-dze). Chi. **Dates.**

zapallo (zah-PAHL-loh). Spa. **Calabaza.**

zarda (ZAHR-dah).   Ind. A sweet **rice pilaf,** with **nuts, raisins, saffron,** and spices.

zarzamora (thaht-thah-MOA-rahss). Spa. **Blackberry.**

zarzuela (thahr-THWAY-lah). Spa. A **seafood stew,** flavored with wine or liquor.

zactar (ZAHK-tahr).   Ara. Plant found in the Middle East used as seasoning; also refers to a seasoning blended from **zactar, thyme, majoram, simmaq,** and **salt.**

zayt (zeyt). Ara. Oil.

zaytun (zey-TOON). Ara. **Olives.**

zayt zaytun (zeyt zey-TOON). Ara. **Olive oil.**

zanahoria (sah-nah-OH-ryah). Mex. **Carrot.**

Zeeland oysters (ZE-lahnd OYI-sturs). USA. Very fine **oysters** from Zeeland Province of the Netherlands; sweet, succulent.

zeevis (ZAH-ves). Dut. **Seafood.**

zensai (ZEHN-sah-e). Jap. **Appetizers.**

zenzai (ZEH-zah-e). Jap. A chunky, sweet **soup** used as a pick-me-up and a **dessert soup.**

zènzero (DZEHN-dzeh-roa). Ita. **Ginger.**

zephire (za-fer). Fre. A small oval-shaped **forcemeat dumpling,** a kind of **quenelle, poached** and **served** with a rich **sauce.**

zephyr (ZEH-fuhr). USA. A very light, airy, delicate **cornmeal** puff, served with **salad** or **luncheon.**

zeppole (tse-POHL-lah). Ita. A kind of **doughnut.**

zest (zehst). USA. The outer rind of **citrus fruit** which is thinly pared off (without pith) for flavoring and **garnishing.**

zeste (zehst). Fre. The peel of **citrus fruits** which contains aromatic oil; used to flavor foods.

zhá (dzah). Chi. To **deep-fry.**

zhá gezi (dzah ge-dzi). Chi. **Deep-fried pigeon.**

zhá yú qíu (dzah yu chiu). Chi. **Deep-fried** fish squares, Sichuan style.

zhàcài tang (dza-tsai tang). Chi. Spicy **vegetable soup.**

zhangchá ua (dzong-cha ya). Chi. **Duck smoked** in camphor and **tea.**

zheng (dzeng). Chi. To **steam.**

zhi má yóu (dzai mah yoh). Chi. Chinese **sesame oil;** darker color, stronger taste than western sesame oil; used for seasoning.

zhi-má hú (dzi-ma hoo). Chi. **Sesame cream.**

zhoud (dzoh). Chi. **Porridge.**

zhou fàn (dzoh). Chi. **Congee rice.**

zhú (dzoo). Chi. **Pork.**

zhu jidàn (dzoo je-dan). Chi. **Boiled eggs.**

zhú rou (dzhoo row). Chi. **Pork** meat.

zibd (ZIB-dah). Ara. **Butter.**

zibeth (ze-beht). Fre. A variety of **chive** from tropical Asia; seasons **ragouts, salads, sauces.**

Ziegel (Ze-gehl). Aus. A cow's whole-milk cheese, sometimes with 15% **cream** added.

Zigeuner Art (tsi-GOY-nehr art). Ger. "In the gypsy style."

Zigeunerspies (tsi-GOY-nehr-shpes). Ger. A **kabob** of meat cubes, **peppers,** and **onions, grilled** over open fire.

zik de venado (thek day bay-NAH-dhoa). Mex. **Shredded** cooked **venison;** served with **onions,** hot chili **peppers, cilantro,** and **Seville oranges.**

zimino (tse-ME-noa). Ita. **Fish stew.**

zimt (tsimt). Ger. **Cinnamon.**

Zimtplatzchen (tsimt-PLETS-khehn). Ger. **Cinnamon cakes.**

zingara (zen-gahr-rah). Fre. Gypsy style; a garnish of **julienne** of **ham, tongue mushrooms, truffles** in **demi-glace,** with **Madeira, tomato purée,** and **tarragon.**

ziste (zest). Fre. The bitter white pith found in **citrus fruits** just under the peel.

ziti (TSET-te). Ita. Large tube **pasta** cut in pieces.

Zitrone (tsi-TROA-ner). Ger. **Lemon.**

zitronenschaum (tsi-TROA-ner-showm). Aus. **Lemon** foam, frothy **dessert.**

Zomma (Zoh-mah) Tur. A plastic curd, **Caciocavallo-type cheese** that is very like **Katschkaval.**

zosui (ZOO-swe). Jap. **Rice gruel** made from leftover, already cooked rice.

zout (zowt). Dut. **Salt.**

zucca (TSOOK-kah). Ita. **Squash; pumpkin.**

zucchini (zoo-KEN-ne). Ita. A slender green or green-striped **summer squash** about five inches long; known worldwide as **marrow** or **marrow squash.**

zucchero (TSOOK-kay-roa). Ita. **Sugar.**

zuccoto (tsook-KOHT-toa). Ita. A **dessert** of dome-shaped **cake,** sprinkled with **liqueur,** filled with **whipped cream, chocolate, nuts.**

Zucker (TSUK-kerr). Ger. **Sugar.**

Zuckererbsen (YSUK-kerr-ehr-psern). Ger. **New green peas.**

Zuckerrübe (TSUK-kerr-rewb). Ger. Sugar **beet.**

Zuckerwähe (TSUK-kerr-vaier). Ger. Swiss **sugar tart.**

Zuger Kirschtorte (TSUK-kerr KERSH-tor-ter). Ger. A Swiss **Kirsch-**soaked **cake** frosted with pink **sugar.**

zumo (THOO-mo). Spa. Juice.

Zunge (TSUN-ger). Ger. **Tongue.**

Zungenwürst (TSUN-gerr-voorst). Ger. **Tongue sausage.**

zuppa (TSOOP-pah). Ita. A **soup,** usually **vegetable,** meat or fish, poured over **fried** or oven-**toasted** bread.

zuppe di pesce (TSOOP-pah dee PAY-shay). Ita. The generic name for fish **soup.**

zuppa inglese (DZOOP-pah eng-GLAY-say). Ita. A type of **trifle;** rum-soaked **sponge cake** layered with **custard** and **cream.**

zuppa rustica (TSOPP-pah roo-STEK-kah). Ita. A hearty, peasant-style **soup** with **potatoes, beans,** and **sausages.**

zuurkool (ZEWR-kohl). Dut. **Sauerkraut.**

Zwetschgen (TSVEH-tsh-gern). Ger. Damson **plums.**

Zwetschkenknödel (TSVEH-tsh-kern-knur-derl). Ger. An Austrian **plum dumpling dessert.**

zwieback (TSVE-bahk). Ger. **Toasted bread,** crisp and slightly sweet.

Zwiebeln (TSVE-berln). Ger. **Onions.**

Zwiebelgrün (TSVE-berl-grewn). Ger. **Scallion.**

Zwiebelkuche (TSVE-berl-koo-ker). Ger. **Onion tart.**

Zwischenrippenstück (TSVI-shehn-RIP-pern-shtayk). Ger. **Rib** steak.

zwitserse kaas (SWEHT-seh-zer KAI-zer). Dut. **Swiss cheeses: Gruyère** or **Emmenthal.**

zwitserse karbonade (SWEHT-seh-zer KAHR-bohn-ahde). Dut. **Swiss steaks.**

Wine Terms

acetic (ah-SE-tehck). All wines contain some acetic acid; any wine with an excessive amount will have a vinegary smell; has a thin, white film on the surface.

acidity (ah-SIHD-eh-te). Natural acidity provides a fresh, **lively** taste; excessive acidity makes the wine **tart** and sour, and renders the wine unfit to drink.

aftertaste (AHF-tehr-tast). The taste that lingers in the mouth after the wine is swallowed. The longer a pleasant taste lingers, the finer the quality of the wine.

aging (AG-eng). The time needed to bring a wine to its prime for drinking.

aggressive (ah-GREH-sehv). Applies to wines with high **acidity,** harsh **tannins,** or both.

Aglianico (Ahg-le-ah-NE-kah). An Italian **grape** used to produce red wines such as *Aglianico del Vulture* and *Taurasi.*

aigre (I-greh). An acidic taste or undertone.

Albana (Ahl-BAH-nah). An Italian **grape** used to produce semisweet white wine.

Albanello (Ahl-bah-NEHL-loh). A Sicilian **grape** that produces a white wine, high in alcohol, and is at times **dry** and coarse, yet sometimes sweet.

aldehyde (AHL-de-hid). A liquid byproduct of alcohol **fermentation** which is volatile, colorless, and pungent.

Aleatico (Ahl-le-ah-TE-koh). An Italian **grape** of the Muscat family that produces a sweet red wine.

Alicante-bouschet (Ah-le-KAHN-tah Bou-shay). A red-wine grape used to produce cheap, bulk wine in Algeria, France, Spain, and California.

Aligoté (Ah-le-GAH-tah). A widely grown, highly productive **grape** of France that produces a short-lived white wine of little distinction.

amontillado (ah-mohn-tel-LAH-doh). A matured **fino sherry,** naturally **dry;** generally sweetened to be mellow in taste.

angelica wine (ahn-JEHL-eh-kah wiyn). A sweet **dessert** wine produced in California.

angular (AHN-gu-lahr). Lacks roundness and **depth.**

Ansonica (Ahn-SOHL-ne-kah). A Sicilian white-wine **grape** used to make Corvo and Marsala.

apéritifs (ahp-re-TEFS). Drinks before a meal.

Aramon (Ah-RAH-mohn). A very productive French and Californian **grape** that makes a low-grade red wine used for **blending** with other wines.

aroma (ah-ROA-mah). The smell of a relatively young wine before it has had time to develop its smell; in a mature wine it is called **bouquet.**

astringent (ah-STREHN-gent). **Harsh** and coarse to the taste because of the amount of **tannin** in the wine; a **dry** quality.

Aurora (or Aurore) (a-ROAR-a, oh-ROAR). Pale yellow **grape** that turns a spectacular pink at harvest; produces a white wine; usually semisweet, can be **dry;** rather neutral when young, takes on a distinct flavor when aged in oak such as a cross between American **Chablis** and **Sauterne.**

austere (aw-STER). A **hard, dry** wine that lacks richness, needs **aging.**

Baco Noir (BAH-ko NWAHR). Blue-black, early-ripening hybrid **grapes** of French-American descent make full-bodied, deep red wine; of **Cabernet Sauvignon** descent, Baco grapes produce wine that ages well.

balance (BAHL-lahnc). The harmonious concentration of **fruit,** level of **tannins,** and **acidity** creating symmetry; wines with good **balance** tend to age gracefully.

Balthazar (bahl-THAH-zahr). Extra-large **champagne** bottle that holds 16 regular bottles or 415 ounces.

Banyuls (bahn-YULZ). Sweet **dessert** wines: reds, **rosés,** and whites.

Barbera (Bahr-BAR-a). A California **grape** of northern Italian descent that makes a robust, deep red, Italian-style wine with a fresh, quite **tart** and **fruity** taste; when aged is very mellow but puckers the taste buds.

barnyard (BAHRN-yawrd). An unclean, farmyard, fecal aroma caused by unsanitary wine-making facilities or unclean barrels.

beeswing (BEZ-wehng). A type of deposit sometimes found in **port,** so named because of the veined pattern it forms.

berry-like (BEH-re-lik). Wines that have intense berry characteristics, such as suggests **blackberry, mulberry, strawberry.**

Biancolella (Beh-ahn-koh-LEHL-lah). A white-wine **grape** of Italy used to produce Ischia Bianco.

big (behg). A full-bodied wine that gives an intense feel on the palate.

Black Hamburg (Blahk HAHM-behrg). A black **grape** of Germany occasionally used to produce wine of poor taste and color.

blackcurrant (blahk-KERR-hent). The smell commonly associated with red Bordeaux wines; varies in intensity.

blanc (blawnk). White.

Blaue Spatburgunder (Blaoh Spaht-buhr-GOON-dehr). Red-wine **grapes** of Baden-Wurttemberg, Germany that produce the best red wine of the area.

blended (BLEHN-dehd). The mixing of wines from different regions, or the addition of **brandy** or rectified alcohols as in **fortified** wines.

blush (bluhsh). A more savory wine than **rosé** with less color incorporated from **grape** skins.

body (BAH-de). The weight and fullness of the wine as it crosses the palate.

Boal Madeira, also Bual Madeira (Bah-ole Mah-DEH-drah). One of **Madeira's** principal wine **grapes;** greenish in color, but produces the fine, golden wine for which **Madeira** is famous.

Bombino Bianco (Bohm-BE-noh Be-AHNK-kah). A white-wine **grape** of Italy used to produce **Trebbiano** d'Abruzzo and San Severo Biaanco.

Bombino Nero (Bohm-BE-noh NEH-roh). A red-wine **grape** produced in Italy used to make Castel del Monte.

Bonarda (Boh-NAHR-doh). A red-wine **grape** of the Piedmoint Region of Italy.

Botrytis cinerea (boh-TRE-tes sin-eh-RE-ah). **Noble rot,** a fungus that attacks **grapes,** forming a mold that concentrates their flavor and sugar, producing sweet wines, high in alcohol and with a unique **bouquet.**

bottle-age (BOWT-tl-ajgd). The length of time a wine is kept in a bottle, rather than in a cask.

bottle-sickness (BOWT-tl-SEHK-ness). Usually a temporary setback in the wine's flavor lasting for weeks or months after bottling, a result of the filtration and bottling.

bottle-stink (BAHT-tl-stenk). A bad smell that eminates from an old bottle upon opening; almost always dissipates instantly; not to be confused with corky.

bouquet (bo-KAY). The distinctive and characteristic fragrance or smell of a matured wine; technically different from **aroma,** which applies to a young wine.

brawny (BRAW-ne). A muscular, hefty, full-bodied wine; has plenty of flavor and weight; inelegant and unrefined.

breathing (BRETH-eng). What a wine does upon decanting it for a few hours.

breed (bred). Great distinction and polish in describing a wine impeccably made from very good vineyards.

briary (BRY-ah-re). **Aggressive,** rather than spicy.

brilliant (BRYLL-yuant). A wine of clear color, not hazy or cloudy.

browning (BROWN-eng). When red wines age, their color changes from a ruby/purple through various color changes to ruby with a brown edge; they are then fully matured and not likely to get better.

Brunello di Montalcino (Broo-NELL-o de Mownt-tahl-CHE-roh). A red-wine **grape** in the Tuscany region of Italy that is used to produce wine by the same name.

brut (broot). Extremely **dry;** unsweetened; a term used to describe **Champagne.**

Burger (BURR-gehr). A Hungarian white wine **grape** that produces wine which is rather dull and low **acidity;** used to make cheap grades of California "chablis" and "sauterne."

Burgundy (BUHR-guhn-de). A generic term as used in the USA for any blended red table wine; as used in France, it is red wine of **Pinot Noir** grapes or white wine made of **Chardonnay** grapes, both expensive grapes and not used to make the inexpensive burgundies of the USA; usually **dry, mellow,** and **soft;** can be sweet; an everyday wine with many different tastes.

butt (buht). A **sherry** or whisky cask holding approximately 491 litres or 519 quarts.

Cabernet Sauvignon (Kahb-ehr-nay SO-ven-you). In the Bordeaux region of France, this great, small, thin-skinned, black **grape** produces the world's most celebrated wines; in the cool coastal regions of California, these vines produce wines so fine they have a respected place in the wine world; an aged Cabernet Sauvignon produces a **deep,** rich wine that is **velvety smooth,** but when young can be rather **harsh** and bitter.

Cabernet Franc (Kahb-ehr-nay Fronc). A more productive variety of the **Cabernet grape** that produces scented wines.

Canaiolo Nero (kahn-ah-O-loa NE-ro). A red-wine **grape** of Tuscany, Italy used to make **Chianti.**

carafe (kah-RAHF). A stopperless container used to decant wine and serve it at table.

Carignane (CAR-e-nyon; incorrectly pronounced "Kerrigan"). A red wine **grape** with no distinctive flavor of its own; grown extensively in Spain, southern France, and California; used to help stretch wine yield from scarcer grapes; taste is **dry** and a bit **fruity;** the addition of **Merlot** gives it a more interesting flavor.

cask (kahsk). A wooden barrel used for storing wine and spirits.

Catarratto (Kah-tah-RAHT-to). A Sicilian yellow **grape** used to produce wine for blending wines such as Marsala.

Catawba (Kuh-TAW-buh). Native eastern purplish-red **grape** that produces red, white, or pink wine; used to make **sparkling** wines as well as **still** wines; sweet with a strong grapy flavor and **aroma.**

caudalie (KAU-dur-le). The length of time the aftertaste lingers in the mouth.

cedar (SE-dahr). The smell of cedarwood, faint or overt, usually part of the **bouquet** of Bordeaux reds.

Chablis (shah-BLE). In the USA a pale, pale burgundy not to be confused with true *French Chablis*, which is a white Burgundy wine made from **Chardonnay** grapes, aristocrat of the dining table; *California chablis* is a blend of various white grape varieties which may include **French Colombard** and **Chenin Blanc** or **Delaware** and **Seyval Blanc** in Eastern chablis; is a **dry**, fresh, **fruity** white wine whose taste varies from winery to winery.

chambrer (SHAHM-bray). To bring wine to room temperature.

Champagne (sham-PAN). A white, pale-pale amber, or pale pink **sparkling** wine; variously described as **brut, extra-sec, sec, demi-sec;** in the USA *champagne* is a generic, all-inclusive name for **sparkling,** effervescent, fizzy white wines; also, sparkling burgundy (red) and **cold duck** (various colors).

Chancellor (CHAHN-sehl-lohr). A deep red, high-quality American hybrid **grape** that makes a dry, full bodied wine in the style of **Cabernet Sauvignon.**

chaptalization (shap-tahl-lee-zah-see-aw). The addition of **sugar** to **grape must** during **fermentation** to increase the alcoholic content.

character (KAHR-eck-tuhr). Indicates that a wine has a distinctive and individual stamp.

Charbono (Shar-bo-no). An Italian-style robust, red wine from California wine producers; quite pungent in flavor with body; **tart, dry;** when ages it is **softer.**

Chardonnay or Pinot Chardonnay (PEA-no SHAR-don-nay). The noblest **grape** variety for making **dry** white wines; makes magnificent but costly wine in Napa Valley, California, also grown in Burgundy, Central Europe, and Australia; produces a pale, straw-colored wine sometimes with a hint of green, and an **apple** or **peach** flavor; can be fresh and fruity when not aged in oak; one of the two most important grape varieties in the making of **Champagne.**

Chasselas (Chahs-soh-lay). A French table **grape** used to produce both red and white wines of common quality.

chateau (SHAH-to). Refers to the wine-producing properties in Bordeaux.

Chelois (SHELL-wah; Shell-OY). French-American hybrid **grapes** that produce a crimson, robust wine that is somewhat **harsh** when young; mellows in oak casks and the bottle.

Chenin Blanc (SHEN-in BLAWN). A white wine from grapes originally from Loire Valley of France, one of California's most delightful; taste is a little sweet, though normally **dry, fruity,** refreshing; has a perfumed **aroma.**

chewy (CHEW-e). Having a dense, viscous texture from a high glycerine content; wines of great vintages can often be **chewy.**

Chianti (Key-ON-te). A fine red wine in Italy, but in America quite ordinary, tending to be sweeter than burgundy; **smooth** and **mellow** ranging downward to bland; lacks a pronounced flavor.

Cinsaut (SAN-so). A red **grape** variety, also called Hermitage, that makes rich, **tannic,** sometimes slightly **jammy** red wine.

Clairet (Klahr-ray). Specially vinified red Bordeaux wines, soon ready to drink, without much color or **tannin;** have a very slight alcoholic content; can be consumed as innocently as lemonade.

Clairette Blanc (Klair-het Blawn). A French white-wine **grape** that produces a good quality neutral wine that is well balanced and pleasant.

Claret (KLAHR-eht). Red **table wine** of Bordeaux.

closed (klozd). Denotes that a wine is not showing its potential, which remains locked in because it is too young; **aging** up to a decade or so may be required.

cognac (KONE-yahk). French word for **brandy.**

Cold Duck (kold duhk). A combination of **sparkling** red and white wines; usually quite sweet; bubbly, even foamy; little distinct flavor; the "pop wine" of American **champagnes.**

Colombard (Koh-LUM-bahrd). A French **grape** that produces quality white wine that is **dry** and full-bodied; in California the wine is tart and well-balanced and is marketed as *French Colombard* or *Chablis.*

complex (KOHM-plex). A term to describe a wine whose taste never gets boring and is interesting to drink; has a variety of subtle scents and flavors to holds one's interest in the wine.

concentrated (KOHN-shin-tra-tehd). Denotes that the wine has depth and richness of fruit to give it appeal and interest.

Concord (KOHN-kord). A native American blue "juice-and-jam" **grape;** not a fine winemaking wine, heavy, sweet, red; very grapy of smell and taste; White Concord is made by removing the grape skins before fermentation.

Corinth (KOR-renth). An almost seedless Italian **grape** with thick-skin that yields an inferior wine.

corked (korkd). Flawed; wine has taken on the smell of a musty cork, resulting from an unclean or faulty cork; also referred to as **corky.**

Cornichon (Cohr-ne-shawng). A **grape** grown in France and California that produces an inferior wine with poor color and aroma.

Cortese (Cohr-TAH-ze). Grown in Lombardy, Italy, this **grape** yields a superior quality white wine that is fresh, light and pale.

Corcino (Kor-VE-no). A red-wine **grape** grown in Veneto region of Italy.

coulant (koo-LAHN). "Flowing"; easy-to-drink wines.

crémant (kreh-mawng). Indicates a degree of sparkle, between **perlant** and **mousseaux.**

crust (kruhst). A heavy deposit found in some bottles of vintage **port.**

De Chaunac (Duh-show-NOK). A French hybrid **grape** used for making red and rosé wines that tend to be light in color unless blended; aging in oak casks improves the flavor.

deep (dep). A rich, full-bodied, mouth-filling wine; synonymous with **concentrated.**

Degoutant (Deh-goo-tawng). A medium-sized black French **grape** that yields an ordinary red wine.

Delaware (DEL-ah-wehr). This native Delaware, Ohio **grape** has pinkish-red fruit that yields white juice used for blending of Eastern **sparkling** wines; pale golden in color; dry or semisweet; pleasantly **soft** and **fruity.**

delicate (DEHL-e-kuht). A light, subtle, understated, shy wine; usually white wines.

demi (DEH-me). Half.

demijohn (DEH-me-john). A large bottle encased in wickerwork and holding at least a gallon.

demi-sec (DEHM-me sehk). Relatively sweet; too sweet for most palates; a term to describe a **champagne.**

deposit (deh-POHS-eht). Fallout from chemical changes that give high-quality wines maturing in bottle greater character, **complexity,** and **bouquet.**

Diana (Di-AHN-nah). An American **grape** that produces a wine light in color.

diffuse (deh-FUSZ). Unstructured and unfocused smell and taste; warm red wines often diffuse.

disgorge (dehs-GOHRJ). The **champagne** method of making **sparkling** wines; at one point the bottle has to be opened to remove a deposit of yeasty sediment.

Dolcetto (Dohl-SEHT-ta). An Italian **grape** that produces a soft, red wine that matures quickly.

domaine (doa-main). Refers to the wine-producing properties in Burgundy.

dosage (DO-sauge). Sweetening added to **sparkling** wine before the final corking.

double-magnum (DUH-bull-MAHG-num). A four-bottle bottle; holds three liters.

dry (dri). The opposite of **sweet.**

dumb (duhm). A dumb wine is a **closed** wine, but whereas a closed wine may only need time to reveal its richness and intensity, a dumb wine will never get better.

Dutchess (DUH-chehs). American native **grape** with yellow-green fruit; has an agreeable **fruity** taste with a lingering aftertaste; usually moderately sweet; does not have the unwanted "grape jelly" **aroma** and flavor.

earthy (UHRTH-e). A positive aroma of rich, clean soil, rather than **woodsy** or **truffle** scents.

Elbling (Ehl-beng). The German version of the **Burger grape;** yields a full, flat wine of poor quality; it goes into cheap, **sparkling** wines.

elegant (ELL-eh-gahnt). Graceful, splendid, high-quality; unmistakable, but indefinable.

Elvira (El-VI-rah). An American native hybrid **grape** that produces a fresh and attractive white wine with a "foxy" **aroma.**

Emerald Riesling (M-ehr-rawld REZ-ling). A variety of **grapes** developed at University of California at Davis; not a true **Riesling;** crisp, clean, refreshing, has a touch of sweetness; a very good, inexpensive white wine.

Erblauce (E-BLU-che). A **grape** grown in the Italian Piedmont which produces **passito** (a sweet dessert wine).

extra-sec (X-tra sehk). Slightly sweetened; a term describing a **champagne.**

extract (x-STRAHK). Soluble solids from the **grape;** contributes to the weight and fullness of the wine.

exuberant (x-ZOO-behr-rahnt). Gushy, nervous, vigorous.

fat (faht). A super sort of maturity; **fat** wines are quite rich with low **acidity.** If a wine is being too fat, a flaw, then it is called **flabby.**

Feber Szagos (Feh-behr Zohs). A **grape** that originated in Hungary that is grown in California and is used to make **sherry.**

fermentation (fehr-mehn-TA-shun). The conversion of **grape** juice into wine through the process of converting sugar into alcohol by action of certain **yeasts** present in the juice.

feuillette (feh-yet). A **Chablis** barrel.

fiasco (ve-ASK-ko). A **Chianti** flask.

fine (fin). Denotes overall quality.

finesse (fe-NESS). Implies subtlety and distinction.

fining (FIN-eng). A method of clarifying wine by pouring a coagulant on top and letting it settle to the bottom.

finish (FEHN-esh). The final taste left after swallowing the wine.

fino (FE-no). The finest **sherry, delicate, dry,** pale.

flabby (FLAHB-be). A wine that is too **fat,** lacks structure, tastes heavy.

Flame Tokay (Flame To-KAY). Important as a table **grape,** this grape is used in California to make sweet wines, both red and white.

fleshy (FLEHSH-e). Synonymous for **chewy** or **meaty;** has lots of **body,** alcohol, and extract and has a high glycerine content.

fliers (FLY-ehrs). Specks of sediment.

Flora (FLOW-rah). An American hybrid white **grape** based on the **Gerürztramiener** stock, which is quite "flowery" and pleasant.

floral (FLOW-ruhl). Having a flowery **bouquet** or **aroma.**

Foch or **Maréchal Foch** (Mar-ay-shahl FOSH). Of Alsatian France origin, these blue-black hybrid **grapes** produce a superior garnet wine that is subtle; harsh and biting when young, but a softer, hearty wine emerges with **aging** in oak and bottle; somewhat spicy in flavor.

focused (FOH-kuhssd). The scents, aromas, and flavors are precise and clearly delineated.

Folle Blanche (Foa-yeah Blahnk). A California **grape** that produces wine which is light and crisp; in France this grape has been traditionally used to make **cognac.**

fortified (FOUR-teh-fid). Wine to which **brandy** or rectified alcohol has been added, sometimes halting **fermentation** before all the **sugar** is converted into alcohol.

forward (FOR-wahrd). A wine that fully reveals its charm and character.

Freisa (Freh-ZE-ah). An Italian red-wine **grape** used to make a dry, fruity wine; also used in a slightly sweet, slightly **sparkling** wine.

Fresia (Frehz-E-ah). American mispelling of the Italian **Freisa grape** often seen in California.

French Colombard (French ko-LOHM-bahrd). A prolific white wine **grape** in California that makes a delicious everyday pale, green-gold wine; juicy, fresh, **light,** enjoyable.

fresh (frehsh). Cleanly made and lively.

frizzante (freh-SAHN-te). Slightly **sparkling,** as opposed to **spumante,** which is fully **sparkling.**

fruity (FROO-te). Said of a wine that has the pleasant taste and **aroma** of **fruit;** a vague term.

full-bodied (fuhl-BOHD-ehd). Rich in **extract,** alcohol, and glycerine; feels weighty and substantial in the mouth.

Fumé Blanc, Blanc Fumé, Napa Fumé. (Foo-may BLAWN). Alternate names for **Sauvignon** Blanc; **fumé** means "smoked" in France; in USA Fumé Blanc is not smoked, nor is it smoky in taste or appearance; a delightful, very **dry** white wine.

Furmint (Fehr-mehnt). The famous Hungarian white-wine **grape** used in making **Tokay;** in California and Germany this grape is high in sugar and gives a high alcohol content.

Gamay, Napa Gamay, Gamay Noir. (Gam-MAY NWAR). In California these red wine **grapes** are descendants of the true Gamay grapes of the French Beaujolais region, and related to the **Pinot Noir** grape of French Burgundy; Gamay wine needs no **aging** and is best consumed fresh; taste is **light, fruity,** fresh, and pleasant; "happy wine."

Gamay Beaujolais. (Gam-MAY BO-zho-lay). A **Pinot Noir** grape, not a Beaujolais; often very fresh and fruity, for immediate consumption; some are labeled "nouveau" or "primeur" and are to be consumed in six months of **fermentation;** other Gamay Beaujolais will keep well two to three years.

Gargenega (Gahr-gahn-NE-gah). A white-wine **grape** of Italy's Veneto region used to produce Gambellara and Soave.

Gewürztraminer (Geh-vertz-tru-MEAN-er, or as in France, Geh-woors-tra-mean-AIR). A pinkish-blue **grape** with tough-skin of the French Alsace region and the USA West Coast; a little sweet in USA; fairly **dry** in France; decidedly spicy; unmistakably "perfumy."

Giro (E-roh). A Sardinian red-wine **grape** that produces a **dessert** wine similar to a light **port** called Giro Cagliari.

Greco (Greh-koh). An Italian white-wine **grape** grown near the toe of the Italian peninsula.

green (green). Made from underripe **grapes;** lacks richness and generosity; **vegetal** in character.

Green Hungarian (gren Huhn-GAHR-e-uhn). A white **grape,** not from Hungary, that is fairly bland, yet pleasant; also used in blends for **California chablis;** fruity and fragrant; a white wine most people like.

Grenache (Greh-NAHSH). Dark, reddish-purple **grapes** that make a light red wine; from Provence region in France, and also Spain; used in California as a blending wine, and for **rosé** wines; deliciously **fruity** and fresh; should be **dry** rather than **sweet.**

Grey Riesling (Gra Reez-ling). An American white wine grape (not a true **Riesling** and not to be confused with the German Schloss Johannisberg wine family) that makes a **soft** wine that is agreeable, usually pleasantly **dry.**

Grignolino (Gren-yo-LEAN-o). Italy's Piedmont district produces this **grape** that gives a light-bodied, **light** red wine with piquant flavor and perfumed **aroma;** used as a **rosé** wine in California; color is unusual— it is tinged with **orange;** aroma of flowers and fruit, dry, tart, pungent.

Grillo (GRE-yoh). A white-wine **grape** of Sicily used in the production of Marsala.

gris (grez). Pale, pinkish-red.

Gropello (Gro-FEHL-loh). An Italian red-wine **grape.**

Gutedel (GOOT-dehl). A German **grape** that produces an ordinary **table wine.**

hard (hahrd). Abrasive, astringent with **tannins,** high **acidity;** a young vintage can be hard but should never be **harsh.**

harmony (HAHR-mo-ne). Balanced attributes; a highly desirable quality.

harsh (harsh). Too **hard,** a flaw in the wine.

herbaceous (hehr-BAY-shush). Has a distinctive herbal smell; usually **thyme, basil, fennel, lavender, rosemary,** and **oregano.**

Hermitage (air-me-tahj). A South African red **grape** variety, also called Cinsault, that makes a rich, **tannic,** sometimes slightly **jammy** red wine.

hollow (HOHL-low). Shallow, dilute, lacks **depth** and **concentration.**

honeyed (HOHN-ned). Has the taste and smell of honey.

hot (hoht). Too high in alcohol content, leaving a burning sensation in the back of the throat when swallowed; usually above 14.5% alcohol content.

hybrid (HIY-brehd). A cross between French and American vines; used for hardiness.

Iona (I-O-na). A native American red-purple **grape** that produces a white wine; in New York it is used to make **champagne.**

Ives (eyevz). A native American **grape;** yields a red "foxy" flavored wine; in New York state it is used in Burgundies and **sparkling** wines.

jammy (JAHM-me). Has a great intensity of fruit from excellent ripeness; very concentrated; flavorful with superb **extract.**

Jeroboam (jeh-ruh-BOW-uhm). Large wine bottle with the capacity of four ordinary bottles, about ⅘ of a gallon.

Johannisberg Riesling (Yo-HON-iss-berg REZ-ling). Also called **White Riesling.** Both names refer to the noble grape of Germany's Mosel and Rhine Rivers; these small green grapes make what is considered one of the two best white wines in the world (the other is **Chardonnay**); as these grapes ripen they may be afflicted with **noble rot** which causes the grapes to shrivel and concentrates the juices, making the wine rich and luscious; young and fresh **White Riesling** has a clean fruity taste with floral **aroma;** Late Harvest White Riesling is heavier of body, richer, and a honeyed fragrance, and is best served alone without food.

kosher wine (KOA-shur win). Wine for Jewish religious occasions made under the supervision of a rabbi, usually very sweet.

Labrusca (Lah-BRU-skah). A native American **grape** (vitis labrusca) that produces a wine quite "grapey" in flavor with a bit of fizz.

Lagrein (Lah-grain). An Italian Tyrolian **grape** used to make red and **rosé** wines.

Lambrusco (Lahm-BROO-sko). An Italian **grape** that produces a very bright, dry red wine with slight sweetness, and a thick but short-lived sparkling froth.

leafy (LE-fe). Smells of **leaves,** rather than **herbs; vegetal** or green.

lean (len). Slim, streamlined; lacks generosity and **fatness;** can still be pleasant and enjoyable.

lees (lez). The solid residue left in the cask after drawing off the wine.

legs (lehgs). The rivulets that run down the side of a wine glass after swirling indicating, when pronounced, that the wine is rich in **body** and **extract.**

length (lenkth). Long; relates to a wine's finish. Its presence is sensed long after being swallowed, from thirty seconds to several minutes; a very desirable trait.

light (lit). Having a low degree of alcohol, or lacking body.

liquoreux (le-quor-roh). A wine that is rich, sweet, and strong, as a **Sauterne.**

lively (LIV-le). Fresh, exuberant; a young wine of good **acidity;** has a thirst-quenching personality.

long (lohng). **Length;** relates to a wine's finish; its presence is sensed long after being swallowed, from thirty seconds to several minutes; a very desirable trait.

lunel (loo-NEHL). A sweet **dessert** wine with a delicate **bouquet.**

lush (luhsh). Velvety, soft, richly fruity; **concentrated** and **fat;** never **astringent** or **hard.**

Madeira (Mah-DEH-rah). One of the great wines of Portugal; the American cousin bears little resemblance to the Portugese; it is heavy, sweet, **fortified,** and dark.

maderisé (ma-dar-e-zay). Refers to the brown color and flat taste of a white wine that has been overexposed to air during production or maturation, giving an aroma and flavor reminiscent of **Madeira** wine.

Malbac (Mohl-baahk). An excellent French red-wine **grape** of the Bordeaux that is well-balanced and often used for blending.

Malvasia Bianca (Mul-va-ze-a Be-AHN-ka). Of the family of **Muscat grapes;** used to make "Malmsey," a famous **fortified** wine of the island of **Madeira;** rich, heavy, "ripe fruit" fragrance of **Muscat grapes;** originally grown in Greece.

Malvoisie (Mahl-voz-e-zay). French for **Malvasia.**

marc (mahr). The pulpy mass of grape skins and pips that remain after the fermented grapes are pressed. Also refers to the **brandy** made from this pulpy mass.

Marsanne (Mahr-sahn). A French **grape** of the Rhone Valley used for blending; used alone it produces a coarse, badly balanced white wine, inferior even to **Burger.**

massive (MAHS-sehv). High degree of ripeness and superb **concentration;** full-bodied and rich.

Mataro (Mahr-TAH-roh). A Spanish **grape** that is black and is grown in California; it produces a coarse red wine used for **blending.**

May Wine (ma win). A semisweet **appetizer** wine of light **body.**

meaty (MET-te). **Chewy, fleshy.**

Merlot (mar-LO). A very fine red wine **grape;** once grown for blending with **Cabernet Sauvignon;** today, in California it is used to make a varietal red wine; a rich, ruby wine with **herb**-like overtones in its **fruity** flavor.

Methuselah (Meh-THUS-eh-lah). A large **champagne** bottle whose capacity equals eight normal bottles.

Mission (MEH-shion). A European **grape** introduced in California by Mission Fathers in the 19th century which produce very sweet wines; used today to make **port** and Angelica.

moelleux (mweh-luh). **Sweet, soft, rich.**

monbazillac (maw-baz-ze-yak). A sweet, golden wine.

Montepulciano (Moht-tah-puhl-che-AHN-noh). A good red-wine **grape** of Southern Italy that produces a wine of passable quality.

Moursetel, mourastel (Moos-seh-tehl).   Grown chiefly in California, this red-wine **grape** yields a wine of undistinguished quality that is pleasant, **soft,** but common.

mousseux (moos-sur).   **Sparkling;** not usually used for first-class wines.

mouth-filling (mowth-FIHL-eng).   Big, rich, concentrated with fruity **extract;** high in alcohol and glycerine; **chewy, fleshy, fat.**

Muller-Thurgau (Meu-lehr-Thur-gau).   A cross between the **Riesling** and the **Sylvaner,** this German **grape** variety yields a pleasing, low-acid white wine.

Muscadel, Muscadelle (Mus-kah-DEHL).   A French white-wine **grape** of the Bordeaux that is used to blend with sweeter whites.

Muscadine (MUS-kah-din).   A native American **grape** used in making **Scuppernong** wine.

Muscat, Moscato, or Moscatel (MUS-kaht, Mus-KAHT-o, or MUS-kaht-tel).   **Muscat grapes** produce a wide variety of white or amber wines with alcohol contents from 11–12% (unfortified, usually dry) to 17–18% (**fortified,** always sweet); flowery and fragrant with **aroma** of "ripe fruit."

must (muhst).   Unfermented grape juice or crushed grapes.

nature (NA-chur).   Means that nothing has been added, in particular, **sugar.**

Nebbiolo (NEHB-be-eh-lo).   An Italian red-wine **grape,** also grown in California, Switzerland, and Uruguay, which is a moderately **sweet, dry wine.**

Nebuchadnezzar (nehb-uh-kahn-NEHZ-zahr).   The largest of **champagne** bottles; holds the equivalent of 20 ordinary bottles.

nerveux (nehr-vo).   Implies fineness with firmness and vitality, a term of praise.

Niagara (Ni-AHG-rah).   Light green native Eastern **grape;** makes a pale yellow wine; quite **fruity;** "grape juicy."

noble rot (NO-bul roht).   See **Botrytis cinerea.**

nose (noz).   Smell, whether **bouquet** or **aroma.**

nouveau (neu-vo).   The wine of the last harvest, during its first winter.

oaky (OK-e).   A toasty, **vanillin** flavor and smell to the wine, imparted by new oak barrels.

off (owff).   Not showing its true character; flawed, spoiled in some way.

oeil de perdrix (uhy der pehr-dre).   "Eye of the **partridge**"; describes the pink color of certain **rosé** wines, some pink **champagnes,** and whites with a pinkish tinge.

oloroso (o-loh-ROH-soh).   One of two basic types of Spanish **sherry.**

ordinaire (or-de-nahr).   Inexpensive, common; of unknown or unstated origin.

overripe (O-vehr-rip). From **grapes** left too long on the vine causing loss of **acidity;** produces **heavy,** imbalanced wines; not a desirable characteristic.

oxidized (OHX-eh-dizd). Excessively exposed to air during making or **aging** causing loss of freshness; gives old, stale smell and taste.

palo cortado (PAHL-o kor-TAH-doh). A rare and excellent style of **sherry;** between **fino** and **oloroso.**

Palomino Fino (Pahl-ah-ME-no Fe-no). This Italian and Californian **grape** is the classic and finest grape for producing **dry** or sweet **sherry.**

passito (pah-SE-toh). An Italian sweet **dessert wine;** made from grapes that have had a short drying period after picking.

Pedro Ximenez (PAY-dro YIM-e-nez). Spanish **grapes** that are very sweet and yield a fine, **dry** white wine with a high alcohol content; for **sherry** making, these grapes are sun-dried, pressed, then fermented to produce a very sweet wine used as the sweetening agent.

pelure d'oignon (peh-lewr on-yawng). "Onion skin," a description of the pale, orange-brown color of certain **rosé** wines and some old red wines.

peppery (PEHP-pehr-re). Has **aroma** of black pepper and a pungent flavor.

perfumed (PEHR-fumd). Fragrant, aromatic; has strong perfume smell.

perlant (payr-yaw). Showing a little sparkle; less than **crémant** and much less than **mousseux.**

Perricone (Pehr-re-KOHN-nay). A red-wine **grape** of Sicily used to produce the wine Corvo Rosso.

pétillant (pay-te-yaw). Having a natural sparkle; less than a **perlant** wine.

Petite Syrah, Petite Sirah (Puh-TET Sear-RAH). A heavily pigmented **grape** once thought to be the **Syrah** grape of the Rhone Valley in France, but now believed to be the **Duriff** grape; widely grown in California; makes a full-bodied deep-colored varietal wine that ages well; **light** and **fruity;** can be very **astringent** when young, but smooths out when aged; a pungent, **peppery** flavor; very **aromatic.**

Pinot Blanc (Pe-no BLAWN). A white wine **grape** of excellent quality; **dry** with a faint hint of **apple, pear,** or **melon.**

Pinot Chardonnay (Pe-no SHAR-don-nay). American designation for **Chardonnay,** though not related to the **Pinot** group; produces some of California's finest white wines.

Pinot Gris (Pe-no Gre). A grayish rose **grape** of Germany, Alsace, and Italy that yields some distinguished wines, but also others that are low in acid and rather flat.

Pinot Noir (Pe-no NWAR). One of the two grape aristocrats (the other being **Cabernet Sauvignon**) from which the world's finest red wines are made; needs several years **aging** in cask and bottle; **silky** and **complex** in character, perfumed **aroma;** taste of ripe **plums.**

Pinot Saint George (Pe-no Sahnt Gorg). An inferior California **grape,** not a true **Pinot,** which yields an ordinary red varietal wine often labeled "Red Pinot."

Pinotage (pe-no-tahjgze). A **grape** that makes wines with highly individual taste and **aroma;** is a crossing of **Pinot Noir** and **Hermitage** (Cinsaut); found in South Africa and New Zealand.

Piquepoul (Pek-ah-poul). This **grape** of the French Armagnac country yields a **thin,** acidic wine, as well as an outstanding **brandy.**

plastering (PLAHS-tehr-eng). Boosting the acid content of a wine, usually **sherry,** by the addition of calcium sulphate.

plonk (plohnk). Slang for everyday wine.

plummy (PLUHM-me). Smell and taste of ripe **plums.**

ponderous (POHN-dehr-us). **Heavy** and tiring to drink.

Port (pohrt). A **fortified wine,** both red and white forms, produced in northern Portugal and matured in Vila Nova de Gaia; California Port is produced in three basic styles: white, which has a fruity **aroma** and golden color; tawny, which is amber-colored; and ruby, deep red and **fruity .**

Portugieser (Pohr-tuh-GAY-zah). A German red-wine **grape.**

pricked (prihkd). The unpleasantly sharp quality caused by too much volatile **acidity.**

Prosecco (Pro-SEHC-koh). An Italian **grape** of the Veneto region that yields a fine white wine.

pruney (PROO-ne). Has character of **prunes,** is a flawed wine.

punt (puhnt). The hollow mound inside the bottom of certain wine bottles.

racking (RAHK-eng). Transferring fermented wine from one cask to another to separate it from its lees.

raisiny (RAY-sihn-e). A late-harvested wine with character of **raisins;** desirable in some **ports** and **sherries,** a major flaw in other wines.

rasteau (rass-to). Sweet, amber, **fortified** wine; similar to a light, white **Port.**

ratafia (rah-TAH-fyah). **Brandy** mixed with sweet unfermented **grape** juice.

Refosco (Re-FOSS-koh). An Italian red-wine **grape** that has been transplanted to California; yields an ordinary burgundy.

Rehoboam (Re-ah-BOH-um). A large **champagne** bottle holding the capacity of six normal bottles.

remuge (ray-mew-ahz). A technique for removing the deposit in **champagne** without removing the sparkle by shaking and progressively inclining the bottle until the sediment is on the cork, then removing the cork and extracting the deposit.

réserve (ray-sehrv). An uncontrolled term implying superior quality.

Rhine (Rin). A white wine with a fresh, juicy flavor; a good base for white wine punch.

Rhine Riesling (Rin Rez-lehng). One of the classiest white **grape** varieties in the world; makes wine that can be slightly sweet to very sweet.

rice wine (ris win). Wine made from the **grain rice** instead of **grapes;** called **saké;** technically a **beer.**

rich (rehch). High in **extract,** flavor, and intensity of the **fruit.**

riddling (REHD-leng). Same as **remuage.**

Riesling (REZ-ling). The classic, white-wine grape of Germany; produces small, yellow, round **grapes** that turn red-brown at maturity; produces the best German wines; successfully transplanted to California and produces "White Riesling" or "Johannesberg Riesling"; also see **Emerald Riesling** and **Gray Riesling.** This classic grape is also grown in Chile, Austria, and Italy.

ripe (rip). **Grapes** have reached the optimum level of maturity.

Rondinella (Rhon-deh-NELL-o). A second rank Italian red-wine **grape** used to produce Bardolino and Valpolicella.

Rosé (Ro-ZAY). Pink wine made from black grapes pressed quickly to allow only the slightest tinge of color, varies from pale, pale pinks to deep, almost-red pinks; the finest are **dry, fruity,** fresh tasting, but may be sweet.

rosso (roh-soh). Red.

rouge (rooug). Red.

round (rawnd). Fully matured, having lost youthful, **astringent tannins;** a very desirable character.

Ruby Cabernet (ROO-be Kab-er-NAY). A **grape** that makes very good ordinary red wines; **dry, fruity,** and refreshing; an everyday wine, not an elegant wine; very pleasant.

Rulander (Roo-LAHN-dehr). German designation of the **Pinot Gras grape.**

Salmanazar (SAHL-mah-nah-zuhr). Third largest size of **champagne** bottle; holds 12 normal bottles.

Salvador (SAL-vah-dor). A California red-wine **grape** used to make **port.**

Sangiovese (Sahn-joh-VEY-zeh). An excellent quality red-wine **grape,** it is the most widely planted red grape variety in Italy; it produces **Chianti** as well as San Gioveto, Elba Rosso, Torgiano Rosso, Riviera del Garda.

Sangria (San-GRE-ah). Essentially a Spanish "lemonade" with a red wine base flavored with a blend of **citrus,** usually **lemons** and **oranges;** may use white wine.

Sauterne (saw-TEHRN). A sweet, white wine of Bordeaux region of France. In California this is a generic term for wines with quite variable results; sometimes sweet but usually **dry.**

Sauvignon Blanc (SO-ve-nyawn BLAWN). An excellent white wine of classical quality; dry, crisp, aromatic, a little spicy, very fruity, sometimes smoky; also known as **Fumé Blanc** and **Blanc Fumé.**

Sauvignon Vert (SO-ve-nyawn Vehrt). A white-wine **grape** of California.

savory (SAY-vah-re). Denotes a round, sweet, flavorful, and interesting wine.

Scheurebe (Shor-RAY-be). A white-wine **grape** grown in the Rheinhassen area of Germany.

Schiava (SHE-vah). An excellent Italian red-wine **grape** that yields early maturing wine that are low in **tannin** and light in color.

Schwarzriesling (Schahrtz-res-zleng). A German white-wine **grape.**

Scuppernong (SKUHP-perr-nohng). A native American **grape** with a strong, somewhat bitter flavor; looks and tastes like **sherry,** being light amber color and sherry-like **aroma.**

sec (sehk). **Dry** or fermented out. In describing **champagne** it means sweet. When describing other wines, it means **dry** or unsweetened.

sediment (SEHD-eh-mehnt). Solid matter deposited in the bottle during maturation, nearly always a good sign.

Semillon (SAY-me-yawn). An excellent white **grape** used to blend with **Sauvignon Blanc** to make the great, lusciously sweet wines; some plantings in California; fruity, often has an aroma of ripe **figs;** when mixed with Sauvignon, makes top sweet **Sauternes.**

Seyval Blanc (SAY-voll BLAWN). French-American hybrid **grape;** makes excellent white wine (**Chardonnay** is in its parentage); good when young and fresh; tastes crisp, fresh, and **fruity;** has **aroma** of **apples.**

shallow (SHAHL-lo). Weak, feeble, watery, lacking **concentration.**

sharp (shawrp). Bitter, unpleasant with **hard,** pointed edges.

Sherry (SHEHR-re). Sherry is a **fortified wine;** there are two types: **dry sherry** to be used as an **appetizer** before meals, and **cream sherry** which is a **dessert** wine; dry sherry has a rich, **heavy** flavor tasting of **nuts** or woody from its casks; cream sherry is sweeter, but not overwhelmingly so; both fill the mouth with wine **aromas** and **bouquets.**

silky (SIHL-ke). Velvety, lush; sometimes **fat,** but never **hard** or angular.

Shiraz (sheh-rahz). A grape variety of the northern Rhône that makes big, dark wines of depth; also called Syrah.

smoky (SMO-ke). Has a distinctive smoky characteristic, because of soil or barrels used to age the wine.

soft (sawft). Round, fruity, low acidity; absence of **aggressive, hard tannins.**

sparkling (SPAHR-kleng). Has undergone a secondary **fermentation** in vat or bottle and has become effervescent through the formation of bubbles of carbon dioxide gas.

spicy (SPI-se). Aromas of **pepper, cinnamon,** and other well-known spices.

spritzer (SPEHT-zehr). White wine diluted with **soda** or **mineral water.**

spumante (spoo-MAHN-te). Fully **sparkling.**

stale (stal). Dull, **heavy** wines that lack balancing **acidity** for freshness or are oxidized.

stalky (STAHL-ke). Synonymous with **vegetal;** green character.

still (stihl). Nonsparkling, as are the majority of table wines.

sulphur (SUHL-fuhr). When the flavor of sulphur is present in a wine, it is due to the careless use of this common disinfectant for wine, which is used to destroy harmful bacteria.

supple (SUHP-pul). **Soft, lush, velvety, round** and **tasty;** a highly desirable characteristic.

Sylvaner (Syl-VAHN-ner). A superior white-wine **grape** of German origin; transplanted to California and Chile; yields a wine that is lighter, softer, and shorter-lived than the **Riesling.**

Syrah (se-rahz). A **grape** variety of the northern Rhône that makes big, dark wines of depth; Also called Shiraz.

table wine (TA-bul win). Any nonfortified wine.

tannin (TAHN-nehn). A substance of grape skins, stalks, and pips; gives the wine firmness, roughness when young; gradually falls away and dissipates with age; important in wine to be matured over a long period.

tart (tahrt). **Sharp, acidic,** lean, unripe; not pleasurable.

tartaric (tahr-TAHR-eck). A naturally occurring acid in **grapes** and the main constituent of the **acidity** in wine.

tawny (TAHW-ne). **Port** aged in wood until it has acquired a warm, sandy color.

thick (thehk). **Rich, ripe, concentrated,** low in **acidity.**

thin (thehn). **Shallow,** watery, lacking in body; diluted; an undesirable characteristic.

Thompson Seedless (TAHM-son sed-less). A renowned table **grape** that is used to make **sherry** in California.

tightly knit (TIT-le neht). Wines that are tightly knit have good **acidity** levels, good **tannin** levels, and are well made. They have yet to open up and develop.

Tinta Cao (TEHN-tah CAH-o). A red-wine **grape** of Portugal used to produce **table wines;** in California this grape produces wine used in **port.**

Tinta Madeira (TEN-tah Mah-der-rah). This **grape** is part of the same family as **Tinta Cao** that is grown chiefly in **Madeira;** used to produce red **table wines** and sweet **dessert** wines.

toasty (TOAS-te). The smell of **grilled toast;** aged in barrels that are charred or toasted on the inside.

tobacco (to-BACK-kah). Scent of fresh burning tobacco; a distinctive and wonderful smell in wine.

Tokay (to-ka). An American **grape** that produces a wine based on an original Hungarian wine; **heavy,** sweet, **fortified;** similar to **Madeira.**

Traminer (Thdrahm-meh-ner). A white-wine grape of the Rhine Valley, the Tyrol, and California; produces a **soft** white wine with a trace of sweetness and a distinctive **aroma.**

Trebbiano (Trehb-be-AHN-no). An Italian white-wine **grape** that produces a good but not distinctive wine; grown in France and California; it is the white wine of **Chianti,** plus other labels.

Trollinger (Trahl-eng-gehr). A German red-wine **grape** that produces a rather **light** wine.

Trousseau (Tru-so). A red-wine **grape** that produces Bastardo of Portugal; in California is used to produce **port;** in France yields a dry red **table wine** while in California the wine is **tawny** and has a low acid content.

Ugni Blanc (Uh-ne Blawn). A white-wine **grape** also called **Trebbiano** that gives a wine that is a well-balanced, sound wine; used to make **Cassis** and, in California, **Chianti.**

ullage (UHL-lahg). The amount that a container lacks of being **full;** the air space above the wine.

unctuous (UNK-choo-us). **Rich, lush,** intense with layers of **concentrated,** soft, velvety fruit, such as **Sauternes.**

Uva di Troia (OO-vah day Tray-yah). An Italian white-wine **grape.**

Valdepenas (Vahl day-PEHN-yahs). Spanish red-wine **grapes** that produce wines of moderately good quality; also planted in California with similar results.

varietal (vah-RI-ah-tuhl). Wine that is named after the **grape** variety from which it is made.

Verdicchio (vehr-DEK-key-o). An Italian white-wine **grape** of superior quality.

Verdot (Vehr-do). A small black **grape** of France that produces full-bodied, deep bodied, slow-maturing wines.

Verduzzo Friulano (Vehr-DUZ-zoh Fre-oo-LAHN-no). Italian white-wine grapes of the Veneto and Friuli-Venezia-Giuia regions.

vegetal (VEHG-eh-tahl). Smell of stems from green, unripe **grapes;** undesirable characteristic, a major flaw.

Veltliner (Veht-LEHN-ner). An Austrian white-wine grape that produces a wine of lesser **bouquet** and flavor.

velvety (VEHL-veht-te). **Lush, silky, rich, soft, smooth** to taste; a desirable characteristic.

Vermouth (Ver-MOOTH). An **appetizer** wine of two kinds: **dry,** which is white and highly perfumed with **herbs** and spices, and sweet, which is red and **mellow.**

Vernaccia (Vehr-nahc-CHE-ah). A white-wine **grape** of Sardinia that produces an unusual wine that is dry, aromatic, and high alcohol content.

Vespaiolo (Vehs-pie-OH-lah).   An Italian white-wine **grape** of the Veneto region.

Vespolina (Vehs-poh-LE-nah).   An Italian red-wine **grape** of the Piedmont region.

Vidal Blanc (Ve-dahll BLAWN).   A French-American hybrid **grape** of excellent quality; makes white wine that is **crisp, dry,** fruity, refreshing.

Vignoles or Ravat 51 (Ven-yole or Rah-VAHT).   This **grape** has **Chardonnay** parentage; is a hybrid; makes light-bodied white wine that is **dry** and **crisp;** an excellent **appetizer.**

vin (vehn). Wine.

vin nouveau (vehn noo-vo). New wine, made to be drunk just after the vintage, such as Beaujolais.

vinho verde (veh-no vehr-de).   A light, tangy wine of Portugal. Verde refers to its newness, not its color, which can be reds or whites.

vintage (VEHN-tahj).   A vintage wine is one that bears the date of the vintage on the label.

viscous (VEHS-kos).   Relatively **concentrated, fat,** almost thick with a density of **fruit extract,** plenty of glycerine and high alcohol content; if **acidity** is balanced, can be very flavorful and exciting; if lacks **acidity, flabby** and **heavy.**

volatile (VOHL-eh-tehl).   Smells of **vinegar** caused by acetic bacteria; a serious flaw.

Walschriesling (wahlsh-re-slieng).   A grape grown in Central Europe of French origin; makes **soft,** easy to drink wines; not a **Riesling.**

White Burgundy (Whit BURR-gun-de).   An American white version of the generic burgundy; usually of higher quality than the red burgundy.

White Muscat (whit Muhs-kat).   A white-wine **grape** of California used to produce White Muscat.

wood-aging (wuhd-AJ-eng).   Maturation of wine in casks or barrels that permits minute amounts of air to interact with the components of the wine.

woody (WOOD-de).   Overly **oaky.**

yeast (yest).   Micro-organisms that produce **fermentation;** occur naturally in grape skins, but special **yeasts** are also used.

Zibibbo (Ze-BE-bow).   A white-wine **grape** of Sicily with the designation of Muscat of Alexanderia, used to produce Marsala.

Zinfandel (ZIHN-fahn-dehl).   A Californian red-wine grape that may be made in at least three ways: as a fresh, young wine; as a wine to be aged several years for complexity of flavor; and as a late-harvest wine for meal time; young and fruity, it has a berry-like flavor and aroma; aged, the **bouquet** is complex and suggests spices, **herbs, black currants.**

What to drink with cheeses

Appenzell light fruity reds, Merlot, Beaujolais

Asiago lively full-bodied Piedmontese reds

Banon dry delicate Provençal whites, reds or rosés, Cassis, Gigondas, Côtes de Provence, Chinon

Bel Paese light rosés, Valpolicella, Barbera, Chianti

Bleu d'Auvergne Saint Pourçain, Cornas, Châteauneuf-du-Pape

Blue Cheshire reds from Burdundy or the Médoc, Australian reds, Chilean Cabernet, port

Blue Stilton tawny port, good amontillado sherry, Dão, red Rioja, Barolo, Hermitage

Blue Wensleydat St. Emilion, lesser Médocs

Bondon Tourine Sauvignon, (Normandy) cider

Brick full fruity reds, beer

Brie Sancerre, Frascati, Médoc, Bordeaux reds, Côtes du Roussillon

Brinza beer

Caciotta Chianti

Camembert white Burgundy, Rhine wines, claret

Cantel Gaillac red, Chinon

Cheddar any red wine—the better the Cheddar the better the wine— Burgundies, Châteauneuf-du-Pape, Barolo, Zinfandel, tawny ports, beer, real ale

Cheshire Beaujolais Villages, Loire Gamay

Chévre French country reds

Coulommiers Nuits-St-Georges

Crottin Sancerre, Chablis

Danablu full-bodied reds, clarets, Burgundies, Rhône reds, Rioja

Edam light fruity reds or whites, beer

Emmental fruity reds or whites, Nierstein, Bourgogne-Mâcon, Champigny, Fendant

Esrom any light to solid red depending on age of cheese

Feta dry Greek whites, retsina, ouzo

Fontina Merlot, Pinot Grigio

Fourme d'Ambert Condrieu

Friese Nagelkaa beer, whiskey

Fromage Frais Soave, Anjou Blanc, Vinho Verde

Gammelost   strong reds
Gaperon   Corbières
Gjetost   strong black coffee, akevitt
Gorgonzola   Barbera, Barolo, robust Sardinian or Provençal reds
Gouda   Beaujolais Villages for young cheeses, full-bodied reds for mature ones, beer
Gruyère Rhône white or red, light fruity Neuchâtel, Pinot Noir
Handkäse   beer, cider, apfelwein
Havarti   dry light wines, lager
Herve   full-bodied reds, Cornas
Kashkaval   light dry whites, beer
Leiden   Beaujolais Villages, strong dry whites, gin, beer
Liederkrantz   powerful reds, Rhônes, Riojas, beer
Limburger   full-bodied reds, Châteauneuf-du-Pape, beer
Livarot   Morgon, Calvados, cider
Manchego   Rhône reds, Riojas
Maroilles   Champigny
Mascarpone   Moselle, light sweet whites
Mont d'Or   Cabernet
Monterey Jack   Chardonnay, light whites, dry reds
Mozzarella   Chianti
Munster   Gerwürztraminer, Pinot Noir
Mycella   strong full reds
Olivet   Gigondas, Morgon
Parmesan   Chianti, Lambrusco, Sangiovese
Peccorino   full Sicilian reds
Piora   Pinot Noir
Pont l'Evêque   Corbières, Côtes du Roussillon, cider
Port-Salut   white Rhône, Fronsac reds
Raclette   dry whites, Savoie Blanc, Fendant, beer
Reblochon   Beaujolais, Muscadet, Chablis
Rollot   St. Emilion
Roquefort   minor Sauterns, Monbazillac, Rhône reds
Royalp   fruity reds, rosés
Sage Derby   strong bitter beer
Samsø   light reds and whites
Serra   Vinho Verde
Taleggio   light reds, Valpolicella, Chianti
Tête de Moine   Fendant
Tilsit   light fruity reds, fresh whites, tawny port, beer
Vacherin   light reds, rosés, Chinon, Côtes de Beaune
Valençay   dry whites, light fruity reds
Weinkäse   Moselles, Rhine wines

Bibliography

A Salute to Cheese
Betty Watson
Hawthorn Books, Inc
New York

Bordeaux: The Definitive Guide for the Wines Produced Since 1961
Robert M. Parker, Jr
Simon and Schuster
New York

Cheeses of the World
US Department of Agriculture
Dover Publications
New York

Everyday Cooking With Jacques Pepin
Jacques Pepin
Haper and Row, Publishers
New York

Food for Fifth, 6th Edition
West, Shugart, Wilson
Macmillan
New York

Food for Fifth, 7th Edition
Shugart, Molt, and Wilson
Macmillan
New York

How to Eat Better for Less Money
Jomes Beard and Sam Aaron
Simon and Schuster
New York

How to Enjoy Wine
Hugh Johnson
Simon and Schuster
New York

Italy: The Beautiful Cookbook
Lorenza De' Medici
The Knapp Press
Los Angeles, CA 90036

Japanese Cooking: A Simple Art
Shizuo Tsuji
Kodansha International
Tokyo, New York, and San Francisco

Knight's Foodservice Dictionary
John B. Knight
Van Nostrand Reinhold Co.
New York

Lebanese Cuisine
Madelain Farah
Portland, Oregon

Mexican Cook Book
Sunset Books
Lane Publishing Co
Menlo Park, Californis

Mrs. Beeton's English Cookery
Crown Publishers, Inc.
New York

Southern Herb Growing
Madalene Hill & Gwen Barclay
Shearer Publishing
Fredericksburg, TX

The Chef's Companion: A Concise Dictionary of Culinary Terms
Elizabeth Riely
Van Nostrand Reinhold Co
New York

The Complete Seafood Book
James Wagenvoord and Woodman
Harris
Macmillan
New York

The Dictionary of American Food &
Drink
John E. Mariani
Ticknor & Fields
New Haven and New York

The Encyclopedia of Fish Cookery
A.J. McClane
Holt, Rinehart and Winston
New York

The Good Housekeeping Cookbook
Harcourt, Brace & World, Inc.
New York, NY

The Italian Cookbook
Staff Home Economists
Culinary Arts Institute
Chicago, Illinois

The Only Texas Cookbook
Linda West Eckhardt
Texas Monthly Press, Inc.
Austin, Texas

The Prudhomme Family Cookbook
Paul Prudhomme
William Morrow and Company, Inc.
New York

The Vegetarian Epicure
Anna Thomas
Vintage Books/Random House
New York

The Vegetarian Epicure Book 2
Anna Thomas
Alfred A Knopf, Inc.
New York

The Wine Handbook
Serena Sutcliffe
Simon and Schuster
New York

The World Encyclopedia of Food
L. Patrick Coyle
Facts On File, Inc.
New York

Uncommon Fruits & Vegetables: A
Commonsense Guide
Elizabeth Schneider
Harper & Row
New York

Webster's Collegiate Dictionary

World-of-the-East Vegetarian
Cooking
Madhur Jaffrey
Alfred A Knopf, Inc.
New York, NY

The many dictionaries and phrase books of Berlitz, Berlitz, Barron's, and Harrap's for help with pronunciations.

VAN NOSTRAND REINHOLD VNR

Your Name_____
Title_____
Function_____
Company_____
Date of book purchase_____

Address_____
City/State/Zip_____
Phone_____
Fax_____
E-Mail_____

Thank you for your interest in Van Nostrand Reinhold publications. To enable us to keep you abreast of the latest developments in your field, please complete the following information.

1. With respect to the topic of this book, are you a:
a. student in this field
   name of your institution: _____
b. working professional in this field
c. hobbyist in this field

2. For how many years have you worked/studied in this field?
_____

3. Of which professional associations are you a member?
_____
_____
_____

4. To which industry or general food-related publications/resources do you subscribe for important information?
_____
_____
_____

5. Describe your professional title:
a. chef
b. caterer
c. restaurant owner/manager
d. food and beverages manager
e. student
f. professor/teacher
g. pastry chef

h. sommelie
i. consulting services
j. government
k. librarian
l. education/research
m. other (please specify)
_____

6. How/where was this book purchased? (circle one)
a. bookstore
b. publisher's outlet
c. through offer in mail
d. through book club
e. other _____

7. How/where do you usually purchase professional books? (please circle all that apply)
a. bookstore
b. publisher's outlet
c. through offer in mail
d. through book club
e. other_____

8. Do you own or have access to a computer with a modem?
a. yes   b. no

9. To which electronic on-line services do you have access? (please circle all that apply)
a. America On-Line
b. Prodigy
c. Compuserve
d. Internet
e. World Wide Web
f. other (please specify)
_____
g. none

10. Do you own or have access to a computer with a CD-ROM reader?
a. yes   b. no

11. Would you purchase updates, supplements and/or additional chapters to this book in an electronic format?
a. yes   b. no

12. Which format would you prefer?
a. disk (circle one)   Mac   Dos   Windows
b. CD-ROM
c. online
d. other_____

13. What was the primary reason for purchasing this book?
a. professional enrichment
b. academic coursework
c. personal interest/hobby
d. other_____

14. Would you be interested in or subscribe to a Professional Chef's Newsletter?
a. yes   b. no
If yes, which do you prefer?
a. online   b. print

15. In which of the following areas would you be interested in new books?
a. International cuisine
b. catering
c. baking and pastry
d. beverage management
e. buffets
f. wines
g. other (please specify)
_____

16. Please indicate author/title and ISBN# of book purchased:
_____
_____

VNR is constantly evaluating its services to better meet your needs. If you need further information please contact us by fax at **212-475-2548**.
BE SURE TO VISIT US AT OUR WEB SITE
http://www.vnr.com/vnr.html

I(T)P

BUSINESS REPLY MAIL
FIRST CLASS MAIL   PERMIT NO. 704   NEW YORK NY

POSTAGE WILL BE PAID BY ADDRESSEE

VAN NOSTRAND REINHOLD
Culinary and Hospitality
115 FIFTH AVENUE
4th Floor
NEW YORK, NY 10211-0025

Weights and Measures Equivalencies

dash	less than 1/8 teaspoon
3 teaspoons	1 tablespoon *(1/2 fluid ounce)*
2 tablespoons	1/8 cup *(1 fluid ounce)*
4 tablespoons	1/4 cup *(2 fluid ounces)*
5 1/3 tablespoons	1/3 cup *(2 2/3 fluid ounces)*
8 tablespoons	1/2 cup *(4 fluid ounces)*
10 2/3 tablespoons	2/3 cup *(5 1/3 fluid ounces)*
12 tablespoons	3/4 cup *(6 fluid ounces)*
14 tablespoons	7/8 cup *(7 fluid ounces)*
16 tablespoons	1 cup *(8 fluid ounces)*
1 jigger	1 1/2 ounces *(3 tablespoons)*
1 gill	1/2 cup
1 cup	8 fluid ounces *(240 milliliters)*
2 cups	1 pint *(480 milliliters)*
2 pints	1 quart *(approximately 1 liter)*
4 quarts	1 gallon *(3.75 liters)*
8 quarts	1 peck
4 pecks	1 bushel
1 ounce	28.35 grams *(rounded to 30)*
16 ounces	1 pound *(453.59 grams rounded to 450)*
1 kilogram	2.2 pounds